Great Lives from History

Notorious Lives

Great Lives from History

Notorious Lives

Volume 2
Salvatore Giuliano - Juan Perón

Editor
Carl L. Bankston III
Tulane University

SALEM PRESS

Pasadena, California   Hackensack, New Jersey

Editor in Chief: Dawn P. Dawson

Editorial Director: Christina J. Moose	*Production Editor:* Joyce I. Buchea
Acquisitions Editor: Mark Rehn	*Graphics and Design:* James Hutson
Research Supervisor: Jeffry Jensen	*Layout:* William Zimmerman
Manuscript Editors: Sarah M. Hilbert	*Photo Editor:* Cynthia Breslin Beres
Elizabeth Ferry Slocum	*Editorial Assistant:* Dana Garey

Cover photos (pictured clockwise, from top left): Richard Nixon (Dennis Brack/Landov); Lizzie Borden (The Granger Collection, New York); Saddam Hussein (Hulton Archive/Getty Images); Adolf Hitler (Hulton Archive/Getty Images); Timothy McVeigh (Jim Bourg/Reuters/Landov); Rasputin (The Granger Collection, New York)

Library of Congress Cataloging-in-Publication Data

Great lives from history. Notorious lives / editor, Carl L. Bankston III.
    v. cm.
  Includes bibliographical references and index.
  ISBN-13: 978-1-58765-320-9 (set : alk. paper)
  ISBN-13: 978-1-58765-321-6 (vol. 1 : alk. paper)
  ISBN-13: 978-1-58765-322-3 (vol. 2 : alk. paper)
  ISBN-13: 978-1-58765-323-0 (vol. 3 : alk. paper)
1. Criminals—Biography. 2. Terrorists—Biography. 3. War criminals—Biography. 4. Dictators—Biography.
5. Political corruption.
I. Bankston, Carl L. (Carl Leon), 1952- II. Title: Notorious lives.

HV6245.G687 2007
364.1092′2—dc22
[B]

2006032935

First Printing

CONTENTS

Key to Pronunciation xlv
Complete List of Contents. xlvii
List of Sidebars. lv

Salvatore Giuliano 413
Arthur de Gobineau 415
Nathuram Vinayak Godse 416
Joseph Goebbels 418
Magda Goebbels 421
Bernhard Goetz. 423
Emma Goldman 424
Baruch Goldstein. 427
Hermann Göring 428
John Gotti. 431
Jay Gould. 433
Sammy Gravano 434
Che Guevara 436
Charles Julius Guiteau 439

al-Ḥākim 441
H. R. Haldeman 442
Matthew F. Hale 444
Robert Philip Hanssen 445
John Wesley Hardin 447
Jean Harris 448
Bill Haywood. 450
Linda Burfield Hazzard 453
Patty Hearst. 454
George Hennard 456
Herod Antipas 458
Herod the Great. 459
Rudolf Hess 460
Reinhard Heydrich 462
Henry Hill 465
Susanna Mildred Hill. 466
Marie Hilley 467
Heinrich Himmler 468
John Hinckley, Jr. 470
Hirohito. 473
Alger Hiss 475
Adolf Hitler. 477
Jimmy Hoffa 480
Abbie Hoffman 483
Doc Holliday 485
H. H. Holmes. 486
Karla Homolka 488

J. Edgar Hoover 489
Elmyr de Hory 492
Enver and Nexhmije Hoxha 493
L. Ron Hubbard 495
James Oliver Huberty 497
Laud Humphreys 498
E. Howard Hunt 499
Qusay Saddam Hussein 501
Saddam Hussein 503
Uday Hussein. 505

Megan Louise Ireland 508
Irish Invincibles 509
Clifford Irving 510
David Irving 512
Ivan V 514
Ivan VI 515
Ivan the Terrible 517

Jack the Ripper. 519
Shoeless Joe Jackson 521
Jesse James 523
Wojciech Jaruzelski 525
Jezebel 527
Jiang Qing 528
Jing Ke 530
Joan the Mad 531
Alfred Jodl 533
King John. 534
John Parricida 536
Jim Jones 537
Margaret Jones 540
Flavius Josephus 541
William Joyce 542
Judas Iscariot 544
Justin II 546

Theodore Kaczynski 547
Lazar Kaganovich 549
Meir Kahane 551
Fanya Kaplan. 552
Radovan Karadžić 554
Alvin Karpis 556
Yoshiko Kawashima 558
Tom Keating 559
Machine Gun Kelly. 561

Ned Kelly 562
Jack Ketch 565
Tom Ketchum 566
Jack Kevorkian 567
Khieu Samphan 569
Ayatollah Khomeini 571
Nikita S. Khrushchev 574
William Kidd 576
Kim Il Sung 578
Kim Jong-il 581
Sante Kimes 584
Rodney King 585
Kuniaki Koiso 587
David Koresh 589
Reginald Kray 591
Ronald Kray 593
Richard Kuklinski 595
Béla Kun 596
Lady Alice Kyteler 598

Jean Laffite 600
Leonard Lake 602
Henri Désiré Landru 603
Meyer Lansky 604
Lyndon H. LaRouche, Jr. 606
Pierre Laval 609
Marie Laveau 610
Anton Szandor LaVey 612
John Law 614
Richard Lawrence 615
Kenneth Lay 617
Timothy Leary 619
Charles Lee 621
Daulton Lee 623
Nick Leeson 624
Henri Lemoine 627
Vladimir Ilich Lenin 628
Leo X 630
Leopold II 632
Nathan F. Leopold, Jr. 634
Jean-Marie Le Pen 636
Marc Lépine 638
Mary Kay Letourneau 640
Dennis Levine 642
G. Gordon Liddy 643
John Walker Lindh 645
Richard A. Loeb 647
Huey Long 649
Harry Longabaugh 651
Bill Longley 653

Byron Looper 654
Roderigo Lopez 655
Seventh Earl of Lucan 657
Tommy Lucchese 658
Lucky Luciano 660
Ludwig II 662
Jeffrey Lundgren 664
Victor Lustig 665
Trofim Lysenko 667

Joseph McCarthy 669
James W. McCord, Jr. 671
Jeffrey MacDonald 673
Donald Duart Maclean 674
Virginia McMartin 676
Daniel M'Naghten 677
Aimee Semple McPherson 679
Timothy McVeigh 681
Horst Mahler 684
Mary Mallon 685
Winnie Mandela 686
Frederika Mandelbaum 688
Charles Manson 689
Mao Zedong 691
Salvatore Maranzano 694
Jean-Paul Marat 696
Carlos Marcello 698
Ferdinand Marcos 699
Imelda Marcos 702
Marie-Antoinette 704
Marozia 706
Jean Martinet 707
Joe Masseria 708
Mata Hari 710
Robert Jay Mathews 712
Gaston Bullock Means 713
Ulrike Meinhof 715
Josef Mengele 717
Mengistu Haile Mariam 719
Ramón Mercader 721
Jacques Mesrine 723
Ioannis Metaxas 724
Tom Metzger 726
Mijailo Mijailovic 727
Stanley Milgram 729
Michael Milken 731
Wilbur Mills 733
Slobodan Milošević 735
John Mitchell 737
Ratko Mladić 739

Mobutu Sese Seko 740
Mohammad Reza Shah Pahlavi 742
Khalid Shaikh Mohammed. 744
Molly Maguires 745
Vyacheslav Mikhailovich Molotov 746
Sun Myung Moon 749
Bugs Moran 751
Sir Henry Morgan 753
Sir Oswald Mosley 755
Mou Qizhong. 757
Zacarias Moussaoui 758
Robert Mugabe. 761
Elijah Muhammad 763
John Allen Muhammad and Lee Boyd Malvo . . . 765
Joaquín Murieta 767
Benito Mussolini 769

Nadir Shah 772
Ne Win 773
Baby Face Nelson 774
Leslie Nelson 776
Nero 777
Bonnie Nettles 779
Florence Newton 781
Huey Newton. 782

Charles Ng 784
Madame Nhu 786
Nicholas I. 788
Terry Nichols. 790
Eligiusz Niewiadomski. 792
Richard Nixon 793
Saparmurat Niyazov 796
Manuel Noriega 797
Nostradamus 799

Titus Oates 802
Dion O'Banion 803
Grace O'Malley 805
Arthur Orton 806
Lee Harvey Oswald 807

Eusapia Palladino. 810
Bonnie Parker 811
Ante Pavelić 813
Charles Peace. 815
Thomas Joseph Pendergast. 817
Dolly Pentreath 818
Leander Perez 819
Eva Perón. 821
Juan Perón 823

KEY TO PRONUNCIATION

Many of the names of personages covered in *Great Lives from History: Notorious Lives* may be unfamiliar to students and general readers. For all names, guidelines to pronunciation have been provided upon first mention of the name in each essay. These guidelines do not purport to achieve the subtleties of all languages but will offer readers a rough equivalent of how English speakers may approximate the proper pronunciation.

Vowel Sounds

Symbol	Spelled (Pronounced)
a	answer (AN-suhr), laugh (laf), sample (SAM-puhl), that (that)
ah	father (FAH-thur), hospital (HAHS-pih-tuhl)
aw	awful (AW-fuhl), caught (kawt)
ay	blaze (blayz), fade (fayd), waiter (WAYT-ur), weigh (way)
eh	bed (behd), head (hehd), said (sehd)
ee	believe (bee-LEEV), cedar (SEE-dur), leader (LEED-ur), liter (LEE-tur)
ew	boot (bewt), lose (lewz)
i	buy (bi), height (hit), lie (li), surprise (sur-PRIZ)
ih	bitter (BIH-tur), pill (pihl)
o	cotton (KO-tuhn), hot (hot)
oh	below (bee-LOH), coat (koht), note (noht), wholesome (HOHL-suhm)
oo	good (good), look (look)
ow	couch (kowch), how (how)
oy	boy (boy), coin (koyn)
uh	about (uh-BOWT), butter (BUH-tuhr), enough (ee-NUHF), other (UH-thur)

Consonant Sounds

Symbol	Spelled (Pronounced)
ch	beach (beech), chimp (chihmp)
g	beg (behg), disguise (dihs-GIZ), get (geht)
j	digit (DIH-juht), edge (ehj), jet (jeht)
k	cat (kat), kitten (KIH-tuhn), hex (hehks)
s	cellar (SEHL-ur), save (sayv), scent (sehnt)
sh	champagne (sham-PAYN), issue (IH-shew), shop (shop)
ur	birth (burth), disturb (dihs-TURB), earth (urth), letter (LEH-tur)
y	useful (YEWS-fuhl), young (yuhng)
z	business (BIHZ-nehs), zest (zehst)
zh	vision (VIH-zhuhn)

COMPLETE LIST OF CONTENTS

VOLUME I

Contents. v
Publisher's Note ix
Contributors. xiii
Key to Pronunciation xix
Complete List of Contents xxi
List of Sidebars xxix

Sani Abacha. 1
Frank W. Abagnale, Jr. 3
Abu Nidal 4
Joe Adonis 6
Mehmet Ali Ağca 8
Said Akbar. 10
Alcibiades of Athens. 11
Alexander VI 14
Aldrich Ames 16
Oakes Ames 18
Idi Amin 20
Yigal Amir. 22
Albert Anastasia 23
Ion Antonescu 25
Apache Kid 27
Marshall Applewhite 28
Eugene Aram 30
Roscoe Arbuckle. 32
Johnnie Armstrong. 35
Benedict Arnold 36
ʿAruj 38
Shoko Asahara. 40
Mohammed Atta al-Sayed. 43
Attila. 45

Andreas Baader 47
Bobby Baker. 48
Jim Bakker. 50
Joe Ball 52
Margita Bangová 54
Barabbas 55
Klaus Barbie. 57
Velma Margie Barfield 59
Ma Barker 61
Clyde Barrow 62
Sydney Barrows 64

Omar al-Bashir. 66
Sam Bass. 68
Jean-Marie Bastien-Thiry 69
Elizabeth Báthory 70
Fulgencio Batista y Zaldívar. 73
Dave Beck 75
Elisabeth Becker. 76
Byron De La Beckwith 78
Tom Bell. 80
Samuel Bellamy 81
John Bellingham. 83
Bambi Bembenek 84
Maurycy Beniowski 85
David Berg. 87
Lavrenty Beria 89
David Berkowitz. 91
Paul Bernardo 93
Charlotte de Berry 94
Kenneth Bianchi 95
Ronnie Biggs 97
Theodore G. Bilbo 99
Osama Bin Laden 101
William Bligh 104
Tamsin Blight 106
Lou Blonger 107
Anthony Blunt 109
Ivan Boesky 110
Jean-Bédel Bokassa 113
Boniface VIII. 115
Stede Bonnet 117
William H. Bonney. 118
Jules Bonnot 120
Anne Bonny 122
John Wilkes Booth 123
Lizzie Borden. 125
Cesare Borgia. 127
Lucrezia Borgia 129
Martin Bormann 131
Christopher John Boyce 133
Belle Boyd 135
Eva Braun 137
Arthur Bremer 139
John R. Brinkley 141

Curly Bill Brocius 143
William Brodie 145
Marcus Junius Brutus 146
Louis Buchalter 148
Ted Bundy 149
Angelo Buono, Jr. 151
Guy Burgess 152
William Burke 154
Aaron Burr 155
Richard Girnt Butler 157
Joey Buttafuoco 159
Mary Butters 160
Samuel Joseph Byck 162

John Cairncross 164
Caligula 165
William Calley 168
Roberto Calvi 170
Simon Cameron 171
Billy Cannon 173
Al Capone 175
Willis A. Carto 177
Cartouche 178
Sante Jeronimo Caserio 180
Butch Cassidy 181
Paul Castellano 183
Fidel Castro 185
Catiline 188
Nicolae Ceauşescu 190
Beatrice Cenci 192
Cassie L. Chadwick 193
Cassius Chaerea 195
Houston Stewart Chamberlain 196
Whittaker Chambers 198
Mark David Chapman 200
Charles II 201
Charles VI 203
Henri Charrière 204
Cheng I Sao 205
Andrei Chikatilo 207
Christian VII 208
John Reginald Halliday Christie 210
Benjamin Church 211
Clement VII 212
Jacques Clément 214
Dorothy Clutterbuck 215
Roy Cohn 217
Schuyler Colfax 219
Vincent Coll 221
Frank Collin 222

Joe Colombo 224
Charles W. Colson 225
Commodus 227
Anthony Comstock 229
Janet Cooke 231
D. B. Cooper 233
Charlotte Corday 235
Frank Costello 237
Charles E. Coughlin 239
Bettino Craxi 241
Aleister Crowley 242
Andrew Cunanan 245
Pauline Cushman 246
George A. Custer 248
Moll Cutpurse 250
Cypselus of Corinth 251
Leon Czolgosz 252

Jeffrey Dahmer 255
Bob Dalton 257
Emmett Dalton 258
William Dampier 260
François Darlan 262
Joseph Darnand 264
Richard Walther Darré 266
Richard Allen Davis 267
Tino De Angelis 268
Léon Degrelle 270
Eugene de Kock 271
John DeLorean 272
Albert DeSalvo 274
Phoolan Devi 275
Legs Diamond 277
Porfirio Díaz 278
John Dillinger 281
Françoise Dior 283
Thomas Dixon, Jr. 284
William Dodd 286
Samuel K. Doe 288
Domitian 289
Karl Dönitz 292
Black Donnellys 294
Bill Doolin 296
Jacques Doriot 298
Diane Downs 299
Francis Drake 301
David Duke 303
John E. du Pont 305
Claude Duval 306
François Duvalier 307

Jean-Claude Duvalier. 309
Reginald Dyer 311
Felix Dzerzhinsky 312

Wyatt Earp 315
Bernard Ebbers 317
Dietrich Eckart 319
John D. Ehrlichman 320
Adolf Eichmann 322
Ira Einhorn 324
Elagabalus 326
Ruth Ellis. 327
Werner Erhard 329
Erik XIV 331
Pablo Escobar 332
Ferdinand Walsin Esterhazy 334
Billie Sol Estes 336
Ada Everleigh 338
Julius Evola. 339
Judith Campbell Exner 340

Albert B. Fall. 342
Wallace Dodd Fard. 344
Father Divine 346
Orval E. Faubus 348
Guy Fawkes 350
John Felton 352
Giuseppe Fieschi 353
Albert Fish 355
Jim Fisk. 357
Heidi Fleiss. 359

Pretty Boy Floyd 360
Jim Folsom 362
Larry C. Ford 363
Nathan Bedford Forrest 365
Elisabeth Förster-Nietzsche 367
Abe Fortas 369
Francisco Franco 371
Antoinette Frank 373
Hans Michael Frank 374
Martin Frankel 376
Lynette Fromme 377
Klaus Fuchs 379
Alberto Fujimori 382
Fulvia. 384
Fyodor I 385

John Wayne Gacy 387
Carmine Galante 389
Galerius. 390
Joe Gallo 392
Leopoldo Galtieri. 394
Carlo Gambino 396
Gilbert Gauthe 397
Ed Gein 399
Genghis Khan 400
Vito Genovese 402
Balthasar Gérard 404
Sam Giancana 405
Vincent Gigante 407
Mildred Gillars 409
Gary Gilmore 411

VOLUME 2

Contents xli
Key to Pronunciation xlv
Complete List of Contents. xlvii
List of Sidebars. lv

Salvatore Giuliano 413
Arthur de Gobineau 415
Nathuram Vinayak Godse 416
Joseph Goebbels 418
Magda Goebbels 421
Bernhard Goetz. 423
Emma Goldman 424
Baruch Goldstein 427
Hermann Göring 428

John Gotti. 431
Jay Gould. 433
Sammy Gravano 434
Che Guevara 436
Charles Julius Guiteau 439

al-Ḥākim 441
H. R. Haldeman 442
Matthew F. Hale 444
Robert Philip Hanssen 445
John Wesley Hardin 447
Jean Harris 448
Bill Haywood. 450
Linda Burfield Hazzard 453

Patty Hearst 454
George Hennard 456
Herod Antipas 458
Herod the Great 459
Rudolf Hess 460
Reinhard Heydrich 462
Henry Hill 465
Susanna Mildred Hill 466
Marie Hilley 467
Heinrich Himmler 468
John Hinckley, Jr. 470
Hirohito 473
Alger Hiss 475
Adolf Hitler 477
Jimmy Hoffa 480
Abbie Hoffman 483
Doc Holliday 485
H. H. Holmes 486
Karla Homolka 488
J. Edgar Hoover 489
Elmyr de Hory 492
Enver and Nexhmije Hoxha 493
L. Ron Hubbard 495
James Oliver Huberty 497
Laud Humphreys 498
E. Howard Hunt 499
Qusay Saddam Hussein 501
Saddam Hussein 503
Uday Hussein 505

Megan Louise Ireland 508
Irish Invincibles 509
Clifford Irving 510
David Irving 512
Ivan V 514
Ivan VI 515
Ivan the Terrible 517

Jack the Ripper 519
Shoeless Joe Jackson 521
Jesse James 523
Wojciech Jaruzelski 525
Jezebel 527
Jiang Qing 528
Jing Ke 530
Joan the Mad 531
Alfred Jodl 533
King John 534
John Parricida 536
Jim Jones 537

Margaret Jones 540
Flavius Josephus 541
William Joyce 542
Judas Iscariot 544
Justin II 546

Theodore Kaczynski 547
Lazar Kaganovich 549
Meir Kahane 551
Fanya Kaplan 552
Radovan Karadžić 554
Alvin Karpis 556
Yoshiko Kawashima 558
Tom Keating 559
Machine Gun Kelly 561
Ned Kelly 562
Jack Ketch 565
Tom Ketchum 566
Jack Kevorkian 567
Khieu Samphan 569
Ayatollah Khomeini 571
Nikita S. Khrushchev 574
William Kidd 576
Kim Il Sung 578
Kim Jong-il 581
Sante Kimes 584
Rodney King 585
Kuniaki Koiso 587
David Koresh 589
Reginald Kray 591
Ronald Kray 593
Richard Kuklinski 595
Béla Kun 596
Lady Alice Kyteler 598

Jean Laffite 600
Leonard Lake 602
Henri Désiré Landru 603
Meyer Lansky 604
Lyndon H. LaRouche, Jr. 606
Pierre Laval 609
Marie Laveau 610
Anton Szandor LaVey 612
John Law 614
Richard Lawrence 615
Kenneth Lay 617
Timothy Leary 619
Charles Lee 621
Daulton Lee 623
Nick Leeson 624

Henri Lemoine 627
Vladimir Ilich Lenin 628
Leo X 630
Leopold II 632
Nathan F. Leopold, Jr. 634
Jean-Marie Le Pen 636
Marc Lépine 638
Mary Kay Letourneau 640
Dennis Levine 642
G. Gordon Liddy 643
John Walker Lindh 645
Richard A. Loeb 647
Huey Long 649
Harry Longabaugh 651
Bill Longley 653
Byron Looper. 654
Roderigo Lopez 655
Seventh Earl of Lucan 657
Tommy Lucchese. 658
Lucky Luciano 660
Ludwig II. 662
Jeffrey Lundgren 664
Victor Lustig 665
Trofim Lysenko 667

Joseph McCarthy. 669
James W. McCord, Jr. 671
Jeffrey MacDonald 673
Donald Duart Maclean 674
Virginia McMartin 676
Daniel M'Naghten 677
Aimee Semple McPherson 679
Timothy McVeigh 681
Horst Mahler 684
Mary Mallon 685
Winnie Mandela 686
Frederika Mandelbaum. 688
Charles Manson 689
Mao Zedong 691
Salvatore Maranzano. 694
Jean-Paul Marat 696
Carlos Marcello 698
Ferdinand Marcos 699
Imelda Marcos 702
Marie-Antoinette 704
Marozia. 706
Jean Martinet 707
Joe Masseria 708
Mata Hari. 710
Robert Jay Mathews 712

Gaston Bullock Means 713
Ulrike Meinhof 715
Josef Mengele 717
Mengistu Haile Mariam 719
Ramón Mercader 721
Jacques Mesrine 723
Ioannis Metaxas 724
Tom Metzger 726
Mijailo Mijailovic 727
Stanley Milgram 729
Michael Milken. 731
Wilbur Mills 733
Slobodan Milošević 735
John Mitchell 737
Ratko Mladić 739
Mobutu Sese Seko 740
Mohammad Reza Shah Pahlavi 742
Khalid Shaikh Mohammed. 744
Molly Maguires 745
Vyacheslav Mikhailovich Molotov 746
Sun Myung Moon 749
Bugs Moran 751
Sir Henry Morgan 753
Sir Oswald Mosley 755
Mou Qizhong. 757
Zacarias Moussaoui 758
Robert Mugabe. 761
Elijah Muhammad 763
John Allen Muhammad and Lee Boyd
    Malvo 765
Joaquín Murieta 767
Benito Mussolini 769

Nadir Shah 772
Ne Win 773
Baby Face Nelson 774
Leslie Nelson 776
Nero 777
Bonnie Nettles 779
Florence Newton 781
Huey Newton. 782
Charles Ng 784
Madame Nhu 786
Nicholas I. 788
Terry Nichols. 790
Eligiusz Niewiadomski. 792
Richard Nixon 793
Saparmurat Niyazov 796
Manuel Noriega 797
Nostradamus 799

Titus Oates 802
Dion O'Banion 803
Grace O'Malley 805
Arthur Orton 806
Lee Harvey Oswald 807

Eusapia Palladino 810
Bonnie Parker 811

Ante Pavelić 813
Charles Peace 815
Thomas Joseph Pendergast 817
Dolly Pentreath 818
Leander Perez 819
Eva Perón 821
Juan Perón 823

VOLUME 3

Contents lxvii
Key to Pronunciation lxxi
Complete List of Contents lxxiii
List of Sidebars lxxxi

Philippe Pétain 825
Peter the Cruel 827
Scott Peterson 828
Marcel Petiot 831
Symon Petlyura 832
Phalaris 834
Kim Philby 836
William Luther Pierce III 838
Pontius Pilate 840
Augusto Pinochet Ugarte 842
Konstantin Petrovich Pobedonostsev 845
Pol Pot 846
Jonathan Pollard 849
Polycrates of Samos 850
Charles Ponzi 852
James Porter 854
Adam Clayton Powell, Jr. 856
Lewis Powell 858
Miguel Primo de Rivera 860
Gavrilo Princip 861
Joseph Profaci 863
Puyi 864

Muammar al-Qaddafi 867
William Clarke Quantrill 869
John Quelch 871
Vidkun Quisling 873

Puniša Račić 876
John Rackham 877

Dennis Rader 879
Gilles de Rais 880
Thenmuli Rajaratnam 882
Ilich Ramírez Sánchez 883
Grigori Yefimovich Rasputin 885
François Ravaillac 888
James Earl Ray 889
Mary Read 891
Madame Restell 892
Joachim von Ribbentrop 894
Richard III 896
Johnny Ringo 898
Efraín Ríos Montt 899
George Rivas 901
Rob Roy 902
Bartholomew Roberts 905
Robespierre 907
Robin Hood 909
George Lincoln Rockwell 911
Ethel Rosenberg 913
Julius Rosenberg 915
Arnold Rothstein 917
Darlie Routier 918
Jack Ruby 919
Eric Rudolph 921

Nicola Sacco 924
Marquis de Sade 926
António de Oliveira Salazar 928
Yolanda Saldívar 930
Salome 932
Savitri Devi 934
Elizabeth Sawyer 935
Baldur von Schirach 937
Dutch Schultz 938

Assata Olugbala Shakur 940
Clay Shaw 941
Jack Sheppard 943
Sam Sheppard 945
Shi Huangdi 947
Fusako Shigenobu 949
Harold Shipman 950
Mother Shipton 952
Muhammad Siad Barre 953
Bugsy Siegel 954
William Joseph Simmons 957
O. J. Simpson 958
Miles Sindercombe 961
Beant Singh 962
Satwant Singh 963
Sirhan Sirhan 965
Jeffrey Skilling 967
Otto Skorzeny 969
Pamela Ann Smart 971
Gerald L. K. Smith 973
Madeleine Smith 975
Susan Smith 977
Ruth Snyder 979
Charles Sobraj 980
Valerie Solanas 982
Anastasio Somoza García 984
Richard Speck 986
Albert Speer 987
Joseph Stalin 990
Charles Starkweather 993
Belle Starr 994
Henry Starr 996
Alexandre Stavisky 998
J. B. Stoner 999
Julius Streicher 1001
Alfredo Stroessner 1004
Robert Franklin Stroud 1005
Suharto 1007
Lucius Cornelius Sulla 1010
Mary Surratt 1012
Willie Sutton 1014
Michael Swango 1015

Ta Mok 1017
Roger Brooke Taney 1018
Charles Taylor 1021
Edward Teach 1023
Than Shwe 1026
Harry Kendall Thaw 1027
Theodora 1028

Benjamin Tillman 1030
Tito 1032
Sweeney Todd 1033
Hideki Tojo 1034
Tokyo Rose 1036
Tomás de Torquemada 1038
Leon Trotsky 1040
Rafael Trujillo 1042
Karla Faye Tucker 1044
Dick Turpin 1045
William Marcy Tweed 1047
John Tyndall 1050

Vasili Vasilievich Ulrikh 1052
Urban VI 1053

Volkert van der Graaf 1055
Bartolomeo Vanzetti 1056
Getúlio Vargas 1059
Hank Vaughan 1060
Veerappan 1062
Hendrik Frensch Verwoerd 1064
Jorge Rafael Videla 1066
Eugène François Vidocq 1067
Pancho Villa 1069
Vlad III the Impaler 1072
Andrey Andreyevich Vlasov 1074
Claus von Bülow 1075
Anastase Vonsiatsky 1077
Andrey Vyshinsky 1079

Winifred Wagner 1081
James J. Walker 1082
William Walker 1084
Rachel Wall 1086
George C. Wallace 1087
Carolyn Warmus 1090
Randy Weaver 1091
Joseph Weil 1094
Carl Weiss 1095
Hymie Weiss 1096
Horst Wessel 1097
Dan White 1099
Charles Whitman 1101
Jonathan Wild 1102
James Wilkinson 1103
Henry Wirz 1105
Adam Worth 1107
Aileen Carol Wuornos 1108
Joan Wytte 1110

Genrikh Yagoda. 1112
Andrea Yates 1113
Nikolay Ivanovich Yezhov 1115
Dominique You 1117
Cole Younger 1118
Ramzi Yousef 1121
Yuan Shikai 1122
Yakov Mikhailovich Yurovsky 1124
Felix Yusupov. 1126

Giuseppe Zangara. 1128
Emiliano Zapata. 1129
Abu Musab al-Zarqawi 1132

Ayman al-Zawahiri 1135
Andrey Aleksandrovich Zhdanov. 1137
Grigory Yevseyevich Zinovyev. 1138

Appendixes

Chronological List of Entries 1143
Bibliography 1152
Electronic Resources 1199

Indexes

Category Index. III
Geographical Index IX
Personages Index XVII

LIST OF SIDEBARS

VOLUME I

Abu Nidal Organization, The 5
Amin, Statements Attributed to Idi 21
Appeal of June 18, Charles de Gaulle's 263
Are the Children of God a Sect?. 87
Aum Shinrikyo. 41
Bakker's Prosperity Gospel 51
Ballad of Mary Butters, The 161
Barabbas, Give Us. 56
Barbarity, Barbie's. 58
Barbie's Barbarity 58
Báthory in the Movies, Elizabeth 71
Batista, Books by 74
Battlefield, Belle on the 136
Belle on the Battlefield 136
Beria's Stature Among the Communist Elite . . . 90
Beware a Beautiful Smiler 220
Biddle Family, The 64
Biggs, Nabbing 97
Bill Gets a Bullet 143
Bin Laden's Vengeance 102
Books by Batista. 74
Booth's Four Chances 124
Brother's View, The 333
Bullet, Bill Gets a 143
Burr-Hamilton Duel, The. 156
Butch Cassidy Rides Again . . . and Again. . . . 182
Butters, The Ballad of Mary 161
Caligula, Suetonius on 166
Car Coups, DeLorean's Two 273
Cassidy Rides Again . . . and Again, Butch . . . 182
Censor's Nemesis, The. 230
Chain of Command, The 169
Chamberlain's Views on Civilization 197
Changing Reputation, A 147
Charles de Gaulle's Appeal of June 18. 263
Children of God a Sect?, Are the 87
Ching, The Widow 206
Circumnavigation, The Dragon's 302
Civilization, Chamberlain's Views on 197
Clemency, Cruelty and 128
Clericis laicos: Heavy Burdens 116
Coffin, Too Much for His 15
Colson, Nixon on 226
Command, The Chain of 169

Commodus, Machiavelli on 228
Communist Elite, Beria's Stature Among the . . . 90
Confession, Deathbed 234
Conscience Tells Me," "This My 81
Controlled Schizophrenia 380
Cop vs. Robber 61
Coughlin's Credos, Father 239
Crazy After All These Years, Still. 29
Credos, Father Coughlin's 239
Cruelty and Clemency 128
Dampier in the New World. 261
Dangerous at the Top, It's 186
Deathbed Confession. 234
De Gaulle's Appeal of June 18, Charles 263
DeLorean's Two Car Coups 273
Desperado, How to Face Down a 316
Díaz, Justice, According to Porfirio 279
Disappearance of Persons, National
   Commission on the 394
Do What Thou Wilt 243
Domitian, Suetonius on 290
Dragon's Circumnavigation, The 302
Duel, The Burr-Hamilton. 156
Duvalierville 308
Elizabeth Báthory in the Movies 71
Everleigh Girl, How to Be an 338
Evil Wears a Smile. 150
Fard, FBI File on 345
Fascism, Franco's 372
Father Coughlin's Credos 239
Fawkes in Rhyme 351
FBI File on Fard 345
Forrest on the Ku Klux Klan 366
Franco's Fascism. 372
Free Enterprise, Scarface and 176
Gardner on Witchcraft 216
Gaulle's Appeal of June 18, Charles de 263
Genghis, Great Granddad 401
Gilmore and the Golden Gloves Girl. 412
Give Us Barabbas 56
Golden Gloves Girl, Gilmore and the 412
Granddad Genghis, Great 401
Great Granddad Genghis 401
Great Persecution, The 391

Hamilton Duel, The Burr- 156
Hays Code, The 33
How to Be an Everleigh Girl. 338
How to Face Down a Desperado 316
If Not Lizzie, Who? 126
"Insider Trading"?, What Is 111
It's Dangerous at the Top 186
Justice, According to Porfirio Díaz 279
Ku Klux Klan, Forrest on the 366
Letter, A Tell-Tale 356
Little Bighorn, Sitting Bull's. 249
Little Rock Nine, The 349
Lizzie, Who? If Not 126
Lucrezia: A Mixed Reputation 130
Machiavelli on Commodus. 228
Man More Sinned Against, A 119
Men of an Ugly Pattern 46
Movies, Elizabeth Báthory in the 71
Nabbing Biggs. 97
National Commission on the Disappearance
    of Persons 394
Nemesis, The Censor's. 230
New World, Dampier in the 261
Nieman, No Man 253
Nixon on Colson 226
No Man, Nieman, ... 253
Organization, The Abu Nidal 5
Party Crasher 13

Persecution, The Great 391
Prosperity Gospel, Bakker's. 51
Reputation, A Changing 147
Reputation, Lucrezia: A Mixed. 130
Right Tartar, A 105
Robber, Cop vs. 61
Scarface and Free Enterprise 176
Schizophrenia, Controlled 380
Sect?, Are the Children of God a 87
Sinned Against, A Man More 119
Sitting Bull's Little Bighorn 249
Smile, Evil Wears a 150
Smiler, Beware a Beautiful. 220
Spy vs. Spy 16
Statements Attributed to Idi Amin. 21
Still Crazy After All These Years 29
Suetonius on Caligula 166
Suetonius on Domitian 290
Tartar, A Right 105
Tell-Tale Letter, A 356
Text of Treachery, The 37
"This My Conscience Tells Me" 81
Too Much for His Coffin 15
Treachery, The Text of 37
Vengeance, Bin Laden's 102
What Is "Insider Trading"?. 111
Widow Ching, The 206
Witchcraft, Gardner on. 216

Volume 2

According to LaRouche 607
Air, Trees, Water, Animals, ATWA: 690
Al-Anfal Campaign Against Iraqi Kurds,
    The 504
Amnesty," Liddy Today: "No 643
Anfal Campaign Against Iraqi Kurds,
    The al- 504
Apocalypse, Waiting for the 590
Atrocities, First Reports of 633
ATWA: Air, Trees, Water, Animals 690
Authority, Göring on. 429
"Autobiography," Laffite's. 600
Ayatollah's Farewell, The 573
Barbecue, Madame Nhu's 787
Beer Hall Putsch, The 461
Before the Firing Squad 711
Black Panther Party Platform, The. 783

Capturing Mary Mallon 685
Charges Against Lady Kyteler, The 599
Che's Farewell to Cuba 437
Chicago Seven Trial, Sentencing at the 484
Cocktail, Molotov's 748
Communism, Hoover on 490
"Cosa Nostra 'til I die". 431
Cuba, Che's Farewell to 437
Death Rehearsal 539
Decency?," "Have you no sense of. 670
Elijah Muhammad on the Races 763
Evita's Postmortem Odyssey. 822
Faith and Resolution 680
FBI on Hubbard, The. 496
Firing Squad, Before the 711
First Reports of Atrocities 633
First Resignation of a President, The. 794

Four—or Six, The Gang of 529

Fourth of August Régime, Proclamation
of the 725

Front National, The. 637

Gang, The James-Younger 524

Gang of Four—or Six, The. 529

Goebbels Argues for Total War 419

Göring on Authority 429

Gospel of Judas, The 545

Haldeman Theory, The. 443

"Have you no sense of decency?" 670

Haymarket Riot, The 426

Hearst on Domestic Terrorism 455

Heydrich's Power 464

Himmler's Inhumanity 469

Hinckley's Other Victims 472

Hirohito Surrenders 474

Hitler's Proclamation on Invading Russia 479

Hoffa, The Hunt for 482

Holocaust, Irving's Statement on the. 513

Hoover on Communism 490

Hubbard, The FBI on. 496

Huey Long, President 650

Hunt for Hoffa, The 482

Industrial Unionism 451

Inhumanity, Himmler's. 469

Iraqi Kurds, The al-Anfal Campaign
Against 504

Irving's Statement on the Holocaust 513

Jackson's Confession. 522

James-Younger Gang, The 524

Jerilderie Letter, The 564

Judas, The Gospel of 545

Ken Lay on Ken Lay. 618

Kevorkian Verdict, The 568

Kidd's Buried Treasure. 577

King and the Law, Rodney. 586

Kurds, The al-Anfal Campaign Against
Iraqi. 504

Kyteler, The Charges Against Lady 599

Laffite's "Autobiography" 600

LaRouche, According to 607

Law, Rodney King and the. 586

Lay on Ken Lay, Ken. 618

Lenin's Last View of Soviet Government . . . 629

Letter, The Jerilderie 564

Liddy Today: "No Amnesty". 643

Long, President, Huey 650

McVeigh's Reasons 682

Madame Nhu's Barbecue 787

Magna Carta 535

Mallon, Capturing Mary 685

Manifesto, The Unabomber's 548

Mao's Fable of Perseverance. 693

Marie-Antoinette 705

Mengele on the Run 718

Milošević Becomes President of Serbia 736

Molotov's Cocktail. 748

Moussaoui Trial, Three Assessments of the 759

Muhammad on the Races, Elijah. 763

Murder, Inc. 661

Mussolini on the War's Progress. 770

Nero's Idea of Fun 778

Nhu's Barbecue, Madame 787

Nine Satanic Statements, The 613

No Turning Back. 635

Nostradamus Predicts His End 800

Oswald Re-Corpsed 809

Panther Party Platform, The Black. 783

Party Platform, The Black Panther. 783

Perseverance, Mao's Fable of 693

Postmortem Odyssey, Evita's 822

Power: Shoes and Jewels, The Rewards of . . . 703

President, The First Resignation of a. 794

President of Serbia, Milošević Becomes. 736

Principles of the Ustaše Movement 814

Proclamation of the Fourth of August
Régime 725

Putsch, The Beer Hall 461

Races, Elijah Muhammad on the. 763

Resignation of a President, The First. 794

Resolution, Faith and. 680

Rewards of Power: Shoes and Jewels, The . . . 703

Riot, The Haymarket. 426

Rodney King and the Law 586

Russia, Hitler's Proclamation on Invading. . . . 479

Satanic Statements, The Nine 613

Sense of decency?," "Have you no. 670

Sentencing at the Chicago Seven Trial. 484

Serbia, Milošević Becomes President of. 736

Shoes and Jewels, The Rewards of Power: . . . 703

Soviet Government, Lenin's Last View of. . . . 629

Surrenders, Hirohito 474

Terrorism, Hearst on Domestic. 455

Three Assessments of the Moussaoui Trial . . . 759

Total War, Goebbels Argues for 419

Totalitarianism Fatigue. 582

Treasure, Kidd's Buried 577

Trial, Sentencing at the Chicago Seven 484

Trial, Three Assessments of the Moussaoui . . . 759

Unabomber's Manifesto, The 548
Unexpected Outcome, An 730
Unionism, Industrial 451
Ustaše Movement, Principles of the 814
Verdict, The Kevorkian 568

Victims, Hinckley's Other 472
Waiting for the Apocalypse 590
War, Goebbels Argues for Total 419
War's Progress, Mussolini on the 770
Younger Gang, The James- 524

VOLUME 3

Alex Haley Interviews the American
  Führer 912
Amber and Scott: A Telephone
  Conversation 830
American Führer, Alex Haley Interviews
  the 912
Assassination, Rasputin Foresees His 886
Ayala, The Plan of 1131
Bin Laden Fatwa, The Zawahiri- 1135
Black Hand, Unification or Death: The 862
Blackbeard by Franklin 1024
Carlos the Jackal and Islam 884
Chandler, Siegel and Raymond 955
Children, Teaching Hate to 1002
Cold War, Seeds of the 991
Colonel Qaddafi Advises the West 868
Conscience, The Emperor's 1029
Conspiracy, Ray and 890
Conspiracy Theory, The Cover-up 966
Constitution, Guatemalan 900
Cover-up Conspiracy Theory, The 966
Dance, Salome's 933
Death, The Why of Dr. 951
Death House, From the 1057
Death of Zarqawi, The 1133
De Sade's Golden Rule 927
Destiny, The Gray-Eyed Man of 1085
Dr. Death, The Why of 951
Doesn't Fit . . ., If It 960
Dred Scott Decision, Reactions to the 1020
Emperor's Conscience, The 1029
Expedition, The Punitive 1070
Fatwa, The Zawahiri-Bin Laden 1135
Female Serial Killers 1109
Fifteenth Century Serial Killer, Trial of a 881
Fit . . ., If It Doesn't 960
France, Pétain's Plan to Revive 826
Franklin, Blackbeard by 1024
From the Death House 1057
From Univerism to Universism 874

Führer, Alex Haley Interviews the
  American 912
Golden Rule, De Sade's 927
Grave," "Rob Roy's 903
Gray-Eyed Man of Destiny, The 1085
Guatemalan Constitution 900
Haley Interviews the American Führer,
  Alex 912
Hate to Children, Teaching 1002
High School Speech, The Hollywood 974
Hollywood High School Speech, The 974
Horiuchi, State of Idaho v. 1093
Horst Wessel Song, The 1098
If It Doesn't Fit 960
Interview with Cole Younger, An 1119
Islam, Carlos the Jackal and 884
Jackal and Islam, Carlos the 884
Killer, Trial of a Fifteenth Century Serial 881
Killers, Female Serial 1109
Kudos for Ponzi's Scheme 853
Liquor, The Worse for 1061
Lucian on Phalaris 835
Male-Free Society: The *SCUM Manifesto* 982
Man of Destiny, The Gray-Eyed 1085
Multitude, Pilate and the 841
Nicaragua, Private Property 984
Notoriety, A Woman of Some 995
Parishioners' Views 855
Patriotism, Pol Pot's 848
Permanent Revolution 1041
Pétain's Plan to Revive France 826
Phalaris, Lucian on 835
Pilate and the Multitude 841
Plan of Ayala, The 1131
Pol Pot's Patriotism 848
Police Statement, Sheppard's 946
Policy, Terror as Public 908
Ponzi's Scheme, Kudos for 853
Proscriptions, Sulla's 1011
Public Policy, Terror as 908

Punitive Expedition, The 1070
Qaddafi Advises the West, Colonel 868
Rasputin Foresees His Assassination. 886
Ray and Conspiracy 890
Reactions to the Dred Scott Decision. 1020
Revolution, Permanent 1041
Revolutionary Party, Vonsiatsky on the
    Russian. 1078
"Rob Roy's Grave". 903
Rosenbergs' Sentence, The. 916
Roses, The Wars of the. 897
Russian Revolutionary Party, Vonsiatsky
    on the. 1078
Sade's Golden Rule, De 927
Salome's Dance 933
Schoolhouse Door, Wallace at the 1088
Scott: A Telephone Conversation, Amber
    and. 830
Scott Decision, Reactions to the Dred 1020
SCUM Manifesto, Male-Free Society:
    The 982
Seeds of the Cold War 991
Selena Forever 931
Sentence, The Rosenbergs'. 916
Serial Killer, Trial of a Fifteenth Century 881
Serial Killers, Female 1109
Sheppard's Police Statement 946
Siegel and Raymond Chandler. 955

Society: The *SCUM Manifesto*, Male-Free 982
Song, The Horst Wessel 1098
Speech, The Hollywood High School 974
State of Idaho v. Horiuchi. 1093
Sulla's Proscriptions 1011
Teaching Hate to Children 1002
Telephone Conversation, Amber and
    Scott: A 830
Terror as Public Policy. 908
Tokyo Rose, Veterans Honor. 1037
Trial of a Fifteenth Century Serial Killer 881
Tweed in Word and Deed. 1048
Unification or Death: The Black Hand. 862
Univerism to Universism, From 874
Veterans Honor Tokyo Rose 1037
Vonsiatsky on the Russian Revolutionary
    Party 1078
Wallace at the Schoolhouse Door. 1088
Wars of the Roses, The. 897
Wessel Song, The Horst 1098
West, Colonel Qaddafi Advises the 868
Why of Dr. Death, The. 951
Witchcraft Act, The 936
Woman of Some Notoriety, A 995
Worse for Liquor, The 1061
Younger, An Interview with Cole. 1119
Zarqawi, The Death of 1133
Zawahiri-Bin Laden Fatwa, The 1135

Notorious Lives

SALVATORE GIULIANO
Sicilian outlaw

BORN: November 16, 1922; Montelepre, Palermo province, Sicily (now in Italy)

DIED: July 6, 1950; Castelvetrano, Sicily, Italy

ALSO KNOWN AS: King of the Mountain

CAUSE OF NOTORIETY: Giuliano was famous for his kidnappings, robberies, and extortion of money from the rich. He advocated the independence of Sicily and successfully fought the Italian police forces until he was betrayed by one of his chief lieutenants.

ACTIVE: 1943-1950

LOCALE: Sicily, Italy

EARLY LIFE

Salvatore Giuliano (sal-vah-TOHR-ee zhyew-LYAH-noh) was born in 1922 to a poor peasant Sicilian family on the Western coast of Sicily; he was the fourth child of Salvatore Giuliano and Maria Lombardo. He received little schooling, and in 1935 he dropped out of school in order to help his family earn a living following the draft of his father into the Italian army. Giuliano's first encounter with the law occurred at a location called Quattro Molini (Four Mills) on September 2, 1943. Giuliano, active in the black market, was carrying two sacks of flour from San Giuseppe Jato to Montelepre and was stopped at a checkpoint by the carabinieri, the semimilitary Italian police. He pleaded with the carabinieri to let him go, but an officer kept his identity card and pulled a gun, at which point Giuliano shot him and ran away. Giuliano had became involved in black market activities largely because of the dire conditions in which the people of the island lived: Fascist rule and the retreat of the German invaders had further impoverished an already poor Sicily. Under the Allied command of the island, the black market flourished, especially under the direction of the Mafia and corrupt politicians.

CRIMINAL CAREER

Following the September 2 shooting, the police did not look for Giuliano until Christmas Eve of 1943, when, not having found him at home, they took his father into custody. Giuliano, who had been watching from a secure post, was angered and attempted to free his father by shooting at the carabinieri; one of them was shot and others were wounded. This event resulted in several arrests. Giuliano succeeded in freeing his friends and cousin from the jail at Monreale a few weeks later, assisted by

the Mafia. The locals and political and criminal forces abided by Omerta (the Mafia code of silence), thereby protecting Giuliano as he engaged in a series of robberies, extortions, and kidnappings; his crimes provided financial support to many and brought fame to himself and his band of men. Throughout 1944, Giuliano engaged in banditry and illegal activities: He attacked police stations and ambushed police patrols with success and with immunity from charges. He and his band were well armed with automatic rifles and hand grenades—items even the local carabinieri did not possess until they captured members of the band.

Giuliano soon became the most popular and well-known bandit of Italy. In the eyes of Sicilians, he became a figure much like Robin Hood: His robberies and extortions provided aid to the peasants and poor people and pitted him against the rich landowners, the *latifondisti*. One legendary episode, in November, 1944, involved the

Salvatore Giuliano in 1948. (AP/Wide World Photos)

413

duchess of Pratameno, whom Giuliano robbed. While despoiling her of her jewels, he asked to borrow the book she was reading; he later returned it with a thank-you note. Giuliano's generosity in rewarding peasants and his spectacular deeds made him a national folk hero. He granted newspapers interviews and became the subject of conversations in every Sicilian café. In September, 1945, the daily *La Sicilia del popolo* declared him a celebrity and a folk hero.

During this period, Giuliano became an ardent supporter of the Sicilian Independence Movement (MIS), a group that believed fervently in the secession of Sicily from Italy. Some supporters of MIS even wanted Sicily to become the forty-ninth state of the United States. This sentiment was influenced by the many Sicilians who were living in America and, at one point, by the American Mafia, which had strong connections to Sicily. Giuliano was made a colonel in this separatist army, but soon the complexity of the Italian political establishment squashed its plans: The Christian Democratic Party, the United Left (combining socialists and communists), and the Mafia itself abandoned the separatist idea.

Giuliano's most spectacular and bloodiest crime was the massacre that occurred at Portella della Ginestra on May Day of 1950. Peasants and workers were commemorating the electoral victory of the United Left in April, 1947, after it had obtained 30 percent of the vote versus the 21 percent of the Christian Democrats. Giuliano's band opened fire on the crowd, perhaps out of confusion, because this was not his intent. A massacre ensued, and eleven workers were killed and thirty-three more were wounded. After this bloody and criminal event, Giuliano continued living as an outlaw, hiding in his territory and protected by his armed followers, as well as political and organized crime figures.

Giuliano suffered a violent death on July 6, 1950. He had become larger than life to many Sicilians, but to others—such as leftist parties, the Christian Democratic Party, the Americans, and the Mafia itself—he had become a national embarrassment and a nuisance. His own followers were beginning to feel this pressure, and several left the band. Giuliano's most trusted friend and cousin, Gaspare Pisciotta, made a deal with the police to obtain amnesty. Pisciotta and Giuliano had moved, under the protection of a Mafia connection, to Castelvetrano in the house of Gregorio De Maria, a law school graduate. They were convinced that they could hide there while negotiating an eventual deal to leave the country.

However, this arrangement, set up with the help of Pisciotta, proved to be a trap: Giuliano was shot dead by police.

IMPACT

The official version of Salvatore Giuliano's death is that he was gunned down by the carabinieri in the house of Gregorio De Maria in Castelvetrano. However, many people believe that Giuliano was killed while he slept. Pisciotta confessed to his role in the killing of his comrade almost a year after Giuliano's death. The official version was likely concocted with the pure intent of protecting police informers at the time. Pisciotta was fatally poisoned in 1954 while he was detailed in jail. It is said that Pisciotta's own father administered the strychnine-laced espresso coffee, as vengeance for the betrayal of Giuliano.

The story behind Giuliano's career and death remains one of the unresolved mysteries of Italian history. The people of Sicily and many others, however, believe that he became a bandit only out of necessity because of the economic conditions of Sicily and the corruption of the ruling classes. It is also believed that he was used as a puppet by many groups.

FURTHER READING

Chandler, Billy Jaynes. *King of the Mountains: The Life and Death of Salvatore Giuliano.* De Kalb: Northern Illinois University Press, 1988. The most comprehensive English-language account of Giuliano story. It is unbiased, precise, and historically accurate and gives a thorough analysis of the political and social forces that helped create this most notable bandit of modern Italy.

Lewis, Norman. *The Honoured Society: The Sicilian Mafia Observed.* London: Eland, 2003. Provides good context for the era in which Giuliano operated, describing, for example, the role that the U.S. Army played in returning the Mafia to power in 1944.

Stille, Alexander. *Excellent Cadavers.* New York: Random House, 1995. The book investigates and unravels the lengthy relationship between the Mafia and the Italian state.

—*Giuseppe Di Scipio*

SEE ALSO: Carmine Galante; Carlo Gambino; Tommy Lucchese; Lucky Luciano; Salvatore Maranzano; Joe Masseria; Robin Hood.

ARTHUR DE GOBINEAU
French writer, diplomat, and white supremacist

BORN: July 14, 1816; Ville-d'Avray, France
DIED: October 13, 1882; Turin, Italy
ALSO KNOWN AS: Joseph Arthur Comte de Gobineau (full name)
CAUSE OF NOTORIETY: In his treatise *Essai sur l'inégalité des races humaines* (1853-1855, 6 volumes; *The Inequality of Human Races*, 1915), Gobineau postulated his belief that of the three "races"—black, yellow, and white—the white race was superior and could be traced back to its Aryan or Teutonic roots.
ACTIVE: 1850's-1882
LOCALE: Europe, Iran, Egypt, Greece, Persia, and East Asia

EARLY LIFE

Born near Paris into an aristocratic family, Arthur de Gobineau (ahr-tur duh goh-bee-noh) was raised as a Roman Catholic royalist. His tutor, from the University of Iena, taught him German and introduced him to *Alf layla wa-layla* (fifteenth century; *The Arabian Nights' Entertainments*, 1706-1708). This book became his favorite for the rest of his life. He was sent to school in Bienne (French-speaking Switzerland), where he studied Latin and Greek.

With the revolution of 1830, Gobineau's aristocratic world burst. There was no more money, and being a member of the nobility was no longer an asset. Gobineau's father tried to persuade him to join the military, but Gobineau found this to be a distasteful prospect and instead persuaded his ornery Parisian uncle to take him in. Gobineau frequented Parisian social circles and wrote feverishly. His first published work appeared in the respected *Revue des Deux Mondes* (review of two worlds); it led to his becoming an aide to French essayist and diplomat Alexis de Tocqueville.

Gobineau married Clémence Monnerot (from whom he would separate thirty years later), and they had two girls, Diane and Christine. In his family, he remained close to his sister Caroline, who became a Benedictine mother in the Abbey of Solesmes. They maintained a long and rich correspondence.

POLITICAL CAREER

Gobineau's service to Tocqueville during the days of the French Constituent Assembly of 1848 ended abruptly when Napoleon III fired Tocqueville a few months later. Through his connections, Gobineau entered the diplomatic corps and was sent first to Berne, Switzerland, and then to Hanover and Frankfurt, Germany; he resided in Frankfurt from 1851 to 1854. The first two volumes of his famous *Essai sur l'inégalité des races humaines* (1853-1855) appeared in 1853 and the remaining four volumes were published in 1855 after his departure for Tehran, Iran. Back in Paris in 1857, he was sent to Newfoundland and the Savoy before returning to Tehran in 1861 for two years. Athens was the next post, from 1864 to 1868. Gobineau was most displeased when Paris recalled him to go to Rio de Janeiro, where he became ill. He returned home in 1870. During the Franco-Prussian War (1870-1871), Louis-Adolphe Thiers, president of the French Republic, sent Gobineau to Stockholm until 1877, when he returned to France to reside permanently.

Gobineau's notoriety resulted from his astounding theories on race, aristocracy, and civilization. His claims in *Essai sur l'inégalité des races humaines* both that the white race emanated from the so-called Aryan race and was superior to the black and yellow races and that intermingling of blood caused degeneration were novel arguments and provoked strong reactions. The inevitable mixing of races, Gobineau held, would eventually bring all races into the melting pot, resulting in egalitarianism and the end of any purity in the races, an utter shame for the human species. Later, Gobineau modified his stance somewhat by claiming that in individuals, the father's strong hereditary traits could be passed to the son.

IMPACT

Gobineau's entire work represents the antithesis to all that the French Revolution of 1789 symbolized and ran counter to many of the new French social mores. It did, however, come at a time of intense interest in and speculation about the origins of humankind and the place and biological and social role of human beings. In 1859, Charles Darwin published his theory of natural selection, *On the Origin of Species by Means of Natural Selection: Or, The Preservation of Favoured Races in the Struggle for Life* (1859), a work that was followed by Darwin's treatise on human evolution, *The Descent of Man and Selection in Relation to Sex* (1871). These works gave life to unscientific theories such as those of Gobineau and, at the same time, fueled speculations about the "survival of the fittest" in a nonevolutionary time frame, which led to the unfortunate and misguided notions of "social Darwinism." Gobineau, then, must be seen in the context of this period, when anthropology and paleontology were not yet grounded in rigorous scientific methodologies. Nevertheless, his notions of racial purity—and of race in general—both reflected and propagated the xenophobia and dehumanization of others that justified racism and colonial imperialism.

FURTHER READING
Boissel, Jean. *Gobineau biographie: Mythes et réalités.* Paris: Berg International, 1993. Assesses Gobineau's reputation in nineteenth century Europe. Anti-Enlightenment, anti-progress, anti-patriotic, and anti-bourgeois, Gobineau was also a romantic who invented himself as a participant in medieval chivalry and a descendant of a Norwegian pirate. A penetrating study. In French.

Dreyfus, Robert. "La Vie et les prophéties du comte de Gobineau." *Cahiers de la Quinzaine* 16 (1905). In the sixth of a series of university lectures, Dreyfus discusses Gobineau's life, voyages, diplomatic career, and writings in a colorful and poignantly moral, social, and literary portrait.

Gobineau, Arthur, Comte de. *The Inequality of Human Races.* Preface by George L. Mosse. New York: H. Fertig, 1999. A reprint of the original 1915 translation by Adrian Collins, including an informative preface, bibliographical references, and an index.

Valette, Rebecca. *Arthur de Gobineau and the Short Story.* Chapel Hill: University of North Carolina Press, 1969. For literature aficionados, the introduction is an excellent synopsis of the life, thought, and literary techniques of a master storyteller.

—*Patricia J. Siegel*

SEE ALSO: Houston Stewart Chamberlain; Julius Evola; Elisabeth Förster-Nietzsche; Winifred Wagner.

NATHURAM VINAYAK GODSE
Hindu nationalist assassin

BORN: May 19, 1910; Baramati, India
DIED: November 15, 1949; New Delhi, India
MAJOR OFFENSE: Assassination of Indian independence leader Mohandas Gandhi
ACTIVE: January 30, 1948
LOCALE: Birla House, New Delhi, India
SENTENCE: Death by hanging

EARLY LIFE
Nathuram Vinayak Godse (NAHTH-ew-rahm VIHN-ah-yahk GAWD-say) grew up in a strict Brahman family in colonial India in the Poona District of Maharashtra. His father was employed in the post office, where he earned fifteen rupees a month. Godse began his primary education at Barainatri, but after completing the fourth grade he moved to Poona, a larger city, to live with an aunt and study in an English-language school. As a student, Nathuram developed a strong interest in politics and oratory and was noted for his ability to memorize long Marathi (the local language) poems. While still a youngster, Nathuram saved the life of an untouchable (the lowest caste) child who had fallen into a well, an

event that might have influenced his later becoming a strong opponent of the caste system.

POLITICAL CAREER
In 1929, Godse's father was transferred to the coastal town of Ratnagiri, where he moved his family. There Nathuram dropped out of high school and became a disciple of a Hindu scholar and revolutionary, Veer Savarkar, whom the government had just released from confinement in Ratnagiri because of his advocacy of armed rebellion to liberate India from the British. Godse become an activist with a political party espousing Hindu nationalism, the Hindu Mahasabha, and started a Marathi newspaper, *Agrani* (later called *Hindurashtra*), for that organization. He settled in Poona, traveled widely with Savarkar, wrote articles for newspapers, and swayed crowds with his fiery speeches.

Godse also was active in the Rashtriya Swayamsevak Sangh (R.S.S.), a fundamentalist Hindu organization that sought to protect the Hindu masses from "cultural invasions" and to protect and advance Hindu civilization.

The R.S.S. was especially opposed to the separatist politics of the All India Muslim League.

Godse soon became a devoted follower of Mohandas Gandhi, one of the principal figures in the movement for Indian independence, and participated in Gandhi's campaigns of civil disobedience. After leading a "passive resistance" demonstration in Hyderabad in 1938, Godse was arrested and imprisoned for one year. Gandhi and Godse had some characteristics in common. Both were extreme ascetics pledged to celibacy, although Godse admitted to enjoying two luxuries in life: coffee and Perry Mason films.

As India moved toward independence after World War II, Godse and his mentor Savarkar criticized what they believed to be Gandhi's sacrificing of Hindu interests in efforts to appease minority groups. They blamed Gandhi for the partition of India, even though he had strongly opposed it. In scathing articles in *Hindurashtra*, Godse condemned Gandhi for his "pro-Muslim bias" and even found fault with the doctrine of *ahimsa*, or nonviolence.

The massive population exchange of Hindus and Muslims between the new nations of India and Pakistan resulted in violence and bloodshed. Godse and his allies blamed Gandhi for the deaths of hundreds of thousands of Hindus in this exodus and demanded revenge.

On January 13, 1948, Gandhi announced that he would fast to the death unless the Indian government paid Pakistan 550 million rupees (a sum that had been specified in the partition agreement but the Indian government had refused to pay because of the ongoing war in the disputed state of Kashmir). The Indian government immediately agreed to pay, a decision that infuriated Godse and his cohorts. Gandhi's hunger strike also caused divisions within the ruling Indian Congress Party as well as the general public. Refugees whose families had been killed in the partition chanted "Let him die!" outside Gandhi's lodging.

Godse decided to assassinate Gandhi as the Mahatma made his way to evening prayers at Birla House, the mansion of an industrialist millionaire in New Delhi. On January 30, 1948, as Gandhi made his way through a garden to the prayer grounds, Godse approached him and, after making obeisance, shot him three times at close range with a Beretta pistol.

LEGAL ACTION AND OUTCOME

The assassin did not try to escape and was immediately arrested. Seven other men, including Savarkar, were rounded up and, along with Godse, tried for conspiracy.

Godse claimed sole responsibility for the politically motivated murder. During his trial before a three-judge court, Godse read for five hours a ninety-page treatise justifying his decision to kill Gandhi as a moral, though illegal, act. He was condemned to die and was hanged in the courtyard of Ambala prison on November 15, 1949. Savarkar was acquitted for lack of evidence.

Millions of Indians mourned Gandhi's assassination. Rioters attacked Hindu activists in Maharashtra, and the R.S.S. was banned for a year, even though there was no evidence that the organization was involved in Godse's plot. Godse's writings explaining his motives for killing Gandhi were subsequently banned by the government of India for many years.

IMPACT

In 1951, Hindu nationalists organized a political wing that eventually became the Bharatiya Janata Party (BJP) in 1980. The BJP ruled India in 1996 and again from 1998 to 2004, when it was defeated by a revived Congress Party. Fundamentalist Hindus played a larger role in the new political climate, and historical revisionists reevaluated Nathuram Vinayak Godse's place in Indian history. In July, 1998, a Marathi drama titled *I, Nathuram Godse Speaking* opened in Mumbai and was shortly thereafter banned by the government. The play, based on Godse's defense in court, highlighted what many observers believe was a deepening struggle over the meaning of Gandhi's principles. Passive resistance had been replaced by nuclear arms; relations between India and Pakistan remained strained; secularism had been replaced by Hindu nationalism. After ultraconservative political parties claimed significant power, Godse was no longer dismissed as a fanatic killer.

FURTHER READING

Collins, Larry, and Dominique Lapierre. *Freedom at Midnight*. London: HarperCollins, 1997. A highly readable account of the year 1947, when India gained its freedom from the British Raj. The concluding six chapters give a detailed account of Gandhi's assassination.

Godse, Gopal. "His Principle of Peace Was Bogus." *Time Asia* 155, no. 6 (February 14, 2000). The brother of the assassin and coconspirator in Gandhi's assassination, who was sentenced to life imprisonment but released after eighteen years, talks about the murder, without regret.

Godse, Nathuram. *Why I Assassinated Mahatma Gandhi*. Delhi, India: Surya Bharti, 2003. The impassioned courtroom plea of the assassin, long banned in India.

Khosla, Gopal Das. *Murder of the Mahatma and Other Cases from a Judge's Notebook.* Bombay: Jaico, 1968. The former chief justice of the Punjab High Court in India reminisces about ten cases, including the trial of Godse for the murder of Gandhi.

Wolpert, Stanley. *Nine Hours to Rama.* New York: Ran-

dom House, 1962. A gripping novel based on the nine hours leading up to the assassination of Gandhi; another book that was banned in India.

—*Theodore M. Vestal*

SEE ALSO: Reginald Dyer; Thenmuli Rajaratnam; Beant Singh; Satwant Singh; Ramzi Yousef.

JOSEPH GOEBBELS
German Nazi propaganda leader

BORN: October 29, 1897; Rheydt, Germany
DIED: May 1, 1945; Berlin, Germany
ALSO KNOWN AS: Paul Joseph Goebbels (full name); Little Doctor
CAUSE OF NOTORIETY: As a high-ranking official in the Nazi Party, Gobbels was a fanatic supporter of total war and the extermination of Jews.
ACTIVE: 1924-1945
LOCALE: Germany

EARLY LIFE

Joseph Paul Goebbels (GURB-uhls) was born in the small industrial town of Rheydt in Rhineland, Germany. He was the son of devout Roman Catholic, lower-middle-class parents. Although physically handicapped by a crippled foot as a result of illness, Goebbels excelled in school, graduating in 1917. Exempt from military service because of his handicap, he then studied Germanics, literature, and history in five different universities. Goebbels completed his doctorate degree under the guidance of a Jewish professor in Heidelberg. After graduation, his career as a litterateur was a failure: He could not get his plays accepted by a Berlin theater, and he failed to obtain a job as a journalist for the distinguished liberal newspaper *Berliner Tageblatt*. For a few months in 1923, he worked in a bank in Cologne but then concentrated on writing his novel, *Michael*, which was not published until 1929.

NAZI CAREER

Unsuccessful in his literary career, Goebbels found a place within the Nazi movement beginning in the summer of 1924 in Weimar. On August 21, 1924, he established a local outpost of the Nazi movement in München-Gladbach in western Germany. Moreover, he discovered that he was an effective speaker. After editing a small weekly Nazi newspaper in 1924, he joined Gregor Strasser the following year to publish the *National-sozialistischen Briefe* (Nazi letters), a newspaper espousing views from the leftist faction of the Nazis. In November, 1926, Adolf Hitler appointed Goebbels *Gauleiter* (Gau leader) of Berlin, and by the next year Goeb-

Joseph Goebbels. (Library of Congress)

GOEBBELS ARGUES FOR TOTAL WAR

On February 18, 1943, Joseph Goebbels spoke before a specially selected audience to rally the nation after losses on the Russian front. Here is the anti-Semitic nub of his speech:

The paralysis of the Western European democracies before their deadliest threat is frightening. International Jewry is doing all it can to encourage such paralysis. During our struggle for power in Germany, Jewish newspapers tried to conceal the danger, until National Socialism awakened the people. It is just the same today in other nations. Jewry once again reveals itself as the incarnation of evil, as the plastic demon of decay and the bearer of an international culture-destroying chaos. This explains, by the way, our consistent Jewish policies. We see Jewry as a direct threat to every nation. We do not care what other peoples do about the danger. What we do to defend ourselves is our own business, however, and we will not tolerate objections from others. Jewry is a contagious infection. Enemy nations may raise hypocritical protests against our measures against Jewry and cry crocodile tears, but that will not stop us from doing that which is necessary. Germany, in any event, has no intention of bowing before this threat, but rather intends to take the most radical measures. . . .

The war of mechanized robots against Germany and Europe has reached its high point. In resisting the grave and direct threat with its weapons, the German people and its Axis allies are fulfilling in the truest sense of the word a European mission. Our courageous and just battle against this world-wide plague will not be hindered by the worldwide outcry of International Jewry. It can and must end only with victory. . . .

Total war is the demand of the hour. . . . The time has come to remove the kid gloves and use our fists. We can no longer make only partial and careless use of the war potential at home and in the significant parts of Europe that we control. We must use our full resources, as quickly and thoroughly as it is organizationally and practically possible. Unnecessary concern is wholly out of place. . . . Those who today do not understand that will thank us tomorrow on bended knees that we courageously and firmly took on the task.

Source: Joseph Goebbels, "Nun, Volk steh auf, and Sturm brich los! Rede im Berliner Sportpalast," in *Der steile Augsteig* (Munich, Germany: Zentraverlag der NSDAP, 1944). Translated by Randall Bytwerk for the German Propaganda Archive, http://www.calvin.edu/academic/cas/gpa.

leader. This new position gave him power not only over propaganda but also over all cultural facets of German society and mass media. On September 22, 1933, Goebbels organized the Reichskulturkammer (Reich Chamber of Culture), which was divided into separate chambers devoted to radio, press, literature, music, films, and theater. Anyone denied membership in one of the professional chambers was then barred from his or her profession. In effect, this allowed Goebbels to control the news, the arts, and films in Germany and helped him purge Jews from these fields. Also in 1933, he organized the April 1 boycott of Jews in Germany, and in May of that year, he orchestrated a massive burning of undesirable books by Jews and Marxists. In 1937 and 1938, he viciously attacked the Catholic clergy and monks for alleged moral and financial violations.

Goebbels was also in charge of the Winter Relief Program, which provided food and heating material to the needy. The funds for this program were raised by massive public donation drives initiated in the fall of each year. Goebbels and the Nazi regime used these campaigns both to generate and to measure public support for the regime.

On November 9, 1938, Goebbels convinced Hitler to unleash a violent attack on Jews, allegedly as a retaliation for the murder of a German official in Paris by a Jewish youth. Addressing party leaders gathered in Munich to commemorate the Beer Hall Putsch of 1923, Goebbels launched a poisonous attack on Jews. After the meeting, party formations throughout Germany launched a vicious attack on Jewish businesses and synagogues during what came to be known as the *Kristallnacht* (the night of broken glass). Windows of Jewish businesses were smashed, synagogues were burned, and a number of Jews were murdered.

During World War II, Goebbels strove to remove all Jews from Berlin, and he supported the "final solution"

bels launched another weekly, *Der Angriff* (the Attack), in Berlin in order to expand the party's influence. Because of Goebbels's propaganda successes, in 1930 Hitler then named him Reich propaganda leader of the party, a position Goebbels used both to advance the Nazi cause in elections and to help create the "Hitler myth" of a caring and dedicated national leader.

On May 10, 1933, barely six weeks after Hitler became chancellor of Germany, Goebbels was appointed Reich minister for public enlightenment and propaganda while still retaining his post as Nazi Party propaganda

to the Jewish problem implemented by Hitler and Heinrich Himmler. In early 1943, he published an article in his paper *Das Reich* (the Reich) in which he admitted that the annihilation of Jews was a Nazi goal. On February 18, 1943, he launched a massive propaganda campaign for total war, which not only helped to prolong the war but also ensured that the mass murder of Jews would continue.

During this time, Goebbels repaired the damage that his affair with a Czech actress had caused to his relationship with Hitler, who adored Goebbels's wife, Magda. He also played a critical role on July 20, 1944, in helping to crush the attempted coup by Klaus von Stauffenberg and some German officers who had attempted to kill Hitler.

Goebbels was appointed general plenipotentiary for total war in July, 1944, with enormous powers to harness the population to the war effort. During the last weeks of the war, he moved his family into Hitler's bunker complex. On May l, 1945, one day after Hitler's death and after having already poisoned his six children, Goebbels and his wife also committed suicide.

IMPACT

Joseph Goebbels played a crucial role in helping Hitler gain total control over German culture, and he purged Jews from the arts and entertainment industry after 1933. His anti-Semitism and his tight control over all artistic expression in Germany helped create an atmosphere in Germany that made it possible for the Nazis to commit terrible atrocities against Jews, homosexuals, and other minorities.

FURTHER READING

Fröhlich, Elke. "Joseph Goebbels, the Propagandist." In *The Nazi Elite*, edited by Ronald Smelser and Rainer Zittelmann, translated by Mary Fischer. New York: New York University Press, 1993. A short, perceptive summary of Goebbels's career by the editor of Goebbels's massive diaries, which are available only in German. Includes a convenient bibliography of primary and secondary sources.

Knopp, Guido. *Hitler's Henchmen*. Translated by Angus McGeoch. London: Sutton, 2000. Includes a chapter on Goebbels, which offers numerous interviews with his associates and other contemporaries. A documentary film version is available from cable television's History Channel.

Lemmons, Russel. *Goebbels and Der Angriff*. Lexington: University Press of Kentucky, 1994. Demonstrates how Goebbels used the newspaper *Der Angriff* successfully for propaganda in Berlin in order to expand Nazi influence.

Reuth, Ralf Georg. *Goebbels*. Translated by Krishna Winston. New York: Harcourt Brace, 1993. Using Goebbels's complete diaries, this account by a journalist attributes Goebbels's behavior to his frustrations in childhood and adolescence. The author maintains that Goebbels's propaganda was crucial for the Nazi triumph.

—*Johnpeter Horst Grill*

SEE ALSO: Klaus Barbie; Adolf Eichmann; Magda Goebbels; Hermann Göring; Rudolf Hess; Reinhard Heydrich; Heinrich Himmler; Adolf Hitler; Alfred Jodl; Josef Mengele; Joachim von Ribbentrop.

MAGDA GOEBBELS
Prominent Nazi

BORN: November 11, 1901; Berlin, Germany
DIED: May 1, 1945; Berlin, Germany
ALSO KNOWN AS: First Lady of the Third Reich; Johanna Maria Magdalena Goebbels (full name); Magda Rietschel (birth name); Magda Ritschel (also spelled this way for birth name)
CAUSE OF NOTORIETY: Held up by Hitler as the wife and mother of the premier family of the Third Reich, Goebbels was a powerful force in spreading Nazi propaganda. As Germany's defeat in World War II loomed, she murdered her six children in Hitler's bunker.
ACTIVE: 1930's-1945
LOCALE: Germany

EARLY LIFE

Magda Goebbels (MAHG-duh GURB-uhlz) was born on November 11, 1901, in Berlin, Germany, to Auguste Behrend and Oskar Rietschel. Her mother was a servant to a private family, and her father was an engineer. Magda's parents divorced when she was three years old, and two years later her mother married Richard Friedlander, a Jewish man who would later die in a Nazi concentration camp. After the marriage, Magda was sent to live with her father in Cologne. Rietschel took her to Brussels, and she was enrolled in the Ursuline convent of Sacré Cœur, an extremely strict Catholic boarding school. Goebbels's mother and stepfather moved to Brussels as well and lived there until the outbreak of World War I, at which point all Germans were deported and the family was relocated temporarily to a refugee camp in East Prussia. During the war, the highly intelligent and precocious Magda became deeply interested in Buddhism.

After World War I, she returned to Berlin, where she attended Kollmorgen Lycée, followed by the prestigious Holzhausen Ladies' College near Goslar, Germany. While in school, she met industrialist Günther Quandt, a millionaire who was nearly twice her age. Magda dropped out of college to marry Quandt on January 4, 1921. The marriage lasted until 1929, and the couple had one son, Harald, who would be Magda's only child to survive World War II.

CRIMINAL CAREER

Encouraged by a friend to attend a Nazi rally, Magda Quandt became spellbound by the attractive, charis-matic, and engaging speaker, Joseph Goebbels. Although she was not particularly interested in politics, Goebbels joined the Nazi Party on September 1, 1930, and began volunteering where needed, quickly being promoted from the local branch to party headquarters. She became the secretary of Dr. Hans Meinshausen, who was a close associate of Joseph Goebbels. Once thoroughly ensconced in the party, Magda acquired a reputation as a valuable presence and attracted the attention of top officials, including Goebbels and Adolf Hitler.

Because Hitler would not marry, partly because his vast support and admiration came from German women, he arranged for Magda and Joseph Goebbels to wed, promoting the Goebbelses as Germany's premier family and thus elevating Magda Goebbels to the status of the first lady of the Third Reich. The Goebbelses were married December 19, 1931, in Mecklenberg, Germany, with Hitler serving as their witness. Magda willingly did anything that would win her favor with Hitler. She was quoted as saying "Love is meant for husbands, but my love for Hitler is greater, I would give my life for it. . . . [W]hen it became clear Hitler can love no woman, but as they say, only Germany, I consented to the marriage with Dr. Goebbels, because I can be close to the Führer."

The Goebbelses, in fact, did not have a loving marriage, partially because of Joseph's notorious womanizing. At one point Magda asked Hitler to grant her a divorce but was refused. Although it is reported by eyewitnesses and close friends that Magda did not agree with the philosophy of her husband and the Nazis, she fulfilled her title and position perfectly and, in doing so, promoted Nazi propaganda and agendas.

In 1945, with the Russian army closing in, Magda, Joseph, and their six young children, who ranged in age from four through twelve, took refuge in Hitler's underground bunker in Berlin. With defeat at hand, Hilter and his recent bride, Eva Braun, committed suicide on April 30. The next day, May 1, Goebbels drugged her five daughters and one son with morphine. While the children were in a drug-induced sleep, she fed them cyanide capsules, killing them all. She was said to have reverted to her Buddhist beliefs before killing her children, believing that because they died innocent, they would be born into a better life through reincarnation. Goebbels had talked of killing her children in the event of Germany's fall in the months leading up to that day—refusing offers to smuggle the children out of Germany. Bruises on the eldest daughter suggested that she might have resisted her mother's plan.

Accounts vary regarding how the Goebbelses killed themselves. Some say they, too, took cyanide capsules and then had Schutzstaffel (SS) troops shoot them. Others say they were shot with machine guns at their request, and still others say they shot each other. Their bodies were found in an open field above the bunker, partially burned. Their bodies, along with their children's, were cremated and scattered over the Elbe River.

IMPACT

The shock that followed the discovery of the murdered Goebbels children added to the horrors of the Holocaust. The murders affected Germans and non-Germans alike on a basic human level, causing them to wonder what could cause an educated woman from a good family to lose herself so completely in Hitler's ideology and, more haunting, how she was able to commit the inconceivable act of murdering her own children.

Magda Goebbels's crime strengthened Germany's and Europe's resolve to create and uphold strict laws regulating neo-Fascist and neo-Nazi policies, including banning the publication and distribution of materials deemed pro-Fascist or pro-Nazi and creating very harsh laws against denying that the Holocaust occurred.

Theories behind what led Goebbels to murder her children have become the foci of many books and films, as well as psychological studies. She has been the subject of several books about Hitler and the Holocaust and the subject of many biographies. In film, Magda Goebbels has been portrayed by Corinna Harfouch, Barbara Jef-

ford, Piper Laurie, Eva Mattes, Hanna Schygulla, Emma Buckley, and Elke Sommer.

FURTHER READING

Klabunde, Anja. *Magda Goebbels*. New York: Time Warner Trade, 2004. Klabunde's well-researched account of Goebbels's life traces how an extremely intelligent and well connected woman fell so deeply into the propaganda consuming Nazi Germany.

Knopp, Guido. *Hitler's Women*. New York: Routledge, 2003. A detailed look at the lives of Goebbels and five other women closely associated with Adolf Hitler and the Nazis.

Meisner, Hans-Otto. *Magda Goebbels: First Lady of the Third Reich*. New York: The Dial Press, 1980. A comprehensive biography of Goebbels, beginning with her childhood and continuing with her involvement in the Nazi Party. Well researched and filled with first-person accounts.

Sayer, Ian, and Douglas Botting. *The Women Who Knew Hitler: The Private Life of Adolf Hitler*. New York: Carroll & Graf, 2004. Filled with eyewitness testimonies, interrogation reports, and government documents, this work examines the personal dimension of the Nazi Party.

Sigmund, Anna Maria. *Women of the Third Reich*. Richmond Hill, Ont.: NDE, 2000. A personal look at the top women of the Nazi Party. The book explores their involvement in the movement and the circumstances that led them there.

—*Sara Vidar*

SEE ALSO: Eva Braun; Joseph Goebbels; Adolf Hitler.

BERNHARD GOETZ
Accused assailant

BORN: 1947; Kew Gardens, Queens, New York
ALSO KNOWN AS: Bernie Goetz; Subway Vigilante; Bernhard Hugo Goetz (full name)
MAJOR OFFENSE: Unlawful possession of a firearm
ACTIVE: December 22, 1984
LOCALE: New York City subway car
SENTENCE: One year in prison; served approximately eight months

EARLY LIFE

Born in Queens to German immigrant parents, Bernhard Goetz (gehtz) was raised in rural Rhinebeck, north of New York City. His father was a strict disciplinarian. For a time Goetz attended private school in Switzerland with one of his sisters. He graduated from New York University with a degree in engineering and worked as a nuclear engineer on submarines.

In New York City in 1981, three men mugged Goetz, who was injured during the assault. He soon applied for a gun permit but was denied. Nevertheless, Goetz managed to purchase a gun.

THE SUBWAY SHOOTINGS

On December 22, 1984, four young black men, Barry Allen, Troy Canty, James Ramseur, and Darrell Cabey, were riding the subway to an arcade where they intended to steal money from video game machines. Goetz entered the subway and sat near the four. Two of the men approached Goetz and asked for, or demanded, five dollars. Goetz asked them to repeat themselves, and Canty ordered Goetz to give him five dollars. Goetz responded by pulling a .38-caliber five-shot Smith & Wesson pistol from his jacket. He hit each man once and left a bullet in the subway car wall. When Goetz saw Cabey moving on the seat where he landed, he walked toward Cabey and said, "You don't look too bad; here, have another," and pulled the trigger, aiming at Cabey's stomach. There were no bullets left in the gun.

LEGAL ACTION AND OUTCOME

Goetz fled the subway, rented a car, and drove to Vermont, where he buried the gun. On December 31, 1984, he turned himself in to police in Concord, New Hampshire. All four of the men survived their wounds, but Cabey was permanently brain-damaged. As the media attention on him grew, Goetz became a divisive figure, regarded by some as a hero and by some as a racist. Goetz

admitted to the shooting, arguing that his actions were in self-defense. The four men maintained they were panhandling for money to play video games.

In the months leading up to the trial, false and leaked information was published in several newspapers. Goetz did not testify during his eight-month trial, which attracted national attention. In 1987, a jury acquitted Goetz of attempted murder and assault charges but convicted him of criminal possession of an unlicensed weapon.

During an interview with a reporter after the criminal trial, Cabey admitted to approaching Goetz because Goetz appeared to be an easy target. Goetz demonstrated no remorse when he testified about the shooting during the civil trial more than a decade after the incident. In April, 1996, Cabey was awarded $43 million in damages by a jury that found that Goetz had acted recklessly and

Bernhard Goetz. (AP/Wide World Photos)

deliberately inflicted emotional distress. Soon after, Goetz declared bankruptcy.

IMPACT

Bernhard Goetz gained notoriety as a symbol of "white fright" during a time when crime plagued New York City. Once the fanfare around the shooting incident diminished, he periodically appeared in public. He even ran (unsuccessfully) for New York City mayor in 2001 and for public advocate in 2005. His mayoral platform included a call for vegetarian meal options in all city-funded facilities and the decriminalization of marijuana.

On the twentieth anniversary of the shootings, Goetz appeared on Larry King's cable television show, where he put the shooting within the context of New York City's precipitous reduction in crime during the 1990's. He also appeared in several B movies and eventually opened a business selling and repairing electronic equipment through his "Vigilante Electronics" company, operated from his New York City apartment. While Cabey remains confined to a wheelchair, each of the other three men who were shot has committed serious crimes since the 1984 shooting.

FURTHER READING

Fletcher, G. *A Crime of Self-Defense: Bernhard Goetz and the Law on Trial*. Chicago: University Of Chicago Press, 1990. The author, a law professor at Columbia University, presents an objective legal examination of the case and explores the meaning and implications of self-defense.

Gladwell, Malcolm. *The Tipping Point*. New York: Back Bay Books, 2002. Chapter 4 of this work about how small changes can lead to large results is titled "The Power of Context: Bernie Goetz and the Rise and Fall of New York City Crime."

Lesley, Mark. *Subway Gunman: A Juror's Account of the Bernard Goetz Trial*. Latham, N.Y.: British American, 1988. Written by a juror at Goetz's trial, this work describes the evidence presented during the trial and the jury's decision-making process.

—*Gennifer Furst*

SEE ALSO: John E. du Pont; Marc Lépine; Byron Looper; Leslie Nelson; Yolanda Saldívar; Charles Whitman.

EMMA GOLDMAN
American anarchist

BORN: June 27, 1869; Kovno, Lithuania, Russian
  Empire (now Kaunas, Lithuania)
DIED: May 14, 1940; Toronto, Ontario, Canada
ALSO KNOWN AS: Mrs. E. Brady; Miss E. G. Smith;
  Mrs. Niedermann; Red Emma
MAJOR OFFENSES: Inciting a riot, publicizing birth
  control, conspiring to violate the Draft Act,
  immigration code violations
ACTIVE: October 17, 1893; August, 1914; July 9,
  1917; November, 1919
LOCALE: United States
SENTENCE: One-year term at Blackwell's Island
  Penitentiary; 15 days in the Queens County
  Penitentiary; two-year term in the Missouri
  Penitentiary at Jefferson City; deportation from
  Ellis Island

EARLY LIFE

Born in Kovno, Russia (now Kaunas, Lithuania), to Abraham and Taube Goldman, Emma Goldman (GOHLD-man) grew up during a period of political repression fol-

lowing the assassination of Czar Alexander II. Her father moved his family first to Köninsberg, East Prussia (now Kalingrad, Russia), and then to St. Petersburg, Russia. There Goldman took a job in a factory. Revolutionary sentiment was spreading throughout the region, and Goldman was introduced to revolutionary ideas at her workplace. Reading Nicolay Chernyshevsky's *Chto delat'* (1863; *What Is to Be Done?*, c. 1863) aroused her interest in anarchical ideas.

She was fifteen when her father decided that she should marry. In opposition to his wishes, she decided to accompany her sister Helena to the United States, and together they journeyed to Rochester, New York, to live with another sister, Lena. Goldman quickly discovered that life for laborers in the United States was little better than in Russia. She took a job working for $2.50 per day in a factory but soon discovered that the factory owner sexually harassed the women he employed. She took another job, and soon her parents arrived from Russia, and Goldman went to live with them. She became engaged to Jacob Kersner, a boarder in her parents' home. The two married, but Kersner was sexually impotent, and Goldman divorced him within a year. She left for New York City, but Kersner followed her and persuaded her to remarry him. She returned to Rochester with him, but their second marriage was also short-lived.

ANARCHIST CAREER

In 1889, Goldman began her career as a political activist and anarchist upon her second arrival in New York City. She went immediately to Sach's Café, a gathering place for radicals. There she met Alexander Berkman, and later, Johann Most. Most recognized Goldman's talent, taught her oratorical skills, and encouraged her to write. Goldman began an affair with Berkman, which would result in a lifelong attachment. When Berkman decided to kill Henry Clay Frick in the aftermath of the Homestead Steel Mills strike, Goldman supported his decision. Berkman wrote to her that he needed a gun for the assassination, and she decided to sell her body to raise the needed funds. Her attempt at prostitution was a failure, but she borrowed the requested fifteen dollars to buy the gun and sent it to him. Like Goldman's prostitution career, Berkman's attempt to kill Frick failed, and Berkman was sentenced to fourteen years in prison. While he was in prison, Goldman visited him, posing as a Mrs. Niedermann, his sister.

Goldman was evicted from her apartment in the wake of Berkman's conviction, but she continued to speak, defending Berkman and actually horsewhipping Most in public for criticizing him. In 1893, after addressing a large crowd in New York, she was arrested and convicted of inciting a riot, even though no riot had occurred. She served a one-year sentence at Blackwell's Island Penitentiary. After her release, she began a liaison with Ed Brady, traveling to Europe on a passport that listed her as Mrs. Ed Brady. In 1899, a Czech anarchist, Hippolyte Havel, became Goldman's new lover.

In 1901, a Polish immigrant named Leon Czolgosz shot and killed President William McKinley. Czolgosz said he had been inspired to assassinate the president by one of Goldman's speeches. The police tried to implicate Goldman in the murder but were unable to do so because of lack of evidence. Goldman expressed sympathy for Czolgosz, and then suddenly found that she could not find work or even rent a room in New York City. She was forced to live under the assumed name of Miss E. G. Smith.

In 1906, she launched a magazine, *Mother Earth*, which she published from 1906 until 1917. Under the direction of her new lover and manager, Ben Reitman, she

Emma Goldman. (Library of Congress)

engaged in a coast-to-coast speaking tour. She supported birth control rights, presenting a lecture in 1916 that resulted in her arrest and a fifteen-day jail sentence. She never endorsed feminists who were fighting for suffrage, however, as she advocated the overthrow, not modification, of the existing government.

LEGAL ACTION AND OUTCOME

In 1917, shortly after the United States entered World War I, she and Berkman established the No-Conscription League to support young men who had refused military service. Goldman was arrested and charged with inducing "persons not to register" for conscription. She was brought to trial, found guilty, and sentenced to two years in the Missouri State Penitentiary located in Jefferson City.

Shortly after her release in 1919, Goldman was targeted for deportation during the Red Scare. Along with Berkman and more than two hundred others who were considered subversives, she was deported to the Soviet Union, leaving on the USS *Buford* on December 21, 1919. After her arrival in the Soviet Union, Goldman soon discovered that the Bolshevik Revolution had not brought freedom to the Russian people. Within two years, she left that country, living and writing in various

THE HAYMARKET RIOT

The Haymarket Riot triggered the radicalization of Emma Goldman: May, 1886, was a momentous month for the American labor movement. On May 4 in Chicago's Haymarket Square, police attempted to disperse a group of workers demonstrating for labor causes when a dynamite bomb was thrown into the crowd. The blast killed seven police officers. In the resulting melee with the crowd, later known as the Haymarket Riot, the police shot and killed a number of demonstrators. More than one hundred people were injured. This bloodshed precipitated a wave of antiradicalism in the United States.

Five men were arrested for the bomb murder of several Chicago policemen during the riot. Four were executed, and the fifth committed suicide, in 1887. Goldman found inspiration in the story of martyred radicals: What especially angered her was that the authorities never ascertained who threw the bomb, making it seem clear that the men who had been arrested were really being tried for their beliefs. If injustices similar to those that occurred in Russia could also take place in the United States, reasoned Goldman, it was time for her to align herself with the opponents of capitalism and of its tools, the state and the church.

European nations until she finally settled in the French village of Saint-Tropez, where she wrote her autobiography. In 1934, Goldman returned to the United States for a ninety-day book tour. She traveled to Canada in 1939, where she suffered a massive stroke and died on May 14, 1940. Her body was buried in Chicago near the Haymarket Square martyrs in Waldheim Cemetery.

IMPACT

Emma Goldman was notorious for her methods as an anarchist and proto-feminist during her time, but today she is applauded as a freethinker and a woman perhaps ahead of her time. Above all, she was an iconoclastic critic of modern society, bringing anarchistic ideas into the discussion of culture during the heyday of anarchism in the United States.

Goldman wrote several books documenting her political and social thought, including *Anarchism and Other Essays* (1910), *The Social Significance of the Modern Drama* (1914), *My Disillusionment in Russia* (1923), and *Living My Life* (1931). She took her ideas to Americans of all classes across the continent and provided an insightful critique of early Soviet government. She has been criticized for her lack of commitment to feminism; nonetheless, her critiques of male domination were reexamined during the second wave of feminism in the 1960's. She inspired the founding of the American Civil Liberties Union, and she remains one of the most flamboyant original thinkers and orators of the late nineteenth and early twentieth centuries.

FURTHER READING

Falk, Candace Serena. *Love, Anarchy, and Emma Goldman.* New York: Holt, Rinehart & Winston, 1984. Reveals a woman searching for a love that mirrored her vision of social and economic freedom.

Goldman, Emma. *Anarchism and Other Essays.* 1910. Reprint. Mineola, N.Y.: Dover, 1969. Essays on anarchism, direct action, the prison system, and woman suffrage, among other topics.

_____. *Living My Life.* 1931. Reprint. New York: Da Capo Press, 1970. Traces Goldman's life from her arrival in New York City in 1889 to her disillusionment with the Bolshevik government in Russia.

Zinn, Howard. *Emma.* Cambridge, Mass.: South End Press, 2002. Focuses on Goldman's U.S. crusade against marriage and in favor of birth control.

—*Yvonne Johnson*

SEE ALSO: Leon Czolgosz; Nicola Sacco; Bartolomeo Vanzetti.

BARUCH GOLDSTEIN
Brooklyn-born Israeli doctor

BORN: December 9 or 12, 1956; Brooklyn, New York
DIED: February 25, 1994; Hebron, West Bank, Israel
ALSO KNOWN AS: Baruch Kappel Goldstein (full name)
CAUSE OF NOTORIETY: Goldstein, who was killed before he could be brought to trial, is believed responsible for the deaths of 29 Arab worshipers and the injury of 125 others in a shooting attack.
ACTIVE: February 25, 1994
LOCALE: Cave of the Patriarchs, Hebron, West Bank, Israel

EARLY LIFE

Baruch Goldstein (bah-ROOK GOHLD-steen) was raised in an Orthodox Jewish family in Brooklyn, New York, and attended Yeshiva University and Albert Einstein Medical School. He was one of the original members of a group called the Jewish Defense League, which was founded by Rabbi Meir Kahane to protect Jews from violent assaults in their Brooklyn neighborhoods. Goldstein moved to Israel and served as a doctor in the army there. After army service, he continued to work as a doctor (as part of a terrorist attack response team) and lived in the city of Kiryat Arba, located next to Hebron on the West Bank.

TERRORIST CAREER

Goldstein had no previous criminal record. In the weeks leading up to the incident at the Cave of the Patriarchs—a biblical burial site in Hebron where both Jews and Arabs regularly pray—there were numerous indications of an impending attack by Arabs on Jewish worshipers in the cave. The preceding months were also filled with Arab terrorist attacks on Jews within Israel, especially in the area where Goldstein lived. As part of his emergency medical work, he was often one of the first on the scene of such attacks. There are news photographs of him attending to victims in a concentrated effort to save their lives.

On February 5, 1994 (coinciding with the Jewish holiday of Purim, which commemorates Jewish resistance to persecution in ancient Persia), Goldstein entered the Cave of the Patriarchs. According to a commission report issued by then-president of the Israel Supreme Court, Justice Meir Shamgar, Goldstein was wearing an army uniform and began shooting. After being subdued, Goldstein was then killed by the Arab worshipers present at the time of his act. A pathologist's report indicated that Goldstein died of a smashed skull from numerous blows to his head. Eyewitness reports confirm that Goldstein's rifle was wrested away from him and that he was attacked by ten Arabs who used metal poles and a fire extinguisher to beat him to death.

It has been reported that the metal detector at the Arab entrance point to the Cave of the Patriarchs had been damaged the night before the shooting and that eight hundred Arab men and women were present that morning. Only a small percentage of the men were searched for weapons when they entered, and three weapons other than Goldstein's gun were subsequently found at the scene, including one wrapped in an Arab keffiya (headscarf). Some speculated that Goldstein may have actually been trying to preempt a rumored attack by Arabs against Jewish worshipers in the same place on the same day. The terrorist organization Hamas had circulated a leaflet to Arab residents of Hebron advising them to stock up on basic supplies in light of a predicted curfew that would likely follow a massive attack on the Jews. A commission of inquiry was established, called the Shamgar Commission, which found that Goldstein acted on his own; the case was never adjudicated in a court of law. No Arabs were ever charged or prosecuted for Goldstein's murder.

IMPACT

An immediate government and media uproar (both in Israel and abroad) followed the events at the Cave of the Patriarchs. There were also numerous riots, and an additional thirty people were killed during the next week. Most mainstream commentators condemned the act, classifying it as a terrorist incident. Some of the circumstances, however, continued to be unclear. For example, in the weeks preceding the incident, there were numerous documented Arab threats to the lives of Jews praying at the Cave of the Patriarchs.

Baruch Goldstein's burial site is in Kiryat Arba and has become a shrine for those sympathetic with his right-wing views, although the Israeli government has attempted to dismantle the site because of ongoing controversy; in particular, authorities have said that they would like to revise the laudatory inscription on his tombstone.

FURTHER READING

Juergensmeyer, Mark. *Terror in the Mind of God: The Global Rise of Religious Violence.* Berkeley: University of California Press, 2000. A comparative analysis of the use of violence by fringe elements of groups from five major religions, including Judaism.

Shahak, Israel, and Norton Mezvinsky. *Jewish Fundamentalism in Israel*. London: Pluto Press, 1999. Promotes the thesis that Jewish fundamentalist attitudes toward non-Jews and sovereignty over the land of Israel helped some to try to justify Yitzhak Rabin's assassination and Goldstein's attack at the Cave of the Patriarchs in Hebron, Israel.

Simons, Chaim. *Did or Did Not Dr. Baruch Goldstein Massacre Twenty-Nine Arabs?* Kiryat Arba, Israel: Chaim Simons, 2003. A detailed analysis of the political atmosphere and events preceding the Goldstein incident, as well as its aftermath, including the Shamgar Commission report.

—*Eric Metchik*

SEE ALSO: Yigal Amir; Meir Kahane.

HERMANN GÖRING
Commander of the German Luftwaffe and the Four Year Plan

BORN: January 12, 1893; Rosenheim, Germany
DIED: October 15, 1946; Nuremberg, Germany
ALSO KNOWN AS: Hermann Wilhelm Göring (full name); Iron Man
CAUSE OF NOTORIETY: Göring commandeered Jewish industries, plundered the economies of occupied European countries, and delegated to Reinhard Heydrich the task of planning for the "final solution" to the Jewish question.
ACTIVE: 1936-1945
LOCALE: Europe, mainly Germany
SENTENCE: Death by hanging; committed suicide on the eve of his execution

EARLY LIFE
Hermann Göring (GER-ing) was born January 12, 1893, in Rosenheim, Bavaria. His father was a member of the German consular service, and many of his male ancestors had served in the Prussian bureaucracy over the past two centuries. Between 1905 and 1911, Hermann attended military schools in Karlsruhe and in Berlin and earned a commission in the German army in 1912. During World War I, he served as an infantry officer in 1914 and was then transferred to the German air force. On June 2, 1918, he was awarded the highest German decoration, the Pour le Mérite, for his service as a fighter pilot in the famous Manfred von Richthofen fighter unit. After the war, he spent time in Denmark and Sweden. Göring married a Swedish woman, Karin von Kantzow, on February 3, 1922. After Karin's death, he married Emmy Sonnenmann, an actress, in 1935.

In 1922, Göring returned to Germany and met

Joseph Goebbels, left, and Hermann Göring. (Library of Congress)

Adolf Hitler, the head of the Nazi party in Munich. Disillusioned with postwar Germany and the Versailles Treaty, Göring joined Hitler's movement, was appointed head of the Nazi Sturmabteilung (SA), and participated in Hitler's unsuccessful Beer Hall Putsch in Munich in November, 1923. Wounded in the attempted coup in Munich, he had to flee to Austria and Italy to escape arrest. In the spring of 1925, Göring returned to Sweden, where he was hospitalized and cured of a morphine addiction.

POLITICAL CAREER

After a political amnesty was issued in Germany, Göring returned to that country in 1927 and joined Hitler's party again in Munich. He found employment as a salesman for the Bavarian Motor Works company in Berlin. In early 1928, Hitler visited Berlin and placed Göring on the Nazi Party's election slate for the national election in that year. Elected first to the Reichstag in May, 1928, Göring became president of the Reichstag in July, 1932, after the Nazi Party won a plurality in the election. In that position, he played an important part

---

GÖRING ON AUTHORITY

On April 18, 1946, Gustave Gilbert, a prison psychiatrist, interviewed Hermann Göring in his cell during a break in the Nuremberg Trials. Göring's own trial was not going well, and he was defensive. He claimed that he had never been anti-Semitic and in fact he would have tried to stop the atrocities had he been able. Göring dismissed his own statements to the contrary as unimportant "temperamental utterances" and insisted that he had lacked sufficient power to help the Jews. However, his comments about power grew boastful when concerning the populace in general:

We got around to the subject of war again and I said that, contrary to his attitude, I did not think that the common people are very thankful for leaders who bring them war and destruction.

"Why, of course, the people don't want war," Göring shrugged. "Why would some poor slob on a farm want to risk his life in a war when the best that he can get out of it is to come back to his farm in one piece? Naturally, the common people don't want war; neither in Russia nor in England nor in America, nor for that matter in Germany. That is understood. But, after all, it is the *leaders* of the country who determine the policy and it is always a simple matter to drag the people along, whether it is a democracy or a fascist dictatorship or a Parliament or a Communist dictatorship."

"There is one difference," I pointed out. "In a democracy the people have some say in the matter through their elected representatives, and in the United States only Congress can declare wars."

"Oh, that is all well and good, but, voice or no voice, the people can always be brought to the bidding of the leaders. That is easy. All you have to do is tell them they are being attacked and denounce the pacifists for lack of patriotism and exposing the country to danger. It works the same way in any country."

Source: Gustave Gilbert, *Nuremberg Diary* (New York: Farrar, Straus, 1947).

---

in the Nazi Party's parliamentary maneuvers aimed at undermining the democratic system and obtaining the chancellorship for Hitler.

On January 30, 1933, when Hitler became chancellor of Germany, Göring was rewarded for his service and appointed minister without portfolio and Reich commissioner for the Prussian Ministry of Interior. From 1933 until the end of the Third Reich, Göring accumulated more offices than anyone else in Germany except Heinrich Himmler. By August, 1933, he was appointed Reich minister for air travel and made a general in the infantry. After Germany openly rearmed in 1935, Göring became commander in chief of the Luftwaffe (air force).

On October 18, 1936, he was put in charge of the Four Year Plan, which gave him enormous power over the German economy. After July, 1938, the Hermann Göring Werke (factory) became the largest steel concern in Europe. In December of 1934, Hitler had signed a secret

document that designated Göring his successor in case of Hitler's death, although this was not officially announced until 1939.

Until the Allied bombing offensive against Germany undermined Göring's influence with Hitler, he enthusiastically supported Germany's aggressive expansion between 1938 and 1941. By early 1943, when Allied air attacks increased markedly and the Luftwaffe had failed to supply Germany troops in Stalingrad, Hitler lost all confidence in Göring. Increasingly, Göring became more lethargic and retreated to his Karinhall estate, where he indulged himself. In April, 1945, when Hitler was trapped in his bunker in Berlin, Göring notified him that he would assume power in Germany according to the law of succession. Hitler flew into a rage and removed Göring from all of his offices. In his last will and testament, dictated on April 29, 1945, Hitler officially barred Göring from the Nazi Party and all state offices.

LEGAL ACTION AND OUTCOME

Captured by American troops on May 9, 1945, Göring was tried, convicted, and sentenced to death in Nuremberg in 1946. Hours before his official execution on October 15, 1946, Göring cheated the hangman by taking poison.

IMPACT

Hermann Göring played a part in Hitler's successful rise to power before 1933, and he helped him consolidate his power after January, 1933, particularly in Prussia. Göring established the Gestapo, the secret state police in Prussia, which under Himmler's direction after 1934 played a key role in persecuting political opponents and Jews. Göring played a key role in the murderous purge of the SA and Ernst Röhm in June, 1934. As head of the Luftwaffe and the Four Year Plan, Göring supported Hitler's rearmament and future aggression. In March, 1938, his role was crucial in the invasion and annexation of Austria. Beginning in 1938, with each German expansion Göring's Reichswerke plundered more foreign industry. For his personal pleasure, he also plundered artworks in the conquered areas.

Beginning in 1938, he played a decisive role in "Aryanizing" Jewish property, first in Germany and then in conquered areas. He gained control over the economic expropriation of Germany's and Europe's Jews. At first he favored the expulsion of Germany's Jews to Madagascar or other regions. In July, 1941, he delegated to Reinhard Heydrich, Himmler's deputy, the task of producing a plan for the "final solution" to the Jewish "problem," which he implemented at the infamous Wannsee Conference on January 20, 1942. Göring also colluded with the Schutzstaffel (SS) in recruiting slave labor for his Reichswerke from European countries and SS concentration camps.

FURTHER READING

Knopp, Guido. *Hitler's Henchmen.* Translated by Angus McGeoch. Phoenix Mill, England: Sutton, 2000. Includes a chapter on Göring, based on testimony of eyewitnesses and associates of this major Nazi leader. The author has also produced a documentary film available from the History Channel.

Kube, Alfred. "Herman Göring: Second Man in the 'Third Reich.'" Translated by Mary Fischer. In *The Nazi Elite*, edited by R. Smelser and R. Zitelmann. New York: New York University Press, 1993. A summary of the author's major monograph on Göring in German. Kube views Göring as a conservative authoritarian who supported the role of the state over the Nazi Party.

Lee, Asher. *Goering: Air Leader.* New York: Hippocrene, 1972. The author, who served in the British Air Ministry during World War II, appraises Göring's role as head of the Luftwaffe.

Overy, Richard. *Goering: The "Iron Man."* London: Routledge and Kegan Paul, 1984. Concentrates on Göring's influence over the Luftwaffe (air force) and the economy between 1936 and 1942. The author views him as a dedicated Nazi and not as a mere opportunist.

—*Johnpeter Horst Grill*

SEE ALSO: Klaus Barbie; Karl Dönitz; Adolf Eichmann; Hans Michael Frank; Joseph Goebbels; Magda Goebbels; Rudolf Hess; Reinhard Heydrich; Heinrich Himmler; Adolf Hitler; Alfred Jodl; Josef Mengele; Benito Mussolini; Joachim von Ribbentrop.

JOHN GOTTI
American organized crime boss

BORN: October 27, 1940; New York, New York

DIED: June 10, 2002; Springfield, Missouri

ALSO KNOWN AS: John Joseph Gotti, Jr. (full name); Teflon Don; Dapper Don

MAJOR OFFENSES: Murder, conspiracy, racketeering, robbery, loan-sharking, obstruction of justice, illegal gambling, and tax evasion.

ACTIVE: May, 1969-April, 1992

LOCALE: New York, Queens, and Manhattan, New York

SENTENCE: Life in prison without the possibility of parole

EARLY LIFE

John Gotti (GOT-tee) grew up in a large Italian family, one of thirteen children. He emerged in high school as a student who demonstrated above-average intelligence; however, he showed little interest in academic endeavors. His criminal interests developed early when he initiated a high school gambling operation. He eventually organized his own street gang and was involved in several minor crimes after dropping out of school.

CRIMINAL CAREER

Gotti eventually sought membership in Italian organized crime, also called among insiders La Cosa Nostra (meaning "this thing of ours"). A high-ranking member of Carlo Gambino's crime family, Aniello Dellacroce, eventually served as Gotti's mentor, sponsoring young Gotti as a member of organized crime. Gotti established himself as a regular at popular mob locales, including Bergin Hunt and Fish Club in Queens and the Ravenite Social Club in Manhattan. Gotti initially became a soldier in the Gambino family, serving as a hit man, among other roles. His first major arrest and conviction took place in 1967 for hijacking trucks at New York's Kennedy Airport, and he served half of a seven-year plea-bargain sentence.

Gotti's use of violence escalated during the 1970's and 1980's. He pleaded guilty to the charge of manslaughter of John McBrantney in 1974 and served two

years. The victim was a suspect in the killing of Carlo Gambino's nephew. Gotti then planned several armored-car hijackings during the 1980's. The first robbery netted $300,000; the second, $700,000. Gotti escaped prosecution even though he was recognized by one of the armored-car drivers.

Gotti was charged with assault and robbery in 1984. The victim initially claimed that he was robbed of $325 during an argument over a double-parked car. However, the victim claimed a memory lapse and could not identify Gotti; charges against Gotti were dropped. Next, Gotti was arrested and prosecuted for the murder of John O'Connor; the verdict of not guilty enhanced Gotti's moniker, Teflon Don (in reference to Teflon pans because criminal charges did not "stick" to him).

Gotti represented the blue-collar members of organized crime. His cronies viewed mobster activity in the old Mafia tradition (that is, through the use of robbery, extortion, and murder). His faction resented Paul Cas-

---

"COSA NOSTRA 'TIL I DIE"

The following is taken from an FBI wiretap of Gotti in 1990 as he spoke to his subordinates in an apartment above Manhattan's Ravenite Social Club on Mulberry Street.

I'm not in the mood for the toys, or games, or kidding [unintelligible]. I'm not in the mood for clans. I'm not in the mood for gangs. I'm not in the mood for none of that stuff there. This is gonna be a Cosa Nostra 'til I die. Be it an hour from now, or be it tonight, or a hundred years from now when I'm in jail. It's gonna be a Cosa Nostra. This ain't gonna be a bunch of your friends, they're gonna be friends of ours. But at the same time would be friends of ours, it's gonna be the way I say it's gonna be, [unintelligible] a Cosa Nostra. A Cosa Nostra. You might, because a guy's nice to you, and I'm not talking about you, I'm just sayin' you might [unintelligible] makes him a good guy. It makes him a m***f*** to me. It don't make him a good guy. It makes him a good guy if he's one of us and he proves he's part of us. And I'm the best judge of that, I think, right now.... I wanna see an effort. I gotta see an effort for [unintelligible] a Cosa Nostra. How many of these guys come, come tell me I feel sorry you got trouble. I don't, I don't need that. I ain't got no trouble, I ain't got no trouble. I'm gonna be all right. They got the f***in' trouble. And I don't mean the cops, I mean the people. The people who coulda made this a joke, you know what I mean. That's not a f***in' joke [unintelligible] guys. Even, even, even some guys, some people downstairs now who I know whose f***ing stomach is rotten. I know whose stomach ain't rotten. You could, I, I could smell it the way a dog senses when a guy's got fear.

---

tellano's appointment as head of the Gambino family in 1976; to Gotti and colleagues, Castellano represented the white-collar faction involved in legal business fronts. In addition, Castellano always demanded a lucrative cut of his members' profits. His disdain for direct involvement in street crimes angered those who earned their living the "old-fashioned" way. Gotti's mentor, Dellacroce, was a restraining figure in any attempt to eliminate Castellano, but when Castellano did not attend Dellacroce's funeral in early December, 1985, his display of disrespect angered Gotti and his blue-collar faction. Later that month, Gotti and his cohorts assassinated Castellano in front of Sparks Steak House. Shortly thereafter, the Gambino family greeted Gotti as their new boss.

Gotti reveled in media attention and wore expensive suits (thus his nickname Dapper Don); many in the crime family felt that his arrogant style drew too much attention to the Mafia. An attempt was made to kill Gotti with a car bomb; however, only his underboss, Frank DiCiccio, was killed. After DiCiccio's death, Sammy Gravano became underboss in the Gambino organization.

LEGAL ACTION AND OUTCOME

In the late 1980's, the Federal Bureau of Investigation (FBI) was determined to prosecute the Mafia. The FBI used electronic surveillance to watch Gotti around the clock and collected a great deal of evidence, including that which implicated both Gravano and Gotti in a number of murders. Authorities arrested the men on multiple counts of violating the Racketeer Influenced and Corrupt Organizations (RICO) Act, as well as loan-sharking, conspiracy to commit murder, and murder.

An exhaustive effort by the federal government during the criminal investigation ensured the conviction of Gotti at trial. Moreover, authorities received the help of Gravano, who violated the Mafia's code of Omerta (silence) by serving as a government witness against Gotti. His damaging testimony assured Gotti's last conviction. On April 2, 1991, he received a sentence of life imprisonment at the Federal Maximum Security Penitentiary in Marion, Illinois. Gotti received consecutive, rather than concurrent, sentences for racketeering and murder. Gotti died of throat cancer at the U.S. Medical Center for Federal Prisoners in Springfield, Missouri, in June, 2002.

IMPACT

The death of Paul Castellano and imprisonment of John Gotti disorganized the Gambino crime family. Gotti appointed his son, John, Jr. (known as Junior), and his brother as his heirs apparent. Gotti tried to maintain control of the family's business from inside federal prison, but Junior never measured up to his father's charismatic leadership.

Senior Mafia leadership was reluctant to step forward and seize power. After the successful targeting and prosecution of Gotti, they feared the limelight and media attention one earns as Mafia boss. While Gotti's imprisonment was an important setback for the Gambino family, his leadership holds lasting impact for modern-day Mafia ventures, whose emerging leadership cannot seem to resist the temptation to seize control and maximize organized crime profits.

FURTHER READING

Abadinsky, Howard. *Organized Crime*. Belmont, Calif.: Wadsworth/Thomson Learning, 2006. An in-depth analysis of organized crime from a historical and theoretical perspective.

Lyman, Michael D., and Gary W. Potter. *Organized Crime*. Upper Saddle River, N.J.: Pearson/Prentice Hall, 2004. A comprehensive textbook, including the essentials of organized crime theory and practice.

Mustain, Gene, and Jerry Capeci. *Mob Star: The Story of Gotti*. Royersford, Pa.: Appha Books, 2002. An insightful, popular book on the life and times of Gotti.

—*Thomas E. Baker and James C. Roberts*

SEE ALSO: Paul Castellano; Carlo Gambino; Sammy Gravano.

JAY GOULD

American railroad financier

BORN: May 27, 1836; Roxbury, New York
DIED: December 2, 1892; New York, New York
ALSO KNOWN AS: Jason Gould (full name)
CAUSE OF NOTORIETY: Gould's unscrupulous business practices included insider trading and speculation.
ACTIVE: 1867-1892
LOCALE: Eastern United States

EARLY LIFE

As the sixth child born to John Burr Gould and Mary Moore, Jay Gould (gewld) spent his formative years working on his father's farm and received his education at local schools. At the age of five, his mother died, and as a young adult, Gould held jobs as a clerk and completing county surveys in New York, Ohio, and Michigan. He wrote and published *History of Delaware County and Border Wars of New York* in 1856. A few years later, he started a tannery business with Zadock Pratt in northern Pennsylvania, but by 1859 Gould had bought out his partner. Gould became a leather merchant in New York City for a short time. He then began to speculate in the securities of small railroads such as the Rutland and Washington but later sold them for a large profit. At the height of the Civil War, he became manager of the Rensselaer and Saratoga Railway. He married Helen Day Miller on January 22, 1863, and the couple had six children—four boys and two girls. Described as a taciturn individual, Gould often enjoyed reading, gardening, and spending time with his family on their estate, Lyndhurst, in Tarrytown.

BUSINESS CAREER

Gould's early financial successes opened opportunities for him to meet influential businessmen such as Daniel Drew, who owned and operated the Erie Railroad. Drew soon partnered with Gould and James Fisk to prevent Cornelius Vanderbilt, railroad tycoon and president of the New York Central Railroad, from taking control of the Erie by dumping 100,000 fraudulent shares onto the market in defiance of a court order. Vanderbilt received an arrest warrant, but the three men fled and set up headquarters at Taylor's Hotel in Jersey City. Vanderbilt realized Gould was a shrewd business adversary, and he reluctantly compromised with him on this issue. Subsequently, Drew sold off his shares of the railroad, and Gould became director of the Erie in 1867. Gould bribed prominent New York legislators and received support from the infamous political machine controlled by William "Boss" Tweed and Peter B. Sweeney to validate the illegal shares.

Two years later, Gould and Fisk then conspired with President Ulysses S. Grant's brother-in-law, A. H. Corbin, to corner the gold market. The price of gold specie skyrocketed and then plummeted, causing Black Friday on September 24, 1869. The ramifications of this event were immense. The downfall of Tammany Hall, Fisk's death, and the public outcry over this affair cost Gould his reputation.

Gould then turned to railroad speculation in the West by becoming the director of seventeen major lines and president of five over the next two decades. In 1873, he took control of the Western Telegraph because of the company's lucrative contracts with the railway system, and a year later, he bought the Kansas Pacific and became director of the Union Pacific Railroad. Gould improved the management of the line but sold the Union Pa-

Jay Gould. (Library of Congress)

cific holdings after attempting to build a competing transatlantic line. He continued to expand his power base by assuming ownership of the Manhattan Elevated Railway and *New York World* newspaper from 1879 to 1883. The tycoon then purchased the Wabash and Missouri Pacific, the major railroad network in the Southwest; at one point, he owned 15,800 miles of track in this region. However, the panic of 1884-1885 caused Gould to lose heavily, and he barely avoided bankruptcy. Gould evolved into a man who had to protect his holdings rather than rely on his speculative skills in the marketplace. He died of complications from tuberculosis at the age of fifty-seven, leaving a fortune estimated at $72 million to his children. His eldest son, George Jay, followed his father's example; he became the owner and president of several railways.

IMPACT

Jay Gould was the master of insider trading, exploitation, and stock manipulation. He took advantage of underdeveloped corporate laws and political monopolies that existed during the late nineteenth century. He also became the favorite target of newspaper reporters and political cartoonist Thomas Nast as a person who typified lavish excesses found in American capitalism. His aggressive policy of reducing rates and building extensions for railroad lines caused rate wars, yet such practices paved the way for decreasing costs for passengers and lowered shipping rates. However, the lines were not maintained well and did not provide good customer service, and Gould failed to introduce technological innovation.

FURTHER READING

Ackerman, Kenneth D. *The Gold Ring: Jim Fisk, Jay Gould, and Black Friday, 1869*. New York: Dodd & Mead, 1988. Recounts political and economic events as Gould and Fisk attempted to corner the gold market, which led to Black Friday.

Grodinsky, Julius. *Jay Gould: His Business Career, 1867-1892*. Philadelphia: University of Pennsylvania Press, 1957. Although not a biography of Gould, the book examines the business practices in American capitalism from 1860 to 1900 by showcasing the career and financial schemes of Gould.

Klein, Maury. "In Search of Jay Gould." *Business History Review* 52 (Summer, 1978): 166-199. Examines Gould's image and his business acumen in an era of railroad and oil tycoons.

_____. *The Life and Legend of Jay Gould*. Baltimore: The Johns Hopkins University Press, 1986. A scholarly biography that addresses Gould's private life and business operations. The author reinterprets the Gould image as a robber baron, revealing him to be a complex man.

Renehan, Edward. *Dark Genius of Wall Street: The Misunderstood Life of Jay Gould, King of the Robber Barons*. New York: Basic Books, 2005. Renehan contends that Gould was a financial wizard whose business strategy of market manipulation and assembling capital still influences the corporate world.

—*Gayla Koerting*

SEE ALSO: Oakes Ames; Schuyler Colfax; Jim Fisk.

SAMMY GRAVANO
Mafia underboss and hit man

BORN: March 12, 1945; Brooklyn, New York
ALSO KNOWN AS: Salvatore Gravano (full name); Sammy the Bull
MAJOR OFFENSES: Racketeering, trafficking, and murder
ACTIVE: 1960's to 2000
LOCALE: New York, New York
SENTENCE: Five years for racketeering; nineteen years for drug trafficking

EARLY LIFE

Salvatore Gravano (grah-VAH-noh) was the youngest of five, born to Sicilian immigrants in Brooklyn, New

York. His parents were law-abiding and hardworking, but Gravano would not follow in their footsteps. He had trouble with school and was picked on because of it. Gravano retaliated with violence and would often fight children who were bigger and older than he. He was nicknamed "the Bull"; his fighting style and his looks were similar to those of a bull. In his teen years, Gravano got involved with gang life and had many run-ins with the police.

Gravano's first arrest was for assaulting an officer, but thanks to a good lawyer, he avoided jail time. In 1964, Gravano was drafted. While in the army, he started a craps circuit and engaged in loan-sharking, which was easy and profitable for Gravano—he even had the military police involved. After two years, he received an honorable discharge and moved back to Brooklyn. There, Gravano joined an old gang called the Rampers, and he continued his shady activities. He and another gang member were shot in a botched car theft. Gravano was shot in the head, his friend in the stomach; both survived.

CRIMINAL CAREER

By the time Gravano was twenty-three, he had made a name for himself and soon found himself involved with Tommy Spero, a member of the Colombo crime family. Gravano soon went to work for the Colombos, loan-sharking money out of a club in Brooklyn. Gravano began robbing stores and banks and beating owed money out of people. Soon he would make his first "hit." After the murder, rumors began that Gravano was the work-horse of the group, and he himself said that this first hit was his stepping-stone into the mob. Shortly thereafter, however, Gravano was moved to the Gambino crime family because of problems he had with Spero's brother and nephew.

Gravano was now working for Toddo Aurello, a Gambino family "capo," or leader. As Gravano soon discovered, income from mob life proved sporadic, and he lived from score to score: He would have plenty of money one month and nothing the next. He decided to leave crime and try to make an honest living. Gravano's mob life, however, would come back to haunt him. Roughly a year later, he received a phone call that he was being indicted for murder. Gravano had no choice but to go back to work for the Gambinos. He could not pay his lawyer fees and had to turn again to a life of crime to pay the bills.

Gravano would eventually be acquitted of the murder charges, but he had once again become deeply involved in the Mafia. In 1975, he would become a made member of the Gambino crime family. The Gambino family was run by Paul Castellano, but when Castellano failed to attend his underboss's wake, rumors started that he needed to be murdered. John Gotti, a capo for the Gambinos, asked Gravano to help with the deed. Gravano agreed, and Castellano was killed. Castellano's death put Gotti in charge of the Gambinos. Soon after Gotti took charge, Aurello resigned, and Gravano became capo. Gotti was flashy and drew too much attention to the Mafia. This upset bosses in other families, and an attempt was made to kill Gotti with a car bomb; however, only his underboss, Frank DiCiccio, was killed. After DiCiccio's death, Gravano became underboss in the Gambino organization.

LEGAL ACTION AND OUTCOME

Under Gotti, Gravano's mob activities escalated. He killed increasingly more people. Gravano allegedly had nineteen hits under his belt—eleven under Gotti and eight from before. During Gotti's reign, the Federal Bureau of Investigation (FBI) was moving closer and closer to bringing down the Mafia. Gotti was charismatic and careless and earned the nickname Teflon Don because charges against him never stuck. However, the FBI eventually was able to bug his headquarters, and the government collected a great deal of evidence from its surveillance, evidence that implicated both Gravano and Gotti in a number of murders. This evidence would prove to be too much for the Mafia: The authorities had them on multiple counts of violating the Racketeer Influenced and Corrupt Organizations (RICO) Act, as well as loan-sharking, conspiracy to commit murder, and murder.

Gravano was loyal to the mob, but when he heard some of the tapes in which Gotti was trying to make it sound like Gravano had made the hits on his own, he decided to cooperate with the FBI. Gravano violated Omerta, the Mafia's code of silence, and testified against Gotti. Despite admitting to nineteen murders, Gravano received a much lesser sentence for his cooperation against Gotti. On April 2, 1991, Gotti was found guilty of the racketeering and murder charges and received a life sentence without the possibility of parole. Gotti later died in prison.

IMPACT

Sammy Gravano's testimony was responsible for the indictments and convictions of dozens of Mafia figures and the downfall of the Mafia. For his efforts, Gravano received a reduced sentence: five years in prison plus three years of supervised release. Gravano was released early and entered the witness protection program. In 2000, however, Gravano and his son Gerard were charged with distribution of the drug Ecstasy in Arizona. In 2001, they pleaded guilty, and Gravano began serving a nineteen-year sentence. In 2003, while in prison, Gravano was indicted for the 1980 murder of Peter Calabro, a New York police detective. This indictment arose from a plea agreement made by Richard Kuklinski, who was also involved in the detective's death. In June of 2005, Gravano was back in court for a hearing; his current lawyer was stepping down as his representative because of a conflict of interest.

In March, 2006, Kuklinski died of unknown causes at the age of seventy. Medical authorities believe that he died of natural causes, but some view his death as suspicious given that he was scheduled to testify in the

Calabro case. A few days after Kuklinski's death, authorities dropped all charges against Gravano because, without Kuklinski's testimony, they had insufficient evidence against him.

FURTHER READING

Jacobs, James J., Coleen Friel, and Robert Radick. *Gotham Unbound: How New York City Was Liberated from the Grip of Organized Crime*. New York: New York University Press, 1999. Addresses Mafia realities, the Cosa Nostra's control of New York City, and how the government finally broke down that control.

Maas, Peter. *Underboss: Sammy the Bull Gravano's Story of Life in the Mafia*. New York: HarperCollins, 1997. Discusses the innermost sanctums of the Cosa Nostra and Sammy the Bull's place in the underworld of power, greed, betrayal, and deception.

Raab, Selwyn. *Five Families: The Rise, Decline, and Resurgence of America's Most Powerful Mafia Empires*. New York: Thomas Dunne Books, 2005. Traces the rise of the Genovese, Gambino, Bonnano, Colombo, and Lucchese families and the roles they have played in American crime.

—Richard D. Hartley

SEE ALSO: Paul Castellano; Joe Colombo; Carlo Gambino; John Gotti; Richard Kuklinski.

CHE GUEVARA
Latin American revolutionary leader

BORN: June 14, 1928; Rosario, Argentina
DIED: October 9, 1967; La Higuera, Bolivia
ALSO KNOWN AS: Ernesto Guevara de la Serna (full name)
CAUSE OF NOTORIETY: Guevara, working with Fidel Castro, orchestrated the Cuban Revolution in 1959 and supported many other rebellions throughout Latin America and in Africa.
ACTIVE: 1954-1967
LOCALE: Argentina, Cuba, Mexico, Bolivia, African Congo, and Guatemala

EARLY LIFE

Ernesto Guevara de la Serna, known to history as Che Guevara (chay gay-BAH-rah), was born in 1928 in Argentina to a middle-class family of Spanish Irish descent. In 1945, he began studying medicine at the University of Buenos Aires. During his studies in 1949 and into the early 1950's, he traveled throughout Argentina and South America on a motorcycle, experiencing the poverty and misery of many people. Along the way, he also worked with people afflicted with leprosy. It was on this journey and through his readings in university that Guevara's social conscience awakened. He began to have increasingly critical opinions of capitalist economics.

In 1953, Guevara graduated with a degree in medicine. After graduation, he traveled to Bolivia, Peru, Ecuador, and finally Guatemala, where he met Hilda Gadea, whom he would marry in 1955; the couple had one child. Guevara's revolutionary persona would arise out of the 1954 U.S. invasion of Guatemala, in which the Central Intelligence Agency and a small group of Guatemalan citizens overthrew the democratic socialist regime, which had been freely elected. Guevara backed

Che Guevara.

the overthrown, pro-communist regime in Guatemala. After the coup, Guevara fled to Mexico and decided that the only way to fight capitalism and imperialism was through violence and armed revolution. While in Mexico, Guevara met Fidel Castro, who turned out to be just the kind of man Guevara was looking for to help him spawn revolution.

REVOLUTIONARY CAREER

While in Mexico, Guevara and Castro planned an expedition to Cuba to fight against Fulgencio Batista y Zaldívar, who had assumed dictatorship through a coup before the 1952 Cuban presidential elections. In 1956, Guevara, Castro, and roughly eighty others boarded a yacht named *Granma* bound for Cuba. They arrived on December 2 and formed a base in the Sierra Maestra. Batista's forces proved formidable, and not many of Guevara's rebels survived. They began to grow in strength, however, because of increasing support from Cuba's peasantry and middle class; more rebels joined Guevara's forces. Because he had high self-esteem and commanded respect from his subordinates, Guevara was said to be a good leader. He also executed many men accused of informing, spying, or deserting his forces. Guevara, Castro, and the rebels finally overthrew Batista on January 1, 1959, and forced him to flee Cuba.

After this victory, Guevara became second in charge of the new Cuban government after Castro, the country's new leader. He became director of the Instituto Nacional de la Reforma Agraria and head of the department of industries; he also became the president of the National Bank of Cuba. Guevara later wrote about the overthrow of the Cuban government in a series of articles published in a revolutionary armed forces publication, *Verde Olivo*. He also became a Cuban citizen, divorced his first wife, and married Aleida March, a rebel he met in the Sierra Maestra mountains of Cuba. He had four more children with March.

As minister of industry, Guevara traveled to many countries, including India, Japan, Egypt, and Pakistan. In 1960, Guevara signed a trade agreement with the Soviet Union, which freed the Cuban sugar industry from rely-

---

CHE'S FAREWELL TO CUBA

On April 1, 1965, Che Guevara wrote a farewell letter to his friend Fidel Castro as he set out for the Congo to spread their brand of revolution.

I have lived magnificent days, and at your side I felt the pride of belonging to our people in the brilliant yet sad days of the Caribbean crisis. Seldom has a statesman been more brilliant as you were in those days. I am also proud of having followed you without hesitation, of having identified with your way of thinking and of seeing and appraising dangers and principles.

Other nations of the world summon my modest efforts of assistance. I can do that which is denied you due to your responsibility as head of Cuba, and the time has come for us to part.

You should know that I do so with a mixture of joy and sorrow. I leave here the purest of my hopes as a builder and the dearest of those I hold dear.... I carry to new battlefronts the faith that you taught me, the revolutionary spirit of my people, the feeling of fulfilling the most sacred of duties: to fight against imperialism wherever one may be. This is a source of strength, and more than heals the deepest of wounds.

I state once more that I free Cuba from all responsibility, except that which stems from its example. If my final hour finds me under other skies, my last thought will be of this people and especially of you. I am grateful for your teaching and your example, to which I shall try to be faithful up to the final consequences of my acts.

I have always been identified with the foreign policy of our revolution, and I continue to be. Wherever I am, I will feel the responsibility of being a Cuban revolutionary, and I shall behave as such. I am not sorry that I leave nothing material to my wife and children; I am happy it is that way. I ask nothing for them, as the state will provide them with enough to live on and receive an education.

I would have many things to say to you and to our people, but I feel they are unnecessary. Words cannot express what I would like them to, and there is no point in scribbling pages.

---

ing on the U.S. market. He also represented Cuba on many delegations to other nations, led Cuba down its socialist path, and was highly outspoken against U.S. foreign policy practices in Asia, Africa, and Latin America. However, Guevara began to move away from Soviet Communist Party ideals and toward Maoist ideals. Guevara set forth his own view for Cuba and Cubans in many articles, speeches, and writings. His philosophy on fighting was described in his 1961 book, *Guerrilla Warfare*, as well as *Guerrilla Warfare: A Method*, published in 1964. He proposed revolutionary movements in developing countries that relied on the peasantry. He wrote that with a limited number of guerrillas, one could move a whole populace against a government by using violence as their means.

DOWNFALL

Following the 1961 American attack on the Bay of Pigs and the Cuban Missile Crisis in 1962, Guevara became increasingly disillusioned. His outright criticism of the Soviet Union as an accomplice of imperialism sealed his departure from Cuban politics. After his withdrawal from the Cuban government, Guevara wrote Castro a letter outlining his intentions to continue the revolutionary fight for the cause in other nations. Guevara's whereabouts were a mystery, and there were even rumors of his death. However, in March, 1965, Guevara, backed by Castro, led a group of revolutionaries into the African Congo in an attempt to stop neocolonialism. This attempt failed miserably because Guevara had underestimated the Congolese army. He returned to Cuba under the condition that his return be secret and with the understanding that it was only temporary in order to organize a revolutionary revolt in Latin America.

In October, 1966, Guevara began to train a group of forces in the Bolivian jungle on land given to him by communists in that country. When the president of Bolivia, René Barrientos, got word of Guevara's presence, he sent the Bolivian army to hunt for Guevara. Guevara believed that the overthrow of Bolivia's government would be easy because its army was ill equipped. What Guevara did not know, however, was that the United States, upon hearing of his plans, had sent special forces to train and aid the Bolivian army. This fact, coupled with Guevara's inability to rally the Bolivian peasantry, led to the failure of the campaign. On October 8, 1967, Guevara and his followers were surrounded and captured. Guevara was taken to La Higuera, a small Bolivian village, where he was executed on October 9. His fingerprints were taken, his hands were severed and sent back to Cuba, and his body was taken to an undisclosed location.

IMPACT

Che Guevara's death dealt an overwhelming blow to socialist revolutionary movements throughout the world and especially within Latin America. Many demonstrations protesting his death took place around the globe. In the late 1960's and in succeeding decades, Guevara remained an icon of revolution for many. He is admired by some both for shunning a comfortable life in order to fight for those less fortunate and for his willingness to die for the cause. Guevara's body lies entombed in a mausoleum in Santa Clara, Cuba.

FURTHER READING

Anderson, Jon Lee. *Che Guevara: A Revolutionary Life.* New York: Grove Press, 1997. A definitive work on Guevara's life.

Castañeda, Jorge G. *Compañero: The Life and Death of Che Guevara.* New York: Knopf, 1997. A substantial biography of Guevara, which attempts to debunk the many myths that have grown about him.

Guevara, Che. *Guerrilla Warfare.* 1961. Reprint. Lincoln: University of Nebraska Press, 1998. Explores Guevara's Marxist ideology and his philosophy about war.

_____. *The Motorcycle Diaries: A Latin American Journey.* Edited and translated by Alexandra Keeble. Rev. ed. New York: Ocean Press, 2003. Guevara chronicled his motorcycle trip throughout Latin America, and his tales give the reader a sense of his burgeoning political awareness. The 2004 film of the same name was based on the book.

Sandeson, David. *Che Guevara.* New York: Octopus, 1997. An account of the student, the rebel, the revolutionary, the diplomat, the guerrilla, and the legend Guevara.

—Richard D. Hartley

SEE ALSO: Fulgencio Batista y Zaldívar; Fidel Castro.

CHARLES JULIUS GUITEAU
American assassin of U.S. president

BORN: September 8, 1841; Freeport, Illinois
DIED: June 30, 1882; Washington, D.C.
MAJOR OFFENSE: Shot President James A. Garfield, who later died of his injuries
ACTIVE: July 2, 1881
LOCALE: Washington, D.C.
SENTENCE: Death by hanging

EARLY LIFE

Born to Luther and Jane (Howe) Guiteau on September 8, 1841, Charles Julius Guiteau (GEE-toh) was the fourth of six children raised in Freeport, Illinois. His mother died when he was seven, but his father soon remarried. Luther, a banker and local politician who practiced the theological teachings of John H. Noyes, was a strict disciplinarian who physically abused his son to correct a speech impediment. After receiving a small inheritance, the young Guiteau spent the Civil War years in Oneida, New York, in a colony dedicated to Noyes's teaching of Bible Communism, the belief in plural marriages, perfectionism, and the second coming of Christ.

Guiteau left the community in 1865 for New York City. He tried his hand at journalism and publishing religious tracts, but he soon ran out of money. He moved in with his sister, Frances, who began to notice his erratic behavior, but before she could commit him to a sanatorium, he left for Chicago in 1869. Because of the laxity of the bar exam, Guiteau was admitted to the Illinois bar. He failed to make an effective courtroom attorney and ended up as a debt collector. During his time in the city, he married Annie Bunn, a teenager who worked in the library at the Young Men's Christian Association (YMCA). He became an itinerant preacher for the next three years and sold a series of publications titled *The Truth: A Companion to the Bible*, based largely on Noyes's beliefs. Eventually, meager earnings, poor living conditions, and the emotional strain caused Annie to seek a divorce in 1873.

CRIMINAL CAREER

Guiteau had turned his attention to politics by the 1880's. He offered to help James Garfield's presidential campaign in New York City by passing out copies of a speech titled "Garfield Against Hancock" (Winfield Scott Hancock was Garfield's Democratic opponent). Guiteau then moved to Washington, D.C., once Garfield assumed the presidency and began appearing at State Department offices saying that he should be given a consulate post in

A historical composite of images documenting Garfield's assassination by Guiteau. (Library of Congress)

Paris or Vienna. After being spurned by Secretary of State James G. Blaine, Guiteau turned away from the liberal "Half-Breeds" faction of the Republican Party (represented by Garfield) and toward the conservative "Stalwart" faction. The Stalwarts originally backed Ulysses S. Grant for a third term in office, opposed the civil service reform policies of President Rutherford B. Hayes, and opposed his attempts to reconcile with the South. Republican Party divisions increased when New York senators Roscoe Conkling and Thomas C. Pratt resigned in protest of Garfield's nomination for collector of customs in their state. Guiteau began to believe that Garfield's death was a political necessity that would return the Stalwarts, represented by Vice President Chester A. Arthur, to power.

Guiteau bought a .44 British caliber gun with an ivory handle because he thought it would make a good museum exhibit. He began to practice with the handgun in a local park. He made two attempts on Garfield's life, the first being in a church on Vermont Avenue in mid-June. The plan was abruptly halted when the president left the church to go visit his recuperating wife in New Jersey. The next attempt took place in a train depot, but Guiteau took pity on seeing the feeble form of the First Lady.

On July 2, 1881, Garfield, accompanied by Blaine, was about to board a train to attend the twenty-fifth reunion of his college class when Guiteau intercepted him in the ladies' waiting room. He fired two shots; one bullet hit the president in the back and lodged near his spinal column. Garfield lingered for a few months. Doctors were unable to find and extricate the bullet, and the president died on September 19.

LEGAL ACTION AND OUTCOME

Guiteau's trial began on November 14 in the Supreme Court of the District of Columbia with Walter S. Cox presiding. Guiteau's brother-in-law, George Scoville, was his attorney throughout the trial. The defense case relied heavily on the insanity plea, but Scoville also maintained that Garfield died as a result of physician negligence. Guiteau's actions in court led to questions of his mental state. He constantly disrupted court proceedings by making long speeches and reading aloud newspaper accounts of the trial. Nevertheless, the jury found Guiteau guilty, and he was hanged in late June, 1882.

IMPACT

The assassination of President James Garfield caused the passage of widespread civil service reform. Charles Guiteau's trial represented one of the most famous cases using insanity as a defense argument; legal ramifications involving such pleas still persist. According to Guiteau, divine inspiration had convinced him that the president must die, but he was found to be a troubled man possessed by an enormous ego who craved recognition and fame.

FURTHER READING

Ackerman, Kenneth D. *Dark Horse: The Surprise Election and Political Murder of President James A. Garfield.* New York: Carroll & Graf, 2003. Author recounts the important political figures in the Republican Party, Garfield's presidency, and how his assassination impacted the country and politics.

Clark, James C. *The Murder of James A. Garfield: The President's Last Days and the Trial and Execution of His Assassin.* Jefferson, N.C.: McFarland, 1993. Clark interweaves the lives and events of Guiteau and Garfield, addressing the political climate, legal system, and medical establishment of the late nineteenth century.

Peskin, Allan. "Charles Guiteau of Illinois: President Garfield's Assassin." *Journal of the Illinois State Historical Society* 70, no. 2 (May, 1977): 130-139. The author provides a brief biographical account of Guiteau.

Rosenberg, Charles E. *The Trial of Assassin Guiteau.* Chicago: University of Chicago Press, 1968. Rosenberg examines the public reaction and legal implication of mental illness during the Gilded Age by focusing on Guiteau's trial.

—*Gayla Koerting*

SEE ALSO: John Wilkes Booth; Leon Czolgosz; Daniel M'Naghten; Lee Harvey Oswald; Giuseppe Zangara.

AL-ḤĀKIM
Imam and the sixth Fāṭimid caliph (996-1021)

BORN: August 14, 985; Cairo, Egypt
DIED: February 13, 1021?; Cairo, Egypt
ALSO KNOWN AS: Al-Ḥākim bi-Amrih Allāh (full name); Abu 'Ali al-Mansūr al-Ḥākim; Mad Caliph; Caligula of Islam
CAUSE OF NOTORIETY: During his rule, al-Ḥākim abused his power by promoting religious intolerance, committing atrocities, destroying monuments, and claiming personal divinity.
ACTIVE: 996-1021
LOCALE: Mainly North Africa and Cairo, Egypt

EARLY LIFE

Al-Ḥākim (ahl HAH-keem) was the first Fāṭimid imam-caliph born in Egypt. He was only eleven years old when his father, the fifth imam-caliph, al-'Azīz (r. 975-996), died. His tutor and regent became the eunuch Bardjawan al-Maghribī. In 996, al-Ḥākim was crowned a new caliph following a conspiracy to murder Bardjawan and thus became the absolute ruler of the state at age eleven.

POLITICAL CAREER

Al-Ḥākim was a controversial ruler of the Fāṭimid Dynasty who was accused of notorious crimes. It is believed that he was mentally unbalanced, an opinion based on numerous examples of illogical and bizarre behavior. His prosecution of Christians and Jews resulted in destruction of monuments and cemeteries; he also imposed torture and forceful conversion on the non-Muslim population.

In 1009, he ordered the destruction of the Church of the Holy Sepulcher at Jerusalem. In addition, he appropriated territorial possessions of the churches, synagogues, and monasteries in Egypt. In 1020, he plundered and burnt al-Fustāt (a part of modern-day Cairo and the economic center of the city) and imposed harsh measures against Sunni and Shiite minorities. His prohibitions included laws such as the order against women appearing in public, limited access to particular food, and complete restriction on the consumption of beer and wine.

Before his disappearance on February 13, 1021, during one of his solitary walks in the Muqattam hills near Cairo, al-Ḥākim began to assume an ascetic lifestyle based on the newly established Druze religion. He believed that he was not only an incarnation of divinity but also God himself. This belief caused the opposition of administrative and religious authorities, who rejected his claim of divine status. Al-Ḥākim punished his opponents by burning al-Fustāt. This act was the final evidence of his madness; it led to a conspiracy to remove him from power. Although his body was never found, it is believed that he was murdered on the order of his sister Sitt al-Mulk, who was, according to some sources, Christian. After al-Ḥākim's death, she was appointed to reign on behalf of his minor son.

IMPACT

Although many believe al-Ḥākim to have been a dictatorial tyrant during his rule because of his arbitrary and harsh policies, historians have noted some positive aspects of his tenure as a result of his interest in education and learning. He was one of the strongest supporters of the Druze theological system and the founder of the first Muslim university in Cairo, the so-called House of Knowledge. A large comprehensive library was established to collect rare manuscripts and books and the access to the institution was free for all. Unfortunately by 1074, the library was completely destroyed and the building was used for other purposes.

Al-Ḥākim was also a patron of visual arts, especially architecture, and was behind the completion of the second largest Fatimid mosque in Cairo, known in modern times as the Mosque of al-Ḥākim, which was started by his father al-'Aziz in 990. The mosque was rebuilt in 1980.

FURTHER READING

Halm, Heinz. *The Fatimids and Their Traditions of Learning*. London: I. B. Tauris, 1997. A rather positive assessment of al-Ḥākim's reign with a special emphasis on his cultural achievements.

Kennedy, Hugh. *The Prophet and the Age of the Caliphates: The Islamic Near East from the Sixth to the Eleventh Century*. Edinburgh Gate, Harlow, Scotland: Pearson Education, 2004. A comprehensive study of the age of caliphates with an emphasis on al-Ḥākim and early Fāṭimids. An excellent selected bibliography is included.

Walker, Paul E. *Exploring an Islamic Empire, Fatmid History and Its Sources*. London: I. B. Tauris, 2002. Another comprehensive study with an extensive list of sources from general to very specific topics.

—*Rozmeri Basic*

SEE ALSO: Shi Huangdi.

H. R. HALDEMAN
White House chief of staff under President Richard M. Nixon

BORN: October 27, 1926; Los Angeles, California
DIED: November 12, 1993; Santa Barbara, California
ALSO KNOWN AS: Harry Robbins Haldeman (full
name); Bob Haldeman
MAJOR OFFENSES: Conspiracy, perjury, and
obstruction of justice
ACTIVE: 1970-1973
LOCALE: Washington, D.C.
SENTENCE: One to four years' imprisonment; served
eighteen months

EARLY LIFE
H. R. Haldeman (HAWL-deh-man) grew up in Los Angeles, the child of a well-to-do heating and air-conditioning contractor. His father, Harry F. Haldeman, was a supporter of the Republican Party, a political loyalty that was passed on to his son. Haldeman attended public schools in California. He was active in the Boy Scouts, attaining the rank of Eagle Scout. He attended the University of Redlands for two years while enrolled in the Navy's reserve program and then, when World War II ended, transferred to the University of California at Los Angeles, graduating in 1948. One of his classmates was John Ehrlichman.

In 1949, Haldeman became an account executive in an advertising agency in New York. He moved back to California in 1959 to manage the California office of his firm. He had already begun to take an active role in Republican politics, supporting Richard Nixon's vice presidential campaign in 1952. He was one of Nixon's earliest political supporters and worked on his behalf in five political campaigns—first as an advance man and ultimately as campaign chief of staff in Nixon's successful race for the presidency in 1968. Shortly after election day, Nixon selected Haldeman to be his chief of staff in the White House.

By 1970, under Haldeman's direction, the administrative structure of the White House staff had assumed the pattern that it was to follow for the most of the remainder of Nixon's presidency. Haldeman, as chief of staff, directed a small staff of his own, substantially controlled the president's scheduling for both trips and appointments, and met almost daily with the president's chief policy advisers—Ehrlichman on the domestic policy side and Henry Kissinger on the foreign policy side. As decisions were made, Haldeman attempted to coordinate them with the federal bureaucratic departments out-side the White House. Most presidents since Nixon have utilized this organizational pattern or a very similar one, although few chiefs of staff have wielded as much power as Haldeman did.

CRIMINAL CAREER
On June 17, 1972, five burglars, later shown to be affiliated with and to have been paid by the Committee to Re-elect the President (CRP), broke into the offices of the Democratic National Committee in the Watergate Hotel. Their purpose was to bug the telephones and offices in order to obtain political intelligence. They were caught and arrested by the District of Columbia police.

Soon after the Watergate burglary occurred, Haldeman was drawn into the administration's attempt to cover up its connections to the burglars. Nixon himself had restricted access to information about the burglary and its genesis, and Haldeman was probably unaware

A 1971 portrait of H. R. Haldeman. (NARA)

THE HALDEMAN THEORY

In his book The Ends of Power *(1978), Haldeman relates his theory of the motives and methods behind the Watergate break-in:*

The Haldeman Theory of the break-in is as follows: I believe Nixon told Colson to get the goods on [Democratic National Party chair Larry] O'Brien's connection with [Howard] Hughes at a time when both of them were infuriated with O'Brien's success in using the I.T.T. case against them.

I believe Colson then passed the word to [E. Howard] Hunt who conferred with [G. Gordon] Liddy who decided the taps on O'Brien and [Democratic operative Spencer] Oliver, the other Hughes' phone, would be their starting point.

I believe the Democratic high command knew the break-in was going to take place, and let it happen. They may even have planted the plainclothesman who arrested the burglars.

I believe that the C.I.A. monitored the Watergate burglars throughout. And that the overwhelming evidence leads to the conclusion that the break-in was deliberately sabotaged. (In this regard, it's interesting to point out that every one of the Hunt-Liddy projects somehow failed, from the interrogation of DeMotte, who was supposed to know all about Ted Kennedy's secret love life and didn't, to Dita Beard, to [Daniel] Ellsberg, to Watergate).

that the president himself was in on the plan. The basic scheme of the cover-up was to buy silence from the burglars by funneling campaign funds to them while trying to divert the Federal Bureau of Investigation (FBI) inquiry into the matter by getting the Central Intelligence Agency (CIA) to claim that the investigation would disclose foreign intelligence secrets. By concealing his role in these plans and by subsequently lying to the Senate Watergate Investigating Committee, Haldeman committed perjury and obstructed justice. He, Ehrlichman, and John Dean, the real architect of the cover-up, were all forced to resign from their White House positions in 1973.

LEGAL ACTION AND OUTCOME

On January 1, 1975, Haldeman was convicted of one count of conspiracy, one count of obstruction of justice, and three counts of perjury, the latter for his false testimony to the Senate Watergate Investigating Committee.

He was initially sentenced to two and a half to eight years' imprisonment, but the sentence was later reduced to one to four years. He was released by order of the trial judge after serving only eighteen months of his sentence at the minimum security federal prison at Lompoc, California.

IMPACT

H. R. Haldeman's resignation crippled the Nixon administration; Nixon was forced to endure the remainder of the Watergate struggle with a less coordinated staff who were unfamiliar with the details of Watergate and the cover-up. However, the organizational structure for the White House staff that emerged during Haldeman's tenure as chief of staff has become the starting point for subsequent presidents. Haldeman's fate in the Watergate affair has served as a warning to later administrations that the people who occupy the position of chief of staff have to be selected for their familiarity with the legal and political constraints that operate in American government.

FURTHER READING

Ambrose, Stephen. *Nixon.* 3 vols. New York: Simon & Schuster, 1987-1991. This is an illuminating and balanced discussion of Nixon, his personality, career, and presidency. The Watergate material is found in volume 3, *Ruin and Recovery.*

Dean, John W. *Blind Ambition: The White House Years.* New York: Simon & Schuster, 1976. Dean recounts his career and his involvement with the Watergate conspiracy and admits his participation in the cover-up.

Haldeman, H. R. *The Ends of Power.* New York: Times Books, 1978. Haldeman's memoir of his White House service. In it he takes responsibility for creating the atmosphere in which Watergate took place.

Safire, William. *Before the Fall: An Inside View of the Pre-Watergate White House.* Garden City, N.Y.: Doubleday, 1975. A fascinating but laudatory view of the accomplishments of the Nixon administration before Watergate destroyed it.

White, Theodore H. *Breach of Faith: The Fall of Richard Nixon.* New York: Atheneum, 1975. Excellent history of the Watergate affair; Haldeman's role thoroughly discussed.

—*Robert Jacobs*

SEE ALSO: Charles W. Colson; John D. Ehrlichman; E. Howard Hunt; G. Gordon Liddy; James W. McCord, Jr.; John Mitchell; Richard Nixon.

MATTHEW F. HALE
American white supremacist

BORN: July 27, 1971; East Peoria, Illinois
ALSO KNOWN AS: Matt Hale
MAJOR OFFENSES: Solicitation of murder and obstruction of justice
ACTIVE: 1996-2005
LOCALE: Peoria, Illinois
SENTENCE: Forty years in prison at the Administrative Maximum United States Penitentiary, Florence, Colorado

EARLY LIFE

Matthew Hale (hayl) was the youngest son of Evelyn Ackerson Bowshier and Russell Hale, Jr. When he was nine years old, his parents were divorced. His father, a police officer, subsequently raised him. Hale claimed that he experienced a political awakening when he was eleven. A year later, he read Adolf Hitler's *Mein Kampf* (1925-1927; English translation, 1933) and other works by the German leader. Within a year, Hale formed a short-lived group called the New Reich. After graduation from high school, Hale attended Bradley University, where he majored in political science and music. At Bradley, he started an organization called the American White Supremacist Party. Hale dissolved the group after it failed to attract more than seven or eight members. Hale then unsuccessfully attempted to start a chapter of David Duke's National Association for the Advancement of White People. Hale graduated from Bradley in 1993. In 1995, he was a candidate for the East Peoria City Council; however, he received only 14 percent of the vote. He graduated from Southern Illinois University School of Law in 1998.

CRIMINAL CAREER

On July 27, 1996, at a meeting in Montana, Hale was elected Pontifex Maximus, or supreme leader, of the World Church of the Creator (WCOTC), a racist and neo-Nazi organization. Ben Klassen, a onetime Florida legislator, founded the WCOTC in 1973. Klassen rejected Judeo-democratic Marxist values and called for a new religion based on race. The so-called Creativity movement considered the white race as nature's highest creation and white people as the creators of all worthwhile culture and civilization. To Klassen, the most dangerous enemy was the Jews. He claimed that Jewish scriptwriters wrote the Bible. Nonwhites were the second most dangerous enemy, and, according to Klassen, the laws of nature did not approve of miscegenation or "mongrelization" of the races.

After Klassen committed suicide in 1993, the Creativity movement was left without an effective spokesperson; Hale took over this position in 1996. Hale, who called Hitler the greatest white leader that ever lived, stressed that the Creativity movement was different from German national socialism in several ways. First, the Creativity movement was a religious movement, not a political one. Second, it was concerned with the entire white race, not just the Germans. The Creativity movement recognized the importance of white solidarity, while the Nazis were hostile to their white racial neighbors. Third, Creativity denounced Christianity, while Hitler did not address Jewish Christianity. Finally, Creativity would not form alliances with any nonwhite race, while Hitler allied his movement with the Japanese.

Hale operated the WCOTC out of an office in his parents' home in East Peoria, Illinois. He used an Israeli flag as a doormat and had swastika stickers decorating the walls. He began to publicize his movement through dozens of Internet sites, newsletters, a public cable television program, public meetings, and interviews. One of the most common methods he used was the distribution of racist and anti-Semitic literature on lawns and at libraries.

As his notoriety increased, Hale was interviewed by national media figures, including Jerry Springer, Ricki Lake, Leeza Gibbons, and Tom Brokaw. He was able to attract more members, mostly young men from blue-collar backgrounds, through this publicity. While Hale claimed to have eighty thousand members, the WCOTC had only a few hundred hardcore followers in twenty-two states. He also had nine international contacts. While Hale publicly claimed that his church did not condone violence, he called on his followers to fight a racial holy war.

In 1999, Hale passed the Illinois Bar; however, the Committee on Character and Fitness denied him a law license because of his bigotry. Following this decision, Hale said he could no longer advise his supporters to obey the laws of the United States. Shortly thereafter, one of Hale's followers, Benjamin Smith, went on a shooting rampage in Illinois and Indiana, killing two persons and wounding nine others. All of the victims were African American, Asian American, or Jewish.

In 2002, the WCOTC lost a trademark infringement

suit brought against it by the Te-Ta-Ma Truth Foundation. Hale was ordered to stop using "Church of the Creator" as part of both his organization's name and his Internet addresses and to turn over all printed materials bearing that phrase. When he refused, U.S. federal judge Joan Lefkow charged him with contempt.

LEGAL ACTION AND OUTCOME
In January, 2003, Matt Hale was charged with solicitation of murder of a federal judge and for obstruction of justice. The charges were brought after Hale sent an e-mail to his security chief asking for Judge Lefkow's address. The security chief, who was working for the Federal Bureau of Investigation (FBI), later tape-recorded Hale ordering the murder of the judge.

Hale's trial began on April 6, 2004, in Chicago, Illinois. His defense team called no witnesses, gambling that the jury would not convict him; however, on April 26, 2004, Hale was convicted of solicitation of murder and three counts of obstruction of justice. On April 6, 2005, Hale was sentenced to forty years in prison and sent to the Administrative Maximum United States Penitentiary in Florence, Colorado.

IMPACT
Following Matthew Hale's imprisonment, the Creativity movement split into several factions and virtually ceased to exist. Although he personified the racism of the white

separatist movement that continued to be present in the United States in the twenty-first century, he was never able to develop the WCOTC into a significant political movement. While he was college educated and articulate, his two hundred followers were mostly young men from blue-collar backgrounds. Hale garnered media publicity merely because his was a sensationalist story about neo-Nazism.

FURTHER READING
Anti-Defamation League. *Poisoning the Web: Hatred Online.* New York: Anti-Defamation League, 1999. This work looks at the use of the Internet by hate groups, including the WCOTC.

Dobratz, Betty A., and Stephanie Shanks-Meile. *The White Separatist Movement in the United States.* Baltimore: Johns Hopkins University Press, 1999. This work is based on interviews with white separatists, including Hale. It provies an excellent analysis of the ideology of the WCOTC.

Swain, Carol M. *The New White Nationalism in America.* New York: Cambridge University Press, 2002. A comprehensive description and analysis of white nationalist groups in the United States, including the WCOTC.

—*William V. Moore*

SEE ALSO: Frank Collin; David Duke.

ROBERT PHILIP HANSSEN
American FBI agent and convicted spy

BORN: April 18, 1944; Evergreen Park, Illinois
ALSO KNOWN AS: B; Ramon; Ramon Garcia
MAJOR OFFENSE: Espionage
ACTIVE: 1979, 1985-2001
LOCALE: New York, New York; Washington, D.C.
SENTENCE: Life in prison without parole

EARLY LIFE
Robert Philip Hanssen (HAN-suhn) was the only child of a police officer who routinely denigrated his son's abilities and occasionally abused him physically. Hanssen grew up in Chicago, where he attended William Howard Taft High School and was remembered by teachers and classmates as bright but socially awkward.

Hanssen excelled in science and won a scholarship to prestigious Knox College in Galesburg, Illinois. He

graduated with a degree in chemistry in 1966, but when a hiring freeze prevented his getting a job as a cryptographer with the National Security Agency (NSA), he entered dental school at Illinois's Northwestern University. This step not only accorded with his father's hope that he enter a medical field but also assured him a draft deferment during the burgeoning Vietnam War. However, Hanssen switched programs within a few years and earned a master's degree in accounting and information systems in 1971.

At first, Hanssen worked for the well-known accounting firm Touche Ross & Company but found the job boring. He joined the Chicago police department in 1972 and, ultimately, the Federal Bureau of Investigation (FBI) in 1976. Hanssen's first bureau assignment was to the Gary, Indiana, office, but subsequent assignments

Robert Philip Hanssen. (AP/Wide World Photos)

moved him back and forth between New York City and Washington, D.C.

CRIMINAL CAREER

Over the years, Hanssen's duties gave him access to a variety of highly classified information. He acted as liaison to the State Department Office of Foreign Missions and was responsible for tracking espionage agents working in the United States under diplomatic cover. He was also the liaison to the State Department's Bureau of Intelligence and Research. Nevertheless, he quickly grew disillusioned with the FBI, which he felt underestimated his talents.

In his initial act of betrayal, Hanssen turned over the name of an important Russian double agent in 1979 to the GRU (the Soviet military intelligence agency) in return for twenty thousand dollars. He took a more decisive step in 1985 by approaching agents of the better-known Soviet intelligence agency the KGB (the GRU's rival). For the next sixteen years, Hanssen functioned as a "mole," or embedded double agent, for the KGB, trading yet more secrets for cash, diamonds, and deposits in a Russian bank account. He utilized a system known as the

"dead drop," which allowed him to leave documents and agents to leave payment at a prearranged site without the need for face-to-face meetings. In his communications, Hanssen identified himself variously as "B," "Ramon," and "Ramon Garcia."

Although Hanssen eventually collected as much as $1,400,000 for his work, monetary gain does not seem to have been his primary motive. Instead, he seems to have delighted in fooling those closest to him. Moreover, despite being a seemingly devoted family man, a Roman Catholic, and a member of the conservative Catholic organization Opus Dei, Hanssen was obsessed with sex and pornography. Sworn to uphold the ideals of the FBI and the United States, he nevertheless sold his country's secrets with no apparent compunction.

LEGAL ACTION AND OUTCOME

The FBI was finally able to identify Hanssen through information provided by a former KGB officer in return for seven million dollars. Hanssen was reassigned to the Washington office, where he could be kept under closer observation, and was arrested on February 18, 2001, at one of his customary dead drop sites. In order to avoid the death penalty, he pleaded guilty on July 6, 2001, to fifteen counts of spying and conspiracy. He was sentenced to life in prison without parole on May 10, 2002.

IMPACT

Robert Philip Hanssen is regarded as one of the most damaging spies in American history. By the time he was arrested, he had passed on some six thousand pages of documents and twenty-seven computer disks of highly sensitive information to the Russians. The information he sold came from the FBI, the Central Intelligence Agency (CIA), the Pentagon, and the NSA, the last of which probably suffered the most damage.

Among many other secrets, Hanssen revealed the names of Soviet agents actually working for the United States (several of whom were then executed by the Soviets); U.S. estimates of Soviet missile strength; specific American plans for retaliation in case of war and for protecting top U.S. officials; and details of electronic eavesdropping and surveillance techniques. He also provided the Soviets with software used to track intelligence cases—software that, in turn, a Russian agent may have sold to the terrorist organization al-Qaeda. Intelligence officials realized after the fact that they should have recognized signs of danger in Hanssen's often erratic behavior and work habits and consequently tightened their procedures.

FURTHER READING

Havill, Adrian. *The Spy Who Stayed Out in the Cold.* New York: St. Martin's Press, 2001. Psychological study of Hanssen and one of the few on its subject to include a bibliography.

Schiller, Lawrence. *Into the Mirror: The Life of Master Spy Robert P. Hanssen.* New York: HarperCollins, 2002. Lightly fictionalized biography based in part on a screenplay by acclaimed author Norman Mailer. Includes a chronology of Hanssen's life and activities.

Vise, David A. *The Bureau and the Mole: The Unmasking of Robert Philip Hanssen, the Most Dangerous Double Agent in FBI History.* New York: Atlantic Monthly Press, 2002. Account by a reporter for The *Washington Post.* Includes a valuable appendix summarizing the secrets that Hanssen sold but no index.

Wise, David. *Spy: The Inside Story of How the FBI's Robert Hanssen Betrayed America.* New York: Random House, 2002. Study by a noted expert on U.S. intelligence services, written with the help of Dr. David L. Charney, a psychiatrist who interviewed Hanssen extensively after his arrest.

—*Grove Koger*

SEE ALSO: Anthony Blunt; Christopher John Boyce; Guy Burgess; John Cairncross; Robert Philip Hanssen; Alger Hiss; Daulton Lee; Donald Duart Maclean; Kim Philby; Jonathan Pollard.

JOHN WESLEY HARDIN
American gunfighter and outlaw

BORN: May 26, 1853; Bonham, Texas
DIED: August 19, 1895; El Paso, Texas
ALSO KNOWN AS: James W. Swain; J. H. Swain
MAJOR OFFENSES: Robbery and murder
ACTIVE: 1868 to July 23, 1877
LOCALE: Northern Texas, southern Kansas, southern Alabama, and northern Florida
SENTENCE: Twenty-five years in prison; served sixteen years

EARLY LIFE

John Wesley Hardin (jahn WEHS-lee HAHR-dihn) was the second of two sons born to Elizabeth and James G. Hardin, a schoolteacher and a Methodist preacher. Events associated with the Civil War embittered young Hardin against Union soldiers and freed slaves. At the age of fourteen, he stabbed a schoolmate during a fight.

As a young man, Hardin worked as a cowboy on a ranch and a schoolteacher in Navarro County, Texas. At the request of his father, Hardin earned a diploma from Landrum's Academy in 1870. In 1871, he participated in a cattle drive along the Chisholm Trail and spent some time in Abilene, Kansas, where he met and reportedly had an uneventful confrontation with U.S. marshall Wild Bill Hickok. Hardin married Jane Bowen in 1872. They had three children.

CRIMINAL CAREER

In 1868, Hardin killed a black man and then killed one or more Union soldiers who attempted to take him into custody. He and a friend killed two more soldiers in 1869. Shortly thereafter, Hardin killed a circus worker. During a gambling dispute, he killed gunfighter Jim Bradley in 1870. After escaping from jail and killing a guard, Hardin killed three more Union soldiers who were tracking him.

In August, 1871, Hardin and a friend killed gunfighter Juan Bideno. Near the end of 1871, Hardin killed Gonzales County law officer Green Paramoor. While participating in the Sutton-Taylor range war in DeWitt County, Texas, in 1873 and 1874, Hardin killed lawman J. B. Morgan and was also involved in the killing of Sheriff Jack Helm. On May 26, 1874, Hardin killed Brown County sheriff Charles Webb in a gunfight. As he fled to Florida, he reportedly robbed some trains in Louisiana, Alabama, and Florida.

LEGAL ACTION AND OUTCOME

Hardin was arrested in Longview, Texas, in the spring of 1871 and charged with murder. Shortly thereafter, he escaped and killed a jail guard. In the fall of 1872, he spent time in jail but again escaped.

The law caught up with Hardin again on July 23, 1877, in Pensacola, Florida, where he was arrested on a train by Texas Ranger John B. Armstrong. On September 28, 1877, Hardin was tried and convicted of murder and sentenced to twenty-five years of hard labor at Rusk Prison in Huntsville, Texas. After good behavior, he was pardoned and released from prison on March 16, 1894. He was killed by Sheriff John Selman over a verbal dispute in El Paso, Texas, on August 19, 1895.

IMPACT

John Wesley Hardin became known as one of the most notorious gunfighters and vigilante heroes in the Old West. His career paralleled that of Jesse James and William Bonney (Billy the Kid). Hardin killed at least twenty-three men in gunfights. Many historians rank him as having the fastest gun and sharpest eyes of any Old West gunfighter. His criminal activities increased the intensity with which law officers hunted down outlaws.

Hardin has been portrayed in many television and film Westerns. His life was explored on the television series *Death Valley Days* and in the film *Streets of Laredo* (1949). Country musician Johnny Cash wrote and recorded a song about Hardin titled "Hardin Wouldn't Run." The title song of one of folksinger Bob Dylan's albums was also about Hardin. Most of the films and songs include legends and myths that tend to glamorize Hardin or the man who finally killed him.

FURTHER READING

Block, Lawrence, ed. *Gangsters, Swindlers, Killers, and Thieves: The Lives and Crimes of Fifty American Villians.* New York: Oxford University Press, 2004. This work includes an account of the life of Hardin, including truths and myths.

Hardin, John Wesley, Jo Stamps, and Roy Stamps. *The Letters of John Wesley Hardin.* Austin, Tex.: Eakin Press, 2001. A collection of 281 letters that were written by Hardin, his wife, and friends between September 8, 1876, and July 28, 1895, which reveal insights about the life and legend of Hardin.

Pryor, Alton. *Outlaws and Gunslingers: Tales of the West's Most Notorious Outlaws.* Roseville, Calif.: Stagecoach, 2001. Explores the lives of twenty-seven of the most famous gunfighters known in the Old West, giving a detailed account of the outlaw life of Hardin.

—*Alvin K. Benson*

SEE ALSO: William H. Bonney; Jesse James.

JEAN HARRIS
American murderer

BORN: April 27, 1923; Cleveland, Ohio
ALSO KNOWN AS: Jean Struven (birth name); Scarsdale Diet Murderess
MAJOR OFFENSE: Murder
ACTIVE: March 10, 1980
LOCALE: Purchase, New York
SENTENCE: Fifteen years to life in prison; received clemency after twelve years

EARLY LIFE

Born Jean Struven in 1923, Jean Harris (HAR-ihs) was the child of a wealthy Cleveland, Ohio, family. Raised in a strict Christian Science household, she was an excellent student and graduated from Smith College. She married Jim Harris, a sales engineer. At first, Jean worked as a schoolteacher, but later she quit teaching to become a full-time homemaker. Her marriage ended in divorce in 1965.

Harris began dating Dr. Herman Tarnower, a high-society cardiologist, well known for his charming and promiscuous ways. He proposed in 1967, but he and Harris never married. Resuming her career as an educator, Harris in 1977 became administrator at Springside, a fe-

male academy outside Philadelphia. She later became headmistress of the exclusive Madeira School in McLean, Virginia.

CRIMINAL CAREER

In 1980, Harris learned of drug use in a Madeira School dormitory. During the investigation, she telephoned Tarnower, who was her physician. She requested more of the medication he had been prescribing to treat her chronic depression. After promising to send the medicine, he also asked her about some missing books. Harris took this as an accusation of stealing. Tarnower also informed her that she would not be his date at an upcoming banquet in his honor.

Meanwhile, at the Madeira School, drug paraphernalia was discovered, as well as marijuana seeds and stems. Harris called an emergency meeting of faculty, students, and four suspects. The tense meeting resulted in the four students' expulsion from the school.

The campus situation and her depressive state led Harris to thoughts of suicide. Wanting to say good-bye to Tarnower, she drove to his home with a gun, ready to take her own life. Once at his house, she found evidence

Jean Harris, left, with television journalist Barbara Walters. (AP/Wide World Photos)

of another woman, Lynne Tryforos, whom Harris felt was her rival for Tarnower's attentions. What began as a conversation with the doctor escalated into a scuffle, and Harris shot Tarnower four times.

LEGAL ACTION AND OUTCOME

In a high-profile trial, Harris pleaded temporary insanity, saying the shooting was accidental. Her trial raised a number of legal questions and divided public opinion. In 1981, she was found guilty of second-degree murder and sentenced to fifteen years to life in prison. She was sent to Bedford Hills Correctional Facility in New York.

Harris was a model prisoner and became known as an authority on the problems faced by children of incarcerated women. She taught parenting and sex education classes and encouraged pregnant inmates to participate in a program that allowed inmates to keep their infants in the prison nursery. Harris established the Children's Center, where incarcerated mothers could spend time with their children. She also wrote three books about her experiences.

After serving twelve years, Harris was granted clem-

ency on December 29, 1992, on the grounds of ill health. Paroled in 1993, she was in her early seventies. Harris settled in the Northeast and continues to raise money and lecture on behalf of the children of incarcerated women.

IMPACT

Jean Harris's crime and conviction took place in the years after the Civil Rights movement swept through the United States. Among the movement's many effects was the more equal treatment of offenders within the criminal justice system. Harris was not a typical murderer. She was upper-class, educated, and older than most female offenders. Her trial raised a number of issues, including the fact that her jury was never given the option of determining her crime to be voluntary manslaughter. Harris, then, became emblematic of an offender condemned by a seemingly nondiscriminatory, newly enlightened justice system.

While in prison, Harris was somewhat able to reform her reputation: She contributed positively to the lives of incarcerated women, especially those with children. As an author, she was able to open a window on the world of women in prison. Her legacy at Bedford Hills Correctional Facility remains positive years after her release.

FURTHER READING

Alexander, Shana. *Very Much a Lady: The Untold Story of Jean Harris and Dr. Herman Tarnower.* Canada: Simon and Schuster, 2006. Examines the early lives of Harris and Tarnower and the trial following Tarnower's death, including mistakes made by Harris's defense team.

Harris, Jean. *They Always Call Us Ladies.* New York: Macmillan, 1988. Provides an excellent discussion of life in prison and the history of women's prisons.

_____. *Stranger in Two Worlds.* New York: Macmillan, 1986. The story of Harris's life in and outside of prison, based on her memory and trial testimony.

—*Janice G. Rienerth*

SEE ALSO: Bambi Bembenek; Ira Einhorn; Seventh Earl of Lucan; Scott Peterson; Sam Sheppard; Pamela Ann Smart; Madeleine Smith; Ruth Snyder; Carolyn Warmus.

BILL HAYWOOD
American labor leader

BORN: February 4, 1869; Salt Lake City, Utah
DIED: May 18, 1928; Moscow, Soviet Union (now in Russia)
ALSO KNOWN AS: William Dudley Haywood (full name); Big Bill Haywood
MAJOR OFFENSE: Violation of the Espionage and Sedition Act
ACTIVE: 1918
LOCALE: American Midwest
SENTENCE: Thirty years in prison; jumped bail and fled to the Soviet Union

EARLY LIFE

The son of a former Pony Express rider who died when his son was only three years old, Bill Haywood (HAY-wood) left school before his tenth birthday and went to work in the mines to help support his family. After trying his hand as a cowboy and homesteader, Haywood returned to mining, where he would become one of the most radical and feared leaders of the American labor movement.

CRIMINAL CAREER

In 1896, while working in a silver mine in Idaho, Haywood witnessed how the Western Federation of Miners (WFM) organized workers, and he joined the union. By 1899, he was on the WFM's general executive board. He quickly became the editor of the union's magazine, and in 1901 he became the union's secretary-treasurer.

That same year, mines in Colorado erupted in violence, resulting in the deaths of thirty-three union and nonunion workers. The WFM launched a series of strikes to protest brutal working conditions and starvation wages. Thirteen out of every fourteen days, underground miners had to work ten hours a day, not counting the time to travel up and down the mine shafts. As a result of WFM efforts, Utah became the first state in the country to enact an eight-hour workday for miners.

Bill Haywood, left, with Charles Moyer and George Pettibone, awaits the start of the Steunenberg murder trial. (Library of Congress)

In 1904, Haywood met with thirty other prominent labor leaders and wrote a manifesto urging the creation of what he called One Big Union. On June 27, 1905, at Brand's Hall in Chicago, Haywood spoke to nearly two hundred delegates at the founding convention of the Industrial Workers of the World (IWW). In his speech, Haywood described "a working-class movement" that would be in possession of "the economic powers, the means of life" and would be "in control of the machinery of production and distribution without regard to capitalist masters."

In the same year that the IWW was established, Frank Steunenberg, former governor of Idaho, was killed by a bomb at his home. Haywood was arrested and charged with conspiracy in the murder. In 1907, Haywood went to trial represented by famous defense lawyer Clarence Darrow. The highlight of what the press called "the trial of the century" was Haywood's own testimony asserting his innocence and claiming that the owners and the government had conspired to destroy the union movement and silence Haywood as a voice for the workers. On July 28, 1907, Haywood was found not guilty and turned his energies back to unionism.

INDUSTRIAL UNIONISM

Bill Haywood defined the aims of the labor movement, as he saw it, in a speech during the IWW founding convention, July 7, 1905:

Now, are there any of you who feel that your interests and the capitalists' interests are identical? Don't you know that there is not an employing capitalist or corporation manufactory in this country that if it were possible would not operate his or its entire plant or factory by machines and dispose of every human being employed? The corporation does not hire you. The employer never looks at your face; he never looks you in the eye. He cares nothing about your feelings. He does not care anything about your surroundings. He cares nothing about your twinges of anguish or your heartaches. He wants your hands and as much of your brain as is necessary to attach yourself to a machine. . . . The machine is rapidly taking your place, and it will have you entirely displaced pretty soon, and it is a question as between you and the capitalist as to who is going to own and control and manipulate and supervise that machine.

That is the purpose of this industrial union. . . . We propose to say to the employing class what the hours of labor shall be and what the remuneration shall be. We are the people who do the work, and we have got tired of those who do nothing but shirk, reaping all of the benefits. That is the definition of industrial unionism; the absolute control and supervision of industry. And when the working class are sufficiently well organized to control the means of life; why then . . . the ownership of legislatures and senates and, militias and police will be of little avail to them. . . . We are going to say to the employer: You must take your place in the productive system of this country or you will starve. . . .

So I have come back to Chicago, and am still on the frontier; that is, on the frontier of this industrial union movement, which I hope to see grow throughout this country until it takes in a great majority of the working people, and that those working people will rise in revolt against the capitalist system as the working class in Russia are doing to-day.

Source: "Big Bill, IWW Leader," in *The 1905 Proceedings of the Founding Convention of the Industrial Workers of the World* (New York: New York Labor Company, 1905).

By 1915, he had become general secretary-treasurer of the IWW and organized massive textile strikes in Massachusetts and New Jersey. An outspoken atheist, Haywood peppered his speeches with attacks on Christianity and the Bible, prompting condemnation from clergy around the country. Haywood relentlessly organized strikes in various industries. At various times, the IWW had more than three million members. It gained its greatest strength in the American West, appealing to that region's rugged individualism. The IWW welcomed men and women, black and white workers, immigrants, and native-born Americans.

Haywood, like many radicals at the time, was a socialist and supported the Bolshevik Revolution in Russia. After the United States entered World War I, Haywood criticized the war effort, calling it a means to make capitalists rich and send young men to die. He openly urged workers not to join the army and to slow down their work in defense industries.

LEGAL ACTION AND OUTCOME

In 1918, Haywood was charged with violating the Espionage and Sedition Act for calling a strike during wartime. He was convicted and sentenced to twenty years in prison. He served a year at the Leavenworth Penitentiary in Kansas, but in 1921, while out on bond pending his appeal, he fled to Moscow, where he became a trusted adviser to the revolutionary Bolshevik government and often appeared as a spokesperson promoting the success of the workers under the Marxist regime.

Suffering from bad health, Haywood soon faded from the public eye. Some historians claim that he became disillusioned that the Soviet Union under Vladimir Ilich Lenin had become more a police state than a "workers' paradise."

In 1928, at the age of fifty-nine, Haywood died in Moscow. Half his ashes were buried in the Kremlin and the other half in Chicago near a monument to the Haymarket anarchists who had inspired Haywood to devote his life to his fellow workers.

IMPACT

Bill Haywood played a pivotal run in the early days of the American labor movement. Bold and outspoken, he demanded better treatment for workers and pushed for the right of unions to organize and to strike. By advocating "direct action" and both being charged (yet acquitted) for the murder of Steunenberg and being convicted of espionage and sedition, Haywood's reputation would forever be linked to the violent and lawless side of the American labor movement.

In many ways, Haywood was ahead of his time. Years later, it would have been unheard of for a labor leader to be imprisoned for organizing a strike, even during wartime. However, in the era of World War I, marked by the Red Scare and the infamous Palmer Raids (raids on American citizens between 1918 and 1921 based on their political beliefs), Haywood's radicalism proved intolerable to the establishment.

FURTHER READING

Brissenden, P. F. *The I.W.W.* 1920. Reprint. New York: Russell & Russell, 1957. An authentic, contemporary chronicle of the creation and expansion of the most radical American labor union, with attention paid to the theoretical and strategic underpinnings of the IWW.

Carlson, Peter. *Roughneck: The Life and Times of Big Bill Haywood*. New York: W. W. Norton, 1983. A colorful and comprehensive biography of Haywood, filled with details of his personal and public life, seen from the perspective of his impact on the labor movement.

Conlin, Joseph R. *Big Bill Haywood and the Radical Union Movement*. Syracuse, N.Y.: Syracuse University Press, 1969. A useful work that employs the life of Haywood to examine the broader question of the goals, purposes, tactics, and impact of the radical wing of the American labor movement.

Lichtenstein, Nelson. *State of the Union: A Century of American Labor*. Princeton, N.J.: Princeton University Press, 2002. A sweeping study of the labor movement in the United States during the twentieth century, examining the legacy of Haywood and his labor movement.

Lukas, J. Anthony. *Big Trouble: A Murder in a Small Western Town Set Off a Struggle for the Soul of America*. New York: Simon & Schuster, 1997. A gripping account of Haywood's trial for murder, which vividly brings the players to life, despite published concerns over possible inaccuracies, which contributed to the author's suicide.

—*Stephen F. Rohde*

SEE ALSO: Dave Beck; Jimmy Hoffa; Vladimir Ilich Lenin.

LINDA BURFIELD HAZZARD
American physician and murderer

BORN: 1868; Carver County, Minnesota
DIED: 1938; place unknown
ALSO KNOWN AS: Lana Burfield (birth name); Linda Perry
MAJOR OFFENSES: Manslaughter and violating the medical practice acts of California and Washington
ACTIVE: November, 1902-May, 1935
LOCALE: Minneapolis, Minnesota, and Seattle and Olalla, Washington
SENTENCE: Hard labor for two to twenty years at Walla Walla, Washington, penitentiary; served two years before being pardoned

EARLY LIFE

Linda Burfield Hazzard (HAZ-uhrd) was brought up as a vegetarian in rural Minnesota. Her father had his seven children treated annually by a doctor typical of the era, and meat was forbidden as part of her medical treatment. Poorly educated and possessing a limited array of diagnostic techniques, the doctor treated intestinal problems, thought typical of all children, by prescribing blue mass pills. The mecurous chloride in the pills was so toxic that the U.S. Army stopped using it during the Civil War. Memories of the pain and sickness suffered by Hazzard and her siblings made her a lifelong foe of conventional medicine. Burfield attended two schools, training osteopathic nurses and studying with Dr. Edward Hooker Dewey for one term. In her book *Scientific Fasting* (1927), Burfield claimed to "throw new light upon [what Dewey] termed the 'New Gospel of Health.'"

CRIMINAL CAREER

In 1898, Burfield opened an office in Minneapolis, Minnesota, and began calling herself Dr. Burfield, D.O., a doctor of osteopathy. Minnesota law allowed the title. She treated hopeless conditions such as diabetes, syphilis, and kidney disease by using a combination of prolonged fasting, frequent enemas, and osteopathic manipulations. This last treatment, generally considered unacceptable, consisted largely of rapping the patient's head, back, stomach, and thighs.

Burfield sought to become the leading authority on "starvation therapy." Medical authorities appear not to have examined her methods until Gertrude Young died in 1902. The coroner, U. G. Williams, M.D., then obtained an autopsy at the University of Minnesota. Although the cause of death was listed as starvation, no charges could be made under the law of the time, and Burfield characterized the outcome of the investigation as a justification of her methods.

In 1903, Burfield met Samuel Christman Hazzard and wanted him both as a husband and as a business manager. Unfortunately, Mr. Hazzard was married to two other women and had fled service in the U.S. Army. While the couple was never married, she adopted the name Dr. Linda Burfield Hazzard for the rest of her life. In 1907, the couple moved to Olalla, Washington, near Seattle, where Dr. Hazzard established her practice and began to develop Wilderness Heights, her sanatorium.

On February 8, 1908, Daisy Maud Haglund died after a fifty-day fast at Wilderness Heights. A number of fatal cures followed, some of which may have involved actual homicide. It also appears that the Hazzards began relieving their victims of money, jewels, and property. The most celebrated outcome of Hazzard's treatments, described in her book, *Fasting for the Cure of Disease* (1912), was the death of Claire Williamson on May 18, 1911.

LEGAL ACTION AND OUTCOME

Claire's sister, Dorothea, persuaded the local attorney to bring a first-degree murder charge against Hazzard. Dorothea had been rescued from Wilderness Heights by Miss Conway, a lifetime friend. Hazzard was arrested on August 5, 1911, and the trial began on January 15, 1912. The trial involved more than one hundred witnesses and fifteen doctors. Hazzard was found guilty of manslaughter and sentenced to between two and twenty years of hard labor. During her appeal process, the Washington State Board of Medical Examiners revoked her medical license. At least two more persons died of starvation before her appeal was rejected in fall 1913. Hazzard served two years in prison at Walla Walla, Washington, and was pardoned by the governor on condition that she leave the United States.

IMPACT

Linda Burfield Hazzard was one of many medical "quacks" whose practices undoubtedly contributed to the eventual tightening of educational standards, examinations, and laws governing all aspects of health care. It appears that her story, with two exceptions, has been unnoticed in the extensive literature devoted to women professionals. However, there are still pseudomedical treatments widely available, and excerpts of Hazzard's works can be found readily on the Internet.

FURTHER READING

Iserson, Kenneth V. *Demon Doctors: Physicians as Serial Killers*. Tucson, Ariz.: Galen Press, 2002. Chapter 4 relies heavily on Olsen but is clearly written from a knowledgeable doctor's point of view.

Olsen, Gregg. *Starvation Heights*. New York: Warner Books, 1997. Detailed description of the years at Olalla with most attention to the Williamson sisters. The author claims to have consulted "every scrap published about Dr. Hazzard" but was unable to determine either her birth or death dates or places. Many references, but phrased very generally. Includes photographs.

—*K. Thomas Finley*

SEE ALSO: William Burke; Marcel Petiot; Michael Swango.

PATTY HEARST

American heiress, kidnapping victim, and urban guerrilla terrorist

BORN: February 20, 1954; San Francisco, California
ALSO KNOWN AS: Patricia Campbell Hearst (birth name); Patricia Hearst Shaw (married name); Tania
MAJOR OFFENSES: Bank robbery and use of a firearm in the commission of a felony
ACTIVE: February 4-May 17, 1974
LOCALE: Berkeley, San Francisco, and Los Angeles, California
SENTENCE: Seven years in prison; served two years

EARLY LIFE

Patricia "Patty" Campbell Hearst (huhrst), the granddaughter of publishing magnate William Randolph Hearst, was the third of five daughters. Her father, Randolph Apperson Hearst, was chairman of the board of the Hearst Corporation, a media conglomerate; her mother, Catherine Campbell Hearst, was a conservative University of California regent. Patty was reared primarily in the wealthy San Francisco suburb of Hillsborough and attended several private Roman Catholic schools. She graduated from high school one year early and entered Menlo College, where she excelled academically and earned a "best student award" her freshman year. As a sophomore art history major, Hearst transferred to the University of California at Berkeley to follow Steven Weed, her former high school math teacher, who had received a graduate teaching fellowship there. The pair became engaged and moved into an apartment in Berkeley with plans to marry in the summer of 1974.

CRIMINAL CAREER

Hearst's wealthy, sheltered life changed forever on the evening of February 4, 1974. Three members of the Symbionese Liberation Army (SLA)—a left-wing, urban guerrilla terrorist group—broke into Hearst's apartment. After beating Weed, the SLA members seized the

Patty Hearst in 1976. (AP/Wide World Photos)

noncompliant, nineteen-year-old heiress from her home at gunpoint, locked her into the trunk of a car, and drove her to a hideaway south of San Francisco. In exchange for her release, the SLA demanded that authorities release two SLA members who were arrested in the 1973 killing of Marcus Foster, Oakland's first African American school superintendent. After authorities refused to exchange Hearst for the jailed SLA members, the SLA made ransom demands, resulting in a donation by the Hearst family and the Hearst Foundation of two million dollars in food for needy persons in the Bay Area. However, negotiations broke down when the SLA sought an additional four million dollars. The Hearst family's efforts, negotiated dependent on Hearst's release, were fruitless, and the SLA continued to hold Hearst captive.

Hearst was imprisoned fifty-seven days in a closet and deprived of light, food, and sleep. Concurrently, she was subjected to almost constant ravings concerning the SLA's causes, as well as physical abuse and rape. Under the continuous threat that she would be killed if she did not cooperate, Hearst was "brainwashed" by escaped convict Donald DeFreeze (also known as General Field Marshal Cinque Mtume) and his small group of white, middle-class, college-aged radicals.

In time, Hearst said she was given the option of becoming an SLA member or being killed. She agreed to join the SLA and began calling herself "Tania," after the girlfriend of Cuban revolutionary leader Che Guevara. A taped communiqué, one of several messages sent to the media, announced that Hearst had taken up the SLA's cause. The SLA publicized a photograph of Hearst with a machine gun in her hand, standing in front of the group's emblem, an apparently willing revolutionary. Then, on April 15, 1974, during a San Francisco robbery at the Sunset branch of the Hibernia Bank, surveillance cameras showed Hearst holding an assault rifle. Witnesses heard "Tania" identify herself just before DeFreeze shot two people in a heist netting little more than ten thousand dollars for the group.

One month later, during a shooting on May 16, 1974, Hearst fired approximately thirty rounds outside a Los Angeles sporting goods store in order to thwart the arrest of SLA member Bill Harris for shoplifting. Police found the ditched getaway van containing a parking ticket, which ultimately led them to the SLA's location. The following day, Los Angeles police surrounded the house in which several SLA members were hiding. Six members of the SLA, including leader DeFreeze, died in the shootout and the subsequent fire that consumed the hideout; Hearst watched the melee on television from a motel.

HEARST ON DOMESTIC TERRORISM

During a January 22, 2002, edition of Cable News Network's Larry King Live, *King interviewed Patty Hearst. He focused on her participation in a 1975 bank robbery as a member of the Symbionese Liberation Army (SLA). In the course of the robbery, Myrna Opsahl, a customer, was shot and killed.*

KING: What did you think of the fact—when did you learn that someone had been killed? . . .

HEARST: It's unspeakable. Well, Larry, for them capital crimes, everything they did was considered a capital crime because they had declared war against the United States. So, you know, if—for them—if they had, you know, stolen a wallet that would have been a capital crime in their minds. It's a mind-set that's kind of difficult to understand. . . .

KING: To the young in our viewing audience, what was the aim of the SLA? What did they want?

HEARST: They wanted to overthrow the government of the United States and . . .

KING: With eight people?

HEARST: Well, yes. They called themselves an army. They were planning on recruiting more armies. They were planning on splitting up and forming smaller cells and going into different areas, recruiting more members and just growing until they had started a full scale war in this country.

Source: "Interview with Patty Hearst," CNN.com/Transcripts.

LEGAL ACTION AND OUTCOME

For more than a year, Hearst remained at large, staying mostly in Pennsylvania and New York. However, while back in San Francisco, Hearst was arrested by the Federal Bureau of Investigation (FBI) on September 18, 1975. In her trial, beginning in January of 1976, Hearst argued that she was intimidated into taking part in the bank robbery. Hearst's defense attorney, F. Lee Bailey, claimed an extreme case of the Stockholm syndrome, in which captives become sympathetic with their captors. In March of 1976, a jury found Hearst guilty of bank robbery and the use of a firearm while under the commission of a felony. Hearst was sentenced to seven years in prison. In a second case involving the store shoot-out in Los Angeles, Hearst pleaded no contest and received probation.

On February 1, 1979, after serving nearly two years in prison and five years after her odyssey had begun,

Hearst's sentence was commuted by President Jimmy Carter, and she was released. She was granted a full pardon by President Bill Clinton on January 20, 2001.

Just two months after Hearst's release from prison, she married former bodyguard Bernard Shaw. Out of the limelight, she became a mother, author, and occasional actor. She settled in Connecticut with her husband and two daughters.

IMPACT

Patty Hearst's saga offers insights into American cultural and political shifts in the late 1960's and early 1970's, which included widespread disillusionment with government policies surrounding such events as the Vietnam War, President Richard Nixon's resignation in the wake of the Watergate scandal, and official responses to dissent. Her tribulations are key to understanding the use of media in reporting violent acts, including kidnappings, the use of violence and terror to promote a cause, law enforcement responses to terrorism, and hostage psychology.

FURTHER READING

Hearst, Patty, with Alvin Moscow. *Patty Hearst: Her Own Story.* New York: Avon, 1998. A detailed account of the events from before Hearst's kidnapping through her clemency.

Rollings, Harry, and Jim Blascovich. "The Case of Patricia Hearst: Pretrial Publicity and Opinion." *Journal of Communication* 27, no. 2 (1977): 58-64. A discussion of pretrial publicity, its impact on a trial processes, and Americans' disenchantment with the U.S. justice system.

Third, Amanda. "Nuclear Terrorists: Patty Hearst and the Terrorist Family." *Hecate* 28, no. 2 (2002): 82-100. Explores the kidnapping of Hearst by the SLA and its relationship to terrorism as a threat to the structure of modern society.

—*Patricia K. Hendrickson*

SEE ALSO: Jules Bonnot; Che Guevara; Huey Newton.

GEORGE HENNARD
American mass murderer

BORN: October 15, 1956; Sayre, Pennsylvania
DIED: October 16, 1991; Killeen, Texas
ALSO KNOWN AS: George Pierre Hennard (full name); Jo-Jo Hennard
CAUSE OF NOTORIETY: Hennard murdered twenty-four people in a crowded restaurant during the noon hour; he committed suicide before being arrested.
ACTIVE: October 16,1991
LOCALE: Belton and Killeen, Texas

EARLY LIFE

The son of a U.S. Army doctor, George Hennard (HEHN-ahrd) moved frequently as a child, finally settling in Belton, Texas. His parents often had screaming fights, which were heard by neighbors. While Hennard's relationship with his father appears to have been distant, his relationship with his mother was highly contentious. As an adult, he often talked of killing her and drew a picture with her head on a rattlesnake's body.

CRIMINAL CAREER

Hennard was convicted of marijuana possession in 1981. On October 17, 1989, he was expelled from the Merchant Marine for flagrant public use of marijuana. He listened obsessively to the Steely Dan song "Don't Take Me Alive," which was about a gunman making a last stand against the police. He also studied every detail of James Oliver Huberty's mass murder at a McDonald's restaurant in 1984. In May, 1991, he was charged with driving while intoxicated and with illegally carrying loaded guns in his car.

On June 5, 1991, he went to a Federal Bureau of Investigation (FBI) office in Nevada, where his divorced mother lived, to complain about a white woman's conspiracy against him. That summer, he stalked two teenage girls in his neighborhood, screamed obscenities at women and girls, threw rocks at children, and made threatening phone calls. The Belton police refused to intervene. His request for clemency and reinstatement in the Merchant Marine was denied on October 11.

During lunchtime on October 16, 1991, Hennard drove his meticulously maintained Ford Ranger pickup truck through the window of a Luby's Cafeteria in Killeen, Texas. He jumped out of the truck and began killing people. Using a 9-millimeter Glock 17 with seventeen round magazines and a 9-millimeter Ruger P89 pistol with fifteen round magazines, he fired ninety-six shots in about four minutes. One patron, chiropractor

Suzanne Gratia, had a clear shot at Hennard while his back was turned, but she had left her handgun in her car in compliance with Texas law, which forbade carrying handguns. Gratia's parents were among the twenty-four people whom Hennard killed; Hennard wounded twenty-two more. Five police officers rushed to the scene, began shooting at Hennard, and entered the cafeteria. Wounded, Hennard retreated to a hallway, where he fatally shot himself in his head after a fierce gun battle with the officers. It was the deadliest mass shooting in the United States.

IMPACT

The George Hennard case had important ramifications for legislation passed at the state and national levels. In 1993, Texas substantially strengthened its antistalking laws to help cover cases such as that of Hennard in 1991. In 1992, the national Democratic Party specifically cited the Luby's massacre in its gun-control platform during the presidential election. Democratic congressman Chet Edwards, who represented Central Texas, switched sides on the assault weapon issue, and his support helped the 1994 federal assault weapon ban pass by a one-vote margin. The ban, which ended in 2004, would not have applied to Hennard's guns but did ban the manufacture of new magazines holding more than ten rounds.

Gratia (who married and took the name Gratia-Hupp) was instrumental in helping convince the Texas legislature to pass a "shall issue" bill to allow adults with a clean criminal record and who passed a safety class to obtain a license to carry a concealed handgun for lawful protection. Texas governor Anne Richards vetoed the bill, a move that subsequently played a role in the loss of her reelection campaign to George W. Bush, who, a few months after taking office, signed the "shall issue" bill into law. In 1996, Gratia-Hupp was elected as a Texas state representative on a strong pro-gun platform. She continued to serve in the legislature into the twenty-first century and to speak around the country in support of "shall issue" laws.

FURTHER READING

Cramer, Clayton E. "Ethical Problems of Mass Murder Coverage in the Mass Media." *Journal of Mass Media Ethics* 9, no. 1 (Winter, 1993-1994). Analyzes coverage of mass murders in the periodicals *Time* and *Newsweek* from 1984 to 1991 and shows that mass murders involving firearms receive far more media coverage. Also explores evidence that widespread coverage of mass murders by firearms provides an important motivation for publicity-seeking sociopaths to commit murder.

France, Alan W. *Composition as a Cultural Practice.* Westport, Conn.: Bergin & Garvey, 1994. A writing instructor explains how students reacted to an assignment asking them to analyze the media theme that Hennard's crimes were motivated by his poor relationship with his mother.

Karpf, Jason, and Elinor Karpf. *Anatomy of a Massacre.* Waco, Tex.: WRS, 1994. Excellent analysis of Hennard's failed adult life, his stalking of two teenagers, and information about the Killeen residents and victims.

—*David B. Kopel*

SEE ALSO: Baruch Goldstein; James Oliver Huberty; Marc Lépine; Charles Whitman.

HEROD ANTIPAS
Tetrarch of Galilee (r. 4 B.C.E.-39 C.E.)

BORN: Before 20 B.C.E.; possibly Sepphoris, Galilee
(now Zippori, Israel)
DIED: After 39 C.E.; probably Lyon, Gaul (now in
France)
ALSO KNOWN AS: Antipas (birth name)
CAUSE OF NOTORIETY: Antipas ordered the execution
of John the Baptist and mocked Jesus Christ.
ACTIVE: 4 B.C.E.-39 C.E.
LOCALE: Ancient Judea

EARLY LIFE

Herod Antipas (HEH-rod AN-tee-pas) was a son of Herod the Great (r. 37-4 B.C.E.) by his fourth wife, Malthace (a Samaritan). He was raised and educated in Rome along with his brother Archelaus. Antipas became Herod's favorite son after Herod executed his three eldest sons. However, just before his death, Herod altered his will to make Archelaus his successor. Antipas challenged the will, and though the Emperor Augustus upheld Archelaus's title, he divided the kingdom of Judaea between the four surviving sons. Antipas became tetrarch (one-fourth governor) of Galilee and Perea, probably in about 4 B.C.E.

POLITICAL CAREER

At the start of his rule, Antipas began an extensive building program, restoring Sepphoris as his capital following its destruction by the Romans after a Jewish rebellion. However, unlike his father, Antipas had weak judgment and was easily influenced by strong women. The later years of his reign are seen as a sequence of increasingly poor decisions. In 17 C.E., he created a new capital at Rakkath, which he renamed Tiberias in honor of the new emperor, Tiberius. However, he built part of the site on a Jewish cemetery, causing the Jews to shun the city, which further isolated Antipas from his subjects. Although Antipas effected Jewish customs, such as celebrating Passover, he was an Idumaean and thus never fully accepted by the Jewish population. Jesus later referred to him as "that fox," that is, both cunning and unclean.

Antipas's notoriety grew after 28 C.E., when he fell under the influence of Herodias, the wife of his recently deceased brother, who was also his niece. Antipas was married to Phasaelis, daughter of Aretas, king of the Nabataeans at Petra (Arabia), but he divorced her, sent her home, and married Herodias. For this action, he was rebuked by John the Baptist, and though Antipas was fearful of John, Herodias convinced him to have John arrested and imprisoned. The Gospel of Mark indicates that at his birthday celebrations, Antipas was delighted by the dancing of Herodias's daughter Salome and promised her anything up to half his kingdom. Herodias told Salome to ask for the head of John the Baptist. Ancient historian Flavius Josephus does not record that episode in *Antiquitates Judaicae* (93 C.E.; *The Antiquities of the Jews*, 1773), but he does confirm that Antipas had John executed.

When Jesus was arrested in Jerusalem, the procurator Pontius Pilate could see no wrong in him but, after learning that Jesus was Galilean, he sent him to Antipas, who was then in Jerusalem. Antipas had heard much about Jesus and was keen to see him, but when Jesus remained silent, Antipas mocked him and sent him back to Pilate; therefore, through inaction, Antipas became instrumental in Jesus's death.

The insult of divorcing his first wife brought Antipas into conflict with her father, Aretas, and a war ensued, which led to the eventual near-destruction of Herod's army in 36 C.E. Tiberius had favoured Antipas, but following the emperor's death in 37 C.E., his successor, Caligula, was less enamoured of him. Herodias encouraged Antipas to go to Rome to be made king, as had happened with her brother, Agrippa. However, Agrippa accused Antipas of conspiracy, and Caligula had him banished to Lyon in Gaul. Herodias joined him there, and Antipas died in exile, probably in Gaul and not Spain as Josephus later asserted.

IMPACT

Although Herod Antipas was not as gross a tyrant as his father, his desire to appeal to Rome made him an ineffective ruler. By executing John the Baptist and not releasing Jesus, he may be seen as one of the catalysts in the birth of Christianity.

FURTHER READING

Harlow, Victor E. *The Destroyer of Jesus*. Oklahoma City, Okla.: Modern, 1954. One of the first serious studies to understand the historical Herod.
Hoehner, Harold W. *Herod Antipas*. Cambridge, England: Cambridge University Press, 1972. Reprint as *Herod Antipas: A Contemporary of Jesus Christ*. Grand Rapids, Mich.: Zondervan, 1983. A thorough

study of Herod's life, using a critical evaluation of contemporary documents to assess and determine Herod's role.

Josephus, Flavius. *Josephus: The Complete Works*. Translated by William Whiston. Nashville: Thomas Nelson, 1998. *The Antiquities of the Jews* is available in this collection of Josephus's works.

Kokkinos, Nikos. *The Herodian Dynasty: Origins, Role in Society, and Eclipse*. Sheffield, England: Sheffield Academic Press, 1998. Covers the entire Herodian family with a reassessment of roles and responsibilities.

—Mike Ashley

SEE ALSO: Caligula; Herod the Great; Flavius Josephus; Judas Iscariot; Pontius Pilate; Salome.

HEROD THE GREAT
King of Judaea (r. 37-4 B.C.E.)

BORN: 73 B.C.E.; Ashkelon, Palestinian coast between Jaffa and Gaza (now in Israel)

DIED: Spring, 4 B.C.E.; Jericho, Judaea (now in Palestine)

ALSO KNOWN AS: Herod I; Herodes Magnus

CAUSE OF NOTORIETY: Herod, a pro-Roman ruler of Judaea, was capable of startling brutality, even against members of his own family.

ACTIVE: 37-4 B.C.E.

LOCALE: Judaea (now in Israel)

EARLY LIFE

Herod (HEHR-uhd) I was the second son of Antipater, a wealthy, influential Idumean, and Cypros, the daughter of an Arabian sheikh from Petra in Nabatea (modern-day Jordan). Antipater served as adviser to the Jewish high priest and ethnarch of Judaea, Hyrcanus II. In 47 B.C.E., Gaius Julius Caesar appointed Antipater procurator over Judaea. Antipater then made Herod governor of Galilee.

In 43 B.C.E., Antipater was poisoned, and anti-Roman factions promoted the nephew of Hyrancus II, Antigonus, as an alternative high priest. Herod and his brother Phasael, the governor of Jerusalem, drove off Antigonus, and Hyrcanus II rewarded Herod by giving him the hand of his granddaughter, the Hasmonean princess Mariamne, in marriage. In 40 B.C.E., the Parthians invaded Jerusalem and made Antigonus king. Herod fled to Rome, where he successfully persuaded Octavian and the Senate to restore him. In 37 B.C.E., two Roman legions drove the Parthians from Jerusalem, executed Antigonus, and established Herod as king over Judaea.

POLITICAL CAREER

Herod proved himself a skilled administrator, politician, and builder, but his high taxes and ruthless cruelty caused his subjects to hate him deeply. In the New Testament, Herod the Great is mentioned in chapter 2 of the Gospel of Matthew. In the Gospel, the Magi from the East visit Herod after the birth of Jesus to determine the location of the "king of the Jews." This alarms Herod, who, after consulting the "chief priests and scribes," learns that Bethlehem is the birthplace of the Messiah. Herod informs the Magi and charges them to report back to him. However, after visiting Jesus in Bethlehem, the Magi are warned in a dream not to report back to Herod. Jesus's father, Joseph, is similarly warned and flees with his family to Egypt to escape Herod. Herod then orders the massacre of all infants under the age of two in Bethlehem, an event known as the slaughter of the innocents.

Because neither the other Gospels nor the works of the Jewish historian Flavius Josephus, who was eager to portray Herod as negatively as possible, mention the Magi or the slaughter, the majority of historians doubt that these events ever occurred. However, Flavius Josephus mentions that in 6 B.C.E. Herod dealt harshly with some Pharisees who prophesied the end of his rule. Thus Herod's displaying concern toward the inquiry of the Magi is historically believable. Furthermore, the slaying of the infants in a small town like Bethlehem would have been an insignificant addition to the atrocities that Herod had already committed. The fourth century pagan philosopher Macrobius mentions the slaughter of the innocents, but it is possible that his words merely reflect the narrative from the Gospel of Matthew.

IMPACT

Herod the Great governed the very difficult province of Judaea with skill and won Roman favor for the Jews. Most of the exemptions and favors the Jews had under the Roman rule were secured and maintained by Herod.

However, his brutality prevented him from being loved by his subjects, despite their debt to him. Josephus sums up Herod's life with these words: "A man he was of great barbarity towards all men equally."

FURTHER READING

Brown, Raymond E. *The Birth of the Messiah*. New York: Anchor Bible Reference Library, 1993. Exhaustive historical and theological analysis of the birth narratives of the New Testament Gospels.

Josephus, Flavius. "Antiquities of the Jews." In *The Works of Josephus*, translated by William Whiston. Lynn, Mass.: Hendrickson, 1984. Standard English translation and annotation of the extant works of the Jewish historian Flavius Josephus, friend and biographer of the Roman emperor Vespasian and his son, Emperor Titus. Josephus relied on the now-lost works of Nicolas of Damascus, Herod's biographer and friend, for his material on Herod.

Kokkinos, Nikos. *The Herodian Dynasty*. Sheffield, England: Sheffield Academic Press, 1998. Describes the Herodian dynasty in the context of the political structure of Judaea and life in Greco-Roman Palestine.

Richardson, Peter. *Herod*. Columbia: University of South Carolina Press, 1996. A thorough and somewhat sympathetic analysis of the life of Herod the Great.

Witherington, Ben. *New Testament History*. Grand Rapids, Mich.: Baker Academic, 2001. Highly readable and reliable summary of the political and social backdrop of the New Testament world.

—*Michael A. Buratovich*

SEE ALSO: Herod Antipas.

RUDOLF HESS

German Nazi deputy to Adolf Hitler

BORN: April 26, 1894; Alexandria, Egypt

DIED: August 17, 1987; Spandau Prison, West Berlin, West Germany (now Berlin, Germany)

ALSO KNOWN AS: Walter Richard Rudolf Hess (full name)

MAJOR OFFENSE: Conspiracy and crimes against peace as defined by the International Military Tribunal at Nuremberg

ACTIVE: April 21, 1933-May 10, 1940

LOCALE: Berlin, Germany

SENTENCE: Life imprisonment

EARLY LIFE

Rudolf Hess (REW-dawlf hehs) was the son of a wealthy wholesaler and exporter living in Alexandria, Egypt. His parents were from the German middle class and had their home in Württemberg. However, Hess did not live in Germany until the age of fourteen. His father refused his request to go to a university and pressured him to join the family business. In 1914, at the outbreak of World War I, Hess joined the German Army in order to escape his undesired vocation. He served with distinction, was twice wounded in combat, rose to the rank of lieutenant, and became a pilot in the German Army Air Service.

Hess left the army at the end of the war and entered the university in Munich, where he studied history, political

Rudolf Hess. (Courtesy, USHMM)

science, and economics. He joined the Thule Society, an organization based on a belief in Nordic supremacy and strongly anti-Semitic in its focus. He studied under geographer and professor Karl Haushofer, who was the formulator of the notion of lebensraum (increased living space for Germans at the expense of other nations). While in Munich, Hess met Ilse Prohl, his future wife.

NAZI CAREER

On July 1, 1920, Hess met Adolf Hitler at a meeting of the National Socialist German Workers' Party, better known as the Nazi Party. The meeting was held in a Munich beer hall. After hearing Hitler speak, Hess joined the party as its sixteenth member and began his lifelong adoration of Hitler. In 1923, Hess joined Hitler and other Nazi Party members in the Beer Hall Putsch, an unsuccessful attempt to seize control of the German government, which was ruled as the Weimar Republic. Imprisoned with Hitler at Landsberg, Bavaria, Hess assumed the role of Hitler's personal secretary. He took dictation of *Mein Kampf* (1925-1927; English translation, 1933), Hitler's book detailing his plan for German expansion, and made editorial suggestions regarding lebensraum. Hess and Hitler were released from Landsberg in 1925.

After prison, Hess continued his role as Hitler's secretary. In 1932, Hitler made him chairman of the Central Political Commission of the Nazi Party, which put him in control of party organization and operation. On April 21, 1933, after Hitler's takeover of Germany, Hess was given the largely ceremonial title of deputy führer. Although many writers question the actual role of Hess with Nazi policy making, Hitler acknowledged Hess's loyalty by making him second in succession at the beginning of World War II in 1939.

Hess shocked the world on May 10, 1941, at the apex of war between Germany and Great Britain, by flying a fighter plane over Scotland and bailing out. His full motive remains a mystery, but his public account was that he wanted to meet with the peace faction of Great Britain, a move that he hoped would lead to peace between the two

---

THE BEER HALL PUTSCH

On November 8, 1923, Rudolf Hess accompanied Adolf Hitler, Hermann Göring, Jules Streicher, and Nazi storm troopers as they burst in on a meeting of three thousand people gathered in a large beer hall outside Munich to hear Prime Minister Gustav von Kahr. Hitler fired a shot at the ceiling and took charge of the meeting room, announcing that his men had surrounded the building. He declared that he was deposing Kahr's administration and told Kahr that he was about to march on Berlin and form a new national government.

With the help of the radical nationalist General Erich Ludendorff, Hitler forced Kahr to announce to the gathered crowd that he recognized the new government. Hitler followed the announcement with his own: "The National Revolution has begun!" Hess took Kahr and his entourage into custody. While this was happening outside Munich, Ernst Röhm was attempting to capture the German Army headquarters in Munich, and other fascist paramilitaries were assuming command at police headquarters. These attempts were not entirely successful and, combined with Hitler's lack of a follow-through plan, led to chaos as event spiraled out of Hitler's control and he succumbed to a nervous collapse.

Despite several later attempts to rally the public, Hitler failed to mount a full-blown revolution. Kahr, released by Ludendorff, regrouped and was able to muster police to meet Hitler's flailing onslaught. In the melee that followed, Göring suffered a gunshot wound to the leg and Hitler, a dislocated shoulder. The police took Hitler, Ludendorff, and others into custody.

The event went down in history as a failed coup, but it made Hitler a celebrity as a self-styled "patriot" and paved the way for his takeover of Germany a decade later.

---

nations. Hess spent the remainder of the war imprisoned in Great Britain; he was returned to Germany to face charges of war crimes charges at the end of the conflict.

LEGAL ACTION AND OUTCOME

The International Military Tribunal at Nuremberg, Germany, began on November 20, 1945, and ended on October 1, 1946. Hess was one of twenty-four Nazi leaders put on trial. He was indicted on all four counts: conspiracy, crimes against peace, war crimes, and crimes against humanity. He ultimately was convicted of the first two of these counts.

Hess's flight over Scotland saved him from the death penalty. He could not be connected to the most serious crimes of other Nazi leaders. Instead, he was sentenced to life imprisonment. He spent the next forty-one years at the Spandau Military Prison in West Berlin, the last twenty-one years as the sole occupant of Spandau Prison and as the most expensive prisoner in the world. He committed suicide by strangling himself with an electric cord on August 17, 1987.

IMPACT

Rudolf Hess's impact on history is far less than he anticipated. Because he was a key leader of the Nazi Party, the crimes of the party were also Hess's crimes. His legacy was tarnished within the Nazi ranks by his mysterious flight into Scotland; even his codefendants at Nuremberg, such as Hermann Göring, ridiculed Hess because of it. Hess died thinking he would be remembered as a martyr to the cause of German National Socialism. However, by irrevocably helping to connect that socialism to Hitler, Hess failed to comprehend that even modern Germans would reject Hitler as a madman and National Socialism as a fallacy.

FURTHER READING

Kater, Michael. *The Nazi Party: A Social Profile of Members and Leaders, 1919-1945.* Cambridge, Mass.: Harvard University Press, 1983. Integrates the impact of Hess on the party with that of other Nazi leaders. Good coverage of the rise of Hess to leadership and his role in party organization.

Manvell, Roger, and Heinrich Fraenkel. *Hess: A Biography.* New York: Drake, 1973. A full-length biography of Hess, one of several books by this author on Nazi Germany. Good coverage of the Nuremberg trial and Hess's years at Spandau Prison.

Reed, Anthony. *The Devil's Disciples: Hitler's Inner Circle.* New York: W. W. Norton, 2003. Details Hess's role in the Beer Hall Putsch, his taking of Hitler's dictation of *Mein Kampf*, and his personal relationship to Hitler.

Schmittroth, Linda, and Mary Kay Rosteck. *People of the Holocaust.* Detroit: UXL, 1998. Covers three groups of people: Nazi leaders, world leaders, and those who aided the Jews. The profiles of Nazi leaders include Hess.

Smelser, Ronald, and Rainer Zitelmann. *The Nazi Elite.* Translated by Mary Fischer. New York: New York University Press, 1993. Biographical sketches of top Nazi leaders. Questions the influence of Hess on Hitler but strongly supports the traditional view of Hess's loyalty to his führer.

—*Glenn L. Swygart*

SEE ALSO: Hermann Göring; Adolf Hitler.

REINHARD HEYDRICH
German Nazi official

BORN: March 7, 1904; Halle, Saxony-Anhalt, Germany

DIED: June 4, 1942; Prague (now in the Czech Republic)

ALSO KNOWN AS: Reinhard Tristan Eugen Heydrich (full name); Butcher of Prague; Blond Beast; der Henker (the Hangman)

CAUSE OF NOTORIETY: Heydrich was instrumental in implementing the Holocaust and was at the forefront of atrocities committed by the Schutzstaffel (SS)/Gestapo.

ACTIVE: 1933-1942

LOCALE: Europe, mainly Germany and what is now the Czech Republic

EARLY LIFE

Reinhard Tristan Eugen Heydrich (HI-drihk) was the son of Bruno Richard Heydrich, a musician, and Elisabeth Anna Amalia Kranz, a musician's daughter. While still in school, he briefly joined the Freikorps, but in 1922, he enlisted in the German Navy. His passions were music and physical exercise; he became one of Germany's most accomplished fencers. For two years he was in the Naval Intelligence Service under the command of Admiral Wilhelm Canaris and by 1929 had attained the rank of first lieutenant. According to a disputed story, Heydrich left the navy in 1931 because of a scandal involving the daughter of an officer (or shipyard director). Having impregnated the girl, he then abandoned her to marry Lina von Osten, and a naval court of enquiry dismissed him for conduct unbefitting an officer. It is known that Lina was an ardent Nazi and persuaded Heydrich to join the Nazi Party and to go for an interview with Heinrich Himmler, head of the Schutzstaffel (SS). Himmler named Heydrich to direct his Intelligence Service (later to be dubbed the SD).

NAZI CAREER

At the helm of the SD, Heydrich's cold, ruthless efficiency and accelerated energy level propelled him rapidly into a leadership position, particularly after Adolf Hitler's appointment as German chancellor on January

30, 1933. By March, 1933, Heydrich had become an SS brigadier general. Heydrich's intelligence network was noted for its intrusiveness and penchant for the minutest detail; he became one of the Third Reich's most feared functionaries. His bureau was said to have kept dossiers on all Nazi Party officials, including Hitler himself. Heydrich played a key role in the Night of the Long Knives (June 30, 1934), assisting Hitler and Himmler in the SS's liquidation of the leadership of the SA (Sturmabteilung, or stormtrooper unit), the rival Nazi paramilitary force; the listing of names that he compiled determined who was to be killed. Heydrich had by October, 1934, risen to a position of power within the SS second only to that of Himmler.

The official German justification for the attack on Poland on September 1, 1939, was orchestrated by Heydrich in what was dubbed Operation Canned Goods (some sources call it Operation Himmler). Heydrich arranged for a group of concentration camp prisoners to be outfitted in Polish uniforms and murdered, their bodies photographed at a frontier radio transmitting station at Gleiwitz, and offered as "evidence" of a Polish attack on Germany. After Poland fell, it was Heydrich who proclaimed the "ghettoization" of the Jewish population as the first step toward genocide. Heydrich and Himmler created the Einsatzgruppen as special mobile killing

Heinrich Himmler, left, and Reinhard Heydrich. (AP/Wide World Photos)

squads to seize Jews and other so-called undesirables and murder them as German forces swept through Eastern Europe. Used first during the Nazi occupation of Czechoslovakia on March 15, 1939, the Einsatzgruppen were the major agents for extermination until the time of the Wannsee Conference and would be utilized extensively during the campaigns in Poland, Yugoslavia, and the Soviet Union.

WANNSEE AND ASSASSINATION

In 1941, Hitler appointed Heydrich as Acting Reich Protector of Bohemia and Moravia (formerly part of Czechoslovakia), and he arrived at its capital, Prague, on September 21 of that year. The subsequent reign of terror and repression earned him the sobriquet Butcher of Prague. Heydrich set up the ghetto of Terezin (Theresienstadt),

from which thousands of Czech Jews were to be deported to the death camps. On January 20, 1942, Heydrich, assisted by his subordinate Adolf Eichmann, presided over the Wannsee Conference, where a more systematic policy of exterminating the Jews of Europe through gas chambers in death camps, labeled the "final solution" (now known as the Holocaust), was discussed, mapped out in detail, and approved.

The effectiveness of Heydrich's regime in suppressing resistance and increasing war production in the Protectorate led to the decision by the exiled Czech government to assassinate the SS leader. The plan was known as Operation Anthropoid. Four special resistance officers were parachuted in from London and on May 27, 1942, ambushed Heydrich, who was riding in his Mercedes convertible through the streets of Prague. A bomb hurled by one of the officers, Jan Kubis, sent fragments of metal and fabric into Heydrich's spleen, and he died on June 4, 1942, of blood poisoning.

IMPACT

Reinhard Heydrich's assassination set off a series of retaliatory atrocities that included the deaths of ten thousand Czechs and the physical eradication of the village of Lidice. With Heydrich out of the way, Himmler tightened his grip on the SS. The Wannsee Plan was implemented during the remainder of World War II, and Heydrich's role in its planning was acknowledged by the code-naming of genocidal procedures at Treblinka, Sobibor, and Belzec as Operation Reinhard.

FURTHER READING

Berenbaum, Michael. *The World Must Know: The History of the Holocaust As Told in the United States Holocaust Memorial Museum.* Boston: Little, Brown, 1993. An indispensable guide to the evolution and workings of the Holocaust; the role of Heydrich and the Wannsee Conference is closely examined.

Botwinick, Rita Steinhardt. *A History of the Holocaust: From Ideology to Annihilation.* Upper Saddle River, N.J.: Pearson Prentice Hall, 2004. Even though, in a book of vast scope such as this, Heydrich is denoted as a secondary figure, the crucial nature of his participation is clearly evidenced.

Butler, Rupert. *An Illustrated History of the Gestapo.* Osceola, Wisc.: Motorbooks International, 1992. One of the most incisive accounts of the organization and its administrators. Includes a characterization of Heydrich as both nefarious and enigmatic.

Goldhagen, Daniel Jonah. *Hitler's Willing Executioners: Ordinary Germans and the Holocaust.* New York: Vintage Books, 1997. Heydrich is distinctly identified as having taken initiative in decreeing ghet-

---

HEYDRICH'S POWER

Those who gather information gather power. Furthermore, those who misuse information condemn themselves. Reinhard Heydrich was the chief gatherer of information for the Nazi Party from 1936 to 1941, and he did not hesitate to use it to intimidate, distort, and murder, and to organize genocide.

In 1931, Heinrich Himmler organized the Sicherheitsdienst (SD, or security service) as the autonomous intelligence branch of the Schutzstaffel (SS). Heydrich was put in charge of the SD. His authority expanded greatly when Adolf Hitler became chancellor in 1933, and even greater power came to him in 1936 when he was given control of the Geheime Staatspolizei (Secret State Police, better known by its abbreviation, Gestapo) as well as the SD in the newly organized Reichssicherheitshauptamt (RSHA, Reich Department of Security), which also controlled the criminal police (Kripo).

In 1936, a new law essentially freed Heydrich and his Gestapo from any judicial oversight. He could use any means whatsoever to do the bidding of Himmler and Hitler. While the SD watched all political opponents (or Nazi Party rivals) and collected information on them, the Gestapo tracked, bullied, tortured, and killed anyone detected in any activity deemed subversive to National Socialism. The Gestapo also took over the duties of border police in order to catch spies and saboteurs.

In September, 1939, the functions of the security police and SD were combined, and groups of officers were transferred to each occupied country. They formed Einsatzgruppen (mobile task forces), which sought out Jews and political enemies for *schutzhaft* (protective custody), a euphemism for imprisonment without trial. Eventually, these task forces simply murdered any Jews and "undesirables" that they found. The Gestapo was also charged with establishing the system of concentration camps, where murder was later carried out with efficiency on an industrial scale.

To cover these extensive duties, RSHA had some forty-five thousand Gestapo officers during World War II. After the war, the International Military Tribunal at Nuremberg declared the Gestapo and SD to be criminal organizations. Its members were thereafter candidates for prosecution as war criminals. Had Heydrich survived that long, he would certainly have been executed along with the other chief Nazis.

---

toization and in organizing the Einsatzgruppen in Goldhaven's controversial work on the degree of culpability of average Germans.

Snyder, Louis L. *Hitler's Elite: Shocking Profiles of the Reich's Most Notorious Henchmen.* New York: Berkley Books, 1989. Heydrich is presented here as an extremely paranoid, self-loathing individual who compensated through sadistic actions.

—Raymond Pierre Hylton

SEE ALSO: Adolf Eichmann; Heinrich Himmler; Adolf Hitler.

HENRY HILL

American gangster and government informant

BORN: June 11, 1943; Brooklyn, New York

MAJOR OFFENSES: Extortion and possession of narcotics

ACTIVE: 1972-2005

LOCALE: New York, New York; Tampa, Florida; and Nebraska

SENTENCE: Ten years' imprisonment for extortion; paroled after six years

EARLY LIFE

Henry Hill (hihl) was born June 11, 1943, in Brooklyn, New York, to an Irish father and Sicilian mother. Hill was fascinated by the power and lifestyles of the local Lucchese crime family "soldiers" and became an associate of the organization at a young age. Still in his boyhood, Hill began to work for Lucchese leaders Paul Vario and Jimmy Burke, as well as other neighborhood gangsters who ran their operation out of Vario's cabstand and pizzeria. As a youngster, Hill helped run credit card scams and other extralegal errands for the older gangsters. After a stint in the U.S. Army as a paratrooper and being stationed at Ft. Bragg (during which time he ran numerous scams), Hill returned to New York in 1963 to continue his criminal career as a mob affiliate with Vario's crew.

CRIMINAL CAREER

Hill partnered with Burke and Tommy DeSimone in a variety of criminal enterprises, including truck hijacking, extortion, and other rackets. He was also involved in the infamous 1978 Boston College basketball point-shaving scheme. A 1972 two-million-dollar Air France heist and a six-million-dollar Lufthansa (German airline) robbery in 1978 are two operations in which Hill was reported to have been involved, along with several other crew members. Hill apparently received no money from the Lufthansa scheme and remained the only living member of the six criminals who were involved in the scheme. Hill later noted that he believed that most of the money went to the Mafia bosses.

LEGAL ACTION AND OUTCOME

Hill and Burke were arrested in 1972 for extortion and sentenced to ten years in prison. Hill then became heavily involved in narcotics trafficking and remained so after his release on parole six years later. Hill reportedly had heavy substance abuse problems of his own, and his womanizing and alleged abusiveness strained his family life with his wife Karen and two children, Gregg and Gina. In 1980, Hill was arrested for trafficking and turned government witness to save himself both from prosecution and from vengeful Mafia colleagues. His testimony sent Burke, Vario, and other associates to prison.

Hill continued to find trouble with the law: He got arrested in 1987 and again in 2004 for narcotics-related charges. He was expelled from the Witness Protection Program and moved to the West Coast, where he lived into the twenty-first century. He was convicted in March, 2005, of cocaine possession and sentenced to six months in jail.

IMPACT

Henry Hill was never "made" as a Mafia soldier because of his Irish heritage, but he serves as a good example of the many "connected" associates who work and earn money with the notorious crime families, paying "tribute," extending their own influence, and operating under the boss's protection. Hill achieved wide-ranging fame for the book *Wiseguy: Life in a Mafia Family*, written by Nicholas Pileggi and based on Hill's life. *Wiseguy* was later made into the popular 1990 film titled *Goodfellas*, with actor Ray Liotta portraying Hill. Hill has attempted to popularize and cultivate his public persona in the last decade, appearing on the *Goodfellas* DVD "special features" commentary section and marketing his own cookbook. However, in 2004, Gregg and Gina, Hill's children, projected a different side of Hill, publishing a book about their tumultuous childhoods with him and excoriating him for his self-centeredness, substance dependence, instability, and violent abuse. Nonetheless, Hill remains an important figure in modern criminal justice lore for his exposition of Mafia life, for making his lifestyle part of popular culture, and for his visibility as a surviving Mafia turncoat.

FURTHER READING

Hill, Gregg, and Gina Hill. *On the Run: A Mafia Childhood*. New York: Warner, 2004. Hill's children recount their tumultuous childhood and provide a damning account of their father as a violent, unstable, and self-centered criminal.

Hill, Henry, with Gus Russo. *Gangsters and Goodfellas: Wiseguys, Witness Protection, and Life on the Run.*

New York: M. Evans, 2004. Hill reports his version of living as a protected witness and his life since entering the program.

Pileggi, Nicholas. *Wiseguy: Life in a Mafia Family*. New York: Simon & Schuster, 1985. Pileggi recounts Hill's life and provides a story of the American Mafia experience, often in Hill's own words.

—*David R. Champion*

SEE ALSO: Tommy Lucchese.

SUSANNA MILDRED HILL
American con artist

BORN: c. 1880; place unknown
DIED: Date and place unknown
ALSO KNOWN AS: Mildred Hill
MAJOR OFFENSE: Mail fraud
ACTIVE: 1942-1945
LOCALE: Washington, D.C.
SENTENCE: Five years in prison

EARLY LIFE
Not much is known about the early life of Susanna Mildred Hill (hihl) before her crimes became known to the American public. A mother of ten children living in Washington, D.C., she was in her sixties when she began to deceive men in distant cities with whom she would correspond through the U.S. mail. Sometimes her children would assist her in setting up her scams.

CRIMINAL CAREER
Hill, a sixty-one-year-old woman, began sending pictures of her very attractive twenty-one-year-old daughter through the mail to lonely men who were looking for companionship and maybe even a promise of her hand in marriage. These men, thinking that the attractive young woman in the photograph was Susanna, would carry on a long-distance correspondence for some time, assuming that there was a romantic connection between Susanna and themselves. Once a strong bond was in place, Hill would begin asking her "pen pals" for money.

She wrote that she needed funds desperately in order to attain medical attention for her ailing mother. In turn, her lonely victims would send her cash and checks. She took thousands of dollars from unsuspecting men. Hill always chose men who were at least five hundred miles away in order to protect herself and her true identity. If, by chance, one of the victims would show up at her home—and quite a few of them eventually did—she would pose as the "ailing" mother, or she would tell the potential suitor that "Susanna" was not at home at the time. She actually told some of the men that Susanna had left home or that she had eloped with a used-car salesman.

LEGAL ACTION AND OUTCOME
Finally, in Chicago, Susanna's ruse was discovered by a suspicious suitor, and she came under investigation by law enforcement authorities. Hill was quickly arrested, tried, and convicted of mail fraud. She spent five years in prison. Little is known about her time there or what happened to her once she was released.

IMPACT
Susanna Mildred Hill's case was made public in the 1940's. Duplicated many times, this type of fraud has since become known as the lonely hearts scam. The case may have influenced present-day computer frauds that are very similar. Today, there are many ongoing cases that involve women or girls who claim via e-mail to be moving from country to country and that they need money to help defray their expenses. They usually prey on lonely men, hoping to part them from their money after spending some time communicating by e-mail. These men believe that they are helping to pay the women's expenses to come to America, or for personal visits or the like. After the scam artists collect the money, they disappear, never to be heard from again.

FURTHER READING
Kohn, George C. *Dictionary of Culprits and Criminals*. 2d ed. Lanham, Md.: Scarecrow Press, 1995. Contains interesting facts and short biographies of many criminals in American history.

—*Jerry W. Hollingsworth*

SEE ALSO: Frank W. Abagnale, Jr.; Billy Cannon; Janet Cooke; Tino De Angelis; Billie Sol Estes; Megan Louise Ireland; Clifford Irving; Victor Lustig; Arthur Orton; Alexandre Stavisky; Joseph Weil.

MARIE HILLEY
American murderer

BORN: June 4, 1933; Blue Mountain, Alabama
DIED: February 26, 1987; Anniston, Alabama
ALSO KNOWN AS: Audrey Marie Frazier (birth name);
   Audrey Marie Hilley; Lindsay Robbi Hannon;
   Robbi Homan; Teri Martin
MAJOR OFFENSE: Murder by poisoning
ACTIVE: 1975-1979
LOCALE: Anniston, Alabama; Fort Lauderdale,
   Florida; and Marlow, New Hampshire
SENTENCE: Life sentence for first-degree murder plus
   twenty years for attempted murder

EARLY LIFE

Audrey Marie Hilley (HIHL-ee) was the daughter of Huey Frazier and Lucille Meads Frazier, who worked at Linen Thread Company near Anniston, Alabama. Her grandmother and great-aunt often cared for her while her parents worked. Marie attended Anniston public schools, familiarizing herself with that community's social elite and aspiring to become wealthy. In seventh grade, she met Frank Hilley, who was four years older. She married him on May 8, 1951. Serving in the U.S. Navy in Guam, Frank sent his paychecks to Marie to deposit while completing her high school education. Instead, she spent the money before her discharged husband returned to Anniston.

CRIMINAL CAREER

During the spring of 1975, Frank began suffering nausea and numbness. He died on May 25. Doctors attributed his death to infectious hepatitis and failed kidneys. Marie spent the $31,140 in life insurance benefits. Then, in August, 1979, Marie's daughter was hospitalized with similar symptoms. Blood tests revealed substantial arsenic in her hair and urine. The county coroner ordered the exhumation of Frank's body on October 3, 1979. The state toxicologist said his body contained deadly amounts of arsenic. Police arrested Marie on October 8 for attempting to murder her daughter, for whom she had bought life insurance.

LEGAL ACTION AND OUTCOME

A Calhoun County, Alabama, grand jury indicted Marie of attempted murder of her daughter on October 25, 1979. After friends posted her fourteen-thousand-dollar bond on November 16, the freed Marie vanished. While she was missing, a Calhoun County grand jury, on Janu-

ary 11, 1980, indicted her of murdering her husband.

As a fugitive, Marie reinvented herself. Traveling to Fort Lauderdale, Florida, she met John Homan and introduced herself as Lindsay Robbi Hannon. The couple moved to Marlow, New Hampshire, where they married on May 29, 1981. Marie then concocted a bizarre story: While traveling alone to Texas, she telephoned Homan and identified herself as Lindsay's twin sister, Teri Martin. Teri told Homan that Lindsay had died. Then, pretending to be Teri, Marie traveled back to New Hampshire to comfort Homan. However, coworkers investigated items in Lindsay's obituary that Marie (as Teri) had written and discovered that it was fraudulent. They alerted authorities, who arrested Marie on January 12, 1983.

Marie's nine-day trial began on May 30, 1983. Her two children, sister-in-law, and cellmate testified against her. The state toxicologist confirmed that bottles seized from Marie's home had contained arsenic. After deliberating for almost three hours, the jury declared Marie guilty, convicting her of first-degree murder and attempted murder. Judge Sam Monk sentenced her to life imprisonment plus twenty years in Julia Tutwiler State Prison for Women in Wetumpka, Alabama.

Marie received a three-day pass from prison on February 19, 1987, and disappeared. On February 26, police found her seeking shelter from heavy rain on a porch near her birthplace. Suffering from hypothermia, she died en route to the hospital.

IMPACT

Marie Hilley's criminal activities shocked the people in Anniston who knew her. Nationwide, her case received a great deal of media attention, and Americans were dismayed that a seemingly normal housewife could act so lethally against her family. Marie's evasive techniques, elaborate lies, and years as a fugitive mystified many people. Some, including her second husband, remained in denial about her murderous nature. Marie's actions influenced the way in which many physicians interpreted possible poisoning situations, while criminal analysts studied her case to profile other females who kill using poisons. Marie defended her innocence, refusing to offer reasons for her behavior. In 1991, a television film titled *Wife, Mother, Murderer: The Marie Hilley Story* depicted Marie's bizarre behavior and multiple identities.

FURTHER READING

Douglas, John, and Mark Olshaker. *The Anatomy of Motive.* New York: Scribner, 1999. Douglas profiled Hilley when she was a fugitive to help Federal Bureau of Investigation (FBI) agents find her, describing her as a complex psychopathic personality motivated by control, anger, and greed.

Ginsburg, Philip E. *Poisoned Blood: A True Story of Murder, Passion, and an Astonishing Hoax.* New York: Charles Scribner's Sons, 1987. In-depth depiction of Hilley, her victims, case investigators, and people associated with her. Includes photographs of Hilley and her family.

Kelleher, Michael D., and C. L. Kelleher. *Murder Most Rare: The Female Serial Killer.* London: Praeger, 1998. Categorizes Hilley as an unexplained serial murderer, noting that she was sane and that she never clarified the motives for her murderous behavior.

McDonald, R. Robin. *Black Widow: The True Story of the Hilley Poisonings.* Far Hills, N.J.: New Horizon Press, 1986. A detailed account written by an *Anniston Star* reporter, providing background information concerning Hilley's family and the Anniston community.

—*Elizabeth D. Schafer*

SEE ALSO: Velma Margie Barfield; Madeleine Smith; Susan Smith; Andrea Yates.

HEINRICH HIMMLER
German high-ranking Nazi

BORN: October 7, 1900; Munich, Germany
DIED: May 23, 1945; Lüneburg, Germany
ALSO KNOWN AS: Reichsführer SS
CAUSE OF NOTORIETY: During the reign of Adolf Hitler and the Nazi Party, Himmler controlled the SS and the Gestapo and became the party's leading organizer and overseer of the Holocaust.
ACTIVE: 1923-1945
LOCALE: Germany and Eastern Europe

EARLY LIFE

Heinrich Himmler (HIN-rihk HIHM-luhr) grew up in a comfortable and conservative Roman Catholic, middle-class family. He excelled in high school in Munich and in Landshut, Lower Bavaria, particularly in classical languages and history. However, physically he was frail, and he suffered from a series of health problems, including lung infections, typhoid fever, and chronic gastrointestinal ailments.

In 1918, Himmler finished an officer candidate course, but he did not see combat before World War I ended on November 11, 1918. After the war, he returned to Landshut to obtain his high school degree before earning a degree in agriculture at the Institute of Technology in Munich. Neither farm work nor employment with a fertilizer company satisfied Himmler, who was disillusioned with conditions in postwar Germany.

NAZI CAREER

In 1921, Himmler noted in his diary that within two years he would emigrate from Germany. Instead, he became involved in right-wing politics and participated in the November, 1923, Beer Hall Putsch—a failed attempt at a coup led by Adolf Hitler and others of the Weimar Republic. After the putsch, Himmler moved back to Landshut and continued his support of Hitler's movement by becoming the deputy party leader in Lower Bavaria under Gregor Strasser, the head of the German National Socialist Workers' Party (the formal name of the Nazi Party). In 1926, Himmler followed Strasser to Munich and became the deputy Nazi Party propaganda leader until 1930. During this period, he married Margarete Boden, with whom he had one daughter.

Although Himmler played a key role in organizing Nazi propaganda and election campaigns between 1926 and 1929, during this period he focused his attention primarily on the Schutzstaffel (SS), initially a small battalion serving the Nazi Party. Having already served as deputy leader of the SS both in Lower Bavaria and in Germany, Himmler was given control of the national SS in 1929. Between 1929 and 1933, he transformed the SS into an elite paramilitary organization within the Nazi Party, and he created the Sicherheitsdienst (SD, or security service) within the SS to carry out secret surveillance operations.

After Hitler assumed power in Germany in January, 1933, Himmler first gained control of the political police in Bavaria and established a concentration camp in Dachau, Bavaria, for political prisoners. By 1934, he had expanded his control over the political police in all other states in Germany, including Prussia, where Hermann Göring had created the Gestapo (the secret state police) the previous year. After the purge of Ernst Röhm, the leader of the Sturmabteilung (SA, or storm troopers), in 1934, the SS became an independent organization and was no longer subordinated to the SA.

In 1936, Himmler was given command of all German police forces, and he assumed the title of Reich leader of the SS and chief of the police. On the eve of World War II, Himmler and his deputy Reinhard Heydrich organized the Reichssicherheitshauptamt (RSHA, or Reich Main Security Office), which combined the Gestapo, criminal police, and SD into one department. The RSHA played a key role in the Holocaust during World War II.

Beginning in 1939, Himmler's powers expanded dramatically. He was appointed Reich commissioner for the consolidation of ethnic Germans, which gave him control over ethnic Germans in Eastern Europe. Four years later, Himmler became Germany's minister of interior, and after July, 1944, he was given control of the German Home Army. Between December, 1944, and March, 1945, he also commanded army groups on the Upper Rhine and the Vistula. Only during the last weeks of the war did Himmler break with Hitler by attempting to negotiate with the western Allies. On April 19, 1945, Hitler dismissed him from all of his SS and police offices. After being captured by the British, Himmler committed suicide at Lüneburg, Germany, on May 23, 1945.

HIMMLER'S INHUMANITY

On October 4, 1943, Heinrich Himmler spoke to one hundred of his elite Schutzstaffel (SS) group leaders in Posen, occupied Poland, about the attitude he expected from his special troops toward non-Aryans and Jews:

One principle must be absolute for the SS man: we must be honest, decent, loyal and friendly to members of our blood and to no one else. What happens to the Russians, what happens to the Czechs, is a matter of utter indifference to me. Such good blood of our own kind as there may be among the nations we shall acquire for ourselves, if necessary by taking away the children and bringing them up among us.

Whether the other races live in comfort or perish of hunger interests me only in so far as we need them as slaves for our culture; apart from that it does not interest me. Whether or not 10,000 Russian women collapse from exhaustion while digging a tank ditch interests me only in so far as the tank ditch is completed for Germany.

We shall never be rough or heartless where it is not necessary; that is clear. We Germans, who are the only people in the world who have a decent attitude to animals, will also adopt a decent attitude to these human animals, but it is a crime against our own blood to worry about them and to bring them ideals. . . . I shall speak to you here with all frankness of a very serious subject. We shall now discuss it absolutely openly among ourselves, nevertheless we shall never speak of it in public. I mean the evacuation of the Jews, the extermination of the Jewish race.

We have taken from them what wealth they had. I have issued a strict order, which SS-Obergruppenführer Pohl has carried out, that this wealth should, as a matter of course, be handed over to the Reich without reserve.

We had the moral right, we had the duty to our people, to destroy this people which wanted to destroy us.

Altogether, however, we can say, that we have fulfilled this most difficult duty for the love of our people. And our spirit, our soul, our character has not suffered injury from it.

Source: "Speech to the SS Officers," in *International Military Tribunal, The Trial of German Major War Criminals* (London: The Authority of H.M. Attorney-General by H.M. Stationery Office, 1946-1951).

IMPACT

Heinrich Himmler's police and SS operations played a crucial role in consolidating Nazi power after January, 1933. The concentration camp established in Dachau became the training camp and model for other SS concentration camps. A number of the commanders and officers of extermination camps in Eastern Europe during the Holocaust received their training in Dachau. Before 1938, the majority of concentration camp victims were political prisoners and other Germans who had made critical remarks about Hitler. After 1939, however, the concentration camp system became a massive SS empire, inflicting pain and suffering on Jews, Gypsies, homosexu- als, political opponents, and social outsiders. Himmler's control of the police, particularly the Gestapo, allowed him not only to persecute opponents but also to punish Jews who violated Nazi restrictions or the Nuremberg laws after 1935.

Himmler's SS organization began a reign of terror in 1939 in Poland with the murder of Polish elites and selected Jews. Using SS Einsatzkommandos (special task units), the SS murdered thousands in the annexed areas of Poland. Moreover, by 1940, major Jewish ghettos were organized in Eastern Europe. In addition, beginning in 1939, Himmler's SS officers also participated in the euthanasia program, which was responsible for the murder of several hundred thousand people with real and imagined handicaps. A much more massive murder campaign was initiated by SS and police units in Einsatzgruppen (special task forces) in Russia after the German invasion in June, 1941.

By the late summer of 1941, Himmler, with the approval of Hitler, had organized plans for the total elimination of Jews in Europe. By 1942, three major extermination camps in eastern Poland, staffed by veterans of the euthanasia program, implemented the Reinhard Action, which decimated the Jewish population of Poland. In addition, the massive complex at Auschwitz in Upper Silesia was responsible for the extermination of Jews from a variety of Western and Eastern European countries. Himmler's SS and police apparatus murdered almost six million Jews and large numbers of non-Jews during World War II.

FURTHER READING

Breitman, Richard. *The Architect of Genocide: Himmler and the Final Solution*. New York: Alfred A. Knopf, 1991. The author argues that Himmler envisioned gas chambers as early as December, 1939, and that by March, 1941, key decisions for the "final solution" had been made.

Knopp, Guido. *Hitler's Henchmen*. Translated by Angus McGeoch. Stroud, England: Sutton, 2000. Includes a chapter on Himmler based on interviews with Himmler's contemporaries, which was used for a documentary film on Himmler available from the History Channel.

Padfield, Peter. *Himmler, Reichsführer*. London: Macmillan, 1991. A popular but reliable general biography based on secondary sources.

Smith, Bradely F. *Heinrich Himmler: A Nazi in the Making, 1900-1926*. Palo Alto, Calif.: Hoover Institution Press, 1971. Relying on Himmler's diary, the author describes in detail Himmler's youth and formative years, which reveals his petty obsession with minor details.

Waller, John H. *The Devil's Doctor: Felix Kersten and the Secret Plot to Turn Himmler Against Hitler*. New York: John Wiley and Sons, 2002. Includes a chapter titled "Himmler, the Man," which is based on the observations of Felix Kersten, Himmler's masseur.

—*Johnpeter Horst Grill*

SEE ALSO: Hermann Göring; Rudolf Hess; Reinhard Heydrich; Adolf Hitler.

JOHN HINCKLEY, JR.
Would-be assassin of President Ronald Reagan

BORN: May 29, 1955; Ardmore, Oklahoma
ALSO KNOWN AS: John Warnock Hinckley, Jr. (full name)
CAUSE OF NOTORIETY: Hinckley was found not guilty by reason of insanity in the attempted assassination of President Ronald Reagan, a verdict that subsequently had important impact on the criminal justice system.
ACTIVE: March 30, 1981
LOCALE: Washington, D.C.

EARLY LIFE

John Hinckley (HIHNK-lee), Jr., was born into a wealthy family. His father was the chairman and president of the Vanderbilt Energy Corporation. His mother was a homemaker. Hinckley was the youngest of three children. He grew up in Texas, and later his family moved to Colorado. As a young child, he excelled in football and basketball, and he was elected president of his seventh and ninth grade classes.

During high school, Hinckley became reclusive. In 1973, after graduating from high school, he enrolled in Texas Tech University, which he attended intermittently until 1980; he never received a college degree. In 1976, he traveled to Los Angeles to pursue his dream of becoming a songwriter. However, his efforts were not successful. During his stay in Los Angeles, he saw the film *Taxi Driver* (1976) several times and became obsessed with Jodie Foster, a child actor who played a prostitute in the film. After living in Los Angeles for a few months, he became disillusioned with Hollywood and returned to his parents' home in Colorado. In 1979, Hinckley bought his first gun, and in 1980 he bought another gun, which was later used in the assassination attempt.

CRIMINAL CAREER

In 1980, Hinckley read an article about Foster's enrollment at Yale University, and he decided to enroll in a writing course at Yale so that he could be near her. He slipped poems and messages under her door and repeatedly tried to contact Foster by telephone. However, Hinckley failed to develop any meaningful contact with Foster. He then decided that he could gain her respect and love if he achieved notoriety by assassinating the president.

In the fall of 1980, Hinckley decided to stalk President Jimmy Carter. He traveled to two locales during Carter's campaign trips; during his second trip, he was arrested at the airport when security officials detected handguns in his suitcase. Hinckley returned home, and his parents convinced him to see a psychiatrist in order to receive treatment for depression.

Hinckley's mental health failed to improve, and he decided to target the newly elected president, Ronald Reagan. He boarded a bus and checked into the Park Central Hotel in Washington, D.C., on March 29, 1981. On Monday, March 30, 1981, Hinckley wrote a letter to Foster describing his plan to assassinate Reagan, and on that same day he took a cab to the Washington Hilton Hotel, where Reagan was scheduled to speak to a labor convention. Hinckley fired a Rohm RG-14 revolver six times at Reagan as he left the Hilton Hotel. The bullets from Hinckley's gun struck Reagan in the left chest; stray bullets also wounded Press Secretary James Brady in the left temple, as well as police officer Thomas Delehanty and Secret Service agent Timothy J. McCarthy. Hinckley was immediately arrested. Surgeons successfully operated on Reagan at George Washington University Hospital; however, Brady was permanently disabled by the bullet lodged in his brain.

LEGAL ACTION AND OUTCOME

The trial of Hinckley took place in 1982. Hinckley claimed the defense of not guilty by reason of insanity. At the time that Hinckley shot Reagan, the law of insanity in the District of Columbia provided that a person was not criminally responsible for his or her acts if, at the time of the commission of the crime, the defendant, as a result of mental disease or defect, lacked substantial capacity to appreciate the wrongfulness of his or her conduct or to conform conduct to the requirements of the law.

The word "appreciate" became a critical issue in the trial of Hinckley. The defense argued successfully that "appreciate" not only meant cognitive awareness but also included an emotional understanding of the consequences of his actions. The defense maintained that Hinckley did not have the capability to emotionally understand the consequences of his actions at the time of the shooting. The defense utilized medical experts at trial

John Hinckley, Jr. (AP/Wide World Photos)

who could testify in support of Hinckley's mental condition. They also presented writings that Hinckley had generated in the months preceding the shootings, including the letter to Foster, in order to portray him as a man who was totally without the mental capacity to appreciate the wrongfulness of his conduct or to conform his conduct to the requirements of the law. The prosecution also presented medical experts as witnesses who testified that Hinckley did indeed know what he was doing at the time of the shootings and was therefore legally sane. However, on June 21, 1982, the jury found Hinckley not guilty by reason of insanity.

Although Hinckley was found not guilty, the court ordered him to St. Elizabeths Hospital for treatment of his mental illness. Beginning in 1999, Hinckley was permitted to leave the hospital for brief periods of time in order to have supervised visits with his parents in the Washington area, as well as to take day trips to local places. In 2005, a federal judge granted his request to make several overnight visits to his parents' home.

IMPACT

The acquittal of John Hinckley, Jr., by reason of insanity sparked public concern about the abuse of the insanity defense and created pressure for reform. At the federal level, Congress passed the Insanity Defense Reform Act of 1984. The act's provisions included changing the phrase "lacks substantial capacity to appreciate" to "unable to appreciate," thereby raising the standard of proof. It further specified that the mental disease or defect in a defendant must be severe. Moreover, the Insanity Defense Reform Act of 1984 required defendants to plead insanity as an affirmative defense. This meant that the act shifted the burden of proof to the defense, which must prove that the defendant is insane. In addition, the standard of proof that the defense must meet is the standard of "clear and convincing" evidence—a standard of proof in between the standard of preponderance of the evidence (more likely than not) and beyond a reasonable doubt (a reasonable certainty). While the prosecution must prove the defendant's guilt using the standard of beyond a reasonable doubt, the act requires that the defense must prove a plea of not guilty by reason of insanity with clear and convincing evidence.

At the state level, as a result of the Hinckley case, thirty-four states made some type of alteration to their insanity defenses between 1982 and 1985. The changes to the defense of insanity at the state level were similar to the ones made under the Insanity Defense Reform Act of 1984. In addition, in some states, "guilty but mentally ill" became a possible verdict in addition to not guilty by reason of insanity. Although these statutes remained in effect into the twenty-first century, many researchers have questioned whether the changes had any substantial impact on the criminal justice system.

FURTHER READING

Bonnie, Richard, Joseph Jeffries, and Peter Low. *A Case Study in the Defense of John W. Hinckley, Jr.* New York: Foundation Press, 2000. Provides a thorough analysis of why the Hinckley defense was successful.

HINCKLEY'S OTHER VICTIMS

The six shots that John W. Hinckley fired at President Ronald Reagan on March 30, 1981, wounded three other people as well:

- **James Brady**, the president's press secretary, received the most damaging wound. Shot in the head, Brady was erroneously reported dead at first. Surgeons were able to save him, but he was left partially paralyzed for life. Even though he never again was able to perform the job, he kept the title of press secretary until the end of the Reagan presidency. In the meantime, he was far from idle. With his wife, Sarah, he launched the Brady Campaign to Prevent Gun Violence and the Brady Center to Prevent Gun Violence, both dedicated to gun control. He lobbied relentlessly for it, and after a fierce political fight in Congress the Brady Handgun Violence Prevention Act, now known as the Brady Bill, passed and was signed into law by President Bill Clinton in 1993. Three years later President Clinton awarded Brady the Presidential Medal of Freedom for his advocacy.
- **Thomas K. Delehanty** had been a District of Columbia police officer for seventeen years when one of Hinckley's bullets hit him in the back and he fell to the sidewalk beside James Brady. He recovered from his wound but later retired on a disability pension.
- **Timothy J. McCarthy** was a secret service agent assigned to guard the president. (That day, however, he was not originally scheduled for duty; he was added to the entourage at the last minute after losing a coin toss with another agent.) The job description requires an agent literally to throw himself or herself between the president and danger—even if that means "taking the bullet" for the president. McCarthy is the only agent ever to do precisely that, and he was shot in the stomach. After surgery he made a full recovery and returned to duty, directing the Secret Service's Chicago Division until retiring in 1993. He then became chief of the Orland Park Police Department in Illinois. He ran unsuccessfully as a Democrat for Illinois secretary of state in 1997 and then returned to school and earned a master's degree in criminal and social justice in 1999. In 2005, the Illinois State Bar Association awarded McCarthy its Law Enforcement Award, for service that brings honor to the profession.

Caplan, Lincoln. *The Insanity Defense and the Trial of John W. Hinckley, Jr.* Boston: David R. Godine, 1984. Discusses the history of the case and pays special attention to the relationship between law and psychiatry.

Simon, Rita, and David Aaronso. *The Insanity Defense: A Critical Assessment of Law and Policy in the Post-Hinckley Era.* New York: Praeger, 1988. Provides a review of the insanity defense in other countries, how the defense has been treated in literature and the theater, and the results of a survey of legal and mental health experts.

Steadman, Henry, et al. *Before and After Hinckley: Evaluating Insanity Defense Reform.* New York: Guilford

Press, 1993. Examines insanity defense reform by focusing on the states of California, New York, Georgia, and Montana.

—*Patricia E. Erickson*

SEE ALSO: Mehmet Ali Ağca; Arthur Bremer; Samuel Joseph Byck; Mark David Chapman; Lynette Fromme; Richard Lawrence; Lewis Powell; Yolanda Saldívar.

HIROHITO
Japanese emperor (r. 1926-1989)

BORN: April 29, 1901; Tokyo, Japan
DIED: January 7, 1989; Tokyo, Japan
ALSO KNOWN AS: Shōwa Tennō; Shōwa Emperor
CAUSE OF NOTORIETY: The emperor of Japan during World War II, Hirohito personally opposed the war, but he failed to oppose militarists in the government.
ACTIVE: 1931-1945
LOCALE: Korea, China, Pacific Islands, and Japan

EARLY LIFE

The firstborn son of the Taishō emperor Yoshihito, Hirohito (hee-roh-hee-toh) was born at the dawn of the twentieth century in Tokyo. He attended private schools organized specially for the heir apparent to the throne and was reared with military ideals. However, the ritual suicide in 1912 of the Japanese hero of the 1904 Russo-Japanese War, General Marusuke Nogi, caused Hirohito to doubt military ethics. A tour of Europe in 1921 gave Hirohito an interest in science and Western culture. He officially assumed the throne in 1926 after his father's death, when he acquired the official Imperial name Shōwa, which means "enlightened ruler of peace."

POLITICAL CAREER

Although never convicted of war crimes, Hirohito ruled over the bloodiest and most turbulent period of East Asian history. Trying to expand its access to natural resources and to create the Greater East Asian Co-Prosperity Sphere, Japan invaded Manchuria, China, in 1931. Japan wanted to continue modernization and avoid the humiliation endured as a result of unequal trade pacts written by the European powers. Britain, France, Germany, and Russia had carved up China in the nineteenth century. Japan wanted to avoid this embarrassment and become the Asian leader of modernization, industrialization, and Western science. Many Japanese felt that an aggressive military was the ticket to future greatness for Japan, but Hirohito quietly opposed militarism and wanted to prevent the rise of a military dictatorship in the gov-

ernment. However, during the 1930's, the military established effective control over the government of Japan and placed military personnel in most of the high offices, including that of prime minister, a position held by former general Hideki Tojo.

In theory, as the emperor of divine origin, Hirohito had unlimited powers and could take a strong stand against rising militarism advocated by leaders of the army and navy. However, Hirohito was a shy, unassuming person even though he cautioned the military leaders

Hirohito. (Library of Congress)

HIROHITO SURRENDERS

On August 14, 1945, Emperor Hirohito announced over the radio Japan's surrender to Allied forces. For many of his subjects, it was the first time that they heard his voice.

We have ordered our Government to communicate to the Governments of the United States, Great Britain, China and the Soviet Union that our empire accepts the provisions of their joint declaration.

To strive for the common prosperity and happiness of all nations as well as the security and well-being of our subjects is the solemn obligation which has been handed down by our imperial ancestors and which we lay close to the heart.

Indeed, we declared war on America and Britain out of our sincere desire to insure Japan's self-preservation and the stabilization of East Asia, it being far from our thought either to infringe upon the sovereignty of other nations or to embark upon territorial aggrandizement.

But now the war has lasted for nearly four years. Despite the best that has been done by everyone—the gallant fighting of our military and naval forces, the diligence and assiduity of our servants of the State and the devoted service of our 100,000,000 people—the war situation has developed not necessarily to Japan's advantage, while the general trends of the world have all turned against her interest.

Moreover, the enemy has begun to employ a new and most cruel bomb, the power of which to do damage is, indeed, incalculable, taking the toll of many innocent lives. Should we continue to fight, it would not only result in an ultimate collapse and obliteration of the Japanese nation, but also it would lead to the total extinction of human civilization. . . .

Let the entire nation continue as one family from generation to generation, ever firm in its faith of the imperishableness of its divine land, and mindful of its heavy burden of responsibilities, and the long road before it. Unite your total strength to be devoted to the construction for the future. Cultivate the ways of rectitude, nobility of spirit, and work with resolution so that you may enhance the innate glory of the Imperial State and keep pace with the progress of the world.

by Allied atomic bombs dropped on Hiroshima and Nagasaki, Hirohito finally made a decisive stand against war and issued an official surrender while the war cabinet still debated the pros and cons of surrendering. Millions of Japanese gathered around radios to listen to the voice of their emperor issuing an unconditional surrender. Japanese citizens had been taught to worship Hirohito as a god, and most were hearing his voice for the first time. Supreme Commander of the Allied Powers General Douglas MacArthur accepted the formal surrender of Japan in a ceremony onboard the USS *Missouri* in Tokyo Bay on August 28, 1945. In the decades following that event, controversy erupted about Hirohito's knowledge of and ineffective resistance against the militarists in the Japanese government.

TOKYO WAR CRIMES TRIBUNAL

During the postwar American occupation of Japan, the International Military Tribunal for the Far East (also known as the Tokyo War Crimes Tribunal) met for two and a half years, beginning on May 3, 1946, and lasting until November 12, 1948. The trials were modeled after the war crimes trials held at Nuremberg, Germany, but they aimed for a grander scale. The prosecuting lawyers representing eleven Allied nations (Australia, Canada, China, France, Great Britain, India, the Netherlands, New Zealand, the Philippines, the Soviet Union, and the United States) tried more than 5,000 war criminal suspects; 920 were found guilty. The tribunal also removed "ultranationalists" from political offices, discontinued Shinto as the Japanese state religion, disbanded the largest multilevel industrial companies (*zaibatsu*), and initiated rural land redistribution. However, General MacArthur granted Hirohito immunity from prosecution on secret orders from President Harry S. Truman. The prosecution, led by American Joseph Keenan, attributed ultimate responsibility for the war to "a common plan or conspiracy" of the Japanese government. MacArthur believed that Hirohito's popu-

against being overly aggressive in Korea and China. The Japanese army had become notorious for cruel and barbaric treatment of prisoners of war, including the mass execution of innocent civilians at Nanjing, China, in 1937. The forces that would lead Japan to World War II were already in place as the United States enforced an embargo on Japan and demanded withdrawal from Manchuria. This led to the inevitable conclusion in the military that Japan needed to stage a preemptive attack on the United States at Pearl Harbor, Hawaii. Hirohito attempted to express his reservations against all-out war, but the militarists in the government were entrenched. The Japanese attacked Pearl Harbor on December 7, 1941, and the United States entered World War II.

On August 14, 1945, after thousands had been killed

larity could be used to rally support for restructuring the government as a democracy and rebuilding Japan following the devastation of World War II.

IMPACT

Hirohito's involvement in World War II war crimes and planning is debatable. He was not convicted along with the Class-A war criminals at the Tokyo War Crimes Tribunal, but many felt he should have been sentenced to death. MacArthur was more interested in using Hirohito to move the citizens of Japan toward rebuilding their social and governmental institutions.

FURTHER READING

Bix, Herbert P. *Hirohito and the Making of Modern Japan*. New York: HarperCollins, 2000. Vast work of modern scholarship based on sources that did not become available until after Hirohito's death in 1989. Argues that the emperor was more actively involved and knowledgeable about the preparations for war than previously believed. Hirohito carried out his role as head of state and commander of the military knowing about plans for Japanese expansion and conquest.

Buruma, Ian. *Inventing Japan*. New York: Modern Library, 2003. Focusing on the period from 1853 to 1964, this book documents how Japan, in just over one hundred years, modernized through a process of cultural reinvention, borrowing, and imagining a shared mythology. Buruma argues that Emperor Hirohito played a major role in the rush toward modernization and militarism.

Duus, Peter, ed. *The Twentieth Century*. Vol. 6 in *The Cambridge History of Japan*. New York: Cambridge University Press, 1988. This authoritative work is the standard in the field of Japanese history. This volume expertly brings together the best scholars in the modern period while the other volumes cover Japan from its origins to the present.

—*Jonathan L. Thorndike*

SEE ALSO: Adolf Hitler; Benito Mussolini; Joseph Stalin.

ALGER HISS
Lawyer and U.S. State Department appointee

BORN: November 11, 1904; Baltimore, Maryland
DIED: November 15, 1996; New York, New York
MAJOR OFFENSE: Perjury
ACTIVE: Late 1930's, 1940's
LOCALE: United States, mainly Washington, D.C.
SENTENCE: Five years in prison; served forty-four months

EARLY LIFE

Born the fourth of five children into a financially stable family, Alger Hiss (AL-juhr hihs) experienced emotional trauma throughout his early years. His father committed suicide when Hiss was only three. When he was twenty-five, his sister committed suicide, and his older brother died later from alcoholism.

Despite his emotionally troubled youth, Hiss became successful at an early age. In 1926, he graduated from the Johns Hopkins University, where he had been an outstanding student, both academically and socially. He was voted most popular student by his peers, was a cadet commander in the Reserve Officers' Training Corps (ROTC), and was a member of Phi Beta Kappa. He graduated from Harvard Law School in 1929. At Harvard, he had become acquainted with U.S. Supreme Court Justice Felix Frankfurter, who recommended him as a private law clerk to U.S. Supreme Court Justice Oliver Wendell Holmes. Hiss later credited Holmes with having the most profound influence on his career. In 1929, Hiss married Priscilla Hobson, a divorced editor and writer. Unlike many women of the time, she continued to work.

POLITICAL CAREER

An intelligent, well-educated, and handsome man, Hiss quickly made an impact as a lawyer and government employee. After working in law firms in Boston and New York, he began his government career in 1933, working as an attorney for the Agricultural Adjustment Administration, for the Nye Committee investigating the munitions industry, and for the Justice Department. In 1936, he joined the State Department. Hiss later played major roles in creating the United Nations and in serving as a member of the American delegation at Yalta in 1945, during the meeting of the "Big Three" Allied powers at the end of World War II. In 1947, he became president of the Carnegie Endowment for International Peace.

Hiss had gained prominence during a tumultuous time

Alger Hiss. (AP/Wide World Photos)

in American history. After World War II, another Red Scare exacerbated fears that communists had infiltrated U.S. government agencies at the highest levels and resulted in government investigations of suspected radicals. In this volatile climate, Hiss was accused of being a member of the Communist Party by Whittaker Chambers, a writer and journalist who, by his own admission, had been a member of the Communist Party. In 1942, Chambers met with the Federal Bureau of Investigation (FBI) regarding his membership in the Communist Party. He contended that he had recanted his membership in the late 1930's, having become disillusioned by the purges in the Soviet Union orchestrated by dictator Joseph Stalin. During the questioning, Chambers accused Hiss of being a Communist, but the FBI did not pursue the matter immediately. However, after interviewing Chambers again in 1945 and following other tips, the FBI tapped Hiss's phones and put him under surveillance. When Hiss met with FBI officials, he denied any connection with the Communist Party.

THE HUAC HEARINGS

Chambers appeared at congressional hearings held by the House Committee on Un-American Activities (HUAC) in 1948, and he again accused Hiss of being a member of the Communist Party.

Hiss demanded an appearance before the HUAC and unequivocally denied being a member of the Communist Party or knowing Whittaker Chambers. HUAC members, including a young Richard Nixon, continued to harbor suspicions regarding Hiss's denials. Chambers

continued supplying committee members with additional information, such as describing receiving a car from Hiss and identifying Hiss as an avid bird-watcher. Although some of the information was inaccurate—for example, that the Hisses did not drink—the new information convinced the HUAC to continue its investigation.

At a face-to-face meeting, Hiss admitted knowing Chambers but by a different name. Later, Chambers accused Hiss of espionage activities and supplying him with secret State Department documents, some of which Chambers kept to protect himself. These new revelations escalated the charges from Hiss being a Communist to being a spy and incriminated Chambers, as he earlier had denied espionage activities. Chambers gave these documents—all dating from 1938 and some containing Hiss's signature and notes—as well as the infamous Pumpkin Papers (microfilm rolls), to the HUAC. Hiss declared the documents were fraudulent.

LEGAL ACTION AND OUTCOME

A grand jury indicted Hiss in December, 1948, for perjury. His trial began in New York City in May, 1949, and lasted six weeks. The prosecution produced the typewriter, which was owned by Hiss, on which State Department documents had been copied. The defense argued that Hiss had disposed of the typewriter, after which others copied the documents. The defense also called several notable character witnesses, including two U.S. Supreme Court justices, a governor, and diplomats, as evidence of Hiss's impeccable loyalty to the United States. Chambers was portrayed as a liar and a person of ill repute. The trial ended in a hung jury—eight jurors for conviction, four against—and a second trial began in November.

At this trial, lasting only three weeks, Hiss was found guilty on two counts of perjury. The prosecution produced another witness who corroborated Chambers's accusations. Additionally, Hiss had less public support, resulting from enhanced Red Scare fears at home and the Cold War intensifying abroad.

Hiss continued to proclaim his innocence by using documents he acquired through the Freedom of Information Act (1966) and requesting Russian authorities to search their archives for documents. Indeed, in the 1990's a former Soviet general declared he found no evidence of Hiss's espionage in Soviet archives, but he later withdrew his statement. Further released archival documents, including the valuable Venona Papers, seem to weaken Hiss's denials.

IMPACT

The case of Alger Hiss became emblematic of the 1950's "witch hunts" against Communist sympathizers that threatened to undermine civil liberties in the United States. The trial of and denials by Alger Hiss reflect the hysteria of the Red Scare and Cold War attitudes in post-World War II America. Hiss's opponents and supporters remain divided on whether he was a guilty as charged or a victim of this era that witnessed attacks on political and civil rights.

FURTHER READING

Chambers, Whittaker. *Witness*. New York: Random House, 1952. In his best-selling autobiography, Chambers discusses his turbulent life and defends his accusations against Hiss.

Hiss, Alger. *In the Court of Public Opinion*. New York: Alfred A. Knopf, 1957. Hiss presents his side of the story, claiming complete innocence. In 1988, he pub-lished another book, *Recollections of a Life*, which presented additional information on his life and career.

Tanenhaus, Sam. *Whittaker Chambers: A Biography*. New York: Random House, 1997. A highly favorable account of Chambers, who the author believes is a significant American intellectual.

Weinstein, Allen. *Perjury: The Hiss-Chambers Case*. New York: Alfred A. Knopf, 1978. Weinstein originally set out to prove that Hiss was innocent, but based on evidence he uncovered, he concluded that Hiss was guilty as charged.

White, G. Edward. *Alger Hiss's Looking-Glass Wars: The Covert Life of a Soviet Spy*. New York: Oxford University Press, 2004. A study that examines and interprets Hiss's struggle to deny accusations made against him.

—*Sharon Wilson and Raymond Wilson*

SEE ALSO: Aldrich Ames; Anthony Blunt; Whittaker Chambers; Richard Nixon; Ethel Rosenberg; Julius Rosenberg; Joseph Stalin.

ADOLF HITLER
German chancellor (1933-1945)

BORN: April 20, 1889; Braunau am Inn, Austria
DIED: April 30, 1945; Berlin, Germany
ALSO KNOWN AS: The führer
CAUSE OF NOTORIETY: In addition to his goal of complete Germanic domination, Hitler aspired to rid the world of Jews. Although no specific order from Hitler authorizing the extermination of the Jews exists, evidence does suggest that in the fall of 1941, Hitler and his deputy Heinrich Himmler agreed in principle to mass extermination. Between 1939 and 1945, the Schutzstaffel (SS), under Himmler's direction, systematically killed approximately eleven million people (some estimates are twice or three times as high), six million of whom were Jews; in addition, non-Jewish Poles, alleged communists or political opponents, Roman Catholics, Protestants, physically and mentally handicapped persons, Roma (Gypsies), and trade unionists were also killed in the Holocaust.
ACTIVE: 1939-1945
LOCALE: Germany; Europe

EARLY LIFE

Adolf Hitler (AY-dawlf HIHT-luhr) was the fourth of Alois and Klara (née Pölzl) Hitler's six children. The Hitler family moved frequently while Adolf was a child, and although he was reportedly a good student, he failed the sixth grade and eventually left school at the age of sixteen. Hitler later tried unsuccessfully to enroll in the Academy of Arts in Vienna, where he was rejected for "lack of talent." Bitter and discouraged, he refused to seek other employment avenues and instead continued to work as a struggling painter in Vienna, where it was estimated that he produced more than two thousand paintings and drawings before enlisting in the Bavarian army in 1914. Poverty-stricken, Hitler temporarily resided in a homeless shelter in 1909 and eventually moved into a house for poor working men in 1910. The early roots of Hitler's anti-Semitism are traceable to his time spent in Vienna, where resentment and dislike of Jews was common among Austrians.

After previously escaping military service in Austria (a crime for which he was arrested by the Austrian army), he enlisted in the Sixteenth Bavarian Reserve Infantry regiment during the early days of World War I. Hitler saw considerable action during World War I; he served in France and Belgium and received several military distinctions, including the Iron Cross Second Class and the Iron Cross First Class. Although described as a somewhat sloppy soldier, Hitler displayed fearlessness in battle, often volunteering for dangerous missions and eventually receiving the Wound Badge (equivalent to an American Purple Heart) for injuries sustained in October of 1916. Two years later, in October, 1918, Hitler was admitted to a military field hospital for temporary blindness brought on by a poisonous gas attack. Historians now believe that Hitler's blindness may in fact have been the result of a hysterical reaction to Germany's defeat. Military physicians and a psychiatric specialist who examined Hitler found him unfit to command subordinates and suggested that he was dangerously psychotic.

Hitler's experiences in World War I greatly influenced him and served as the catalyst for his belief that he was Germany's savior. Although not a German citizen until 1932, he had become a fanatical German patriot

Adolf Hitler. (Library of Congress)

during the war and was appalled by the surrender and subsequent conditions of the 1919 Treaty of Versailles. Most Germans, Hitler in particular, perceived the harsh stipulations of the treaty as imposing humiliation and degradation on the German people and nation. Germany's discontent with the terms of Versailles proved an important factor in the sociopolitical conditions under which Hitler began to operate during the 1920's.

POLITICAL CAREER

During 1919, Hitler became involved with the small nationalist political organization, the German Workers' Party (DAP), which espoused anti-Marxist and anti-Semitic philosophies. He quickly rose through the ranks of the DAP to become the party's spokesperson and leading propagandist. In July of 1921, after an attempted ousting by the DAP's original members, Hitler's demands for dictatorial power were met: He was anointed führer (leader) of the party, the name of which Hitler changed from DAP to the Nationalist Socialist German Workers' Party, or Nazi Party. In 1923, inspired by fascist Italian leader Benito Mussolini's March on Rome, Hitler attempted a coup, known now as the Beer Hall Putsch; it failed and resulted in his arrest and conviction for conspiracy to commit treason, a crime for which he was sentenced to five years' imprisonment. While at Landsberg Prison, Hitler dictated his infamous autobiography *Mein Kampf* (1925-1927; English translation, 1933) to his deputy Rudolf Hess (who would later become deputy führer, third in command of Nazi Germany). This book would later serve as the political platform of the Nazi Party.

When Hitler was released early from prison in December of 1924, he faced a dwindling Nazi Party in desperate need of rebuilding. Hitler attempted to incorporate nationalistic sentiments with accusations against "international Jewry" in order to garner electoral support. However, he was largely unsuccessful. The party soon learned to utilize subtler propaganda techniques, blaming Germany's problems on the failures of the Weimar Republic. These messages and their subtext resonated better with the populace. While rebuilding his party, Hitler also introduced a new method of party organization that included unquestioning obedience to superiors and devolution of power and authority from the top down.

With Hitler at the helm, the Nazi Party found itself in politically advantageous circumstances when the Great Depression hit Europe. The Nazis rose from relative obscurity to win 107 seats in the Reichstag in September,

1930, becoming the second largest party in Germany. Not quite three years later, on January 30, 1933, Germany's president, Paul von Hindenburg, appointed Hitler as chancellor. Following Hindenburg's death on August 2, 1934, Hitler seized absolute power, refusing to hold new presidential elections and instead passing a law that combined the offices of president and chancellor. Shortly thereafter, Hitler ordered every member of the military to swear an oath of personal allegiance to him.

Hitler's government pushed through sweeping reforms during the first several years of his reign, which buttressed the campaign for absolute control. Nazi Germany also instituted policies, to be enforced by Hitler's Gestapo (secret state police), that targeted Jews, communists, and habitual criminals. During the early to mid-1930's, several pieces of legislation were passed restricting the civil rights of Jews and limiting their economic opportunity. These policies fueled the emigration of thousands of Germany's Jews and led to increasingly violent tactics, such as *Kristallnacht* (the night of broken glass) in November, 1938, when Jewish businesses and synagogues were destroyed. Hitler's vision of world domination became increasingly apparent after he reoccupied the Rhineland and invaded Poland on September 1, 1939, effectively starting World War II. Hitler would threaten Europe throughout the war until his death by suicide in his Berlin bunker with his mistress Eva Braun, on April 30, 1945. Allied victory in the European theater was declared one week later.

IMPACT

There is perhaps no other individual whose name is more synonymous with evil than that of Adolf Hitler. Hitler's legacy is one of racism, hatred, and destruction, and he remains vilified across time and space. The effects of World War II and the Holocaust are almost incalculable and the level of destruction wrought on the world by Hitler's vision almost incomprehensible.

On a global level, Hitler's world war set the stage for what would come to define the remainder of the twentieth century—the battle for military and economic supremacy between the newly created superpowers, the United States and Soviet Union. The events of World War II opened a political vacuum on the European continent that was filled by the Soviets, consequently triggering a reaction formation from the United States, which manifested itself across a range of issues and events, from the space race to the proposal of a Strategic Defense Intiative (Star Wars) in the early 1980's, to ongoing troubles in Korea and Vietnam. Had Europe been less susceptible to foreign meddling in the years immediately following World War II, the Cold War may not have unfolded in such a manner. European weakness was ultimately traceable to the actions engaged by Hitler.

HITLER'S PROCLAMATION ON INVADING RUSSIA

On June 22, 1941, Adolf Hitler announced to the German people his intention to invade Russia, as usual mixing truth with lies. He ended his speech with typical Hitlerian stridency:

Today something like 160 Russian divisions are stranding at our frontiers. For weeks constant violations of this frontier have taken place, not only affecting us but from the far north down to Rumania. Russian airmen consider it sport nonchalantly to overlook these frontiers, presumably to prove to us that they already feel themselves masters of these territories. During the night of June 17 to June 18 Russian patrols again penetrated into the Reich's territory and could only be driven back after prolonged firing. This has brought us to the hour when it is necessary for us to take steps against this plot devised by the Jewish-Anglo-Saxon warmongers and equally the Jewish rulers of the Bolshevist center in Moscow.

German people! At this moment a march is taking place that, as regards, extent, compares with the greatest the world hitherto has seen. United with their Finnish comrades, the fighters of the victory of Narvik are standing in the Northern Arctic. German divisions commanded by the conqueror of Norway, in cooperation with the heros of Finnish freedom, under their marshal, are protecting Finnish soil. Formations of the German eastern front extend from East Prussia to the Carpathians. German and Rumanian soldiers are united under Chief of State Antonescu from the banks of the Pruth along the lower reaches of the Danube to the shores of the Black Sea. The task of this front, therefore, no longer is the protection of single countries, but the safeguarding of Europe and thereby the salvation of all.

I therefore decided today again to lay the fate of the future of the German Reich and our people in the hands of our soldiers.

May God help us especially in this fight!

Source: "Hitler's Proclamation on Invading Russia, 1941," *The Great Documents of Western Civilization*, edited by Milton Viorst (New York: Grosset & Dunlap, 1965).

FURTHER READING

Davidson, Eugene. *The Unmaking of Adolf Hitler.* Columbia: University of Missouri Press, 1996. Follows the author's *The Making of Hitler* (1977), which addressed Hitler's rise to power. The second volume focuses on Hitler from the Nazi seizure of power through his death, with an emphasis on events prior to 1939. Dissects the various relationships between Hitler and his political allies and foes, cleverly demonstrating that these were often one and the same over time. Academic historians will be disappointed in the lack of incorporation of leading sources and documents such as the Nazi archives. Hitler's cult of personality is portrayed in great detail in a somewhat positive manner that seems to minimize the vast social harm and devastation to humanity normally attributed to Hitler.

Giblin, James Cross. *The Life and Death of Adolf Hitler.* New York: Clarion, 2002. A biography that focuses heavily on the dictator's early life experiences, particularly his troubled family life during his formative adolescent years. In-depth coverage is also given to Hitler's military experiences prior to World War II and how they influenced the development of the Nazi political party in prewar Germany. Numerous reviews cite the chapter on anti-Semitism as a leading academic reference source. Little attention is given to the rise of the Nazi Party and Hitler's ascension to political and social dominance. Rather, the emphasis is on the lingering effects of Hitler and the Nazi experience. Includes eyewitness accounts that support the author's contention that world politics continue to reflect Nazi history.

Rosenbaum, Ron. *Explaining Hitler: The Search for the Origins of His Evil.* New York: Random House, 1998. This portrayal of Hitler examines the psychological basis of his personality and wicked conduct. The work is a meta-analysis in that the author relates the thoughts of the wide range of commentators—journalists, filmmakers, historians, and philosophers—he has interviewed, all of whom have sought to unravel Hitler's psyche. He examines a number of competing hypotheses regarding why Hitler subscribed to the ideology of supremacy and, ultimately, the reasons for the Holocaust. Accordingly, various Hitlers are illustrated, ranging from ladies' man to homosexual, con man to patriot, and brutal gangster to artist.

—J. Mitchell Miller

SEE ALSO: Klaus Barbie; Karl Dönitz; Adolf Eichmann; Hans Michael Frank; Joseph Goebbels; Magda Goebbels; Hermann Göring; Rudolf Hess; Reinhard Heydrich; Heinrich Himmler; Alfred Jodl; Josef Mengele; Benito Mussolini; Joachim von Ribbentrop.

JIMMY HOFFA
American Teamsters Union president (1957-1971)

BORN: February 14, 1913; Brazil, Indiana
DIED: Possibly July 30, 1975; Bloomfield Hills, near Detroit, Michigan
ALSO KNOWN AS: James Riddle Hoffa (full name)
MAJOR OFFENSES: Misuse of union funds
ACTIVE: 1957-1975
LOCALE: Detroit, Michigan
SENTENCE: Eight years' imprisonment for jury tampering; five years' imprisonment for misuse of union funds; commuted by President Richard Nixon in 1971

EARLY LIFE

James "Jimmy" Riddle Hoffa (HAW-fah) was born on Valentine's Day in 1913 in Brazil, Indiana. His father was a coal miner who died seven years after Hoffa's birth, leaving Jimmy and his mother impoverished. At fourteen, Hoffa left school to work in a Detroit warehouse. Concerned over the mistreatment of the workers, he participated in organizing his first strike at the age of twenty. Shortly thereafter, he was hired as a business agent by the local International Brotherhood of Teamsters (commonly called the Teamsters), a labor union that organizes truck drivers nationwide, and was quickly promoted.

UNION CAREER

Hoffa was elected the international Teamsters vice president in 1952; he became president in 1957, succeeding Dave Beck after Beck was imprisoned. Hoffa allegedly had ties to the Republican Party and the Mafia, who assisted his ascension to presidency of the Teamsters. Hoffa guided the Teamsters in assisting truckers with securing better contracts through coordinating strikes and

Jimmy Hoffa. (AP/Wide World Photos)

LEGAL ACTION AND OUTCOME

As a result of the Teamsters' alleged ties with the Mafia, in 1957 Robert Kennedy directed a federal investigation into the union via the McClellan Committee, the abbreviated name for the Senate Select Committee on Improper Activities in the Labor or Management Field, headed by Arkansas senator John L. McClellan. Explosive confrontations occurred between Kennedy and Hoffa during the hearings, with Hoffa insisting that he did not remember events or individuals. National media provided extensive coverage of the events. Ultimately, the three-year investigation by the committee found, among other things, approximately ten million dollars of Teamsters Union money misappropriated by Hoffa. Over the course of five different trials, Hoffa was ultimately sentenced to eight years' imprisonment for jury tampering in 1962 and five years' imprisonment for misuse of union funds in 1964.

Although he was imprisoned, Hoffa refused to resign his Teamsters presidency, and he continued to lead the union. After Hoffa had served four years in prison, President Richard M. Nixon commuted his sentence. (Hoffa had contributed financially to Nixon's campaign.) Hoffa was released on December 24, 1971, on the condition that he refrain from any union activities for ten years. Because of this restriction, Hoffa was forced to give up his Teamsters presidency.

DISAPPEARANCE

Despite Hoffa's popularity as the president of the Teamsters Union and his publicized conviction and prison time, Hoffa is perhaps best remembered for the mysterious circumstances surrounding his disappearance in 1975. At that time, Hoffa was contesting the ban on his union activities and attempting to regain his Teamsters leadership. He was scheduled to meet two Mafia leaders at the Machus Red Fox Restaurant in Bloomfield Hills, Michigan. Hoffa was last seen in the parking lot on July 30, 1975. His body was never found, and investigators assumed he was killed by the Mafia, as he had incriminating information on many high-ranking mob bosses. However, no one was ever convicted for Hoffa's murder. Several years later, he was declared legally dead, and a death certificate formalized his death on July 30, 1982.

IMPACT

After Jimmy Hoffa's disappearance, the trucking industry was deregulated, countering many of the achievements made by Hoffa for truck drivers under the National Master Freight Agreement. However, despite his success

boycotts. The union was also criticized for using illegitimate means (such as violence and alleged ties to organized crime) in order to control workers and companies.

The Teamsters expanded quickly under Hoffa's lead, with increasing membership that reached more than two million. Hoffa developed the union nationally by negotiating the first national master freight contract among trucking companies. He later attempted to expand the union to include employees of other transportation industries, such as the airlines. Despite improved working conditions for truck drivers, many local Teamsters Unions created deals that continued to exploit workers in order to make money for the union officials. In some industries, organized crime took control, with union officials receiving kickbacks. The corruption of the Teamsters under Hoffa was exemplified by the Central States Pension Fund—retirement money of union members meant to be invested for high returns. From this fund, the Teamsters loaned money to those in the underworld, including Morris "Moe" Dalitz, who then used the money in part to build hotels in Las Vegas.

within the union, Hoffa is remembered by most Americans for his disappearance and the speculation surrounding his presumed death, which, in turn, created further myths and investigations over the ensuing decades. With the technological advancements of evidence analysis, police were able to use deoxyribonucleic acid (DNA) evidence in 2001 to contradict the claims of Teamster Charles O'Brien that Hoffa never was in his car, although this evidence did not lead to any indictments. Three years later, Mafia hit man Frank Sheeran confessed to Hoffa's murder in the 2004 book *I Heard You Paint Houses*, authored by former prosecutor Charles Brandt; the confession was not substantiated. Many films, television series, and books have focused on Hoffa's life and alleged mob ties, while references to his unfound remains are used for comedic effect within American popular culture.

FURTHER READING

Brandt, Charles. *I Heard You Paint Houses: Frank "the Irishman" Sheeran and the Inside Story of the Mafia, the Teamsters, and the Last Ride of Jimmy Hoffa*. Hanover, N.H.: Steerforth Press, 2004. Sheeran, a Mafia hit man and Delaware Teamsters official, confesses to the murder of Hoffa in great detail.

Franco, Joseph, with Richard Hammer. *Hoffa's Man: The Rise and Fall of Jimmy Hoffa As Witnessed by His Strongest Arm*. New York: Prentice Hall, 1987. A contract killer's account of Hoffa's expansion of the Teamsters with the help of the Mafia and his path to prison.

Kennedy, Robert. *The Enemy Within: The McClellan Committee's Crusade Against Jimmy Hoffa and Corrupt Labor Unions*. 1960. Reprint. Westport, Conn.: Greenwood Press, 1982. Kennedy details the inner workings of labor and trade unions, including Hoffa's role within them, and examines how Hoffa was caught attempting to tamper with the findings of the McClellan Committee.

—*Jennifer C. Gibbs*

SEE ALSO: Dave Beck; Bill Haywood.

THE HUNT FOR HOFFA

On May 30, 2006, the Detroit office of the Federal Bureau of Investigation (FBI) released the following statement after failing to find Jimmy Hoffa's body when a tip led federal agents to search for it near the Hidden Dreams Farm in Milford Township, Michigan:

On May 17th, the FBI, in conjunction with the Bloomfield Township Police Department, commenced the search of this property acting on the authority of a federal search warrant. The warrant was based on specific information indicating there was probable cause to believe that the body of James Hoffa might be buried here. The information was specific. The information also contained certain details that were never made available to the FBI before. That information was then investigated by agents and corroborated in several ways. The details of the information and the steps taken to verify it to the extent possible were drawn up into a sworn affidavit and presented to a federal judge who found that there was indeed probable cause to go forward with this search. That affidavit remains sealed because the investigation remains ongoing. There are still prosecutable defendants who are living, and they know who they are. . . .

This search commenced May 17, 2006, in Milford Township, Michigan. After a thorough and comprehensive search, no remains of Mr. Hoffa have been located and absent any additional new information, our work here has concluded.

In the course of this search, we engaged the assistance of experts such as anthropologists, archeologists, and graduate students from Michigan State University, and Detroit Police Department cadaver canines were utilized at the site as well as a geologist and archeologist from FBI Headquarters. . . . In total, approximately 15 to 20 FBI Special Agents and command post supervisors were onsite during daylight hours to assist with the search and evidence collection. Five to seven additional Special Agents were assigned 24 hours a day for security purposes. . . . We do not put a price tag on kidnapping/murder investigations, as we treat all human life on an equal basis. We do not make moral judgments on the victims of crimes, we do our job. We go where the investigation takes us.

This search is where the evidence led us and we will continue to follow up and pursue all leads in an effort to resolve this investigation and all other ongoing organized crime matters. We hope this sends a message to those involved in organized crime activities, that the FBI does not give up and will pursue all logical investigation, no matter how much time has passed.

ABBIE HOFFMAN
American political activist

BORN: November 30, 1936; Worcester, Massachusetts
DIED: April 12, 1989; New Hope, Pennsylvania
ALSO KNOWN AS: Abbott Howard Hoffman (full name)
CAUSE OF NOTORIETY: Co-founder of the Youth International Party or "Yippies," Hoffman staged "guerrilla theater" to direct media attention to his causes.
ACTIVE: 1960's
LOCALE: United States

EARLY LIFE

Abbie Hoffman (HAWF-man) was the firstborn son of John and Florence Schanberg Hoffman. His father, a druggist, was a Russian Jew who had come to the United States in 1906. Abbie Hoffman graduated from Worcester Academy and attended Brandeis University, where he was influenced by Marxist philosopher Herbert Marcuse and psychologist Abraham Maslow. While Marcuse affected Hoffman's political beliefs, Hoffman said Maslow's teachings became his personal code. Maslow, a founder of humanist psychology, counseled that conformity was not necessarily a sign of social adjustment and that rebellion against an unjust society was a psychological good.

After graduating from Brandeis in 1959, Hoffman attended the University of California at Berkeley. In July, 1960, he married Sheila Karklin. They had two children, a son, Andrew, born in 1960 and a daughter, Amy, born in 1962. Hoffman and his first wife were divorced in November, 1966. He married Anita S. Kushner in July, 1967. They named their one child america (the small "a" was meant to denote patriotism but also non-jingoistic intent). In 1980 he and Kushner were divorced.

POLITICAL CAREER

In 1964 and 1965, Hoffman worked as an organizer for the Student Nonviolent Coordinating Committee in the American South. He later opened a store in New York City and sold products made by Mississippi cooperative enterprises in support of the Civil Rights movement. He left the store in 1967, moved to the lower East Side of New York City, and became involved with the counterculture movement.

It was during this period that Hoffman developed his own methods of protest using techniques that he felt fit the time, the place, and his own personality. His techniques of guerrilla, or street, theater attracted media attention to Hoffman and the causes with which he was in-

volved. Hoffman garnered his first national publicity in August, 1967, when he and a group of supporters threw dollar bills from the gallery of the New York Stock Exchange onto the trading floor below. In October, 1967, Hoffman announced that antiwar activists were going to levitate the Pentagon and exorcise it of the evil spirits that were killing both Americans and Vietnamese. While his group failed to raise the Pentagon, Hoffman did receive the desired media attention.

On December 31, 1967, Hoffman and his friends decided to call their movement the Yippies, or Youth International Party. While the Yippies had no organization or formal membership, the activists now had a name and embraced the techniques of guerrilla theater. Throughout the spring and summer Hoffman and his followers were involved in various protests and activities in New York City. They also announced that they would hold a Festival of Life in Chicago while the Democratic Party was holding its presidential nominating convention. In Chicago the Yippies nominated a pig for president, which they named Pigasus. ("Pigs" at that time was a derogatory term for law enforcement in particular and authority figures of the "establishment" in general.)

LEGAL ACTION AND OUTCOME

Hoffman was later charged with and convicted of conspiracy to cross state lines to incite a riot because of his Chicago activities. His conviction was overturned on appeal. In 1973, Hoffman was arrested for smuggling and selling cocaine. He skipped bail and went into hiding. In 1980 he surrendered to authorities and served a short prison term. Following his release from prison, he continued to be involved in various environmental and political causes. At the same time, he became a popular figure on the United States lecture circuit. On April 12, 1989, he died of a deliberate drug overdose.

IMPACT

Abbie Hoffman was one of the New Left leaders of the 1960's who challenged the status quo and fought for social justice. His use of guerrilla theater resulted in media coverage of antiwar and other causes with which he was involved. In contrast, government and law enforcement overreacted to Hoffman and his pronouncements. While Hoffman was not an organizational leader, he succeeded in attracting the attention of the public to the causes espoused by the New Left during this era.

SENTENCING AT THE CHICAGO SEVEN TRIAL

On February 20, 1970, at the sentencing of the Chicago Seven, the judge, Julius Hoffman, asked each of the defendants—Abbie Hoffman, Jerry Rubin, David Dellinger, Rennie Davis, Tom Hayden, John Froines, Lee Weiner, and Bobby Seale—if he wished to make a statement before the court passed sentence. Here is Hoffman's statement:

THE COURT: Mr. Hoffman, the law gives you the right to speak in your own behalf. I will hear from you if you have anything to say.

MR. HOFFMAN: Thank you.

I feel like I have spent fifteen years watching John Daly shows about history. You Are There. It is sort of like taking LSD, which I recommend to you, Judge. I know a good dealer in Florida. I could fix you up.

[Prosecutor Thomas] Foran says that we are evil men, and I suppose that is sort of a compliment. He says that we are unpatriotic? I don't know, that has kind of a jingoistic ring. I suppose I am not patriotic.

But he says we are un-American. I don't feel un-American. I feel very American. I said it is not that the Yippies hate America. It is that they feel that the American Dream has been betrayed. That has been my attitude.

I know those guys on the wall [portraits of past U.S. presidents]. I know them better than you, I feel. I know Adams. I mean, I know all the Adams. They grew up twenty miles from my home in Massachusetts. I played with Sam Adams on the Concord Bridge. I was there when Paul Revere rode right up on his motorcycle and said, "The pigs are coming, the pigs are coming. Right into Lexington." I was there. I know the Adams. Sam Adams was an evil man.

Thomas Jefferson. Thomas Jefferson called for a revolution every ten years. Thomas Jefferson had an agrarian reform program that made Mao Tse Tung look like a liberal. I know Thomas Jefferson.

Hamilton: Well, I didn't dig the Federalists. Maybe he deserved to have his brains blown out.

Washington? Washington grew pot. He called it hemp. It was called hemp them. He probably was a pot head.

Abraham Lincoln? There is another one. In 1861 Abraham Lincoln in his inaugural address said, and I quote "When the people shall grow weary of their constitutional right to amend the government, they shall exert their revolutionary right to dismember and overthrow that government."

If Abraham Lincoln had given that speech in Lincoln Park, he would be on trial right here in this courtroom, because that is an inciteful speech. That is a speech intended to create a riot.

I don't even know what a riot is. I thought a riot was fun. Riot means you laugh, ha, ha. That is a riot. they call it a riot.

I didn't want to be that serious. I was supposed to be funny. I tried to be, I mean, but it was sad last night. I am not made to be a martyr. I tried to sign up a few years, but I went down there. They ran out of nails. What was I going to do? So I ended up being funny.

It wasn't funny last night sitting in a prison cell, a 5 × 8 room, with no light in the room. I could have written a whole book last night. Nothing. No light in the room. Bedbugs all over. They bite. I haven't eaten in six days. I'm not on a hunger strike; you can call it that. It's just that the food stinks and I can't take it.

Well, we said it was like Alice in Wonderland coming in, now I feel like Alice in 1984 [a reference to George Orwell's dystopian novel *Nineteen Eighty-Four*], because I have lived through the winter of injustice in this trial.

And it's fitting that if you went to the South and fought for voter registration and got arrested and beaten eleven or twelve times on those dusty roads for no bread, it's only fitting that you be arrested and tried under the civil rights act. That's the way it works.

Just want to say one more thing.

People—I guess that is what we are charged with—when they decide to go from one state of mind to another state of mind, when they decide to fly that route, I hope they go youth fare no matter what their age.

FURTHER READING

Hoffman, Abbie. *The Autobiography of Abbie Hoffman.* 2d ed. New York: Four Walls Eight Windows, 2000. A reprint of Hoffman's autobiography, which was originally titled *Soon to Be a Major Motion Picture.* It has a new afterword by Howard Zinn.

Raskin, Jonah. *For the Hell of It: The Lives and Times of Abbie Hoffman.* Berkeley: University of California Press, 1996. A well-researched and documented biography of Hoffman and the era in which he lived.

—*William V. Moore*

SEE ALSO: Timothy Leary; Huey Newton.

DOC HOLLIDAY
American gambler and gunfighter

BORN: August 14, 1851; Griffin, Georgia
DIED: November 8, 1887; Glenwood Springs,
Colorado
ALSO KNOWN AS: John Henry Holliday (birth name);
Tom Mackey
MAJOR OFFENSES: Assault and battery, murder
ACTIVE: January 2, 1875, to August 19, 1884
LOCALE: North-central Texas; southwestern Colorado;
southeastern Arizona
SENTENCE: Jailed October, 1880; March, 1881;
October to November, 1881; May, 1882

EARLY LIFE
John Henry Holliday (HAHL-ih-day) was the second
child of Alice Jane and Henry Burroughs Holliday.
John's father was a pharmacist who became a wealthy
planter and lawyer in Georgia. John's beloved mother
died of tuberculosis on September 16, 1866.

In 1870, Holliday attended dental school in Pennsylvania and earned the degree of doctor of dental surgery in
March, 1872. Later in 1872, he started a dental practice in
Atlanta. After developing tuberculosis, he moved to Dallas, Texas, where he practiced dentistry for a short time
prior to taking up gambling. A man with a quick temper,
"Doc" became very proficient with a gun and a knife.

CRIMINAL CAREER
After killing a prominent citizen in Dallas in 1875,
Holliday fled to Jacksboro, Texas, and worked as a faro
dealer. In the summer of 1876, Holliday killed a U.S. soldier from nearby Fort Richardson. In order to avoid the
law, Holliday headed for Denver, Colorado, where he
dealt faro. After a fight with a prominent gambler in Denver, Holliday eventually wound up in Fort Griffin,
Texas, where he met the woman of his life, Kate Elder
Haroney.

While in Fort Griffin, Holliday also met U.S. Mar-
shall Wyatt Earp, who was in Texas tracking an outlaw.
After stabbing a man over a gambling dispute in Fort
Griffin, Holliday was jailed. Haroney helped him escape.
The two headed to Dodge City, Kansas, where Holliday
dealt faro at the Long Branch Saloon. While in Dodge
City, Holliday saved Earp from a band of Texas ruffians.
The two became lifelong friends.

Holliday killed gunfighter "Kid" Colton in 1879 in
Colorado. He drifted to Tombstone, Arizona, in 1880.
Earp and his brothers had also moved there. The Earps

and Holliday became fierce enemies of the lawless group
of cowboys in Tombstone, which led to the famous gunfight at the O.K. Corral on October 26, 1881. Holliday
killed two men in the battle.

LEGAL ACTION AND OUTCOME
In October, 1880, Holliday was arrested and charged
with assault with a deadly weapon for a brawl in the Ori-
ental Saloon in Tombstone. In 1881, he was arrested for a
stagecoach robbery but later released when witnesses
testified that he was elsewhere when the stage was
robbed. After the gun battle at the O.K. Corral, Holliday
and the Earps were arrested and tried for murder. They
were later freed when it was determined that they had
acted within the law.

In May, 1882, Holliday was accused of murder, arrested, and jailed in Denver for the killing of Tombstone
outlaw Curly Bill Brocius. The governor of Colorado refused to honor a request for extradition from Arizona,
and Holliday was set free. In August, 1884, he was ac-

Doc Holliday.

quitted of shooting charges during a gunfight in Leadville, Colorado, since he had acted in self-defense.

IMPACT

Known as one of the most fearless men on the Western frontier, Doc Holliday became a close personal friend of Earp and the Earp brothers. Doc and the Earps helped clean up the lawless element in Tombstone, Arizona. Doc was a primary participant in the gunfight at the O.K. Corral, one of the most famous gunfights in the history of the Old West. He killed two of the three men who were slain in the battle.

Earp claimed that Doc was the fastest six-gun that he ever saw. Beginning in the 1940's, Holliday's fame grew as a result of numerous Western novels and magazines, television Westerns, and at least eight films. He is also featured in computer games, particularly the "Fallout" series.

FURTHER READING

Brooks, L. T. *The Last Gamble of Doc Holliday.* Raleigh, N.C.: Pentland Press, 2004. Biography that investigates the truths and myths about Holliday's life.

Pryor, Alton. *Outlaws and Gunslingers: Tales of the West's Most Notorious Outlaws.* Roseville, Calif.: Stagecoach, 2001. Explores the lives of twenty-seven of the most famous gunfighters known in the Old West, giving a detailed synopsis of the life of Holliday.

Tanner, Karen Holliday. *Doc Holliday: A Family Portrait.* Norman: University of Oklahoma Press, 2001. Tanner reveals many intriguing insights into the life, times, and experiences of Holliday.

—*Alvin K. Benson*

SEE ALSO: Wyatt Earp.

H. H. HOLMES
American serial killer

BORN: May 16, 1861; Gilmanton, New Hampshire
DIED: May 7, 1896; Moyamensing Prison, Philadelphia, Pennsylvania
ALSO KNOWN AS: Herman Webster Mudgett (birth name); Henry Howard Holmes; H. M. Howard; O. C. Pratt; Harry Gordon; Monster of Sixty-Third Street; Torture Doctor; Modern Bluebeard
MAJOR OFFENSES: Fraud, bigamy, and murder
ACTIVE: c. 1890-1895
LOCALE: Chicago, Illinois; Philadelphia, Pennsylvania; Toronto, Canada; and Irvington, Indiana
SENTENCE: Jailed for stock fraud; death by hanging for murder

EARLY LIFE

Herman Webster Mudgett, later known as H. H. Holmes (hohmz), was born to a religious mother who could not protect him from his strict, harsh father. A bright child, he was harassed by bullies; once they chased him into a doctor's office, terrifying him with a skeleton. He also performed experimental operations on neighborhood pets before he was eleven years old.

In 1878, Holmes married Clara Lovering. After working as a schoolmaster, he attended the University of Michigan Medical School in Ann Arbor; then he en-sconced his wife and son with her parents in New Hampshire. He practiced medicine briefly in Mooers Falls, New York, then moved to Chicago, using the name Henry Howard Holmes. Holmes became partner in a pharmacy in Englewood, then a suburb and later incorporated into the city. In 1887, he bigamously married Myrta Belknap.

CRIMINAL CAREER

How many people Holmes murdered remains a mystery. His multiple and unreliable confessions vary widely in their facts. Contemporary newspapers speculated that he had murdered as many as two hundred; modern historians estimate the number to be between nine and about fifty.

Holmes's first murder victim was probably Mrs. E. S. Holton, Holmes's partner in the Englewood pharmacy. Her disappearance in 1890 left him the business's sole owner. Ned Conner managed a jewelry counter in Holmes's store; in late 1891, his wife Julia disappeared with their daughter, Pearl. Other likely victims were his fourth simultaneous wife, Minnie Williams; her sister Nannie; and Holmes's mistress, Emeline Cigrand. He may have sold some of his victims' remains to medical schools.

When the Chicago World's Columbian Exposition

opened in 1893, Holmes rented out rooms in a huge building he had erected on Sixty-Third Street. The building, called The Castle, had three stories with hidden passageways, an insulated, room-sized vault, gas jets in some rooms, and peepholes in all. In 1895, police discovered that the basement held a dissection and a torture table, mysterious wooden tanks, and an iron stove—eight feet tall by three feet wide—containing remains such as jewelry, clothing, and bones. Holmes may have murdered many visitors; he imprisoned guests and spied on them, gaining a sense of power and sexual thrills. He may have used the gas to incapacitate women and molest them.

Holmes clearly also murdered for financial reasons. Under many names, he committed various swindles, from defaulting on credit to selling faked inventions. His motive in the 1894 murder of longtime assistant Benjamin Pitezel seemed to be insurance fraud; he received ten thousand dollars in Pietzel's benefits. Holmes murdered three of Pitezel's children, perhaps to prevent discovery of their father's death.

LEGAL ACTION AND OUTCOME

In 1894, Holmes was jailed for stock fraud. In 1895, Pinkerton detectives arrested Holmes for insurance fraud. Tireless and clever work by Detective Frank Geyer proved Holmes's culpability for the Pitezel deaths. In an internationally publicized trial, Holmes—primarily serving as his own lawyer—presented his defense but was convicted on four counts of murder; he was hanged.

IMPACT

Arguably America's first well-documented serial killer, H. H. Holmes represents the dark side of the Gilded Age, when commerce and invention boomed and Americans admired the self-made tycoon. Chicago, especially, was growing from the ashes of its great fire and offered local opportunity and the glamour of the World's Fair. Moreover, Holmes's crimes eerily mirror the burgeoning technological sophistication of the United States as it prepared to enter a new century, both in his killing "factory" and in the "mass production" of his crimes. His exploits scandalized post-Victorian America, receiving far more publicity than his English contemporary, Jack the Ripper. He also inspired a reporter to coin the term "multi-murderer," a forerunner of the current concept of the serial killer. Many books on the Holmes case were published, including Holmes's own self-serving autobiography. For a time, Holmes was largely forgotten, but attention to his story was revived during the 1970's and 1980's with a concomitant rise in interest concerning serial killers.

FURTHER READING

Franke, David. *The Torture Doctor*. New York: Hawthorn Books, 1975. Well-researched and detailed discussion about Holmes.

Geary, Rick. *The Beast of Chicago: The Murderous Career of H. H. Holmes*. New York: NBM Comics, 2003. A graphic novel, impeccably researched both factually and visually.

Holmes, H. H. *Holmes' Own Story*. Philadephia: Burk & McFetridge, 1895. Holmes's autobiography.

Larson, Erik. *The Devil in the White City: Murder, Magic, and Madness at the Fair That Changed America*. New York: Vintage, 2004. Well-researched and well-written analysis, with a useful index, that places Holmes within the context of the Chicago World's Columbia Exposition and turn-of-the-century Chicago.

Schechter, Harold. *Depraved: The Shocking True Story of America's First Serial Killer*. New York: Pocket, 1994. Another accessible, detailed account of Holmes's criminal career.

Wilson, Colin. "H. H. Holmes: The Torture Doctor." In *The Mammoth Book of Murder*, edited by Richard Glyn Jones. New York: Carroll & Graf, 1989. Brief but useful, with minor errors.

_____. *The History of Murder*. New York: Carroll & Graf, 2000. Contains a slightly revised version of the essay in the book edited by Jones.

—*Bernadette Lynn Bosky*

SEE ALSO: Joe Ball; William Burke; Albert Fish; Jack the Ripper; Henri Désiré Landru; Marcel Petiot; Sweeney Todd.

KARLA HOMOLKA
Canadian murderer

BORN: May 4, 1970; Port Credit, Ontario, Canada
ALSO KNOWN AS: Karla Leanne Teale (birth name); Karla Leanne Homolka (full name)
MAJOR OFFENSE: Manslaughter
ACTIVE: December 23, 1990; June 15, 1991; and April 16, 1992
LOCALE: Port Dalhousie, Ontario, Canada
SENTENCE: Twelve years in prison

EARLY LIFE
Karla Homolka (KAHR-lah HOHM-ohl-kah) was born in Port Credit, Ontario, Canada, and attended high school at Sir Winston Churchill, in St. Catherines, Ontario, where she had lived most of her life. After high school, she worked for a veterinarian, and in 1987, while only seventeen, she met Paul Bernardo in Toronto at a convention. She fell in love with him, and he would regularly visit on weekends from Toronto and stay with her at her parents' home. Everyone seemed to like Bernardo, and in 1990, Homolka announced that they were engaged.

CRIMINAL CAREER
In the summer of 1990, Bernardo told Homolka that he wanted to have sex with other women and that he found Homolka's thirteen-year-old sister, Tammy, attractive. He persuaded Homolka to help him have sex with her. Homolka obtained drugs from the veterinary clinic where she worked. She laced Tammy's drink with Halcion (sleeping pills) and made sure that Tammy would not wake up by placing a cloth soaked in halothane (an anesthetic) over her sister's mouth. Tammy was stripped, and while Bernardo ran a video recorder, he had intercourse with her and then demanded that Homolka have oral sex with her. Tammy later died from choking on her own vomit, and at that time the death was ruled an accident.

On June 15, 1991, Bernardo kidnapped a teenager named Leslie Mehaffey and locked her in the guest bedroom of his and Homolka's house. The couple then raped, tortured, and abused her. Homolka gave Mehaffey some sleeping pills and made her swallow them. Afterward they strangled her, dismembered her body with a power saw, placed the body parts in concrete, and threw the body into a lake.

On April 16, 1992, they abducted Kristen French from a parking lot and took her back to their home, where she was locked in the guest bedroom for four days. There

the couple tortured, raped, and abused her, also recording the acts on video. On Easter Sunday, French was strangled, and Bernardo and Homolka dumped her body in a field, after they tried to remove any physical evidence from the body.

On January 5, 1993, Homolka left Bernardo after he delivered a series of beatings that left her severely bruised. Meanwhile, Bernardo was coming under intense scrutiny for a series of rapes in Toronto, known as the Scarborough serial rapes. On February 17, 1993, Bernardo was arrested in connection with those rapes, and after the police interviewed Homolka, she provided information that caused them to arrest Bernardo for the murders of Mehaffey and French.

LEGAL ACTION AND OUTCOME
During interviews with police investigators, Homolka stated she was severely beaten by her husband and forced to take part in the rapes and murders of their victims. On July 6, 1993, Homolka pleaded guilty to the manslaughter of both Leslie Mehaffey and Kristen French and was later found liable for the murder of her own sister as well. Even though videotape evidenced showed that Homolka participated willingly in the sexual activities, she had already struck a plea bargain in agreement for testifying against Bernardo. Her trial, then, was brief, and she received a sentence of twelve years in prison. She served her time and was released from prison in 2005.

IMPACT
The criminal justice system in Canada came under intense scrutiny during the Karla Homolka trial for offering a plea bargain that was later termed a "deal with the devil." It was called the worst plea bargain in Canadian history because the prosecution, in offering Homolka a deal for testifying against Bernardo (on whom they felt their case was centered), failed to see the role that Homolka played in the deaths. Homolka had quickly accepted the terms of the deal, and it was not until the police investigated the tapes more fully that they became aware of her cooperation in the sexual assaults of the victims. The courts also struggled with the public's right to know during the media blitz that centered on the case. For the first time, Canada's justice system was scrutinized before an international audience.

After her release from prison in 2005, Homolka again became the center of much media attention. In a newspaper article an employer stated that she had violated parole, and in an Internet "death pool," people were taking bets on the date in which Homolka would be killed.

FURTHER READING

Burnside, Scott, and Alan Cairns. *Deadly Innocence.* New York: Warner Books, 1995. Thorough account of the Bernardo-Homolka case from various perspectives, with pictures.

Pron, Nick. *Lethal Marriage: The Unspeakable Crimes of Paul Bernardo and Karla Homolka.* New York: Seal, 1995. A *Toronto Star* crime reporter for more than thirty years, Pron investigates the reasons behind and the impact of the Bernardo-Homolka murders.

Williams, Stephen. *Karla: A Pact with the Devil.* Toronto: Random House of Canada, 2003. Although focusing on Homolka, this follow-up to Williams's previous book *Invisible Darkness* (1998) provides a different perspective on Bernardo's behavior.

—*Jerry W. Hollingsworth*

SEE ALSO: Paul Bernardo.

J. EDGAR HOOVER
Director of the FBI (1924-1972)

BORN: January 1, 1895; Washington, D.C.
DIED: May 2, 1972; Washington, D.C.
ALSO KNOWN AS: John Edgar Hoover (full name)
CAUSE OF NOTORIETY: Revelations of Hoover's lying, double-dealing, and lawbreaking helped to weaken the faith of twentieth century Americans in their government.
ACTIVE: 1924-1972
LOCALE: United States, mainly Washington, D.C.

EARLY LIFE

John Edgar Hoover (HEW-vur) was the youngest child in his family and the apple of his mother's eye. His father would be forced out of his job as head of the printing division of the U.S. Coast and Geodetic Survey in 1917 because of the mental illness he suffered. Edgar, as the son was known, had to mature quickly, in part to support his mother in the face of his father's depression. Hoover was precociously disciplined and active for a teenager, becoming a gifted debater, delivering groceries, and joining the Central High School Brigade of Cadets.

Against his Lutheran mother's wishes, Hoover became a Presbyterian and almost considered becoming a pastor. Deciding instead to practice law, he chose to stay close to his family, turning down a place at the University of Virginia's law school. Instead, in the fall of 1913, Edgar eventually matriculated as an evening student at George Washington University, which offered night classes designed to be convenient for government employees and other nontraditional students who had to work. At the same time, he became an entry-level gofer in the Order Division of the Library of Congress. Three years later he rose to the position of clerk. Passing the Washington, D.C., bar in 1917 with his master's degree in tow, Hoover first started work in the U.S. Department of Justice on July 26 of that year. He would serve that agency for the following fifty-four years.

J. Edgar Hoover. (Library of Congress)

CAREER

Hoover epitomized, long after it was fashionable, the political and moral prerogatives of the Progressive Era. Early on, he championed merit and hard work over connections and corruption at the Department of Justice, leading to his eventual and, at first, temporary appointment as director of what would become the Federal Bureau of Investigation (FBI) in 1924. Steering clear of the open graft of the Warren Harding administration, Hoover tried to make the fledgling agency more professional, adapting the use of fingerprint, crime lab, and other modern forensic technologies.

Such dedication to hard work and creativity became more rhetorical than real as the years passed. The glamour of being FBI director, coupled with the increasingly expected perquisites of office, shortened his workdays and stymied his initial receptive embrace of reform. His FBI became reactive rather than proactive, missing vital clues before the 1941 bombing of Pearl Harbor and the 1963 assassination of President John F. Kennedy. Hoover publicly denied that the Mafia existed until its presence was too obvious to ignore, then touted the single episode in which he personally apprehended a suspect in New Orleans as evidence that the FBI would inevitably and always prevail. The G-men, as Hoover's agents came to be called, also became overly concerned with crediting all of the agency's accomplishments to Hoover, making the FBI a personal reflection of its director rather than an efficient agent of criminal justice. Hoover's jealousy of Bill Donovan, the head of the agency that would become the Central Intelligence Agency, set the stage for the strained relations and poor communications between the two agencies that persisted for many years.

For Hoover, sacrificing the civil rights of some miscreants made possible the maintenance of freedom for middle-class, white America, which he and his milieu provincially considered the real nation. During World

---

HOOVER ON COMMUNISM

J. Edgar Hoover testified before the House Committee on Un-American Activities on March 26, 1947, about the threat from domestic communists:

. . . The communist movement in the United States began to manifest itself in 1919. Since then it has changed its name and its party line whenever expedient and tactical. But always it comes back to fundamentals and bills itself as the party of Marxism-Leninism. As such, it stands for the destruction of our American form of government; it stands for the destruction of American democracy; it stands for the destruction of free enterprise; and it stands for the creation of a "Soviet of the United States" and ultimate world revolution. . . . One thing is certain. The American progress which all good citizens seek, such as old-age security, houses for veterans, child assistance, and a host of others, is being adopted as window dressing by the communists to conceal their true aims and entrap gullible followers. . . . The Communist Party of the United States is a fifth column if there ever was one. It is far better organized than were the Nazis in occupied countries prior to their capitulation. They are seeking to weaken America just as they did in their era of obstruction when they were aligned with the Nazis. Their goal is the overthrow of our government. There is no doubt as to where a real communist's loyalty rests. Their allegiance is to Russia, not the United States. . . . I would have no fears if more Americans possessed the zeal, the fervor, the persistence and the industry to learn about this menace of Red fascism. I do fear for the liberal and progressive who has been hoodwinked and duped into joining hands with the communists. I confess to a real apprehension so long as communists are able to secure ministers of the gospel to promote their evil work and espouse a cause that is alien to the religion of Christ and Judaism. I do fear so long as school boards and parents tolerate conditions whereby communists and fellow travelers, under the guise of academic freedom, can teach our youth a way of life that eventually will destroy the sanctity of the home, that undermines faith in God, that causes them to scorn respect for constituted authority and sabotage our revered Constitution.

Source: Records of the U.S. House of Representatives, "Investigation of Un-American Propaganda Activities in the United States," in Record Group 233, "Records of the House Un-American Activities Committee, 1945-1969" (Center for Legislative Archives, National Archives and Records Administration, Washington D.C.).

War I, Hoover tracked German sympathizers or potential spies. Then, immediately after the war, he helped to usher in the Palmer raids in search of suspected radicals or Bolsheviks. At the height of the Joseph McCarthy era in the early 1950's, Hoover led the charge to purge the government of Communists. Finally, he tried to smear the leaders of the Civil Rights and antiwar movements of the 1960's via semilegal or illegal wiretaps and surveillance. Only when President Richard Nixon requested illegal break-ins—which by then were no longer palatable even by FBI standards—did Hoover say no to collecting personal information for political gain.

Hoover thought that African Americans were inherently inferior to members of the white race and that homosexuals were detrimental to the social order. His racism infected the early FBI; while Hoover reigned, the only African Americans hired by the agency were personal servants for the director. Later, discrediting Martin Luther King, Jr., with taped evidence of King's sexual improprieties became an almost pathological priority for Hoover.

On the other hand, Hoover's homophobia made him particularly sensitive to any rumors that he might be gay, which arose from the facts that he had never married and had lived with his mother until he was forty-three. It was also rumored that he and Clyde Tolson, his assistant and only friend, were intimately involved. Ordinary Americans who casually discussed the sexual orientation of the director were often quickly placed on FBI surveillance. Hoover's actual personal life was much more boring than notorious, perhaps explaining his obsession with the sexual behavior of others and his own collection of pornography that had been confiscated by the FBI from others.

IMPACT

J. Edgar Hoover served under ten presidents, from Woodrow Wilson to Richard Nixon, creating the framework of the modern national security state. Working with Franklin D. Roosevelt and Lyndon B. Johnson proved fulfilling for him because of those presidents' use of gossip and wiretaps. Hoover hated presidents Harry S. Truman and Kennedy, in part because they insisted on his adherence to the protocol of acting through the U.S. attorney general, Hoover's nominal boss. Nixon, on the other hand, tried to get rid of Hoover because the latter refused to go even further in his abuses of power by wiretapping prominent journalists. Nixon's effort to dump Hoover would ironically return to him when one of Hoover's protégés, Mark Felt, angered over not being selected to succeed Hoover as FBI director, became the Deep Throat of the Watergate scandal.

In some important ways, Hoover's image was much more important to the FBI than his negligible effectiveness in combating crime or espionage. During the De-

pression, Hoover became a celebrity, exploiting high-profile crimes such as the kidnapping of aviator Charles Lindbergh's child and the shooting of four unarmed FBI agents at the 1933 Kansas City Massacre. Reports of the FBI's tracking and killing of outlaw John Dillinger were exaggerated in order to hype the role of the director. Indeed, from the 1930's through the 1960's, feature-length films, documentaries, books, and eventually a television show starring Efrem Zimbalist, Jr., sanitized and glorified Hoover and his agency as patriotic crime fighters who could do no wrong.

Hoover's keeping of personal secrets served him well in life, but it damaged his posthumous reputation. After his death in 1972, his loyal secretary tried to destroy Hoover's personal and confidential files, but some of their contents surfaced anyway. Particularly harmful to the righteous image he sought to project were the revelations of venality, blackmailing, officially sanctioned burglaries, lying to Congress and to presidents, and alliances with gangsters. The nation's top cop for most of the twentieth century was, in reality, a criminal when it suited his agenda. The public exposure of that array of secrets, in conjunction with the debacle of the Vietnam War and the Watergate scandal, greatly weakened the American faith in government.

FURTHER READING

Gentry, Curt. *J. Edgar Hoover: The Man and His Secrets.* New York: W. W. Norton, 1991. Analyzes Hoover's relationships with attorneys general and presidents.

Hack, Richard. *Puppetmaster: The Secret Life of J. Edgar Hoover.* Beverly Hills, Calif.: New Millennium Press, 2004. Hack argues that Hoover, however homophobic, was not gay.

Summer, Anthony. *Official and Confidential: The Secret Life of J. Edgar Hoover.* New York: Putnam, 1993. Delves into the celebrity gossip gathered by and about the director.

—*Charles H. Ford*

SEE ALSO: John Dillinger; Joseph McCarthy; Richard Nixon.

ELMYR DE HORY
Hungarian art forger

BORN: 1906; Hungary
DIED: December 11, 1976; Ibiza, Spain
ALSO KNOWN AS: Elemér Horthy; Louis Cassou; Baron de Hory; Joseph Dory; Elmyr Dory-Boutin (birth name); Baron Herzog; Elmyr Hoffman; L. E. Raynal; Elmyr von Houry
CAUSE OF NOTORIETY: De Hory forged more than one thousand works of art, including paintings by Pablo Picasso, Henri Matisse, and Amedeo Modigliani; in some cases his forged art was evaluated as superior in quality to that of the imitated artist.
ACTIVE: 1946-1976
LOCALE: Europe, South America, North America

EARLY LIFE
According to Elmyr de Hory (el-MEER dih HOHR-ee) himself, he was born into a wealthy family in Hungary in 1906. His parents divorced when he was sixteen, at which time the young man began attending art school in the Hungarian capital of Budapest. He enrolled in a German school two years later and went on to study at the Académie la Grande Chaumière in Paris.

In the late 1930's, de Hory returned to Hungary, where he was imprisoned briefly as a result of his contacts with suspect foreigners. He was later arrested as a Jew and sent to a concentration camp in Germany. After escaping and returning to Hungary, de Hory discovered that his parents had been murdered during World War II and the family fortune confiscated. Hoping to make a living as a painter, he made his way back to Paris in 1945.

These and other details about de Hory's life must be treated with caution, as the standard biography (by Clifford Irving) was written with de Hory's cooperation and may not be reliable. A later researcher has found evidence that the artist may have been born Elemér Horthy in 1905 in very modest circumstances.

CRIMINAL CAREER
De Hory's life of crime apparently began in 1946 when a friend mistook an unsigned de Hory drawing for the unsigned work of Pablo Picasso. De Hory did not disabuse the woman in question and instead sold her the drawing.

Subsequently, de Hory began producing other "Picassos," as well as works ostensibly by Henri Matisse and Amedeo Modigliani. He toured Europe with a young companion who handled all the selling, visited South America briefly, and in 1947 turned to the United States, where he remained for twelve years. There he tried unsuccessfully to live as a legitimate artist but soon reverted to forgery on a large scale.

By 1959 de Hory believed that he was in legal jeopardy and returned to Europe, where he made an arrangement with shady "art dealers" Fernand Legros and Réal Lessard. By now de Hory had added forgeries of many more nineteenth and twentieth century artists to his repertoire, and although his partners kept most of the profits, de Hory lived comfortably on the Spanish island of Ibiza. However, his actions had drawn the attention of Spanish authorities, and in 1968 he was imprisoned for two months—for homosexuality, consorting with criminals, and having no visible means of support—and exiled for two years.

De Hory returned to Ibiza in 1969, but during the following decade he was investigated by French authorities. Upon learning on December 11, 1976, that he was to be extradited to France to face multiple charges of forgery, de Hory killed himself with an overdose of barbiturates.

IMPACT
Elmyr de Hory is regarded as the most successful known art forger of the twentieth century. He is thought to have forged more than one thousand works, defrauding dealers, collectors, and art galleries of as much as one million dollars. He remains a fascinating figure, as art forgery is regarded by many as a glamorous crime, and de Hory was by all accounts a genial and even generous man. Some experts have declared his works as good as or even better than the works of the artists he copied, and such a market developed for his forgeries (identified as such) that other forgers began to produce their own "de Horys."

FURTHER READING
Irving, Clifford. *Fake: The Story of Elmyr de Hory, the Greatest Art Forger of Our Time.* New York: McGraw Hill, 1969. Entertaining, if unreliable, biography by a writer later jailed for faking a biography of Howard Hughes.
Jackman, Ian, ed. *Con Men: Fascinating Profiles of Swindlers and Rogues from the Files of the Most Suc-*

cessful Broadcast in Television History. New York: Simon & Schuster, 2003. Includes a chapter about de Hory based on material from the television program *60 Minutes*.

Kleiner, Carolyn. "Artful Dodgers." *U.S. News and World Report* 133, no. 8 (August 26, 2002): 54-56. Discusses de Hory, his involvement with Clifford Irving, and Irving's later notoriety.

—*Grove Koger*

SEE ALSO: Clifford Irving; Tom Keating; Gaston Bullock Means.

ENVER AND NEXHMIJE HOXHA
Albanian communist leader (1944-1985) and his wife

ENVER HOXHA

BORN: October 16, 1908; Gjirokastër, Albania
DIED: April 11, 1985; Tiranë, Albania

NEXHMIJE HOXHA

BORN: February 7, 1921; Monastir, Macedonia (Nexhmije Hoxha)

CAUSE OF NOTORIETY: As the paranoid dictator of Albania, Hoxha, along with his wife, isolated his country from the rest of Europe and emulated the autocratic, oppressive policies of Joseph Stalin.
ACTIVE: 1944-1985
LOCALE: Albania

EARLY LIFE

Enver Hoxha (EHN-vuhr HOH-jah) was born in 1908, the year after the Young Turk rebellion in the Ottoman Empire, which then included Albania. As a result of the Balkans War (1912-1913), his native Albania gained independence in 1913. His father, a Muslim traveling merchant, was often abroad, so Enver's uncle, Hysen Hoxha, cared for and influenced Enver with his revolutionary and democratic ideas. Hoxha studied at the French lycée at Korcë and at the university in Montpellier, France, on a state scholarship. He later worked in the Albanian consulate in Brussels. When he returned to Albania, he reenrolled in the Korcë lycée and became a schoolteacher there. After Albania was annexed by Italy in 1939, Hoxha was dismissed because of his refusal to cooperate with the new rulers. He opened a tobacco shop in Tiranë, which soon became a meeting ground for Albanians with radical ideas.

Nexhmije (NEHZH-mee-yee) Hoxha was born in what later became the Republic of Macedonia. She attended high school in Tiranë, Albania, and when World War II broke out, she joined the Communist Party and fought as a partisan in the National Liberation Army. She also served on the general council of the National Liberation Front and the secretariat of the Albanian Women's League. She and Hoxha married after the war.

POLITICAL CAREER

In 1941, Hoxha and his comrades formed the Albanian Communist Party (whose name was later changed to the Albanian Party of Labor). They joined in the resistance against the Italians and, after May, 1943, when Italy fell, against the Germans. During the war, Hoxha maintained links with other communist guerrillas, especially Josip Broz (Tito) in Yugoslavia and Nikolaos Zachariadis in Greece. In the late 1940's, Hoxha and the Communist Party managed to gain control of the country in opposition to the Balli Kombëtar (a nationalist organization of Albanians fighting for ethnic Albania) and the monarchists despite the support that American and English covert groups, such as the Central Intelligence Agency (CIA) and Britain's Military Intelligence Section 6 (MI6), gave to his opponents.

After the war, Albania found itself threatened by its prewar rivals in the region, Yugoslavia and Greece. Hoxha feared that Tito had designs on the country and wanted to make it a republic of the Yugoslav federation. When the Greek Communists lost the Greek Civil War (1946-1949) and the Yugoslav city of Belgrade broke ideologically with Moscow, Hoxha looked to Soviet leader Joseph Stalin for support.

However, after Stalin's death in 1953 and the new Soviet leader Nikita Khrushchev's reconciliation with Belgrade, Hoxha found himself isolated. He defiantly decided to follow his own path, completely isolating his country from the rest of the world. For a while, Hoxha moved close to China, after Beijing also began quarreling with Moscow, but he did not entirely approve of Chairman Mao Zedong's policies either.

Hoxha was determined to turn Albania into a true

Marxist state, stressing the equality of individuals. He eliminated all forms of public worship both because of the Marxist belief that religion is an opiate of the masses and because he wanted to avoid religious conflict as a source of division in the country: Albania's citizens were Muslims, Roman Catholics, and Eastern Orthodox Christians. Moreover, Greece, capitalizing on Albania's ethnic and religious divisions, claimed that many of Albania's Orthodox citizens were really Greek nationals even if their native language was Albanian. However, in un-Marxist fashion, nationalism also became an important focus of the Albanian state. People in Tiranë, for example, engaged in historical disputes over medieval heroes claimed by both the Albanians and the South Slavs. Historical figures, such as the legendary military hero Skanderbeg (1405-1468), were praised by the Albanian government and Party of Labor. National literature was hailed.

Hoxha also confiscated farmland from wealthy landowners and consolidated it into collectives. As this process continued, Hoxha boasted that Albania had become self-sufficient in food production. He also claimed that his administration brought a great degree of modernization to Albanians, by bringing electricity to rural areas, increasing literacy, and eliminating disease.

Throughout his tenure, Hoxha eliminated any opposition to his hard-line policies; even his closest comrades were not spared. In 1949, he accused Koçi Xoxe of "pro-Yugoslav activities" (namely espionage) and had him purged. One of Hoxha's closest associates, Mehmet Shehu, committed suicide in 1981 after a falling out with Hoxha and being accused of working for the CIA. Shehu most likely wanted to ease some of Hoxha's restrictions and bring greater contact with the West.

After marrying Hoxha after World War II, Nexhmije stood firmly beside him during his dictatorship. She was elected to the Albanian National Assembly in 1948 and the Central Committee of the Albanian Party of Labor in 1952. In 1966, she was appointed director of the Albanian Institute of Marxist-Leninist studies. In 1985, Nexhmije became chair of the Communist-led Democratic Front.

After Hoxha died in 1985, Ramiz Alia succeeded him in 1989, and Albania, like most of the Eastern European countries during this period, found itself freed of Soviet control and introduced to a Western style of democracy. A staunch supporter of her husband's orthodox communist principles and policies, Nexhmije was removed from office by the leaders of the post-1990 reforms. In 1994, she was arrested for corruption during her husband's reign; she was released in 1998 without being brought to trial. However, while imprisoned and after, she continued to defend her husband's views.

IMPACT

Under the rule of Enver and Nexhmije Hoxha, Albania prided itself for decades on not relying on economic assistance from the outside world. Thus, despite being the country with the lowest standard of living in Europe, Albania resisted raising the level of consumer production that began all over Eastern Europe during the 1960's and 1970's. Following the collapse of Hoxha's communist regime in the late 1980's, Albania was found to lack any means of modernization and agricultural wealth, contrary to what Hoxha had claimed repeatedly throughout his rule. Telephone communication was nonexistent; collectives used nineteenth century farming methods; and working wages were the lowest of Eastern Europe, leading to Albanian workers' mass immigration in the early 1990's into Greece because of its higher wages. Although Hoxha and his wife created their own personality cult among Albanians, their human rights record was dismal, and most civil and personal liberties had been suspended. As a national leader, perhaps the only achievement Hoxha could claim was the fact that Albania, one of the oldest nations in Europe, had not had a span of independence as long as the one it had under his leadership.

FURTHER READING

Jones, Lloyd. *Biografi: A Traveller's Tale*. San Diego: Harcourt Brace, 1994. An account of Albania written by a New Zealand author who visited there after the fall of communism.

O'Donnell, James S. *A Coming of Age: Albania Under Enver Hoxha*. Boulder, Colo.: East European Monographs, 1999. Examines and evaluates Hoxha's rule, noting both positive and negative accomplishments.

Orizio, Riccardo. *Talk of the Devil: Encounters with Seven Dictators*. Translated by Avril Bardoni. New York: Walker, 2003. Derived from interviews by the author, an Italian journalist, this is an engrossing account of seven dictators from around the world. Nexhmije Hoxha is among them.

—*Frederick B. Chary*

SEE ALSO: Nicolae Ceauşescu; Mao Zedong; Slobodan Milošević; Benito Mussolini; Ante Pavelić; Joseph Stalin; Tito.

L. RON HUBBARD
Founder of the Church of Scientology

BORN: March 13, 1911; Tilden, Nebraska
DIED: January 24, 1986; Creston, California
ALSO KNOWN AS: Lafayette Ronald Hubbard (full name)
CAUSE OF NOTORIETY: Hubbard was the founder of Dianetics and the religion Scientology, which has been both praised for its contributions to adherents' success and criticized as a quasi cult.
ACTIVE: 1930's-1986
LOCALE: Camden, New Jersey; Sussex, England; Rhodesia (now Zimbabwe); California

EARLY LIFE

L. Ron Hubbard (HUHB-ahrd) was the son of a career U.S. Naval veteran and a high school teacher. He attended but did not graduate from George Washington University in Washington, D.C. Hubbard began making a living as an author during the 1930's writing short stories and novellas; two of his early works include *Final Blackout* (1940) and *Fear* (1951). He married Margaret Grubb in 1933. They had two children, L. Ron, Jr., and Katherine May, in 1934 and 1936.

Hubbard joined the Navy, following his father's footsteps, in 1941. He left active service in 1945 and resigned his commission in 1950. There are many inconsistencies between his own accounts of his military service and official accounts of the Navy.

In 1950, he published *Dianetics: The Modern Science of Mental Health*, which was designed as a self-improvement program. It included the concept of "auditing," in which two individuals conduct a question-and-answer session regarding difficult times and painful memories. The book sold 150,000 copies in its first year of publication.

In 1952-1953, Hubbard worked to expand Dianetics into a philosophy and then a religion. He founded the Church of Scientology in 1953 in Camden, New Jersey. Hubbard moved to England shortly thereafter and bought a manor in Sussex, where he set up the world headquarters of Scientology. Members of the church paid for expensive courses of study and other services, and the church and Hubbard had a very positive cash flow. He often implied that forming a church was a good way to succeed in business.

However, while his success as an author was thriving, his private life was in difficulty. He was accused of bigamy, and his wife sought divorce. The divorce papers included a number of accusations, including kidnapping, torture, and beatings; no criminal charges were filed, however.

RELIGIOUS CAREER

In the 1960's, Scientology became highly scrutinized by governments of many countries. Its controversial concept of "fair game"—supporting the use of aggressive means against "suppressive persons" who actively seek to oppress Scientology—made church members suspect of committing crimes against those who opposed them. In the name of fair game, it is alleged, individuals have been harassed and abused for criticizing the church. Hubbard moved several times to avoid the controversy, living in Rhodesia for a while and then commanding a fleet of ships on the Mediterranean.

The Church of Scientology's offices were raided in the 1970's by the Federal Bureau of Investigation (FBI) because of suspicion of espionage. Hubbard's third wife

L. Ron Hubbard. (AP/Wide World Photos)

and some top officials were charged with conspiracy against the U.S. government in 1979. Hubbard was named an "unindicted coconspirator."

Hubbard wrote extensively in the science-fiction genre during the 1980's and continued to receive a good income from the Scientology organization, although he was officially separated from the Church of Scientology's management at that time. He died at his ranch in Creston, California, on January 24, 1986. Controversy followed his death, with questions about cause of death, last-minute changes to his will, and high levels of Vistaril, a psychotropic drug, found by the coroner in his system.

IMPACT

Judgments about the impact of L. Ron Hubbard's life are full of controversy, as his supporters make many claims about his accomplishments and almost superhuman abilities. He has been depicted as a hero by some and an unscrupulous individual by others. He has written and influenced people in many realms of life, including psychology and education. Those who have documented his life have painted him either as a world-changing visionary or as a scoundrel. Hubbard's books continued to sell well in the twenty-first century. The Church of Scientology has many followers worldwide, including many famous people, who say they owe him much for providing a way of thinking that changed their lives.

FURTHER READING

Atack, Jon. *A Piece of Blue Sky*. New York: Lyle Stewart, 1990. A history of Hubbard and Scientology that takes a critical view of Hubbard, Dianetics, and Scientology.

Corydon, Bent. *L. Ron Hubbard: Messiah or Madman?* Fort Lee, N.J.: Barricade Books, 1992. Although the title might lead one to believe that this book offers a balanced perspective, the discussion is very critical of Hubbard as a person and a leader of people.

Hubbard, L. Ron, ed. *What Is Scientology?* Los Angeles: Bridge, 1993. A discussion of Scientology and Hub-

---

THE FBI ON HUBBARD

The files of the FBI contain many documents on L. Ron Hubbard, including this one, dated February 15, 1963:

. . . L. Ron Hubbard was the founder and president of Hubbard Dianetic Research Foundation Inc. (HDRF), which was incorporated in New Jersey during April, 1950.

The December 5, 1950, issue of "Look" magazine contained an article entitled "Dianetics—Science or Hoax?" which related that L. Ron Hubbard was an obscure writer of pseudoscientific pulp fiction prior to the publishing of his book entitled "Dianetics." Hubbard's book asserts that "the creation of dianetics is a milestone for Man comparable to the wheel and the arch . . . the intelligent layman can successfully and invariably treat all psychosomatic ills and inorganic aberrations," according to Hubbard. "These psychosomatic ills, uniformly cured by dianetic therapy, include such varied maladies as eye trouble, bursitis, ulcers, some heart difficulties, migraine headaches and the common cold." According to the article, Hubbard's book has "outraged scores of psychiatrists, biochemists, psychologies, physicians and just-plain-ordinary scientists, who look upon the astounding claims and growing commercial success of this strange new phenomenon with awe, fear and . . . disgust. . . . Hubbard's greatest attraction to the troubled is that his erzatz psychiatry is available to all. It's cheap. It's accessible. It's a public festival to be played at clubs and parties."

During March, 1951, the Board of Medical Examiners, State of New Jersey, had a case against the HDRF . . . on the grounds that the organization was conducting a school, teaching a branch of medicine and surgery, without a license.

---

bard's life, written and published by the Church of Scientology's own publishing house.

Melton, J. Gordon. *The Church of Scientology*. Salt Lake City: Signature Books, 2000. Melton, a religious scholar, produced a concise book that summarizes Scientology and Hubbard's contributions. The book attempts not to take sides.

Monsma, Stephen. *When Sacred and Secular Mix: Religious Nonprofit Organizations and Public Money*. Lanham, Md.: Rowman & Littlefield, 2000. Hubbard made a major business from charging fees for Church of Scientology publications and training materials. This book examines that concept in depth.

—*Mary C. Ware*

SEE ALSO: Werner Erhard.

JAMES OLIVER HUBERTY
American mass murderer

BORN: October 11, 1942; Canton, Ohio
DIED: July 18, 1984; San Ysidro, California
CAUSE OF NOTORIETY: Huberty entered a busy McDonald's restaurant and shot and killed twenty-one people before being killed by law enforcement officers.
ACTIVE: July 18, 1984
LOCALE: San Ysidro, California

EARLY LIFE

When James Oliver Huberty (HEW-buhr-tee) was seven, his mother abandoned the family to become a Pentecostal missionary. He was frequently teased by other children for coming from a broken home and for having spastic paralysis from polio. After graduating from the Pittsburgh Institute of Mortuary Science, Huberty got a job in a funeral home. Although his embalming skills were good, he was fired because of his unsympathetic demeanor toward the bereaved. Around 1976, Huberty began hearing disembodied voices. A successful career as a welder in Ohio ended in 1982, when he was laid off by the Babcock and Wilcox Company. Huberty, his wife Etna, and his children moved to Mexico briefly and then to San Ysidro, California (near the Mexican border), where Huberty earned a meager income as a security guard. He sometimes hit his wife, who did her best to shield the increasingly reclusive and hot-tempered Huberty from the rest of the world.

CRIMINAL CAREER

On July 17, 1984, after being fired from his security guard position, Huberty called a mental clinic, and an employee promised to get back to him in two days to schedule an appointment. Worried that her husband might kill someone in the interim, Etna called every mental clinic in the area in an attempt to determine which clinic Huberty had called and to plead for an immediate appointment. However, because the clinic had misspelled Huberty's name, there was no record of his call. Etna ignored one clinic's suggestion that she call the police.

The next day, Huberty told Etna that his life was over and that he was "going to hunt humans." Etna did nothing. A little before 4:00 P.M., Huberty entered a McDonald's in a Mexican American neighborhood. Huberty had expressed his hatred for children and for Mexicans; he felt that Mexicans were to blame for the loss of some of his jobs. Using a 9 millimeter Browning pistol, a 9 millimeter Uzi pistol, and a Winchester 12-gauge shotgun, he began killing people. An assistant manager at the McDonald's called the operator and reported a shooting in progress. The operator told her to dial 911; only after extensive pleading from the manager (noting that if she reached for the wall phone to dial 911, she would be killed) did the operator connect her to the police. Several officers finally arrived but did not enter the restaurant. The commander of the Special Weapons and Tactics (SWAT) team took almost an hour to arrive because of rush-hour traffic, and the SWAT officers would not act without a commanding order. Finally, at 5:17 P.M., a SWAT sniper, following orders, took a clear rifle shot at Huberty's head and instantly killed him. In 77 minutes, Huberty had fired approximately 150 shots, murdered 21 people and wounded 19. Many of those who died bled to death while the police officers remained outside the building.

IMPACT

James Oliver Huberty's life and murders were later carefully studied by George Hennard, who would commit a similar but deadlier mass murder in a restaurant in Killeen, Texas, in 1991. Gun control groups attempted to use the McDonald's Massacre, as the event came to be called, to promote their cause; they met with little success. Furthermore, no changes occurred in the law enforcement policies of refusing to enter a building in order to confront an "active shooter" or of not allowing police snipers to act except in response to a command.

In 1987, several survivors filed a lawsuit, *Lopez v. McDonald's Corporation*, accusing McDonald's of failing to provide adequate security within the restaurant, but their litigation efforts failed. Also in 1987, Etna Huberty sued McDonald's and Babcock and Wilcox Company, claiming that a combination of the monosodium glutamate in the restaurant's food and Huberty's long years of working with poisonous metals contributed to his delusions and episodes of rage. Her lawsuits were also unsuccessful.

FURTHER READING

Foreman, Laura, ed. *Mass Murderers*. Alexandria, Va.: Time-Life Books, 1993. Chapter 4 serves as an excellent survey of Huberty's childhood, lifelong interest in guns, and descent into mental illness. Also provides extensive information about the victims, as well as the police department's response to the killings.

Kohl, James. "Foreseeing One's Duty to Protect." *Security Management* 33, no. 9 (September, 1989). Analyzes the unsuccessful lawsuit, *Lopez v. McDonald's*, that a few San Ysidro victims brought against McDonald's for allegedly failing to provide adequate security.

Salva-Ramirez, Mary-Angie. "The San Ysidro Massacre, Ten Years Later: McDonald's Actions Spoke Louder than Words." *Public Relations Quarterly* 40,

no. 1 (1995). Explains how the reaction of the McDonald's Corporation to the massacre focused on providing all possible assistance to the victims and their families without regard for possible legal liability and how the compassionate approach left the positive corporate image of McDonald's as strong as ever.

—*David B. Kopel*

SEE ALSO: Baruch Goldstein; George Hennard; Marc Lépine; Charles Whitman.

LAUD HUMPHREYS
American sociologist and author

BORN: October 16, 1930; Chickasha, Oklahoma
DIED: August 23, 1988; Van Nuys, California
ALSO KNOWN AS: Robert Allan Humphreys (full name)
CAUSE OF NOTORIETY: Humphreys, after studying anonymous male homosexual behavior in public restrooms, was criticized for unethical research, although some credited him with dispelling stereotypes about homosexuals.
ACTIVE: 1965-1970
LOCALE: St. Louis, Missouri, and Claremont, California

EARLY LIFE
Robert Allan Humphreys (HUHM-freez) adopted the first name "Laud" (lawd) in 1955 upon his successful completion of studies at the Seabury-Western Theological Seminary in Evanston, Illinois, where he was ordained as an Episcopalian priest. Five years later, in 1960, Humphreys married Nancy Wallace. He continued his education, earning a doctoral degree from Washington University in St. Louis, Missouri.

SOCIOLOGY CAREER
Humphreys learned after his father's death that his father had traveled frequently to New Orleans in order to engage in sex with other men. This knowledge perhaps influenced Humphreys: He focused his dissertation research on the characteristics of men who engaged in anonymous homosexual acts in public places. During Humphreys' tenure as a graduate student at Washington University, most arrests of homosexual men were for engaging in fellatio in public restrooms, also called "tearoom sex."

In order to study tearoom behavior, Humphreys posed as a "watchqueen" (a guard who warns the participants when others, especially the authorities, approach) at the tearooms, thereby observing hundreds of men in sexual acts. However, unbeknownst to his subjects, Humphreys also recorded detailed descriptions of them, as well as their license plate numbers. Using a contact with the police, Humphreys later secured the identities and addresses of most of the men. Then, changing his appearance and claiming to be conducting a health study (for which he truly was a researcher, although these particular men were not subjects), Humphreys interviewed the men in their homes.

A small minority fit the cultural homosexual stereotype; however, most of the men Humphreys had observed were married with children. Humphreys' research was criticized by some fellow academics for his follow-up interviews with the men. Because his research occurred before the advent of institutional review boards and human subjects committees, Humphreys neither revealed the true nature of his study nor requested consent to participate. Instead, he asked the men about their attitudes toward homosexual behavior, couching his questions in the context of a health study. Many academics and researchers argued that Humphreys' approach was psychologically harmful to the subjects, partly because it was potentially threatening to their marriages and social standing. However, to a small group of men at the tearoom, Humphreys did reveal his true identity as a researcher and was able to gain a rich body of knowledge about the "tearoom trade."

After the publication of *Tearoom Trade: Impersonal Sex in Public Places* in 1970, Humphreys went to Pitzer

College in Claremont, California, in 1972 to teach sociology. After realizing his own homosexual preference and "coming out" publicly as a gay man in 1980, Humphreys left his wife and children. He retired from the college in 1986 and died two years later.

IMPACT

Initially, Laud Humphreys' tearoom studies led to a moral outrage about the privacy of research subjects. Other professors in the Washington University sociology department learned of the research afterward—some opposed the research as unethical, some left Washington University, while some petitioned the university president to repeal Humphreys' degree. Humphreys' research and the publicity surrounding *Tearoom Trade* contributed to the establishment of institutional review boards and human subjects committees in American university departments.

Humphreys' study of the tearoom trade challenged many public perceptions about homosexual behavior and gay men. Most men in his sample were married and respectable members of their communities—a difference from the prevailing stereotype of homosexuals as dangerous deviants. Some people credit Humphreys with reduced arrests for tearoom activity. In subsequent decades, sociologists reflected more positively on the

benefits of Humphreys' work and recognized that he helped build a better understanding of male sexuality, which in turn became helpful for the understanding of the transmission of human immunodeficiency virus (HIV).

FURTHER READING

Galliher, John F., Wayne Brekhus, and David P. Keys. *Laud Humphreys: Prophet of Homosexuality and Sociology*. Madison: University of Wisconsin Press, 2004. A solid biography of Humphreys' life and career.

Humphreys, Laud. *Out of the Closets: The Sociology of Homosexual Liberation*. Englewood Cliffs, N.J.: Prentice-Hall, 1972. Another piece of Humphreys' famed research.

_____. *Tearoom Trade: Impersonal Sex in Public Places*. Chicago: Aldine, 1970. The product of Humphreys' controversial research on tearooms.

Schacht, Steven P., ed. Special issue of *International Journal of Sociology and Social Policy* 24, nos. 3-5 (2004). This issue is devoted to analyzing with a series of essays the impact of Humphreys' research.

—*Jennifer C. Gibbs*

SEE ALSO: Stanley Milgram.

E. HOWARD HUNT
American CIA operative (1949-1970) and consultant to the Nixon White House

BORN: October 9, 1918; East Hamburg, New York
ALSO KNOWN AS: Edward Howard Hunt (full name);
    John Baxter; Gordon Davis; Robert Dietrich
MAJOR OFFENSES: Burglary, conspiracy, and
    wiretapping
DATE: 1949-1974
LOCALE: Latin America and Washington, D.C.
SENTENCE: Thirty-three months in prison

EARLY LIFE

Edward Howard Hunt (huhnt) was born in East Hamburg, New York, on October 9, 1918. He graduated from Brown University in 1940 with a degree in English literature and then joined the Naval Reserve. During World War II, Hunt served in the U.S. Navy, U.S. Army Air Force, and the Office of Strategic Services, the predecessor to the Central Intelligence Agency (CIA). In 1949, he joined the CIA and, while stationed in China, met and

married Dorothy Hunt. He remained in the CIA from 1949 to 1970. He began writing fictional books in 1942 and continued to do so throughout his life.

ESPIONAGE AND ADMINISTRATIVE CAREER

As a CIA operative, Hunt initially served in China and then in Latin America, blazing the trail of CIA involvement there. In 1949, he established the first postwar CIA station in Mexico City. During this period, the U.S. government feared communist influence on Latin American politics and the possible takeover of Latin American nations. CIA missions against communist-influenced governments, even when democratically elected, were therefore considered justified. Hunt was the architect of the 1954 U.S.-backed coup in Guatemala, which deposed President Jacobo Arbenz Guzmán. He was also a major participant in the 1961 Bay of Pigs operation—the failed attempt to overthrow Cuban revolutionary leader Fidel

Castro. This episode is regarded as one of the biggest disasters in the history of U.S. foreign policy.

Hunt retired from the CIA in 1970 and joined a Washington public relations firm. A year later, he accepted a part-time consultancy in the Nixon White House. He became a member of President Richard Nixon's Plumbers group, a special investigations unit so called because it was established to stop leaks of information from the administration to the media. Hunt also was one of the White House operatives who broke into the office of the psychiatrist who was treating Daniel Ellsberg. The Nixon administration wanted to find material with which Ellsberg could be discredited, because he had given the Pentagon Papers—a classified government study of the origins of the war in Vietnam—to *The New York Times*. The Pentagon Papers revealed that the U.S. government understood early in the war that it was probably unwinnable and that continuing the war would likely lead to exponentially more casualties than were being admitted publicly.

Hunt secured his notoriety, however, on June 17, 1972, when five men broke into the Democratic Party's National Committee office at the Watergate Hotel in Washington, D.C. The men were discovered in the office and arrested for breaking in. While Hunt was not one of the five men arrested, he and G. Gordon Liddy were the architects of the plan.

LEGAL ACTION AND OUTCOME

Hunt was convicted of burglary, conspiracy, and wiretapping and served thirty-three months in prison. The Rockefeller Commission of the U.S. Congress in 1974 regarded Hunt and Watergate burglar Frank Sturgis as suspects in the 1963 assassination of President John F. Kennedy. Witnesses placed Hunt in Dealey Plaza at the time that Kennedy was killed nearby. Attorney Mark Lane's theory about Hunt's and the CIA's role in Kennedy's murder can be found in the 1991 book *Plausible Denial*.

IMPACT

The Watergate scandal led to the resignation of President Richard Nixon, contributed to changes in campaign

E. Howard Hunt. (AP/Wide World Photos)

finance reform, and was a major factor in the passage of amendments to the Freedom of Information Act in 1986. The U.S. presidency would never again engage the automatic trust and respect it had enjoyed earlier in the century. Moreover, Watergate led to the news media becoming far more aggressive in reporting and investigating the activities of politicians. The scandal also resulted in a substantial loss of confidence of the public in political leaders and government agencies.

The criminal and subversive activities of E. Howard Hunt and others like him also contributed to the scaling back of the CIA's prerogatives following hearings by the Church Committee in 1976.

Throughout his career as a soldier and spy, Hunt remained a prolific author of spy thrillers. His novels mix fact and fiction, with details altered, locations blurred, and identities changed so that they cannot be recognized. The books he wrote while working for the CIA always had to be submitted to his superiors for approval. In his later years, he continued to enjoy fame tinged with notoriety, occasionally appearing as a guest on television shows and maintaining his own Web site.

FURTHER READING

Blight, James, and Peter Kornbluh. *Politics of Illusion: The Bay of Pigs Invasion Reexamined.* Boulder, Colo.: Lynne Rienner, 1998. Blends declassified documents and firsthand accounts of participants into an interesting and updated analysis of the Bay of Pigs disaster.

Cullather, Nick. *Secret History: The CIA's Classified Account of Its Operations in Guatemala, 1952-1954*. Palo Alto, Calif.: Stanford University Press, 1999. Describes the involvement of the CIA and Hunt in overthrowing the Guatemalan government of Arbenz, despite its being democratically elected.

Olson, Keith. *Watergate: The Presidential Scandal That Shook America*. Lawrence: University Press of Kansas, 2003. Olson calls his book a "layman's guide to Watergate," and as such, it provides a complete and readable analysis of the scandal and its aftermath.

Woodward, Bob, and Carl Bernstein. *All the President's Men*. New York: Simon & Schuster, 1974. The definitive book on the Watergate scandal by the *Washington Post* reporters who investigated and broke the story. In addition to crucial information on the scandal itself, this book is also an invaluable look into the process of investigative journalism.

—*Jerome L. Neapolitan*

SEE ALSO: Charles W. Colson; John D. Ehrlichman; H. R. Haldeman; G. Gordon Liddy; James W. McCord, Jr.; John Mitchell; Richard Nixon.

QUSAY SADDAM HUSSEIN
Iraqi government official and son of dictator Saddam Hussein

BORN: May 17, 1966; Baghdad, Iraq
DIED: July 22, 2003; Mosul, Iraq
ALSO KNOWN AS: Qusay Saddam Hussein al-Tikriti (full name)
CAUSE OF NOTORIETY: While serving as deputy chairman of the Special Security Committee of the Iraqi National Security Council, Hussein presided over a network of spies and informers in the Iraqi security services. He likely authorized torture, interrogation, jailing, and execution of thousands of political prisoners and their families.
ACTIVE: 1991-2003
LOCALE: Iraq

EARLY LIFE
Qusay Saddam Hussein (kew-SAY sah-DAHM hew-SAYN) was the second and youngest son of future president of Iraq Saddam Hussein. He and Saddam's other son, Uday, were educated at the Al Khararkh al Namouthajiya. The school reportedly provided a high-quality education. Both boys received special treatment and security protection while at the school. Later, Qusay studied law at Baghdad University. He was the quieter of the two sons and initially was less favored by Saddam. However, as Uday became more vulgar and less reliable, the more calculating and serious Qusay emerged as Saddam's heir apparent. In 1985, Qusay married Sahar, daughter of General Maher al-Rashid, a Sunni Muslim. The marriage produced three children but was dissolved after the birth of the third child.

POLITICAL CAREER
Qusay kept a low profile throughout most of his early life. He first emerged as a key actor in Iraq after the liberation of Kuwait by American-led forces in 1991. He oversaw the brutal suppression of an uprising against the Hussein regime by Shiite Muslims in the south of Iraq. After proving himself against the Shiite in 1991, Qusay quickly rose through the ruling Ba'th Party structures, taking command of Iraq's intelligence, security forces, and the elite of the Republican Guard.

The Iraqi security directorate that became Qusay's personal power base included the hated *mukhabarat* (secret police), which claimed a higher percentage of the national budget than any similar service in the world. Qusay was willing and able to use blackmail, and he forced confessions in order to control and prevent threats to Saddam's regime. Reports indicate that he ordered the interrogation, jailing, and execution of political prisoners and their families. He was alleged to have ordered mass executions of thousands of prison inmates.

After the 1991 Persian Gulf War, Qusay's Special Security Organization was responsible for hiding Iraq's weapons of mass destruction programs. During this period, Qusay's power and influence increased greatly. While Saddam retained formal control of the Iraqi military machine, Qusay regularly presided over the military in the late 1990's. He led a crackdown against the al-Dulaymi tribe in 1995 and another against a local Shiite revolt in 1997. His reputation for brutality was undoubtedly the cause for several attempts by opponents of the regime to kill him; in 2001, he was wounded in the arm during one such attempt.

Qusay had attained the height of his power just prior to the start of the Iraq War in 2003 and had clearly become the heir apparent to Saddam. Just days before the war, he was given absolute charge of four key regions, including the capital and the family seat of Tikrit. Until his death, he was Saddam's main strategist during the war. On July 22, 2003, troops of the American 101st Airborne, aided by U.S. Special Forces, killed Qusay and his older brother Uday in a fierce three-hour gunfight in the town of Mosul in northern Iraq.

IMPACT

Qusay Saddam Hussein was a key target of the coalition forces, just behind his father. Many military and political leaders believed that Saddam's sons were behind the daily attacks on American troops, both in practical and in symbolic terms. Thus, it was thought that their deaths would contribute to demoralizing the resistance and perhaps even result in its demise. To this end, on July 24, 2003, gruesome photographs of the killed brothers were released to the press and shown on television and in newspapers.

Many people—within and outside Iraq—criticized the United States for having a double standard in releasing the photos of the dead brothers, since the administration of George W. Bush had condemned Saddam Hussein for releasing photos of dead American soldiers during the conflict. The Bush administration responded by arguing that it was necessary to combat rumors that the brothers were still alive and that confirmation of the deaths would bring "closure" to the Iraqi people.

The deaths of the brothers failed to have the desired effect, as the days following the deaths saw some of the deadliest attacks against American personnel since the insurgency had begun. Although the deaths appeared to have little effect on the ongoing insurgency in Iraq, they may have contributed to the eventual capture of Saddam Hussein in December, 2003.

FURTHER READING

Aburish, Said. *Saddam Hussein: The Politics of Revenge.* New York: Bloomsbury USA, 2000. Aburish worked with Saddam Hussein in the 1970's, and thus his personal experiences and access to inside sources lend depth and veracity to this book. It provides a compelling and sometimes frightening biography and psychological profile of Saddam Hussein.

Cerf, Christopher, and Micah Sifry, eds. *The Iraq War Reader: History, Documents, Opinions.* Carmichael, Calif.: Touchstone, 2003. This book provides historical documents, speeches, essays, and commentaries that cover the history and politics that led to war in Iraq. It is divided into four sections, which cover relevant information from 1915 to 2003.

Johnson, James Turner. *The War to Oust Saddam Hussein: The Context, the Debate, the War, and the Future.* Lanham, Md: Rowman & Littlefield, 2005. This book attempts a moral analysis of the war in Iraq, asking questions about the justifications for, and implications of, the war.

Keegan, John. *The Iraq War.* New York: Knopf, 2004. John Keegan is recognized as one of the top military writers of the past fifty years. Here he provides valuable insight into the social and political history of Iraq and, in particular, Saddam Hussein and his closest supporters. The book does not address the insurgency that followed the initial invasion.

—Jerome L. Neapolitan

SEE ALSO: Saddam Hussein; Uday Hussein.

SADDAM HUSSEIN
Iraqi dictator (1979-2003)

BORN: April 28, 1937; al-Awja, near Tikrit, Iraq
ALSO KNOWN AS: Saddam Hussein al-Tikriti
CAUSE OF NOTORIETY: Hussein was dictator of Iraq until his defeat by U.S.-led forces in 2003.
ACTIVE: 1979-2003
LOCALE: Iraq
SENTENCE: Death by hanging

EARLY LIFE

Saddam Hussein (sah-DAHM hew-SAYN) was born in 1937, six miles south of Tikrit. His early years were marked by extreme poverty and an unstable family life. Hussein never knew his biological father, and his stepfather physically abused him. This cruelty no doubt had a negative impact upon Hussein's character development. At ten years of age, he left his mother's home to live with an uncle by the name of Kharillah Talfah; this man later played a vital role in Hussein's political life. During the mid-twentieth century, Tikrit was known as a lawless place, where violence was viewed as a virtue and where inhabitants often resorted to the knife or gun as a means of resolving disputes. Hussein's formative years in this city furthered his predilections for violence and authoritarian personality.

POLITICAL CAREER

Through his uncle's influence, Hussein joined the Ba'th Socialist Party while still a teenager. In 1959, he was recruited by the party to join a team of assassins and kill the country's military dictator, General Abdul Karim Qassim. The attempt failed. Wounded, Hussein managed to escape. He spent the following four years in exile, first in Damascus and later in Cairo. During February, 1963, with Hussein in exile, the Ba'thists engineered a second, and this time successful, coup.

General Qassim was executed, and Hussein returned to Iraq to serve the new regime as the Ba'th Party's enforcer. Soon, Hussein developed a brutally efficient secret police and intelligence network that eventually became the foundation for the Mukhabarat, Iraq's feared security agency.

Initially, the Ba'th Party's reign was short-lived; it was ousted in November, 1963—barely ten months after taking power. However, the Ba'th returned to power in 1968 with General Ahmed Hassan al-Bakr as president and Hussein as vice president. Hussein's political ascendancy at such a young age (he was only thirty-one), is a testament to his penchant for power as well as his exceptional organizational skills. Instrumental, too, were connections facilitated through Hassan al-Bakr, a well-positioned relative.

By 1975, Hussein had used the Mukhabarat to consolidate his power and become Iraq's de facto ruler. Four years later, Hassan al-Bakr resigned as president, ostensibly for health reasons. Hussein now officially took that post. Although the term "president" may suggest parliamentary procedures that are common in liberal democracies, in reality, Hussein wielded absolute authority. Through systematic demagoguery and terror, his presidency exercised nearly totalitarian power over the lives of the Iraqi people. No opposition would be tolerated.

Hussein's reign of terror was unleashed immediately following his assumption of the presidency. When, during the summer of 1979, the Regional Command convened, a legislative body that included the Ba'th Party's highest ranking leaders, many members were stunned to find themselves framed in an imaginary plot against Hussein and Iraq. Charged with treason, these supposed plotters were publicly identified and immediately ushered from the congressional chamber. Several days later, these officials were summarily executed by Hussein and his henchmen. A video of the arrests was mailed to members of the Ba'th Party throughout Iraq to serve as warning that dissent from any quarters could mean death.

During his twenty-four-year reign, Hussein demonstrated over and over again the extreme means he would invoke to ensure the preservation of his regime. The Mukhabarat spied on high officials and ordinary citizens alike, constantly seeking to uncover plots against the Iraqi leader or his government. As a result of this intensive surveillance, thousands of people were arrested for crimes, both real and imaginary, against the state. Many were tortured and executed just for making derogatory remarks about Hussein or members of his family. Anyone who was viewed as a challenge to Hussein's authority, even in a very small measure, could expect a visit of terror. Therein, Hussein also implemented systematic purges of the Iraqi army, executing high-ranking officers whose only offense was that they were too competent or too highly regarded by their troops.

In 1980, Iraq invaded Iran, inaugurating a costly eight-year war. During this conflict, Hussein repeatedly employed chemical weapons against Iranians. By the time the killing finally subsided, the two countries to-

THE AL-ANFAL CAMPAIGN AGAINST IRAQI KURDS

From 1986 until 1989, Saddam Hussein gave his cousin Ali Hassan al-Majid, later known as "Chemical Ali," extensive powers (including use of chemical weapons) to quash a revolt among the Kurds in northern Iraq. The result was the mutilation of a whole society. In 1993, Human Rights Watch accused the Iraqi regime of the following "gross violations of human rights":

- Mass summary executions and mass disappearance of many tens of thousands of noncombatants, including large numbers of women and children, and sometimes the entire population of villages.
- Widespread use of chemical weapons, including mustard gas and the nerve agent Sarin, or GB, against the town of Halabja as well as dozens of Kurdish villages, killing many thousands of people, mainly women and children.
- Wholesale destruction of some two thousand villages, which are described in government documents as having been "burned," "destroyed," "demolished," or "purified," as well as at least a dozen larger towns and administrative centers.
- Destruction of civilian objects by army engineers, including all schools, mosques, wells, and other nonresidential structures in the targeted villages as well as a number of electricity substations.
- Looting of civilian property and farm animals on a vast scale by army troops and progovernment militia.
- Arrest of all villagers captured in designated "prohibited areas," despite the fact that these were their own homes and lands.
- Arbitrary jailing and warehousing for months, in conditions of extreme deprivation, of tens of thousands of women, children, and elderly people, without judicial order or any cause other than their presumed sympathies for the Kurdish opposition. Many hundreds of them were allowed to die of malnutrition and disease.
- Forced displacement of hundreds of thousands of villagers upon the demolition of their homes, their release from jail or return from exile; these civilians were trucked into areas of Kurdistan far from their homes and dumped there by the army with only minimal governmental compensation, or none at all, for their destroyed property, or any provision for relief, housing, clothing, or food, and forbidden to return to their villages of origin on pain of death. In these conditions, many died within a year of their forced displacement.
- Destruction of the rural Kurdish economy and infrastructure.

In 2005, an international court in the Hague ruled that the al-Anfal campaign was an act of genocide.

Source: Genocide in Iraq: The Anfal Campaign Against the Kurds (New York: Human Rights Watch, 1993).

Two years after the war with Iran, Hussein decided to invade Kuwait. The attack against the wealthy oil state prompted an immediate and unequivocal response from the United States. Hussein's bravado response was that any attempt to repulse his maneuvers would result in the "mother of all wars" and countless American casualties. In fact, a U.S.-led coalition (Operation Desert Storm) quickly routed the Iraqi army in February, 1991, and evicted it from Kuwait. Even more than in 1988, Hussein's political position again seemed assailable; during the early spring of 1991, popular uprisings developed in the north, led by Kurdish rebels, and in the south of Iraq, led by Shiite Muslims. Through an unrelenting campaign of terror, Hussein managed to regain his control; approximately forty-five thousand Kurdish and Shiite people were killed in the process.

LEGAL ACTION AND OUTCOME

After a decade of repeated U.N. Security Council resolution violations, the United States invaded Iraq in March, 2003, and overthrew Hussein that April. He was tried in 2005-2006 for ordering the torture and murders of more than 140 Iraqis in Dujail in 1982 and was convicted of crimes against humanity. His sentence, death by hanging, was announced on November 5, 2006.

IMPACT

The hallmarks of Saddam Hussein's character that took him to the apex of Iraqi society were ambition, decisiveness, and mercilessness. Upon achieving power, he systematically transformed Iraqi society so as to extend and secure his political authority. Through that process, Iraq became a police state that brutally repressed all forms of dissidence and discouraged any type of independent thinking, analysis, or development. After more than forty years of Ba'th Party rule ended, post-Hussein Iraq struggled with

gether had lost more than one million people, and Iraq was left with eighty billion dollars in debt. Now the Kurdish people of northern Iraq rebelled. Hussein's response was to turn his chemical weapons upon them, murdering or wounding approximately ten thousand civilians.

the consequences of his authoritarian dictatorship. U.S. troops lingered in Iraq for years as the nation collapsed into a de facto civil war between religious and ethnic factions.

One important reason the Bush administration saw its efforts for installing a democratic government in Iraq repeatedly thwarted was that the people there possessed very limited experience with the design and function of republican institutions. They lived within a political culture that had been denied access to the collective democratic values and norms that citizens in democratic societies routinely take for granted. Respect for the rule of law, minority rights, rights of the accused, freedom of speech, and freedom of religion remained foreign concepts to most Iraqis. Such institutions would require at least a generation or two before they could become dominant within the political culture. Thus, through his tyrannical exclusion of key democratic principles and practices, Hussein's legacy to his people, at least in the short term, could be characterized by continued sectarian violence, strong-armed police tactics in dealing with "criminal" suspects, and suspicion and distrust by the Iraqi people of their government and of their fellow citizens.

FURTHER READING

Coughlin, Con. *Saddam: King of Terror*. New York: HarperCollins, 2002. Biographical sketch examines the dictator's life from his youth to late adulthood.

Karsh, Efraim, and Inari Rautsi. *Saddam Hussein: A Political Biography*. 1991. Reprint. New York: Grove Press, 2002. Shows how Hussein and the Ba'th Party came to power in 1968 and provides insight into the major geopolitical issues of the Middle East.

Miller, John, and Aaron Kenedi, eds. *Inside Iraq: The History, the People, and the Politics of the World's Least Understood Land*. New York: Marlow, 2002. A collection of essays by scholars and journalists about the history of Iraq and Hussein's role in shaping modern Iraq.

—*Randall D. Swain*

SEE ALSO: Qusay Saddam Hussein; Uday Hussein; Ayatollah Khomeini; Kim Jong-il; Mohammad Reza Shah Pahlavi; Muammar al-Qaddafi; Suharto; Than Shwe.

UDAY HUSSEIN
Iraqi official and son of dictator Saddam Hussein

BORN: June 18, 1964; Baghdad, Iraq
DIED: July 22, 2003; Mosul, Iraq
ALSO KNOWN AS: Uday Saddam Hussein al-Tikriti (full name); Odai Hussein
CAUSE OF NOTORIETY: Uday Hussein was dictator Saddam Hussein's oldest son and was probably hated and feared more than his father, whose viciousness and ruthlessness he exceeded.
ACTIVE: c. 1982-2003
LOCALE: Iraq

EARLY LIFE
Uday Hussein (AW-day hew-SAYN) al-Tikriti was born in 1964 in Baghdad, the capital city of Iraq. He had a privileged and pampered childhood as the eldest son of the second most powerful man in Iraq. It seems that his mother had the most influence in young Uday's life. Because Saddam was busy with the affairs of state and was rarely home, it is doubtful that Uday had a normal relationship with his father, and throughout his life, Uday's only meaningful attachment was to his mother. In all likelihood, he was spoiled and indulged, and it is doubtful that any restrictions were placed on him.

POLITICAL CAREER
In keeping with an Arabic tradition that bestows a family's inheritance on the oldest son, Uday was the rational choice to succeed his father as ruler of Iraq when time came for Saddam to step down. Indeed, Uday's importance in the regime and Iraqi society was derived from his status as Saddam's son and heir apparent. After receiving his college degree, Uday was placed in charge of Iraq's Olympic Committee.

Over time, however, Uday's character flaws would prove his undoing. Whereas Saddam was ruthless in his dealings with real or imagined enemies—he often tortured and killed as a means of self-preservation—Uday, on the other hand, tortured and killed for entertainment and sport. Furthermore, he was imprudent and erratic, and often his friends were as likely to be tortured, imprisoned, or even killed, as his enemies, for wholly capricious reasons.

Uday, Saddam, and Qusay Hussein. (AP/Wide World Photos)

An incident that illustrates Uday's cruel vindictiveness and imprudence occurred in 1988 and ultimately caused a rift between father and son that was never fully healed. While attending a state-sponsored party, Uday noticed his father's favorite bodyguard in attendance. Some time earlier, this bodyguard had introduced Saddam to a woman who later became Saddam's second wife. The bodyguard had acted as a go-between for Saddam and his mistress and arranged trysts between the two of them. Uday was offended for his mother's honor and blamed the bodyguard for introducing Saddam to the woman.

Noticing the man at the party, Uday summoned him but was contemptuously slighted by the bodyguard. Uday then assaulted the bodyguard with a nightstick that was equipped with electric prods and bludgeoned him to death. The incident caused an international stir because

Suzanne Mubarak, the wife of Egyptian president Muhammad Hosni Mubarak, was also in attendance at the party. She witnessed the episode and was horrified at what she saw. Saddam was furious at his son and imprisoned him, had him tortured for forty days, and threatened to execute him. His mother's pleas effected a change of mind for Saddam, and Uday was sent into exile for two years. The damage was permanent, however, as Uday's status as heir apparent was gradually supplanted by his younger brother Qusay.

Prior to the first Persian Gulf War in 1990, Uday returned to Iraq and was put in charge of the *Babel*, a major newspaper in Iraq. He took control, with his father's blessing of the newspaper and a radio station that played American popular music. Uday used the paper to distribute the regime's propaganda. Uday's time in exile did not temper his malignant barbarity and greed. He profited from the first Persian Gulf War by looting Kuwait of valuable paintings and expensive automobiles, and he used economic sanctions placed on Iraq by the international community to make a fortune on the black market.

He also resumed his place as head of Iraq's Olympic Committee. In this capacity, Uday often imprisoned and tortured athletes for not performing as expected. On one occasion, he imprisoned and tortured Iraq's soccer team for losing a match.

In 1996, Uday was shot several times in an assassination attempt that left him severely disabled for the remainder of his life. He was so widely hated and feared that it was difficult to determine who the potential assassins could be or where the search for the plotters should begin. Some have speculated that only Saddam or his younger brother Qusay could have assembled the assets and personnel required to make an attempt on the life of someone as closely guarded as Uday.

After the assassination attempt, Uday continued to flaunt his status as a central figure in his father's regime. If anything, his actions became more depraved, eccentric, and violent as he tried to prove that he was as virile and in control as he had been before being shot. The extent of his injuries was so systemic, however, that he was never fully capable of doing the things he did before his injuries. Therefore he became more depraved and exhibited more brutality, taking out his frustrations on those around him.

LEGAL ACTION AND OUTCOME

Saddam's regime was toppled and Uday's despotic aspirations with it in March, 2003, after U.S. forces and an international coalition overthrew the dictatorship and ended Saddam's twenty-four-year reign. Uday's life of rape, torture, and murder came to an end in July, 2003, in a firefight with U.S. forces in the city of Mosul after the military received an anonymous tip concering Uday and Qusay's hideout.

IMPACT

Uday Hussein liked to boast that when he succeeded his father, the people of Iraq would look back with nostalgia on Saddam's reign because of the terror he, Uday, planned to unleash on the country.

Uday's political impact, however, is not as systemic as his father's. Even if the Hussein regime had somehow been able to placate the George W. Bush administration and maintain its hold on Iraq, it is unlikely that Uday would have succeeded his father as president of Iraq. By the time of the U.S. invasion, Qusay was considered his father's heir. Uday's eccentric and violent behavior, coupled with the loss of his father's trust, all but assured that the best that he could have hoped for was to be Iraq's number-two man.

Nevertheless, Uday's name will go down in history as ignominious. Years after the fall of the Hussein regime, the world was continuing to discover the extent of the Husseins' depravity and the lengths to which they would go to stay in power. While the father's depravity may be explained by political expediency, Uday's excesses—the torture and murder of real and imagined enemies and the rape of an untold number of Iraqi women—can only be explained by uncontrolled urges. Uday's life serves as a warning of the potential dangers of nepotism where politics are concerned.

FURTHER READING

Coughlin, Con. *Saddam: King of Terror*. New York: HarperCollins, 2002. Although the book is mostly about Saddam, it provides detailed accounts of Uday's sadistic nature.

Global Security.org. *Uday Saddam Al-Tikriti*. http://www .globalsecurity.org/military/world/iraq/uday.htm. Online account of the life and death of Uday Hussein. Accessed May, 2006.

Miller, John, and Aaron Kenedi, eds. *Inside Iraq: The History, the People, and the Politics of the World's Least Understood Land*. New York: Marlow, 2002. A collection of essays by scholars and journalists about the history of Iraq and Hussein's role in shaping modern Iraq.

Yahyá, Latif, and Karl Wendl. *I Was Saddam's Son*. New York: Arcade, 1997. Latif Yahyá served as a body double for Uday Hussein. He chronicles Uday's life and the atrocities that were commonplace in Iraq's corridors of power.

—*Randall D. Swain*

SEE ALSO: Qusay Saddam Hussein; Saddam Hussein.

MEGAN LOUISE IRELAND
Australian con artist

BORN: August 18, 1967; Lismore, New South Wales, Australia
MAJOR OFFENSES: Fraud, theft, and blackmail
ACTIVE: Ended 2003
LOCALE: Worldwide
SENTENCE: Imprisonment

EARLY LIFE
Megan Louise Ireland (IEHR-land) was born in New South Wales, Australia, on August 18, 1967. She began her career as a schoolteacher and continued to teach until 2003, when it was alleged that she had sexually propositioned a student.

CRIMINAL CAREER
Ireland's criminal activities were discovered in 2003, while she was a high school teacher. A parent complained that Ireland had sexually propositioned a male high school student. The allegations were made after a tutor found letters Ireland had written to the student. Following the police inquiry into Ireland's activities, it was discovered that she had been banned by the University of Sydney after it was determined that she had forged a letter of reference to gain admission into a masters of education program there. Despite her banishment, she was still teaching in state schools in Australia, which was illegal.

Ireland was also found knowingly to have harbored an illegal immigrant from Shanghai, China, in her home. She subsequently blackmailed him into giving a false statement during a police interview. Insurance investigators discovered that Ireland had also been involved in an insurance compensation fraud involving faked back pain following a minor traffic accident.

She was also involved in a worldwide lottery "Lotto" scam. This type of fraud was derived from well-known chain-letter scams and so-called Nigerian 419 scams. Ireland's Lotto scam contacted individuals, telling them that they had won millions of dollars. The catch was that the victims were asked to provide their bank account details and then later asked for various fees in order to release the winnings.

LEGAL ACTION AND OUTCOME
Ireland was apprehended by New South Wales detectives, but not before she had defrauded an estimated sixty people. She was incarcerated at the Grafton Correctional Centre in New South Wales.

IMPACT
Worldwide Lotto scams such as Megan Louise Ireland's successfully duped individuals out of millions of dollars. The Lotto scam also developed into a phishing scam, an attempt to lure victims through e-mails that claimed that the recipient had won the lottery, then asked for personal information—names, addresses, and bank account numbers—so that supposedly the money could be transferred electronically into the victim's account. The information was then used to perpetrate fraud and theft. As of 2006, there were allegedly more than 380 Lotto scams throughout the world.

FURTHER READING
Davia, Howard R. *Fraud 101: Techniques and Strategies for Detection.* New York: John Wiley, 2000. Written by an accountant with more than thirty years of proactive, fraud-specific auditing experience. Provides a guide, drawing on the author's expertise and knowledge, to how to detect and protect oneself from fraud.

Mizell, Louis R. *Masters of Deception: The Worldwide White-Collar Crime Crisis and Ways to Protect Yourself.* New York: J. Wiley & Sons, 1997. This book, written by a former special agent and intelligence officer, addresses the growing problem of white-collar crime in America, using actual cases. Mizell exposes numerous perpetrators and their methods as well as offering invaluable advice on what to look for, how to avoid being a victim, and how to fight back.

Shover, Neal, and John Paul Wright, eds. *Crimes of Privilege: Readings in White-Collar Crime.* New York: Oxford University Press, 2001. This book examines knowledge and debate concerning white-collar crime. White-collar crime differs fundamentally from street crime because those who commit it typically lead lives of privilege.

—*Carly M. Hilinski*

SEE ALSO: Billie Sol Estes; Susanna Mildred Hill; Joseph Weil.

IRISH INVINCIBLES
Irish terrorist group

FORMED: Late 1881; London, England
ALSO KNOWN AS: Irish National Invincibles; the Invincibles
MAJOR OFFENSE: Assassinations of the chief secretary of Ireland Lord Frederick Cavendish and his undersecretary, Thomas Henry Burke
ACTIVE: May 6, 1882
LOCALE: Phoenix Park, Dublin, Ireland
SENTENCES: Death by hanging for five members; prison for eight others

EARLY LIFE
On May 6, 1882, the bodies of the newly installed chief secretary of Ireland, Lord Frederick Cavendish, and his undersecretary, Thomas Henry Burke, were found brutally stabbed along a footpath in Dublin's Phoenix Park. A group calling itself the Irish Invincibles left notes in Dublin newspaper offices claiming responsibility for the murders. The murders were a manifestation of the struggle between Irish militant groups and constitutional parties, and the sometimes tenuous links between them. This tension became a hallmark of late nineteenth and twentieth century Irish and Northern Irish political struggles.

Knowledge of the Invincibles, their membership, and organization remains vague. The group's core was composed of disgruntled members of the Irish Republican Brotherhood (IRB), also known as the Fenians. Founded in 1858, the IRB/Fenians were devoted to armed insurrection in order to gain Irish independence from Great Britain. With cells in New York, Ireland, and Britain, the IRB maintained international connections and secret fund-raising operations.

By 1879, some IRB leaders, such as John Devoy and Michael Davitt, supported Irish Home Rule leader Charles Stewart Parnell's National Land League in the attempt to garner political power. Termed the New Departure, this shift in the IRB leadership from militant action to political involvement caused a split within the group. The more militant Fenians refused purely political means to gain Irish independence. A leader affiliated with the IRB, Clan na Gael leader Jeremiah O'Donovan Rossa, continued to call for violent tactics against the British government and officials, especially bombings and assassinations.

Though unconnected to the Invincibles, O'Donovan Rossa had a significant influence on the Invincibles' message and tactics. The British government's crackdown on and imprisonment of Parnell and other Land League/Home Rule leaders in October, 1881, brought the Invincibles to fruition.

POLITICAL CAREER
According to information provided by Invincible-turned-police-informant James Carey, the Invincible leadership included several high-ranking members of Parnell's Land League in Britain, including Secretary Frank Byrne, Treasurer Patrick Egan, and organizer J. P. Sheridan. All three men maintained Fenian connections, and all were outraged at the British government for Parnell's imprisonment. Organized by Byrne and Carey sometime in late 1881, the group met at Carey's home in London. The reported leader of the Dublin cell was Irish American James McCafferty. Besides Carey and McCafferty, the core members included Daniel Delaney, Daniel Curley, and Edward McCafferty. Little is known of their backgrounds.

The main target for the Invincibles was Irish undersecretary Thomas Henry Burke. Burke, an Irish Roman Catholic, was perceived as a traitor for working with the British government. Plans were made for Burke's assassination in spring, 1882.

LEGAL ACTION AND OUTCOME
After murdering both Burke and Lord Cavendish in Phoenix Park in May, 1882, the Invincibles were tracked down by Dublin police investigators using evidence from Carey. Five murderers were tried and hanged by January, 1883, and eight others were sentenced to long terms in prison. Carey was given amnesty for identifying the others, but in 1883 he was shot dead by another Invincible while trying to flee Ireland.

IMPACT
The Invincibles were broken as an organization by 1883, but terror tactics against the British government and officials continued throughout the 1880's. As late as 1887, *The Times* of London attempted to connect Parnell with the Phoenix Park murders in a series of forged letters. Parnell was cleared of the charges, but this episode highlighted the difficulty in separating the Irish Home Rule movement from Irish militant violence.

FURTHER READING
Comerford, R. V. *Fenians in Context: Irish Politics and Society, 1848-1882.* Dublin, Ireland: Wolfhound

Press, 1985. Comerford's analysis emphasizes the nonviolent, social-communal aspects of the Fenian organization and development.

Kee, Robert. *The Green Flag: A History of Irish Nationalism*. London: Penguin Books, 2000. Kee's analysis of Irish independence movements and organizations broadly questions the formation of a purely "Irish" political-national identity.

O'Broin, Leon. *Revolutionary Underground: The Story of the Irish Republican Brotherhood, 1858-1924*.

Totowa, N.J.: Rowman and Littlefield, 1976. A narrative of the changing role of the Irish Republican Brotherhood.

Townshend, Charles. *Political Violence in Ireland: Government and Resistance Since 1848*. Oxford, England: Clarendon Press, 1983. An analysis of Irish militant violence in an international perspective.

—Tyler T. Crogg

See also: Molly Maguires.

Clifford Irving
American novelist

Born: November 5, 1930; New York, New York
Also known as: Clifford Michael Irving (full name)
Major offense: Fraud
Active: 1970-1972
Locale: New York, New York
Sentence: Thirty months in a federal prison; served fourteen months

Early Life

Clifford Irving (UHR-vihng) developed an interest in the arts early in life. He grew up in New York, the only son of illustrator and cartoonist Jay Irving and his wife, Dorothy Irving. Irving's father, who had created a popular newspaper cartoon called *Pottsy*, had high ambitions for his son and sent him to New York's High School of Music and Art, where Irving enjoyed considerable success. After graduation, he enrolled at Colgate University and began keeping company with a group of aspiring writers. His popularity there led him toward an epicurean lifestyle, and over the following twenty years he traveled across Europe, had numerous affairs and several unsuccessful marriages, and eventually settled in Spain, where he met and married Edith Sommer, who would later play a role in his downfall.

Irving published his first novel at the age of twenty-six, and by the time he turned thirty, in 1960, he had established a relationship with the prestigious New York publishing company McGraw-Hill. Through the 1960's, Irving found considerable success with the publisher. One of his works, titled *Fake* (1969), tells the story of an infamous art forger, Elmyr de Hory, whom Irving had come to know while living in Spain.

Criminal Career

In 1971, Irving told executives at McGraw-Hill that reclusive billionaire Howard Hughes had asked him to assist in writing Hughes's autobiography. Irving produced several letters purportedly written by Hughes confirming the request and demanding that the arrangement be kept confidential. The McGraw-Hill executives could hardly contain their enthusiasm for the project and eventually agreed to an advance of $750,000, most of it handed to Irving in checks written to Hughes.

In actuality, Irving had engineered the entire affair himself, forging the letters and inventing the circumstances around Hughes's unlikely request, including a claim of hundreds of hours of secret interviews with Hughes. He recruited a friend and colleague, Richard Suskind, to assist him in researching the book, and had his wife, Sommer, launder the checks written to Hughes through a Swiss bank account. In a stroke of good fortune, Irving was invited to help rewrite a biography of Hughes that had been cowritten by one of Hughes's former associates and rejected by numerous publishers. Instead, Irving made a copy of the work and used much of the material to write his own book.

When McGraw-Hill announced the book, Hughes's business colleagues challenged its authenticity, and Hughes himself broke his seclusion to conduct a telephone interview with seven journalists in which he denied any involvement in the work. Irving continued to defend the book, even appearing on the popular television newsmagazine *60 Minutes*, but when Hughes sued McGraw-Hill, subsequent investigations revealed the similarities between Irving's book and the manuscript from which he had stolen the material, as well as discrepancies in the dates of Irving's purported interviews with Hughes. Around the same time, Swiss police were investigating the Swiss bank account Irving had used to launder the checks written to Hughes. By the end of January, 1972, Irving was forced to confess to the hoax.

LEGAL ACTION AND OUTCOME

The state of New York charged Irving, Sommer, and Suskind with fourteen criminal counts, including possession of forged documents, intent to defraud, grand larceny, perjury, and conspiracy, and the U.S. government indicted Irving and Sommer on two counts of mail fraud. All three defendants were convicted. Irving served fourteen months of a thirty-month sentence in federal prison and was forced to reimburse McGraw-Hill a total of $765,000. Sommer served two months in the Nassau County Jail and Suskind five months in a New York state prison.

IMPACT

After fourteen difficult months in three different federal prisons, Clifford Irving was released on parole and eventually settled in Mexico. Though many publishers were hesitant to work with him following the Hughes affair, he eventually built a successful career as a novelist, primarily writing thrillers, such as *The Death Freak* (1976) and *The Sleeping Spy* (1979), but also several historical novels, such as *Tom Mix and Pancho Villa* (1982) and *The Angel of Zin* (1984). Ironically, though Irving's notoriety came from his fraudulent research in the Hughes episode, he became so invested in researching the facts for his book *Daddy's Girl* (1985), on a lurid 1980's murder trial in Houston, that he eventually was called as a witness in the trial.

Shortly after his release from prison in 1974, Irving sued for the rights to what he would publish as *The Autobiography of Howard Hughes* and entertained contacts from several publishers hoping to benefit from the widespread publicity generated by the incident. Though he won the suit, he lost interest in the project after deciding that the book's appeal was primarily as a novelty item rather than a literary work. *The Autobiography of Howard Hughes* was eventually published over the Internet in 1999, but in spite of the historical significance of the book, the event attracted little attention.

FURTHER READING

Ambrosius, Lloyd E. *Writing Biography: Historians and Their Craft.* Lincoln: University of Nebraska Press, 2004. A compilation of essays on the challenges of historiography in the writing of biographies, with a focus on the personal and psychological connections between biographer and subject.

Bartlett, Donald L., and James Steele. *Howard Hughes: His Life and Madness.* New York: W. W. Norton, 2004. A detailed examination of Hughes's life with an emphasis on his financial dealings and his technological innovation. Includes an extensive summary of the Clifford Irving affair.

Fay, Stephen, Lewis Chester, and Magnus Linklater. *Hoax: The Inside Story of the Howard Hughes-Clifford Irving Affair.* New York: Viking Press, 1972. A contemporaneous exploration of the literary world's fascination with the reclusive Hughes and the role Hughes's lifestyle played in enabling Irving's fraudulent claims.

Irving, Clifford. *The Hoax.* New York: Permanent Press, 1981. Irving's detailed account of the hoax, from its fabrication through the complex web of deception and international intrigue that enabled Irving to fool the literary world.

—*Devon Boan*

SEE ALSO: Elmyr de Hory; Tom Keating.

DAVID IRVING
English author and Holocaust denier

BORN: March 24, 1938; Essex, England
ALSO KNOWN AS: David John Cawdell Irving (full name)
MAJOR OFFENSES: Libel, fraud, and denying the Holocaust
ACTIVE: Beginning in the 1960's
LOCALE: North America, Europe, Australia, and Canada
SENTENCE: Three years' imprisonment in Austria; banned from four countries

EARLY LIFE

David Irving (UHR-vihng) was born in Essex, England, to John James Cawdell Irving and Beryl Irving. His father was a commander in the Royal Navy, and his mother worked as an illustrator. During World War II, Irving's father was on the light cruiser HMS *Edinburgh*, which was sunk May 2, 1942. He survived the disaster but cut off all communication with his wife and children.

David Irving, a gifted student, continued his education in physics at the Imperial College, London. He did not complete his degree because of financial difficulties. While in college, Irving was the editor for the London University Carnival Committee's journal, *Carnival Times*, and began publishing racist and anti-Semitic cartoons and editorials, which cost him his position.

Irving relocated to Germany, where he worked as a steelworker and became fluent in German. He then moved to Spain, doing clerical work at an air force base near Madrid, under Francisco Franco's regime. Throughout his time traveling and working in Europe, Irving began to develop ties with the European extreme right.

CRIMINAL CAREER

In 1963, Irving published *The Destruction of Dresden*, an examination of the atrocities that befell Dresden during the carpet bombing raids of World War II. Irving weighs the morality of the Allied forces' bombings of German nonmilitary targets against the horrors perpetuated by the Nazis. He concludes that the Allies, who knew they were bombing innocent civilians, were responsible for far worse acts than were the Nazis, as Irving believes that Adolf Hitler and his upper-ranking officers were unaware of the genocide and that there were no concentration camps, only work camps. The book's release coincided with the rise of questions surrounding the bombings, making it an international best seller.

Following the success of his first book, Irving went on to write *Hitler's War* (1977), a two-part biography that examines World War II from Hitler's point of view. The book portrays Hitler in a positive light, insisting that the German leader did not know the Holocaust was occurring. Irving maintains that Heinrich Himmler and Reinhard Heydrich masterminded the genocide and that Hitler was actually a friend to the Jews. In the 1991 edition, Irving deleted all references to the systematic murder of Jews, claiming that it never happened. Irving wrote a follow-up, *Churchill's War* (1987), in which Winston S. Churchill is portrayed as a drunk and a warmonger who destroyed all ties between England and Germany.

Many former Nazis saw Irving as an ally and donated memoirs, diaries, and artifacts to him, some of which Irving translated and published. In addition to his numerous writings, Irving also made a name for himself by associating with racist and anti-Semitic groups, including

David Irving. (AP/Wide World Photos)

IRVING'S STATEMENT ON THE HOLOCAUST

In February, 2000, David Irving, in his libel suit against Penguin Books and Deborah Lipstadt, outlined his views on the killing of Jews during World War II:

I am asked by the Court to state my position on Hitler, the Einsatzgruppen, and the killings of Jews behind the eastern front.

Eastern European and Russian Jews

1. Hitler issued orders from March 1941 to his military chiefs which authorised the summary execution of unspecified numbers of captured Jewish/Bolshevik intelligentsia and leaders, including political officers and commissars. These orders were requested by the military for rear-area security (i.e. military reasons).

2. This was one of the "special tasks" assigned to Himmler's responsibility as chief of the SS and police and added to the anti-partisan and Intelligence gathering operations of his SS task forces (Einsatzgruppen). Hitler was probably informed of the "anti-partisan" operations, though not on a regular basis, and there is evidence that no secret was made of the inclusion of large numbers of (non-German) Jews in the resulting body-counts of "partisans."

Western European and German Jews

3. Beginning in the late summer of 1941 train transports of German Jews were deported eastwards to Nazi-occupied Russia and the Baltic states. Jews from other European countries were later also deported. The intention of the police authorities in the Reich who dispatched them was that they were being deported to new existences in the east—i.e. to anywhere but within the Reich—and they did not care under what conditions. This transport movement, which continued until 1943, was done on Hitler's authority.

4. In the occupied eastern territories including the Baltic states the German occupation authorities treated the arriving transports of German and West European Jews with a variety of methods which of itself suggests a lack of system and co-ordination. Some were housed in ghettos or concentration camps. Others were murdered immediately on arrival or soon after.

5. We have been shown no clear or unambiguous evidence that Hitler was aware of this latter fate (mass murder). There is however unambiguous evidence (a) that when word of the liquidation of the Berlin Jews at Riga (November 30, 1941) reached the Wolf's Lair, an immediate verbal reprimand was issued to the culprit; and (b) that an order went through the appropriate channels to Riga that this kind of mass shooting was to stop. The mass murder of German Jews then halted for some months.

6. This position does not differ materially from that set out in *Hitler's War* (1977), and in *Goebbels: Mastermind of the Third Reich* (1996).

DAVID IRVING
Wednesday, February 23, 2000

and rallies for these and similar hate groups across the world.

In 1967, Irving published *The Destruction of Convoy PQ-17*, in which he blames British convoy commander Captain Jack Broome for the heavy losses of Convoy PQ-17. Broome sued Irving for libel in October of 1968 and was awarded four thousand British pounds in February, 1970. The book was pulled from circulation and subsequently banned in Great Britain.

In 1993, Deborah Lipstadt and Penguin Books published *Denying the Holocaust*, in which Lipstadt refers to Irving as a falsifier and history revisionist, a bigot, a racist, and one of the most dangerous Holocaust deniers alive. Irving waited until the book was released in England in 1996 to sue Lipstadt and Penguin for libel, because in English courts the burden of proof would lie upon the defendant. Irving chose to represent himself; he presented a freedom of speech case and missed the focus of the lawsuit. He ignored the defense's evidence against him, which proved that Irving knowingly included forged documents in his writings, misrepresented facts, and was consistently inaccurate. Irving claimed he had been a victim of an international conspiracy for more than three decades and went as far as calling the judge "Mein Führer" on March 15, 2000. Irving lost the case and all attempts at appeals; he was ordered to pay Lipstadt more than two million pounds, bankrupting him and ruining his career.

LEGAL ACTION AND OUTCOME

On November 11, 2005, Irving was arrested in Styria, Austria, on a 1989 warrant for denying the Holocaust, a crime punishable by up to ten years in prison. He was incarcerated in Graz, Austria, until his trial on February 20, 2006, at which he was found guilty and sentenced to three years in prison.

the Neo-Nazi Alliance and the California-based Institute for Historic Review, the top Holocaust denial organization in the United States. He has spoken at conventions

IMPACT

David Irving's hate speech and Holocaust denial have resulted in his being banned from Austria (early 1980's), South Africa (1992), Australia (1992), Germany (1993), and New Zealand (2004), as well as being arrested and deported from Canada and the United States. He is also on hate group watch lists.

Irving has been proven to be a misinterpreter of history, and his career as a legitimate historian has been destroyed by lawsuits as well as the outrageous statements he has made. As a result, the way history is interpreted and manipulated has been revisited by scholars and is the subject of many books concerning Irving and other hatemongers.

FURTHER READING

Evans, Richard J. *Lying About Hitler: History, Holocaust, and the David Irving Trial.* New York: Basic Books, 2002. Evans differentiates between interpreting and misrepresenting history and how those definitions affected the Irving-Lipstadt case.

Guttenplan, D. D. *The Holocaust on Trial.* New York: W. W. Norton, 2002. Guttenplan, a reporter at the *Irving v. Lipstadt* trial, offers his point of view of the proceedings, which proved Irving a Holocaust denier and anti-Semite.

Lipstadt, Deborah E. *Denying the Holocaust: The Growing Assault on Truth and Memory.* New York: Free Press, 1993. This is the book that spurred the trial that ultimately discredited Irving's career, sending him into bankruptcy.

_____. *History on Trial: My Day in Court with David Irving.* New York: Ecco, 2005. A firsthand account of the libel suit that put Irving, Holocaust denial, and historic interpretation on trial.

Shermer, Michael. *Denying History: Who Says the Holocaust Never Happened and Why Do They Say It?* Berkeley: University of California Press, 2002. Shermer explores the theories Holocaust deniers hold as truths, refutes them, and questions deniers on their beliefs.

—*Sara Vidar*

SEE ALSO: Willis A. Carto; Francisco Franco; Reinhard Heydrich; Heinrich Himmler; Adolf Hitler; Savitri Devi.

IVAN V
Russian co-czar (r. 1682-1696)

BORN: September 6, 1666; Moscow, Russia
DIED: February 8, 1696; Moscow, Russia
ALSO KNOWN AS: Ivan Alekseyevich; Ivan the Ignorant
CAUSE OF NOTORIETY: The simpleminded Ivan was able to reign as co-czar alongside his half brother Peter the Great, first through the auspices of Ivan's sister Sophia, then through Peter's beneficence.
ACTIVE: 1682-1696
LOCALE: Kremlin, Moscow, Russia

EARLY LIFE

Ivan (ih-VAHN *or* I-van) V was one of thirteen children born to Czar Alexis I of Russia (r. 1645-1676) by his first wife, Maria Miloslavskaia, who died when Ivan was only three years old. Ivan, like many of his siblings, was a sickly child. Partially blind and with a heavy speech impediment, Ivan was not expected to live to adulthood.

Czar Alexis married Natalya Naryshkina, with whom he had three healthy children, including the future leader of the Romanov Dynasty, Peter the Great (r. 1682-1725). The Muscovite rule of Russia deteriorated after the death of Alexis in 1676, leaving the czar's children to rule a tumultuous period of Russian history fraught with familial rivalry, military rebellion, religious fanaticism, and xenophobia. Ivan and his siblings received Western-style educations, which went against the staunch tradition of the Russian Orthodox Church, creating further upheaval as Alexis's successors took their respective thrones.

POLITICAL CAREER

Ivan V's reign is really a misnomer; he held a title with no political activity of his own will. His physical and mental ailments left him to rule Russia in title alone, not in action or policy, situating Ivan as a puppet czar.

Upon the early death of Alexis's heir to the throne, Ivan's older brother Fyodor III (r. 1676-1682), a dilemma of succession arose. The Miloslavskaia and Naryshkina families each wanted the next czar to be from their lineage. In a pathetic comparison of the incapable Ivan against the vibrant young Peter, brother was pitted against brother. The decision of succession was put to the Russian people.

Peter was named czar at the age of nine, with his German mother, Natalya Naryshkina, appointed as regent. Ivan's older sister Sophia quickly rallied support for the adoption of Ivan as czar. Rumors conveniently circulated among the musketeers (streltsy) that Fyodor had been murdered by the Naryshkinas and that Ivan, if not already dead, was in grave danger. The streltsy stormed the Kremlin on Ivan's behalf, demanding that Ivan be named co-czar and that Sophia replace Natalya as regent, due to Peter's age and Ivan's simplemindedness.

Ivan Alekseyevich took the title Ivan V (1682-1689), co-czar of Russia, in late May, 1682. Sophia ascended to the regency, ruling Russia through Ivan, who served as a mere pawn in her plans, until 1689. During this time Sophia arranged a marriage for Ivan with a politically prominent family in the hope of producing a male heir in the Romanov/Miloslavskaia bloodline, which would have continued her role as regent. However, the birth of Ivan's children—two daughters—ended Sophia's hope of retaining power. In 1689, Peter deposed Sophia as regent. In a kind gesture, Peter allowed Ivan to maintain the title of co-czar, although Ivan's official participation was limited to religious events. Peter, who truly loved his half brother, went on to care for Ivan for the remainder of his life and supported Ivan's wife and daughters, including Anna II (r. 1730-1740).

IMPACT

Paradoxically, Ivan V's lack of robustness in the role of co-czar set the stage for the rise of one of Russia's most revered and absolutist rulers, Peter the Great, and the flourishing of the Romanov Dynasty. Peter ushered the Age of Reason into Russia with the resurgence of traditional religion and the adoption of a new capital in St. Petersburg.

FURTHER READING

Bushkovitch, Paul. *Peter the Great: The Struggle for Power, 1671-1725*. New York: Cambridge University Press, 2001. An in-depth look at the political struggle surrounding Peter the Great's reign, with emphasis on his early years as co-czar with Ivan V.

Riasanovsky, Nicholas V. *A History of Russia*. 7th ed. New York: Oxford University Press, 2004. A book of monumental importance in the discourse of Russian history, with excellent historical references, thorough summaries of events, and political and cultural development.

Warnes, David. *Chronicle of the Russian Tsars: The Reign-by-Reign Record of the Rulers of Imperial Russia*. London: Thames & Hudson, 1999. Interesting examination of the reign of Ivan V, intermingled with those of his siblings.

—*Emilie B. Sizemore*

SEE ALSO: Fyodor I; Ivan the Terrible; Ivan VI.

IVAN VI
Russian czar (r. 1740-1741)

BORN: August 23, 1740; St. Petersburg, Russia
DIED: July 16, 1764; Shlisselburg, Russia
ALSO KNOWN AS: Ivan Antonovich (birth name)
CAUSE OF NOTORIETY: Ivan VI was made the Russian czar while still an infant. Following a plot to remove him from power, he spent the rest of his life in a prison cell, where he became mentally feeble.
ACTIVE: 1740-1764
LOCALE: St. Petersburg and various prisons in Russia

EARLY LIFE

Ivan (ih-VAHN *or* I-van) was the son of Anna Leopoldovna and Anton Ulrich, duke of Braunschweig. On October 5, 1740, his great-aunt, Russian czarina Anna Ivanovna, named him to be her successor as the future ruler of the Russian state. Upon her death the same month, two-month-old Ivan was officially declared to be the new Russian monarch. Because Ivan was a baby, Ernst Johann Biron led the government as the regent for the infant ruler. Shortly after, a palace coup ousted Biron, and Ivan's mother became regent for her son. However, she provided poor guidance and leadership, which led to her arrest and the ouster of her son as Russia's monarch.

Palace intrigues and power plays typified Russian politics at the time. Elizabeth Petrovna, the daughter of Peter the Great and a distant relative of the infant czar, plotted to take power for herself. She succeeded in this plan with the nighttime arrest of Ivan and his mother in a bloodless coup in November, 1741.

POLITICAL CAREER

For the rest of his life, Ivan remained a state prisoner under the control of three Russian monarchs: Elizabeth (r. 1741-1761), Peter III (r. 1761-1762), and Catherine the Great (r. 1762-1796). He was incarcerated in several prisons, including Kholmogory for twelve years (1744-1756), before being sent to the Shlisselburg fortress, where he would spend his remaining years. Ivan lived in squalid conditions in a dark dungeon cell, not allowed visitors or medical care, and his guards treated him badly. Catherine the Great visited him briefly in 1762. By the time of his murder at the age of twenty-three in 1764, his warped personality and mental condition showed the negative effects of his harsh treatment for more than two decades.

During his years of incarceration, the three rulers gave strict orders that if any attempt to free Ivan was made, his guards should immediately kill him. In July, 1764, when army officer Vasily Mirovich made the effort to free the young man, Ivan's guards followed their long-standing orders and stabbed Ivan to death in his cell. Following his military trial, Mirovich was beheaded.

Upon being told of the murder, Catherine the Great allegedly expressed her satisfaction, glad that a potential rival had been eliminated. She also issued a public manifesto in mid-August explaining her version of the incident and justifying the elimination of an illegal pretender to the Russian throne.

IMPACT

Ivan VI was a pathetic infant ruler who became a pawn in the power politics of the period. Russian politics during the eighteenth century reveal numerous examples of instability, confusion, and uncertainty. Eight monarchs—four men and four women—led the country during a period of internal development, foreign expansion, wars, and increasingly harsh conditions for the population.

Several of these rulers became famous in Russia's history: Peter III, Elizabeth Petrovna, and Catherine the Great.

Never able to govern in his own name as an adult, Ivan VI's brief appearance in Russian history is far surpassed by the successful rulers of the century. His brutal treatment and violent death were common elements of that age. It is curious, however, that those who kept him in prison might have strengthened their claims to the throne if he had been killed earlier. It is one of the fascinating quirks of Russian history that Ivan was held for many years as the mysterious prisoner inside Shlisselburg, barely alive but still to be feared if he ever came to power.

FURTHER READING

Alexander, John T. *Catherine the Great: Life and Legend.* New York: Oxford University Press, 1989. Describes Ivan's years in prison and his murder.

Grey, Ian. *Catherine the Great: Autocrat and Empress of All Russia.* Philadelphia: Lippincott, 1962. Provides details of Mirovich's failed scheme to free Ivan.

Paxton, John. *Leaders of Russia and the Soviet Union: From the Romanov Dynasty to Vladimir Putin.* New York: Fitzroy Dearborn, 2004. Includes a section devoted to Ivan VI's life and political significance.

Troyat, Henri. *Catherine the Great.* New York: Meridian, 1994. Covers the 1741 coup, Ivan's imprisonment, and his murder at Shlisselburg.

Warnes, David. *Chronicle of the Russian Tsars: The Reign-by-Reign Record of the Rulers of Imperial Russia.* New York: Thames and Hudson, 1999. Illustrated volume includes a summary of the life and significance of Ivan VI

—*Taylor Stults*

SEE ALSO: Ivan the Terrible; Ivan V.

IVAN THE TERRIBLE
Russian czar (r. 1533-1584)

BORN: August 25, 1530; Moscow, Russia
DIED: March 18, 1584; Moscow, Russia
ALSO KNOWN AS: Ivan IV Vasilyevich
CAUSE OF NOTORIETY: Ivan's cruel dictatorial rule
  included murder and torture.
ACTIVE: c. 1533-1584
LOCALE: Russia

EARLY LIFE

When Vasily III, the prince of Moscow (1505-1533), died in 1533, his wife, the Grand Princess Elena Glinskaia, and her uncle Mikhail Lvovich Glinsky, dominated a Regency Council to guard against the rivals of three-year-old Ivan (ih-VAHN *or* I-van) IV, Vasily and Elena's son and heir. Elena's death allowed Prince Vasily Vasilevich Shuisky to bully Ivan IV until the Shuisky brothers died. At his coronation in 1547, Ivan assumed the title of czar, meaning either a king or an emperor with functions that expressed the charisma of power. In the same year, Ivan married Anastasia Romanova Zakharina, the first of his seven wives.

Ivan the Terrible. (Library of Congress)

The czar's personal servant and the priest Sylvester probably checked the young czar's impulse to cruelty and advised him in his governance. In a large public gathering in 1549, Ivan warned the aristocratic boyars against oppressing their inferiors, and a year later, he revised the laws to abolish maladministration and corruption. The khan of Kazan died the same year; his death encouraged the young czar to undertake a Crimean campaign that culminated in 1552 in a brutal victory for Russia.

POLITICAL CAREER

A serious and suspicious illness befell Ivan in 1553, soon followed by the accidental drowning of his six-month-old son. Even worse, Russian troops were crushed in a battle at the Baltic city of Dorpat in 1559, and a year later, the czarina died. These events set off a terrible intensification of the czar's innate cruelty and an admonishment from his intimate friend, Prince Andrey Mikhailovich Kurbsky, about his dissipation, fornication, and cruelty. When Prince Dmitri Obolensky-Ovchinin complained about Ivan's latest catamite, Fedor Basmanov, the czar stabbed Ovhininin to death. Ivan's heartless persecution of the boyars prompted Kurbsky to desert to Livonia in 1564, and in the same year, Ivan's swelling paranoia caused him to plunder the churches and move with his new czarina to Aleksandrovskaia Sloboda, his hunting lodge northeast of Moscow.

With the people of Moscow imploring him to return, the czar announced he was creating for himself a large *oprichnina*, or tract of land, and leaving the remaining land, the *zemshchina*, to the rule of the boyars. Under his command, Ivan's *oprichniki*, or mercenaries, then mounted an orgy of senseless arrests and murders, a reign of terror that only worsened when the boyars in 1566 begged the czar to abolish the mercenaries. Between 1567 and 1572, the butchery grew until thousands died at the hands of the *oprichniki* in towns such as Novgorod and Pskov. July 25, 1570, was an especially horrific day, as Ivan had 116 victims publicly executed in numerous painful ways. Kurbsky attributed the death by torture of three prominent boyars in 1573 to the malign influence of the mysterious astrologer Dr. Eliseus Bomelius, who later also died horribly at the czar's hands.

A series of failures dogged Ivan's last decade. He lost his effort to be named king of Poland; the new king of Poland, Stephen Báthory, thwarted his aggression in

517

Livonia; and Sweden captured Narva and three other Baltic towns in 1581. A measure of the czar's frustration emerged in a sudden outburst against his son, Ivan Ivanovich, whom he accidentally killed by a blow to the head with a staff. Brokenhearted, Ivan soon fell ill and died, probably, as biographer Isabel de Madariaga believes, by choking or suffering a heart attack.

IMPACT

Madariaga identifies several results of Ivan's rule. He broke the power of the princes and established a unified authority that spread into every corner of his realm. He enlarged Russian rule enormously by his conquest of Kazan and Astrakhan, and he extended Russian domination deep into western Siberia. As a necessary aspect of this extension, he modernized his military forces and built a line of fortified towns and fortresses to guard against predators from the Crimea. However, these military accomplishments occurred only at a great cost to his people, whose finances were drained by the heavy expenditures. By the 1580's, war, taxation, confiscation of peasant land, and other brutal social policies had devastated and depopulated the villages. Madariaga believes that Ivan's cruel rule slowed the development of a modern state by making impossible the growth of independent political structures. Moreover, the provincialism of the czar's crude approach to foreign policy, Madariaga asserts, isolated Russia from the powerful European states with their linguistic and cultural sophistication. The notion of chivalry, for instance, which advanced civilized manners in Europe, however "meretricious" the concept may have been, never penetrated Russian thinking.

In her analysis of Ivan's psychology, Madariaga finds the root of his cruelty in the religious elements of his personality. Specifically, he claimed a divine right to punish derived from several medieval works on Orthodox spirituality, and Madariaga's explanation deserves quotation:

> It was this self-identification of Ivan with the idea of sacred violence which opened the way for the Czar's belief in the purificatory value of his cruelty, and enabled him to accept as divine in origin the sadism which made life a hell for his subjects.

FURTHER READING

Keenan, Edward L. *The Kurbskii-Groznyi Apocrypha: The Seventeenth Century Origin of the "Correspondence" Attributed to Prince A. M. Kurbskii and Tsar Ivan IV*. Cambridge, Mass.: Harvard University Press, 1971. Argues that the correspondence is a forgery, a position rejected by Madariaga.

Kurbsky, Prince A. M. *The Correspondence Between Prince A. M. Kurbsky and Tsar Ivan IV of Russia, 1564-1579*. Translated and edited by J. L. I. Fennell. Cambridge, England.: Cambridge University Press, 1963. Presents the disputed letters.

Madariaga, Isabel de. *Ivan the Terrible: First Tsar of Russia*. New Haven, Conn.: Yale University Press, 2005. A comprehensive scholarly biography with detailed accounts of Ivan's butchery, his creation of the *oprichnina*, and his foreign policy undertakings.

Perrie, Maureen. *The Cult of Ivan the Terrible in Stalin's Russia*. London: Palgrave, 2001. A minority view of Ivan.

—Frank Day

SEE ALSO: Fyodor I; Ivan V; Ivan VI.

JACK THE RIPPER
British serial killer

FLOURISHED: 1888

ALSO KNOWN AS: Leather Apron; Whitechapel Murderer

CAUSE OF NOTORIETY: During a period of four months in 1888, the person who became known as Jack the Ripper murdered and mutilated five women in London's East End.

ACTIVE: c. 1888

LOCALE: London, England

EARLY LIFE

Because the criminal known as Jack the Ripper (RIH-puhr) was never caught, nothing is known of his early life. Investigators in the nineteenth and twentieth centuries have speculated that the killer was from a respectable family. Because of the skill that the murderer exhibited in eviscerating his victims, some have suggested he was trained as a physician, surgeon, or butcher. Experts have concluded further that Jack the Ripper suffered some traumatic experience that drove him to commit atrocities on prostitutes, possibly gaining some perverse sexual pleasure from their murders.

CRIMINAL CAREER

London's East End, a notorious center of poverty and squalor, had already seen more than its share of crime by the fall of 1888 when the murderer who would become known at Jack the Ripper first struck. On August 31 in Bucks Row, the body of Mary Ann Nicholls, a known prostitute, was found with her throat cut and stomach mutilated. The particularly vicious nature of the crime shocked both the neighborhood's inhabitants and the police, and the level of alarm was raised significantly just days later when, on September 8, Annie Chapman, another prostitute, was discovered on Hanbury Street, throat slit and body parts removed and placed by the corpse.

After Chapman's murder, Detective Inspector Frederick Abberline of Scotland Yard was called in to handle the investigation; he remained the chief investigator for the remaining murders. Because a leather apron was found near Chapman's body, a leatherworker was picked up for questioning but later released. At the same time, the London press became an active participant in the investigations—its sensational reporting, based largely on speculation and innuendo, fueled a panic in the area and complicated police efforts. Interagency squabbles and meddling by senior police officials did not help matters either; in one instance, the commissioner of the metropolitan police force erased a note thought to have been written by the killer on a wall near a victim; the commissioner feared it might spark anti-Semitic riots.

After the second victim was discovered, the police, the press, and the Whitechapel Vigilance Committee began receiving numerous letters offering tips about the murderer. In one letter sent to "The Boss" at London Central News agency, the killer identified himself as

Jack the Ripper, as imagined in a contemporary cartoon.

"Jack the Ripper"; the sobriquet was immediately adopted by police and populace. Many notes ostensibly sent from the Ripper were eventually proven to be hoaxes. One chilling piece of correspondence, however, generated special attention. Addressed "From Hell" to Vigilance Committee head George Lusk, it was accompanied by a piece of kidney that the writer said was from one of the victims.

The third and fourth murders attributed to Jack the Ripper occurred on September 30. Shortly after 1:00 A.M., Elizabeth Stride's body was found on Berner's Street, still warm but not mutilated. Later the same evening, just blocks away in Mitre Square, police found the body of Catherine Eddowes, disfigured in the same ways as earlier victims. Police speculated that the Ripper had been interrupted during his attack on Stride and had gone off to commit another murder and complete his ritual eviscerations. Because all four victims were known prostitutes, police efforts were focused on men who had expressed hatred of such women. Unfortunately, despite numerous tips from the public, Abberline could not compile sufficient evidence to make an arrest. Jack the Ripper's final victim was the prostitute Mary Kelly, slain in her own room in Miller's Court. Her mutilations were worst of all.

Mysteriously, however, months went by without another such incident, and both the police and the populace began to think the murderer had been imprisoned for a different crime, had fled the city, or perhaps had died. In the years immediately after the killings stopped, investigators identified more than a dozen suspects who possessed one or more of the characteristics of the Ripper's profile; none was indicted, however, and eventually police dropped their active investigation.

IMPACT

The killings caused an immediate panic in the East End of London; women were especially terrified that they might be the Ripper's next victim. The news media seized on the killings as a means of building readership; the refusal of police officials to cooperate with the media fed the frenzy of speculation about the murderer and generated additional publicity for these crimes. An important positive impact of the killings, however, was the heightened attention given to the appalling environment in the East End. Reform efforts were undertaken to improve living conditions there, although these were only modestly successful.

As time passed, additional murders were attributed to Jack the Ripper, enhancing a legend that would only grow during the coming decades. Because the Ripper was never caught, a series of after-the-fact investigations by professionals and amateurs were launched to identify the killer from the scant clues available. Among those later identified as the Ripper were physicians, surgeons, artists, quite a number of foreigners who had been living in the East End, and even Queen Victoria's personal physician and her grandson, the duke of Clarence. Efforts to solve the Ripper mystery lasted well into the twentieth century and beyond, as Jack the Ripper became the subject of books, plays, and films.

FURTHER READING

Begg, Paul. *Jack the Ripper: The Definitive History*. London: Longman, 2003. Begg considers each murder in detail and offers information on the most likely suspects; he also explores reasons for the British public's morbid fascination with the Ripper.

Cornwell, Patricia. *Portrait of a Killer: Jack the Ripper, Case Closed*. New York: G. P. Putnam, 2002. Novelist and criminalist Cornwell reviews the evidence in the Ripper murders using modern forensic techniques, explaining why she believes she has identified the murderer and then describing his life in detail.

Curtis, L. Perry. *Jack the Ripper and the London Press*. New Haven, Conn.: Yale University Press, 2001. Curtis provides insight into the cultural and moral values of Victorian Britain by focusing on ways that the media influenced both the investigation and the public perceptions of the killer.

Gordon, R. Michael. *Alias Jack the Ripper: Beyond the Usual Whitechapel Suspects*. Jefferson, N.C.: McFarland, 2001. Gordon reviews evidence from each murder to identify persons most likely to have committed these crimes; he includes facsimiles of reports and maps and a useful chronology.

—*Laurence W. Mazzeno*

SEE ALSO: William Burke; John Reginald Halliday Christie.

SHOELESS JOE JACKSON
American baseball player

BORN: July 16, 1887; Brandon Mills, South Carolina
DIED: December 5, 1951; Greenville, South Carolina
ALSO KNOWN AS: Joseph Jefferson Wofford Jackson (full name)
CAUSE OF NOTORIETY: Jackson was among the eight baseball players suspected of fixing the 1919 World Series; though acquitted, all eight were banned thereafter from the sport.
ACTIVE: 1919
LOCALE: Chicago, Illinois, and Cincinnati, Ohio

EARLY LIFE

Shoeless Joe Jackson (JAK-suhn), the son of a textile mill worker, entered the workforce at an early age. He never learned to read or write. Various mills he worked for fielded baseball teams in a "textile league," and Joe was such a good athlete that he starred on his mill's team at age thirteen. Later, starring for Greenville's minor league team, he got the name "Shoeless Joe" by playing part of one game without shoes. A new pair had given him blisters, so he played part of the game in his socks. He was so good that Connie Mack, manager of the Philadelphia Athletics, signed him to a contract while he was still in his late teens.

MAJOR LEAGUE CAREER

In Philadelphia, Jackson was homesick, and the other Athletics players mocked his illiteracy. He played in only five games each of two years for the Athletics and did not do well in those games. He was traded and played in twenty games for Cleveland in 1910, hitting .387. In 1911 he batted .408 in 147 games, a sensational performance. He had three more great years with Cleveland. During the 1915 season he was traded to the Chicago White Sox, with whom his performance over the following five years was outstanding.

Jackson's career batting average (.356) is the third best in baseball history, behind those of Ty Cobb (.367) and Rogers Hornsby (.358). Cobb called him baseball's greatest natural hitter. Babe Ruth copied his swing. Jackson was also a superb outfielder with the best throwing arm in baseball. Many thought of him as the greatest natural player of all time.

In 1919, the Chicago White Sox won the American League pennant but lost five of eight games to the Cincinnati Reds in the World Series. That year the series was decided on the basis of nine games, instead of seven

as it is today. The White Sox were such overwhelming favorites to win, and there were so many suspicious events during the series, both on and off the field, that a fix was suspected. Gamblers were suspected of paying the White Sox players to lose the series (fixing it) while the gamblers bet on Cincinnati.

LEGAL ACTION AND OUTCOME

In 1920, the suspicion led to an investigation in which eight Chicago players, called the Black Sox ever since, were accused of fixing the series. Jackson was one of the eight players accused. The eight were tried in 1921, but evidence disappeared, stories changed, and a cascade of legal problems occurred. All eight players were acquitted. Despite the acquittal, the new commissioner of baseball, Kenesaw Mountain Landis, banned them all from baseball forever.

IMPACT

The Black Sox scandal is credited with initiating reforms in baseball. Betting on and suspected fixing of baseball

Shoeless Joe Jackson.

games had been present since the sport's inception. Both had been escalating in the years leading up to 1919. Landis's unyielding banishment of the eight Black Sox is thought to have enhanced confidence in the honesty of the institution.

However, in many eyes, Shoeless Joe Jackson became a mistreated hero. He produced excellent statistics for the series and claimed until he died that he had played an honest series. A number of books have been written about his life and the 1919 World Series. Two, Eliot Asinof's *Eight Men Out* (1963) and W. P. Kinsella's *Shoeless Joe* (1982), were made into feature films, *Eight Men Out* (1988) and *Field of Dreams* (1989), respectively. Several Internet sites are dedicated to Jackson. Most of these are sympathetic to Jackson and urge his admission to the Baseball Hall of Fame, for which he is ineligible because he was banned from baseball. It is probably impossible to know the exact role Jackson played in the fix, and so it is probably impossible to interpret his appropriate place in baseball history and the justice of his punishment.

FURTHER READING

Fleitz, David L. *Shoeless: The Life and Times of Joe Jackson*. Jefferson, N.C.: McFarland, 2001. Less supportive of Jackson than most other works. Good bibliography.

Gropman, Donald. *Say It Ain't So, Joe! The True Story of Shoeless Joe Jackson*. New York: Carol, 2001. Very supportive of Jackson. Several appendixes of original material regarding Jackson's life.

Sagert, Kelly Boyer. *Joe Jackson: A Biography*. Westport, Conn.: Greenwood Press, 2004. This overview discusses and references most books and Web sites on Jackson.

—*Carl W. Hoagstrom*

SEE ALSO: Arnold Rothstein.

JACKSON'S CONFESSION

On September 28, 1920, Hartley L. Replogle, assistant state's attorney, questioned Shoeless Joe Jackson before the Grand Jury of Cook County, Illinois. Jackson's testimony implicated him in the scandal. The following excerpts, however, show that he was being bullied and cheated.

REPLOGLE: Did anybody pay you any money to help throw that series in favor of Cincinnati?

JACKSON: They did.

REPLOGLE: How much did they pay?

JACKSON: They promised me $20,000, and paid me $5.

REPLOGLE: Who promised you the twenty thousand?

JACKSON: "Chick" Gandil.

REPLOGLE: Who is Chick Gandil?

JACKSON: He was their first baseman on the White Sox Club. . . .

REPLOGLE: You think Gandil may have gotten the money and held it from you, is that right?

JACKSON: That's what I think, I think he kept the majority of it.

REPLOGLE: What did you do then?

JACKSON: I went to him and asked him what was the matter. He said Abe Attel gave him the jazzing. He said, "Take that or let it alone." As quick as the series was over I left town, I went right on out. . . .

REPLOGLE: Didn't you think it was the right thing for you to go and tell [White Sox owner Charles A.] Comiskey about it?

JACKSON: I did tell them once, "I am not going to be in it." I will just get out of that altogether.

REPLOGLE: Who did you tell that to?

JACKSON: Chick Gandil.

REPLOGLE: What did he say?

JACKSON: He said I was into it already and I might as well stay in. I said, "I can go to the boss and have every damn one of you pulled out of the limelight." He said, "It wouldn't be well for me if I did that. . . ."

REPLOGLE: What did you say?

JACKSON: Well, I told him any time they wanted to have me knocked off, to have me knocked off.

REPLOGLE: What did he say?

JACKSON: Just laughed. . . .

REPLOGLE: Supposing the White Sox would have won this series, the World's Series, what would you have done then with the $5,000?

JACKSON: I guess I would have kept it, that was all I could do. I tried to win all the time.

JESSE JAMES
American outlaw

BORN: September 5, 1847; near Centerville (now Kearney), Missouri
DIED: April 3, 1882; St. Joseph, Missouri
ALSO KNOWN AS: Jesse Woodson James (full name); Dingus James; Thomas Howard; Ed Everhard; Dave Smith; J. T. Jackson; John Davis Howard; J. D. Howard
CAUSE OF NOTORIETY: James, leader of the James-Younger Gang, led a sixteen-year lawless rampage and was suspected of robbing banks, trains, omnibuses, stagecoaches, and a state fair, as well as causing the deaths of ten people.
ACTIVE: February 13, 1866-September 7, 1881
LOCALE: Alabama, Arkansas, Iowa, Kansas, Kentucky, Minnesota, Missouri, Texas, and West Virginia

EARLY LIFE

Jesse James (JEHS-ee jaymz) began his life as the third child of Robert James and Zerelda James. Robert James was a slave-owning, well-to-do, educated minister who cofounded William Jewell College in Liberty, Missouri, and several churches in Clay County, Missouri. When Jesse was three, his father left his family for the goldfields of California, where he died and was buried in an unmarked grave. Zerelda, a mother of three children, married Benjamin Simms but divorced him after a few months. Dr. Reuben Samuels became her third and last husband and stepfather to her children.

Little else is known of James's childhood. His teen years were marked by the bloodshed of the Civil War and its devastation of Missouri. He followed the exploits of William Quantrill's guerrillas, who roamed under the Black Flag, indiscriminately plundering and killing both Union and Confederate sympathizers. Frank James, Jesse's older brother, joined the guerrillas, and Jesse followed when he turned seventeen. He participated in the Centralia (Missouri) Massacre, where twenty-five unarmed Union soldiers were lined up and killed. From his days with Quantrill and Quantrill's lieutenant William "Bloody Bill" Anderson, Jesse James learned guerrilla tactics that would later serve him well as the leader of an outlaw gang. His outlawry did not hamper his marriage to his first cousin, Zerelda Mimms, with whom he had two children, Jesse Edwards James and Mary Susan James.

CRIMINAL CAREER

Following the Civil War, James and Frank, who refused to take the loyalty oath demanded by the United States government, were not granted amnesty for their guerrilla activities. The James brothers gathered their old wartime comrades and formed a gang. Their first target, the Clay County Savings Association in Liberty, is considered the first bank in the United States to experience a daytime robbery during peacetime. Over the following fifteen years, the gang netted more than $175,000 from nine banks, seven trains, two stagecoaches, two omnibuses, and one state fair. Rewards for the arrest and conviction of James ranged from three thousand to five thousand dollars. Although the Pinkerton's National Detective Agency and hundreds of posse members chased James and his gang through eight states, he was never captured. Only after Robert and Charles Ford, members of James's gang, met with Missouri governor Thomas T. Crittenden and agreed to kill James did his outlawry end. The Ford brothers waited until James was unarmed and shot him in the back of the head on April 3, 1882.

Jesse James. (Library of Congress)

IMPACT

For more than one hundred years, Jesse James has been the subject of newspaper and magazine articles, dime novels, ballads, biographies, plays, poems, television series, movies, documentary footage, and an operetta. James, the Missouri farm boy with the alliterative name, became known as an American Robin Hood, an outlaw hero known far beyond his boyhood home. Historians, journalists, and sociologists have pondered how such a man gained such renown.

In post-Civil War Missouri, devastated by guerrilla warfare and Union military actions, James's outlawry resonated with people who had southern sympathies. They believed that James was forced to become an outlaw and that he was merely robbing the rich to give to the poor. Nationally, James appealed to America's sense of individualism, the little man taking on larger forces and escaping to rob another day. James's post-Civil War exploits evidence sociological arguments that societal upheavals are breeding grounds for outlaw hero adulation. In 1927, efforts failed to erect a monument to commemorate James's life, but the number of markers and festivals bearing his name ensure he will not be forgotten.

The violence of the way James lived has been largely forgotten. Beginning with the 1927 film *Under the Black Flag*, the quasi-historical treatments used by Hollywood have served to anchor James more firmly in a world of fiction than reality, where he remains today.

THE JAMES-YOUNGER GANG

At various times during Jesse James's criminal career, forty-one men rode with the James-Younger Gang. The most famous were:

- **Frank James:** He surrendered to Governor Crittenden five months after his brother was murdered. He explained, "I have been hunted for twenty-one years, have literally lived in the saddle, have never known a day of perfect peace. It was one long, anxious, inexorable, eternal vigil." He was indicted for only one of his crimes and found innocent in court. Before he died of a heart attack in 1915, he worked as a shoe salesman, theater guard, and betting commissioner and toured briefly with the Cole Younger and Frank James Wild West Company in 1903.
- **Cole Younger:** After serving twenty-five years for the Northfield, Minnesota, robbery, he was paroled in 1901. He joined with Frank James in a Wild West show and wrote a memoir claiming he was a Confederate diehard rather than an outlaw. In 1912, he espoused Christianity and apologized for his violent past. He died in 1916.
- **Jim Younger:** He was also paroled in 1901 after a twenty-five-year jail sentence for the Northfield robbery. He committed suicide a year later.
- **Bob Younger:** He died of tuberculosis in Stillwater Prison while serving out his sentence for the Northfield robbery.
- **John Younger:** He was shot dead by Pinkerton agents in Missouri in 1874.
- **Robert Ford:** He was "the dirty little coward who shot Mr. Howard and laid Jesse James in his grave" (according to the song "Jesse James"). He died in a barroom brawl in Colorado in 1892.
- **Charlie Ford:** He committed suicide in 1882.

Among the others, many of whom rode with the James boys in Quantrill's Raiders, are Bill Anderson (sentenced to ten years for robbery), Jim Cummins, Andrew Moorman (murdered in 1897), Clarence Hite (served twenty-five years for robbery), Wood Hite (murdered by Bob Ford in 1882), Jack Keene (sentenced twelve years for robbery), Payne Jones (died violently), Andy McGuire (died violently), Thompson McDaniels (killed during a robbery), William McDaniels (sentenced to prison, escaped, and was killed), Ed Miller (died violently), Allen Palmer (James's brother-in-law), Bud Pence (sentenced to prison), Donny Pence (became sheriff of Nelson County, Kentucky), Charley Pitts (killed in shoot-out), Al Shepherd (died violently), William Stiles (died in shoot-out), and James Wilkerson (identified James's body).

FURTHER READING

Brant, Marley. *Jesse James: The Man and the Myth*. New York: Berkley Books, 1998. Historical treatment that attempts to separate the legend from the reality of James's life.

Dyer, Robert L. *Jesse James and the Civil War in Missouri*. Columbia: University of Missouri Press, 1994. A historian documents the role James played in the Civil War and its influence on his outlaw career.

Kooistra, Paul. *Criminals as Heroes: Structure, Power, and Identity*. Bowling Green, Ohio: Bowling Green State University Popular Press, 1989. A sociologist notes the effect societal crises had on the lawless careers of Frank and Jesse James, Billy the Kid, Butch Cassidy, John Dillinger, Bonnie Parker, Clyde Barrow, Charles Arthur "Pretty Boy" Floyd, and Al Capone.

Settle, William A. *Jesse James Was His Name: Or, Fact and Fiction Concerning the Careers of the Notorious James Brothers of Missouri*. Columbia: University of Missouri Press, 1966. The first scholarly treatment of

James's life traces his outlawry through newspapers, ballads, plays, dime novels, and movies.

Stiles, T. J. *Jesse James: Last Rebel of the Civil War.* New York: Alfred A. Knopf, 2002. Well documented, this account depicts James as a nineteenth century terrorist and a public relations hound who politicized and maneuvered his way into infamy.

—Cathy M. Jackson

SEE ALSO: Apache Kid; Tom Bell; William H. Bonney; Curly Bill Brocius; Butch Cassidy; Bob Dalton; Emmett Dalton; Bill Doolin; John Wesley Hardin; Doc Holliday; Tom Ketchum; Harry Longabaugh; Bill Longley; Joaquín Murieta; William Clarke Quantrill; Johnny Ringo; Belle Starr; Hank Vaughan; Cole Younger.

WOJCIECH JARUZELSKI
Polish prime minister (1981-1985) and president (1989-1990)

BORN: July 6, 1923; Kurów, near Puławy, Poland

ALSO KNOWN AS: Wojciech Witold Jaruzelski (full name)

CAUSE OF NOTORIETY: Jaruzelski, in an attempt to solidify Communist rule, ordered Polish soldiers to shoot protesting workers during the 1970 Polish shipyard strikes. In December, 1981, he declared martial law in order to crush the Independent Trade Union, called Solidarity, in Poland.

ACTIVE: 1970's-1980's

LOCALE: Poland

EARLY LIFE

Wojciech Jaruzelski (VOY-syehk yah-roo-ZEHL-skee) was born in the Lublin region of Poland to a gentry family. He and his family were captured by the Soviet Army after its invasion of Poland in September, 1939, as an ally of Nazi Germany. Jaruzelski was sent to Siberia along with thousands of other Poles. His father died in Siberia in 1942.

Jaruzelski worked as a laborer until he enlisted in a Soviet-sponsored Polish military unit known as the Tadeusz Kosciuszko Division (or First Polish Division). Jaruzelski proved to his superiors that he was not only a good soldier but also politically reliable. He was sent to the Polish Officers' Training School at Ryazan, where he received both military and political training. He was given command first of an infantry platoon and then of a regimented field-reconnaissance unit. In January of 1945, Jaruzelski participated in the Soviet liberation of Warsaw. He then joined the fighting in Pomorze (Pomerania). In May of 1945, his unit made contact with American soldiers on the Elbe River.

POLITICAL CAREER

From 1945 to 1947, Jaruzelski aided in the stabilization of Communist control in Poland by eliminating pockets of resistance from the Polish underground army, which was opposed to the Communists and Ukrainian freedom fighters. In 1947, he took part in Operation Vistula, which was meant to vanquish the last remnants of the Ukrainian Resistance Army (UPA). Jaruzelski distinguished himself in the "pacification" of Ukrainian villages.

In 1947, Jaruzelski was sent to the Higher Infantry School at Rembertow to study staff operations. Upon graduation, he became a lecturer in tactics and staff operations. He did postgraduate work at the Świerczewski General Staff Academy and the Voroshylov Academy in Moscow. He was quickly promoted to lieutenant colonel in 1949 and to full colonel by 1954. After his promotion to colonel, Jaruzelski was made head of the Department of Military Academics and Officer Education.

In 1956, Jaruzelski was promoted to general and named chief of the Central Department of Battle Training. The chief's position required extensive cooperation and contact with elements of the Soviet Army leadership. From 1957 to 1960, Jaruzelski commanded the Twelfth Mechanized Division of the Polish People's Army.

For Jaruzelski, party loyalty and military service went hand in hand. He was made chief of the main political board of the Polish Armed Forces in 1960. He was then elected to the Central Committee of the Polish United Workers' Party in 1964. Following his election to the party hierarchy, he rose within a year from deputy minister of national defense to chief of the general staff. In this capacity, he became responsible for integrating Polish forces into Soviet military strategies.

In April of 1968, Jaruzelski was promoted to divisional (two-star) general. This new promotion came while he was planning, along with his Soviet counterparts, to invade Czechoslovakia in order to crush the Prague Spring uprising. He was in charge of the Polish contingent of the Warsaw Pact that invaded and occupied Czechoslovakia in August, 1968. For his loyal service, he was promoted to three-star general in October, 1968, and was named minister of national defense.

In December of 1970, workers' strikes broke out in Poland along the Baltic coast. Jaruzelski ordered Polish troops to open fire on striking workers, resulting in forty-four dead and more than eleven hundred wounded. Jaruzelski also helped negotiate an end to the strikes with the new party leader, Edward Gierek. Gierek rewarded him with a fourth star and associate membership in the Politburo of the party.

When Polish workers rose up again in 1976, Jaruzelski remained on the sidelines, refusing to order Polish soldiers to attack the rioters. After the deaths in 1970 riots, he feared a mutiny within the army if force was again ordered. He wisely chose not to side with Gierek, who was removed in 1980 after workers went on strike again. The Polish workers then created the Communist bloc's first independent trade union, Solidarity.

SOLIDARITY AND MARTIAL LAW

Throughout 1980 and 1981, Solidarity began to undermine the authority of the Communist Party and the Polish government. To give the party an appearance of credibility, Jaruzelski was named first party secretary in June, 1981, and prime minister shortly after. He also maintained the portfolio of minister of national defense. Jaruzelski concentrated power around him in order to weed out unreliable party and military leaders who had sympathies toward Solidarity. Plans for martial law were prepared and approved by Moscow in March, 1981. Jaruzelski then waited for the most opportune time. He struck on December 13, 1981, making mass arrests of union leaders and others associated with the opposition movement in Poland. Detention camps were established, and all civil associations outside the party were declared illegal. The party itself was temporarily suspended. Hunts were carried out for those not arrested in the first wave. Jaruzelski created the Military Council of National Salvation to rule Poland until it returned to "normality." However, Solidarity and other resistance groups simply moved underground and did not yield to martial law.

The period between 1981 and 1988 saw Poland fall into stagnation, both economically and civilly. Workers began striking again in 1988. Jaruzelski saw no alternative but to reopen talks with Solidarity in 1988. These "round table" talks resulted in semifree elections and a Communist defeat at the polls. In a compromise, Jaruzelski was recognized as the president of the People's Poland in 1989 but had to share power with a non-Communist prime minister, Tadeusz Mazowiecki. In 1990, Poland broke from the Communist bloc and became the Third Polish Republic. Jaruzelski stayed as president for the rest of that year and then retired from public office. Although Jaruzelski was tried in 2001 by the Polish government for his participation in the 1970 killings, the court failed to reach a decision. In 2005, he was threatened with a new trial for his part in declaring martial law in 1981.

IMPACT

Wojciech Jaruzelski was the archetype of the Polish army officer under the rule of the Polish United Workers' Party, the nation's communist party. As a party loyalist, he maneuvered himself into successive promotions until he was the major coordinator of Polish military actions. He thus had a major role in crushing the Prague Spring in 1968 and in coordinating Polish soldiers to end the Baltic shipyard strikes in 1970-1971, which resulted in untold worker deaths. Jaruzelski withdrew his support of Edward Gierek in 1976 and the party politicians as a whole in 1980 when he took control of the state. Jaruzelski again used the Polish Army to crush the Solidarity labor movement, in defense of the communist system, which resulted in more deaths. Following 1989, the Polish Army began to return to its pre-World War II historical traditions.

FURTHER READING

Maxwell, Robert. *Jaruzelski*. New York: Pergamon Press, 1985. Presents a very sympathetic portrayal of Jaruzleski which was published by a socialist publisher in England.

Michta, Andrew. *Red Eagle*. Stanford, Calif.: Hoover Institution Press, 1990. Provides an excellent overview of the role of the Polish Army under communist rule from 1944 until 1989. Jaurzelski appears frequently in the work.

_____. *The Soldier-Citizen*. New York: St. Martin's Press, 1997. Traces the undoing of Jaruzelski's work after 1989.

Stefancic, David. *Robotnik*. New York: Columbia University Press, 1992. An overview of the Polish workers movement toward free labor unions from 1945 to 1989. Jaruzelski appears frequently in the descriptions of the era between 1970 and 1989.

Wiater, Jerzy. *The Soldier and the Nation.* Boulder, Colo.: Westview Press, 1988. A Polish socialist sociologist, who comes off as an apologist for the declaration of martial law in 1981, gives a good descrip-

tion of the development of the Polish Army under Jaruzelski.

—*David Stefancic*

SEE ALSO: Nicolae Ceauşescu; Enver and Nexhmije Hoxha; Tito.

JEZEBEL
Queen of the Kingdom of Israel (ninth century B.C.E.)

BORN: Date unknown; Zarephath, Phoenicia (now Sarafand, Lebanon)
DIED: 853 B.C.E.; Israel
CAUSE OF NOTORIETY: Jezebel, who ruled as an absolute monarch, was accused of judicial murder and idolatry, and her name came to be synonymous with wickedness, seduction, and sorcery.
ACTIVE: c. 875-853 B.C.E.
LOCALE: Kingdom of Israel

EARLY LIFE

Jezebel (JEHZ-eh-behl) was the daughter of Ethbaal, the king of Sidon (1 Kings 16:31). She married into the royal family of the Kingdom of Israel. The marriage between Jezebel and King Ahab (r. 875-854 B.C.E.) was probably arranged by Ahab's father Omri and Ethbaal in order to seal a pact of political and economic cooperation between their two kingdoms. Jezebel's status as a royal princess was not merely ceremonial. As the daughter of the king, she was the high priestess of Baal, the principal god of Sidon, while her father the king was the high priest. Together, they held enormous political, economic, and religious authority. Jezebel likely was accustomed to wielding power just as she attempted to do after becoming Ahab's wife and queen.

POLITICAL CAREER

The Old Testament depicts Jezebel in a thoroughly negative fashion. The intensity of the rhetoric of her story as given in 1-2 Kings is evidence that its author recognized that Jezebel was a formidable opponent of ancient Israel's religious beliefs and political practices. Even the Bible's name for this woman is a clear critique. Her name was likely *izebul* (meaning "where is the prince?"). *Zebul* ("prince") was a title of Baal, a Canaanite deity that was the chief rival of Yahweh for the loyalty of the ancient Israelites. The Bible distorts *zebul* into *zebel*, the Hebrew word for dung.

Jezebel promoted the worship of Baal in Israel by providing support for 450 prophets of Baal and 400 prophets of Asherah, another important Canaanite deity (1 Kings 18:19). The Baal-cult had extensive support in ancient Israel since Baal was a god who provided rain, an absolute necessity for agricultural success in Israel, which had no river systems that could provide irrigation. Jezebel also promoted the worship of Canaanite deities in Israel because these deities provided religious support for the hierarchical social and centralized political system that was characteristic of the national states of the Levant. However, the kings of Israel did recognize the rights of individual Israelites despite their preference for a more absolutist political system. The story of Naboth (1 Kings 21) illustrates the clash of these two political systems.

Ahab wished to enlarge his vegetable garden. To do so, he proposed to purchase Naboth's vineyard, which abutted his own holdings. When Naboth refused to sell, Ahab, with great reluctance, respected Naboth's decision. When Jezebel heard of it, however, she mocked what she saw as Ahab's weakness: "A fine ruler over Israel you are indeed!" (1 Kings 21:7). She then took decisive action, coopting the elders of Naboth's village to subvert the judicial system. Naboth was executed for treason, and his land was confiscated. Ahab now had his enlarged vegetable garden. Jezebel's actions and Ahab's complicity were condemned by the prophet Elijah, who predicted a gruesome end for Jezebel (1 Kings 21:23).

Jezebel's death came during a revolution against Joram (r. 853-842 B.C.E.), her son. Resentment against the absolutist tendencies of the Israelite monarchy exploded into a revolution led by Jehu, who was determined to purge of the royal family of Israel. When Jezebel heard that Jehu had arrived at Jezreel, where she was staying, she knew what lay in store for her. However, she faced her fate with a strength characteristic of one accustomed to rule: She "shadowed her eyes and adorned her hair" (2 Kings 9:30). When she saw Jehu, she ridiculed him as a usurper. Jezebel's servants, aware that Jehu would prevail, killed her at his command (2 Kings 9:32-33). Despite Jehu's hatred of Jezebel and her family, he ordered her to be buried since "she was a king's daughter" (2 Kings 9:35).

IMPACT

The Bible portrays Jezebel as an evil foreign woman who promoted the worship of Baal and subverted traditional Israelite religious and social values. Jezebel, however, acted as she was accustomed—as a king's daughter. Undoubtedly, she enjoyed substantial power as queen in the Kingdom of Israel. To eliminate her influence, Jehu had little choice but to execute her along with the rest of the Israelite royal family. The biblical portrait of Jezebel has led to her serving as a paradigm for a conniving, power-hungry female whose determination to control knows no bounds.

FURTHER READING

Beach, Eleanor Ferris. *Jezebel Letters: Religion and Politics in Ninth Century Israel*. Minneapolis: Fortress Press, 2005. A collection of fictionalized, although historically accurate, letters and memoirs which provide insight into the century in which Jezebel ruled. Includes drawings of contemporary artifacts, as well as photographs.

Dutcher-Walls, Patricia. *Jezebel: Portraits of a Queen*. Collegeville, Minn: Liturgical Press, 2004. Intertwines two portraits of Jezebel: the fictionalized character from literature and the historic queen, both of which serve to provide a perspective with which to approach all biblical texts.

Myers, Carol L. *Discovering Eve: Ancient Israelite Women in Context*. New York: Oxford University Press, 1988. Reconstructs the everyday lives of women in ancient Israel and argues that the Bible does not provide an accurate understanding of women's roles during this period.

—*Leslie J. Hoppe*

SEE ALSO: Salome.

JIANG QING
Chinese Communist leader and last wife of Mao Zedong

BORN: 1914; Zhucheng, Shandong Province, China
DIED: May 14, 1991; Beijing, China
ALSO KNOWN AS: Chiang Ch'ing (Wade-Giles); Li Shumeng (birth name); Li Yunhe; Lan Ping (stage name); Madame Mao
MAJOR OFFENSE: Complicity in more than 34,000 deaths and 700,000 additional persecutions
ACTIVE: 1966-1976
LOCALE: China
SENTENCE: Death; commuted to life imprisonment; released after ten years for medical reasons

EARLY LIFE

Jiang Qing (jyong chihng) was born Li Shumeng in 1914 to an alcoholic, abusive innkeeper and his wife in Eastern China. As a girl, she proved headstrong, unbound her feet, and ran away at age fourteen to join an itinerant opera company. When she met Mao Zedong at his remote Yan'an redoubt in 1937, she was known as Lan Ping, a successful Shanghai stage and screen actress of the mid-1930's. To Mao's Communist comrades, she was notorious at age twenty-three for three failed marriages and allegations of recanting her Communist Party membership, held since February, 1933, which had supposedly gotten her out of a Guomindang jail in 1934. Mao gave her the name Jiang Qing ("azure river"). Himself thrice divorced at forty-five, Mao held their marriage ceremony in 1938. His comrades insisted that Jiang stay out of politics.

POLITICAL CAREER

Having remained in the background since her marriage to Mao, in the early 1960's Jiang led a move to rid the Beijing Opera of counterrevolutionary influences. By December, 1964, having proven herself a fierce and radical speaker, she had ascended to China's National People's Congress. In 1965, she was instrumental in launching the brutal Cultural Revolution in mainland China, a cover for repressing all opposition to Mao. Jiang directed the Red Guards to destroy bureaucrats, artists, academics, and all who represented the old order, encouraging zealous dedication to her husband, Chairman Mao.

Appointed by her husband to the Politburo in April, 1969, Jiang used her position to persecute her personal and political enemies. She denounced individuals at will, with disastrous consequences for those she named. She briefly courted American media after meeting American president Richard M. Nixon and his wife, Patricia, during their visit to Beijing on August 12, 1972, but the hard line on which she trod was unrelieved. Until Mao died on September 9, 1976, Jiang was the most powerful and most widely feared woman in China.

LEGAL ACTION AND OUTCOME

On October 6, 1976, less than a month after Mao's death, Jiang and three others, known as the Gang of Four, were arrested by Mao's successor Hua Guofeng. While jailed, Jiang was vilified in the Chinese media. In November, 1980, her trial opened in Beijing. Jiang and her three co-defendants were accused of persecuting to death 34,800 people and of having framed and persecuted 729,511 people during the Cultural Revolution. Jiang admitted no guilt, challenged the legitimacy of her judges, and insisted she had acted only on Mao's orders.

On January 25, 1981, she was sentenced to death but given a reprieve of two years to confess her crimes. In 1983, her death sentence was commuted to life in prison. On May 14, 1991, a few days after her release for medical reasons, Jiang committed suicide in her home. To her death, Jiang remained unrepentant.

IMPACT

As cultural adviser of the army and co-leader of the Cultural Revolution Group in 1967, Jiang Qing exerted absolute power over Chinese social life. Her promotion of the Cultural Revolution and her barbaric persecution of those she deemed enemies of the revolution brought to a halt all higher education in China. Hundreds of thousands were tortured, imprisoned, or sent to harsh labor camps, and many died.

FURTHER READING

Chang, Jung, and John Halliday. *Mao: The Unknown Story*. New York: Alfred A. Knopf, 2005. Chapter 18 tells of Jiang's meeting and marriage to Mao; chapter 56 details her dominant role in the Cultural Revolution.

THE GANG OF FOUR—OR SIX

"I was Chairman Mao's dog. What he said to bite, I bit," Jiang Qing said at her 1981 trial regarding the atrocities she helped commit during China's Cultural Revolution (1966-1976). However, historians believe her influence, and that of the other members of the Gang of Four, was already declining during the mid-1970's. Their excesses had compromised public order and worried both the military and Premier Zhou Enlai. Deluded about their power, the gang expected one of its members to succeed Zhou when he died in January, 1976; however, the party chose Hua Guofeng instead. Hua also was named chairman when Mao himself died on September 9 of the same year. A power struggle ensued, which Hua won. He had Jiang and her partners arrested as "anti-Communists." These partners were:

- **Zhang Chunqiao**, a second deputy prime minister. Formerly a journalist in Shanghai, he helped organize the city's Cultural Revolution committee, during which time he met and worked with Jiang.
- **Yao Wenyuan**, a member of the Politburo of the Central Committee of the Communist Party of China. His specialty was official propaganda. As one of the "proletarian writers for purity," he edited *Liberation Daily*, Shanghai's main newspaper, where he started his career as a literary critic. In fact, it was his article "On the New Historical Beijing Opera 'Hai Rui Dismissed from Office'" (November, 1965) that historians cite as the beginning of the Cultural Revolution. Encouraged by Zhang and Jiang to write the article, Yao attacked the playwright, a deputy mayor of Beijing, as counterrevolutionary.
- **Wang Hongwen**, a deputy president of the Communist Party. He had been a member of the Red Guards, who helped Zhang organize the Shanghai Commune for the Cultural Revolution in 1967.

Two other partners, dead by 1976, had been instrumental during the Cultural Revolution: Kang Sheng, chief of China's security and intelligence community, and Xie Fuzhi, minister of public security.

Min, Anchee. *Becoming Madame Mao*. Boston: Houghton Mifflin, 2000. Fictional account of Jiang's life, basically historically accurate.

Terrill, Ross. *Madame Mao: The White-Boned Demon*. Rev. ed. Stanford, Calif.: Stanford University Press, 2000. Detailed biography focuses on Jiang's rise to power and her struggles within the Communist leadership.

Witke, Roxane. *Comrade Chiang Ch'ing*. New York: Little, Brown, 1977. Sympathetic biography based on the author's interviews of Jiang in 1972; in-depth coverage of her life and worldview. Witke is at times very kind to her subject.

—*R. C. Lutz*

SEE ALSO: Mao Zedong.

JING KE
Chinese would-be assassin

BORN: Mid-third century B.C.E.; Wei, China
DIED: Early 227 B.C.E.; Xianyang, China
ALSO KNOWN AS: Ching K'o (Wade-Giles)
CAUSE OF NOTORIETY: Jing Ke failed in an attempt to assassinate the king of Qin, who would become China's first emperor, Shi Huangdi.
ACTIVE: 227 B.C.E.
LOCALE: Xianyang, China

EARLY LIFE
Jing Ke (jihng keh) was born in the middle of the third century B.C.E. in the state of Wei, one of northern China's independent kingdoms at the time. He studied literature and swordsmanship. He left the kingdom of Wei after failing to get a position there and traveled to the state of Yan.

ATTEMPT TO KILL KING ZHENG
When Yan faced hostilities from the State of Qin in 228 B.C.E., Yan's Prince Dan sought a quick solution. He turned to Jing Ke's local mentor, Tian Guang; the old man recommended Jing Ke, himself committing suicide to prevent the plan's discovery. Jing Ke agreed, after initial reluctance, either to force King Zheng of Qin to create a safe position for Yan or to assassinate the king.

To access his target, Jing Ke asked a fugitive Qin general, Fan Yuqi, for sacrifice. Fan Yuqi killed himself so Jing Ke could offer the general's head to King Zheng. Jing Ke also got an assistant, the murderer Qin Wuyang. Jing Ke planned to present the head of Fan Yuqi and a map of Yan's Dukang region to King Zheng, with a poisoned dagger hidden in the map.

After some hesitation, singing a farewell song that became famous, Jing Ke crossed into Qin in early 227 B.C.E. Arriving at Xiangyang, Qin's capital, Jing Ke announced the (false) submission of the king of Yan as well as his gift of the general's head and the map.

As the two assassins were invited into King Zheng's throne room, Qin Wuyang trembled noticeably. Jing Ke said his assistant was in awe of the king and was permitted to proceed. He showed Zheng the map, and the dagger was revealed. Jing Ke grasped the dagger and Zheng's left sleeve, pressing the weapon to the king's breast without hurting him. Zheng rose and tore off his sleeve. Zheng tried to draw his sword but could not remove it from its vertically worn scabbard, so he ran behind a pillar. As the king's attendants were unarmed and

prohibited to move, and the king failed to alarm his guards outside, Jing Ke chased Zheng around the pillar.

The king's physician, Xia Wuju, struck Jing Ke with his medicine bag, while others shouted to Zheng to move his scabbard horizontally to draw his sword. So doing, King Zheng wounded Jing Ke in the left thigh. Jing Ke threw his dagger but hit only the pillar. King Zheng hit Jing Ke seven more times. Collapsing, Jing Ke explained that he failed only because he wanted to capture the king alive. Zheng's guards appeared and killed Jing Ke.

IMPACT
Jing Ke's failed assassination motivated King Zheng immediately to attack Yan. Prince Dan's father had him killed to appease Zheng, but Zheng conquered Yan in 226 B.C.E. As China's first emperor, titled Shi Huangdi, Jing Ke's target retained a lifelong fear of assassins and executed all involved in the plot.

Throughout Chinese history, the notorious assassination attempt of Jing Ke has fascinated the popular imagination. When public opinion of his target was hostile, Jing Ke was celebrated. Once Mao Zedong named Shi Huangdi as the unifier of China, a different picture emerged. Modern Chinese films portray the assassination attempt in an ambiguous light, including Chen Kaige's *The Emperor and the Assassin* (1999) and Zhang Yimou's *Hero* (2004), in which a positive depiction of the emperor has startled some critics.

FURTHER READING
Crump, J. I. "The Assassins." In *Legends of the Warring States*. Ann Arbor: University of Michigan Press, 1998. Presents a historical account of Jing Ke's notorious act. Illustrated. with preface, notes, and bibliography (Wade-Giles).
Paludan, Ann. *Chronicle of the Chinese Emperors*. London: Thames & Hudson, 1998. Describes Jing Ke's assassination attempt as depicted at a second century C.E. Chinese family shrine. Richly illustrated (Pinyin).
Qian, Sima. "The Biography of Jing Ke." In *Records of the Grand Historian*. Translated by Burton Watson. 3d ed. New York: Columbia University Press, 1995. Originally written in China in the first century B.C.E.; key account of Jing Ke's notorious act (Pinyin).
—*R. C. Lutz*

SEE ALSO: Shi Huangdi.

JOAN THE MAD
Queen of Castile (r. 1504-1555) and queen of Aragon (r. 1516-1555)

BORN: November 6, 1479; Toledo, Castile (now in Spain)

DIED: April 12, 1555; Tordesillas, Spain

ALSO KNOWN AS: Joan of Castile; Joan I; Juana la Loca

CAUSE OF NOTORIETY: The first queen of Spain, Joan was left unfit to rule by a derangement that started after her marriage to Philip I.

ACTIVE: 1504-1555

LOCALE: Spain

EARLY LIFE

Joan (john) of Castile, later known as "the Mad," was the third child of the Catholic monarchs Isabella I and Ferdinand II of Castile and Aragon, and she became heir to the throne of both kingdoms when those who had precedence died one after the other. In October, 1496, Joan married Philip I, archduke of Austria (also known as Philip the Handsome), in Flanders, thus strengthening her parents' alliances in Europe. The couple had six children (one of them being the future emperor Charles V). On Isabella's death, in November, 1504, Joan was proclaimed queen of Castile.

ROYAL CAREER

Contemporary accounts relate Joan's strange behavior following her arrival in Flanders, dwelling on her unremitting and delirious fits of jealousy, her anxiety crisis, her alternating episodes of ire and melancholy, her irreligiousness, and her refusal to eat, sleep, and wash (now believed to have been manic depression, or bipolar disorder). Such mental disability could be genetic (Joan's maternal grandmother, Isabella of Portugal, suffered from dementia). However, Philip's attitude also contributed to the turn that his wife's illness took, with his gruesome game of infidelity, jealousy, and emotional blackmail. In court, he would often present her as a madwoman; he scolded her in public and would even beat her and lock her up in her rooms.

The Catholic queen's will appointed Ferdinand as regent of the lands governed by Joan, whose unsuitability to reign was certified by Philip and Ferdinand in June, 1506, when they signed the Villafáfila Agreement, which split power between them. Following Philip's untimely death in September that same year, Ferdinand rushed to take over the government of Castile. The manic-depressive Joan got worse. She would not shed a tear for her husband or depart from his corpse, accompanying it in a macabre procession across half the country. She also persisted in her refusal to sign any document and exert her authority, in spite of sporadic moments of lucidity. On February 15, 1509, Joan was taken to Tordesillas, where she lived in deplorable physical conditions and completely isolated from the rest of the world until her death. These years in Joan's life are a mystery, but historians know that she continued her passive resistance, obsessive behavior, and deep depression.

IMPACT

When Queen Joan died in Tordesillas after nearly forty years' imprisonment in her palace, few knew who she was. Ignored for centuries, Romanticism rescued her from oblivion, initiating the image of the lovesick queen.

Joan the Mad.

531

Nineteenth century artists tended to idealize Joan's disturbed mind. Francisco Pradilla's painting *Doña Juana la Loca* (1877)—housed in the Prado Museum, Madrid, and depicting the funeral cortège formed by Joan and her retinue accompanying Philip the Handsome's coffin—is a landmark in Spanish painting for its marked realism. Pradilla was awarded the Medal of Honour at the Spanish National Fine Arts Show (1878) and at two World Fairs, Paris (1878) and Vienna (1882).

Juan de Orduña transferred the painting's composition to one of the scenes in his film *Locura de amor* (1948), a romantic drama that marked a turning point in Spanish historical filmography. Orduña based his work on *La locura de amor* (1855); this brilliant study of jealousy, by Manuel Tamayo y Baus and set in sixteenth century Castile, has been in print in Spain continuously since its publication. Also indebted to a large extent to Tamayo's work is Vicente Aranda's successful film *Juana la Loca* (2001), released in the United States as *Mad Love*. An opera was written in 1877 by Emilio Serrano, *Doña Juana la Loca*. More recently, two rock bands have chosen to name themselves after the Spanish queen: the internationally formed Mad Juana and the Argentinian Juana la Loca.

These examples serve to illustrate how Joan's legend has captivated the popular imagination in the generations since her time. Modern scholars, from historians to psychologists, have also made her the object of their analysis, as evidenced by many studies that analyze the true nature of her illness and the true historical role played by the queen who never reigned.

FURTHER READING

Aram, Bethany. *Juana the Mad: Sovereignty and Dynasty in Renaissance Europe*. Baltimore: Johns Hopkins University Press, 2005. The author of this biographical study of Joan analyzes abundant documentation from that period to question the queen's supposed incapacity to reign. Aram's thesis is that it was the lifelong family pressure to which Joan was subjected that prevented her from reaching the throne.

_____. "Juana 'the Mad,' the Clares, and the Carthusians: Revising a Necrophilic Legend in Early Habsburg Spain." *Archiv für Reformationsgeschichte* 93 (2002): 172-191. This article revises the assessment of Joan's relationship with two religious orders, giving it a religious and political import and providing a new dimension to some of the queen's personal actions, traditionally marked as a "heretic."

Beecher, Donald A., and Massimo Ciavolella, eds. *Eros and Anteros: The Medical Traditions of Love in the Renaissance*. Toronto: University of Toronto Italian Studies, 1992. This study of the Renaissance medical philosophy behind lovesickness, though not expressly related to Joan, provides insights into her illness, a mixture of jealousy, melancholy, and depression.

Dennis, Amarie. *Seek the Darkness: The Story of Juana la Loca*. 5th ed. Madrid: Impresores Sucesores de Rivadeneyra, 1969. This historical narrative of Joan's life assumes in many passages the romantic perspective that has characterized her historiography for centuries.

Graham, Thomas F. *Medieval Minds. Mental Health in the Middle Ages*. London: George Allen & Unwin, 1967. A psychological study of some relevant characters in the spirituality and thought of medieval and Renaissance Europe (such as Augustine of Hippo, Moḥammad, Roger Bacon, Thomas Aquinas, and Martin Luther).

—*Avelina Carrera*

SEE ALSO: Charles II.

ALFRED JODL
Chief of Operations staff of the German High Command

BORN: May 10, 1890; Würzburg, Germany
DIED: October 16, 1946; Nuremberg, Germany
MAJOR OFFENSES: Four counts of Nuremberg war crimes
ACTIVE: February, 1938-May 7, 1945
LOCALE: Theaters of German military operation
SENTENCE: Death by hanging; in 1953, he was posthumously exonerated by a German court

EARLY LIFE

Alfred Jodl (YOHD-ehl) was born on May 10, 1890 in Würzburg, Germany. He was educated in local schools and entered the military Cadet School in Munich as a teenager, graduating in 1910. Jodl enlisted as an officer in the artillery service of the German Imperial Army, attaining the rank of *Leutnant* (lieutenant) in 1912. During the first two years of World War I, Jodl served as an officer in a Bavarian artillery battery on the Western Front and was wounded twice. After a short stint on the Russian Front in 1917, he was shifted to a position as a staff officer and returned to the Western Front, where he served until the war's end, having reached the rank of *Hauptmann* (captain). When the victorious Allies reduced the Imperial Army to the rump Reichswehr, Jodl retained his commission, obtaining the ranks of *Oberstleutnant* (major) in 1933 and *Oberst* (colonel) in 1935. In 1935, Jodl was given the position of chief of the national defense section in the High Command of the Armed Forces, in which he served as second-in-command to Wilhelm Keitel. He met Adolf Hitler for the first time in 1923, and the future führer took a liking to the Bavarian officer from Hitler's adopted state. Jodl's rapid advancement and high attainments were probably propelled by the fact that he was not a member of the Prussian *Junker* military aristocracy.

NAZI CAREER

The International Military Tribunal in Nuremberg convicted Jodl of crimes against peace—both "conspiracy to wage aggressive war" and "waging aggressive war"—for actions beginning with the planning of Germany's Anschluss with Austria in early 1938, which he carried out under orders from Keitel and pressure from Hitler. He was also a key figure in the German military plans for occupation of the Sudetenland in Czechoslovakia. After the success of this operation, in October, 1938, Jodl received the commission of artillery commander of the Forty-Fourth Division, which he held until late August, 1939. His promotion to general major was posted on May 1, 1939. Thus, though he did not oversee the planning of the Polish campaign, on its eve he was appointed chief of operations staff of the High Command of the Armed Forces. In this position, he played key roles in the planning of the invasions of Norway, Denmark, Belgium, and the Netherlands in the spring of 1940, and Yugoslavia and Greece in the spring of 1941. Planning for the invasion of the Soviet Union, known as Operation Barbarossa, began as early as July, 1940. In each of these cases Jodl played key roles in preparing the German armed forces for offensive operations against nonbelligerent nations. Though the impetus in each case came directly from Hitler, and Keitel served as Jodl's superior military officer, the tribunal concluded that his complicity in the preparations and directions constituted crimes against peace.

The tribunal also succeeded in finding Jodl guilty of "war crimes," which were generally defined as violations of the traditionally accepted limitations on violence or destruction in the course of war. In Jodl's case it cited specifically his roles in issuing the infamous Commissar and Commando orders, which called for the summary executions of Soviet political officers and partisan leaders by German troops. Wanton destruction of buildings and other property was also grounds for conviction as a war criminal. The court cited the order of October 7, 1941, signed by Jodl, mandating the utter destruction of the Soviet cities of Moscow and Leningrad without regard to their surrender. It also cited his role in ordering the evacuation of northern Norwegians and the destruction of their homes as a measure against their aiding Soviet relief troops. The Norwegian government testified that some thirty thousand houses were damaged or destroyed as a result.

As for the fourth count, "crimes against humanity," Jodl's guilt was restricted to a single speech in November, 1943, given to military governors. In it, he urged them to be vigorous and remorseless in compelling the labor forces in occupied France, Belgium, the Netherlands, and Denmark to aid the construction of the Nazi coastal defenses.

On May 7, 1945, Jodl signed the papers by which the Germans surrendered unconditionally to the Allied forces. Immediately placed under arrest, he was incarcerated in Flensburg and then taken to Nuremberg for trial.

LEGAL ACTION AND OUTCOME

Evidence against Jodl was largely in the form of his signature on key planning documents and orders that directed German military operations. They proved his presence at key meetings and planning sessions, and thus his complicity in the formulations of the various directives. In his defense, Jodl attempted to show how he had opposed the führer's intentions in many of the cases and in others how he attempted to mitigate their effects. The tribunal found none of this compelling. Jodl's key defense claim, that he was only following orders, had been prohibited as a defense by the countries involved in the proceedings. Jodl was condemned to death. Though he requested execution by firing squad, he was hanged with other convicted Nazis in Nuremberg on October 16, 1946. In 1953, a German government arbitration board considered his case and declared him posthumously acquitted of all charges on the grounds that he was only following his superior's orders.

IMPACT

Alfred Jodl's fate paralleled that of dozens of other Nazi German and Imperial Japanese military and political leaders and created the precedent by which victorious nations could impose post factum conditions on defeated enemy leaders, both military and civilian.

FURTHER READING

Barnett, Correlli, ed. *Hitler's Generals*. New York: Grove Press, 2003. Brief but full discussions of twenty-six German generals, including Jodl, with an emphasis on why they allowed Hitler to make the blunders that he did.

Gilbert, G. M. *Nuremberg Diary*. New York: Da Capo Press, 1995. Firsthand observations and records of conversations with Jodl (and others) by a member of the prosecution.

Overy, Richard. *Interrogations: The Nazi Elite in Allied Hands, 1945*. New York: Penguin Books, 2002. Transcripts of formal interrogations with Jodl (and other Nazis) during the course of the Nuremberg war crimes trials.

Warlimont, Walter. *Inside Hitler's Headquarters*. New York: Presidio Press, 1991. Military memoirs of Jodl's assistant.

—*Joseph P. Byrne*

SEE ALSO: Klaus Barbie; Martin Bormann; Léon Degrelle; Adolf Eichmann; Hans Michael Frank; Joseph Goebbels; Hermann Göring; Rudolf Hess; Reinhard Heydrich; Heinrich Himmler; Adolf Hitler; Josef Mengele; Joachim von Ribbentrop; Baldur von Schirach; Otto Skorzeny; Julius Streicher.

KING JOHN
King of England (r. 1199-1216)

BORN: December 24, 1166; Beaumont Palace, Oxford, Oxfordshire, England

DIED: October 18, 1216; Newark Castle, Nottinghamshire, England

ALSO KNOWN AS: John Lackland; Soft-Sword

CAUSE OF NOTORIETY: The territorial losses of England during John's reign incited a rebellion that led him to sign the Magna Carta; in doing so, he signed away significant monarchical rights and powers.

ACTIVE: 1202-1216

LOCALE: London and areas nearby

EARLY LIFE

John (jahn) was born to Henry II, the first of the Angevin-Plantagenet line of English monarchs, and Eleanor of Aquitaine. Through his paternal grandmother, Matilda, he was the great-grandson of William of Normandy. The fourth and favorite son of Henry II, John grew up in the shadow of his brothers Henry, Richard, and Geoffrey. John's nickname "Lackland" referred to the expectation that, as the fourth son, he would inherit nothing from his family.

The Angevins were constantly seeking to enlarge their empire, which already included Aquitaine, Anjou, and Normandy in France as well as England. In 1183 John's oldest brother, Henry the Younger, died. In 1185, Henry II sent the eighteen-year-old John to rule Ireland. John arrived there with a treasury, which he wasted on his own luxuries, and an army of three hundred, which he lost.

POLITICAL CAREER

After John's brother Geoffrey was killed in a tournament, John joined Richard, his oldest living brother and the heir apparent, in rebellion against Henry II. The aging king, broken-hearted, died in 1189.

Monarchial turmoil continued during the reign of Richard I (1189-1199), with John attempting to usurp the throne while Richard was away on the Third Crusade. The efforts of Eleanor, their mother, thwarted John's attempts. In spite of the difficulties between the brothers, Richard forgave John, and on his deathbed in 1199 he named him as his successor.

King John was crowned, at age thirty-one, in Westminster Abbey on May 27, 1199. Turmoil resumed in 1202 when John's nephew, Arthur of Brittany, son of Geoffrey, was murdered. Based on the law of primogeniture, Arthur had claimed the English crown in 1199. Reports that John was responsible for the murder led to a rebellion. John's army, sent to quell the rebellion, was defeated in 1204. Because of this defeat as well as earlier ones, John's barons began losing confidence in him as a military leader. John soon had another nickname, Soft-Sword. His disagreement with the pope in 1207 regarding the appointment of a new archbishop of Canterbury led to his excommunication in 1209. England was put under an interdict until 1213.

MAGNA CARTA

In 1215, King John of England was forced to sign the document now known as the Magna Carta, which laid the foundation for later principles of democracy, including the U.S. Constitution and Bill of Rights. The excerpt below includes rights that remain in effect with only minor modifications.

John, by the grace of God King of England, Lord of Ireland, Duke of Normandy and Aquitaine, and Count of Anjou, to his archbishops, bishops, abbots, earls, barons, justices, foresters, sheriffs, stewards, servants, and to all his officials and loyal subjects, Greeting.

KNOW THAT BEFORE GOD, for the health of our soul and those of our ancestors and heirs, to the honour of God, the exaltation of the holy Church, and the better ordering of our kingdom, at the advice of our reverend fathers Stephen, archbishop of Canterbury, primate of all England, and cardinal of the holy Roman Church . . . and other loyal subjects:

FIRST, THAT WE HAVE GRANTED TO GOD, and by this present charter have confirmed for us and our heirs in perpetuity, that the English Church shall be free, and shall have its rights undiminished, and its liberties unimpaired. . . .

TO ALL FREE MEN OF OUR KINGDOM we have also granted, for us and our heirs for ever, all the liberties written out below, to have and to keep for them and their heirs, of us and our heirs . . .

The city of London shall enjoy all its ancient liberties and free customs, both by land and by water. We also will and grant that all other cities, boroughs, towns, and ports shall enjoy all their liberties and free customs. . . .

No free man shall be seized or imprisoned, or stripped of his rights or possessions, or outlawed or exiled, or deprived of his standing in any other way, nor will we proceed with force against him, or send others to do so, except by the lawful judgement of his equals or by the law of the land. . . .

To no one will we sell, to no one deny or delay right or justice. . . .

Given by our hand in the meadow that is called Runnymede, between Windsor and Staines, on the fifteenth day of June in the seventeenth year of our reign.

Source: G. R. C. Davis, *Magna Carta*, rev. ed. (London: British Library, 1989).

After defeat in Aquitaine in 1214, the English barony was exhausted. A minority declared themselves against the king on May 3, 1215. Negotiations collapsed when London opened its gates to the rebels. The result was a meeting at Runnymede in June, where John was forced to sign the Magna Carta (great charter). The king was denied absolute power, and for the first time English kings were subject to the laws of the land.

John's attempt to renege on the charter prompted the civil war that led to his death by dysentery at Newark on the night of October 18, 1216. He had been abandoned by two-thirds of his barons and had lost his crown jewels in the marshes of East Anglia. He was buried in Worcester Cathedral and was succeeded by his nine-year-old son, Henry III.

IMPACT

King John's reign was a disaster, with England losing its landholdings in France. Reaction to John ranges from utter contempt to a recognition that his intelligence and potential for success were superseded by personality faults. The positive legacy of King John is the Magna Carta. Although signed under duress, it remains the foundation of the English constitution.

FURTHER READING

Church, S. D., ed. *King John: New Interpretations.* Rochester, N.Y.: Boydell Press, 1999. Essays on John's reign and on the problems facing England during the time period. Includes John's problems involving Ireland, Scotland, and the Roman Catholic Church.

Danziger, Danny, and John Gillingham. *1215: The Year of the Magna Carta.* New York: Simon and Schuster, 2004. Concentrates on the events leading up to the signing of the charter by King John, especially the opposition and actions of the English barons. Also summarizes the impact that the Magna Carta had on the future English monarchy.

Jones, J. A. P. *King John and the Magna Carta.* London: Longman, 1971. Puts John and the Magna Carta in the context of the Angevin-Plantagenet period of the English monarchy (1154-1399). Provides detailed chronological accounts from 1205 to 1215.

—*Glenn L. Swygart*

SEE ALSO: Richard III; Robin Hood.

JOHN PARRICIDA
Swabian prince and assassin

BORN: 1290; Habichtsburg, Swabia (now in Switzerland)

DIED: December 13, 1312 or 1313; probably Pisa (now in Italy)

ALSO KNOWN AS: John the Parricide; John of Swabia; John the Landless; John of Swabi; Johann Parricida von Habsburg

MAJOR OFFENSE: Murder of his uncle, Albrecht I, emperor-king of Austria

ACTIVE: May 1, 1303

LOCALE: Switzerland, across the Seusse River from Brugg

SENTENCE: Outlaw in Empire, sentenced to death a year later

EARLY LIFE

John Parricida (pah-rih-SEE-dah) was born in the manorial castle Habichtsburg (source of the dynastic name "Habsburg") in present-day Switzerland after the death of his father, Rudolf II, successor to Rudolf I, the first Holy Roman emperor (r. 1276-1291). John spent his early years at the Habsburg court and later lived at the Prague court of his Bohemian uncle, King Wenceslas I. Upon his maturity he became a ward of his paternal uncle, Emperor-King Albrecht I. At repeated points John advanced his incontrovertible and legal claims and demanded of his uncle title and rule over the territories bequeathed him by his emperor father.

CRIMINAL CAREER

Albrecht continually denied John's requests for territory, title, and rule as well as monetary compensation. At an assembly of nobles on May 1, 1308, partly convened to deal with the beginnings of Swiss resistance to Austrian domination, John again demanded his inheritance; again his uncle refused. John succeeded in separating Albrecht from his retinue. He crossed the Seuss River with his uncle. In sight of the retinue, John's accomplices stabbed Albrecht in the throat, slashed him with a halberd, and split his head open with an axe. John's co-assassins headed north. (One would die an agonizingly slow death on the wheel in response to Albrecht's widow's thirst for revenge.) John headed south.

According to the definitive research of Johannes von Mueller (1752-1809), dramatist Friedrich Schiller (1759-1805), himself a professional historian, incorporated Mueller's account into his historical drama *Wilhelm Tell* (1804), act 5, scene 1. In the following scene, Schiller created a mythical encounter between John and Wilhelm Tell in Tell's alpine hut, in which John pleads for sanctuary. Tell denies it to him on the grounds that John's murder was committed for personal reasons, unlike Tell's murder of the Austrian representative who had forced him to shoot the apple off his son's head, thus freeing the Swiss from Austrian tyranny. Tell insists that John must make a pilgrimage to Rome and seek absolution for his deed from the pope. As an alpine huntsman, Tell knows all the passes through the Alps and orally maps out for John an escape route to Italy.

From this point, history loses trace of John until his end four or five years later. He did manage to avoid detection and capture. Some sources believe that he became a monk and died in a Pisan monastery; others that he died in Pisa, in the custody of local authorities, having been denied clemency by the German king Henry VII, who had descended into Italy.

LEGAL ACTION AND OUTCOME

A year after the assassination of Albrecht, a murder warrant was issued for John. As he was neither apprehended nor extradited from Italy for trial and execution, he escaped punishment.

IMPACT

John Parricida's murder of his uncle had historical repercussions. First, the murdered emperor's brother and successor, Ferdinand the Fair, who was not the powerful figure that Albrecht had been, was unsuccessful in securing for himself the imperial crown. It would not return to a Habsburg head until Maximilian I in 1493. Second, the commander of the army sent by Ferdinand to subjugate the Swiss was defeated at the Battle of Mansfeld in 1313, forcing Austria to renounce further claim to the origin of the Swiss Federation, which marked the beginning of Switzerland's stature as oldest European democracy.

FURTHER READING

Bishop, Morris. *The Middle Ages*. New York: Mariner Books, 2001. A widely used, classic history of the period, with relevance to the emergence of the Habsburg Dynasty.

Cantor, Norman F. *The Civilization of the Middle Ages*. New York: HarperCollins, 1993. Cantor's revised and expanded magisterial portrait of major factors in medieval history was published ten years before his death. Particularly relevant to John's claims on his emperor-uncle is part 3 of chapter 11, "The German Investiture Question," pages 265-277. From section 2 of chapter 9, "The Rise of Europe," through chapter 10, pages 228-242, can be found compelling background information on the historical lead-up to the dissension in the House of Habsburg.

Herde, Peter. "The Empire from Adolf of Nassau to Lewis of Bavaria, 1292-1347." Vol. 6 in *The New Cambridge Medieval History*, edited by Michael Jones. New York: Cambridge University Press, 2000. The sub-chapters "[Ausust's] Final Years and Death" and "The Swiss Confederation" are richly informative about the events and players of the period.

Killy, Walter, and Rudolf Vierhaus, eds. "John Parricida." In *Dictionary of German Biography*. Munich: K. G. Saur, 2002. A biographical sketch of John, his provenance, homicidal act, and end.

Tapié, Victor L. *Rise and Fall of the Habsburg Monarchy*. Translated by Stephen Hardman. New York: Praeger, 1971. Good source of information on the rise of the longest-lived European dynasty and the state of the infant dynasty at the time of John's homicide and the breakaway of Switzerland from the incipient Empire.

Wandruszka, Adam. *The House of Habsburg: Six Hundred Years of a European Dynasty*. Translated by Cathlee and Hans Epstein. Westport, Conn.: Greenwood Press, 1975. Translation of the German-language classic on the Habsburg monarchy from its origins. Good explanation of the two-century setback for the dynasty owing to John's murder of his uncle Albrecht. Contains relevant maps.

—*Robert B. Youngblood*

SEE ALSO: John Bellingham; Jacques Clément; Charlotte Corday; Guy Fawkes; Balthasar Gérard; Jack Ketch; François Ravaillac; Miles Sindercombe.

JIM JONES
American minister and cult leader

BORN: May 13, 1931; Crete, Indiana
DIED: November 18, 1978; Jonestown, Guyana
ALSO KNOWN AS: James Warren Jones (full name); the Reverend Jim Jones
CAUSE OF NOTORIETY: The founder of a cultlike church called the Peoples Temple, Jones led its members in a mass murder-suicide in Guyana.
ACTIVE: 1952-1978
LOCALE: Indianapolis, Indiana; Redwood Valley, California; and Guyana

EARLY LIFE

James Warren Jones (commonly known as the Reverend Jim Jones) was born into an impoverished family in rural Indiana during the Great Depression. He was the only child born to his parents, James and Lynetta Jones. His father was a disabled military veteran. His mother supported the family and was primarily responsible for rearing Jones.

During high school, Jones was employed as an orderly at a hospital, where he met his future wife, Marceline Baldwin, who was a nursing student. They married on June 12, 1949. The marriage produced one child, Stephan, who was born in 1959. When Jones married Marceline, he was a freshman at Indiana University. However, he did not complete college until 1961, when he obtained a bachelor's degree in education from Butler University.

MINISTRY CAREER

Jones's career in the ministry began as a student pastor at Sommerset Southside Methodist Church in 1952 in Indianapolis, Indiana. His ministry emphasized racial integration at a time when the United States was still racially segregated, and he sought to bring African Americans into his all-white church. His differences with the Sommerset church over segregation led to his dismissal. Afterward, he became involved with several Pentecostal churches before founding the Peoples Temple Full Gospel Church in 1955 in Indianapolis. In 1959, the Peoples Temple became an affiliate of the Disciples of Christ denomination, but Jones was not ordained as a minister for the Disciples of Christ until 1964.

Jones's ministry included staged faith healings and other faked miracles. His theology emphasized socialist political views and racial integration. He encouraged his followers to practice communal living and communal rearing of children. In 1964, Jones relocated the Peoples Temple to Redwood Valley, California, where he believed his political and social views would be more welcomed. Jones's ministry grew in California, and addi-

Jim Jones. (AP/Wide World Photos)

tional Peoples Temple churches opened in San Francisco and Los Angeles in the early 1970's. In 1974, the Peoples Temple leased a plot of land in the South American nation of Guyana. Jones's stated intention was to create a socialist and racially integrated community, free of what he saw as the evils of modern American capitalist society. The community came to be called Jonestown and was later the site of the mass murder-suicide for which Jones became infamous.

TRAGEDY IN JONESTOWN

As the congregation of the Peoples Temple grew in California, so did Jones's political influence and media presence. While media attention toward the Peoples Temple was initially positive, several exposés of the organization alleged financial misconduct, faked faith healings, and abusive practices toward members. In the wake of these exposés, as well as a potential tax problem, Jones relocated to Jonestown in July, 1977; his followers were encouraged to relocate as well. By September, 1977, more than one thousand members lived in Jonestown. The majority of the residents of Jonestown were African American, more than a quarter of the residents were children, and many were senior citizens.

The factors that ultimately led Jones to advocate suicide among his followers may not ever be fully understood, but biographers have noted that Jones perceived himself as persecuted by the media and that he had developed an addiction to prescription narcotics, both of which intensified in Jonestown.

In November, 1978, a delegation from the United States led by Congressman Leo Ryan arrived in Guyana to investigate allegations that Peoples Temple members were being abused and held in Jonestown against their will. Fifteen members opted to leave with the delegation but were attacked along with members of the delegation as they boarded a plane to leave. Five people were killed, including Ryan. Ten people were wounded.

After the attack, Jones called a meeting of the entire Jonestown community, where he announced that their community would be destroyed because of the attack on the delegation. He argued that they must commit an act of "revolutionary suicide," by taking their own lives before the military and police could launch a counterattack. Jonestown's medical staff distributed fruit punch containing a mixture of cyanide and sedatives to the Peoples Temple members. More than nine hundred of Jones's followers, including Jones's wife and several of their adopted children, were forced to drink or voluntarily drank the poisoned punch. Jones was killed by a gunshot wound to the head. It is unclear if he fired the fatal shot himself or if one of his followers fired the shot.

IMPACT

Jim Jones is less well known for his ministry than for the tragedy in Jonestown, which remains the largest mass murder-suicide in American history. The Jonestown tragedy was widely reported in the national and international media and spurred debate about the dangers of cults and other extremist organizations. Subsequent study of Jones and the Peoples Temple by academicians, as well as memoirs by former members, has provided insights into how cults and other extremist organizations control their followers and how these members can make destructive choices that they may have never considered prior to their involvement in the group. The lingering impact of Jonestown on American popular culture is reflected in the expression "drink the Kool-Aid," a term that indicates an individual has conformed to the demands of a larger social group without considering the consequences of his or her conformity.

FURTHER READING

Hall, John R. *Gone from the Promised Land: Jonestown in American Cultural History.* New Brunswick, N.J.: Transaction, 1987. Contains a biography of Jones and a history of the Peoples Temple; compares Peoples Temple practices to those of other religious movements.

Kilduff, Marshall, and Phil Tracy. "Inside People's Temple." *New West.* June, 1977. The original exposé that drew critical attention to Jones's ministry.

Lalich, Janja. *Bounded Choice: True Believers and Charismatic Cults.* Berkeley: University of California Press, 2004. Discusses a theory, Bounded Choice, to explain how cult members come to make destructive and irrational decisions that diverge from their behavior prior to cult membership.

DEATH REHEARSAL

On June 15, 1978, Deborah Layton Blakey, a Jonestown survivor, recorded a sworn affidavit about her experience:

I was eighteen years old when I joined the People's Temple. I had grown up in affluent circumstances in the permissive atmosphere of Berkeley, California. By joining the People's Temple, I hoped to help others and in the process to bring structure and self-discipline to my own life. . . . I watched the organization depart with increasing frequency from its professed dedication for social change and participatory democracy. The Reverend Jim Jones gradually assumed a tyrannical hold over the lives of Temple members. Any disagreement with his dictates came to be regarded as "treason." . . . He steadfastly and convincingly maintained that the punishment for defection was death. The fact that severe corporal punishment was frequently administered to Temple members gave the threats a frightening air of reality. . . .

He convinced black Temple members that if they did not follow him to Guyana, they would be put into concentration camps and killed. White members were instilled with the belief that their names appeared on a secret list of enemies of the state that was kept by the CIA and that they would be tracked down, tortured, imprisoned, and subsequently killed if they did not flee to Guyana. . . .

During one "white night," we were informed that our situation had become hopeless and that the only course of action open to us was a mass suicide for the glory of socialism. We were told that we would be tortured by mercenaries if we were taken alive. Everyone, including the children, was told to line up. As we passed through the line, we were given a small glass of red liquid to drink. We were told that the liquid contained poison and that we would die within forty-five minutes. We all did as we were told. When the time came when we should have dropped dead, Reverend Jones explained that the poison was not real and that we had just been through a loyalty test. He warned us that the time was not far off when it would become necessary for us to die by our own hands.

Source: "Affadavit of Deborah Layton Blakey," Rick A. Ross Institute, http://www.rickross.com.

Maaga, Mary M. *Hearing the Voice of Jonestown: Putting a Human Face on an American Tragedy.* Syracuse, N.Y.: Syracuse University Press, 1998. Focuses on the female leadership of the Peoples Temple; analyzes the causes of the Jonestown tragedy from a sociological perspective.

—*Damon Mitchell*

SEE ALSO: Marshall Applewhite; David Koresh; Bonnie Nettles.

MARGARET JONES
Massachusetts Bay Colony midwife and lay healer

BORN: Date unknown; place unknown
DIED: June 15, 1648; Charlestown, Massachusetts Bay Colony (now Massachusetts)
MAJOR OFFENSE: Witchcraft
ACTIVE: c. 1648
LOCALE: Charlestown, Massachusetts Bay Colony
SENTENCE: Death by hanging

EARLY LIFE

Very little documentation of Margaret Jones's life exists before her indictment for practicing witchcraft. At the time of her trial in 1648, she was married to Thomas Jones and was a practicing midwife and lay healer. Jones used herbal medicine and other simple remedies to aid her friends' and neighbors' physical complaints, with varying degrees of success. According to records of her statements prior to her execution, Jones admitted to stealing early in life, although the specifics of this incident were omitted.

WITCHCRAFT CAREER

Jones was accused of witchcraft, and numerous pieces of evidence related to her role as a midwife and lay healer were brought against her at trial. Jones was accused of having a malignant touch, which locals claimed could cause deafness, vomiting, or severe pains and sickness. Jones's use of common herbs in her treatment of ailments was deemed supernatural because her concoctions sometimes produced violent reactions in those using them. Jones was also accused because she often accurately predicted that those who refused her herbal treatments would not get better, despite seeking help from physicians. Under a physical examination, Jones was said to have a witch teat on her genitals, from which a demon had recently suckled. It was also claimed that Jones could accurately predict the future in an unnatural way. A final piece of evidence was presented by a prison guard, who claimed to see Jones in her cell holding a child who then ran into another room and disappeared. This same child was independently reported in two other places before vanishing.

LEGAL ACTION AND OUTCOME

Jones was convicted of practicing witchcraft in Charlestown, Massachusetts Bay Colony, in May, 1648. Although she was encouraged by neighbors and friends to confess to her crimes and thus avoid execution, Jones ad-

amantly maintained her innocence until her death at the gallows. Her husband Thomas was similarly accused of witchcraft and brought before the court, but he was never formally tried. On the day of Jones's execution, Thomas fled the Massachusetts Bay Colony by sea.

IMPACT

Margaret Jones's indictment, trial, and subsequent guilty verdict were a first for the Massachusetts Bay Colony and signaled the advent of the "witch craze" that would culminate in the witch trials held by John Hathorne in Salem Village, Massachusetts, in 1692. Before the Salem witch trials and hysteria were over, nineteen men and women were tried and executed for practicing witchcraft. Many others were spared execution both by confessing to the crimes of which they had been accused and by naming others in the community who were also presumed guilty of practicing witchcraft.

Jones's trial is particularly notable within the context of witch trials because it consisted entirely of evidence that had been verified by witnesses and victims, however false it might have been. Later trials, most famously those in Salem Village, allowed spectral evidence, meaning evidence in the form of dreams, hallucinations, visions, or vague feelings. Many jurors and townspeople claimed unsubstantiated spectral evidence to be the most damning indicators of witchcraft at work.

The witch trials of the seventeenth century captured the interest of the public in the following centuries and have been the subject of historical novels, films, and award-winning plays. Modern literature, such as Arthur Miller's play *The Crucible* (pr., pb. 1953), has drawn parallels between witch hysteria in the seventeenth century and the Red Scare and McCarthyism during the 1950's.

FURTHER READING

Demos, John. *Entertaining Satan: Witchcraft and the Culture of Early New England.* New York: Oxford University Press, 2004. Provides detailed historical data on the accused, including birth, death, marriage, and court documents, as well as a multidisciplinary analysis of the events leading up to the witch hysteria that plagued New England in the 1600's.

Hill, Francis. *The Salem Witch Trials Reader.* Cambridge, Mass.: Da Capo Press, 2000. Hill explores the historical backdrop surrounding the trials using original court records and testimony and provides a good overview of how facts of the trials have been sometimes distorted but widely embraced by popular culture in the form of plays, novels, and film.

Karlsen, Carol F. *The Devil in the Shape of a Woman: Witchcraft in Colonial New England*. New York: W. W. Norton, 1998. Karlsen uses historical data to examine the commonalities among the accused and

possible motivations behind accusations of witchcraft.

—*Sally A. Lasko*

SEE ALSO: Tamsin Blight; Mary Butters; Dorothy Clutterbuck; Lady Alice Kyteler; Dolly Pentreath; Elizabeth Sawyer; Mother Shipton; Joan Wytte.

FLAVIUS JOSEPHUS
Jewish historian

BORN: c. 37 C.E.; Jerusalem, Palestine (now in Israel)
DIED: c. 100 C.E.; probably Rome (now in Italy)
ALSO KNOWN AS: Joseph ben Matthias (Jewish name)
CAUSE OF NOTORIETY: Josephus survived and recorded the destruction of Jerusalem by Romans in 70 C.E., an account that led Jews to accuse him of treason.
ACTIVE: 66-100 C.E.
LOCALE: Roman Palestine (now in Israel)

EARLY LIFE

Flavius Josephus (FLAY-vee-uhs joh-SEE-fuhs) was the son of a priestly family and born in the year of the accession to the throne of the emperor Caligula. Since his own writings are the only source for most of the information on his life, there is little way to check his claim that he was already being consulted on points of interpretation of Jewish law in his early teens. He was sent off to Rome while still in his twenties to negotiate the release of prisoners (the relations between the Jewish inhabitants of Palestine and its Roman overlords were often uneasy), and his diplomatic skills accomplished the desired result. He did not return to Palestine until 66 C.E.

POLITICAL CAREER

Upon his return, Josephus found himself amid popular discontent with the Roman government. In his later historical writings, he claimed that the majority of the Jewish inhabitants were not so unhappy with Roman leadership as to want to turn to arms, but there was enough pressure for armed resistance that Josephus found himself in control of an army designed to resist the Romans in the Galilee region. Josephus tried to avoid combat but, in the face of Roman attacks, he found himself with the remains of his troops in the fortress of Jotapata. There, as Josephus describes it, the decision was made to commit mass suicide (each soldier killing the one next to him),

but Josephus managed to arrange the sequence so that he and another soldier survived.

On surrendering to the Romans, Josephus was taken to the Roman general Flavius Vespasian and prophesied that Vespasian would subsequently become emperor. When Vespasian did in fact gain power, he became a generous patron of Josephus and took him on a trip as far as Alexandria. (The name "Flavius" that Josephus added to his own name was in honor of the emperor's family.) Josephus returned to his homeland in the company of Vespasian's son Titus, who was to lead the final assault on the Temple in Jerusalem. While he was in Titus's company, Josephus addressed his fellow Jews within the walls of Jerusalem and urged them to lay down their weapons. His claim was that he was trying to save lives, but the Jewish reaction then, as well as for centuries afterward, was to regard him as a traitor. After the Roman victory, Josephus was granted land in Palestine but decided to spend the rest of his life in the safer setting of Rome. His date of death is unknown.

IMPACT

Flavius Josephus's picturesque story would be little known if he had not spent his later years writing the history both of the period and of his own activities. His first work carried a Greek title (the language of the intelligentsia), *Peri tou Ioudaikou polemou*, which in Latin is *Bellum Judaicum* (75-79 C.E.; *History of the Jewish War*, 1773). He later wrote another expansive history of Judaism titled *Antiquitates Judaicae* (93 C.E.; *The Antiquities of the Jews*, 1773). In both works, he set forth his own actions, even when they were not always to his advantage, as well as a history of the Jewish people. One of the reasons for writing these stories may have been to refute the claim made by anti-Semites that military heroism was not to be found among the Jews. He may also have been providing material for the non-Jewish population of Rome to understand Jewish history and religion.

A surprising consequence of his writing about that period was the popularity of his work with the Christian population over the centuries. He gave background for the setting of the birth and rise of Christianity that appeared nowhere else. Until the nineteenth century, Christian readers of Josephus were more common than Jewish readers, although the rise of Jewish scholarship restored Josephus to a more central place. His actions are seen in the context of the Pharisaic tradition in Judaism, while his work remained a guide for archaeologists in modern-day Israel.

FURTHER READING

Feldman, Louis H. *Josephus's Interpretation of the Bible.* Berkeley: University of California Press, 1998. Explains the non-Jewish audience whom Josephus was addressing.

Hadas-Lebel, Mireille. *Flavius Josephus: Eyewitness to Rome's First Century Conquest of Judea.* New York: Macmillan, 1993. A popular account that tries to analyze the basis for Josephus's decisions.

Mason, Steve, ed. *Understanding Josephus: Seven Perspectives.* Sheffield, England: Sheffield Academic Press, 1998. Mason's own essay examines the reactions to Judaism within the wealthy classes of Rome when Josephus was living there.

Rajak, Tessa. *Josephus.* Rev. ed. London: Duckworth, 2002. A sympathetic portrait that recognizes Jewish aspects in Josephus's life and writings.

Williamson, G. A. *The World of Josephus.* London: Secker and Warburg, 1964. A Christian portrait of the environment in which Josephus lived and about which he wrote.

—*Thomas Drucker*

SEE ALSO: Caligula; Domitian; Herod Antipas.

WILLIAM JOYCE
British broadcaster for the Nazis during World War II

BORN: April 24, 1906; Brooklyn, New York
DIED: January 3, 1946; Wandsworth Prison, London, England
ALSO KNOWN AS: Lord Haw Haw
MAJOR OFFENSE: Treason
ACTIVE: September, 1939-September, 1940
LOCALE: Germany
SENTENCE: Death by hanging

EARLY LIFE

William Joyce (joys) was born in New York City. His parents were native Britons who had emigrated to the United States. Joyce's father, Michael, who left Ireland as a teenager, was naturalized as a U.S. citizen in 1894. The Joyce family eventually returned to the British Isles, first to Ireland in 1909 and then England in 1921. It became clear when he was enrolled in university that Joyce's heart lay not in academe but rather in politics. Beginning in 1923, Joyce was an active participant in a British fascist group that lionized Benito Mussolini and, later, Adolf Hitler.

BROADCAST CAREER

About a year after Oswald Mosley began the British Union of Fascists (BUF) in 1932, Joyce signed on, soon

becoming propaganda director. He and Mosley fell out in 1937, with Joyce forming his own National Socialist League (NSL). Joyce proved a mesmerizing speaker, though he never was as well known as Mosley.

During the 1930's, Joyce obtained a British passport and renewed it several times. His purposes in traveling to the Continent were political; he wanted to observe Hitler at close hand. In the summer of 1939, as tensions mounted between Britain and Germany, Joyce decided he could not continue to live in England. On August 24, 1939, he applied for a one-year passport renewal, repeating an earlier affirmation that he was a British subject. Joyce and his wife Margaret departed from England by boat on August 26, 1939.

Upon arrival in Germany, Joyce quickly put himself at the service of the Nazi apparatus. Soon he secured a job with the Reichsrundfunk (RRF), the radio propaganda operations headed by Joseph Goebbels. Joyce remained the Germans' favorite English-language radio spokesperson throughout the war. In addition, he directed the process of recruiting British POWs (usually under duress) as radio speakers.

Through radio broadcasts and recordings, Joyce became quite well known as a personality in English-speaking areas of the world, including Canada and the

United States. His sneering and pseudo-aristocratic speaking style earned him the derisive nickname "Lord Haw Haw."

The Allies captured Joyce in late May, 1945, in a village near the Danish border. Despite the fact that the British were actively searching for him, the Joyces were identified by accident. Joyce was gathering firewood, and some Allied soldiers nearby engaged him in casual conversation. When he replied to them, one of the Englishmen recognized his voice.

LEGAL ACTION AND OUTCOME

The most important charge against Joyce was that he had violated the Act of Treason of 1351. That law defined treason as giving aid and comfort to the king's enemies. The act also made clear that treason could consist of committing such an offense not only within England but also outside the geographical confines of the realm.

The allegation against him that proved most critical in Joyce's conviction was the charge that he had committed treason between September 18, 1939, and July 2, 1940 (the date of his first known employment at the RRF and the date that his last British passport expired). Joyce's alleged offense was the radio broadcasting of propaganda.

As the trial began, the issue of Joyce's American birth was raised immediately by the defense as a barrier to his being convicted. The judge, however, ruled that because he held a British passport, Joyce was required to refrain from adhering to Britain's enemy. The jury—who remembered the horrors of the Blitz and Joyce's radio taunting—clearly were unsympathetic to Joyce. He was sentenced to hang.

Joyce's case went as far as the House of Lords and there garnered one famous, if narrow, judicial argument for the conviction's being overturned. However, in the end, Joyce's appeals failed. He was executed in early January, 1946.

IMPACT

In the immediate wake of William Joyce's execution, several legal and historical experts maintained in books and law journal articles that the prosecution and execution of Joyce were troubling. To these scholars, Joyce's trial and execution did not have to be an inevitable outcome of his capture by Allied forces. They frequently echoed a vital point that was raised by Joyce's attorneys: Since Joyce was by birth an American citizen, he should not have been required to show allegiance to the British government. In the 1940's, as well as in the decades since his death, the fate of Lord Haw Haw has inspired discussions among scholars about the definition of treason and the nature of citizenship.

FURTHER READING

Cole, J. A. *Lord Haw Haw and William Joyce: The Full Story*. New York: Farrar, Strauss, and Giroux, 1964. Filled with illustrative detail, Cole's biography of Joyce explores his relationship with Fascists in England and on the Continent.

Hall, J. W., ed. *The Trial of William Joyce*. London: W. Hodge, 1946. Hall's study of the Joyce case was published as a number of the prestigious Notable British Trials series. Hall includes detailed records of the original trial as well as arguments and decisions on appeal.

Joyce, William. *Twilight over England*. Berlin: Internationaler Verlag, 1940. Joyce provided justification for his own actions in this autobiographical account.

Kenney, Mary. *Germany Calling*. Dublin: New Island Books, 2003. In her biographical study of Joyce, Kenney places emphasis on Joyce's Irish roots and his style as a broadcaster.

Martland, Peter. *Lord Haw Haw: The English Voice of Nazi Germany*. London: National Archives, 2003. Using government files opened in the early twenty-first century, Martland carefully pieces together a picture of what British intelligence knew about Joyce.

West, Rebecca. *The Meaning of Treason*. London: Macmillan, 1949. West wrote as a reporter who sat in on Joyce's trials and who also recalled the horrors of the war. She argued passionately for Joyce's conviction.

—*Elisabeth Cawthon*

SEE ALSO: Charles E. Coughlin; Mildred Gillars; Sir Oswald Mosley; Tokyo Rose.

JUDAS ISCARIOT
Jewish apostle of Jesus Christ

BORN: First century B.C.E.; Kerioth, Judaea (now in Israel)

DIED: c. 30 C.E.; Jerusalem, Judaea (now in Israel)

ALSO KNOWN AS: The One Who Betrayed Christ

CAUSE OF NOTORIETY: According to the New Testament, Judas was the apostle who betrayed Jesus Christ to arresting Roman soldiers, an act that ultimately led to the crucifixion of Jesus.

ACTIVE: c. 30 C.E.

LOCALE: Jerusalem, Judaea (now in Israel)

EARLY LIFE

No historical information exists that documents details about the early life of Judas Iscariot (JEW-duhs ihs-KAHR-ee-uht). The Gospels of John and Matthew in the Bible's New Testament are the primary source for the story of Judas. John records Judas's father's name as Simon but nothing else. Debate has occurred about the designation "Iscariot." One suggestion is that the term is derived from a Greek word for dagger, which lent its name to the Sicarii, a group of Jewish nationalists and assassins who opposed the Roman occupation of Judaea. As Jesus attracted other revolutionaries, such as Simon the Zealot, speculation suggests that Judas may have had a similar background. Traditionally, however, New Testament scholars derive "Iscariot" from a Hebrew word that means "man of Kerioth," a town located in southern Judah.

APOSTOLIC CAREER

Judas joined the ministry of Jesus and became one of the Twelve Apostles; he should not be confused with another Judas, the son of James. He held a prominent leadership role among the disciples as their treasurer, but within the Gospels, he remains anonymously linked with the other eleven men. However, during the Passion Week, he moved to the forefront of the group. He clashed with Jesus over the use of expensive perfume when a woman of questionable reputation anointed his head. Judas next made his way to the chief priests and agreed to betray Jesus for thirty pieces of silver.

The opportunity to complete his bargain came after what is known as the Last Supper. Jesus indicated his knowledge of Judas's duplicity during an earlier defection of other disciples from his ministry, but during the meal, Jesus explicitly announced the presence of a traitor. In the midst of the ensuing uproar, Jesus revealed to the apostle John that Judas was the culprit by means of passing him a piece of bread. When Jesus sent Judas away, the others believed that he went to perform an act of benevolence. In actuality, Judas gathered soldiers and took them to the Garden of Gethsemane, a customary retreat for Jesus. Judas identified Jesus with a traditional kiss of greeting, alerting the soldiers to the identity of the man whom they were seeking.

Remorse led Judas to return the money and hang himself. The Jewish leadership took the money and purchased a potter's field, known as the Field of Blood. In

Judas leaves the high priests.

the story's recounting in the New Testament's book of Acts, however, Judas purchased the field himself and fell upon it, perhaps from a precipice, and his bowels burst forth. Later, Saint Augustine attempted to reconcile these passages by claiming that Judas's corpse was left hanging until it rotted and split open.

IMPACT

Judas Iscariot's motivations have been the subject of speculation. The biblical account indicates Satanic possession, but more psychological explanations have been put forth, such as simple greed, based on the apostle John's accusation of theft. A more complex motivation is that Judas became disenchanted with Jesus. Thus, an arrest might force Jesus to call his followers to revolution in order to rescue him. That the disciples misunderstood the nature of Jesus' "kingdom" is evident in their debates about their status. The texts, however, do not offer enough evidence to substantiate such speculation.

Judas became known as the archetype for betrayal. The use of "Judas" as a label is synonymous with an accusation of treachery. Ironically, Judas's actions inevitably shaped a theological understanding of Jesus' death as an atoning sacrifice for the sins of humanity and laid the foundation for Christianity.

THE GOSPEL OF JUDAS

In 2004 a scholar announced the existence of the gospel of Judas at a conference. This nonbiblical gospel was already known from scattered references among early Christian writers, but no copy had come to light until one appeared on the antiquities "gray market," and the National Geographic Society eventually bought it. It was edited and translated by Rodolphe Kasser, Marvin Meyer, and Gregor Wurst, and published by the Society in 2006.

The manuscript dates from between 220 and 340 C.E., but the text itself was written sometime between 130 and 180 C.E. It belongs to an ancient tradition of secret spiritual knowledge that was supposed to lead its adepts to salvation. The tradition, called Gnosticism, combined ideas from ancient religions, Greek philosophy, and, eventually, Christianity. Specifically, it comes from the Sethian branch of Gnosticism, which considered Adam's son Seth as humanity's spiritual leader, the Christ.

The text is fragmentary. Large sections of the gospel are missing. However, several matters are evident. The gospel concerns a series of conversations with the Apostles that took place three weeks before Jesus celebrated his last Passover. In one, the disciples relate to Jesus a dream vision of a temple, and to their dismay and anger, he interprets it as evidence that they do not understand his teaching. He suggests that they "have planted trees without fruit, in my name, in a shameful manner." Jesus laughs a good deal during these conversations, apparently amused at the pretension and waywardness of those seeking knowledge beyond their abilities.

Only Judas is singled out as capable of understanding. To him alone Jesus offers special explanations in cryptic (and fragmentary) numerological and astrological language. He does so, however, only after laughing at Judas and affectionately teasing him for his eagerness to please: "You thirteenth spirit, why do you try so hard?"

Jesus and Judas also appear to plan together Jesus's betrayal to the Roman authorities. Judas carries it out even though Jesus hints that the other disciples will stone him for it. The gospel concludes:

[S]ome scribes were there watching carefully in order to arrest [Jesus] during the prayer, for they were afraid of the people, since he was regarded by all as a prophet. They approached Judas and said to him, "What are you doing here? You are Jesus' disciple."

Judas answered them as they wished. And he received some money and handed him over to them.

FURTHER READING

Beasley-Murray, George. *John*. 2d ed. Waco, Tex: Word Books, 1999. One of the best commentaries, albeit technical, on the Gospel of John; it uses Greek within the comments.

Edersheim, Alfred. *The Life and Times of Jesus the Messiah*. Grand Rapids, Mich.: Eerdmans, 1981. Although somewhat dated and occasionally devotional in nature, Edersheim's analysis attempts to put events in a historical context and discuss Judas's motivations.

McBirnie, William. *The Search for the Twelve Apostles*. Wheaton, Ill.: Tyndale House, 1982. A dated work but valuable for its collection of Roman Catholic traditions about the lives of the Apostles within the New Testament and afterward.

Morris, Leon. *The Gospel According to John*. Rev. ed. Grand Rapids, Mich.: Eerdmans, 1995. A commentary that examines the book of John and makes it accessible to the general reader.

—*Todd W. Ewing*

SEE ALSO: Barabbas; Herod Antipas; Jezebel; Pontius Pilate; Salome.

JUSTIN II
Byzantine emperor (r. 565-578)

BORN: c. 520 C.E.; Balkans
DIED: October 5, 578 C.E.; Constantinople, Byzantine Empire (now Istanbul, Turkey)
ALSO KNOWN AS: Flavius Justinus (birth name)
CAUSE OF NOTORIETY: Justin's policies contributed to the beginnings of the downfall of Byzantine Empire; his reign was marred by his mental illness.
ACTIVE: 565-578
LOCALE: Constantinople, Byzantine Empire

EARLY LIFE
Very little is known of the childhood or youth of Justin (JUHS-tihn). His exact date of birth and birthplace are unknown. His mother was Vigilantia, sister of the famous Byzantine emperor Justinian. Justin married Sophia, niece of the empress Theodora, Justinian's wife. The first mention of Justin in history describes his involvment in a diplomatic mission in 552 to Pope Vigilius (537-555).

POLITICAL CAREER
Most contemporary histories cover Justin's life once he became emperor. His reign immediately followed that of Emperor Justinian and the infamous Empress Theodora. Justin began his imperial career by overturning some of Justinian's unpopular decrees, which helped Justin's own popularity. Because of his lack of military experience, he relied heavily on others to direct his foreign endeavors. These were largely unsuccessful, and Justin lost many of the gains Justinian had achieved in Africa, Italy, and Spain. Part of the reason for these reversals was Justin's failure to supply his troops adequately. He also decided to attack Persia, an empire that most of his advisers (and earlier emperors) felt was better to leave alone.

Justin's ecclesiastical conflicts were contradictory to Justinian's policies of diplomacy and reconciliation. Justin exacerbated several problematic situations, for example with the various Monophysite bishops and their followers. Justin eventually jailed most of those bishops, outlawed Monophysitism, and stopped all further attempts at reconciliation.

In 573 Justin decided to attack Dara (a border city between the Byzantine and Persian Empires, today in southeastern Turkey, near Oğuz). He put his cousin Marcian in charge but again failed to support the troops with enough personnel and supplies. By November, 573, the Persian king Khusrau took the city. This failure may have caused Justin to lapse into mental illness; among his many reac-

tions to losing Dara were hiding under his bed, barking like a dog, and crowing like a rooster. More than once he tried to throw himself out windows. His attendants could calm him down by pulling him around in a wagon or by telling him that a sort of Byzantine boogeyman (called Bogle) was looking for him, at which Justin would become quiet, then run and hide. His wife, Sophia, took over Justin's duties for him until she could get Justin, during a brief period of lucidity, to grant his friend and military commander Tiberius the titles of caesar and regent of the empire. Tiberius then ruled for Justin until Justin's death.

IMPACT
Most contemporary historians blamed Justin II for the beginnings of the downfall of the Byzantine Empire, although a few praised him extensively. Justin did lose a great amount of land that Justinian had reconquered for the empire, land that the Byzantines would never fully recover. This could be viewed as the beginnings of the decline of the Byzantine Empire; it certainly would never again be as large as it had been. Justin's conflict with the Monophysites was inconclusive; the religion would survive until the time of the Fourth Crusade (1204).

FURTHER READING
Kroll, Jerome, and Bernard Bachrach. "Justin's Madness: Weak-Mindedness or Organic Psychosis?" *Journal of the History of Medicine and Allied Sciences* 48 (1993): 40-67. Examines possible origins and causes of Justin's mental instabilities by reference to modern psychoanalysis. Excellent footnotes on other aspects of Justin's political and personal life.
Menander. *The History of Menander the Guardsman.* Translated with an introduction and notes by R. C. Blockley. Liverpool, England: F. Cairns, 1985. This work contains Manander's Greek text, preceded by textual analysis. Although only fragments remain of Menander's history, it covers the years 557-582, including accounts of Justin's entire reign.
Treadgold, Warren. *A History of the Byzantine State and Society.* Stanford, Calif.: Stanford University Press, 1997. Covers in detail the history of the Byzantine Empire. Includes an excellent, succinct chapter on Justin. Examines political and ecclesiastical conflicts as well as Justin's later madness.

—Michael T. Martin

SEE ALSO: Theodora.

THEODORE KACZYNSKI
American murderer

BORN: May 22, 1942; Chicago, Illinois
ALSO KNOWN AS: The Unabomber; Theodore John Kaczynski (full name)
MAJOR OFFENSES: Murder and attempted murder
ACTIVE: 1978, 1979, 1980, 1981, 1982, 1985, 1987, 1993, 1994, and 1995
LOCALE: Illinois; Washington, D.C.; Utah; Tennessee; California; Washington State; Michigan; Connecticut; and New Jersey
SENTENCE: Life in prison without the possibility of parole

EARLY LIFE

Theodore Kaczynski (KA-zihn-skee) was born in 1942 in Chicago, Illinois, the eldest of two children. From an early age he demonstrated that he was an exceptionally bright and gifted child. His intelligence allowed him to skip two grades in school and eventually enter Harvard University at the age of sixteen to study mathematics. While at Harvard he became part of a psychological experiment linked to mind control that may have been a contributing factor to his future criminality.

After completing his undergraduate degree, he went to the University of Michigan in 1962, where he would finish a Ph.D. in mathematics. His brilliance was acknowledged again with awards, and he soon found himself with a job teaching mathematics at the University of California at Berkeley. Two years after beginning the job in 1967, he suddenly quit and never again held a full-time position.

CRIMINAL CAREER

Over the following nine years, Kaczynski drifted through menial jobs and began living in a primitive shack on land in Montana that he and his brother had bought in 1971. In 1978, Kaczynski launched his bombing campaign, which would continue, off and on, for the following seventeen years. The focus of his attacks would be on those tied in some way to modern technology, which he blamed for, in effect, enslaving individuals and depriving them of freedom and happiness.

His first target in May, 1978, was Northwestern University, where a bomb left in a parking lot injured one person. The following year a bomb exploded in the hold of a passenger jetliner, forcing the plane to make an emergency landing. A major police investigation into the case under the code name "Unabomb" (from "university

and airline bomber") was under way by 1980, when another attack targeted an airline executive. Eventually, Kaczynski would be nicknamed the Unabomber. He proved elusive because he built his own bombs, bombed geographically dispersed targets, and allowed lengthy intervals between attacks.

In December, 1985, his attacks reached a new level of seriousness when one of his bombs killed a Sacramento computer dealer. In 1987, Kaczynski made his first major mistake when a woman spotted him planting a bomb outside a Salt Lake City computer store. Her testimony led to the creation of a composite drawing of the Unabomber, but, fortunately for Kaczynski, sunglasses and a hooded tracksuit obscured his visage.

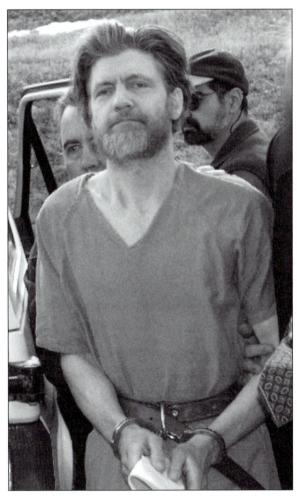

Theodore Kaczynski. (AP/Wide World Photos)

THE UNABOMBER'S MANIFESTO

Ted Kaczynski, the Unabomber, wrote a long, rambling manifesto bewailing the ills of industrial society, excerpted below. The full text was published on September 19, 1995, by both The Washington Post *and* The New York Times *in an attempt to elicit leads to the identity of a domestic terrorist who had been threatening havoc for seventeen years. It begins with an indictment of modern industrial society:*

1. The Industrial Revolution and its consequences have been a disaster for the human race. They have greatly increased the life-expectancy of those of us who live in "advanced" countries, but they have destabilized society, have made life unfulfilling, have subjected human beings to indignities, have led to widespread psychological suffering (in the Third World to physical suffering as well) and have inflicted severe damage on the natural world. The continued development of technology will worsen the situation. It will certainly subject human beings to greater indignities and inflict greater damage on the natural world, it will probably lead to greater social disruption and psychological suffering, and it may lead to increased physical suffering even in "advanced" countries.

2. The industrial-technological system may survive or it may break down. If it survives, it MAY eventually achieve a low level of physical and psychological suffering, but only after passing through a long and very painful period of adjustment and only at the cost of permanently reducing human beings and many other living organisms to engineered products and mere cogs in the social machine. Furthermore, if the system survives, the consequences will be inevitable: There is no way of reforming or modifying the system so as to prevent it from depriving people of dignity and autonomy.

3. If the system breaks down the consequences will still be very painful. But the bigger the system grows the more disastrous the results of its breakdown will be, so if it is to break down it had best break down sooner rather than later.

4. We therefore advocate a revolution against the industrial system. This revolution may or may not make use of violence: it may be sudden or it may be a relatively gradual process spanning a few decades. We can't predict any of that. But we do outline in a very general way the measures that those who hate the industrial system should take in order to prepare the way for a revolution against that form of society. This is not to be a POLITICAL revolution. Its object will be to overthrow not governments but the economic and technological basis of the present society.

5. In this article we give attention to only some of the negative developments that have grown out of the industrial-technological system. Other such developments we mention only briefly or ignore altogether. This does not mean that we regard these other developments as unimportant. For practical reasons we have to confine our discussion to areas that have received insufficient public attention or in which we have something new to say. For example, since there are well-developed environmental and wilderness movements, we have written very little about environmental degradation or the destruction of wild nature, even though we consider these to be highly important.

Then, for reasons that are still not known, Kaczynski went into a hiatus for six years before beginning his attacks again in June, 1993, with two separate bombings. In the following two years his bombs killed two more people. By then he had also begun to attempt to publicize his reasons for committing his crimes by contacting the media. Through the threat of further attacks, Kaczynski pressured both *The Washington Post* and *The New York Times* into publishing a thirty-five-thousand-word manifesto he had written.

Among the readers of this work was his brother, David Kaczynski. Based on the ideas in the manifesto, David suspected that it was the work of Ted and contacted the Federal Bureau of Investigation (FBI) with this information. On April 3, 1996, the FBI arrested the suspected Unabomber at his cabin in Montana.

LEGAL ACTION AND OUTCOME

Soon after his arrest, Kaczynski was officially indicted for the Unabomber attacks. The trial was officially set to begin in January, 1998, but Kaczynski soon found himself at odds with his defense lawyers, who sought to argue that he was not guilty on the grounds of insanity. Kaczynski, on the other hand, wanted to defend his case on political grounds and attempted to fire his lawyers. Eventually, he made a deal with the prosecution and pleaded guilty in order to avoid the death penalty. He later tried to change his mind with respect to his plea, but this was rejected, and he began serving a life sentence.

IMPACT

In addition to the deaths of innocent people caused by Ted Kaczynski's violence, his crimes had a complex impact. Each one generated widespread publicity and fear because of its detailed planning and the mystery surrounding the attacker. Kaczynski's bombings sparked a major police effort that, in the end, demonstrated the powerlessness of the authorities. They did not catch Kaczynski—he was apprehended because his own writings led his brother to turn him in. Finally, his crimes drew more public attention to the issue of terrorism, although his attacks would pale in comparison to those carried out by Timothy McVeigh in Oklahoma in 1995 and by the September 11, 2001, hijackers.

FURTHER READING

Chase, Alton. *Harvard and the Unabomber: The Education of an American Terrorist*. New York: W. W. Norton, 2003. An interesting attempt to explain the cause of Kaczynski's behavior by linking his crimes to his involvement in psychological experiments at Harvard.

Gelernter, David. *Drawing Life: Surviving the Unabomber*. New York: Free Press, 1997. A personal account by a computer scientist who was wounded by a Kaczynski bomb in 1993.

Graysmith, Robert. *Unabomber: A Desire to Kill*. New York: Regnery, 1997. An examination of the Unabomber case written shortly after Kaczynski's capture.

Kaczynski, Theodore. *The Unabomber Manifesto: Industrial Society and Its Future*. New York: Jolly Roger Press, 1995. Kaczynski's manifesto, issued before his capture. It blames technology for the ills of society and calls for its elimination in the name of humanity's survival.

—Steve Hewitt

SEE ALSO: Timothy McVeigh; Terry Nichols; Ilich Ramírez Sánchez; Eric Rudolph.

LAZAR KAGANOVICH
Soviet Politburo member

BORN: November 22, 1893; Kabany, near Kiev, Ukraine, Russian Empire (now in Ukraine)
DIED: July 25, 1991; Moscow, Soviet Union (now in Russia)
ALSO KNOWN AS: Lazar Moiseyevich Kaganovich (full name); Iron Commissar; Wolf of the Kremlin; Zhirovich
CAUSE OF NOTORIETY: A high-ranking Soviet official, Kaganovich enthusiastically supported Joseph Stalin's mass purges and forced collectivization, which resulted in the deaths of millions of Soviet citizens.
ACTIVE: 1917-1964
LOCALE: Soviet Union, mostly Moscow

EARLY LIFE

Lazar Kaganovich (LAY-zur kah-gah-NOH-vihch) was born in 1893 in the Ukraine to Jewish parents; his father was a tailor. At a young age, he worked in a shoe factory. When Kaganovich was eighteen, he heard a speech by the fiery revolutionary Leon Trotsky and joined the Bolsheviks, the most radical of Russia's Marxist parties. He helped foment the Bolshevik revolution of 1917 under the alias "Zhirovich." After the Bolsheviks established the Soviet Union as the world's first communist state, Kaganovich fought in the Soviet Red Army against

counterrevolutionary forces. He then began a rapid rise within the Soviet political system.

POLITICAL CAREER

A talented administrator, Kaganovich was quickly promoted as a favorite of Joseph Stalin, the dictator of the Soviet Union. Advancing swiftly in the ranks of the Soviet Communist Party, Kaganovich became a section leader of the Soviet Secretariat in 1922, a member of the Central Committee in 1924, first secretary of the Ukraine in 1925, and a member of the Politburo—the inner circle of Soviet rulers—in 1930. As a powerful commissar of the people, Kaganovich oversaw transport (1935-1937), heavy industry (1937-1939), and the fuel industry (1939). During World War II, he served as a deputy premier and as a member of the State Defense Committee.

During the 1930's, Kaganovich gained a reputation as Stalin's most loyal, tireless, and efficient subordinate. As head of the Party Control Commission, he helped collectivize Soviet farms and liquidate the class of kulaks (landowners) in the Ukraine and Siberia. During Stalin's great terror of 1936-1938, Kaganovich conducted a ruthless purge of the industrial sector and thus bears responsibility for as many as a half million deaths. Kaganovich opposed any attempt to relax repression for political offenses. Some historians have also assigned him blame for the horrendous famine in the Ukraine between 1932 and 1933.

Throughout the terror, Stalin systematically liquidated the former Bolshevik leadership. Taking their place was a new group of party functionaries who were ruthless and absolutely servile to Stalin: men such as Kaganovich, Secret Police Chief Lavrenty Beria, Nikita S. Khrushchev (a protégé of Kaganovich and eventual leader of the Soviet Union), Georgi M. Malenkov, and Vyacheslav Mikhailovich Molotov. As members of Stalin's inner circle, Kaganovich and the others participated in Stalin's macabre all-night drunken parties. Kaganovich also shared in the cult of personality of Stalin. In charge of the massive reconstruction of Moscow, Kaganovich was honored with the Order of Lenin, the Soviet Union's highest award; he also had a battleship and the Moscow subway named for him.

DE-STALINIZATION

In the vicious power struggle after Stalin's death in 1953, Khrushchev rose to power as party leader. In 1956, Khrushchev, himself a former Stalin loyalist, denounced the cult of Stalin and launched a campaign of de-Stalinization, exposing Stalin's former henchmen to imminent danger. Kaganovich was relegated to the Anti-party Group, and along with Malenkov and Molotov, he was accused of trying to overthrow Khrushchev in June, 1957. Kaganovich was expelled from the Presidium and sent to manage a cement factory in the Urals. In 1964, he was expelled from the Communist Party. He died in 1991 at the age of ninety-seven.

IMPACT

Even in his old age, Lazar Kaganovich remained a private but unabashed defender of Joseph Stalin and Stalinism. In such recorded conversations as those with Feliks Chuev and the disputed interviews with Stuart Kahan, Kaganovich continued to praise Stalin as the leading light of the Soviet Union. Kaganovich's impact can be seen in two spheres: as Stalin's henchman when Stalin was alive and as the continuing true believer following Stalin's death. During Stalin's dictatorship, Kaganovich was third in power, subordinate only to Stalin and Beria in responsibility for carrying out Stalin's campaign of ruthless collectivization, industrialization, purges, and mass murder. Kaganovich combined administrative expertise with absolute devotion to Stalin and an apparent belief that the defense of the Russian Revolution justified any cruelty and loss of life. While Kaganovich always played the role of unassuming toady, his culpability remained unquestionable, as attested by his former protégé Nikita Khrushchev (who discussed Kaganovich in his 1970 memoirs) and by historians such as Robert Conquest.

FURTHER READING

Chuev, Feliks. *Tak govoril Kaganovich*. Moscow: Otechestvo, 1992. Although in Russian, this book, translated as *Thus Spake Kaganovich*, brings together invaluable conversations between Chuev and Kaganovich near the end of Kaganovich's life.

Conquest, Robert. *The Great Terror: A Reassessment*. New York: Oxford University Press, 1991. Conquest, a leading historian of Stalin's reign of terror, records Kaganovich's ruthless role in the purges of the 1930's.

Kahan, Stuart. *The Wolf of the Kremlin: First Biography of L. M. Kaganovich, the Soviet Union's Architect of Fear*. London: Robert Hale, 1989. A controversial biography of Kaganovich, attacked by Kaganovich's heirs for questionable assertions, including that Kaganovich had a sister, Rosa, who became Stalin's third wife.

Khrushchev, Nikita. *Khrushchev Remembers*. Translated and edited by Strobe Talbot. Boston: Little, Brown, 1970. In these memoirs, emanating from various sources, Khrushchev describes his former mentor Kaganovich as a vicious and despicable lackey of Stalin.

Rappaport, Helen. *Joseph Stalin: A Biographical Companion*. Santa Barbara, Calif.: ABC-CLIO, 1999. Organized by topics, an encyclopedic guide to the events and people in the life of the Soviet dictator.

The Stalin-Kaganovich Correspondence: 1931-1936. New Haven, Conn.: Yale University Press, 2003. This collection of 177 letters reveals Stalin's consolidation of his power in the course of receiving information from his perhaps most trusted subordinate—Kaganovich.

—*Howard Bromberg*

SEE ALSO: Lavrenty Beria; Nikita S. Khrushchev; Vyacheslav Mikhailovich Molotov; Joseph Stalin.

MEIR KAHANE
American Israeli activist

BORN: August 1, 1932; Brooklyn, New York
DIED: November 5, 1990; New York, New York
ALSO KNOWN AS: Martin David Kahane (full name); Michael King; David Sinai; Hayim Yerushalmi
CAUSE OF NOTORIETY: Kahane founded the Jewish Defense League in 1968, thus helping to incite racially based hatred of Arabs.
ACTIVE: 1968-1990
LOCALE: United States and Israel

EARLY LIFE
Meir Kahane (MI-yur kah-HAH-neh) was born in Brooklyn, New York, into an Orthodox Jewish family. His father, Rabbi Charles Kahane, had been born in Safed (then Palestine, now Israel), and his grandfather had traveled to Palestine from Poland. Perhaps the most influential event in Meir Kahane's childhood was an ambush in 1938 in Palestine in which Charles Kahane's sister-in-law was among those killed. This event led to Charles Kahane's allying himself with some of the more radical elements trying to create a Jewish state in Palestine, and to Meir Kahane's early antagonism toward Arabs. He tried to avoid mention of the murder in discussing his own history for fear of giving the impression that his hostility to the Arabs was a personal vendetta.

From an early age, Meir Kahane was involved in violent expressions of his political opinions. Even before the creation of the state of Israel in 1948, Kahane took part in a New York-based attack on the British foreign secretary to protest the British government's limitations on Jewish immigration to Palestine. This was to typify Kahane's career as an attempt to publicize protests against groups with which he disagreed (whether it was the British, African Americans, the Soviets, or the Arabs). How Kahane spent the following few decades is not entirely clear, but he was married and had children within the Jewish community during this period. He was also accused of having had extramarital affairs and serving as an informer.

POLITICAL CAREER
Kahane reentered the public sphere with the foundation in 1968 of the Jewish Defense League. This was consciously an echo of the various organizations promoting black power, and the emblem of the group was a Star of David (a six-pointed star) with a clenched fist. With a

motto of Never Again (in reference to the murder of millions of Jews by the Nazis during the Holocaust during World War II), the group claimed to focus on protecting Jews from attacks by blacks in neighborhoods where the two ethnic groups lived together. Kahane also advocated a return to Jewish tradition, although his interpretation of such tradition involved a readiness to use weapons with slight provocation.

From the issue of protecting Jews in New York, Kahane turned the Jewish Defense League's focus to the situation of Jews not allowed to emigrate from the Soviet Union. The group's course of leading protests against the Soviet Union involved several acts of violence, and in 1971 Kahane was tried on charges of conspiracy to violate the Federal Firearms Act. His receiving a suspended sentence of five years probably led to his decision to emigrate to Israel.

Even after moving to Israel, however, Kahane made frequent fund-raising trips to the United States. Subsequent court actions included his conviction after shots were fired at the Soviet Mission to the United Nations. After the massacre of Israeli athletes at the Olympic Games in Munich in 1972, Kahane figured that support could be gained in calling for the expulsion of Arabs from Israel; he ran for the Knesset (the Israeli Parliament) and was narrowly defeated. His second run for office was even less successful, and he was subsequently barred from seeking elected office in Israel.

After Kahane's electoral setbacks, he continued to be vocal in his demands that Israel be a Jewish state, even if that meant its not being democratic. After the Camp David peace accords with Egypt in 1978, Kahane was even less inclined to compromise, and he was placed in administrative detention in 1980 after the discovery of a cache of ammunition at a yeshiva (Jewish academy for study) near the Western Wall in Jerusalem.

Then, in 1984, Kahane's political party broke through, and he was elected to the Knesset with 1.2 percent of the popular vote. The attempt to bar his party from competing for office had been overturned by the Israeli court. Many of the leading figures in the Israeli government were disinclined to have anything to do with a figure who had espoused views as hostile to the Arabs as Kahane's. These politicians pointed to Kahane's willingness to give up majority rule as a feature of government and to his disagreements with the document on which the Israeli government was founded. Legislation was passed, with

Kahane as the target, to prevent parties from running candidates if their platforms included incitement to racism.

After being barred from running in the 1987 elections, Kahane persevered in his protests and his fund-raising while out of office. In November, 1990, he was fatally shot in the streets of New York; his assailant was identified as an Islamic extremist. Various political parties claimed to inherit Kahane's mantle, including one headed by his son, but none could boast a figure quite so able to capture popular attention as Kahane had been.

IMPACT

Some actors in the international political scene had doubts about the ability of Israel to deal satisfactorily with its Arab population. Meir Kahane made his conviction about the impossibility of coexistence the center of his political agenda. This attitude, combined with a readiness to use violence against the Arab community, helped to remind the public that Jewish extremists as well as Palestinian extremists indulged in excesses. In 1994, Baruch Goldstein killed a number of Arabs in Hebron, Israel, claiming to have been inspired by Kahane's ideas. Kahane's legacy is a spiral of violence which created much of the distrust that hung over Israeli-Palestinian negotiations in later years.

FURTHER READING

Cohen-Almagor, Raphael. *The Boundary of Liberty and Tolerance: The Struggle Against Kahanism in Israel.* Gainesville: University Press of Florida, 1994. Offers a scholarly assessment of how Kahane's views were received by Israel and the political and judicial reactions.

Elon, Amos. *A Blood-Dimmed Tide: Dispatches from the Middle East.* London: Penguin, 2000. Reprinting of the journalistic reactions to Kahane while he was alive by an informed observer.

Friedman, Robert J. *The False Prophet: Rabbi Meir Kahane, from FBI Informant to Knesset Member.* Chicago: Chicago Review Press, 1990. Viciously attacks Kahane's personal life but provides details hard to find elsewhere.

Herzog, Chaim. *Living History: A Memoir.* London: Weidenfeld and Nicolson, 1997. Autobiography by the president of Israel when Kahane was elected to the Knesset; presents his efforts to prevent Kahane's views from being given a platform.

Kotler, Yair. *Heil Kahane.* New York: Adama Books, 1986. As the title indicates, the author aligns Kahane with Fascism and criticizes his claims to represent traditional Judaism.

—Thomas Drucker

SEE ALSO: Baruch Goldstein.

FANYA KAPLAN
Anarchist and accused assailant of Vladimir Ilich Lenin

BORN: 1887; Volhynia Province, Ukraine, Russian Empire (now in Ukraine)
DIED: September 3, 1918; Moscow, Soviet Russia
ALSO KNOWN AS: Faiga Khaimovna Roitman (birth name); Fanya Yefimovna Kaplan (full name); Faiga Roitman Kaplan; Mitropolskaia; Dora Kaplan
MAJOR OFFENSES: Armed assault and attempted assassination of Lenin
ACTIVE: August 30, 1918
LOCALE: Moscow, Russia
SENTENCE: Eternal hard labor in the Maltsev prison in Siberia for armed assault conviction; execution for assassination attempt

EARLY LIFE
Fanya Kaplan (FAHN-ya KAP-lahn) was born as Faiga Khaimovna Roitman in 1887 in the Ukrainian rural

province Volhynia in czarist Russia's Settlement of the Pale. One of seven children born to a schoolteacher, Faiga was educated at home. While still in her teens, she left home and found work in Odessa in a women's hat factory. In the early years of the twentieth century, Russia was wracked by labor strikes, pogroms in the Pale, and violent revolutionary activity that increased in intensity with the start of the Russo-Japanese War in 1904. By 1906, Feiga had joined the anarchist movement. Her marriage to a man named Kaplan enabled her to obtain an internal passport that in turn allowed her to move out of the Pale and into the restricted town of Kiev.

CRIMINAL CAREER
Faiga, now using Fanya Yefimovna Kaplan as her revolutionary name, and two other anarchists rented a hotel

room in Podol, the Jewish quarter of Kiev, where they plotted to assassinate the governor general of Kiev. On December 22, 1906, their explosives detonated unexpectedly. The three anarchists fled the hotel, but Kaplan, slightly injured and somewhat disoriented, alone was arrested. Because the blast had killed a hotel maid, Kaplan was tried and convicted of armed assault. On December 31, 1906, because she was only nineteen, her death sentence was commuted to eternal hard labor in the Maltsev prison in Siberia. Women prisoners were not required to work, and the prolonged isolation and confinement caused many to suffer from chronic diseases and mental illnesses. Kaplan developed severe, prolonged headaches and went completely blind. In 1912 and 1913, she was treated in other prison hospitals and recovered some of her sight.

Released from prison after the overthrow of the czar in 1917, Kaplan moved to Moscow in April, 1917, with former terrorist Anna Pigit. One year later, on August 30, 1918, as Bolshevik leader Vladimir Ilich Lenin was leaving the Mikhelson Armaments Factory, someone shot a pistol at him three times. One bullet wounded a woman talking to Lenin, and two bullets hit Lenin in the left shoulder, severely wounding him. The crowd dispersed rapidly except for Kaplan. When approached, she denied having done anything but was taken into custody. In a short time, she declared that she indeed had shot Lenin. She refused to name any accomplices and insisted that she had no affiliation with any political or revolutionary parties.

LEGAL ACTION AND OUTCOME

Kaplan did not request an open trial or clemency. On September 3, 1918, after three days of relatively light questioning, the commandant of the Kremlin executed Kaplan on the orders of Iakov M. Sverdlov, the acting head of the Council of People's Commissars while Lenin was incapacitated.

IMPACT

The assassination attempt against Lenin was used as a pretext to begin the infamous Red Terror, which was decreed within hours of Kaplan's shooting by calling for "a merciless mass terror against all the enemies of the revolution." Although no one could connect Kaplan directly to any organization, the first target of persecution of the terror was the Socialist Revolutionary Party; many believe that Fanya Kaplan was used as a pawn to discredit this party. When Lenin recovered from what were thought to have been mortal wounds, there emerged a Lenin cult, whose glorifications culminated in his mummification and public display following his death on January 24, 1924.

FURTHER READING

Fel'shtinskii, Iurii G. "The Mystery of Lenin's Death." Translated by Liv Bliss. *Russian Social Science Review* 45, no. 3 (July/August, 2004): 37-87. Argues that Kaplan's light interrogation and quick execution indicate that she was a pawn in a campaign to discredit and destroy the Socialist Revolutionary Party.

Lyandres, Semion. "The 1918 Attempt on the Life of Lenin: A New Look at the Evidence." *Slavic Review* 48, no. 3 (Autumn, 1989): 432-448. This seminal article, based on careful examination of all interrogations of Kaplan and the changing depositions of witnesses who testified in the 1922 show trials against members of the Socialist Revolutionary Party, argues that Kaplan could not have been the assailant.

Service, Robert. *A History of Modern Russia: From Nicholas II to Valdimir Putin.* 2d ed. Cambridge, Mass.: Harvard University Press, 2003. Service agrees with Lyandres that it was unlikely that Kaplan was the assailant of Lenin.

—*Paul E. Kuhl*

SEE ALSO: Vladimir Ilich Lenin; Ramón Mercader; Eligiusz Niewiadomski; Puniša Račić.

RADOVAN KARADŽIĆ
Serbian dictator (1992-1996)

BORN: June 19, 1945; Petnjica, Montenegro,
Yugoslavia (now in Serbia and Montenegro)

CAUSE OF NOTORIETY: In 1996, Karadžić became a
fugitive indicted for war crimes, genocide, and
plunder.

ACTIVE: 1991-1996

LOCALE: Bosnia-Herzegovina

EARLY LIFE
Radovan Karadžić (RAH-doh-vahn kah-RAD-jeech)
was born in the mountainous village of Petnjica, near
Šavnik, Montenegro, in Yugoslavia. His father, Vuko, had
been a member of the army of the anticommunist kingdom of Yugoslavia, which fought against the
Communist Tito; as a result Vuko spent the
majority of Karadžić's childhood in prison.
Karadžić's mother, Jovanka, raised her son
alone.

In 1960, Karadžić moved to Sarajevo, in
Bosnia-Herzegovina, to study psychiatry. He
met his wife, Ljiljana, there. After graduating, he worked as a doctor in the psychiatric
unit of the Kosevo Hospital. During his time
in Sarajevo, Karadžić became immersed in
poetry, writing it himself and also following
the nationalistic writer Dobrica Ćosić. He
developed a friendship with Ćosić, who convinced him to enter politics.

POLITICAL CAREER
In 1989, after working briefly with the Green
Party, Karadžić cofounded the Serbian Democratic Party (Srpska Demokratska Stranka)
in Bosnia-Herzegovina. The party's goal was
to bring together the republic's Serbian population and protect its culture and interests.

On March 3, 1992, Bosnia-Herzegovina
(later renamed the Serb Republic of Bosnia,
or Republika Srpska) declared its independence and was recognized by the United Nations (U.N.) as an independent state on April
6, 1992. Karadžić became the first president
of the Bosnian Serb administration on May
13, 1992. The freshly drafted Bosnian Serb
constitution gave Karadžić command of the
army and the authority to appoint and discharge its officers.

Karadžić used his power to begin a campaign to de-
moralize and terrorize the Bosnian Muslim and Bosnian
Croat populations. His armies forced non-Serbs to leave
areas deemed important to the new Serb republic. Those
who did not leave voluntarily were forcibly deported,
placed in deplorable refugee camps, or murdered.

Between April, 1992, and November, 1995, Karadžić's troops attacked Sarajevo. Thousands of civilians,
mainly women, children, and the elderly, were killed by
constant bombings and sniper fire. Those who survived
were forced to live without utilities and could venture
out of their shelters only at great risk to gather water and
supplies.

Posters showing Radovan Karadžić warn against his arrest. (AP/Wide
World Photos)

In 1993 the United Nations established an international war crimes tribunal to indict and prosecute those accused of crimes against humanity in the former Yugoslavia. Refugees, meanwhile, sought safety in rural border areas of Bosnia, which the United Nations had declared as security zones in April, 1993. These areas included Srebrenica, Zepa, Goražde, and Tuzla.

Between May 26 and June 2, 1995, Karadžić ordered his army to detain two hundred military observers and U.N. peacekeepers in Pale and Sarajevo in retaliation against North Atlantic Treaty Organization (NATO) air strikes. The hostages were held in key military sites in order to protect buildings from additional NATO strikes.

On July 6, 1995, Karadžić ordered his troops to raid the security zones and attack the U.N. observation posts. By July 12, the army had carried out a mass slaughter of civilians. An estimated fifteen thousand refugees, mostly men, attempted to flee the horrors but were summarily executed. Those who were spared were forced into detention camps where physical, psychological, and sexual abuse was constant. Thousands died at the hands of the camp guards or were executed en masse.

The United Nations estimated that Karadžić's forces were responsible for the deaths of at least seventy-five hundred Muslim men and boys in Srebrenica alone in 1995. Faced with growing international pressure, war crimes indictments, and impending Western sanctions, Karadžić was forced to resign his position in 1996.

LEGAL ACTION AND OUTCOME

As of the fall of 2006, there was an international arrest warrant for Karadžić, following Rule 61 of the International Criminal Tribunal for the former Yugoslavia (ICTY) in The Hague. Karadžić was accused of ordering his army to enact the "ethnic cleansing" of the Bosnian Muslims and Croats. After a 1996 indictment for war crimes and genocide he became a fugitive. The indictment charges him with two counts of genocide, five counts of crimes against humanity, three counts of violations of the laws or customs of war, and one count of grave breaches of the Geneva Conventions. He was also charged with the shelling of Sarajevo and using U.N. peacekeepers as human shields in 1995.

Karadžić denied all charges made against him and refused to recognize the U.N. tribunal as having any power. The United States government offered five million dollars for Karadžić's arrest.

IMPACT

In 2004, a Norwegian news agency produced a report stating that the Bosnia-Herzegovina war resulted in the deaths of more than 100,000 people, more than half of whom were civilians. These findings exclude those who died of indirect causes such as starvation, exposure, and lack of medical attention. A study by the Sarajevo Research and Documentation Center leaned toward a higher death count of 150,000.

The crimes against humanity that Radovan Karadžić inflicted upon non-Serb populations virtually destroyed a generation and left survivors both homeless and fearful.

After the publication of the final report of the Srebrenica Commission in 2004, detailing the atrocities Karadžić and his administration committed, Republika Srpska issued an apology for the Srebrenica massacre.

In 2005, the Bosnian Serb government made a plea for Karadžić's surrender. The officials stated that as long as he was a fugitive, their country would not be able to advance economically, politically, or psychologically. Because Karadžić and other war criminals remained fugitives, integration talks between Serbia and the European Community ceased in 2006. For his ability to remain a fugitive, Karadžić became something of a folk hero, with many Bosnian Serb supporters. They maintained that Karadžić was no more guilty of criminal acts than any other wartime leader and held public demonstrations in support of him.

FURTHER READING

Dormann, Knut. *Elements of War Crimes Under the Rome Statute of the International Criminal Court.* New York: Cambridge University Press, 2003. A thorough explanation of war crimes and how Karadžić violated laws of war.

Gutman, Roy. *Crimes of War.* New York: W. W. Norton, 1999. An examination of modern warfare and crimes against humanity.

Honig, Jan Willem. *Srebrenica: Record of a War Crime.* New York: Penguin Books, 1997. A detailed look into Bosnian massacre and those who were responsible.

—*Sara Vidar*

SEE ALSO: Slobodan Milošević; Ratko Mladić; Tito.

ALVIN KARPIS
American gangster

BORN: August 10, 1908; Montreal, Quebec, Canada
DIED: August 26, 1979; Torremolinos, Spain
ALSO KNOWN AS: Albin Karpowicz (birth name); Ray;
    Old Creepy
MAJOR OFFENSES: Bank robbery and kidnapping
ACTIVE: 1918-1979
LOCALE: Midwestern United States
SENTENCE: Life in prison; served thirty-four years

EARLY LIFE
Albin Karpowicz (KAHR-poh-vits) was born to Lithuanian immigrants by way of England and Canada. They settled in Topeka, Kansas, where Albin grew up. Albin's father farmed, did odd jobs, and worked as a painter for the Santa Fe Railroad. His mother raised Albin and three sisters. An elementary teacher changed Albin's name to Alvin Karpis (KAHR-puhs) because it was easier to pronounce.

CRIMINAL CAREER
By age ten, Alvin was running errands for petty criminals whom he admired in Topeka. An older boy then talked Karpis into burglarizing a store, a task that Karpis found thrilling. As a teenager, Karpis did honest work, performed the occasional burglary, and rode freight cars while carrying a loaded pistol. In 1926, he burglarized a warehouse and got five-to-ten years' time in a reformatory. He escaped with another prisoner and began a small-time crime wave. Caught and sent to a Kansas penitentiary, Karpis met Freddie Barker, who became his best friend and gang cofounder. Discharged in 1931 and schooled by older cons, Karpis partnered with Barker to rob banks because the larger sums attracted them.

In 1931, Karpis married Dorothy Slayman, the niece of a prostitute friend. They lived together for a few months before Karpis left her. Karpis soon dated sixteen-year-old Dolores Delaney, who gave birth to Raymond Alvin Karpis while she was in police custody in New Jersey. Karpis wrote that he read about the birth of his son while hiding in a Toledo, Ohio, brothel.

Karpis and Barker became professional criminals, taking great care in recruiting partners and planning robberies. They rented safe houses under aliases, parked getaway cars out of sight, plotted escape routes, and worked with "pros" such as Harvey Bailey, Volney Davis, and Barker's brother Doc. They stole more than one million dollars in four to five years' time. Their tricks included

abandoning getaway cars that pointed away from actual escape routes and letting their engines idle until the car ran out of fuel so that police concluded that the robbers had run out of gas while fleeing in that direction. The gang also threw roofing nails out windows to flatten tires on police cars. They robbed exclusively in the Midwest—a lucrative, flat geographic region for robbers in fast cars in the days before two-way police radios.

Karpis wanted as little trouble as possible when stealing, but he admired the fact that Barker never hesitated to kill if threatened. Karpis never admitted to shooting anyone, although it is probable that he did. Even as an old man, he was completely silent on his specific role in the crimes.

In 1933, Karpis and the gang abducted beer brewer William Hamm, Jr., and held him for a ransom of $100,000. The Federal Bureau of Investigation (FBI) arrested the wrong gang for the crime. In 1934, the men kidnapped bank president Edward Bremer, demanding a $200,000 ransom. The Bremers were friends of President Franklin D. Roosevelt, and extra pressure was put on the nascent FBI to catch Bremer's kidnappers. The FBI laboratory found Doc Barker's fingerprint on an empty gas can stashed near the ransom drop-off site. Working backward and sorting out details from other kidnappings and robberies, FBI agents discovered the existence of the Barker-Karpis gang.

LEGAL ACTION AND OUTCOME
In 1935, the FBI in Chicago captured Doc Barker and, from a map in his apartment, deduced the whereabouts of Freddie and his mother, Ma Barker. The FBI surrounded the pair's Lake Weir, Florida, cottage a few days later and shot them to death. J. Edgar Hoover, director of the FBI, encouraged the fiction that Ma was the leader of the gang, perhaps as a way to offset blame for her death at FBI agents' hands. Ma was actually an uneducated Arkansas woman who accepted and benefited from her sons' crimes. Karpis said she was his second mother, and the gang took her with them for cover.

Karpis found new partners and moved constantly—to Chicago; St. Paul, Minnesota; Toledo and Cleveland, Ohio; Hot Springs, Arkansas; and Cuba. He was apprehended in New Orleans in April, 1935, by surprised FBI agents, who saw him getting into his car. Agents had planned to raid Karpis's apartment later and probably kill him. An FBI car cut Karpis off before he pulled away, and an agent stuck a gun to his ear. Hoover told the press that he personally arrested Karpis, but in his 1971 autobiography, Karpis claimed that Hoover waited behind a building until it was safe. Indeed, Hoover was not among the arresting officers who improvised Karpis's capture, but he did appear shortly thereafter.

Karpis was sentenced to life in prison for kidnapping and went to Leavenworth, Kansas, and then to Alcatraz in 1936. He remained at Alcatraz until 1962, becoming the longest-serving inmate on Alcatraz as a result of his twenty-five years there. He was then sent to McNeil Island Penitentiary in Puget Sound, Washington, where he spent another seven years in prison before his release in 1969; he was sent back to his native Canada.

Karpis wrote *The Alvin Karpis Story* with Bill Trent in 1971. He then moved to Spain, where he invested money in a Montreal pizza business that later failed. He wrote *On the Rock: Twenty-Five Years in Alcatraz* (1980) with Robert Livesey in the late 1970's, a book about his years inside Alcatraz. He told Livesey that he amused himself by plotting the robbery of a local Spanish bank. He died in 1979 in Torremolinos, Spain, of an overdose of sleeping pills.

IMPACT

Alvin Karpis was the last Depression-era "public enemy," and his pursuit, along with those of other gangsters in the same era, established the FBI as the United States' chief crime-fighting organization. He was the only public enemy to survive capture. Karpis's alleged "personal arrest" by director J. Edgar Hoover ended congressional criticism of the agency, which had focused on allegations that the director was reckless and ineffectual. After gangster John Dillinger's death and Karpis's arrest, Hoover's position became unassailable to his critics. He remained director of the FBI until his death in 1972—a tenure of more than forty years. Karpis often claimed that he was responsible for Hoover's successful career.

Before his accidental fatal overdose of sleeping pills, Karpis was paid twenty thousand dollars to be the consultant for a film about his life. After he died, the film was scrapped. According to Karpis's ghostwriter, Robert

---

KARPIS ON MA BARKER

Alvin "Old Creepy" Karpis, released from prison in 1969, went on to write his memoirs. He contradicts the official FBI story—retold lovingly in movies and fiction—that Ma Barker was a crime boss:

The most ridiculous story in the annals of crime is that Ma Barker was the mastermind behind the Karpis-Barker gang. . . . She wasn't a leader of criminals or even a criminal herself. There is not one police photograph of her or set of fingerprints taken while she was alive . . . she knew we were criminals but her participation in our careers was limited to one function: when we traveled together, we moved as a mother and her sons. What could look more innocent? . . . Ma was always somebody in our lives. Love didn't enter into it really. She was somebody we looked after and took with us when we moved from city to city, hideout to hideout. . . . It's no insult to Ma's memory that she just didn't have the brains or the know-how to direct us on a robbery. It wouldn't have occurred to her to get involved in our business, and we always made a point of only discussing our scores when Ma wasn't around. We'd leave her at home when we were arranging a job, or we'd send her to a movie. Ma saw a lot of movies.

Source: Alvin Karpis with Bill Trent, *The Alvin Karpis Story* (New York: Coward, McCann & Geoghegan, 1971).

Livesey, Karpis babysat in Toronto for future actors Neve and Christian Campbell when they were in grade school.

FURTHER READING

Burrough, Bryan. *Public Enemies: America's Greatest Crime Wave and the Birth of the FBI, 1933-1934.* New York: Penguin Books, 2004. A hefty study of four public enemies of the 1930's, including much discussion of Karpis.

Esslinger, Michael. *Alcatraz: A Definitive History of the Penitentiary Years.* Carmel, Calif.: Ocean View, 2003. Provides a solid history of "life on the rock" and gives information about Karpis, including his prison mugshots.

Karpis, Alvin, with Robert Livesay. *On the Rock: Twenty-Five Years in Alcatraz.* Toronto, Ont.: Beaufort Books, 1980.

Karpis, Alvin, with Bill Trent. *The Alvin Karpis Story.* New York: Berkley, 1971. Karpis claimed to have a near-photographic memory. Both of his books were written with the assistance of ghostwriters, who taped hours of Karpis reminiscing about robbing banks and surviving a quarter century inside Alcatraz.

—*Jim Pauff*

SEE ALSO: Ma Barker; John Dillinger; J. Edgar Hoover.

YOSHIKO KAWASHIMA
Manchu princess and intelligence agent for the Japanese

BORN: May 24, 1907; Beijing, China
DIED: March 25, 1948; Beijing, China
ALSO KNOWN AS: Aisin Gioro Xianyu (birth name);
  Aisin Gioro Xianwangyu; Aisin Gioro Xianxi; Jin
  Bihui; Dongzhen; Eastern Jewel
MAJOR OFFENSE: Treason
ACTIVE: 1931-1945
LOCALE: Manchuria and Northeast China proper
SENTENCE: Death by shooting

EARLY LIFE

Born as Aisingoro Xianyu, Yoshiko Kawashima (yoh-shee-koh kah-wah-shee-mah) was the daughter of Prince Su (1863-1922), a member of the Manchu family, who ruled China until 1911. Su then became an ally of Japanese forces in North China in exchange for their patronage. In 1913, Su arranged for his daughter's adoption by the childless Kawashima Naniwa, a Japanese agent in China. Renamed Yoshiko Kawashima, she had a Japanese-style upbringing and education. In November, 1927, she married Kanjurjab, son of the Inner Mongolian general Babojab, who had been allied with Prince Su against the Russians. Kawashima divorced Kanjurjab in 1931 but maintained connections with Inner Mongolian leaders. As a member of the old Manchu ruling family and having Mongol contacts and a Japanese education, Kawashima became an agent aiding Japanese expansionist activities in Manchuria, Inner Mongolia, and Northeast China proper.

ESPIONAGE CAREER

Kawashima was a part of secret operations involved in the Japanese military takeover of Manchuria in September, 1931. She then became a powerful figure in the Manchukuo puppet state, nominally ruled until 1945 by another member of the Manchu Aisingoro family, Puyi (1906-1967). She was also involved in the events leading to Japanese military action in Shanghai in 1932, in a premature attempt by the Japanese to gain full control of that city. The Japanese military subsequently gave Kawashima a nominal command in the Japanese-controlled Manchurian forces, but her overbearing attitude and unpredictability led to her loss of this position in 1936. Kawashima then went to Japan, but official displeasure over Kawashima's public remarks concerning Japanese Army excesses in China and her open cohabitation in Tokyo with an unsavory war profiteer led to her being pressured to return to China.

LEGAL ACTION AND OUTCOME

After Japan's defeat in World War II in August, 1945, Kawashima was quickly arrested as a traitor to China by acting as a collaborator with and agent of the Japanese military. She was detained in Beijing by intelligence agents belonging to the Kuomintang Nationalist regime. Kawashima defended herself on the grounds that she was a Japanese citizen and so could not commit treason against China. Despite her Japanese citizenship by adoption, the Chinese authorities regarded her as a traitor since she was Chinese by birth. After two years of appeals and delays, she was finally sentenced to death and executed in Beijing Prison No. 1 on March 25, 1948.

IMPACT

For forty years after her death, Yoshiko Kawashima was regarded as a traitor by most Chinese. She epitomized the duplicity and high-handedness of the Japanese military occupiers of China. In the mid-1980's, however, Kawashima began to be portrayed as a tragic figure by Japanese and Chinese novelists. This revisionist image was reinforced by a Chinese film about her life that was released in 1990 and titled *Chuan dao fang zi*. Some believe that the romanticization of a major collaborationist figure such as Kawashima aids in the mitigation of Chinese hostility felt toward Japan regarding its repeated military incursions into China.

FURTHER READING

Cribb, Robert, and Li Narangoa, eds. *Imperial Japan and National Identities in Asia, 1895-1945*. New York: Routledge, 2003. Includes chapters on Japanese expansionism in Manchuria, imperial Japanese influences on Mongol nationalism, and Japanese military involvement in North China.

Deacon, Richard. *Kempei tai: The Japanese Secret Service, Then and Now*. Tokyo: Tuttle, 1990. The only English-language history of Japan's military intelligence service, including its activities in Manchuria. Extensive bibliography.

Jordan, Donald A. *China's Trial by Fire: The Shanghai War of 1932*. Ann Arbor: University of Michigan Press, 2001. An account of Japanese intelligence machinations and military action in Shanghai in 1932.

Kahn, Winston. *Doihara Kenji and the "North China Autonomy Movement," 1935-1936*. Tempe: Arizona State University Press, 1973. Details Japanese espionage and intrigues in North China as directed by noted Japanese Army Intelligence officer Kenji Doihara.

Lee, Lilian. *The Last Princess of Manchuria*. New York: Morrow, 1992. Written as a historical novel, this is the only biography of Kawashima available in English.

Translated by Andrea Kelly from the 1990 Chinese original, which was the basis of a popular film about Kawashima.

—Michael McCaskey

SEE ALSO: Puyi; Tokyo Rose.

TOM KEATING
British art forger

BORN: March, 1917; London, England
DIED: February 12, 1984; Colchester, Essex, England
ALSO KNOWN AS: Thomas Patrick Keating (full name)
CAUSE OF NOTORIETY: Keating fooled the art and antiques world with his impeccable copies of paintings done by well-known artists. He was charged with conspiracy to defraud by art forgery, but the charges were dropped because of his frail health.
ACTIVE: 1950's-1979
LOCALE: United Kingdom and Tenerife, Spain

EARLY LIFE

Tom Keating (KEET-ihng) was born into poverty in southeast London. His father was a house painter and decorator, and Tom and his brothers learned the trade, though Keating's ambition had always been to be a painter. At the outbreak of World War II, Keating was drafted into the navy as a stoker and sent to Singapore. After the Japanese invasion, he escaped to Australia, returning to Great Britain to work on Atlantic convoys. These wartime experiences caused severe emotional trauma, and he left military service in January, 1944. He married a local woman, Ellen, by whom he had two children. After the war and after working as a house painter and at other jobs, he entered Goldsmiths College on a scholarship to study art. He finished there in 1952 but failed to gain a diploma, a disappointment that always stayed with him.

Unable to earn much as a painter, he supplemented his income by cleaning and restoring frames and paintings, mainly for small-time antiques dealers. Sometimes this restoration meant patching and painting over original parts of the art piece, and Keating soon found he had a facility for re-creating such paintings. This lead him to paint copies or imitations of some of the paintings he had seen or studied in various art galleries, many of which he gave away or sold cheaply to pay for his living expenses. He called these works his "Sexton Blakes" (or just "Sextons"), a slang term rhyming with "fakes."

CRIMINAL CAREER

One of the artists Keating particularly copied was the little-known Canadian artist Cornelius Krieghoff, an early painter of North American scenes. Keating claimed to have produced approximately two hundred copies of Krieghoff's works over the years. In the 1950's, Keating also began to copy British watercolorists and had a particular admiration for Tom Girtin, a contemporary of William Turner. Later, in the 1960's, he came to admire Samuel Palmer, another nineteenth century Romantic British painter. He also copied German Expressionist painting, French Impressionists, and the Dutch masters. In all, he claimed to have produced some two thousand fakes in twenty-five years.

Keating claimed that this copying was not merely a technical feat but involved getting inside the imagination of the artist and even feeling "possessed" by the dead artist's spirit. At such intense times, he could produce ten or twenty paintings over the course of a few days. He relied heavily on friends in the antiques business, who supplied him with old canvases, frames, and drawing paper. Sometimes Keating would try to reproduce old paint techniques; at other times, he used modern acrylics or even household emulsion paint mixed with powder poster paint. He even found old frames discarded from leading auctioneers and repainted the pictures that had once been held in them.

Keating did receive some significant commissions as a restorer, including various collections in ancestral and stately homes in Scotland and East Anglia and even at Marlborough House, London, one of the royal residences.

His marriage fell apart in the 1960's. For a while, he lived with Jane Kelly, whom he had trained as a restorer and cleaner; they moved to East Anglia but spent time in Tenerife, Spain. It was Kelly who took many of Keating's forgeries to dealers and auctions for disposal. The couple broke up in 1974.

In 1976, Geraldine Norman, an art critic for *The Times* of London, was writing a piece on the paintings of Samuel Palmer and the possibility that some were forgeries. She was particularly interested in a group of thirteen Palmers that had been sold through a London antiques dealer, Legers. After careful research involving a number of Palmer experts, Norman, with her husband Frank, published the first of her articles in July, 1976. Further investigation led her to Keating, and a second article, on August 10, 1976, mentioned his name. Keating immediately replied to the charge in a letter published in *The Times* on August 20, admitting not only to the Palmer fakes but also to a number of other forgeries. He contacted the Normans privately and offered to tell them his story.

LEGAL ACTION AND OUTCOME

London-area art dealers initially were not sure how to handle the admissions, but Legers and the Redfern Gallery decided to refer the matter to the metropolitan police force, which investigated their specific complaints. Keating's defense was that he had always introduced deliberate mistakes into his fakes, used modern paint, or in some other way given clues to the paintings' inauthenticity.

The police decided to prosecute. Keating was charged in 1977 with conspiracy to defraud, and the case was scheduled for trial in 1979. However, Keating's health had been badly undermined by years of smoking and drinking, and his lungs were further damaged by the various chemicals used in his paintings, which were often done in cramped, unventilated conditions. The stress of the court case broke Keating's health, and the case was dropped. Despite some improvement to his health, he died in 1984.

IMPACT

The case against Tom Keating turned Keating himself into a celebrity. His interviews with the Normans were chronicled in 1977 as an autobiography titled *Fake's Progress*. He was asked to do a series of television interviews regarding the techniques of the old masters, which were later sold as videotapes. More extraordinary, his forgeries, of which he was never able to give a full list, began to take on a value of their own, fetching up to ten thousand pounds each. In a strange twist, other artists began to forge Keating's works.

The case also exposed the dearth of art expertise in the antiques business and the lack of any self-policing. It also raised questions of the difference between "imitations," which have always occurred in the history of art, and deliberate "forgeries," as well as inflated prices associated with certain artists as opposed to others.

FURTHER READING

Keating, Tom, with Geraldine and Frank Norman. *Fake's Progress*. London: Hutchinson, 1977. Keating's own account of his forgery career, as told to the Normans. It reveals a very self-aware artist who was as much a rebel as a criminal.

Keating, Tom, with Geraldine Norman, ed. *The Tom Keating Catalogue Illustrations*. London: Hutchinson, 1977. The *Times* art correspondent who broke the Keating story introduces some of the paintings Keating produced.

Phillips, David. *Exhibiting Authenticity*. Manchester, England: Manchester University Press, 1997. Raises the same philosophical questions that Keating raised in his defense.

Radnstis, Sandor. *The Fake: Forgery and Its Place in Art*. Lanham, Md.: Rowman and Littlefield, 1999. Puts the Keating story in a wider context and raises some of the artistic, moral, and philosophical questions about integrity and authenticity in art.

—*David Barratt*

SEE ALSO: Elmyr de Hory; Clifford Irving.

MACHINE GUN KELLY
American gangster

BORN: July 17, 1895; Memphis, Tennessee
DIED: July 17, 1954; Fort Leavenworth, Kansas
ALSO KNOWN AS: George Kelly Barnes, Jr. (birth name); George R. Kelly
MAJOR OFFENSES: Bank robbery and kidnapping
ACTIVE: 1928-1933
LOCALE: Various midwestern and southern states
SENTENCE: Life in prison

EARLY LIFE
Machine Gun Kelly (KEHL-ee) was born George Kelly Barnes in 1895 in Memphis. Kelly's father was an insurance executive, and the family was upper-middle-class. Kelly reportedly despised his father for the older man's marital philandering and extorted automobile privileges and an increased allowance from him. Kelly was involved in bootlegging while he was still a student at Memphis's Central High School. His mother, Elizabeth Kelly Barnes, passed away during this time, and young George blamed his philandering father for hastening her death. After graduating from high school, Kelly attended Mississippi A&M (now Mississippi State University) but dropped out within a few months.

After his brief college career, George met Geneva Ramsey, the daughter of a respected Memphis businessman. The couple eloped, and for a short time Kelly apparently tried to make a legitimate living. He was positively influenced by his new father-in-law, whom he liked and respected. After the older man's death, Kelly was unable to hold a job, and he regressed into bootlegging activities. Furthermore, his reported drinking and violent rages eventually resulted in a divorce for the couple, who had two sons by then.

CRIMINAL CAREER
After his divorce from Geneva, Kelly moved to Kansas City and formed a bootlegging gang that spread to multiple states, including Oklahoma, Tennessee, and New Mexico. He began using the name George R. Kelly, dropping the family name of Barnes. He was arrested twice in 1927 for bootlegging and for vagrancy, then sent to Leavenworth Federal Prison in 1928 for selling alcohol on an Indian reservation. After Kelly's release, he married Cleo Brooks (who went by Kathryn), whom he had met prior to his conviction. The thrice-divorced Kathryn Kelly was said to be the main force behind Kelly's "Machine Gun" image and nickname. It was reportedly Kathryn who first purchased a Thompson automatic for her husband and boasted to friends of the bootlegger's supposed prowess with the weapon.

Kelly worked with various accomplices and robbed banks from 1930 to 1932 in Minnesota, Iowa, Texas, and as far west as Colfax, Washington. The last yielded Kelly's biggest haul as a bank robber, netting him seventy-seven thousand dollars. Kelly's final bank heist was in November, 1932, when he and two associates robbed a Mississippi bank of thirty-eight thousand dollars. Kelly may also have robbed banks in parts of Mississippi and Texas as well as Chicago, Kansas City, and Denver. Some sources state that Kathryn might have assisted her husband with the planning and execution of some of the bank jobs.

On 1932, Kelly and an accomplice attempted a couple of failed kidnappings. The second one was of an Indiana banker who convinced the gangsters that he could not pay the ransom. The kidnappers released their hostage under the rather ludicrous promise that the victim would later try to raise the money for his ex-captors, which of course he did not.

Machine Gun Kelly.

In July of 1933, Kelly and his bank-robbing partner Albert Bates kidnapped millionaire Oklahoma oilman Charles Urschel. Urschel, blindfolded and stashed at Kathryn's family ranch in Texas, made keen observations about his whereabouts despite being unable to see. After the ransom was paid and Urschel was released unharmed, he was able to give enough information to authorities to lead to a coordinated sweep and arrest of Kelly associates. By September, 1933, police and federal agents had tracked George and Kathryn to a friend's house in Memphis.

LEGAL ACTION AND OUTCOME

Local police and Federal Bureau of Investigation (FBI) agents apprehended the Kellys in Memphis. It was here that Kelly supposedly uttered his famous plea, "Don't shoot, G-men!" as he surrendered to the agents. Others claim that Kelly actually surrendered to Memphis police and said instead, "I've been waiting for you all night," or alternatively "I give up, ya got me!" Whatever Kelly said during his arrest, it was the end of his gangster career. On October 12, 1933, George and Kathryn Kelly were convicted and sentenced to life imprisonment for kidnapping and conspiracy. Kelly died of a heart attack at the Leavenworth Federal Penitentiary on July 17, 1954. Kathryn was released in 1958, and her last known residence was in Oklahoma.

IMPACT

Many believe that Kathryn Kelly was the architect of the "machine gun" image and that Kelly might not have achieved his notoriety without his wife's passion for public notice. Machine Gun Kelly remains one of the iconic figures of the Prohibition era. The tale of Kelly coining the term "G-Men" (government men) for FBI agents (as romantically portrayed in movies like *The FBI Story* and *G-Men*) certainly served to underscore the colorful history of the war between the FBI and the Depression-era public enemies, embedding them in American popular culture.

FURTHER READING

Barnes, Bruce. *Machine Gun Kelly: To Right a Wrong.* Perris, Calif.: Tipper, 1991. Barnes's account of his father's life sheds a personal light on Kelly, particularly his earlier life and marriage to Geneva Ramsey.

Burrough, Bryan. *Public Enemies: America's Greatest Crime Wave and the Birth of the FBI, 1933-34.* New York: Penguin, 2004. Provides a general historical overview of the most famous of the Prohibition-era gangsters. Also reveals the workings of the fledgling FBI as it expanded to meet the challenge presented by the midwestern public enemies.

Hamilton, Stanley. *Machine Gun Kelly's Last Stand.* Lawrence: University Press of Kansas, 1993. A well-researched, thorough, and exciting account of Kelly's criminal career and the efforts of J. Edgar Hoover's FBI against the 1930's gangsters.

—*David R. Champion*

SEE ALSO: John Dillinger; Pretty Boy Floyd; J. Edgar Hoover; Baby Face Nelson.

NED KELLY

Irish Australian bushranger

BORN: December, 1854; Beveridge, Victoria, Australia
DIED: November 11, 1880; Melbourne, Australia
ALSO KNOWN AS: Edward Kelly (full name)
MAJOR OFFENSES: Murder and bank robbery
ACTIVE: 1878-1880
LOCALE: Stringybark Creek, Eurora, Jerilderie, and Glenrowan, New South Wales, Australia
SENTENCE: Death by hanging

EARLY LIFE

Edward (Ned) Kelly (KEHL-ee) was the oldest son of John Kelly, a former convict, and Ellen (Quinn) Kelly, a free immigrant. After their marriage in Melbourne, the couple moved to Beveridge, Victoria, where Ned was born in 1855. Nine years later, the family moved to Avenel, Victoria, where Ned attended school and learned to read and write. When he was eleven years old, he saved another boy from drowning, and the grateful family gave Kelly a green silk sash with a gold fringe; he wore the sash on important occasions, including the famous shoot-out at Glenrowan years later.

In 1866, his father died, and his mother moved the family to Gretna in northeast Victoria, where she attempted to homestead eighty acres of uncultivated farmland. Kelly soon got into trouble. After serving as a kind of "apprentice" to Harry Power, a notorious bushranger (an outlaw living in the Australian bush), Kelly was charged with being an accomplice, but charges were dropped because of a lack of evidence. He was convicted of assault and indecent behavior and sentenced to six months' imprisonment in 1870. After his release, Kelly worked in a sawmill for three years and stayed out of trouble. However, he became involved in a ring of stock rustlers with his stepfather, George King. He was later arrested for public drunkenness and fined.

CRIMINAL CAREER

Kelly's serious criminal career began when Constable Alexander Fitzpatrick came to the Kelly home, ostensibly to arrest Dan, Kelly's younger brother, but when Fitzpatrick made unwanted advances toward Kelly's sister Kate, the Kelly clan came to her rescue; in the ensuing melee, shots were fired. Fitzpatrick charged the entire family with attempted murder, and Kelly's mother was convicted and given a three-year sentence. Kelly and Dan fled with Joe Byrne and Aaron Sherritt; they were declared "outlaws" by local authorities.

A reward of one hundred pounds was offered for Kelly's capture. When the police finally caught up with the gang at Stringybark Creek, three policemen were killed, and the gang escaped. They later robbed banks at Eurora and Jerilderie, netting forty-four hundred pounds; the reward was then increased to two thousand pounds per gang member.

For protection, the gang had suits of armor made for them. These they put to use at Glenrowan, where they intended to ambush a contingent of police. The gang took hostages and forced the railroad workers there to tear up the railroad ties so that the police would have to leave the cars and be vulnerable to attack. The police, however, were tipped off and surrounded the hotel where the gang took refuge. In the ten-hour gun battle that followed, police killed three gang members and wounded and captured Kelly.

LEGAL ACTION AND OUTCOME

The wounded Kelly was imprisoned in the Benalla jail and then transferred to Melbourne, instead of nearby Beechworth, because the law feared reprisal from Kelly's supporters. Kelly was charged with the murders of constables Thomas Lonigan and Michael Scanlan at Stringybark Creek. Later, the charge was altered, and Kelly was accused only of the murder of Lonigan. At the trial, Kelly was represented by Henry Bindon, an inexperienced lawyer, and the evidence presented related not

Ned Kelly. (Courtesy, State Library of Victoria, Australia)

only to Lonigan's death but also to Kelly's entire career. Kelly's "Jerilderie letter," which would have provided him with a chance to explain his actions and prove he shot Lonigan in self-defense, was ruled not admissible. The two-day trial ended October 29, 1880, with a verdict, returned by the jury after only thirty minutes, of guilty. Judge Sir Redmond Barry, son of a British general, then sentenced Kelly to be hanged. Despite pro-Kelly demonstrations and petitions, the sentence was carried out on November 11, 1880.

IMPACT

The furor over the Ned Kelly trial resulted in a royal commission being appointed to investigate the matter. In 1881, after eighteen months of deliberations, the commission issued its report, which was critical of the police. Several members of the Victoria police, including senior staff, were reprimanded, demoted, or dismissed. For a period, Kelly's supporters caused some problems, but eventually things returned to normal.

Despite his crimes, Kelly continued to represent the quintessential Australian even more than a century later. He is considered a preeminent fighter against British rule and the Irish republican rebel who displayed a few Robin Hood characteristics. The persistent popularity of Kelly is reflected in literature, film, and sports. His image was popularized by J. J. Kenneally, whose *Complete Inner History of the Kelly Gang and Their Pursuers* (1929) portrayed Kelly as a hero and the police as villains. Famous Australian painter Sydney Nolan did a series of paintings depicting the Kelly story, and the Aboriginal people of northwestern Australia included Kelly in their Dreaming stories. The first feature-length film about Kelly appeared in 1906. Two more Kelly films followed, one in 1970—in which singer Mick Jagger played Kelly—and one in 2003, which was based on Robert Drewe's 1991 book titled *Our Sunshine* and starred Heath Ledger in the title role. Finally, the opening ceremonies at the 2000 Olympic Games in Sydney featured scores of Kelly-like figures dancing to Irish music.

FURTHER READING

Drewe, Robert. *Kelly Gang*. New York: Penguin Books, 2003. Originally published in 1991 under the title *Our Sunshine*, this work presents Kelly as both devil incarnate and national hero and stresses his rebelliousness.

Jones, Ian. *Ned Kelly: A Short Life*. Rev. ed. South Melbourne, Vic.: Lothian Books, 2003. One of the best factual accounts of Kelly's story, utilizing primary texts and including the entire text of Kelly's famous Jerilderie letter.

Molony, John. *Ned Kelly*. Rev. ed. Melbourne, Vic.: Melbourne University Press, 2002. Novel focusing on the Kelly clan contrasts their "Irishness" with the behavior of the British overlords.

Morgan, Wendy. *Ned Kelly Reconstructed*. Cambridge, England: Cambridge University Press, 1994. Examines the accounts of the Kelly story, demonstrating that they are the products of their creators' perspectives, rather than the truth.

—*Thomas L. Erskine*

SEE ALSO: Johnnie Armstrong; Harry Longabaugh; Joaquín Murieta; Rob Roy; Robin Hood.

THE JERILDERIE LETTER

In 1879, during a raid on the town of Jerilderie, Ned Kelly dictated an 8,300-word letter in which he defended himself against various accusations. The letter denounces Irishmen who served English authorities as policemen and betrayed their fellow settlers. For this reason the letter is considered to be an early Australian nationalist statement.

What would people say if they saw a strapping big lump of an Irishman shepherding sheep for fifteen bob a week or tailing turkeys in Tallarook ranges for a smile from Julia or even begging his tucker, they would say he ought to be ashamed of himself and tar-and-feather him.

But he would be a king to a policeman who for a lazy loafing cowardly bilit left the ash corner deserted the shamrock, the emblem of true wit and beauty to serve under a flag and nation that has destroyed massacreed and murdered their fore-fathers by the greatest of torture as rolling them down hill in spiked barrels pulling their toe and finger nails and on the wheel. and every torture imaginable more was transported to Van Diemand's Land to pine their young lives away in starvation and misery among tyrants worse than the promised hell itself all of true blood bone and beauty, that was not murdered on their own soil, or had fled to America or other countries to bloom again another day, were doomed to Port Mcquarie Toweringabbie norfolk island and Emu plains and in those places of tyranny and condemnation many a blooming Irishman rather than subdue to the Saxon yoke Were flogged to death and bravely died in servile chains but true to the shamrock and a credit to Paddys land What would people say if I became a policeman and took an oath to arrest my brothers and sisters & relations and convict them by fair or foul means after the conviction of my mother and the persecutions and insults offered to myself and people Would they say I was a decent gentleman, and yet a police-man is still in worse and guilty of meaner actions than that The Queen must surely be proud of such heroic men as the Police and Irish soldiers as It takes eight or eleven of the biggest mud crushers in Melbourne to take one poor little half starved larrakin to a watch house.

Source: Max Brown, *Australian Son* (London: Angus and Robertson, 1948).

JACK KETCH
British public executioner

DIED: November, 1686; London, England
ALSO KNOWN AS: John Ketch (full name); Jack Catch
CAUSE OF NOTORIETY: Ketch was a hangman infamous for his incompetence and brutality.
ACTIVE: c. 1663-1686
LOCALE: London

EARLY LIFE

Little is known about the early life of England's most notorious executioner. Although a real person, Jack Ketch (jak kehch) survives mainly through his infamy. The earliest records of Ketch concern his being a hangman. By some accounts, he received that appointment around 1663; he was known to be a hangman at some point by the time of or shortly after the Great Fire of London (1666).

EXECUTIONER CAREER

Perhaps the most infamous beheading enacted by Ketch was of a French Catholic, Robert Hubert, who was essentially a Catholic scapegoat during a period of oppressive Protestant rule in England. His execution indicates a pattern typical of such proceedings. Ketch led the prisoner to Tyburn following an effigy of the pope containing live cats which, as a prelude to the public ritual, was set on fire, to the delight of the spectators. As usual, the execution took place on a Monday afternoon. Typically, after the requisite hour of dangling from the rope, the victim would be lowered and his or her clothes removed. On this day, a mob rushed forward and tore the corpse apart to express both antipapal sentiments and the desire for war against France.

Most executions were more orderly and followed strict protocol. Chapbooks and broadsides regularly were published with accounts of the victim's composure and last words. Such sources made Ketch become a celebrated personality. The execution of Hubert foreshadowed a trend of executing suspected Catholic sympathizers, especially in the wake of the Popish Plot of 1678, which was a failed attempt to assassinate the king, Charles II, and crown his brother, James Stuart. In this climate, Ketch became the focus of many satirical tracts, notably *The Plotters Ballad, Being Jack Ketch's Incomparable Receipt for the Cure of Traytorous Recusants: Or, Wholesome Physick for a Popish Contagion* (1678) and *The Romanists Best Doctor* (1680). Later, he became a target of derision, largely because of the botched beheadings of his two most eminent victims, William,

Lord Russell, a Whig instigator, and James Scott, duke of Monmouth, illegitimate son of Charles II, whom he had sought to succeed.

In Ketch's defense, hangings and public punishments were his usual charges; beheadings were reserved for persons of quality. The duke of Monmouth's beheading required five chops, with Ketch nearly abandoning his task midway. He finally had to use a knife to sever Monmouth's head completely.

IMPACT

Whether owing to incompetence or simply as a function of the brutal task of discharging the wishes of the crown, Jack Ketch's reputation long outlived him. His name became eponymous for a rough hangman upholding the rule of law. Forty years after Ketch's death, William Hazlitt's "On the Spirit of Obligations" mentioned in passing, "A Jack-Ketch may be known to tie the fatal noose with trembling fingers." The figure of the hangman in the trio of figures outwitted and killed by Punch of puppet-show fame (the others being his wife, Judy, and the Devil) became known as Jack Ketch. The slang phrase "to dance with Jack Ketch," once popular in pirate ballads, still means to hang.

FURTHER READING

An Account of What Passed at the Execution of the Late Duke of Monmouth. London, 1685. Records the duke's giving six guineas to Ketch and promising that his servant would give six more if he did better by him than he had by Lord Russell.

Gatrell, V. A. C. *The Hanging Tree.* New York: Oxford University Press, 1994. Tracks the survival of Ketch as a byword among the English, emphasizing that their experience with the law was never benign.

Ketch, Jack? *The Apologie of John Ketch.* London. 1683. Purportedly by Ketch, this tract seeks to vindicate him for the treatment of Lord Russell, denying that he was drunk at the time of the execution and blaming the victim for flinching when the blow approached.

Stephenson, Neal. *The Baroque Cycle.* 3 vols. New York: HarperCollins, 2003-2005. Although a work of historical fiction, this story richly portrays the likely public responses to executions, recounting the way victims of means would wear expensive clothes as an incentive to Ketch to do his job well, since he would reap the valuable clothing as part of his compensation if his job were done correctly. Poor criminals would arrange for boys to grab their legs to hasten death.

Wales, Tim. "John Ketch." In *Oxford Dictionary of National Biography*. New York: Oxford University Press, 2004. Compiles extant records concerning Ketch's role in the restored Stuart monarchy's efforts to institute conformity to the state's religion and later to Tory policies. Also documents the durability of Ketch's name in puppet shows.

—*William E. Engel*

SEE ALSO: Henry Wirz.

TOM KETCHUM
American outlaw

BORN: October 31, 1863; San Saba County, Texas
DIED: April 26, 1901; Clayton, New Mexico
ALSO KNOWN AS: Thomas Edward Ketchum (full name); Black Jack Ketchum
MAJOR OFFENSES: Murder and robbery
ACTIVE: 1892-1899
LOCALE: Eastern Arizona, northeastern New Mexico, and west Texas
SENTENCE: Death by hanging

EARLY LIFE
Thomas (Tom) Edward Ketchum (KEHT-chuhm) was the youngest of eight children born to Temperance and Green Berry Ketchum. His father died when Tom was only five years old, and his mother died when he was ten. Ketchum then lived off and on with his older brother Berry, Jr., for the next sixteen years. Thomas and another older brother, Samuel, worked as cowboys in Texas and New Mexico, participating in many cattle drives. They worked at the Bell Ranch near Liberty, New Mexico, for many months. However, both preferred to be drifters, a lifestyle that eventually led them to a life of crime.

CRIMINAL CAREER
After failing to appear as a witness in a criminal case, Ketchum was summoned for contempt of court on March 17, 1880. These events signaled the beginning of his defiance of legal authority. However, his first major offense occurred in 1892, when his gang robbed a train just outside Nutt, New Mexico; they stole about twenty thousand dollars. He fled to Arizona and then Texas. On December 12, 1895, Ketchum and others killed John Powers in Tom Green County, Texas. Ketchum was indicted by a grand jury for the murder of Powers in Texas in early 1896, but he managed to escape to New Mexico. There, Ketchum and his gang robbed a store and post office in Liberty in June, 1896. Most of the pursuing posse were killed by Ketchum and his gang during a gunfight along the Pecos River.

After spending some time in Arizona, Ketchum and his gang held up a train near Folsom, New Mexico, on September 3, 1897. They hid for a time in a cave south of Folsom. On December 9, 1897, Ketchum's group robbed a post office and railroad station at Stein's Pass, New Mexico, but were foiled in an attempted train robbery. Heading back to Texas, Ketchum robbed a train near Comstock on April 28, 1898. This was followed by another train robbery near Stanton, Texas, on July 1, 1898.

After a disagreement with his brother Sam and other members of the gang, Ketchum rode to central Arizona, where he robbed a store and killed two men at Camp Verde on July 2, 1899. Back in New Mexico, Ketchum tried to rob a train by himself near Folsom on August 16, 1899. During that attempt, Ketchum was shot in the right arm by the train conductor and captured the next morning.

LEGAL ACTION AND OUTCOME
After Ketchum killed the two men at Camp Verde, a warrant was issued for his arrest. Following Ketchum's arrest for train robbery in New Mexico in August, 1899, the governor of New Mexico denied a requisition order for his extradition to Arizona, claiming that the train robbery took precedence. On October 5, 1900, Ketchum was sentenced to hang in Clayton, New Mexico. The hanging occurred on April 26, 1901, and was particularly gruesome: Because of poorly placed weights, the taut rope tore Ketchum's head from his torso.

IMPACT
Tom Ketchum was known as a dangerous, hardened individual who was fast with his gun and an excellent marksman. He became one of the most notorious outlaws and train robbers in the American Southwest. He is the only person to suffer capital punishment in New Mexico for train robbery and is the only person ever hanged in Union County, New Mexico. According to historical

documents, Ketchum is also the only criminal ever decapitated during a judicial hanging in the United States. Stories of his outlaw adventures, crimes, and death have been exploited in many magazines, particularly *Wild West*. He has also been a featured outlaw in films and televison shows, including the television series *Death Valley Days*.

FURTHER READING

Barton, Barbara. *Den of Outlaws*. San Angelo, Tex.: Rangel Printing, 2000. Barton examines the life, gang, and outlaw days of Ketchum.

Hillerman, Tony. *The Great Taos Bank Robbery, and Other True Stories of the Southwest*. New York: HarperCollins, 2001. This work contains stories surrounding Ketchum's crimes.

Jersig, Shelby. *Black Jack Ketchum*. Clovis, N.Mex.: Jersig Printing, 2001. An excellent account of Ketchum's life, his train robberies, and the other crimes he committed in New Mexico.

—*Alvin K. Benson*

SEE ALSO: Sam Bass; Tom Bell; Ronnie Biggs; Bill Doolin.

JACK KEVORKIAN

American pathologist and advocate of physician-assisted suicide

BORN: May 26, 1928; Pontiac, Michigan
ALSO KNOWN AS: Dr. Death
MAJOR OFFENSE: Second-degree murder and administering a controlled substance
ACTIVE: 1990-1998
LOCALE: Primarily Michigan
SENTENCE: Ten to twenty-five years; concurrent three to seven years for administering a controlled substance

EARLY LIFE

Jack Kevorkian (keh-VOHRK-ee-uhn) was born in 1928 to Armenian immigrants who were survivors of the genocidal holocaust directed against their people by the Turks in 1915. He had two sisters, Flora and Margo. His father, Levon, was an automobile factory worker and later an excavator. Kevorkian was raised in Armenian Orthodoxy, but he later abandoned his religious faith.

As a child, Kevorkian was an avid reader and baseball fan. He was a studious pupil at Pontiac High School and won National Honor Society awards. In 1945, he enrolled in the University of Michigan, graduating from its medical school in 1952 with a speciality in pathology, the study of determining causes of death and disease by investigating the tissue of deceased persons.

Kevorkian then took an internship at Detroit's Henry Ford Hospital, where he was struck by the condition of a terminally ill woman. He later reported feeling an overwhelming empathy for her and attaining an epiphany about the morality and ethics of physician-assisted suicide and euthanasia.

In 1953, Kevorkian served as a medical officer in the Korean War. Upon his discharge, he returned to Michigan to practice at Pontiac General, Detroit Receiving, and the University of Michigan Medical Center. In 1954, he published his research on photographing people's

Jack Kevorkian. (AP/Wide World Photos)

eyes at the moment of death to help physicians distinguish between coma and death. In 1958, he advocated using condemned prisoners for medical research; the resulting controversy led to the loss of his university residency. In 1961, Kevorkian pursued the possibility of using corpses as sources for blood transfusions. In 1968, he published an article in which he praised Nazi physicians for trying to garner some positive outcomes from the concentration camps.

Kevorkian later left Pontiac General and eventually took a position at Saratoga General Hospital in 1970. He decided to remain a bachelor after he broke off an engagement and continued to pursue his artistic interests alongside his professional ones. Kevorkian's interests in art further demonstrated his interest in the morbid and grisly. In an adult education art class, he created graphic and surreal tableaus depicting cadavers, skulls, dismemberment, and cannibalism.

CRIMINAL CAREER

In 1976, Kevorkian quit his job at Saratoga and moved to Los Angeles to make a film of George Frideric Handel's oratorio *Messiah* (1741). The film failed, and by 1979 he was back in Michigan working at various hospitals. He continued to publish his ideas about medical ethics and euthanasia in the German journal *Medicine and Law*. In 1987, he advertised his services as a "physician consultant for death counseling," and he continued to publish his ideas about clinics for planned suicides and medical research on the patients.

In 1989, Kevorkian built his first "suicide machine" to assist the death of David Rivlin, a quadriplegic who had publicly requested to be removed from life support. The machine, which Kevorkian called the Thanatron, allowed the patient to activate a lethal injection through intravenous tubing. Although Rivlin rejected Kevorkian's assistance and eventually had his life support removed by another physician, Kevorkian sought other patients to test the Thanatron.

On June 4, 1990, Janet Adkins, a fifty-four-year-old Alzheimer's patient, was the first person to use Kevorkian's machine to self-inflict death. The state of Michigan brought charges against Kevorkian immediately. A judge enjoined Kevorkian from assisting further suicides, but the murder charge against the pathologist for Adkins's death was dismissed.

LEGAL ACTION AND OUTCOME

Between 1990 and 1998, Kevorkian attended the suicides of 130 people, adding to his armamentarium a gas mask designed to facilitate the inhalation of carbon monoxide. During that time, Kevorkian's license to practice medicine was revoked by Michigan's state board, and charges against the pathologist were brought up and dismissed. He was then acquitted in another case, and he continued his work. Kevorkian was acquitted or had a mistrial on no fewer than four separate occasions during this time. Other judges dismissed charges against him. The social and legal storm about the issues of privacy, individual liberty, value of life, and other core cultural issues continued to surround Kevorkian.

Kevorkian often sought public platforms to espouse his views about assisted suicide. In 1998, he appeared on the television series *60 Minutes* and showed a videotape of the lethal injection of Thomas Youk, a victim of Lou Gehrig's disease. The bold move led to charges against Kevorkian of second-degree murder and administration of a controlled substance. On March 26, 1999, a Michigan jury convicted the former physician. Judge Jessica Cooper sentenced Kevorkian to ten to twenty-five years in prison, with a concurrent sentence of three to seven years for administering a controlled substance. His parole eligibility was scheduled to come up in 2007.

IMPACT

Jack Kevorkian is seen as a serial murderer by some people and as a pioneer for individual liberty by others. His repeated confounding of the Michigan prosecutors certainly added to his appeal for some of his defenders, who consider him a principled advocate for the rights of suffering people to make their own decisions about when they die. His detractors point to his morbid paintings and his death-focused research. Kevorkian's practice of assisting patients in ending their lives has provoked cultural and legal debates about the sanctity of life and self-determinism. He continued to challenge his conviction and in 2000 received an award from the Gleitsman Foundation for Civil Activism.

FURTHER READING

Betzold, Michael. *Appointment with Dr. Death.* Troy, Mich.: Momentum Books, 1993. A journalist with the *Detroit Free Press* covered the Kevorkian story and provides a history of the physician's career and assisted suicide advocacy.

Loving, Carol. *My Son, My Sorrow: A Mother's Plea to Dr. Kevorkian.* East Rutherford, N.J.: New Horizon Press, 1998. A mother of a young man who had Lou Gehrig's disease recounts her story of how her son's death was assisted by Kevorkian. The author supports Kevorkian's efforts.

Nicol, Neal, Harry Wylie, Cheeni Rao, and Jack Kevorkian. *Between the Dying and the Dead: Dr. Jack Kevorkian's Life and the Battle to Legalize Euthanasia.* Madison: University of Wisconsin Press, 2006. Relates personal, firsthand accounts gleaned from interviews with Kevorkian.

—*David R. Champion*

SEE ALSO: Larry C. Ford; Linda Burfield Hazzard; Josef Mengele; Stanley Milgram; Harold Shipman; Michael Swango.

KHIEU SAMPHAN
President of Democratic Kampuchea (1976-1979)

BORN: July 27, 1931; Svay Rieng Province, Cambodia
CAUSE OF NOTORIETY: Khieu Samphan was an obedient, high-ranking supporter of Pol Pot responsible for murderous party purges when the Khmer Rouge ruled Cambodia.
ACTIVE: 1976-1979
LOCALE: Cambodia

EARLY LIFE

Khieu Samphan (kyew sohm-fahn) was born in Svay Rieng Province in 1931. He was the eldest son of the judge Khieu Lung and his wife, Kung. Intelligent and studious, Khieu attended high school in Phnom Penh and earned his baccalaureate from Lycée Sisowath in 1954. On a scholarship, he went to France, attending the University of Montpellier and the University of Paris. In Paris, Khieu associated with Cambodian students like Saloth Sar (later called Pol Pot) who were drawn to Marxism. In 1959, Khieu earned his Ph.D. in economics from the University of Paris.

POLITICAL CAREER

Returning to Phnom Penh in 1959, Khieu sought to reform Cambodian society. He joined Prince Norodom Sihanouk's mass party, Sangkum, and became a professor of mathematics. He also edited the progressive newspaper *L'Observateur*, which angered Sihanouk. On July 13, 1960, Sihanouk's security force accosted Khieu while walking, beat and stripped him naked in public, and photographed him. In August, Khieu was arrested for five weeks, and his paper ceased publication.

In 1962, he was elected to Cambodia's National Assembly and appointed secretary of commerce. Severely criticized as leftist by Sihanouk, Khieu resigned in July, 1963. In 1966, against Sihanouk's wishes, Khieu won re-election to the assembly. Blamed unjustly for a peasant rebellion, Khieu fled to the jungle to join Pol Pot and his fellow Communists on April 24, 1967.

When Sihanouk was deposed on March 18, 1970, Khieu formed an alliance with the Khmer Rouge, as the Communists were now known. Fighting in Cambodia, he was appointed deputy prime minister and minister of national defense in the coalition government and became commander in chief of its armed forces. After the Khmer Rouge's victory in Cambodia's civil war, which ended with their capture of Phnom Penh on April 17, 1975, Pol Pot was the undisputed leader of the new regime, but Khieu himself kept great power among the Khmer Rouge. One of his first acts was to reassure and thus draw out key members of the vanquished Khmer Republic, whom his party then executed.

Beginning in May, 1975, Khieu attended the meetings of the powerful Standing Committee of the Central Committee of the Communist Party of Kampuchea and took minutes. His enthusiastic support for the murderous policies of the Khmer Rouge that turned Cambodia into the "killing fields" is well documented. Khieu also participated in the dismantling of the coalition government, which ended with the execution of former allies. To replace Sihanouk as head of state, on April 14, 1976, Khieu was made president of Democratic Kampuchea.

Khieu's zealous purges, nearly inevitably leading to the deaths of those purged, earned him promotion to chairman of "Office 870," the Center Office Committee of the party's Central Committee, in February, 1977. As chairman, Khieu ceaselessly conducted inquiries and launched more bloody purges. Two men who had fled with him to the jungle in 1967 were among those purged and then executed. As a result of Khieu's visit to the "West Zone" in August, 1977, for example, its secretary, Chou Chet, was identified by Pol Pot as a traitor and executed.

As opposition to Pol Pot rose, Khieu unerringly stood by the leader. The Vietnamese capture of Phnom Penh on January 7, 1979, drove the Khmer Rouge into jungle strongholds close to Thailand. Khieu, like others, was saved by Cold War antagonism, as many nations objected to the new Vietnamese-installed Cambodian government. Khieu became prime minister of a Khmer Rouge rebel government in December, 1979, and foreign minister in the new coalition government with Sihanouk

in 1982. When the United Nations brokered the Paris Peace Agreement of October 23, 1991, Khieu became a member of the Cambodian Supreme National Council. On his return to Phnom Penh on November 27, 1991, demonstrators attacked him and bloodied his head.

In April, 1993, the Khmer Rouge left Phnom Penh, boycotting an election they could not win. Khieu became prime minister of a provisional rebel Khmer Rouge government in July, 1994. After key defections and the death of Pol Pot, Khieu surrendered to the Cambodian government on December 24, 1998. Granted freedom from arrest, he moved into a modest home in Pailin, one mile from the Thai border. In January, 2004, Khieu finally admitted to his knowledge of Khmer Rouge atrocities in a book but claimed he had been powerless to stop them. By late 2006, with a Cambodian/United Nations agreement in place for prosecution of Khmer Rouge leaders, it was still uncertain if Khieu would face trial.

IMPACT

From 1975 to the end of 1978, Khieu Samphan, without discernible reluctance, served to strengthen Pol Pot's notorious rule. As chairman of Office 870, he launched party purges that deepened the horrors of Cambodia's "killing fields," where as many as two million people perished. Khieu zealously acted on his desire to destroy traditional Cambodian society and replace it with a radical alternative.

Although the few Cambodians who escaped while Khieu was president, and many refugees thereafter, reported the atrocities committed by the Khmer Rouge, the West was slow in acknowledging Khmer Rouge crimes. In 1979 the Vietnamese showed the world the notorious torture and execution prison, Tuol Sleng (a former high school code-named S-21), where many victims of Khieu's notorious party purges had been killed.

However, it was only with the triple-Oscar-winning movie *The Killing Fields* (1984), directed by Roland Joffé, that the murders designed by Khieu and his fellow Khmer Rouge leaders became part of the West's public consciousness. A harrowing, historically accurate film about Cambodian journalist Dith Pran (played by Haing S. Ngor), who experienced firsthand the murders of the Khmer Rouge, *The Killing Fields* unflinchingly recreated how the Khmer Rouge left their victims' bodies piled in immense shallow graves. When rain washed away the earth, their skulls and bones were left exposed to the sun.

In spite of this documentation, but because they opposed the Vietnamese-installed government in Cambodia, the West and China supported Khieu and his Khmer Rouge for more than a decade after the atrocities of the killing fields had taken place. Khieu was accepted diplomatically as Khmer Rouge leader and invited to participate in U.N.-sponsored elections in 1993. By 2006, a U.N. tribunal had begun to investigate aging Khmer Rouge leaders in preparation for a trial, but the long delay continued to cast a dark shadow on the global effort to hold accountable those implicated in crimes against humanity.

FURTHER READING

Fawthrop, Tom, and Helen Jarvis. *Getting Away with Genocide?* London: Pluto Press, 2004. Passionate chronicle of the struggle to bring surviving Khmer Rouge leaders such as Khieu Samphan to trial. Annexe A has a short biography of Khieu. Illustrated, with notes, bibliography, and index.

Heder, Stephen. *Pol Pot and Khieu Samphan*. Clayton, Vic.: Centre of Southeast Asian Studies, 1991. Detailed account of Khieu Samphan's notorious purges of fellow Khmer Rouge cadres; makes the case for Khieu's liability.

Kiernan, Ben. *The Pol Pot Regime*. New Haven, Conn.: Yale University Press, 1996. Detailed presentation of people, including Khieu, responsible for the Cambodian genocide; shows their politics. Illustrated, notes, index, bibliography.

Short, Ben. *Pol Pot*. New York: Henry Holt, 2005. Comprehensive biography of Khmer Rouge dictator includes detailed discussion of Khieu Samphan, one of his most loyal allies. Illustrated, with notes, index, and bibliography.

—R. C. Lutz

SEE ALSO: Pol Pot; Ta Mok.

AYATOLLAH KHOMEINI
Islamic cleric and leader of the Iranian Revolution

BORN: May 17, 1900, or September 24, 1902;
   Khomein, Iran
DIED: June 3, 1989; Tehran, Iran
ALSO KNOWN AS: Ruhollah Musawi (birth name);
   Ayatollah Seyyed Ruholla Khomeini (full name)
CAUSE OF NOTORIETY: Ayatollah Khomeini was responsible for the imprisonment, torture, and deaths of thousands of Iranian dissidents, and he stubbornly refused to stop an unwinnable war with Iraq.
ACTIVE: 1963-1989
LOCALE: Primarily Iran

EARLY LIFE

Born in a small village in the Isfahan region of Iran, Ruhollah Khomeini (koh-MAY-nee) was the son of a respected cleric of the Shiite branch of Islam. When he was five months old, his father died, and he moved into the home of a moderately prosperous uncle. He studied at a maktab (traditional religious school), where he reportedly memorized the Qur'ān (Islamic scripture) by the age of six. He completed his theological education at the Fayzieh seminary in Qom, where his primary mentor was Abd al-Karim Haeri, who was an ayatollah (a high Shiite clergyman).

In 1928, Khomeini completed his studies and began his career as a teacher and mullah (Shiite clergyman) at the Fayzieh seminary. He soon gained a reputation as both an outstanding scholar and teacher and a man of great piety. Emphasizing the social teachings of Islam, especially the duty to help the poor, he spent long hours in theological discussions with his students. Khomeini eschewed involvement in political activities through the first decade of his career. Rather, he pursued the path of Islamic mysticism and followed the quietist policies of the esteemed seminary leader Ayatollah Hosayn Borujerdi.

POLITICAL CAREER

In the 1940's, Khomeini gradually became politically engaged. He published his first political book, *Kashf-i asrār* (1944; secrets revealed), which castigated the Iranian government for its secularism and pro-Western policies. In 1955 he tried but failed to convince Borujerdi to participate in a campaign against the unpopular heterodox sect, the Baha'i. When Borujerdi died in 1961, Khomeini was a senior ayatollah and was widely revered as the most charismatic "source of imitation" in Qom.

In 1962, he led a successful campaign against a newly enacted law that would have allowed non-Muslims to participate in local councils. In January, 1963, the Shah of Iran, Mohammad Reza Shah Pahlavi, announced plans for an American-inspired program of reforms called the White Revolution, which was designed to make Iran more liberal and secular. Khomeini was the leading voice opposing the Shah's program. His declarations and speeches denounced the Shah for promoting moral corruption and submitting to America and Israel.

On June 5, 1963, Khomeini was arrested and imprisoned in Tehran, where he remained a prisoner for ten months. When released, he continued to attack the government, and in November, 1964, he was exiled to Turkey. Disliking Turkey's secularism, he moved to Iraq and lived there for the following thirteen years. During this time he formulated the concept of an Islamic republic, to be supervised by a supreme religious leader, called the *faqih*. By late 1977, Khomeini was calling himself "Imam," the highest title of a Shiite teacher-leader.

Throughout 1978, violent confrontations in Iran between pro-Khomeini protesters and the police resulted in heavy loss of life. In January, 1979, the Shah, unable to restore order, left Iran. When Khomeini returned to the

Ayatollah Khomeini in 1979. (AP/Wide World Photos)

country on February 1, gigantic crowds welcomed him with unrestrained emotion. On February 11 the royalist prime minister resigned, marking the triumph of the Iranian Revolution. Khomeini appointed Mehdi Bazargan as political leader of the provisional government.

After receiving approval in a referendum, Khomeini proclaimed the establishment of the Islamic Republic on April 1, 1979. He was named the first *faqih* of the republic. During the following ten years in this position, he crushed opposition groups and consolidated the power of the clerics. The judiciary system was organized according to Islamic law, the sharia, and numerous Iranians opposed to the new regime were sentenced to death or to long prison sentences.

In late 1979, when Khomeini supported the seizure of the U.S. embassy by students in Tehran and the taking of some fifty American hostages, most of the moderates left the government. Soon thereafter, the extreme violence of the Iran-Iraq War (1980-1988) further radicalized the revolution. During the tumultuous year of 1981, Khomeini had Abolhasan Bani Sadr and other moderates removed from the government. After two bombs killed a new president and other political leaders, Khomeini endorsed the use of terror against anyone suspected of disloyalty, and he called on citizens to spy on their neighbors.

According to Amnesty International, at least 5,447 executions had occurred under the regime by the end of 1983. Not long before Khomeini died of a heart attack in 1989, he issued his most infamous fatwa (religious decree), ordering the murder of author Salman Rushdie as punishment for writing a novel disrespectful of the Islamic religion.

IMPACT

Ayatollah Khomeini played a key role in the overthrow of a dictatorial government, and he was the dominant figure in one of the most important revolutions of modern history. He was a complex man firmly committed to a militant version of Islam, which included a progressive conception of social justice, particularly as it related to helping the poor.

Once in power, nevertheless, Khomeini proved to be an intolerant and tyrannical leader. He had disdain for the notion of individual liberty, and he showed no sympathy for religious "heretics" or opponents of the revolution. His stubborn resolve to continue the war with Iraq resulted in the deaths of tens of thousands of soldiers, and his continuing support for the illegal taking of American hostages did considerable harm to the Iranian economy.

THE AYATOLLAH'S FAREWELL

From the Ayatollah Khomeini's last testament, dated February 15, 1983:

You, Mujahid nation, move under an emblem and banner that is waving everywhere in the moral and material world! Whether you are aware of it or not, you are treading in a path that is the path of all prophets and is the only path to happiness and bliss! This is the incentive or motive of the prophets in accepting and embracing martyrdom. This is what makes martyrdom to them sweeter than honey. Your youth have experienced this at the battle grounds and it has made them live in ecstasy ever since. It is reflected in the souls and conduct of their brothers, sisters and parents. We must truly say: "We wish we were with you, perhaps we, too, could be blessed with a great success." May they enjoy the breeze that delights the heart and the "sight" that sets fire to it. We should know that a fragment of that "sight" or "epiphany" is made manifest in the hot, cultivated fields; in enervating factories, workshops; in industrial centres of research, development and inventions; in the nation on the whole; in the bazaar, the streets and rural areas; and in all who serve Islam, the Islamic Republic and work toward progress and self-sufficiency. As long as this spirit of co-operation and dedication prevails in the society, our country shall, God willing, be immune to worldly woes. Thank God, the theological centres, the universities and the young generation in education institutes, have all been blessed with the divine spirit. They have control over all these agencies which, God willing, are safe from encroachment by the saboteurs and perverts. My advice to all is to advance towards self-awareness, self-sufficiency and independence with the remembrance of God. Without a doubt His helping Hand is with you if you be with Him and continue in this spirit of Ta'avon [co-operation] for advancement of the Islamic country. I pray that all that I see in the noble nation of alertness, intelligence, commitment, devotion, spirit of resistance, and courage being employed in the path of God, shall, by His Grace, be transmitted to the successive future generations with increased momentum. With a peaceful mind, a certain heart, a happy spirit, and a conscience hopeful for God's mercy, I take my leave of all brothers and sisters to journey to the eternal abode.

FURTHER READING

Abrahamian, Ervand. *Khomeinism: Essays on the Islamic Republic.* Berkeley: University of California Press, 1993. A revisionist work that portrays Khomeini as a populist leader who defended the lower-middle class.

Bakhash, Shaul. *The Reign of the Ayatollahs: Iran and the Islamic Revolution.* New York: Basic Books, 1984. Includes a very good summary of Khomeini's ideas and career.

Brumberg, Daniel. *Reinventing Khomeini: The Struggle for Reform in Iran.* Chicago: University of Chicago Press, 2001. A scholarly account of the conflict between moderates and radicals after Khomeini's death.

Khomeini, Ruhallah. *Islam and Revolution: Writings and Declarations.* Translated by Hamid Algar. Berkeley: University of California Press, 1981. Collection of Khomeini's writings on political theory and Islamic government.

Moin, Baqer. *Khomeini: Life of an Ayatollah.* New York: St. Martin's Press, 2000. Based on interviews and original sources, this is a readable and scholarly biography that is highly respected by experts in the field.

Rajaee, Farhang. *Islamic Values and World View: Khomeyni on Man, the State, and International Politics.* Washington, D.C.: University Press of America, 1983. An excellent analysis of Khomeini's ideas.

—*Thomas Tandy Lewis*

SEE ALSO: Mohammad Reza Shah Pavlahi.

NIKITA S. KHRUSHCHEV
Soviet premier (1958-1964)

BORN: April 17, 1894; Kalinovka, Russia
DIED: September 11, 1971; Moscow, Soviet Union
ALSO KNOWN AS: Nikita Sergeyevich Khrushchev (full name)
CAUSE OF NOTORIETY: Khrushchev led the Soviet Union during the formative years of the Cold War and made important symbolic revisions to Soviet foreign policy, including the escalation of nuclear weapons development.
ACTIVE: 1953-1964
LOCALE: Moscow, Soviet Union

EARLY LIFE
Nikita Sergeyevich Khrushchev (khroosh-CHAWF) was born to a peasant family and grew up during the last few decades of the Russian Empire. The family moved to Yuzovka in the Ukraine, and while still a teenager, Khrushchev began working in a factory. He became part of a group that pressed for better conditions and organized a strike. Khrushchev was fired from that job, and when he gained employment elsewhere, he continued to press for workers' rights and organized strikes. The 1917 October Revolution brought the Communist Party to power in Russia. Khrushchev joined the party in 1918 and volunteered to serve in the Red Army during the Russian Civil War (1918-1922). After the end of the war, he accepted a position in the Communist Party in the Ukraine.

POLITICAL CAREER
Within a few years, the struggle to succeed the first premier of the Soviet Union, Vladimir Ilich Lenin, was under way, and Khrushchev supported Joseph Stalin in his bid for power. Stalin's victory over his rivals opened many possibilities for Khrushchev. In 1929, he moved to Moscow and proceeded to rise within the party hierarchy. By the mid-1930's, he was entrusted with major construction projects and proved his reliability to Stalin. Khrushchev also actively participated in Stalin's purges, which resulted in the deaths of hundreds of thousands of Soviet citizens, including many party leaders.

Khrushchev went back to the Ukraine in 1938 as the leader of the Communist Party in that republic. In 1939, he became a member of the Politburo, the most important committee of the Communist Party. When the Soviet Union and Germany divided Poland in 1940, Khrushchev was given the task of politically securing the occupied territory. When the Germans attacked the Soviet Union in 1941, he was made a general and led the underground resistance to Germany within the Ukraine. After the war, Khrushchev worked to rebuild the region and was then appointed the Soviet agricultural minister.

During the last few years of Stalin's rule, Khrushchev managed to survive further purges and was strategically placed to move into power at the time of Stalin's death in March, 1953, despite power struggles from several factions of the Communist Party.

Georgi Malenkov was expected to be Stalin's successor for the top posts both in the government and in the Communist Party. However, Khrushchev replaced Malenkov as the first secretary of the party in September, 1953. This move was presented to the world as a time of collective leadership, rather than the power struggle it truly was. When Malenkov resigned as the head of the state, it was clear Khrushchev had won. Unlike Stalin, who had all his rivals executed, Khrushchev had most rivals either removed from the Communist Party or assigned to positions far away from Moscow.

SOVIET LEADER
At the Twentieth Party Congress in 1956, Khrushchev gave what was called his Secret Speech, in which he criticized Stalin's brutal leadership and said he would embark on a series of "de-Stalinization" reforms. Within a year, Khrushchev was at the height of his power, free to make major domestic and foreign policy changes. He released millions from prison camps and decentralized the government's economic planning apparatus. He was also impressed by American methods of agricultural production and tried (unsuccessfully) to use certain aspects of it within the Soviet Union. Khrushchev also claimed the superiority of Soviet over Western science, largely as a result of the Soviets beating the Americans into outer space with the launch of Sputniks 1 and 2 in 1957.

In 1959, Khrushchev announced that there would be a peaceful rivalry between the Communists and the Western countries rather than an antagonistic relationship. It is clear that he was fully convinced that within a few decades the economic power of the Communist states would overwhelm the capitalist system. Many historians point to Khrushchev's emphasis on the buildup of the Soviet space program and focus on nuclear weapon development during this period as key to the beginnings of the Cold War.

Khrushchev was the first Soviet leader to travel widely. This proved to be a mixed blessing for the Soviet Union, as his persona appeared gruff and boorish to many of his hosts. For example, in 1960 during an appearance at the United Nations, Khrushchev pounded the podium with his shoe while shouting in Russian and threatening the West, thus creating an enduring image among Americans of an aggressive leader. Many Americans, fearful of Khrushchev's competitive rhetoric, embraced anticommunism even more fervently.

Cordial diplomatic relations with the United States were stopped short in 1960 when an American U-2 plane was shot down over the Soviet Union. In 1961, the Berlin Wall Crisis—in which a fortification separating East and West Germany was approved by Khrushchev and subsequently built—led to another confrontation with the United States.

CUBAN MISSILE CRISIS

In 1962, the Soviet Union sought to gain a military advantage by placing missiles with nuclear warheads inside Cuba. When U.S. aerial surveillance indicated the construction of the missile site, Khrushchev denied its presence. However, the release of photographs by the United States in October, 1962, showed the world that he had lied. The United States initiated a naval blockade of Cuba and announced it would maintain the blockade until the Soviet Union dismantled the missile site. This event brought the world dangerously close to a nuclear war. After examining his available options, Khrushchev finally announced that he would dismantle the site, withdraw all missiles from Cuba, and agree never to replace them. Within the leadership of the Soviet Union, this was seen as a devastating defeat by the United States. Politically, Khrushchev never was as strong after this episode. This international setback, coupled with a poor agricultural harvest in 1963, gave his rivals the strength to remove him from power on October 14, 1964.

IMPACT

Nikita S. Khrushchev's leadership of the Soviet Union had promise, but it ultimately collapsed. Khrushchev talked about peaceful coexistence with the United States and signed the first Cold War agreements with Americans to ease tensions. However, American leaders recognized that he was in command during the repression of the Hungarian Uprising in 1956, the Berlin Crisis, and the Cuban Missile Crisis. He believed in the agricultural and industrial superiority of the Soviets, while at the same time his policies were responsible for a major collapse in these areas during the early 1960's. Khrushchev did attempt to reform many aspects of Soviet life but never fully moved away from his authoritarian roots. The only Soviet leader not to die in office, his lack of political results and his crude personality led to his removal officially "for health reasons."

FURTHER READING

Khrushchev, Nikita S. *Khrushchev Remembers*. Translated and edited by Strobe Talbot. Boston: Little, Brown, 1970. Published during Khrushchev's lifetime, this book covers his entire political career. While he could not acknowledge his creation of this book at the time, it is authentic.

_____. *Memoirs of Nikita Khrushchev: Commissar,*

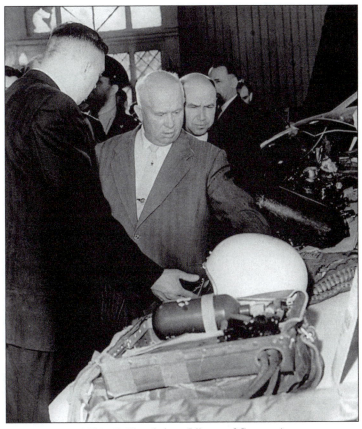

Nikita S. Khrushchev. (Library of Congress)

1918-1945. Translated by George Shriver and Stephen Shenfield. University Park: Pennsylvania State University Press, 2005. This is the first of three volumes from the dictated memoirs of Khrushchev, which are now fully available. This volume deals with the early stage of Khrushchev's political career.

Taubman, William. *Khrushchev: The Man and His Era.* New York: W. W. Norton, 2003. Taubman uses

sources available only since the fall of the Soviet Union to create a full and informed picture of the life, personality, politics, accomplishments, and failures of Khrushchev.

—*Donald A. Watt*

SEE ALSO: Fidel Castro; Vladimir Ilich Lenin; Trofim Lysenko; Joseph Stalin.

WILLIAM KIDD
Scottish pirate

BORN: c.1645; Greenock, Scotland
DIED: May 23, 1701; London, England
ALSO KNOWN AS: Captain Kidd
MAJOR OFFENSES: Piracy on the high seas and murder
ACTIVE: 1697-1698
LOCALE: The Caribbean islands, the west coast of India, and the American East Coast
SENTENCE: Death by hanging

EARLY LIFE
William Kidd (kihd) was reputedly the son of a Covenanting minister, but no historical record of him exists until 1689, when he was among a company of pirates coopted by the governor of the Caribbean Leeward Islands, Christopher Codrington, for service as a privateer against the French in the war between British and French forces. He became captain of the *Blessed William* and

Captain Kidd welcomes a woman aboard his ship in New York Harbor. (Library of Congress)

saw action on the island of Maria Galante and in the relief of Saint Martin before his crew dispossessed him of his ship. They made off with his booty to New York City, at the time a notorious pirate haunt; Kidd gave chase but could not catch them. In New York, Kidd joined the royal forces sent to put down Jacob Leisler's rebellion, an uprising of colonial militia against the policies of King James II. He then settled in the colony and married the twice-widowed Sarah Oort on May 16, 1691; they had two daughters.

CRIMINAL CAREER

Kidd and a merchant named Robert Livingston approached the newly appointed governor of New York and Massachusetts, Richard Coote, earl of Bellomont, with a proposition that he form a corporation with them and raise funding for an expedition to the Indian Ocean, the purpose of which would be to harass the French forces and pirates operating thereabouts. Coote agreed and obtained clandestine funding from several influential Whig peers: the earls of Shrewsbury, Oxford, and Romney and Lord John Somers. Kidd set off in a thirty-gunner ship named the *Adventure Galley*.

After sailing from New York, where he had recruited a crew, Kidd reached Madagascar early in 1697 but then sailed north into the Red Sea and attacked a fleet returning pilgrims from Mecca. *The Sceptre*, an East India Company vessel keeping company with the fleet, defended it. The *Adventure Gunner* then turned for the west coast of India, but Kidd's crew became restless when no ships were captured. Kidd quelled a potential mutiny by killing his gunner, William Moore. He then began attacking ships indiscriminately, perhaps because his enterprise was failing and he was becoming desperate to cover its costs. Of the six vessels he captured, only two were French. The damaged *Adventure Gunner* sank, and Kidd sailed for Europe in the best of his captured ships, the Armenian vessel *Quedagh Merchant*. In the meantime, however, the East India Company had mounted a political campaign against pirates, naming Kidd as an exemplar.

KIDD'S BURIED TREASURE

By Captain William Kidd's own testimony before his trial, he brought back a fortune from the Indian Ocean. Speaking of himself in the third person, he says:

> Whilst he lay at Hispaniola he traded with Mr. Henry Bolton of Antigua and Mr. William Burt of Curacoa, Merchants, to the value of Eleven Thousand Two Hundred Pieces of Eight, whereof he received the Sloop Antonio at 3000 Ps. of eight, and Four Thousand Two Hundred Ps. of Eight in Bills of Lading drawn by Bolton and Burt upon Messers. Gabriel and Lemont, Merchants, in Curacoa, made payable to Mr. Burt who went himself to Curacoa, and the value of Four Thousand Pieces of Eight more in dust and bar gold. Which gold, with some more traded for at Madagascar, being Fifty pounds weight or upwards in quantity, the Narrator left in custody of Mr. Gardiner of Gardiner's Island, near the eastern end of Long Island, fearing to bring it about by sea. It is made up in a bagg put into a little box, lockt and nailed, corded about and sealed. . . . Some of his Sloop's company put two bails of Goods on store at Gardiner's Island, being their own property. The Narrator delivered a chest of Goods, Vizt; Muslins, Latches, Romals, and flowered silk unto Mr. Gardiner of Gardiner's Island to be kept there for him. He put no goods on shore anywhere else.

An inventory of Kidd's booty made after his arrest listed 1,111 ounces of gold, 2,353 ounces of silver, more than 1 pound of rubies and diamonds, 57 bags of sugar, and 41 bags of miscellaneous goods, estimated at approximately six thousand pounds. However, he was rumored to have gathered much more, of which sixteen thousand pounds was his share alone. Where was it? Despite Kidd's statement, rumors also spoke of a "treasure island" where the loot was hidden. Treasure seekers continue to look for it in the modern era. Besides Gardiner's Island, geographic locales that might hold the missing riches include Clark's Island in the Connecticut River near Northfield, Massachusetts; Tenerife in the Indian Ocean; Oak Island near Nova Scotia; and an island in the South China Sea (whose name is a closely kept secret), as well as spots near Plymouth and Cape Cod.

Source: Robert C. Ritchie, *Captain Kidd and the War Against the Pirates* (Cambridge, Mass.: Harvard University Press, 1986).

When Kidd learned that he was an outlaw, he set off for New York, stopping at Hispaniola, an island east of Cuba, to buy a new ship, the *San Antonio*. He spent some time moving up and down the American East Coast, trying to forge another deal with Coote, who dared not support Kidd and eventually had him arrested and shipped to London.

LEGAL ACTION AND OUTCOME

Kidd was held in Newgate Prison in London. On May 8, 1701, he was placed on trial, charged with piracy on the high seas and the murder of Moore. The Tories tried to persuade Kidd to give testimony against the Whig lords who had supported him, but he refused. He was convicted and was hanged on May 23, 1701.

IMPACT

William Kidd's fame, initially promoted by the scurrilous weekly periodical *Newgate Calendar* and a highly fanciful book titled *A General History of the Pyrates* (1724) by Daniel Defoe, was perpetuated by rumors of treasures that he had hidden on remote islands in the Indian Ocean and off the North American coast. The value attributed to his captures was vastly inflated, so what, if anything, he actually buried remains a matter for conjecture. Kidd's legend was given further impetus by Edgar Allan Poe's story titled "The Gold Bug" (1843), and his cause was enthusiastically taken up by supporters who considered him a good American who was manipulated by the British. The six thousand pounds seized by the government upon his conviction were used to purchase the land on which London's Greenwich Hospital now stands.

FURTHER READING

Abbott, John S. C. *The Pioneers and Patriots of America: Captain William Kidd*. New York: Dodd Mead, 1874. An early assertion of the thesis that Kidd was badly treated by the British and that his reputation ought to be rehabilitated, which proved remarkably influential.
Bonner, Willard Hallam. *Pirate Laureate: Life and Legends of Captain Kidd*. New Brunswick, N.J.: Rutgers University Press, 1947. A significant historical examination of Kidd's career and the process of its mythologization, to which subsequent accounts are heavily indebted.
Brooks, Graham, ed. *Notable British Trials: Trial of Captain Kidd*. Edinburgh, Scotland: William Hodge, 1930. Part of a long and relatively respectable series of popular accounts of famous trials, which attempts to correct and counterbalance lurid accounts given in such sources as the *Newgate Calendar*.
Defoe, Daniel. *A General History of the Pyrates*. Edited by Manuel Schonhorn. 1724. Reprint. Mineola, N.Y.: Dover, 1999. A contemporary account of the lives of several pirates, including Kidd.
Ritchie, Robert C. *Captain Kidd and the War Against the Pirates*. Cambridge, Mass.: Harvard University Press, 1986. A historical account that supplements and carries forward the work done by Bonner, paying more attention to the historical context of Kidd's expedition and less to subsequent legend-mongering.

—*Brian Stableford*

SEE ALSO: Samuel Bellamy; Charlotte de Berry; Stede Bonnet; Anne Bonny; William Dampier; Sir Henry Morgan; Grace O'Malley; John Quelch; John Rackham; Mary Read; Bartholomew Roberts; Edward Teach.

KIM IL SUNG
President of the Democratic People's Republic of Korea (1948-1994)

BORN: April 15, 1912; Namri, South Pyongan Province, Korea (now in Mangyongdae, Pyongyang, North Korea)
DIED: July 8, 1994; Pyongyang, North Korea
ALSO KNOWN AS: Kim Song Ju (birth name); Kim Sung Chu; Great Leader; Eternal Leader; Supreme Leader
CASE OF NOTORIETY: Kim invaded South Korea and started the Korean War, which killed millions of Koreans, hundreds of thousands of Chinese, and thousands of Americans. He was also known for harsh treatment of political enemies and for establishing a strict communist regime that defied the world community through its actions and policies.

ACTIVE: 1948-1992
LOCALE: North Korea

EARLY LIFE

Kim Il Sung (kihm ihl soong) was born Kim Song Ju. He was the oldest of three boys born to a middle-class Christian family. Looking to escape Japanese persecution, the family moved to Manchuria, where Kim attended Chinese schools in 1919. He stayed in Korea from 1923 to 1925 in order to continue his education but then moved back to Manchuria. In 1929, Kim was jailed for belonging to a communist youth association. He was released a year later and joined an anti-Japanese guerrilla unit.

In 1932, Kim was made the unit's leader while it operated against the Japanese army in Manchuria. Kim was such an effective guerrilla leader that the Japanese created a special unit to try to capture him. He escaped to the Soviet Union and was forced to join a Soviet military unit made up of Koreans to fight the Japanese.

While in the Soviet Army, Kim changed his name to Kim Il Sung. He received training in communication, espionage, sabotage, and political instruction. During the training in Siberia, Kim and his second wife, Kim Chong Suk, had their first child, Kim Jong-il. Kim served until the end of World War II, achieving the rank of captain.

POLITICAL CAREER

There is no clear official date that Kim began his political career, but his association with the Communist Party and his military ranking during the war contributed to his being appointed head of the provisional government for the North by the Soviets. During the Potsdam Conference in July of 1945, the Americans and Soviets agreed to the invasion of Korea and the split occupation of Korea, divided by the thirty-eighth parallel. The United Nations called for elections to allow the people of Korea to choose a government for a unified Korea. However, when the Soviets and North Korea refused, the establishment of two Koreas began.

As head of the provisional government of North Korea, Kim solidified his power. He introduced a series of reforms, including the establishment of the eight-hour workday and equality of the sexes; redistribution of land from the Japanese, Japanese collaborators, or enemies of the regime; a repression of religions; nationalization of industry; and the introduction of a Soviet style of economic planning. When national elections were not held in 1948 to establish a unified government for the whole of the Korean peninsula, Kim, with the backing of the Soviets, declared the independence of the Democratic People's Republic of Korea and stated that it was the only legitimate government on the peninsula.

After declaring independence, Kim continued purging all opponents within the Korean Workers Party (KWP) and the military. When the United States reduced its military presence in South Korea, Kim began to encourage the Soviets and Chinese to help invade the South. Both the Soviet leader, Joseph Stalin, and Chinese leader, Mao Zedong, denied outright support of Kim but continued to supply weapons and advisers. After constant pleading, both leaders acquiesced to Kim's requests, and on June 25, 1950, Kim's North Korean Army invaded South Korea.

Kim's goal for the invasion was to unite the two Koreas under communist control. After achieving initial success, the North Korean army was defeated by a combined United Nations force led by United States soldiers and commanded by General Douglas MacArthur. By Christmas of 1950, the U.N. forces had pushed past the thirty-eighth parallel and were at the northernmost border of North Korea. Fearing invasion from the American-led U.N. forces, the Chinese government sent hundreds of thousands of its soldiers into North Korea and attacked the U.N. army. This began a two-and-a-half-year struggle that resulted in a draw and restored the original border at the thirty-eighth parallel; the two Koreas were once again separated. An official peace treaty between the United States, South Korea, and North Korea has never been signed.

To try to save political face, Kim declared victory over the "imperialist" Americans and claimed he had protected his people from becoming slaves of the United States. This "victory" was bittersweet: The infrastructure of North Korea was devastated. To curb political dissent, Kim established worker camps to house "political prisoners" based on the Soviet gulag system. By the end of the twentieth century, it was estimated that between 150,000 and 200,000 political and criminal prisoners had been held in these political penal-labor colonies. Many of the inmates faced life sentences for offenses that included singing Western or South Korean pop music, reading a foreign newspaper, or insulting the North Korean government. Kim went so far as to declare that the seed of the enemies of the state must be eradicated through three generations, which condemned the families of political prisoners to life imprisonment without a trial.

POSTWAR POLICIES

Kim's postwar policies included a political ideology that emphasized the need for autonomy and patriotic self-reliance. This policy stressed the benefits of self-sacrifice, discipline, unity, dedication, and patriotism. However, Kim traveled regularly to the Soviet Union, China, and Eastern Europe, asking for financial loans and other forms of aid to rebuild and reconstruct the devastated North Korean economy and infrastructure.

Kim portrayed himself as a strong, always victorious commander who knew what was best for the people, even making the people call him Great Father. Kim had the calendar remade so that the year of his birth was year one and had his birthday declared a national holiday. He forbade all political dissent and even placed himself at the head of the new state religion that all North Koreans had to follow. At his death, there were more than thirty-four thousand statues of Kim around the country.

During the mid-1950's, Kim saw positive results in his Soviet-style economic plan. North Korea was surpassing the South in industrial output. The collectivization of the farming industry also saw a rise in the standard of living in rural areas. This prosperity continued until the late 1970's, when military expenditures began to outpace industrial and food production. North Korea eventually became the first communist country to default on loans from free-market countries.

By the mid-1980's, North Korea had amassed a huge debt that it could not repay. Kim went on a tour of the Eastern bloc nations looking for assistance and economic aid. By 1986, North Korean debt had reached six billion (U.S.) dollars, and Japan officially declared it to be in default. North Korea also began to show signs of food shortage and famine. Kim responded by continuing to pursue nuclear weapons. He established a policy of using his nuclear weapons program as leverage to force other nations to make concessions to North Korea. This policy, continued by his son, Kim Jong-il, has been highly successful.

IMPACT

Kim Il Sung was a defiant guerrilla leader who came of age and governed a country during a difficult and dangerous time of the twentieth century. A master of getting what he wanted, Kim used whatever means he thought necessary to become one of the most ruthless people of the twentieth century. He never gave up on his desire to reunite the Korean peninsula. On many different occasions, North Korean commandos crossed into South Korea to attempt to assassinate the South Korean president. Every occasion failed, though one attempt in 1974 cost the life of South Korea's first lady. Another occasion

cost the lives of seventeen South Korean diplomats in Rangoon, Burma. The North Koreans also kidnapped South Korean citizens and dug infiltration tunnels under the demilitarized zone. In all, South Korean officials believe that, between 1955 and 2006, 454 South Korean and 10 Japanese citizens were kidnapped by the North Korean government.

Furthermore, Kim created a cult of personality that is reminiscent of those created by the likes of Stalin and Adolf Hitler. Under Kim's direction—one that was continued by his son—North Korea ignored the international community and sought goals that met its own specific agenda, regardless of the impact on its neighbors or the world.

FURTHER READING

Lankov, Andrei. *From Stalin to Kim Il Sung: The Formation of North Korea, 1945-1960*. Philadelphia: Rutgers University Press, 2003. A rare look into the early years and formation of the only lasting Stalinist communist regime left in the world. It also describes the only known coup attempt against Kim in 1956.

Sohn, Won Tai. *Kim Il Sung and Korea's Struggle: An Unconventional Firsthand History*. Jefferson, N.C.: McFarland, 2003. A retired doctor and boyhood friend of Kim, Sohn offers a rare and detailed look at the life and sudden death of the North Korean leader.

Suh, Dae-Sook. *Kim Il Sung: The North Korean Leader*. New York: Columbia University Press, 1988. A comprehensive look at the early life, politics, and rise to power of one of Asia's most ambitious leaders of the twentieth century.

—*Karen L. Hayslett-McCall*

SEE ALSO: Adolf Hitler; Kim Jong-il; Joseph Stalin; Suharto.

KIM JONG-IL
Dictator of the Democratic People's Republic of Korea (1994-   )

BORN: February 16, 1941; Vyatskoye, Siberia, Soviet Union (now in Russia)

ALSO KNOWN AS: Kim Chŏng-il; Yuri Iresenowich Kim (Soviet name); Dear Leader; Party Center; Peerless Leader; Great Successor to the Revolutionary Cause

CAUSE OF NOTORIETY: Noted for his eccentricities, Kim Jong-il is best known for his strict enforcement of police state policies in North Korea.

ACTIVE: Beginning in 1994

LOCALE: North Korea, mainly Pyongyang

EARLY LIFE

Kim Jong-il (kim jong-IHL) was born the oldest son of Kim Il Sung and his first wife, Kim Jong-suk. Born in a Russian camp during the middle of World War II, he at-tended school in China during the Korean War and grad-uated from Naman School in Pyongyang, a school spe-cifically for the privileged children of Communist Party members. According to his official biography, Kim grad-uated in 1964 from Kim Il Sung University with a degree in political economics. He is rumored to have learned the English language at the University of Malta during the early 1970's at the invitation of Maltese prime minister Dom Mintoff.

POLITICAL CAREER

Kim Jong-il began his political career after graduation in 1964 from the university by working his way through the ranks of the Korean Workers Party. He began in the party's elite Organization Department before he was named to the Politburo in 1968. He was appointed deputy

South Korean president Kim Dae-jung, front left, holds hands with North Korean leader Kim Jong-il at a summit. (AP/Wide World Photos)

director of the Propaganda and Agitation Department in 1969. He was made party secretary of organization and propaganda in 1972 and was officially named his father's successor in 1974.

Kim asserted himself within the Korean Workers Party during the Seventh Plenum of the Fifth Central Committee in September, 1973, by leading the "Three Revolution Team" campaigns. This earned him the nickname "Party Center" because of his growing influence over the day-to-day operations of the party.

At the time of the Sixth Party Congress in October of 1980, Kim Jong-il had gained complete control of the Communist Party's operations. He advanced through senior posts in the Politburo, the Military Commission, and the party secretariat. By the time of his appointment to the Seventh Supreme People's Assembly in February, 1982, it had become clear to international observers that he was the heir apparent to succeed his father as the supreme leader of the Democratic People's Republic of Korea. Kim consolidated his power with his assumption of control over the civil administration and was named the supreme commander of the Korean People's Army.

This last act was completed by his father, Kim Il Sung, in December of 1991, when he announced that Kim Jong-il would replace him as supreme commander. Upon taking control of the post, Kim Jong-il was given the title of marshal, even though he had never served in the military. This detail is particularly important, as the military is very powerful in North Korea's Communist state.

Kim Jong-il became the supreme leader of North Korea upon the death of his father in 1994. With his ascension to the post of general secretary of the Korean Workers Party, Kim had accomplished a dynastic transfer of power never seen before in a communist country. In September of 1998, Kim was reconfirmed as chairman of the National Defense Commission, and the Supreme People's Assembly declared that his position was the "highest office of state." Kim Jong-il has continued as the official head of the North Korean government ever since.

TOTALITARIANISM FATIGUE

In March, 2006, Andrew Scobell, an associate research professor for the Strategic Studies Institute, published Kim Jong-il and North Korea: The Leader and the System. *His introduction considers the nature and future of Kim's government:*

A variety of labels are given to the North Korean regime. These include likening the regime to an organized crime family and to a corporatist organism. . . . Pyongyang does share some of the attributes of organized crime and certainly engages in criminal activity in a systematic and calculating manner. This pattern of illicit behavior includes the production and distribution of narcotics as well as the counterfeiting of foreign currencies, cigarettes, and pharmaceuticals. But the [Democratic People's Republic of Korea] DPRK is more than a crime family; it possesses a massive conventional military force as well as significant strategic forces. . . .

The most accurate way to characterize North Korea today is as an eroding totalitarian regime. While totalitarianism is a powerful and intimidating system, it places tremendous strain on a state and a society—demanding constant activity and mobilization of personnel and exploitation of resources. The costs of maintaining heightened ideological indoctrination, an ever-vigilant coercive apparatus, and a large national defense organization are high and ultimately debilitating. . . .

An absolute dictator still rules the regime. While the regime continues to hold a monopoly of the instruments of coercion, there has been some slippage or erosion in the defining features of totalitarianism. First of all, Kim Jong Il, although he is virtually an absolute dictator, appears to take into account the opinions of others the way his father did not. And ideology no longer appears to be so focused on transforming the state and society and more on the instrumental goals of economic recovery, development, and firming up regime power. . . . As a result of the shift in ideology and alleviation of the climate of terror, the regime has become corrupted literally as bribery is rampant, and figuratively as the regime seeks to preserve its power and status. . . .

Kim has probably at most 10-15 years in which to pave the way for one of his offspring to succeed him. If he lives long enough, it is possible he could be successful. What is less likely is that totalitarianism could survive another leadership transition. At some point, the totalitarian regime will simply collapse or weaken to the extent that it becomes a post-totalitarianism system.

IMPACT

The family dynasty of Kim Il Sung and Kim Jong-il created a cult of personality that is unrivaled in modern times. The North Korean people have suffered war, food shortages, power shortages, a divided country, and countless human rights violations. For years, reports by

North Korean defectors have described political prisons like the old Soviet-style Gulags. Such prisons allegedly held political prisoners and others who spoke out against Kim Il Sung, Kim Jong-il, or the government.

During the 1980's, Kim Il Sung reinforced a policy of national self-reliance. North Korea discontinued all trade with its two biggest trading partners, China and the Soviet Union. The primary purpose was to fend off foreign criticism and influence in North Korea. This put a great strain on North Korea's already weak economy. Without side markets, the nation's economic crisis worsened. North Korea began to default on its loan repayments to various Eastern and Western countries. Kim Jong-il was forced to take extreme measures to try to raise hard currency to fend off debt collectors. These included state-sanctioned drug dealing and kidnapping of Japanese citizens.

The North Koreans have also been accused of kidnapping citizens from South Korea and Japan to help teach in their espionage schools. A book published by two former captive South Koreans, a film producer and an actress, discussed how they were forced to participate in North Korea's fledgling film industry and propaganda films. Other books published by North Korean defectors describe Kim Jong-il as an insecure man, self-conscious about his height, whose lavish luxuries included a ten-thousand-bottle wine cellar, sports cars like the Mazda RX-7, and parties lasting for days, where guests were forced to overindulge on food and drink. Kim was said to enjoy all of these luxuries while millions of North Koreans suffered food shortages and starvation every year.

North Korea's right to possess nuclear weapons created contention between Kim Jong-il and other world governments, particularly in the West. For years, North Korea tried to be a player in regional and world affairs. Kim Jong-il believed that by becoming a nuclear power, he would be able to influence regional policies. In pursuing his desire to become a nuclear power, Kim Jong-il put the rest of the world in danger and violated many treaties and agreements. China, Japan, South Korea, Russia, and the United States conducted talks with North Korea in an attempt to dissuade Kim Jong-il from pursuing this dangerous goal. In April, 2005, Kim Jong-il nevertheless stunned the world by announcing that North Korea had already developed a nuclear arsenal, and on July 4, 2006, North Korea tested five short-range and one long-range nuclear missiles, followed with underground tests in the fall. These defiant acts aroused international alarm.

FURTHER READING

Becker, Jasper. *Rouge Regime: Kim Jong-il and the Looming Threat of North Korea.* New York: Oxford University Press, 2005. Paints a disturbing picture of North Korea, which is led by a dangerous man supported by a fanatical population. Becker describes the cult of personality around Kim Jong-il as unmatched in modern history.

Breen, Michael. *Kim Jong-il: North Korea's Dear Leader.* New York: John Wiley & Sons, 2004. Takes an in-depth look into one of the world's remaining communist countries. Breen examines how the North Korean people, suffering from food and energy shortages, still support the North Korean leadership.

Harrold, Michael. *Comrades and Strangers: Behind the Closed Doors of North Korea.* New York: John Wiley & Sons, 2004. Harrold served seven years as an English translator and adviser to both Kim Sung Il and Kim Jong-il. His insights into the leadership and youth of North Korea are impressive.

—*Karen L. Hayslett-McCall*

SEE ALSO: Fidel Castro; Saddam Hussein; Kim Il Sung; Pol Pot; Suharto; Than Shwe.

SANTE KIMES
American con artist and murderer

BORN: July 24, 1934; Oklahoma City, Oklahoma

ALSO KNOWN AS: Sante Louise Singhrs (birth name); Sandra Chambers (adopted name); Sondra Chambers; Sandy Chambers; Irene Silverman

MAJOR OFFENSES: Second-degree murder, grand larceny, forgery, possession of forged instruments, eavesdropping, conspiracy to violate slavery laws, illegal weapons possession, and criminal possession of stolen property

ACTIVE: 1961-1998

LOCALE: New York, New York, and Los Angeles, California

SENTENCE: Five years' imprisonment for conspiracy to violate slavery laws, paroled after three years; 120 years and eight months to life imprisonment for death of Irene Silverman; life in prison without parole for murder of David Kazdin

EARLY LIFE

Sante Kimes (SHAWN-tay kimz) was born Sante Louise Singhrs into a sharecropping family in Oklahoma during the Great Depression. After Sante's East Indian father died in 1940, her mother moved the family to Los Angeles. Because Mrs. Singhrs worked as a prostitute and neglected her children, family friends arranged for Sante's adoption by a Nevada couple, Edwin and Mary Chambers, in 1945. As Sandy Chambers, Sante led a typical teenager's life, although later she would claim that Edwin Chambers had molested her.

Sante graduated from high school in 1952. After a brief marriage, she took secretarial courses and found clerical work in California. In 1957, she married architect Ed Walker, with whom she had a son; the couple divorced in 1968. She met Kenneth Kimes in 1970 and began using his name after she claimed to have married him; Kimes, however, told family members that he had never married Sante. Their son Kenny, Jr., was born in 1975. Kenneth Kimes, Sr., died in 1994.

CRIMINAL CAREER

Sante cultivated a flamboyant, glamorous image. She was occasionally mistaken for the actress Elizabeth Taylor and would sign autographs in Taylor's name. Although both Walker and Kimes had provided Sante with substantial material wealth, she was arrested fourteen times between 1961 and 1998 for petty theft, grand theft, auto theft, shoplifting, robbery, forgery, and credit card fraud. She was also suspected of arson. In 1986, Sante was sentenced to five years in prison for conspiracy to violate slavery laws, having smuggled young Mexican women into the United States, forcing them to work as unpaid household servants. She was paroled in 1989.

In July, 1998, Sante and Kenny, Jr., were arrested in New York City for buying a Lincoln Town Car the previous February with a bad check. Among their possessions, police found identification belonging to Irene Silverman, a wealthy eighty-two-year-old widow who had been reported missing. Investigators learned that Sante and Kenny were also suspected in the 1998 shooting death of Los Angeles businessman David Kazdin, a onetime friend of Kenneth Kimes.

LEGAL ACTION AND OUTCOME

Although police did not find Silverman's body, prosecutors showed that Sante had forged Silverman's signature, tried to obtain her Social Security number, wiretapped her telephones, possessed a pistol, and had prepared to dispose of a body. Sante had filled fourteen notebooks with handwritten plans for stealing Silverman's identity and assuming control of her property. In 2002, Sante was convicted of fifty-eight charges related to Silverman's murder and sentenced to 120 years and 8 months to life in prison. Furthermore, in 2004, a California court sentenced Sante to life without parole for ordering Kenny, Jr., to kill Kazdin in 1998.

IMPACT

Sante Kimes captured media attention as a larger-than-life character and the mastermind behind a violent mother-and-son criminal team. To police and courtroom observers, her relationship with Kenny, Jr., seemed inappropriately physical, raising suspicions of incest. Sante and Kenny were compared with the heartless con artists in the motion picture *The Grifters* (1990), while their story inspired several books, two television specials, and a television documentary.

FURTHER READING

Havill, Adrian. *The Mother, the Son, and the Socialite: The True Story of a Mother-Son Crime Spree.* New York: St. Martin's Paperbacks, 1999. This melodramatic account of Sante's life and criminal career provides family background on Sante, Kenneth Kimes, and Irene Silverman.

King, Jeanne. *Dead End—The Crime Story of the Decade: Murder, Incest, and High-Tech Thievery.* New York: M. Evans, 2002. Journalist King's disjointed but detailed account includes time lines tracing Sante's life and the Silverman murder trial, along with a sampling of Sante's bizarre letters to her son.

Walker, Kent, with Mark Schone. *Son of a Grifter: The Twisted Tale of Sante and Kenny Kimes, the Most Notorious Con Artists in America.* New York: William Morrow, 2001. Sante's older son wrote this memoir about growing up with Sante and his attempts to disassociate from her.

—*Maureen Puffer-Rothenberg*

SEE ALSO: Bambi Bembenek.

RODNEY KING
American petty criminal

BORN: April 2, 1965; Sacramento, California

ALSO KNOWN AS: Rodney Glenn King (full name); Glenn King

CAUSE OF NOTORIETY: After King was stopped for a traffic violation, his beating at the hands of police was captured on videotape by a witness and received wide news coverage. The police officers involved stood trial; the not guilty verdict triggered the Los Angeles riots.

ACTIVE: March 3, 1991

LOCALE: Lake View Terrace and south central Los Angeles

EARLY LIFE

Born in Sacramento in 1965, Rodney King (RAHD-nee kihng) went by his middle name, Glenn, until he became famous in 1992 under the name on his police report, Rodney. King showed considerable athletic promise but began drinking at an early age. Teenage friends described him as friendly and gentle but capable of irrationality after drinking. He dropped out of high school his senior year and found construction work in Los Angeles.

CRIMINAL CAREER

On November 3, 1989, King was convicted of assault with a deadly weapon and second-degree robbery of two hundred dollars from a convenience store. He was sentenced to prison for two years but was placed on parole. During a traffic stop by the Los Angeles Police Department (LAPD) on March 3, 1991, King was beaten and then arrested.

This police activity was caught on videotape by a bystander, George Holliday, who was wakened by the noise and lights and began taping from his apartment balcony using his new camcorder. Holliday repositioned the camera to get a better view, at which point he captured the officers in the middle of beating King. Television stations later edited out the earlier, blurred segment (which probably provided some context for the beatings) and began to air the tape repeatedly. Police dispatch tapes recorded the almost cavalier speech of the officers who carried out the beating. LAPD had previously paid millions of dollars to victims of police brutality.

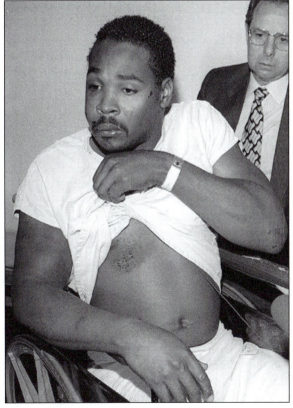

Rodney King shows bruises he sustained after an encounter with L.A. Police Department officers. (AP/Wide World Photos)

RODNEY KING AND THE LAW

Best known as a victim of the police brutality that eventually launched the 1992 Los Angeles Riots, Rodney King became a symbol of the economic disparities and subverted racial hatreds entrenched in America when he asked haltingly why people cannot all "get along." His problems with authorities, however, predated his 1991 arrest and continued well afterward:

- *July 27, 1987:* King's wife complains that he beat her. King is charged with battery and pleads no contest.
- *November 3, 1989:* King attempts to steal cash from a convenience store but becomes a victim of his own weapon, a tire iron, when the store's clerk grabs the iron. King is charged with assault, second-degree robbery, and intent to commit bodily injury. He is sentenced to two years in prison, is paroled on December 27, 1990.
- *March 3, 1991:* California Highway Patrol officers stop King for speeding and failing to stop at speeds exceeding 100 miles per hour. When stopped, King resists an order to lay face-down on the pavement and is beaten and arrested. This incident leads eventually to the Los Angeles Riots a year later, after the officers are acquitted.
- *May 11, 1991:* King is stopped for driving in a car with an overly darkened windshield. He proves to be driving without a license and an expired car registration. He is not charged.
- *May 28, 1991:* King is stopped in Hollywood for a liaison with a transvestite prostitute and, in an attempt to evade arrest, nearly runs over an officer with his vehicle. King is not charged.
- *June 26, 1992:* King's second wife reports domestic violence, and King is transported to the police station. He is later released when his wife refuses to press charges.
- *July 16, 1992:* King is arrested for driving under the influence of an intoxicating substance (DUI). He is not charged.
- *August 21, 1993:* King, driving while drunk, crashes his vehicle in downtown Los Angeles. He is charged with violating parole and is sentenced to sixty days in an alcohol treatment center and twenty days of community service.
- *May 21, 1995:* King is arrested for DUI on his way to Pennsylvania. He is tried and acquitted.
- *July 14, 1995:* King abandons his wife on the freeway. He is charged with assault with a deadly weapon, reckless driving, spousal abuse, and hit-and-run. He is found guilty of hit-and-run driving.
- *March 3, 1999:* King is arrested for injuring his illegitimate teenage daughter and her mother as well as vandalism. He denies guilt.
- *September 29, 2001:* King is arrested for indecent exposure and for using the drug PCP.

LEGAL ACTION AND OUTCOME

Four LAPD officers were charged with using excessive force in subduing King. On April 29, 1992, a California jury acquitted all four of them, which acted as the flash point for the 1992 Los Angeles riots. The verdict had racist overtones: All the officers were white, and they were acquitted in a court located in the mainly white suburb of Simi Valley.

On that day, the verdict triggered growing protests into the late afternoon and evening. Los Angeles television stations began airing live helicopter coverage of mainly young African American and Latino males breaking store windows, looting, and setting fires. Reginald Denny, a white truck driver caught in traffic caused by the mob, was pulled from his truck and beaten. It was clear to those who watched these events live that the lawbreakers—mainly low-income minorities, many of whom would not normally think of crossing such ethical lines—felt justified by what appeared obvious: the political and economic dominance and arrogance of privileged white authorities. Fires burned for three days, and more looting followed. The civil unrest spread throughout the city, making it one of the worst disturbances in Los Angeles history, comparable to the 1965 Watts riots. The LAPD and the California National Guard finally restored order.

IMPACT

Although Rodney King's beating and the attendant trial have been blamed for the riots, the city was suffering from an economic depression caused by the collapse of the aerospace industry and end of the Cold War. The poor—who were largely ethnic minorities—suffered first and suffered most. The repeated vision of white police officers beating a poor black man triggered hostilities fueled by economic stress which aggravated the ethnic divisions and tensions. In south central Los Angeles especially, neighborhoods and small stores had become increasingly ethnically diverse. Much analysis followed, speculating on whether—in the 1990's—racial prejudice or socioeconomic divisions were at the root of the explosive unrest; many concluded that both factors were at fault and that both were deeply intertwined.

The total cost of the riots was estimated at more than one billion dollars. Fifty-five people were killed; 2,387 were injured. Whole neighborhoods looked like war zones. Hundreds of buildings were severely damaged or destroyed. More than eight thousand people were finally arrested.

President George Bush, Sr., and Attorney General William P. Barr ordered the Department of Justice to investigate. A federal grand jury indicted two of the four LAPD officers, and both were sentenced under federal guidelines to thirty months in federal prison for violating King's civil rights. In a civil suit against Los Angeles, a jury awarded King $3.8 million. African Americans, Latinos, and Asian Americans began building working partnerships to reduce friction and began applying for federal development grants.

Rodney King continued to have intermittent trouble with the law for minor infractions. The King beating became a watershed case in the use of force by the police. Many police departments, including the LAPD, changed their practices. The image of Rodney King being interviewed during the riots and asking the question on all Americans' minds—"Can we all get along? Can we all just get along?"—remains a poignant legacy.

FURTHER READING

Abelmann, Nancy, and John Lie. *Blue Dreams: Korean Americans and the Los Angeles Riots.* Cambridge, Mass.: Harvard University Press, 1995. An examination of urban poverty and ethnic conflict between Korean Americans and African Americans in the Los Angeles riots of 1992.

Cannon, Lou. *Official Negligence: How Rodney King and the Riots Changed Los Angeles and the LAPD.* Reprint. New York: Basic Books, 1999. A *Washington Post* journalist's investigation of the LAPD and King beating.

Hunt, Darnell M. *Screening the Los Angeles "Riots": Race, Seeing, and Resistance.* New York: Cambridge University Press, 1997. Combines ethnographic and field research to produce examination of the power of television coverage of the 1992 Los Angeles riots.

Koon, Stacey C., with Robert Deitz. *Presumed Guilty: The Tragedy of the Rodney King Affair.* Washington, D.C.: Regnery, 1992. Biography written by the LAPD sergeant who was in charge of the officers who beat King.

—*William Bourns*

SEE ALSO: O. J. Simpson.

KUNIAKI KOISO
Military officer and prime minister of Japan (1944-1945)

BORN: March 22, 1880; Tochigi Prefecture, Japan
DIED: November 3, 1950; Tokyo, Japan
ALSO KNOWN AS: Koiso Kuniaki; Tiger of Korea
MAJOR OFFENSES: Waging wars of aggression against China, Korea, the United States, and Britain; and barbaric treatment of prisoners of war
ACTIVE: 1937-1945
LOCALE: Korea, China, Pacific islands, and Japan
SENTENCE: Life in prison

EARLY LIFE

Kuniaki Koiso (koo-nee-ah-kee koy-so) was born in 1880 in Tochigi Prefecture at the beginning of the Meiji Restoration. After graduation from a military academy, Koiso fought in the Russo-Japanese War in 1905. He was commander of the Japanese Army in Korea from 1935 to 1938, when Japan embarked on a policy of conquest of the Pacific that helped lead to the global catastrophe of World War II.

MILITARY CAREER

In 1944, as World War II began to show signs of ending, Japan struggled in the face of military losses and huge numbers of casualties in the Philippines and other Pacific islands; defeat was inevitable. Japan's enemies (the United States, Britain, Russia, and China, known collectively as the Allied Powers) were increasing the pressure by winning victories on occupied Pacific islands. The Allies were also increasing their industrial output and growing stronger while the Axis Powers (Italy and Germany) had surrendered or were close to defeat. Prime Minister Hideki Tojo and his cabinet resigned under political pressure on July 14, 1944, opening the way for a new government under Koiso. Japan needed to surrender in order to bring World War II to a swift conclusion, and many Japanese citizens hoped a new government would indeed change course and exit the war.

As governor general of occupied Korea, Koiso had overseen massacres of innocent Chinese and Korean civilians. He was known as the Tiger of Korea because of his extreme cruelty and his management of prisoner-of-war (POW) death camps, in which he failed to change the culture of militarism and aggression. He tortured and killed numerous Chinese and Korean civilians, while Chinese, Korean, and Allied soldiers were forced to march in cruel and inhumane conditions. Japanese army units wantonly destroyed Chinese and Korean villages and private property. Koiso oversaw military forces that routinely carried out atrocities such as rape, mass murder, and arbitrary destruction.

Koiso rose to the status of general in 1942 and served as prime minister of Japan from 1944 to 1945. After he became prime minister, to the frustration of many Japanese, he advocated continuation of an offensive military strategy and supported the policy of fighting to the death. Koiso knew about POW death camps that were operated by the Japanese military and did nothing to stop them.

LEGAL ACTION AND OUTCOME

The International Military Tribunal for the Far East (also known as the Tokyo War Crimes Tribunal) sentenced Koiso as a class-A war criminal in 1948. He was charged with being a leader of a plan to wage wars of aggression in violation of international law, a charge that took into consideration his unprovoked wars against China, the United States, Britain, the Netherlands, and Russia. Koiso and the Japanese military were convicted of carrying out a strategy of conquest that involved murder, torture, and forced labor of POWs and innocent civilians.

IMPACT

Kuniaki Koiso's involvement in World War II atrocities was undeniable. His conviction among twenty-eight class-A war criminals at the War Crimes Tribunal helped to bring major perpetrators to justice and moved Japan toward rebuilding its social and government institutions. With Koiso in prison, Japan could begin to realize its goal of becoming a constitutional democracy under the rule of law.

FURTHER READING

Duus, Peter, ed. *The Cambridge History of Japan.* Vol. 6 in *The Twentieth Century.* Cambridge, England: Cambridge University Press, 1988. This authoritative work is the standard in the field of Japanese history. This volume expertly brings together the best scholars in the modern period while the other volumes cover Japan from its origins to the present.

Rees, Laurence. *Horror in the East: Japan and the Atrocities of World War II.* Cambridge, Mass.: Da Capo Press, 2002. Based on interviews with survivors and military veterans, the book describes the horror of Japanese war crimes. In earlier wars, Japan treated POWs with respect, but the new political climate of tyranny and assumption of racial superiority led to brutal crimes against humanity.

Tanaka, Yuki. *Hidden Horrors: Japanese War Crimes in World War II.* Boulder, Colo.: Westview Press, 1996. The first in-depth and fully researched historical work by a Japanese scholar on Japanese war crimes, including information on the Sandakan POW camp, the Geneva Convention, cannibalism, rape, and civilian massacres.

—*Jonathan L. Thorndike*

SEE ALSO: Hirohito; Hideki Tojo.

DAVID KORESH
American leader of the Branch Davidians

BORN: August 17, 1959; Houston, Texas
DIED: April 19, 1993; Waco, Texas
ALSO KNOWN AS: Vernon Wayne Howell (birth name)
CAUSE OF NOTORIETY: Koresh and his religious followers were involved in a shoot-out with agents of the federal Bureau of Alcohol, Tobacco, and Firearms (ATF). A fifty-one-day standoff ensued, and Koresh and eighty-five Branch Davidian members were killed.
ACTIVE: February 28-April 19, 1993
LOCALE: Waco, Texas

EARLY LIFE

Vernon Wayne Howell, who would later change his name to David Koresh (kohr-EHSH), by most accounts lived a challenging life that was characterized by a tumultuous childhood and indications of violent tendencies in adulthood. Howell was born to a fifteen-year-old single mother in Houston, Texas. He never knew his father and was raised by his grandparents. He described his childhood as lonely and indicated that he suffered abuse at the hands of his stepfather. He also dropped out of high school.

At the age of twenty, Howell joined his mother's church, the Seventh-day Adventists. He became deeply involved in the religious teachings of the church and eventually began to develop his own interpretations of the Scripture to which he was exposed. Howell began to oppose the leaders of the church on various points of Scripture and was eventually asked to leave the church. In 1981, at the age of twenty-two, Howell joined the Branch Davidian religious sect located in Waco, Texas, at a religious compound known as Mount Carmel Center.

RELIGIOUS CAREER

Howell eventually assumed control of the Branch Davidian sect at Mount Carmel. In 1990, Howell legally changed his name, assuming the name David Koresh. His name change had important religious symbolic meaning. Howell maintained that he was now the leader of the biblical house of David and that he was a messiah sent to Earth

by God; hence, he chose the name David. Howell assumed the last name "Koresh" because it is the transliteration of the name Cyrus in Hebrew. Both David and Cyrus are referred to as messiahs in the Hebrew Bible. Howell's new name reflected his belief that he was a messiah and that God had spoken to him and provided him with an interpretation of the Bible that differed from many other interpretations. In essence, Koresh believed that he was the final disciple of Christ who was sent to Earth to spread God's religious teachings.

Koresh also maintained that he was to bear numerous children while the other men in the religious group were to remain celibate. The offspring of Koresh were to represent a good and pure sect of society that would remain intact after a battle between an armed apostate and a group that had remained true to their religious beliefs—in other words, a battle between good and evil. Because of Koresh's views, the members of the religious sect kept firearms at the Mount Carmel Center. There is also evi-

David Koresh in 1998. (AP/Wide World Photos)

WAITING FOR THE APOCALYPSE

The Branch Davidian sect descends from the Baptist preacher William Miller, who prophesied that the Second Coming of Christ would occur in 1844. After the appointed time came and went without incident, some Millerites continued to wait for apocalypse, forming first the Seventh-day Adventist Church and then the Davidian offshoot, which finally became the Branch Davidians. Each branch followed its own succession of prophets (chosen vessels) who foresaw the world's destruction on various dates through the twentieth century. In 1996, the Branch Davidians presented their revelation of the "final event" in March, 2012 A.D.: It All Begins as Foretold. Except for true believers, the book's prediction is grim:

We are living in the last generation that will be hit by a huge comet. This comet's impact shall unleash plagues from a huge exploding crater. All people living in this last generation already perished by the ensuing effects of a comet's impact at the end of the first timeline. Thereafter, Elohiym played over all generations, thereby knowing what will take place in every person's replayed lifetime. Dire events will soon unfold in this last replayed generation. These events were conveyed by Elohiym to the prophets who wrote them in scrolls. Today, many of these scrolls are compiled in the Bible along with the Book of Revelation. The mysteries contained in these divine scriptures can only be revealed by the Chosen Vessel. The conclusion of these mysteries are written in this book. If a person decides not to read the book, his or her fate will be to perish by plagues of sores, anarchy, famine, and death, which he or she experienced in the first timeline. If a person reads this book and rejects its declarations, or believes it, yet fails to allow it to influence a dramatic change in his or her course of life, he or she will again encounter the same fateful end. After a person has diligently studied to comprehend this book's contents and thereafter believes, supports, and forwards its doctrine, then this person's destiny will have changed. This enlightened individual will not perish by the imminent impact of the comet's wrath nor the ensuing effects thereof.

On the morning of February 28, 1993, the ATF planned to execute a raid of the compound to seize the illegal weapons that were believed to be on site. Koresh and his followers knew that they were being investigated by authorities and were tipped off by media that the raid was about to occur, which gave Koresh and his followers time to prepare. As agents approached the compound, shots were fired, and a shoot-out was initiated. Conflicting reports exist concerning who fired first—ATF agents or the Davidians. The shoot-out ended with the deaths of four ATF agents and five Davidian members.

The Federal Bureau of Investigation (FBI) assumed control over the operations in the aftermath of the raid and negotiated with Koresh during a fifty-one-day standoff, during which Koresh claimed to be following the instructions of God, which required him to write religious documents that needed to be completed before he was to surrender. Federal agents worked to make it uncomfortable for the occupants of the compound to stay inside, blasting loud music at the compound for days. The standoff ended on April 19, 1993, when the Branch Davidian compound burned to the ground, killing eighty-five Davidian members, including Koresh.

The burning of the compound proved to be controversial. The official government position was that the Branch Davidians burned down the compound and that at no time during the lengthy standoff did FBI agents fire rounds of ammunition at the Davidians in the compound. However, an independent investigation using infrared technology of film shot from above the compound concluded that FBI agents did indeed fire rounds of ammunition into the compound. Independent accounts of the events at Waco have also countered the government claim that the Davidians started the blaze, asserting that government officials were responsible.

dence that Koresh and his followers engaged in the trade of firearms at gun shows as a method of securing funds to keep the Mount Carmel Center operational.

ATF RAID AND STANDOFF
The activities of the Branch Davidians came under the scrutiny of the federal Bureau of Alcohol, Tobacco, and Firearms. Undercover ATF agents collected evidence suggesting that the Davidians were stockpiling weapons, many of them illegal weapons, and that Koresh had been involved in sexual misconduct involving underage children as young as twelve inside the compound. Subsequent independent investigations would eventually question the veracity of many of the assertions on which these charges were based and question the ATF jurisdictional authority over the sex-based charges.

IMPACT
The ATF standoff with David Koresh and the Branch Davidians initiated questions about the role of government in its regulation of subterranean religious groups

and other subcultures in U.S. society. To many, the siege and standoff at Waco became just one more example of government abuse of authority. Others supported the strong arm of the government to regulate such groups, blaming Koresh and his megalomania for the deaths. The events at Waco also became intricately tied to an event that occurred exactly two years later. On April 19, 1995, Timothy McVeigh and Terry Nichols bombed the Alfred P. Murrah Federal Building in Oklahoma City, killing 168 people. McVeigh claimed that the bombing was a show of retaliation against the government for its handling of the Waco case and a similar standoff that occurred between the AFT and the Randy Weaver family at Ruby Ridge, Idaho, in 1992.

FURTHER READING

Boyle, Peter J. "The Children of Waco." *The New Yorker*, May 15, 1995. Speaks to the ongoing impact of Waco long after it was over.

Linedecker, C. L. *Massacre at Waco, Texas: The Shocking Story of Cult Leader David Koresh and the Branch Davidians*. New York: St. Martin's Press, 1993. Presents the events at Waco in the context of the government's official position: that Koresh was an evil cult leader who was a law violator and needed to be tamed.

Reavis, D. J. *The Ashes of Waco: An Investigation.* Syracuse, N.Y.: Syracuse University Press, 1998. Reavis examines the events of Waco from a multitude of perspectives, including the perspectives of the ATF, the FBI, and the Davidians. Concludes that the government had little reason to investigate the Davidians and lied about key events, including who fired first and allegations of drug and sexual abuse.

Wright, S. A., ed. *Armageddon in Waco: Critical Perspectives on the Branch Davidian Conflict.* Chicago: University of Chicago Press, 1995. Contains critical essays about the history of the Davidians and Koresh and the events at Waco.

—*Kevin G. Buckler*

SEE ALSO: Marshall Applewhite; Jim Jones; Timothy McVeigh; Bonnie Nettles; Terry Nichols; Randy Weaver.

REGINALD KRAY
British gang leader

BORN: October 24, 1933; London, England
DIED: October 1, 2000; Norwich, England
ALSO KNOWN AS: Reggie Kray
MAJOR OFFENSES: Murder and accessory to murder
ACTIVE: 1966-1967
LOCALE: London, England
SENTENCE: Life in prison

EARLY LIFE

Reginald Kray was, along with his identical twin, Ronald, and older brother, Charlie, born and raised in London's East End. His father, Charles, was a peddler who bought and sold goods in the English countryside. During World War II, Charles avoided military service, choosing instead to become a fugitive. Although he provided for the family's financial needs, Charles's occupation and legal troubles meant that he was often absent from family life. Reginald's mother, Violet, was doting, particularly to the twins, and was an influential parent.

Reggie, the first-born twin, and Ronnie were inseparable throughout their lives, but a childhood bout with diphtheria affected their relationship. Reggie was sick for a short time but recovered completely. Ronnie, who nearly died, emerged from the illness slower mentally, more socially awkward, and exceedingly jealous of his twin. Running with childhood gangs and training as boxers, both Reggie and Ronnie were known for their toughness and ferocity, often teaming up to fight older boys in the streets and having their most vicious fights with each other. In the ring, Reggie was the more accomplished boxer, but in the streets Ronnie was known for his rage. From an early age, Reggie spoke of wanting a life of wealth and respectability but instead often followed his younger brother's more violent ways. As teenagers, the twins ran protection rackets but had their first real contact with the legal authorities when, like their father, they refused military service. They spent their late teens as fugitives or locked up in military prisons. It was in these prisons that they began their training as career criminals.

CRIMINAL CAREER

By their early twenties, the Krays were gaining their reputations in the criminal world for their propensity for violence. They bought a billiard hall that became a criminal headquarters, and they began operating as extortionists, offering protection to other criminals in exchange for a fee. The twins surrounded themselves with allies and called their organization "the Firm." Before long, every criminal in the area was paying the twins for protection. Reggie wanted to maintain a low profile, while Ronnie wanted to emulate the gangsters of the Hollywood films, of which he was fond. This tension would remain throughout their criminal career. After Ronnie was arrested and sentenced to three years in prison for his part in an assault, Reggie opened a nightclub. The club attracted celebrities, wealthy Londoners, and others who wanted to rub shoulders with the criminal element. Reggie began thriving as a businessman, but, after his return, Ronnie began to exert control over the organization once again.

In 1960, Reggie was arrested and sentenced to eighteen months' imprisonment for extortion. While on bail, Reggie joined with Ronnie to control a gambling establishment, which became a chief source of income for the brothers. After completing his sentence, twenty-seven-year-old Reggie fell in love with Frances Shea, who was sixteen. During the following five years, the Krays built their empire, providing protection for numerous clubs around London and heading a formidable criminal organization. Their activities brought them to the attention of the authorities, who began investigating and charging the Krays with crimes. During this period, Reggie was charged with breaking and entering, loitering with the intent to steal cars, and demanding money with menaces. In every case, he was either acquitted or the charges were dismissed. These victories made the twins seem invincible to many in the criminal underground, and their reputations continued to grow.

On April 20, 1965, Frances and Reggie were wed, but their marriage would be short-lived. Reggie's criminal activity and the time he spent with his brother and friends were continual sources of tension in the marriage. The two would live together only eight weeks before Frances left. She committed suicide in 1967.

In 1966, Ronnie murdered George Cornell, a criminal rival. This murder put the authorities even more firmly on the trail of the Kray organization. In the wake of his wife's suicide, Reggie became more violent, shooting two men and attacking another with a knife. On October 28, 1967, Reggie committed a murder to match his brother's, killing Jack "the Hat" McVitie, a sometime Firm associate. McVitie had taken money from the Krays to commit a murder, then had kept the money even though he did not carry out the crime. In addition, he had insulted the Krays and their friends. When the Krays confronted McVitie at a bar, Reggie put a gun to McVitie's head and pulled the trigger, but the gun jammed. Reggie then stabbed McVitie repeatedly in the face and neck with a knife, killing him.

LEGAL ACTION AND OUTCOME

Leonard "Nipper" Read, one of Scotland Yard's top detectives, began investigating the Krays' criminal empire and established the twins' pattern of crime dating back over a decade. Although evidence pointed to extortion, bookmaking, assault, and other offenses, the Krays were tried only for the murders of Cornell and McVitie. They were found guilty and sentenced on March 8, 1969, to life in prison with a recommendation that they serve a minimum of thirty years. They were thirty-five years old. In 1997, while still in prison, Reggie married Roberta Jones. He died of cancer in 2000. Ronnie had died in 1995.

IMPACT

Reginald and Ronald Kray, with their Cockney upbringing and celebrity connections, are often viewed as a symbol of swinging London of the 1960's and, like the American Mafiosi, are to some symbolic of a glamorous side to criminal life. Their celebrity grew while they were in prison, as they became the authors and subjects of numerous books and articles and a 1990 feature film by Peter Medak, *The Krays*.

FURTHER READING

Fido, Martin. *The Krays: Unfinished Business*. London: Carlton Books, 2000. Based on public documents. Attempts to discredit much of the Krays' version of events.

Kray, Charlie, and Colin Fry. *Doing the Business*. London: Blake, 1999. The Krays' older brother gives intimate details of their criminal organization.

Pearson, John. *The Cult of Violence: The Untold Story of the Krays*. London: Orion, 2001. Behind-the-scenes story from the Krays' official biographer. Pearson tells secrets here that he could not reveal when the Krays were alive.

_____. *The Profession of Violence: The Rise and Fall of the Kray Twins*. London: HarperCollins, 1995. A famous biography of the Krays, to whom Pearson had access during their criminal days.

—*Bryan Jack*

SEE ALSO: Ronald Kray.

RONALD KRAY
British gang leader

BORN: October 24, 1933; London, England
DIED: March 17, 1995; Slough, Berkshire, England
ALSO KNOWN AS: Ronnie Kray; the Colonel
MAJOR OFFENSE: Murder
ACTIVE: 1966-1967
LOCALE: London, England
SENTENCE: Life in prison

EARLY LIFE

Ronald Kray, along with his identical twin, Reginald, and older brother, Charlie, grew up in London's East End. His father, Charles, a peddler, bought and sold goods in the English countryside. During World War II, Charles avoided military service and instead became a fugitive. Although he provided for the family financially, Charles's occupation and legal troubles meant that he was often absent from family life. Ronnie's mother, Violet, doted on her children, especially the twins.

Reggie, who was born first, and Ronnie were inseparable throughout their lives. As children, both contracted diphtheria. Reggie, who was sick for a short time, made a complete recovery. Ronnie nearly died and emerged from the illness slower mentally, more awkward socially, and very jealous of his twin brother. Running with childhood gangs and training as boxers, both Reggie and Ronnie were known for their toughness and ferocity, often teaming up to fight older boys in the streets and also fighting each other viciously from time to time. Ronnie, while not as skillful a boxer as his brother, was more violent. As teenagers, the twins ran protection rackets, but they had their first real encounters with law enforcement authorities when, like their father, they refused military service. They spent their late teens running from the authorities or locked up in military prisons. It was in these prisons that they began learning the ways of career criminals.

Ronnie, left, and Reggie Kray. (Hulton Archive/Getty Images)

CRIMINAL CAREER

By their early twenties, Reggie and Ronnie were gaining a reputation among East End criminals for their propensity for violence. The billiard hall they bought became a criminal headquarters, and the two brothers began operating as extortionists, selling protection services to other criminals. The twins surrounded themselves with allies and called their organization "the Firm." Before long, every criminal in the area was paying the Kray twins for protection. Reggie wanted to maintain a low criminal profile, while Ronnie wanted to emulate the gangsters of the Hollywood films, of which he was fond. This tension would remain throughout their criminal career.

It was during this time that Ronnie's homosexuality became somewhat of an open secret among the members of the Firm. Ronnie also became obsessed with guns and fantasized about murdering someone. In 1956, Ronnie shot his first victim, wounding a man who had a conflict with a car dealer who paid the Krays for protection. The Krays were able to convince the witnesses not to testify. Later that year, after the Krays assaulted a member of a rival gang, Ronnie was arrested, charged with assault, and began a three-year sentence. In 1958, separated from his brother, Ronnie was diagnosed with schizophrenia. He would battle mental illness the rest of his life, suffering paranoia and delusions.

In 1960, Reggie was arrested and sentenced to eighteen months in prison for extortion. Although Reggie had tried to expand the legitimate side of the Krays' business, under Ronnie's influence, criminal activity took priority. During the next five years, the Krays built their criminal empire, providing protection for numerous clubs around London and heading a formidable criminal organization. Their ability to enlarge their organization, connect with American Mafia groups, and avoid arrest made the twins seem invincible to many in the criminal underground, and their reputations continued to grow. In a nightclub they owned, the Krays attracted celebrities, wealthy Londoners, and others who wanted to rub shoulders with the criminal element.

Ronnie, however, was growing increasingly violent and paranoid. He began keeping a list of people to murder. The authorities were also keeping an eye on the Krays. After a fight involving friends of the Firm and a rival gang turned deadly and a member of the Firm was killed, Ronnie decided he would finally commit the murder he had been planning. In March, 1966, he walked into a pub where George Cornell, longtime rival and a suspect in the Firm member's killing was sitting. Kray shot Cornell in the head at point-blank range, killing him. This murder put the authorities even more firmly on the trail of the Kray organization. In 1967, Ronnie watched and encouraged his brother as Reggie stabbed to death Jack McVitie, a sometime Firm associate. McVitie had taken money from the Krays to commit a murder but had not carried it out.

LEGAL ACTION AND OUTCOME

In the wake of this violence, Leonard "Nipper" Read, one of Scotland Yard's top detectives, took over the investigation of the Krays' criminal empire and established the twins' pattern of crime dating back over a decade. Although evidence pointed to extortion, bookmaking, assault, and other offenses, the Krays were tried only for the murders of Cornell and McVitie. They were found guilty and sentenced on March 8, 1969, to life in prison with a recommendation that they serve a minimum of thirty years. They were thirty-five years old. Ronnie, who identified himself as bisexual, married twice in prison—to Elaine Mildener and Kate Howard. He died of a heart attack in 1995. Reggie died in 2000.

IMPACT

Reginald and Ronald Kray, with their Cockney upbringing and celebrity connections, are often viewed as a symbol of swinging London of the 1960's and, like the American Mafiosi, to some symbolic of a glamorous side to criminal life. Their celebrity grew while they were in prison, as they became the authors and subjects of numerous books and articles and a 1990 feature film, *The Krays*.

FURTHER READING

Fido, Martin. *The Krays: Unfinished Business*. London: Carlton Books, 2000. Based on public documents, attempts to discredit much of the Krays' version of events.

Kray, Charlie, and Colin Fry. *Doing the Business*. London: Blake, 1999. The Krays' older brother, Charlie, gives intimate details of their criminal organization.

Pearson, John. *The Cult of Violence: The Untold Story of the Krays*. London: Orion, 2001. The Krays' authorized biographer tells secrets that he could not reveal when the Krays were alive.

_____. *The Profession of Violence: The Rise and Fall of the Kray Twins*. London: HarperCollins, 1995. A famous biography of the Krays.

—*Bryan Jack*

SEE ALSO: Reginald Kray.

RICHARD KUKLINSKI
Pleasure killer and Mafia hitman

BORN: April 11, 1935; Jersey City, New Jersey
DIED: March 5, 2006; Trenton, New Jersey
ALSO KNOWN AS: The Iceman; the Polack
MAJOR OFFENSE: Murder for hire
ACTIVE: 1949, 1965-1985
LOCALE: New York and New Jersey
SENTENCE: Two consecutive life sentences

EARLY LIFE

Richard Kuklinski (kew-KLIHN-skee) was born on April 11, 1935, in New Jersey. He was raised in a low-income housing project in Jersey City by his strict Catholic parents until the age of sixteen. His father, who was a brakeman for the railroad, and his mother, who worked at a local meatpacking plant, were far from ideal parents; they abandoned Kuklinski and his brother in 1951. Later, after Kuklinski was convicted of murder, he admitted that it was the frequent beatings from his alcoholic father that caused him to become psychologically numb and detached from his victims throughout his murderous career.

At age fourteen, Kuklinski killed his first victim, a local neighborhood bully. At sixteen, Kuklinski began to understand his potential as a fighter when he severely beat six teenage boys with a bar from a neighbor's clothesline. In a 1991 prison interview, Kuklinski openly admitted that he enjoyed the rush and the sense of power that came from beating and killing those who stood in his way or contested him. He also admitted that during his younger years, he had an obsession with torturing and brutally killing neighborhood pets. In one account, he mentioned how he would tie the tails of two cats together and throw them over a clothesline to watch them claw each other to death.

With only an eighth-grade education, Kuklinski took to the streets and became a pool-hall hustler, an enforcer for local bookies, and eventually a film technician, in which capacity he pirated pornographic films for various Mafia members. It was not until the mid-1960's, after he married his wife, Barbara, and began to have children (he would have three), that Kuklinski began his new profession as a contract killer for the mob.

CRIMINAL CAREER

To his family and friends he was a quiet businessman who worked long and sometimes strange hours to support his family. However, to his employers, various Mafia families from both New Jersey and New York, Kuklinski was an enforcer and professional hit man with a tremendous reputation for making his victims suffer. At the pinnacle of his career, Kuklinski was earning nearly fifty thousand dollars a hit and became known as one of the best contract killers in the business.

Kuklinski was known for using numerous heinous methods to kill his victims. His favorite was using liquid cyanide, either lacing his victim's drink or literally throwing the chemical on the victim's skin, to watch him go into cardiac arrest. Kuklinski was also notorious for the various instruments he used to murder his victims, from chainsaws to axes to ice picks. Kuklinski received his nickname the Iceman for his method of freezing his victims' bodies over long periods of time, both to conceal and to prevent discovery of any physical evidence. Kuklinski estimated that in total, he killed more than one hundred people during his criminal career.

LEGAL ACTION AND OUTCOME

Kuklinski was arrested in December, 1986, and was subsequently convicted of four murders in 1988. He received two life sentences, to be served consecutively. He died in March, 2006, in the prison wing of St. Francis Hospital in Trenton. At the time of his death he was scheduled to testify regarding a hit he purportedly made for Mafia boss Sammy Gravano. Authorities, however, considered Kuklinski to have died of natural causes.

IMPACT

Richard Kuklinski is one of the most infamous killers of the twentieth century. He admitted to committing more than one hundred murders. Although this number may never be substantiated, his brutal and heinous tactics gained for him irrefutable notoriety among scholars and clinicians alike. In particular, his contract killings for various Mafia families—in which Kuklinski would torture, kill, and dismember his victims—brought him notable acclaim among his peers. Kuklinski's story was told in two HBO documentary films, one released in 1992, the other in 2001.

FURTHER READING

Bruno, Anthony. *The Iceman: The True Story of a Cold-Blooded Killer.* New York: Dell, 1993. This biography of Kuklinski offers the first look into what some have deemed the most notorious serial murderer in the history of the United States.

Kuklinski, Barbara, and John Driver. *Married to the Iceman: A True Account of Life with a Mafia Hitman and the Inside Story of His Crimes*. New York: E. P. Dutton, 1994. Kuklinski's wife offers a detailed look at the man behind the killer, highlighting his role as a father and husband.

Kuklinski, Richard. *The Iceman Interviews*. Film documentary. HBO Productions, 2004. A unique compilation of interviews conducted with Kuklinski, first in 1992 and then in 2001. He gives a firsthand account of his life as a ruthless role as a hit man for the mob.

—*Paul M. Klenowski*

SEE ALSO: Sammy Gravano.

BÉLA KUN
Hungarian premier (1919)

BORN: February 20, 1886; Szilágycseh, Transylvania, Austro-Hungarian Empire (now Cehu Silvaniei, Hungary)

DIED: November 30, 1939; Moscow, Soviet Union (now in Russia)

ALSO KNOWN AS: Béla Kohn (birth name)

CAUSE OF NOTORIETY: In establishing the short-lived Hungarian Soviet Republic in 1919, Kun became the leader of the first communist state outside the Soviet Union. Later, as leader of the Crimean Soviet Republic, he was responsible for a massacre of opposing troops that surrendered.

ACTIVE: 1917-1939

LOCALE: Hungary and Russia

EARLY LIFE

Béla Kun (BEH-lah koon) was born to a Jewish family in the last decades of the existence of the Austro-Hungarian Empire. Although he is said to have become a Bar Mitzvah at the age of thirteen, the family seems not to have observed any Jewish traditions or customs. This was probably a result of his father's zeal for political liberalism as represented by the Hungarian patriot Lajos Kossuth. Moreover, a powerful assimilationist bent among the Jewish population of Hungary existed at the end of the nineteenth century. Kun was not a successful student, partly because of the faults of his temperament, which were to characterize him throughout his life. Even academic success would not have been a guarantee of employment for one of Jewish background at the time, and Kun turned to journalism for a living.

He also turned to political activity early, inspired by the example of the Hungarian poet Sándor Petőfi, who had given his life to fight oppression. Kun had a sharp literary style, which emerged both in his journalism and in his attacks on his political rivals. After a variety of positions during the period leading up to World War I, he served in the Austro-Hungarian army and was captured by the Russians. During his internment in Tomsk, he was introduced to the writings of Karl Marx and became a devotee of the communist solution to political problems. In particular, he thought that the Marxist analysis would better fit a developed country such as Hungary than a country such as Russia. As a result, when Kun was released after the Bolshevik uprising in Russia in 1917, he was eager to put to work in his homeland the lessons he had learned in prison and from some acquaintance with Russian Bolshevik leader Vladimir Ilich Lenin.

POLITICAL CAREER

Although Kun was not especially well known to the socialists and communists in Hungary when he returned, his claim to know Lenin procured him a hearing and, shortly thereafter, leadership of the coalition of left-wing parties that took over the government in the confusion that prevailed in 1919. While the peace conference that ended World War I was taking place in Versailles, France, the Hungarians were learning with dismay that they were likely to be losing territory to neighbors that had been on the "right" side in the war. The leftist parties seemed to offer the best prospects for military resistance, so they formed a revolutionary governing council on March 22, 1919, without significant resistance; the Hungarian Soviet Republic was formed. Kun displayed a good deal of political adroitness in managing to balance the competing factions within the council, as the communists were pressing for more drastic and more urgent reforms and the socialists were inclined to be more hesitant.

Kun's government proceeded with the nationalization of industries and large sectors of the economy. However, his efforts foundered on two major problems. The nationalizations did not have the effect of improving the lot of the ordinary workers, upon whose goodwill Kun had figured that he could count. One aspect of their resistance was the reluctance to accept the leadership of a Jew, and Kun publicly attacked the anti-Semitism that sparked some of this resistance. The other problem was the perception in the rest of Europe of the danger posed by Kun's Soviet Republic. As a result, the French were almost ready to send troops into Hungary, and the Allies at Versailles encouraged the Romanians and the Czechs to invade. Faced with internal dissension and the arrival of Romanian troops in the Hungarian homeland, Kun and the other commissars on the governing council escaped and took political refuge in Austria. Thus ended, after 133 days, the first communist government in Europe.

Kun claimed to be the interpreter of the lessons of the Hungarian "experiment" when he arrived in Petrograd (now St. Petersburg) in 1920. As chairman of the Crimean Soviet Republic, Kun took advantage of a military victory to order the execution of between ten and twenty thousand White Russian officers and men by firing squad. While there had been some executions during his leadership in Hungary, this was far and away the bloodiest act of his career. The Bolshevik soldiers were not pleased to see their fellow countrymen killed on the orders of a foreigner (and a Jew).

Lenin sent Kun abroad to foment revolution in Berlin in 1921, and Kun saw this as an opportunity to replay his experiences in Hungary. Despite the discouragement of the local communists, he proceeded to organize a putsch (a secret plot to overthrow the government), which failed. Kun abandoned those whom he had led to disaster and returned to the Soviet Union, where he remained active as a member of the Communist administration for many years. Kun, however, had been dependent on the favor of leaders within the party, who eventually fell into disrepute with Soviet premier Joseph Stalin. Kun was left exposed to the fury of Stalin's enmity, and he was imprisoned for subversion in the late 1930's. He may have been tortured while he was in prison, and he was executed in 1939.

IMPACT

Béla Kun's Communist government in Hungary was succeeded by a regime that was close to fascism. The political history of Hungary over the decades that followed veered between political extremes, and Kun deserves at least a share of the blame for rendering moderation dangerous. On the other hand, during the Twentieth Communist Party Congress in the Soviet Union in 1956, Kun's reputation was rehabilitated within the communist world. There have been attempts to see the Hungarian uprising of 1956 and the attempt by Soviet leader Nikita S. Khrushchev to produce a de-Stalinized version of communism during the 1950's as offshoots of Kun's policies and attitudes. It is hard to see this as justified, however, as Kun was never enough of a theoretician to understand the nuances of Marxist thought. His enthusiasm for the Marxist cause was undoubted, but his actions did not benefit even those he sought to serve.

FURTHER READING

Hoensch, Jörg K. *A History of Modern Hungary, 1867-1986.* New York: Longmans, 1988. Describes the political environment in Hungary before, during, and after the Kun years.

Janos, Andrew C., and William B. Slottman, eds. *Revolution in Perspective: Essays on the Hungarian Soviet Republic of 1919.* Berkeley: University of California Press, 1971. Most detailed analysis of the coalition that Kun put together and the difficulties of keeping it intact.

Kontler, László. *A History of Hungary: Millennium in Central Europe.* New York: Palgrave Macmillan, 2002. Assigns blame to the 1919 Peace Conference in Versailles for the conditions Kun had to face.

Molnár, Miklós. *A Concise History of Hungary.* Cambridge, England: Cambridge University Press, 2001. Assesses some of the reasons for the unpopularity of the Kun regime apart from the economic issues.

Tökés, Rudolf L. *Béla Kun and the Hungarian Soviet Republic.* New York: Frederick A. Praeger, 1967. Most detailed work in English on Kun, including his years in the Soviet Union.

—*Thomas Drucker*

SEE ALSO: Vladimir Ilich Lenin; Joseph Stalin; Grigory Yevseyevich Zinovyev.

LADY ALICE KYTELER
Irish witch

BORN: 1280; Kyteler's House, Kilkenny, Ireland
DIED: After 1324; England
ALSO KNOWN AS: Dame Alice Kyteler; Lady Alice
　　Kettle; Alice le Kyteler; Alice Kyteller
CAUSE OF NOTORIETY: First suspected of poisoning
　　some or all of her husbands, Kyteler was accused of
　　sorcery in the first major witch trial in the British
　　Isles.
ACTIVE: 1299-1323
LOCALE: Kilkenny, Ireland

EARLY LIFE
Alice Kyteler (KIT-luh) came from a Norman family that
had settled in Ireland following the conquest of 1169.
Her father died in 1298. Alice, as his only child, inherited
his property and business.

CAREER
In 1299, Alice married one of her father's former associates, William Utlagh (outlaw), a banker twenty years her
senior; they had one son, also named William. She extended her house for use as an inn and became a successful hostess. Following Utlagh's death, Alice married
Adam Le Blond, another banker; after Le Blond's death
in 1310 she married Richard De Valle, a wealthy landlord, and then—in 1320—John Le Poer. Her troubles began when Le Poer sought help at a Franciscan abbey after
falling ill in 1323.

LEGAL ACTION AND OUTCOME
Following Le Poer's death, charges were made against
Alice by her stepchildren that she had murdered some or
all of her husbands by means of poison. These charges
occasioned an enquiry by the Franciscan bishop of
Ossory, Richard Ledrede. The only contemporary record of the affair is an account of that enquiry's findings,
presumably commissioned by Ledrede. Ledrede was
an Englishman, but he had spent considerable time in
France, where the Franciscans were very active in the
persecution of heretics. Ledrede had been there during
the years following the suppression of the Knights
Templars by Philippe le Bel, who had used accusations
of sorcery as a justification for seizing their wealth.
Ledrede was, therefore, well versed in the politics of
slander and pursued Lady Alice's case determinedly.
He had several of Lady Alice's alleged accomplices
flogged, including one of her barmaids, Petronilla of

Meath—who proved quite inventive when suitably encouraged.

Ledrede concluded that ten people were implicated in
the homicides, which had been accomplished by sorcery.
Various apparatuses supposedly used in sorcery were
procured as evidence, and testimony was amassed—
mostly that of Petronilla—regarding the concoction of
poisonous potions whose ingredients included worms,
the fingernails of corpses, and the swaddling-cloths of
unbaptized children. The skull of a decapitated robber
was said to have been used as a mixing bowl, and the
sorcerous proceedings were alleged to have been illumi-
nated by candles made of human fat. Lady Alice, it was
said, had a familiar demon named Robin Artisson who
could appear in the form of a cat, a black dog, or a "negro," and who copulated with her.

Ledrede presented an account of his findings to the
lord chancellor of Ireland, Roger Utlagh—Lady Alice's
brother-in-law—who declined to take any action. The
bishop attempted to institute proceedings on his own authority but was prevented by the seneschal of Kilkenny,
who was related to John Le Poer. The seneschal imprisoned Ledrede, who then excommunicated Lady Alice.
Sued for defamation, Ledrede appeared before the parliament in Dublin—but persuaded them that he was in
the right. With the support of parliament he was able to
take formal legal action against the ten accused, but the
court refused to convict them. By this time, however, the
rumors of sorcery had created a panic, and Petronilla of
Meath was burned on November 3, 1324, in order that
the mob might have satisfaction. Lady Alice allegedly
fled to England, vanishing from the historical record.
Ledrede excommunicated the seneschal but then had to
flee prosecution himself; he spent nine years in Avignon
before returning to lodge charges of heresy against the
archbishop of Dublin.

IMPACT
The Lady Alice Kyteler affair became famous during
the years of the great European witch hunt of the sixteenth century as the first significant sorcery trial in the
British Isles. It became a significant local legend; there
is still a Kyteler Inn in Kilkenny. The peasantry undoubtedly took great delight in the scandal among the
ranks of their Norman overlords, and scholarly fantasists
fascinated by the history of witch trials have taken equal
delight in Petronilla's inventions. Whether Alice actu-

THE CHARGES AGAINST LADY KYTELER

The following, almost certainly spurious, charges were made against Lady Kyteler and her alleged accomplices:

1. They had denied the faith of Christ absolutely for a year or a month, according as the object they desired to gain through sorcery was of greater or less importance. During all that period they believed in none of the doctrines of the Church; they did not adore the Body of Christ, nor enter a sacred building to hear mass, nor make use of consecrated bread or holy water.
2. They offered in sacrifice to demons living animals, which they dismembered, and then distributed at cross-roads to a certain evil spirit of low rank, named the Son of Art.
3. They sought by their sorcery advice and responses from demons.
4. In their nightly meetings they blasphemously imitated the power of the Church by fulminating sentence of excommunication, with lighted candles, even against their own husbands, from the sole of their foot to the crown of their head, naming each part expressly, and then concluded by extinguishing the candles and by crying Fi! Fi! Fi! Amen.
5. In order to arouse feelings of love or hatred, or to inflict death or disease on the bodies of the faithful, they made use of powders, unguents, ointments, and candles of fat, which were compounded as follows. They took the entrails of cocks sacrificed to demons, certain horrible worms, various unspecified herbs, dead men's nails, the hair, brains, and shreds of the cerements of boys who were buried unbaptized, with other abominations, all of which they cooked, with various incantations, over a fire of oak-logs in a vessel made out of the skull of a decapitated thief.
6. The children of Dame Alice's four husbands accused her before the Bishop of having killed their fathers by sorcery, and of having brought on them such stolidity of their senses that they bequeathed all their wealth to her and her favourite son, William Outlawe, to the impoverishment of the other children. They also stated that her present husband, Sir John le Poer, had been reduced to such a condition by sorcery and the use of powders that he had become terribly emaciated, his nails had dropped off, and there was no hair left on his body. No doubt he would have died had he not been warned by a maid-servant of what was happening, in consequence of which be had forcibly possessed himself of his wife's keys, and had opened some chests in which be found a sackful of horrible and detestable things which he transmitted to the bishop by the hands of two priests.
7. The said dame had a certain demon, an incubus, named Son of Art, or Robin son of Art, who had carnal knowledge of her, and from whom she admitted that she had received all her wealth. This incubus made its appearance under various forms, sometimes as a cat, or as a hairy black dog, or in the likeness of a negro (Æthiops), accompanied by two others who were larger and taller than he, and of whom one carried an iron rod.

Source: St. John D. Seymour, *Irish Witchcraft and Demonology* (Dublin: Hodges, Figgs, 1913).

ally poisoned her husbands remains a matter for conjecture.

FURTHER READING

Cohn, Norman. *Europe's Inner Demons: An Inquiry Inspired by the Great Witch-Hunt.* New York: Basic Books, 1975. A general account of the historical, sociological, and psychological origins of the witch hunt, which pays heed to the peculiar circumstances of the Kyteler trial and the significant precedents it set.

Davidson, L. Sharon, and John O. Ward. *The Sorcery Trial of Alice Kyteler: A Contemporary Account.* Binghamton, N.Y.: Center for Medieval and Early Renaissance Studies, 1993. An annotated reprint of the document from which all modern accounts of the trial are taken; the commentary is more conscientious than Wright's, as befits a modern academic study.

Wright, Thomas, ed. *Alice Kyteler. A Contemporary Narrative of the Proceedings Against Dame Alice Kyteler, Prosecuted for Sorcery by Richard de Ledrede, Bishop of Ossory, 1324.* London: Camden Society, 1843. A different and looser translation of the source document, whose tone lends support to a commentary that is far more credulous than the one provided by Davidson and Ward; the source of many subsequent sensational accounts.

—*Brian Stableford*

SEE ALSO: Tamsin Blight; Mary Butters; Margaret Jones; Florence Newton; Dolly Pentreath; Elizabeth Sawyer; Mother Shipton; Joan Wytte.

JEAN LAFFITE
Pirate and sometime patriot

BORN: c. 1780; probably Bordeaux, France
DIED: After 1822; place unknown
ALSO KNOWN AS: Jean Lafitte
CAUSE OF NOTORIETY: Though arrested several times for piracy and smuggling, Laffite was never brought to trial.
ACTIVE: 1812-1823
LOCALE: Louisiana

EARLY LIFE

Little is definitively known about the early years of Jean Laffite (zhehn lah-feet). He and his brother, Pierre Laffite, may have been born in the region of Bordeaux in France. Somehow Jean developed the skills of a fine seaman. He may have been in the French navy, though there are no records of his service. Some authors suggest he turned to piracy in the Indian Ocean before joining his brother in the Louisiana territory in 1809.

PIRACY CAREER

The vast Louisiana territory underwent political and ethnic changes in the early nineteenth century as it was, in rapid succession, ceded from Spain to France and then sold to the United States through the Louisiana Purchase (1803). The uncertainty of these changes and the upheavals in Napoleonic Europe and New World colonies made conditions ripe for privateering in the Caribbean Sea and the Gulf of Mexico. Privateers were not pirates, but only because they held "letters of marque" from one government permitting them to attack the ships of the enemy. Privateers sold captured goods, bypassing customs; they also sold contraband goods, especially slaves.

When Laffite arrived in Louisiana, he established his base at Barataria Bay, which provided a good harbor, protection from pursuing warships, protection from pursuing warships, and easy access to the markets of New Orleans. From this base he captured merchant vessels and smuggled the goods and slaves to his brother, Pierre, in New Orleans for sale. Between 1810 and 1813, the Laffites outfitted a small fleet of armed ships to operate in the Gulf of Mexico. Without valid letters of marque, Jean Laffite was a pirate, but a rich one. He was known for his civility to captives, and he avoided taking American ships.

The Laffite brothers became more sophisticated and bold in their operations, flouting authority by openly

---

LAFFITE'S "AUTOBIOGRAPHY"

In the 1940's a manuscript turned up that was reputed to be the autobiography of the pirate Jean Laffite. Written in French, Le Journal de Jean Laffite *contradicted much of what was thought about Laffite's later life, stating, for example, that he died in 1850 in St. Louis, Missouri, after having raised a family. Scholars are divided about the manuscript's authenticity. If genuine, it reveals a thoughtful man with a radical social outlook, a true scion of the French Revolution. Here is an extract from the book's second half:*

I left Saint Louis for Europe in June 1847, stopping in various interesting places. I returned to America in January 1848. I was always moving about, dissatisfied, and always wishing for a universal change of man by man.

Personally, I never needed anything. I never had hunger for food products at any time. I was never like many other people who could find contentment in living between four walls without searching out what was beyond the horizon. I could not stand the sight of the multitudes, of the masses, suffering among the better off. I was everywhere when I was only a boy: on land, at sea, in prison; wherever my home might be, it was always happy.

There was even a time when I had my own prisons. I have taken part and been a witness to a cycle of changes of the world. I learned that revolutions were never complete, that Europe was not stabilized, that America was not completed. From the two sides of the Atlantic, problems existed within. I saw that persecution had again returned. I went to Europe; I had meetings with many leaders of the Church, the French Government, and some of the lower classes. . . .

No one knew the true motivation for my mission to Europe. I even opened a line of escrow credit in the banks of Paris to finance two young men, Mr. Marx and Mr. Engels, for a revolution of the workers of the world. They are at the task and creating laws in Germany, France, Belgium, and Holland. I hope that the new manifest doctrine will overthrow England and Spain, which is now feeble.

It was always my pleasure and intention to take up any cause of liberty, snatched from monarchies or any kingdom.

Source: The Memoirs of Jean Laffite, translated by Gene Marshall (Philadelphia: Xlibris, 1999).

selling smuggled goods both in New Orleans and at their island base. Government pressure from the newly admitted state of Louisiana mounted, however, between 1813 and 1815. Both brothers were indicted for piracy, smuggling, and receiving illegal goods in 1813, and at the end of that year a bounty was offered for their capture. In 1814, Pierre Laffite was imprisoned, though never tried.

New Orleans was a strategic target in the War of 1812. British naval officers contacted Jean Laffite, offering limited immunity if he served them in attacking the city. Whether out of patriotic feelings for the United States (as he claimed) or out of self-interested desire to free his brother and escape prosecution, Laffite informed President Andrew Jackson of the British move and offered his services and the services of the men of Barataria in the defense of New Orleans. While it is unclear what role he actually played at the Battle of New Orleans, his reputation as a hero was created.

Laffite received a pardon from the president of the United States for his service in 1815. After 1815 he returned to piracy. He ended his days as a legal privateer, commissioned by the government of Colombia. It was in this capacity that he was wounded and died while trying to take a Spanish vessel in the waters off Cuba. Though wanted for piracy by the United States and Spain, and though he was captured several times, Laffite was never brought to trial.

IMPACT

Jean Laffite's participation in the Battle of New Orleans may not have had great impact. His legend, however, grew to be larger than the man. Hailed as a patriot hero in Louisiana and the United States, he became a romantic example of the honorable thief and pirate.

FURTHER READING

Davis, William C. *The Pirates Laffite: The Treacherous World of the Corsairs of the Gulf.* Orlando, Fla.: Harcourt, 2005. An unsensational, extensively researched, and clearly presented history of Jean and Pierre Laffite. Documentary material and sources are clearly presented in bibliography and endnotes.

Konstam, Angus. *The History of Pirates.* Guilford, Conn.: The Lyons Press, 2002. A broad history of pi-

Jean Laffite. (AP/Wide World Photos)

racy from the ancient world to the modern day. Solidly researched with useful maps and illustrations of the times.

Marine Research Society. *The Pirates Own Book: Authentic Narratives of the Most Celebrated Sea Robbers.* 1924. Reprint. New York: Dover, 1993. Contains a chapter on Jean Laffite. Reasonably good use of documentary evidence, though the stilted language presents some difficulty.

—*Jean Owens Schaefer*

SEE ALSO: Samuel Bellamy; Stede Bonnet; Anne Bonny; Sir Henry Morgan; John Rackham; Mary Read; Bartholomew Roberts; Dominique You.

LEONARD LAKE
American abductor, torturer, and murderer

BORN: July 20, 1946; San Francisco, California
DIED: June 6, 1985; San Francisco, California
ALSO KNOWN AS: Tom Meyers; Alan Drey; Paul
Cosner; Charles Gunnar
MAJOR OFFENSES: Drug dealing, voyeurism,
pornography, burglary, and murders.
ACTIVE: 1982-1985
LOCALE: San Francisco and Wilseyville, California

EARLY LIFE
Leonard Lake (layk) was born in 1946, just after World
War II had ended and the United States was struggling to
get back on its economic feet. Lake's family also struggled economically, for a time occupying public housing.
When Lake was of kindergarten age, his father left the
family, and some months later his mother also abandoned him. Lake lived with his grandmother, a strict disciplinarian. His life was now materially better, and he no
longer suffered hunger and poverty. He even enjoyed attending summer nature camps. However, he resented his
mentally impaired brother, Donald. As a youth, Lake
took nude photographs of women, including sisters and
cousins.

Lake was a United States Marine from January, 1964,
to January, 1971. In March, 1969, he married Karen Lee
Mainersman. He served in the Vietnam War as a radar
technician. Although he bragged about killing during the
Vietnam War, he in fact never saw battle. His second tour
in Vietnam ended with his spending two months in a
mental ward back in California. His wife divorced him in
1972.

In 1974, Lake moved in with Venus Salem at The
Ranch, a counterculture enclave north of Ukiah, California. At The Ranch, Lake met Sir Lancelot, a goat surgi-
cally altered to have one horn. Traveling with the "uni-
corn," Lake met women, including his second wife,
Claralyn "Cricket" Balazs, whom he married in September, 1981. However, their marriage would last for little
more than a year.

CRIMINAL CAREER
The number of Lake's crimes is unknown. In late 1981,
he met Charles Ng, age twenty, with whom he committed
his worst. Together they managed a youth camp, but in
1982 both had to flee: Ng was a fugitive from a court-
martial, and Lake had been charged with seventeen felony counts for guns stolen in burglaries. Lake finally settled on Blue Mountain Road in Wilseyville, Calaveras
County, California, in an isolated one-floor house that
Cricket's family owned. Cricket had divorced him in November, 1982, but the two were still close. Like Ng,
Cricket collaborated with Lake, though how much is dis-
putable.

With Ng's help, Lake became serious about "Operation Miranda": a dream, inspired by John Fowles's novel
The Collector (1963), to imprison female sex slaves.
Their most infamous crime was recorded on videotapes
of Lake and Ng stripping, verbally tormenting, and hitting victims Kathy Allen and Brenda O'Connor. The
women were kept in a partly underground bunker; Lake
had built the bunker in 1983, for crime and for survival
after a nuclear holocaust. Ng and Lake's videotapes did
not show their victims' deaths.

However, death did follow. Allen's boyfriend and
O'Connor's husband and son were also killed. The murders all had financial rewards for Lake and Ng, who sold
or used the victims' belongings. Often, Lake found his
victims by answering classified ads, such as Paul Cosner's ad to sell an automobile. Lake also killed his
brother Donald and former best friend Charles Gunnar.
He used their assets, identities, and disability checks.
From remains in Wilseyville, police estimate that Lake
killed twenty-five people, two or three of them children.

LEGAL ACTION AND OUTCOME
In June of 1985, police interrupted Ng while he was
shoplifting a vise. Ng put the vise in the Honda automobile that Lake had stolen from Cosner; Ng escaped, but
police arrested Lake. Lake took cyanide while in police
custody, becoming fully comatose and dying four days
later.

Thus, Lake was never convicted of the abductions and
murders. However, the videotapes, photographs, and
Lake's diary provided damning evidence. Ng's 1999
trial established many of the crimes and Lake's role in
them.

IMPACT
Leonard Lake's misogyny, his desire for female sex
slaves, and his paranoid, paramilitary survivalism both
reflected and exemplified a sense during the 1980's that
society was crumbling and a holocaust was near. Lake
might have felt victimized by women, starting with his

mother, responding with an extreme subjugation of them instead. He stalked women, seduced them, photographed them, and resented them. His entire life was dominated by sex and by fantasies of power that compensated for his unsuccessful life, supported primarily by crime. The videotapes, and their transcripts, are incomparably shocking.

FURTHER READING
Lasseter, Don. *Die for Me!* New York: Pinnacle Books, 2000. Large book on Lake and Ng, overflowing with

details, including those about the trial and victims' lives.

Newton, Michael. *The Encyclopedia of Serial Killers.* New York: Checkmark Books, 2000. Excellent summary of events and insights into Lake's mind.

Norris, Joel. *Serial Killers.* New York: Doubleday Anchor, 1989. Valuable insights into Lake's upbringing and psychology, despite minor errors.

—*Bernadette Lynn Bosky*

SEE ALSO: Charles Ng.

HENRI DÉSIRÉ LANDRU
French serial killer

BORN: April 12, 1869; Paris, France
DIED: February 25, 1922; Versailles, France
ALSO KNOWN AS: Bluebeard of Gambais; Raymond Diard; Lucien Guillet; Monsieur Tric; Monsieur Dupont; Monsieur Petit
MAJOR OFFENSES: Eleven murders (of ten women and the son of one of the women)
ACTIVE: April, 1915-January, 1919
LOCALE: Paris, Gambais, and Vernouillet, France
SENTENCE: Death by guillotine

EARLY LIFE
Henri Désiré Landru (ahn-ree day-zee-ray lahn-drew), the son of a Vulcan Ironworks stoker and a dressmaker, received his early education at the École des Frères. He attended the School of Mechanical Engineering but, lacking financial resources, was unable to complete his studies. He served in the army for four years, becoming a sergeant. During this time, he seduced his cousin Marie-Catherine Remy, who had a daughter by him. They married in 1893 and had three more children. Landru worked for an architectural firm, then as a used furniture dealer. As early as 1900, he was involved in swindling widows and had served two years in prison. The fact that a dishonest employer had cheated him out of money is often mentioned as a factor contributing to his fraudulent activities.

CRIMINAL CAREER
In 1914, Landru began placing advertisements in Paris newspapers, usually representing himself as an affluent widower with two children wishing to meet a widow and remarry. He used many aliases in his correspondence

with the women and kept extensive records of the names. Between 1914 and 1918, Landru met and seduced ten women, all of whom disappeared, as did as the teenage son of one of the women. During this time, Landru rented two villas outside Paris, one near Vernouillet and later Villa Hermitage near Gambais.

Landru sought out women with assets, usually widows. He proceeded to convince them of his affection, promise them marriage, and eventually persuade them to move into his villa. Although the women were no longer seen, he continued to manage their assets. He withdrew money from their bank accounts using various ruses and sold their furniture and other possessions. He also equipped his villa with a new kitchen stove and bought a large supply of coal. He was apparently strangling the women, cutting them up, and burning their bodies in the stove. At his trial, neighbors testified that a great amount of ill-smelling black smoke frequently poured from his chimney.

In 1919, the sister of Célestine Buisson, one of his victims, was attempting to locate Buisson. By chance, she saw Landru in Paris and discovered where he lived; the Paris police began an investigation. At first, the police found only enough evidence to charge Landru with embezzlement. After additional investigation, although no bodies were found, they accumulated enough evidence to charge him with murder.

LEGAL ACTION AND OUTCOME
On November 7, 1921, charged with eleven counts of murder, Landru began trial at the Court of Versailles. He maintained his innocence throughout the trial and refused to cooperate. He made satirical remarks and re-

peatedly demanded that authorities produce the rumored bodies. The prosecutor's speech lasted for an entire day, and the defense spoke for two days. In spite of the eloquence of the defense and the lack of bodies, the jury returned a verdict of guilty on all eleven counts. The trial ended on November 30, 1921. On February 25, 1922, Landru was executed by guillotine.

IMPACT

Upon his arrest, Henri Désiré Landru immediately caught the public's attention. His trial caused a sensation in Paris. The courtroom was filled with women fascinated by him. He received front-page coverage in the newspapers. The journalists reported every detail of the police findings and created discoveries when there were none. Landru became a villain celebrated in popular culture. He was compared to Bluebeard (whose legend may have been inspired by Gilles de Rais) and inspired songs by Charles Trenet and Renaud and films by Charles Chaplin (*Monsieur Verdoux*, 1948) and Charles Chabrol (*Landru*, 1963).

FURTHER READING

Egger, Steven A. *Serial Murder: An Elusive Phenomenon*. Westport, Conn.: Praeger, 1990. Comprehensive investigation of serial murder and its perpetrators as well as law enforcement's response.

Tatar, Marie. *Secrets Beyond the Door: The Story of Bluebeard and His Wives*. Princeton, N.J.: Princeton University Press, 2004. Explores the treatment of the Bluebeard story in literature and film and the reactions of various cultures and time periods.

Walz, Robin. *Pulp Surrealism: Insolent Popular Culture in Early Twentieth Century Paris*. Berkeley: University of California Press, 2000. Chapter 3 gives a detailed account of Landru's trial as it was recounted in Parisian newspapers and discusses the inclusion of Landru in the Paris Dada group's "literary value chart."

—*Shawncey Webb*

SEE ALSO: Joe Ball; William Burke; Albert DeSalvo; Albert Fish; H. H. Holmes; Jack the Ripper; Marcel Petiot; Gilles de Rais; Sweeney Todd.

MEYER LANSKY
American Mafioso

BORN: July 4, 1902; Grodno, Poland, Russian Empire (now Hrodna, Belarus)
DIED: January 15, 1983; Miami Beach, Florida
ALSO KNOWN AS: Maier Suchowljansky (birth name)
CAUSE OF NOTORIETY: A leading underworld figure, Lansky was a bootlegger and then a casino operator in the United States and Cuba.
ACTIVE: 1920-1959
LOCALE: New York; Miami, Florida; and Havana, Cuba

EARLY LIFE

Meyer Lansky (MI-urh LAN-skee) was born in the heavily Jewish city of Grodno, Poland, around 1902. His father moved to the United States in 1909 to escape the pogroms of czarist Russia, and two years later he sent for his wife and sons. Meyer later claimed July 4 as his birthday, even though there is no record of the exact date. The family lived in the Brownsville section of Brooklyn, New York, and Meyer's school records list his name as Lansky from the beginning.

By 1914 the Lansky family had moved from Brooklyn to the lower East Side of Manhattan, a crowded tenement area with many immigrants. Lansky was a good student in school and attended religious training. He soon learned, however, to take part in street-corner dice games and encountered other tough teenagers, such as Benjamin (Bugsy) Siegel and Charlie (Lucky) Luciano. In 1917, Lansky left school and went to work in a tool and die shop.

CRIMINAL CAREER

In 1920, the Eighteenth Amendment to the U.S. Constitution went into effect, prohibiting the manufacture and sale of alcoholic beverages. The unintended consequence of this legislation was to spur illegal bootlegging and speakeasies, which became common throughout urban America. Lansky soon became involved in bootlegging activities under the guidance of Arnold Rothstein, a well-known Jewish gambler and criminal. Throughout the 1920's and early 1930's, Lansky and Siegel worked together with members of Italian gangs in bootlegging activities.

After Prohibition ended and New York authorities began to crack down on criminal activities, Siegel and Lansky went their separate ways. Siegel went to Los Angeles and eventually Las Vegas, and Lansky moved the center of his operations to Florida. He became involved with illegal casinos in Florida (outside Miami) and

Saratoga Springs, New York, as well as other gambling concerns around the United States.

During World War II, Lansky worked with the U.S. Office of Naval Intelligence on anti-Nazi activities, including protecting the New York docks from sabotage. After the war, U.S. senator Estes Kefauver began an investigation of organized crime that caused a sensation across the country. Lansky was called before a Senate committee in 1951 but made few revelations. However, his name was soon made famous across the country in connection with other gangsters, such as Frank Costello and Luciano.

Lansky and his brother Jake had been involved in gambling casinos, including those in Las Vegas. Lansky had invested in Siegel's Flamingo Hotel and the Thunderbird Hotel and was collecting money from them after Siegel's murder in 1947. In 1952, when Fulgencio Batista y Zaldívar became dictator of Cuba, he invited Lansky into the city of Havana; Lansky spent the next several years building up the credibility and clientele of the Cuba casinos. In 1957, he opened the Riviera Casino, one of the largest casinos in Cuba and in the world outside Las Vegas.

By December of 1958, Cuban rebels in the mountains, led by Fidel Castro, had made headway against the corrupt Batista regime. On New Year's Eve, Bastista fled the country, and Castro's rebel army was about to take over Cuba. American gamblers and casino owners quickly became special targets for the revolutionaries. In the early months of 1959, the Castro government had assumed control of all the hotels and ejected the gamblers, including Lansky.

Lansky spent several years after the Cuban fiasco trying to rebuild his personal wealth. He was getting money from the profits skimmed off his interests in Las Vegas casinos, but otherwise Lansky lived in Florida in a state of semiretirement. He also suffered declining health through the 1960's and 1970's. During this period, he was under surveillance by the Federal Bureau of Investigation and was the object of press scrutiny. In 1970, he was briefly detained on a drug charge that was later dismissed (the drugs were a prescription ulcer medicine). He tried to move to Israel in the early 1970's but was refused entry because of his criminal past.

LEGAL ACTION AND OUTCOME

Criminal trials throughout the 1970's occupied much of Lansky's time but brought few results. His age and medical condition prompted delays in litigation, and evidence and witnesses proved to be in short supply. Lansky's

health continued to decline until January 15, 1983, when he died in a hospital in Miami.

IMPACT

Meyer Lansky became a legend during his own lifetime. His character was featured in films and television programs, including in the film *The Godfather II* (in which he was portrayed by actor Lee Strasburg). From the time of the Kefauver hearings to his death, he was portrayed in the media as the slippery brains behind the mob. Later evidence would suggest that Lansky was important in criminal circles from the 1920's to 1950's but was never the leader of any special group or gang. His investments in Las Vegas were comparatively small and sporadic. He had, in fact, staked much of his reputation and personal fortune in the ventures in Cuba, which failed.

Lansky's ability to avoid prison in the 1960's and 1970's was more attributable to the fact he was already out of the mainstream and by then vulnerable to government investigations than to any brilliance on his part. All aspects of American life changed in the 1960's, including its criminal life, and Lansky was simply left behind. Contrary to rumors of vast wealth when he died, Lansky left a relatively small legacy, and his disabled son, Buddy, was soon on welfare. Lansky was the last of the old-time gangsters romanticized in novels and films. His comparatively normal retirement and death only increased his stature in a world of violent death.

FURTHER READING

Cohen, Rich. *Tough Jews*. New York: Simon & Schuster, 1998. Describes the assimilation of Jewish immigrants into American life, with an emphasis on how criminal activities were a part of that assimilation.

Hammer, Richard, "Slicing up the Big Apple." *Playboy* (October, 1973). One installment in a multipart history of organized crime, this article covers the early period of New York crime that influenced Lansky's life. Journalistic and sensational, it is nonetheless informative.

Lacey, Robert. *Little Man: Meyer Lansky and the Gangster Life*. Boston: Little, Brown, 1991. An outstanding account of Lansky's life and the circumstances that surrounded his rise and eventual fall. The detail and research in this book dispel many myths and inaccuracies.

—*Charles C. Howard*

SEE ALSO: Fulgencio Batista y Zaldívar; Fidel Castro; Frank Costello; Lucky Luciano; Arnold Rothstein; Bugsy Siegel.

LYNDON H. LaROUCHE, JR.
Political activist

BORN: September 8, 1922; Rochester, New Hampshire

ALSO KNOWN AS: Lyndon Hermyle LaRouche, Jr. (full name); Lyn Marcus (pseudonym)

CAUSE OF NOTORIETY: Although variously known as an extremist, a writer, an anti-Semite, a cult founder, and a convicted conspirator, fraud, and tax evader, LaRouche is best known for his multiple runs for the U.S. presidency.

ACTIVE: Beginning in 1966

LOCALE: New York, Virginia, and Germany

SENTENCE: Fifteen years in prison; paroled after five years

EARLY LIFE
The parents of Lyndon LaRouche (LIHN-dihn lah-REWSH), shoe salesman Lyndon H. LaRouche, Sr., and Jessie Weir LaRouche, moved with their son to the small industrial town of Lynn, Massachusetts, in 1936. The family belonged to the Society of Friends (Quakers), but in 1941 the Lynn Meeting voted to oust Lyndon senior for defaming the other members.

The younger LaRouche entered Northeastern University in Boston but dropped out in 1942. He enlisted in the Army in 1944 and spent his service in India and Burma as a noncombatant in medical units. Back in the United States, he reenrolled at Northeastern University but dropped out in 1948 and joined the Socialist Workers Party (SWP) in Lynn. He married fellow party member Janice Neuberger and found work as a management consultant in New York City, advising on the use of computers in business production.

POLITICAL CAREER
LaRouche remained in the SWP until his expulsion in 1965. During these years he developed his interests in economics, business management, psychoanalysis, and

Lyndon H. LaRouche, Jr. (AP/Wide World Photos)

ACCORDING TO LaROUCHE

Here are some of Lyndon LaRouche's comments and opionions on various topics of interest:

On AIDS:

So far, the world's leading experts see no way in which the Soviet biological-warfare apparatus could have created AIDS in a test-tube. However, it is in the strategic interests of Moscow to see to it that the West does nothing to stop this pandemic; within a few years, at the present rates, the spread of AIDS in Asia, Africa, Western Europe, and the Americas would permit Moscow to take over the world almost without firing a shot.

—H. LaRouche, Jr., "The Lesson of the Merchant of Venice," *Executive Intelligence Review*, November 1, 1985

On American universities:

Harvard University and Massachusetts Institute of Technology (MIT) are among a handful of leading centers of fascist social engineering research and development throughout the post-war U.S. Other universities of comparable status include Columbia University, Cornell University, University of Pennsylvania, University of Michigan, University of Chicago, University of California at Berkeley, and Leland Stanford University.

—H. LaRouche, Jr., "What Happened to Integration," *The Campaigner*, August, 1975

On The Beatles:

The Beatles had no genuine musical talent, but were a product shaped according to British Psychological Warfare Division (Tavistock) specifications, and promoted in Britain by agencies which are controlled by British intelligence.

—H. LaRouche, Jr., "Why Your Child Became a Drug Addict," *Campaigner Special Report*, 1978

On Adolf Hitler:

The first, and most important fact to be recognized concerning the Hitler regime, is that Adolf Hitler was put into power in Germany on orders from London. The documentation of this matter is abundant and conclusive.

—H. LaRouche, Jr., "Humboldt Versus Hitler," *The Campaigner*, August, 1978

On jazz:

Jazz was foisted on black Americans by the same oligarchy which had run the U.S. slave trade, with the help of the classically trained but immoral George Gershwin and the Paris-New York circuit of drug-taking avant-garde artists.

—H. LaRouche, Jr., "The Racist Roots of Jazz," *The Campaigner*, September-October, 1980

On Judaism:

Judaism is the religion of a caste of subjects of Christianity, entirely molded by ingenious rabbis to fit into the ideological and secular life of Christianity. In short, a self-sustaining Judaism never existed and never could exist. As for Jewish culture otherwise, it is merely the residue left to the Jewish home after everything saleable has been marketed to the Goyim.

—H. LaRouche, Jr., as L. Marcus, "The Case of Ludwig Feuerbach," *The Campaigner*, December, 1973

---

other topics. He and Janice separated in 1963, nine years after the birth of their son, Daniel. In 1966, LaRouche and his new common-law wife, Carol Larrabee, formed a New York branch of the New Left Committee for Independent Action and gathered a group of Columbia University students who attended LaRouche's classes in dialectical materialism at the New York Free School. Together with the Students for a Democratic Society (SDS), LaRouche's group was heavily involved in the 1968 student strike and occupation of the Columbia University campus. LaRouche organized a faction of the SDS called the SDS Labor Committee but criticized the New Left for neglecting labor's role in the counterculture.

After separating from the SDS in 1969, LaRouche's SDS Labor Committee became the National Caucus of Labor Committee (NCLC) and eventually dropped all connections with the labor movement. Members of the NCLC gave up their former jobs and private lives and became fully devoted to LaRouche and his organization. By the early 1970's, LaRouche was using cultlike pressure to consolidate his grip on the NCLC and instigated a series of physical attacks on Communists and Black Nationalists. During the 1970's and 1980's, the NCLC developed an international network for spying and propaganda and infiltrated high levels of government, businesses, and organized crime. In the 1970's it conducted harassment campaigns against the United Auto Workers and the United Steelworkers unions. LaRouche's electoral organization, the United States Labor Party (USLP), published a conspiracy attack on then-president Jimmy Carter. The organization, which had become rabidly anti-Semitic, also attacked homosexuality, globalism, free trade, and international bankers.

In 1984, Larouche helped found the Schiller Institute in Germany with his wife Helga Zepp-LaRouche, whom he had married in 1977, and in following years built an extensive political network in several other countries. Funds for the institute were raised by selling literature, soliciting donations at university campuses and airports, and phone solicitation. These fund-raising activities involved tax law violations, money laundering, and fraudulent solicitation of so-called loans to the elderly.

LEGAL ACTION AND OUTCOME

In 1986, the Federal Bureau of Investigation and Virginia state troopers raided the LaRouche headquarters in Leesburg, Virginia, seeking evidence to support frequent media accusations. LaRouche and six of his associates were charged with conspiracy and mail fraud involving fund-raising. LaRouche was also charged with tax evasion dating back to 1979. In 1988, a federal jury in Alexandria, Virginia, convicted LaRouche of all three charges. He served five years of a fifteen-year prison sentence and was released on parole.

LaRouche continued political activism while in prison. He ran for president in 1992, met with important international figures, and gave interviews. After his release, he again ran for president, toured India, and addressed the Russian Academy of Science. An important development after his release from prison was the Larouche Youth Movement (LYM), created for young people eighteen to twenty-five years old. Members of LYM broke up a debate of the Democratic candidates for president at Morgan State University in Baltimore in September, 2003.

IMPACT

Lyndon H. LaRouche, Jr., and his associates have had an extraordinary effect on American politics, perhaps greater than the impact of any other extremist movement in American history. Most surprising, this was accomplished during a time of prosperity and political stability in the United States. Critics regard the LaRouche group and its associated organizations as a fascist movement based on many elements of Nazi ideology, saying that LaRouche and his associates advocate a dictatorship of elites who would rule in the name of industrial capitalists and that they spread conspiracy theories attacking leftists, environmentalists, Jews, blacks, feminists, gay men, lesbians, and organized labor. In 1986, followers of Larouche won the Democratic Party primaries for lieutenant governor and secretary of state in Illinois.

FURTHER READING

Gilbert, Helen. *Lyndon LaRouche: Fascism Restyled for the New Millennium*. Seattle: Red Letter Press, 2003. Purports to expose the fraud that LaRouche perpetuated; examines the dangers of his political philosophy, placing it in the tradition of fascism.

King, Dennis. *Lyndon LaRouche and the New American Fascism*. New York: Doubleday, 1989. Informative biography examines how LaRouche remained safe from prosecution for so many years, how he inspired so much fear, and why he attracted so many allies including defense scientists, New Right members, foreign dictators, and politicians.

Levitas, Daniel. *The Terrorist Next Door: The Militia Movement and the Radical Right*. New York: St. Martin's Press, 2002. Reveals the origins and ideology of hate groups that pose a serious threat to the security of democracy. Analyzes and discusses the place of the LaRouche group.

—*Sheila Golburgh Johnson*

SEE ALSO: Bobby Baker; David Duke; Jean-Marie Le Pen.

PIERRE LAVAL
Vichy prime minister of France (1931-1932, 1935-1936, 1942-1944)

BORN: June 28, 1883; Châteldon, France
DIED: October 15, 1945; Paris, France
MAJOR OFFENSE: Treason
ACTIVE: 1930's-1940's
LOCALE: France
SENTENCE: Death by firing squad

EARLY LIFE
Pierre Laval (pyehr lah-vahl) was born and raised in the small village of Châteldon, in the Puy-de-Dome département of the Auvergne region of France. Because his family had little money, he took odd jobs as a youth. He attended university and received a law degree, then relocated to Paris in 1907 to begin work as a lawyer. Soon he became a force in politics and was elected to the Chamber of Deputies as a Socialist in 1914.

World War I changed Laval's political views, and he began to side with the right. After leaving the Socialist Party and losing reelection after the war, Laval became the mayor of Aubervilliers in 1924. By 1927 he was elected to the French senate and served as prime minister from January, 1931, to February, 1932, and again in 1935. *Time* magazine named him man of the year in 1931.

POLITICAL CAREER
Laval lost favor and was forced to resign as prime minister on January 22, 1936, after devising a controversial solution to the Abyssinia crisis, which proposed ceding most of Ethiopia to Italy. After leaving politics, Laval began to amass a business empire of broadcasting and print media that debased the left and promoted his right-wing ideology. His propaganda succeeded in ousting the existing government and supporting the prime minister of the Vichy government, Philippe Pétain, who would name Laval as his vice premier during World War II. Laval arranged a meeting with Adolf Hitler, during which he pledged his cooperation, as well as that of the French state, to Germany. Laval's pro-Nazi zeal and demands for a Franco-German alliance caused Pétain to become wary of his associate; Laval was removed from office and arrested on December 13, 1940.

News of Laval's dismissal and arrest caused the German ambassador to France, Otto Abetz, to protest on Laval's behalf. Laval was released and sent to Paris under Abetz's protection. While staying with the Germans, Laval was injured during an assassination attempt. Upon his recovery he was reinstated as prime minister in 1942, under pressure from Abetz.

Under Laval's rule, France began to see a noticeable increase in anti-Semitic policies. Jewish families were identified and watched. Laval arranged and began heavily promoting an exchange program, La Relève, in which skilled French workers would be sent to Germany in exchange for French prisoners of war. By September of 1942, Laval had authorized the German Gestapo to hunt down members of the French Resistance in unoccupied France. Laval was also instrumental in the development of the Vichy Milice in 1943, a wartime police force known for its brutality. The Milice was responsible for gathering Jewish families and left-wing activists and deporting them to Germany. With the Allied invasion of France, the government relocated to Belfort, France, and then to Sigmaringen, Germany, in August, 1944. By May of 1945, Laval had fled to Spain.

LEGAL ACTION AND OUTCOME
Spain deported Laval to Austria, and Austria turned him over to the new French government headed by Charles de Gaulle on July 30, 1945. Once back on French soil, Laval was tried for treason, aiding the enemy, and violating state security. After forcefully defending himself, Laval was found guilty and sentenced to death by firing squad. While awaiting his execution, he attempted to take his life by ingesting a cyanide tablet. The tablet had lost its potency, and Laval went to the firing squad semiconscious. He was executed at Fresnes prison, near Paris, on October 15, 1945.

IMPACT
The name "Laval" became, and remains, synonymous with "traitor" in the French language. Pierre Laval's collaboration with the Nazis not only earned him the contempt of his fellow French but also aroused increased patriotism and appreciation for the Allied forces. After the demise of Laval and the Vichy regime, France encouraged citizens to become vigilant toward fascism, Nazi sympathizers, and neo-Nazi hate movements.

Under the Vichy government, French citizens were divided between those who supported the Vichy government and fascism, and those who supported the French Resistance and the goals of the Allies. After World War II, much of France was left in a state of confusion and shame over what the country had stood and fought for in the war. In trying to rebuild and redefine France, Laval's execution, and those of many other Vichy officials, was seen as a step toward France's regaining its national identity and disassociating itself from a dark past.

FURTHER READING

Alexander, Martin S. *The Republic in Danger: General Maurice Gamelin and the Politics of French Defense, 1931-1940*. New York: Cambridge University Press, 2002. An excellent account of France's involvement in World War II and the internal war that was occurring simultaneously within France. Intended for those who already possess a working knowledge of French politics of the era.

Burrin, Philippe. *France Under the Germans: Collaboration and Compromise*. New York: New Press, 1998. Explores the psychological impact that compromises France made with the Nazis had on its citizens.

Jackson, Julian. *France: The Dark Years, 1940-1944.*

New York: Oxford University Press, 2003. Suggests that, although controversial, the Vichy government was not an oppressive force that was thrust upon France by the Germans but rather a government welcomed by French Fascists and anti-Semites.

Paxton, Robert O. *Vichy France*. New York: Columbia University Press, 2001. An impeccably researched book about the Vichy government and the factors that played into its decision-making processes.

Rousso, Henri. *The Vichy Syndrome: History and Memory in France Since 1944*. Cambridge, Mass.: Harvard University Press, 2004. Young French historian Rousso examines the confusion and division of France under the Vichy government and, based on interviews and documents, records what people chose to remember about those dark years.

—*Sara Vidar*

SEE ALSO: François Darlan; Joseph Darnand; Jacques Doriot; Adolf Hitler; Philippe Pétain.

MARIE LAVEAU
American priestess and practitioner of Voodoo

BORN: 1794; New Orleans, Louisiana
DIED: June 15, 1881; New Orleans, Louisiana
ALSO KNOWN AS: Voodoo Queen of New Orleans
CAUSE OF NOTORIETY: Laveau, using her shrewd knowledge of the social and political system of New Orleans, her Voodoo practice, and her many informants and spies, influenced large numbers of influential and prominent people, as well as many members of the lower classes, in New Orleans society.
ACTIVE: 1830's-1881
LOCALE: New Orleans, Louisiana

EARLY LIFE

Marie Laveau (lah-VOH) was born as a free mulatto in the French Quarter of New Orleans in 1794. Very little about her life is known to be factual, with many of the stories about her simply rumor or speculation. She was said to be the daughter of a wealthy white planter and a mulatto woman with a mix of Indian blood. She was raised as a devout Roman Catholic and was known to be friends with Père Antoine, who was chaplain at St. Louis Cathedral. On August 4, 1819, at age twenty-five, she married a local free black man, Jacques Paris, at St. Louis

Cathedral. His death was recorded in 1820. They apparently had no children.

Laveau next became a hairdresser, serving the elite women of New Orleans in their homes. She took a lover, Louis Christophe Duminy de Glapion, and lived with him until his death in 1835. They had fifteen children. It was sometime in the 1830's that Laveau became a Voodoo priestess. Much of the information about her career is based on newspaper accounts at the time, as well as legend and oral tradition.

PRIESTESS CAREER

It is unknown how Laveau developed her passion for the practice of Voodoo. However, the custom of the time was for women of the elite to talk carelessly and pass confidential information while in the company of black servants. Laveau's position as a hairdresser visiting homes of the wealthy put her in an excellent position to obtain access to information that could easily be used to gain both social and political power. Laveau was also known to have practiced charitable acts among the poor and sick, especially in prisons, and helped nurse the ill during a yellow fever epidemic. However, she was ruthless in exercising power over those who greatly feared

Marie Laveau. (Courtesy, Louisiana State Library)

her, many of them of high social standing. Her power and reputation were earned through her shrewd knowledge of the social and political system and her many informants and spies, as well as her Voodoo spells. Laveau mixed her Catholic beliefs with her Voodoo practice.

Laveau ceased to practice Voodoo late in life and once again apparently became a devout Catholic. The death of Laveau was announced in the New Orleans newspapers on June 16, 1881. People reported seeing her long after that date, but it was probably her daughter, Marie, who looked like her and inherited her position, al-

though she never reached the level of power or influence of her mother.

IMPACT

Marie Laveau, through her notoriety and visibility, became a renowned, influential, and powerful woman at a time when women had very little power. In addition, she was a black woman in a time of slavery, which made her status even more remarkable. While many of the stories told of Laveau are unproven, they have become legend and an important part of the history of New Orleans. Many still visit her tomb in St. Louis Cemetery Number 1 to leave offerings.

FURTHER READING

Asbury, Herbert. *The French Quarter: An Informal History of the New Orleans Underworld*. 1936. Reprint. New York: Capricorn Books, 1968. This history covers many aspects of early infamous New Orleaners and the French Quarter and includes information on both Voodoo and Laveau. Asbury cites contemporary newspaper accounts and publications of the time.

Duggal, Barbara. "Marie Laveau: The Voodoo Queen Reposessed." In *Creole: The History and the Legacy of Louisiana's Free People of Color*, edited by Sybil Kein. Baton Rouge: Louisiana State University Press, 2000. Discusses the role of Laveau as a free mulatto woman and her contributions to Creole history in Louisiana.

Martinez, Raymond. *Mysterious Marie Laveau: Voodoo Queen and Folk Tales Along the Mississippi*. Jefferson, La.: Hope, 1956. Martinez's accounts of Laveau are based on various newspaper stories of the time, public records, and folklore.

—*Martha Oehmke Loustaunau*

SEE ALSO: Dorothy Clutterbuck.

ANTON SZANDOR LAVEY
Founder of the Church of Satan

BORN: April 11, 1930; Chicago, Illinois
DIED: October 29, 1997; San Francisco, California
ALSO KNOWN AS: Howard Stanton Levey (birth name); Black Pope
CAUSE OF NOTORIETY: With a practical yet scandalous philosophy, self-promotion, and cynical but valid insights into human behavior, LaVey created cultural shocks in the 1960's and early 1970's; a comeback in 1987 was less successful.
ACTIVE: 1964-1997
LOCALE: San Francisco, California

EARLY LIFE
Anton Szandor LaVey (AN-ton SAN-dohr lah-VAY) was born in Chicago in 1930 as Howard Stanton Levey. Unsubstantiated legends, some perpetuated by LaVey himself, surround his youth: that his Transylvanian Gypsy grandmother introduced him early to folklore and magic; that in 1945 his uncle took him to postwar Germany, where LaVey collected information on occult rituals; that at age fifteen, he played second oboe with the San Francisco Ballet Orchestra; and that he tamed lions in the Clyde Beatty Circus at age seventeen. An organist at a San Francisco burlesque house, he supposedly had an affair with Marilyn Monroe, then a young dancer there. In

the 1950's LaVey allegedly was a photographer for the San Francisco Police Department and studied criminology at San Francisco City College.

Research by his daughter Zeena, however, has revealed a more reliable account: LaVey was born Howard Stanton Levey to Michael and Gertrude Levey. His grandmother was Ukranian, with no Gypsy ancestry. He spent all of 1945 in suburban Northern California and never played oboe for the San Francisco Ballet. He probably worked for a circus at some time, but the Clyde Beatty Circus has no record of him, and some basic details he gave about his associates there are false. He never knew Marilyn Monroe, never worked for the San Francisco Police Department, and never enrolled at San Francisco City College.

Although some writers accuse LaVey's daughter of lying, her documentation is good. Moreover, some of LaVey's remarks may have been inside jokes: The supposed German occult rituals from 1945 are based on fiction, H. G. Wells's *The Island of Dr. Moreau* (1896) and Frank Belknap Long's "The Hounds of Tindalos" (1929). LaVey's self-mythologizing must always be kept in mind.

LaVey married the fifteen-year-old Carole Lansing in 1951; their daughter, Karla Maritza LaVey, arrived in 1952. By 1959 LaVey had fallen in love with Diane Hagerty, and he and Carole divorced in 1960. His and Hagerty's daughter, Zeena Galatea LaVey, who was born in 1964, was satanically baptized at age three and disowned her father in 1989. Blanche Barton (born Sharon Densley) delivered LaVey's son, Satan Xerxes Carnacki LaVey, in 1993 and assumed control of the Church of Satan after Anton LaVey's death.

SATANIC CAREER
By 1964, LaVey had appeared in *The San Francisco Chronicle* as a ghost chaser. He began delivering weekend lectures on occult and paranormal topics; attendees paid for "witches' workshops," a popular blend of sorcery and seduction. After a friend's suggestion, the Church of Satan was founded, pur-

Anton Szandor LaVey with his wife Diane. (AP/Wide World Photos)

THE NINE SATANIC STATEMENTS

In his last interview in 1997, Anton Szandor LaVey defined "Satanism" as "giving the Devil his due":

The Nine Satanic Statements pretty much spells it out. We want bold, but not pretentious disciples. By employing the S word, the timid and superstitiously frightened stay away. They have good reason to be scared, but not as they surmise.

Here are LaVey's Nine Satanic Statements:

1. Satan represents indulgence instead of abstinence!
2. Satan represents vital existence instead of spiritual pipe dreams!
3. Satan represents undefiled wisdom instead of hypocritical self-deceit!
4. Satan represents kindness to those who deserve it instead of love wasted on ingrates!
5. Satan represents vengeance instead of turning the other cheek!
6. Satan represents responsibility to the responsible instead of concern for psychic vampires!
7. Satan represents man as just another animal, sometimes better, more often worse than those that walk on all-fours, who, because of his "divine spiritual and intellectual development," has become the most vicious animal of all!
8. Satan represents all of the so-called sins, as they all lead to physical, mental, or emotional gratification!
9. Satan has been the best friend the Church has ever had, as He has kept it in business all these years!

Anton LaVey, *The Satanic Bible* (New York: Avon Books, 1969).

portedly on Walpurgisnacht (May Eve) in 1966, which, according to LaVey's calendar, was year one of the age of Satan.

LaVey held rituals in a huge black Victorian house filled with eerie decorations, including a human skeleton. Beginning with what Blanche Barton in her study *The Church of Satan* (1990) describes as "cathartic blasphemies against Christianity," especially the Black Mass, the church developed original rituals to exploit the "grey area between psychiatry and religion." Members could enact curses, raise power for success, or develop themselves through psychodramas. LaVey's writing fluctuates between purely psychological views of ritual and claims of supernatural efficacy.

LaVey's church attained wide publicity over the satanic wedding of journalist John Raymond and socialite Judith Case and the satanic funeral of a naval officer, both in 1967. The archbishop of San Francisco wrote President Lyndon Johnson to protest the funeral. The church was covered by magazines, from *Cosmopolitan* and *McCall's* to *Look* and *Time*; men's magazines published photographs of the provocative Black Masses. LaVey even conducted an on-camera ritual on *The Tonight Show*.

In 1968 a documentary, *Satanis: The Devil's Mass*, was filmed. That year LaVey also recorded a long-playing record album of the Black Mass. He wrote three books: *The Satanic Bible* (1969), *The Satanic Rituals* (1970), and *The Compleat Witch* (1971). In the early and mid-1970's, LaVey spent time in Los Angeles, hobnobbing with Hollywood celebrities.

Apparently LaVey became tired of his fame even before it faded. In 1972, he stopped his weekly public ceremonies. The Church of Satan was reorganized in 1975; LaVey was already withdrawing from publicity. Rumors of his death spread. However, LaVey resurfaced in 1986 with a lengthy interview in the magazine *Birth of Tragedy*. He continued writing and giving interviews until his death from heart disease in 1997.

IMPACT

Anton Szandor LaVey's satanism continued the traditions of a long line of rebellious, antireligious groups, such as the eighteenth century Hellfire Club and Aleister Crowley's occult orders. Offshoots of LaVey's church include the Order of the Black Ram, the Temple of Set, and the Church of Satanic Liberation. LaVey may even have influenced the vampire underground: He reputedly slept during the day, allegedly in a coffin.

The cultural turmoil of the late 1960's was fertile ground for satanism. In April, 1966, *Time* magazine asked "Is God Dead?" Dissent and alienation were in vogue, and flower children (whom LaVey disdained) and businesspersons alike were looking for new spiritual avenues.

LaVey's writings combine humor and misanthropy: His philosophy shows affection for outsiders, music, children, and animals and disdain for television, conformity, religion, and "psychic vampires" (those who emotionally drain others). He advocates elitism, selfishness, and gratification of desires. His philosophy reflects the influences of H. L. Mencken, H. P. Lovecraft, Ayn Rand, Jack London, Friedrich Nietzsche, and the authors of noir detective stories—all of whom, disparate though they may be, champion the exceptional individual over the societal group.

Much of LaVey's thought was more shocking in 1966 than it is now. However, the stories of recovered memory of satanic sexual abuse that were made public in the 1980's made LaVey's choice of "satanism" as the name for his cause once again offensive and taboo.

FURTHER READING

Baddeley, Gavin. *Lucifer Rising: A Book of Sin, Devil Worship, and Rock and Roll.* Medford, N.J.: Plexus, 2006. Covers LaVey's predecessors and successors in satanism, including backlash reactions; contains the last in-depth interview with LaVey.

Barton, Blanche. *The Church of Satan.* New York: Hell's Kitchen Productions, 1990. Some repetition of Barton's other book but more theory, practice, and history of the church itself.

_____. *The Secret Life of a Satanist.* Los Angeles: Feral House, 1992. Unreliable but indispensable; parts are taken from *The Devil's Avenger* by Burton H. Wolfe (1974), a biography authorized by LeVey whose accuracy is suspect. Excellent bibliography.

Church of Satan. http://churchofsatan.org/aslv.html. Accessed December, 2005. The home site of the Church of Satan, which includes a history of the organization.

LaVey, Anton Szandor. *Satan Speaks!* Los Angeles: Feral House, 1998. Essays by LaVey on topics including the fad for stories of satanic sexual abuse and murder.

_____. *The Satanic Bible.* New York: HarperCollins, 1976. First and fullest explication of the satanic philosophy; biographical introduction by Burton H. Wolfe.

—*Bernadette Lynn Bosky*

SEE ALSO: Aleister Crowley.

JOHN LAW
Scottish economist and speculator

BORN: April 21, 1671; Edinburgh, Scotland
DIED: March 21, 1729; Venice (now in Italy)
CAUSE OF NOTORIETY: Law established the Mississippi Company, France's first joint stock enterprise. A scheme involving the company collapsed when it became evident that the company's shares had soared because of Law's fraudulent claims.
ACTIVE: 1719-1720
LOCALE: France and the American colonies

EARLY LIFE

John Law, born in Edinburgh, Scotland, in 1671, was the son of William Law, a goldsmith and successful banker, and his second wife, Jean Campbell. At the age of twenty-three, Law was convicted for the murder of Edward Wilson in a duel that has been inconclusively attributed to various circumstances. Law was sentenced to death. However, probably by bribing his jailers, he escaped and fled to Holland. There, he relied on a brilliant mathematical sense to earn money by gambling. He traveled widely, absorbing the tenets of political arithmetic, the forerunner of modern-day economic theory.

BANKING CAREER

When Law relocated in France, he convinced the regent, Philippe I, duc d'Orléans, to support the establishment of France's first bank, the Banque Générale, which inaugurated the use of paper money. In 1719, the bank, renamed the Banque Royale, was placed under the control of the state, though Law remained its chief officer. Law thereafter formed a joint-stock entity, the Compagnie d'Occident (Company of the West), known popularly as the Mississippi Company. The company sought to settle and trade in a three-thousand-mile swath of the American colonies, from the mouth of the Mississippi River to Canada. At some point, Law began to exaggerate the wealth of the colonies, which subsequently induced wild speculation on the shares of the company. The price of its stock rapidly soared from one hundred livres a share (six hundred dollars in modern-day currency) to ten thousand livres (sixty thousand dollars in modern-day currency). By the summer of 1719, Paris was engulfed in a mania of speculation; on the basis of the extraordinary gains of some investors, the term "a millionaire" was coined.

However, settlers dispatched to the United States were dying from disease, Indian raids, and oppression by the Spanish; anticipated profits were far from being realized. The scheme was kept alive temporarily by printing currency that had inadequate backing. By the summer of 1720, there were 2.5 billion livres of paper money in circulation, while the bank held only 300 million in specie, such as gold and silver, to back up the banknotes.

IMPACT

History has vindicated John Law's pioneering reliance on paper money, as well as many of his other economic insights. Nonetheless, he clearly overextended his reach. When the scheme that became known as the "Mississippi Bubble" collapsed in late 1720, Law fled to England in disgrace, lived there for four years, and then relocated to Venice, where he died in genteel poverty in 1729. The collapse caused an economic crisis in France and Europe.

Later, German philosopher Karl Marx would accurately characterize Law as having the mixed character of a swindler and a prophet. The respected economist Alfred Marshall declared that Law was reckless but a most fascinating genius.

Law pioneered many bank practices, but the disastrous results of his overextended speculation put a damper for some time on the adoption of his innovative designs for public involvement in finance through financial investment in business entities.

FURTHER READING

Gleeson, Janet. *Millionaire: The Philander, Gambler, and Duelist Who Invented Modern France*. New York: Simon & Schuster, 2000. The author maintains that Law's intentions were admirable but that he was overcome by poor judgment and a run of bad luck due to circumstances beyond his control.

Hyde, H. Montgomery. *John Law: The History of an Honest Adventurer*. London: W. Allen, 1969. A writer of numerous biographies, Hyde tells Law's story in fascinating style but lacks the sources that became available to later commentators on Law's career.

Minton, Robert. *John Law: The Father of Paper Money*. New York: Association Press, 1975. Minton claims that Law was a financial genius who careened into disaster after losing his sense of proportion, compounding initial miscalculations by even more reckless tactics.

Murphy, Antoin. *John Law: Economic Theorist and Policy Maker*. Oxford: Clarendon, 1997. A comprehensive scholarly examination of Law's ideas, with a particular emphasis on the relationship between the Mississippi Company and Law's economic principles.

Oudard, Georges. *The Amazing Life of John Law, the Man Behind the Mississippi Bubble*. Translated by G. E. Massé. New York: Payson & Clar, 1928. Oudard relates the story of Law's life and work in melodramatic fashion, inventing dialogue and romanticizing Law and his supporters.

—Gilbert Geis

SEE ALSO: Jim Fisk; Jay Gould.

RICHARD LAWRENCE

American assassin

BORN: 1800 or 1801; England
DIED: June 13, 1861; Washington, D.C.
MAJOR OFFENSE: Attempting to assassinate President Andrew Jackson
ACTIVE: January 30, 1835
LOCALE: The funeral of South Carolina congressman Warren R. Davis.
SENTENCE: Confinement to mental institutions

EARLY LIFE

Richard Lawrence (LAH-rehns) was born in England at the beginning of the nineteenth century and, by the time he became an adult, was diagnosed as insane. He had worked as a painter; some historians argue that the chemicals from the paint may have caused or exacerbated his mental illness. In the 1830's, Lawrence began to have delusions that he was the king of England. He also believed that the United States government and President Andrew Jackson owed him a large amount of money. Lawrence also believed that Jackson had murdered his father in 1832, even though Lawrence's father, who died in England in 1823, had never been to the United States. Lawrence was unemployed most of his life, and he blamed President Jackson and the U.S. government for his personal condition.

CRIMINAL CAREER

Lawrence purchased two pistols in 1835 and began to stalk Jackson. On January 30, 1835, Jackson was in attendance at the funeral of Warren R. Davis, a congressman from South Carolina. As President Jackson entered the service, Lawrence was unsuccessful at obtaining a position close enough from which to shoot Jackson. However, as Jackson left the funeral, Lawrence stepped out from behind a pillar and shot at Jackson's back with one of his two pistols. Lawrence's pistol misfired: The percussion cap exploded, but the bullet did not release. Lawrence tried again with his second pistol, but it also misfired. Investigators later determined that Lawrence's two pistols were extremely sensitive to damp conditions, and the humid weather at the time caused them to misfire.

Lawrence was brought under control by a large crowd who witnessed the assassination attempt. Among those present in the crowd was Congressman Davey Crockett, who assisted in Lawrence's capture. It also was reported that President Jackson played a role in subduing Lawrence by using his own walking stick to strike Lawrence several times.

LEGAL ACTION AND OUTCOME

Lawrence's trial began on April 11, 1835, with Francis Scott Key, author of the U.S. national anthem, acting as the prosecutor. A jury found Lawrence guilty by reason of insanity after only a few minutes of deliberation. Lawrence spent the following two decades in a variety of mental institutions until the government placed him in a newly opened facility in 1855 called the Government Hospital for the Insane in Washington, D.C., which was later renamed St. Elizabeths Hospital.

IMPACT

Richard Lawrence perpetrated the first attempt to assassinate a U.S. president. After the assassination attempt, Vice President Martin Van Buren was known to carry two pistols while presiding in the Senate.

The assassination attempt prompted the first of many conspiracy theories that would become traditional in response to political assassinations. Jackson himself believed that his political enemies, the Whigs, may have been involved in the attempted assassination. He had sought to eliminate the Bank of the United States, which had angered the Whigs. However, no evidence surfaced to indicate a conspiracy, and history has recorded the assassination attempt against Jackson as the act of one delusional man.

In some ways the incident promoted Jackson's reputation as a military hero. Upon the first shot, Jackson had raised his cane to attack his assailant, and in etchings of the incident made for public consumption, this moment was memorialized to underscore Jackson's reputation for courage in the face of fire.

FURTHER READING

Clarke, James W. "Richard Lawrence." In *American Assassins: The Darker Side of Politics*. Rev. ed. Princeton, N.J.: Princeton University Press, 1990. Clarke develops a typology for analyzing sixteen political assassins throughout American history.

Cole, Donald B. *The Presidency of Andrew Jackson*. Lawrence: University Press of Kansas, 1993. Cole briefly documents the assassination attempt on President Andrew Jackson by Lawrence.

Lawrence, Richard. *Shooting at the President!* New York: W. Mitchell, 1835. Lawrence writes for sixteen pages about his assassination attempt on President Andrew Jackson.

                                                                 —*Scott P. Johnson*

SEE ALSO: John Wilkes Booth; Arthur Bremer; Samuel Joseph Byck; Leon Czolgosz; Lynette Fromme; Charles Julius Guiteau; Lee Harvey Oswald; Giuseppe Zangara.

KENNETH LAY
American business executive of Enron Corporation

BORN: April 15, 1942; Tyrone, Missouri
DIED: July 5, 2006; Aspen, Colorado
ALSO KNOWN AS: Kenneth Lee Lay (full name)
MAJOR OFFENSES: Bank fraud, money laundering, securities fraud, insider trading
ACTIVE: 1990's-early 2000's
LOCALE: Houston, Texas

EARLY LIFE

Kenneth Lay was born during the early years of World War II into a financially struggling family in Tyrone, Missouri. Lay's father ran a general store and sold tractors before becoming a Baptist minister. According to all accounts, the young Lay was a hard worker who helped his family by mowing lawns and delivering newspapers. After graduating from Hickman High School in Columbia, Missouri, he enrolled in the University of Missouri. He was elected president of his college fraternity and graduated in 1964 with a B.A. in economics. The following year, he earned a master's degree and went to work at Humble Oil Company, which was later renamed Exxon.

After serving in the Navy, Lay completed a doctorate in economics at the University of Houston in 1970. During the early 1970's, he worked for the federal government, first at the Federal Power Commission and then as undersecretary for energy issues at the Department of the Interior. He took a position as vice president of Florida Gas in 1974 and became president two years later. By 1984, he had become chief executive officer (CEO) of Houston Natural Gas. A year later, Houston Natural Gas merged with InterNorth to become Enron.

CRIMINAL CAREER

Under Lay's leadership, Enron became a successful and increasingly diversified company. At first, most of its activities remained in energy, mostly in distributing gas

Ken Lay, left, with former president George H. W. Bush at a Houston Astros baseball game. (AP/Wide World Photos)

and electricity and in forms of construction, such as building pipelines and power plants. During the 1990's, however, Enron used its assets to move into other fields, eventually trading in more than eight hundred products, including communications and financial instruments.

Lay won praise for Enron's apparent success, and he became a pillar of Houston society, giving large donations to charity and becoming politically involved. He cultivated close ties to the Republican Party in Texas and in the national government. By the end of the twentieth century, Lay had become one of the highest-paid CEOs in the United States.

Signs of Enron's fall appeared behind the apparent success. There were rumors throughout the business world that many of Enron's contracts were results of bribery and political pressure. Following the late 1980's, executives with the company had also been accused of engaging in insider trading, or buying and selling stock by individuals engaged in activities that would influence the price of the stock. During the 1990's, under Chief Financial Officer Andrew Fastow, Enron created companies that were offshore and off the books. This enabled the company both to move currency that could not easily be tracked and to hide losses. Moving currency and assets around gave executives the power to make their company appear more profitable than it actually was and thereby drive up its stock price, bringing more money into the company and enriching Enron executives.

By 2000, Enron stock had reached its highest price. Company executives, who knew about their corporation's hidden losses, sold their own stock. As stock prices began to decline, Lay and fellow Enron executive officer Jeff Skilling assured the public and Enron's employees that the business was basically sound and that stock would rebound. Thus, they encouraged their employees and others to invest money in a declining company. Lay's wife, Linda, sold 500,000 shares of stock just ten minutes before the public announcement of bankruptcy at the end of November, 2001.

LEGAL ACTION AND OUTCOME

On July 7, 2004, a grand jury in Houston indicted Lay on eleven counts of conspiracy, fraud, and making false and misleading statements. Lay's attorneys attempted to delay the legal proceedings and have them moved out of Houston, claiming that the negative publicity their client had received would make it impossible for him to receive a fair trial. However, a jury trial did begin in Houston on January 30, 2006. In this trial, Lay was found guilty on six counts of conspiracy and fraud on May 25. After

---

KEN LAY ON KEN LAY

Shortly after May 25, 2006, when he was found guilty on all six counts against him in the Enron fraud case, Ken Lay mounted this statement on his own Web site. On July 5, 2006, Lay died of a heart attack.

DEAR VISITOR:

Now that my trial has concluded, I would like to offer a few brief comments.

Certainly, we are surprised at the verdict against me. Perhaps it is more appropriate to say we are shocked, as this is not the outcome we expected.

I firmly believe that I am innocent of the charges against me, as I have said from day one. I still firmly believe that to this day. I will continue to work diligently with my legal team to prove this.

In spite of what has happened, I am still a very blessed man. I have a very warm, loving and Christian wife and family that supports me, as well as many, many loving and supportive friends. I'd like to thank all of the people who have shown their concern, support and kept our family in their prayers.

Most of all, my family and I believe that God is in control and, indeed, He does work all things for good for those who love the Lord. And we love our Lord.

Thank you.

KENNETH L. LAY

---

hearing the decision of the twelve jurors, he stated that he was shocked at the verdict and once again asserted his innocence. In the separate bench trial, in which U.S. district judge Sim Lake made the decision, Lay was found guilty on four counts of federal banking violations. On all charges together, the former Enron executive faced a possible 165 years in prison. On July 5, 2006, Lay died of a massive heart attack while on a family vacation in Aspen, Colorado. On Tuesday, October 17, a federal judge, in accordance with the law, vacated Lay's conviction, making it more difficult for the government to seek damages from Lay's estate.

IMPACT

The Enron scandal was one of several widely publicized corporate scandals in the United States in the early twenty-first century. Lawmakers responded to public concern over apparently corrupt practices at Enron, Tyco International, and Worldcom by passing the Sarbanes-Oxley Act, named after Maryland Democratic senator

Paul Sarbanes and Ohio Republican representative Michael Oxley, in July, 2002. The Sarbanes-Oxley Act is generally considered the greatest change to American securities law since the 1930's. It was intended to prevent crimes such as securities fraud by raising accounting requirements, increasing penalties for corporate criminals, and mandating changes in the Securities and Exchange Commission (SEC).

Kenneth Lay's legal problems also had political impact. His company had made substantial contributions to politicians and political parties around the world, especially in the United States and Great Britain. The U.S. Republican Party was one of the largest recipients of these contributions. Lay was a strong supporter of George W. Bush when Bush ran for governor of Texas; he also made one of the largest individual contributions to the successful Bush campaign for the presidency in 2000. This led some critics of the Bush administration and of the Republican Party to raise questions about Republican connections with corrupt corporations.

At the time of its collapse, Enron's bankruptcy was the largest bankruptcy in American history. The affair also produced waves throughout American financial circles. The investigation of Enron led to the trial of the Arthur Anderson accounting firm, which in turn incrimi-nated other companies. The widening investigation helped to uncover fraud at Worldcom; Worldcom's own resulting bankruptcy was even bigger than that of Enron.

FURTHER READING

Eichenwald, Kurt. *Conspiracy of Fools: A True Story.* New York: Random House, 2005. A popular and detailed account of the Enron scandal.

McLean, Bethany, and Peter Elkind. *The Smartest Guys in the Room: The Amazing Rise and Scandalous Fall of Enron.* New York: Portfolio, 2003. The story of the Enron company, written by a *Fortune* reporter who was one of the first to question whether Enron was overvalued.

Skeel, David. *Icarus in the Boardroom: The Fundamental Flaws in Corporate America and Where They Came From.* New York: Oxford University Press, 2005. Inspired by the actions of Lay and other high-profile executives in the early twenty-first century, this book takes a general look at the risk-taking behavior of corporate leaders in American society.

—*Carl L. Bankston III*

SEE ALSO: Bernard Ebbers; Martin Frankel; Michael Milken; Jeffrey Skilling.

TIMOTHY LEARY

American psychologist and promoter of psychedelic drug use

BORN: October 22, 1920; Springfield, Massachusetts
DIED: May 31, 1996; Beverly Hills, California
ALSO KNOWN AS: Timothy Francis Leary (full name)
MAJOR OFFENSE: Drug possession
ACTIVE: 1965-1970
LOCALE: Laredo, Texas; Laguna Beach, California; Poughkeepsie, New York
SENTENCE: Thirty years in prison plus a fine of $30,000; served two years, then escaped; upon recapture, served almost four years

EARLY LIFE

Timothy Leary (LEER-ee) had a conventional childhood, although his father abandoned his family. The young Leary graduated from high school in Springfield, Massachusetts, without distinction. As an adult, he pursued studies at several educational institutions, including Holy Cross College, the U.S. Military Academy at West Point, and the University of Alabama. Then, in the early 1940's, Leary was drafted into the U.S. Army. His military experience was gained at an American hospital, where he met his first wife and became a serious student.

ACADEMIC CAREER

Leary finished his undergraduate degree from the University of Alabama and then continued in psychology, earning an M.A. from Washington State University in 1946, then a Ph.D. from the University of California at Berkeley in 1950. Leary's area of expertise was the developing field of personality and social norms. His first academic appointment was to the position of research director of the Psychiatric Clinic at Kaiser Hospital in Oakland, California (1955-1958). At Kaiser, he published his renowned *The Interpersonal Diagnosis of Personality* (1957).

This professional triumph was followed almost im-

Timothy Leary. (AP/Wide World Photos)

the auspices of his International Foundation for Internal Freedom, which developed into the League for Spiritual Discovery. None of the organizations were characterized by financial viability or long-term stability. His personal life was also scripted by short-term romantic liaisons, interspersed with his four different marriages.

LEGAL ACTION AND OUTCOME

When Leary first began experimenting with psychedelic substances, they were legal in the United States (until 1966, when the federal government imposed regulations). However, in 1965 Leary was arrested in Texas for marijuana possession and ultimately sentenced to thirty years in prison plus a fine of thirty thousand dollars. After a series of legal appeals and additional drug charges, Leary was remanded to a California correctional institution in 1970. He escaped that year, reportedly assisted by the Weathermen revolutionary unit.

Leary spent two years exiled in Algeria and Europe before the American government managed to extradite him from Afghanistan, and he reentered the American penal system. After several years in prison, he was released in 1976 and followed a law-abiding career in software development, complemented by some lecturing, until his death from cancer in 1996.

mediately by family tragedy, when his first wife, Marianne, killed herself in 1958, leaving Leary with two small children. Almost immediately, he quit work. He spent some time living in Cuernavaca, Mexico, where he reportedly ingested his first hallucinogenic substance, *Psilocybe mexicana* mushrooms. The euphoric power of this experience laid the foundation for further experiments with psychedelics and his belief that drug-fueled religious ecstasy could harness personal growth.

The academic venue for his first experiments with synthesized psylocybin, and later lysergic acid diethylamide (LSD), was the staid campus of Harvard University. Leary was offered a position at the Center for Research in Human Personality in 1959. Initially, he performed relatively orthodox teaching and research activities at Harvard but soon moved into experimentation with psychedelic substances, which prompted his departure from Harvard in 1963.

After leaving Harvard, Leary operated several experimental communes in Mexico and near Poughkeepsie, New York. Some of these communities operated under

IMPACT

Timothy Leary was best known for his promotion of psychedelic substances as a means to enlightenment. He played an iconic role in the counterculture movement of the 1960's—coining the phrase, "Turn on, tune in, drop out"—and interacted with all the important personages of the time.

FURTHER READING

Greenfield, Robert. *Timothy Leary: A Biography*. Orlando, Fla: Harcourt, 2006. Substantial and scathing biography.

Henderson, Leigh A., and William J. Glass, eds. *LSD: Still with Us After All These Years*. San Francisco: Jossey-Bass, 1994. Provides information about LSD, including personal accounts documenting its appeal for users.

Leary, Timothy. *Flashbacks: An Autobiography—A Personal and Cultural History of an Era*. New York: G. P. Putnam's Sons, 1990. Leary's own account of his life.

McWilliams, John C. *The 1960's Cultural Revolution.* Westport, Conn.: Greenwood Press, 2000. A historical rendering of the era, including Leary's involvement.

Stevens, Jay. *Storming Heaven: LSD and the American Dream.* New York: Atlantic Monthly Press, 1987. A detailed account by a journalist fascinated with the era; covers Leary's contribution to the times.

Strack, Stephen. "Interpersonal Theory and the Interpersonal Circumplex: Timothy Leary's Legacy." *Journal of Personality Assessment* 66, no. 2 (1996): 212-216. Documentation of Leary's professional contributions.

—*Susan J. Wurtzburg*

SEE ALSO: Abbie Hoffman; Huey Newton.

CHARLES LEE
American Revolutionary War soldier

BORN: February 6, 1732; Cheshire, England
DIED: October 2, 1782; Philadelphia, Pennsylvania
MAJOR OFFENSES: Court-martialed for disobedience of orders and disrespect to his commander; treason
ACTIVE: June 28, 1778 at Battle of Monmouth
LOCALE: Freehold, Monmouth County, New Jersey
SENTENCE: Relieved of command for one year

EARLY LIFE

Charles Lee was born the youngest of seven children of Irish parents in England, where his father was a colonel in the British Army. Lee graduated from a Swiss military school and was commissioned as an ensign in the army at age twelve. In 1748, he completed grammar school, where he had studied military history and learned both to speak and write French and Italian and to read Greek and Latin. Lee entered into regular service in his father's regiment at age fifteen and became a lieutenant in the Forty-Fourth Regiment of Foot at age nineteen. He was then sent to the United States at the beginning of the French and Indian War in 1755.

Lee was of medium height, thin, slovenly, and not handsome. During the French and Indian War, he married the daughter of a Mohawk Indian chief, but little else was reported about the marriage. There were also hints of Lee's homosexual proclivities. He preferred his pack of dogs, which accompanied him everywhere, to associations with people. His disagreeable manners included arrogance, a violent temper, petulance, sarcasm, and vain self-assessment. Offsetting these factors to some degree were his self-confidence, intelligence, and scrupulous honesty. These latter qualities, as well as his extensive military experience, articulate speech, and effective pamphleteering, helped make him a strong competitor to George Washington when the Congress was choosing a commander-in-chief.

MILITARY CAREER

After being wounded in the unsuccessful attack on Fort Ticonderoga in July of 1758 and after some months of recovery, Lee took part in the capture both of Fort Niagara and of Montreal in 1760. Following his return to England, his unit fought in Portugal against the Spanish, and later he served King Stanislaus Leszczyński of Poland. Placed on half-pay in 1772, he retired from the British Army in 1773, went to Virginia to live, and became a promoter of American independence.

When an American Army was formed in 1775, Washington was named commander-in-chief, with Lee third in order after Artemas Ward. Lee served initially at the Siege of Boston, and then in Rhode Island, New York, and Charleston, South Carolina, before returning north to New Jersey, where he commanded an army. On December 12, 1776, Lee spent an evening apart from his army at a local tavern, where he was taken prisoner next morning by a small party of British soldiers. During his captivity, on March 29, 1777, Lee submitted a plan to his captors for ending the revolution. Discovered some time later, this plan was considered treasonous, although Lee asserted that it was intended only to deceive the British. By the spring of 1778, Lee was released in a prisoner exchange and reported to Washington at Valley Forge.

At the Battle of Monmouth on June 28, 1778, Lee failed to perform as ordered: He refused to attack the enemy as directed by Washington and instead ordered a retreat. When he was dressed down by Washington for doing so, he responded disrespectfully. Subsequent letters by Lee to Washington in which he asked for a trial to prove his case were also disrespectful.

LEGAL ACTION AND OUTCOME

Lee was arrested and charged with disobedience of orders and disrespect to his commander; he was found

Charles Lee. (Library of Congress)

guilty of all charges in a court-martial and was removed from command for one year. Lee continued to attack Washington both in words and in print, which caused Colonel John Laurens, an aide to Washington, to challenge Lee to a duel. Lee was wounded in the duel and unable to accept another challenge from Anthony Wayne. He then retreated to his decrepit plantation in Virginia. When Lee's year of suspension was complete, he wrote such an offensive letter to the Continental Congress that they released him from duty in January, 1780. Lee died of pneumonia while visiting in Philadelphia in 1782.

IMPACT

Had Charles Lee succeeded either in his attempt to get Congress to recognize him as superior to George Washington in military capabilities or in his efforts, while in British captivity, to mediate a peace agreement or to promote with his captors a plan to defeat the Americans, the Revolutionary War and the establishment of the United States might have turned out very differently. Lee's lack of success was undoubtedly influenced by his opportunistic, self-serving, egotistical approach in all situations. It eventually became obvious, not only to Washington but also to congressional leaders, that Lee's decisions and actions were primarily dictated by what he saw as beneficial to his own career. In the end, his generalship was not regarded in the same class as that of other well-regarded military figures.

FURTHER READING

Alden, J. R. *General Charles Lee: Traitor or Patriot?* Baton Rouge: Louisiana State University Press, 1951. Examines the life and times of Lee and the impacts of his treason.

Patterson, S. M. *Knight Errant of Liberty; The Triumph and Tragedy of General Charles Lee.* New York: Lantern Press, 1958. Another biography of Lee.

Thayer, T. *The Making of a Scapegoat: Washington and Lee at Monmouth.* Port Washington, N.Y.: Kennikat Press, 1976. This collection from the Lee papers (1754) of the New York Historical Society details the events at Monmouth.

—*Jack H. Westbrook*

SEE ALSO: Benedict Arnold; James Wilkinson.

DAULTON LEE
American drug trafficker and spy

BORN: 1952; Los Angeles, California
ALSO KNOWN AS: Andrew Daulton Lee (full name); the Snowman
MAJOR OFFENSE: Espionage
ACTIVE: 1974-1977
LOCALE: Mexico City, Mexico
SENTENCE: Life in prison; paroled in 1998

EARLY LIFE

Andrew Daulton Lee (DAHL-tuhn lee) is a Los Angeles native and adopted son of a physician. He attended elementary school at St. John Fisher parochial elementary school in California and was an altar boy at a Roman Catholic church. Lee's grades began to fall as he got older, and his teenage years were difficult socially because he was self-conscious about his looks. He only reached five feet, three inches in height and grew his hair long to cover ears that he believed stood out too far. During adolescence, Lee befriended Christopher John Boyce, who had attended the same elementary school and church and was a fellow altar boy. The two became involved in various activities together, including high school football and falconry.

Unlike Boyce, Lee did not achieve high grades and felt alienated from what many considered the mainstream within his school; however, he did excel in woodworking and carpentry. Lee also experimented with drugs and became involved in selling them sometime during high school. After graduating from high school, he went from job to job and expanded his drug-dealing activities. Boyce bounced around from college to college before his father, a former agent of the Federal Bureau of Investigation (FBI), helped him secure a clerk's job at the Los Angeles area aerospace company TRW Defense and Space Systems Group, which was involved in the operation of spy satellites for the United States.

CRIMINAL CAREER

During the 1970's, Lee began to specialize in cocaine dealing and eventually became known as the Snowman (in reference to his dealing "snow," or cocaine). Boyce continued working at TRW and was in close proximity to classified information about United States spy satellites. Boyce managed to gain access to TRW's "vault," where the company conducted classified communications.

Boyce became disillusioned with the spying activities that he witnessed and saw an opportunity to make extra money. He and Lee schemed to sell intelligence to Soviet officials. He began compiling rolls of film of the documents in the vault, including photographs of Rhyolite, a satellite used to detect the telemetry from Soviet missile tests, and other important technologies. Lee served as a courier, delivering the documents to the Soviet embassy in Mexico City.

LEGAL ACTION AND OUTCOME

The espionage committed by Boyce and Lee was uncovered more by accident than by any official investigation. In 1977, Lee was falsely arrested by Mexican police in Mexico City in front of the Soviet embassy; he was suspected of murdering a police officer. At the time of his arrest, Lee had film strips marked "top secret" with him. He was then interrogated by Mexican police and FBI officials, and he admitted to working as a liaison between Soviet officials in Mexico and Boyce in California. Boyce was arrested soon after Lee's confession.

After their arrests, Lee and Boyce were both convicted of espionage. Boyce was sentenced to forty years in prison, while Lee, because of his prior record, was sentenced to life in prison. Both were assigned to the penitentiary in Lompoc, California. In 1980, Boyce escaped and spent nineteen months as a fugitive, robbing banks during his time at large. He was released from prison on parole in March of 2003, but his parole would not end until 2046. Lee remained at Lompoc, where in 2006 he was engaged to marry Kathleen McKenney, a twenty-eight-year-old writer whom he met while she was interviewing him for a book she was writing in relation to the case.

IMPACT

The arrests of Daulton Lee and Christopher John Boyce surprised the intelligence community and eventually exposed the poor security measures existing at TRW. Indeed, investigators later found that alcohol and drug use were occurring among employees in the vault. There were also problems with storage, oversight, and destruction of classified materials. The ease with which the two young men had penetrated TRW's security measures underscored both the need for stricter measures and the difficulty of subverting Soviet espionage. During this same time period, other spies were detected, including some who had infiltrated British and Canadian intelligence agencies and worked closely with the United States.

Lee and Boyce's saga also revealed the nation's spying endeavors to an American public that was largely unaware of the extent of such activities. Following this period, the United States declassified many of the images that were collected in the 1960's and 1970's and acknowledged the existence of the National Reconnaissance Office, which was established in the 1960's to coordinate reconnaissance of foreign territories. Although some feared that declassification could hamper the United States in its eventual war against terrorism, current and ongoing intelligence operations remain largely classified.

The story of Lee and Boyce was popularized in the book *The Falcon and the Snowman: A True Story of Friendship and Espionage* (1979) by Robert Lindsey. A motion picture of the same name, starring Timothy Burton as Christopher John Boyce and Sean Penn as Daulton Lee, was released in 1985.

FURTHER READING

"Andrew Daulton Lee." In *Outlaws, Mobsters, and Crooks: From the Old West to the Internet.* Detroit: UXL, 1998. A reference-book entry that covers Lee's upbringing, involvement in drug dealing and espionage, and the case's outcome.

Lindsey, Robert. *The Falcon and the Snowman: A True Story of Friendship and Espionage.* New York: Simon & Schuster, 1979. Chronicles the lives of Boyce and Lee and their eventual descent into espionage, including the poor security measures in place at TRW Defense and Space Systems Group.

_____. *The Flight of the Falcon.* New York: Simon & Schuster, 1983. The story of Boyce's escape from the Lompoc penitentiary, his year and a half as a fugitive, and the hunt to find him.

Owen, David. *Hidden Secrets: A Complete History of Espionage and the Technology Used to Support It.* Toronto, Ont.: Firefly Books, 2002. Reviews some of the largest cases of espionage in history and how technology was used to solve them.

—*Brion Sever*

SEE ALSO: Christopher John Boyce.

NICK LEESON
British bank trader

BORN: February 25, 1967; Watford, England
ALSO KNOWN AS: Nicholas William Leeson (full name); Rogue Trader
MAJOR OFFENSES: Forgery and fraud
ACTIVE: July, 1992-March, 1995
LOCALE: Singapore
SENTENCE: Six and a half years in jail

EARLY LIFE

Nick Leeson (LEE-suhn) came from working-class origins—his father was a plasterer. After elementary school, he attended Parmiter's School, Watford, studied and played hard, and was made a prefect. He left in 1985 at eighteen years old but with few qualifications. However, he managed to obtain a clerical job at Coutts and Company—an established banking firm in London and bankers to the queen—even though there had been three hundred applicants for the post. Then, in June, 1987, he applied for a job at Morgan Stanley, the international investment bank, and chose to work in the futures and options division. There he earned £20,000 a year, with another £20,000 bonus, far beyond anything his family or friends were earning.

While there, he realized that substantial earnings were to be made on the trading floor rather than in back-room offices. In 1989, he heard that Barings Securities was looking for someone in its settlements division; he applied for the position and was accepted at once. Barings Securities was part of Barings Bank, founded in London in 1763, the oldest surviving British merchant bank. In its time, it had financed famous deals such as the Louisiana Purchase and the floating of Guinness as a Limited Company. Leeson astutely recognized that big opportunities could be found in East Asian economies and so asked to be transferred to the bank's Indonesian office. By Christmas, 1990, he had managed to sort out £100 million worth of share certificates lying unpaid by customers and had earned a reputation as a settlements expert in futures (predicting how the stock market would develop) and options.

CRIMINAL CAREER

Barings had also had an office in the nearby island nation of Singapore since 1987, called Barings Securities (Singapore) Limited (BSS). It had started in ordinary stocks and shares, but a growing amount of trade was develop-

Nick Leeson, at left. (AP/Wide World Photos)

ing in futures on the Singapore International Money Exchange (SIMEX). In 1992, Leeson obtained the position of general manager of the branch, with authority to hire a small team both to do business on the trading floor in the bank's own right at SIMEX and to manage the "back office," as the clearing of accounts was called. In fact, Leeson qualified himself to be both trader and back-office manager. Nearly every other banking firm kept the two activities entirely separate in a system of checks and balances. However, Leeson created for himself the authority not only to trade options and futures for clients and other companies under the Barings umbrella but also to arbitrage price differences between SIMEX and the Japanese stock exchange at Osaka. There existed a small time difference between the two markets, and this could be exploited by lightning-quick decisions to buy or sell on the trading floor. All such deals had to be accompanied at the end of the day by a percentage payment to SIMEX.

Leeson soon discovered that a Barings account existed carrying the number 88888, which had been occasionally used in the past to carry small errors until they could be rectified. It was not used and had not been closed. This account was to prove fatal for Leeson: He used it to hide growing trading losses while requesting various divisions of Barings to supply him with money to cover SIMEX end-of-day payments.

Leeson claims that he began using the 88888 account to cover the mistakes of a newly hired trader. However, other mistakes began to happen, which were dealt with in the same way. The mistakes moved from being straight errors of misunderstanding to taking calculated risks to keep clients and meet their demands. Leeson tried to rectify these losses by taking unauthorized risks in arbitraging on the futures market or by "creative accounting," which led Barings's head office to believe BSS was actually making healthy profits. Leeson achieved such a reputation that when he began to ask for sums of money to be transferred to BSS, they were made without question. Occasional audits were done perfunctorily, but Leeson was able to hide the true state of affairs.

By the end of 1992, the 88888 account was in the red by £2 million; by the end of 1993, £23 million, though BSS declared a £10 million profit, 10 percent of Barings's total profits for the year. By the end of 1994, the account loss was £208 million, though Leeson had declared a £28.5 million profit for the branch.

Leeson also had some bad luck. The Japanese economy, as indexed by the Nikkei (equivalent of the American Dow-Jones stock exchange), which had been growing healthily during the 1980's, began to slow and decline; after the Kobe earthquake on January 17, 1995, it dropped rapidly. This was at a moment when Leeson was gambling that it would start to rise again. In the end, he was making such huge trades that it is probable the rest of the market saw what was happening and worked to bring his downfall. This finally came on February 23, 1995, when the Barings position became completely untenable. Barings's final loss amounted to £827 million ($1.3 billion).

LEGAL ACTION AND OUTCOME

Leeson and his wife, Lisa, fled Singapore, finally emerging a week later at Frankfurt, Germany, hoping to get arrested in Britain. When he fled, Leeson still had no idea how serious the damage was. By the time he was arrested at Frankfurt on March 2, 1995, Barings had been declared bankrupt. The British Serious Fraud Office refused to intervene when the Singaporean authorities issued a request for extradition. After nine months of wrangling, in December, Leeson was finally put on trial in Singapore on two counts of forging a signature to mislead the bank's auditors and cheating the Singapore exchange. He pleaded guilty and was sentenced to six and one half years in jail, the nine months already spent in a German jail counting toward that total.

While Leeson was in Changi Prison, his wife divorced him, and he suffered colon cancer, from which his mother had died earlier, but he was successfully treated. He was released in the summer of 1999.

IMPACT

Barings's assets could not cover its final debts, and the bank was bought by the Dutch Bank ING for £1 plus its debts. A Bank of England report noted failures of accountability in the Barings management. A Singaporean investigation was much more damning, however, simply not believing its senior management when they claimed that they had no idea what Nick Leeson had been doing. All the Barings management finally resigned or were fired. In addition, twelve hundred Barings employees lost their jobs. The notably volatile futures markets had a few more regulations put in place to guard against a repetition of such events. The ability of just one man to bring down an old established banking firm was sensational at the time and a profound shock to the British financial world. Moreover, the ability of the Bank of England to supervise was seriously questioned.

Leeson himself on his release found that he had earned considerable sums on royalties and from a film made about his experiences. He later became a lecture speaker and ran his own seminars on stress management.

FURTHER READING

Braithwaite, John, and Peter Drakes. *Global Business Regulation*. Cambridge, England: Cambridge University Press, 2000. Puts the Barings debacle in a wider context and shows the lessons learned from it.

Hunt, Luke, and Karen Heinrich. *Barings Lost: Nick Leeson and the Collapse of Barings*. London: Butterworth-Heinemann, 1996. Representative of a spate of books written soon after the bank's collapse, all giving slightly varying accounts of causes and effects.

Leeson, Nick, with Ivan Tyrell. *Back from the Brink: Coping with Stress*. London: Virgin Books, 2005. A sequel to Leeson's 1996 book, written after his release from prison and his reinvention of himself as speaker and entrepreneur.

Leeson, Nick, with Edward Whitley. *Rogue Trader*. London: Little, Brown, 1996. Leeson's own account of what happened, written from jail in Singapore. While not excusing himself, he claims he was not trying to make money for himself and that Barings was largely to blame for its own collapse.

—*David Barratt*

SEE ALSO: Ivan Boesky; Roberto Calvi; Bernard Ebbers; Martin Frankel; Michael Milken.

HENRI LEMOINE
French con artist

BORN: Date unknown; France?
DIED: After 1909; place unknown
ALSO KNOWN AS: Henri François Lemoine (full name)
MAJOR OFFENSE: Fraud
ACTIVE: 1905-1908
LOCALE: Paris, France
SENTENCE: Six years of hard labor

EARLY LIFE
Nothing is known about the early life or education of Henri Lemoine (ahn-ree luh-mwawn). He may have been an engineer and an assistant to Henri Moissan, who was France's first Nobel laureate in chemistry (1906).

CRIMINAL CAREER
In the summer of 1905, Lemoine met with Sir Julius Charles Wernher, a director of De Beers Consolidated Mines Ltd., and said that he had discovered a method of making synthetic diamonds. Wernher asked for a demonstration, thinking that even the rumor of such a breakthrough might cause serious financial problems. A few weeks later, the two men met, and Lemoine seemed to produce synthetic diamonds. Most reports indicate that Lemoine mixed his ingredients—most likely iron fillings and coal—in another room and returned in the nude to prove he had hidden nothing. He then placed the ingredients into a furnace to produce the synthetic diamonds. The location has been described as Lemoine's laboratory, a department store basement, an abandoned warehouse, or even somewhere in London. A second demonstration was demanded of Lemoine and was also apparently successful. Some reports say that one of the observers, Francis Oats, was immediately suspicious but went along with the payment for further research.

Accounts also vary concerning the sequence of events and the total amount of money exchanged, but all mention Wernher giving Lemoine sixty-four thousand pounds to set up a laboratory. The most likely location was in the Pyrenees Mountains, for electricity, secrecy, or both. (In 1908, it was discovered that Lemoine was selling electricity to the local people.)

Lemoine's deceit soon began to unravel. Those unwittingly involved with the scheme discovered that Lemoine had put the diamonds into his furnace by sleight-of-hand. One account says that during a third demonstration, a De Beers manager had slipped a diamond into the furnace and found that it did not decompose as Lemoine had predicted. Still another says that a jeweler in Paris admitted to selling Lemoine the gems that Lemoine then claimed to have prepared.

LEGAL ACTION AND OUTCOME
Lemoine was arrested, and while free on bail he fled to Constantinople. Upon his return, he was rearrested and tried. During the trial, he was forced to re-create the diamond synthesis and failed. The description of his process, which Wernher had insisted be placed in a London bank, was opened and found to use only carbon powder and sugar. On July 6, 1909, Lemoine was sentenced to six years of hard labor for fraud. Another account says that while the court was trying to decide the case, Lemoine escaped and disappeared. There is no record of him after 1909.

IMPACT
The Lemoine story has been retold in a several places with a variety of details. The most elaborate of these appeared in a highly regarded journal of chemistry and makes an intriguing link to the French writer Marcel Proust. After losing a substantial sum of money in this scheme, Proust wrote a series of brief works called *pastiches*, or imitations, on the advice of a family friend. Each of these nine works is written in the style of an author of greater reputation, such as Honoré de Balzac or Gustave Flaubert, much as an artist copies famous works to perfect technique. In one *pastiche*, Proust predicted that someday a hotter furnace would be developed that could produce diamonds.

In 1953, both a Swedish and an American firm succeeded in synthesizing gem-size diamonds using higher pressure rather than higher heat. In 2005, an entirely new approach of laying down successive thin films of carbon was announced.

FURTHER READING
Epstein, Edward Jay. *The Rise and Fall of Diamonds.* New York: Simon & Schuster, 1982. Gives brief accounts of the affair.
Krätz, Otto. "The 'Rocky' Road to Literary Fame: Marcel Proust and the Diamond Synthesis of Professor Moissan." *Angewandte Chemie (International Edition)* 40 (2001): 4604-4610. Both scholarly and read-

able, contains many references (mostly in German). A reliable account that ties Lemoine into the contemporary scientific and literary worlds.

—*K. Thomas Finley*

SEE ALSO: Frank W. Abagnale, Jr.; Tino De Angelis; William Dodd; Billie Sol Estes; Victor Lustig; Alexandre Stavisky; Joseph Weil.

VLADIMIR ILICH LENIN
Russian political leader (1917-1924)

BORN: April 22, 1870; Simbirsk (now Ulyanovsk) Russia

DIED: January 21, 1924; Gorki, Soviet Union (now in Russia)

ALSO KNOWN AS: Vladimir Ilich Ulyanov (birth name)

CAUSE OF NOTORIETY: After leading the Bolshevik Revolution that established the Soviet Union, Lenin evolved into a dictator who ruled with repression and ruthlessness.

ACTIVE: 1903-1924

LOCALE: Russia

EARLY LIFE

A son of an educator, the young Vladimir Ilich Ulyanov (VLAD-ee-meer IHL-ihtch LYAY-nyihn) lived in an upper-middle-class home in central Russia. He became interested in politics as a teenager, especially after his father's death and the execution of his brother for radical activities against the government. He moved to St. Petersburg, the Russian capital, in his early twenties and participated in radical movements there. Arrested in 1895, he was sent to a Siberian exile camp for political prisoners from 1897 to 1900. He then traveled to Western Europe in 1900 and helped create the Russian Social Democratic Party (RSDP) in 1903.

Adopting the alias "Lenin," by which he is best known, he led the Bolshevik faction of the RSDP, eventually establishing it as a separate political party committed to the communist theories of Karl Marx. During World War I, he lived in exile in Switzerland before returning to Russia in the spring of 1917. By that time, the Russian monarchy had been overthrown, and numerous political parties vied for power in this confused and difficult period. Lenin and his Bolshevik comrades plotted to overthrow the new democratic government in Petrograd, succeeding in November, 1917.

He became the prime minister of the Russian government while continuing as party leader. Under his direction, the Bolsheviks used forceful methods against their rivals, including banning all political parties and fighting a devastating civil war against their opponents. Lenin created the Cheka, a ruthless Bolshevik secret police organization that used brutal measures against those who opposed Lenin's leadership and policies. The Bolsheviks succeeded in forcibly extending their power over the entire nation by 1921.

POLITICAL CAREER

During his remaining life before dying in early 1924 at age fifty-three, Lenin dominated the Russian political scene. Domestically, he tried to restore the Russian economy that had been ravaged by war. The period of War Communism (1918-1921) attempted to bring the total

Vladimir Ilich Lenin. (Library of Congress)

LENIN'S LAST VIEW OF SOVIET GOVERNMENT

Semiretired because of health issues, Lenin sent three letters recommending changes to the ruling Central Committee of the Communist Party between December, 1922, and January, 1923. He clearly foresaw trouble for the Union of Soviet Socialist Republics and wanted to avert it. According to Leon Trotsky, Joseph Stalin suppressed the letters. Few people ever knew about them. (Stalin later had Trotsky assassinated.)

"Letter to Congress"

- I would urge strongly that at this Congress a number of changes be made in our political structure. . . .
- I think that from this standpoint the prime factors in the question of stability are such members of the C.C. as Stalin and Trotsky. I think relations between them make up the greater part of the danger of a split, which could be avoided, and this purpose, in my opinion, would be served, among other things, by increasing the number of Central Committee members to 50 or 100.
- Stalin is too rude and this defect, although quite tolerable in our midst and in dealing among us Communists, becomes intolerable in a Secretary-General. That is why I suggest that the comrades think about a way of removing Stalin from that post.

"Granting Legislative Functions to the State Planning Commission"

- [T]he State Planning Commission stands somewhat apart from our legislative institutions, although, as a body of experienced people, experts, representatives of science and technology, it is actually in a better position to form a correct judgment of affairs. . . .
- I think that we must now take a step towards extending the competence of the State Planning Commission.

"The Question of Nationalities or 'Autonomisation'"

- It is quite natural that in such circumstances the "freedom to secede from the union" by which we justify ourselves will be a mere scrap of paper, unable to defend the non-Russians from the onslaught of that really Russian man, the Great-Russian chauvinist, in substance a rascal and a tyrant, such as the typical Russian bureaucrat is. There is no doubt that the infinitesimal percentage of Soviet and sovietised workers will drown in that tide of chauvinistic Great-Russian riffraff like a fly in milk. . . .
- [W]ere we careful enough to take measures to provide the non-Russians with a real safeguard against the truly Russian bully? I do not think we took such measures although we could and should have done so.

izens. In foreign affairs, Lenin fought a war against Poland and also created the Comintern (Communist International) in 1919 to promote and assist revolutionary movements in other nations, although Lenin achieved limited success in both instances.

IMPACT

Vladimir Ilich Lenin represents a remarkable combination of a revolutionary who possessed intellectual and theoretical brilliance and one who at the same time took the necessary steps to consolidate political power and create a one-party state that quickly became a dictatorship. The system he established, promoting the ideology of communism, was continued after his death in 1924, first by Joseph Stalin and then by later successors. The nation he led, the Union of Soviet Socialist Republics (USSR), lasted until its dissolution in 1991.

Lenin's strong totalitarian system was sustained at a high price, however: repressive practices, including mass arrests, purges against his opponents, concentration camps, numerous executions, and press censorship. Lenin approved policies to harass and suppress religious life. He demanded absolute obedience within the Bolshevik Party, removing followers who questioned his authority and replacing them with loyalists such as Stalin, who ruthlessly implemented Lenin's policies.

Terrorism became a well-known feature of the communist dictatorship, and Lenin defended those methods without apology. Once in power, Lenin declared: "We are engaged in building up a dictatorship, a regime of violence against the exploiters; whoever does not grasp this simple truth we cast away from us." The leader of the feared Cheka stated:

> We stand for organized terror—this should be frankly admitted. Terror is an absolute necessity during times of

economy under state control. The effort did not meet its objectives, leading to Lenin's tactical decision in 1921 to create the New Economic Policy (NEP) to permit a small degree of private ownership and capitalism. However, he declared that this was only a temporary approach and not a fundamental change in his socialist economic objectives. Russian society also was rigidly controlled under his harsh rule, creating massive hardship for ordinary cit-

revolution. Our aim is to fight against the enemies of the Soviet government and of the new order of life. To these [enemies] we show no mercy.

In addition to governing the communist state, Lenin is important for his extensive writing on political issues. Two works are noteworthy in explaining his concept of a revolutionary party and the means to take and hold political power: *Chto delat* (1902; *What Is to Be Done?*, 1929) and *Gosudarstvo i revolyustiya* (1919; *State and Revolution*, 1971).

Lenin exemplifies the rise of secular totalitarian movements that became a significant characteristic of the twentieth century. He lived very simply, while remaining totally committed to his ideological and political objectives. Even decades after his death, the controversy over the appropriate location for his embalmed body (whether Moscow in the Lenin Mausoleum on Red Square or elsewhere) shows Russians' continued devotion to his mystique. His dynamic personality and powerful leadership mark Lenin as one of the most influential figures of the century and the broader span of history.

FURTHER READING

Gerson, Lennard D. *The Secret Police in Lenin's Russia.* Philadelphia: Temple University Press, 1976. Provides numerous examples of repressive policies and techniques used against Lenin's opponents.

Leggett, George. *The Cheka: Lenin's Political Police—The All-Russian Extraordinary Commission for Combating Counter-revolution and Sabotage.* New York: Oxford University Press, 1981. Detailed scholarly assessment of Lenin's secret police as part of his totalitarian system.

Levytsky, Boris. *The Uses of Terror: The Soviet Secret Police, 1917-1970.* New York: Coward, McCann and Geoghegan, 1972. Provides many examples of the communist dictatorship that Lenin and his successors created.

Pipes, Richard, ed. *The Unknown Lenin: From the Secret Archive.* New Haven, Conn.: Yale University Press, 1998. Secret documents, published in the 1990's, further reveal Lenin's determination to use force against his opponents.

Service, Robert. *Lenin: A Biography.* Cambridge, Mass.: Harvard University Press, 2000. Comprehensive account of Lenin's life, including his justification for a one-party state and the use of terror techniques to achieve his objectives.

—*Taylor Stults*

SEE ALSO: Joseph Stalin; Leon Trotsky.

LEO X
Roman Catholic pope (r. 1513-1521)

BORN: December 11, 1475; Florence (now in Italy)
DIED: December 1, 1521; Rome, Papal States (now in Italy)
ALSO KNOWN AS: Giovanni de' Medici (birth name)
CAUSE OF NOTORIETY: Leo X engaged in simony, nepotism, and an extravagant lifestyle while head of the Roman Catholic Church.
ACTIVE: 1513-1521
LOCALE: Rome, Papal States (now in Italy)

EARLY LIFE

Giovanni de' Medici (jyoh-VAHN-nee deh MEH-dee-chee), who would become Pope Leo X, was the second son of Lorenzo the Magnificent of the powerful Medici clan, which dominated Florentine politics for several generations. Because of the economic and political power this afforded Giovanni, he was tonsured at age seven and made cardinal-deacon at age thirteen. He studied theology and canon law and was later exiled from his native city, Florence, because of the French campaign in 1494. After traveling through parts of Europe, he returned to Rome, where he stayed until sent to Bologna as a legate in 1511. When Florence declared itself for the Pisan cardinals who opposed Pope Julius II, Giovanni led a papal army against the city. He was captured at Ravenna in 1512 but was able to escape. Later that same year, Florence was returned to Medici control in a bloodless coup.

Giovanni was elected pope at age thirty-seven. The conclave to elect the pope after the death of Julius II lasted eight days. In retaliation for their opposition to the recently deceased pope, the Pisan cardinals were excluded. Giovanni was elected on March 9, 1513, in part because he was believed to be in ill health and therefore unlikely to have a long reign. However, he was unable to ascend immediately to the papacy because he was neither a priest nor a bishop. Therefore, he was ordained a priest on March 15, consecrated bishop on March 17, and crowned pope, as Leo X, two days later. The Vatican's official list begins his pontificate on March 9, the day of his election.

PAPAL CAREER

Pope Leo X was known as a Renaissance prince who loved books, music, theater, art, hunting, and lavish feasts. Two of his main concerns were the advancement of his family's interests and the welfare of Florence. These two concerns were intimately related, because Florence had long been under Medici control. In an effort to advance his family, he made his cousin Giulio de' Medici archbishop of Florence and his nephew Lorenzo the duke of Urbino. Later, in 1523, Giulio became Pope Clement VII.

To protect Italy from falling under foreign control, Leo X made a treaty with France in 1515 after it had achieved several victories in Italy. Under the terms of the treaty, France would guarantee Florence independence under Medici control and in return would receive Parma and Piscenza, in addition to a concordat that gave the French crown the right to nominate all bishops, abbots, and priors in France. With the help of Charles I of Spain, France was later driven from Italy, and Leo recovered Parma and Piscenza.

In 1517, a plot to poison Leo was discovered. Cardinal Alfonso Petrucci, the leader of the plot, was executed while four other cardinals were imprisoned. To strengthen his position, Leo elevated thirty-one new members to the College of Cardinals.

In order to finance a projected crusade against the Turks and the construction of St. Peter's Basilica, Leo X authorized the sale of indulgences and the selling of high church offices. He died suddenly of malaria on December 1, 1521. The suddenness of his death caused some speculation that he may have been poisoned.

IMPACT

In response to Leo X's authorization of the sale of indulgences in Germany, the Augustinian monk Martin Luther affixed his Ninety-Five Theses of protest to the door of the church in Wittenberg in 1517, setting off the Protestant Reformation. In addition, Leo X left the Vatican with a large financial debt. The split in the Church resulted in divisions and hostilities in many countries of Europe.

Leo X. (R. S. Peale and J. A. Hill)

A Catholic Counter-Reformation began, culminating in the Council of Trent (1545-1563). The objectives of this body were to clarify Catholic doctrine, which delimited it from Protestantism, and pass legislation for the needed reform of the Church. A standardization of religious rituals and practices resulted in the use of Latin rather than the vernacular. This made the Mass, central in Catholic worship, less understandable to the common people and the spread of the faith more difficult in different cultures. Many people have believed that the actions taken by the Council of Trent deepened the split between Catholics and Protestants, making an eventual reconciliation more difficult.

FURTHER READING

McBrien, Richard. *Lives of the Popes.* San Francisco: HarperCollins, 1997. Presents brief but informative biographies of every pope from Peter to John Paul II.

Also included is an extensive glossary of related terminology.

Rendina, Claudio. *The Popes: Histories and Secrets.* Translated by Paul McCusker. Santa Ana, Calif.: Seven Locks Press, 2002. Biographies of popes from Peter to John Paul II. Includes comments on the list and various anomalies.

Walsh, Michael, ed. *Lives of the Popes.* Gordon, Vic.: Universal International, 1998. Much briefer bibliography of popes from Peter to John Paul II. Contains many black-and-white as well as color illustrations of related people, places, and events, including some photographs.

—*Philip E. Lampe*

SEE ALSO: Alexander VI; Cesare Borgia; Clement VII; Urban VI.

LEOPOLD II
King of Belgium (r. 1865-1909) and the Congo Free State (r. 1885-1908)

BORN: April 9, 1835; Brussels, Belgium
DIED: December 17, 1909; Laeken, Belgium
ALSO KNOWN AS: Léopold-Louis-Philippe-Marie-Victor (full name); Leopold-Lodewijk-Filips-Maria-Victor
CAUSE OF NOTORIETY: Leopold established a personal fiefdom, the Congo Free State, from which he acquired an immense fortune by brutally forcing natives to collect ivory, mineral ore, and rubber; some five million to eight million Congolese died because of his depredation, and countless more had their bodies mutilated when they failed to meet the heartless work quotas.
ACTIVE: 1876-1908
LOCALE: Belgium and Central Africa

EARLY LIFE

Leopold II (LEE-ah-pohld) was a gawky, shy youth with a rather pronounced nose. First cousin to Britain's Queen Victoria and grandson of King Louis-Philippe, Leopold married a Habsburg archduchess, Marie-Henriette. Excluded by his father from state affairs, Leopold dreamed of acquiring colonies for Belgium. Belgians, however, were more interested in their own industrial development and were wary of funding foreign adventures. Moreover, the Revolution of 1830, which had created Belgium and a constitutional monarchy, limited Leopold's ability to force his imperial schemes upon the government.

Thus after becoming king in 1865, Leopold devised a cunning and deceptive plan to acquire a colony by founding an international association to combat the slave trade in Africa (1876). Claiming that neither he nor Belgium, a neutral country, desired any territorial expansion, he enlisted the Welsh explorer Henry Morton Stanley to work for the Association Internationale Africaine in its civilizing mission.

POLITICAL CAREER

In 1879, Stanley was sent to persuade Congolese chiefs to surrender land and rights to the association. Unable to raise money from the Belgian parliament to fund his scheme, Leopold enlisted an American, Henry Shelton Sanford, to set up private concessions for the economic exploitation of central Africa so that the colony would pay for itself. Led to believe that the Congo was a union of "Negro" republics open to free trade, American president Chester A. Arthur gave his blessings to the spurious cause. Negotiating English, French, Portuguese, and German rivalry in Africa, Leopold played up the neutrality of Belgium and had himself recognized as the king of the Congo Free State at the Berlin Conference (1884-1885), creating a state eighty times the size of Belgium itself.

Constitutionally, the Congo Free State, a federation of various tribal areas under the control of Leopold's agents, ended the Arab slave trade but replaced it with a brutally conscripted labor force. In a notoriously hypocritical case, Tippu Tib, who controlled an extensive slaving network on the upper Congo and Lualaba Rivers, was induced to become the governor of Stanleyville. In repressing native rebellion and rounding up laborers, mercenaries were instructed to bring back a human hand for every spent shotgun cartridge, to ensure they did not waste ammunition shooting game.

Severing limbs, along with rape and other forms of carnage, became a means to punish laborers who did not meet their quotas in red rubber. When news leaked of extensive British shareholding in one concession, a potential threat to Belgian commercial interests, the government considered making the Congo into a state colony, but Leopold lied about a loan from one of his concessionaires, Browne de Tiège, to make such a conversion appear too costly for the state to pursue. Leopold also had imperial ambitions in China and the Philippines, and the profits from the Congo were reinvested in a host of private enterprises there and throughout the world.

Leopold's cold and miserly treatment of his three daughters and wife deserves mention. Embittered by the death of his young son, the count of Hainaut, in 1869, Leopold feared that his imperial fortune would be squandered through the decadent dynastic connections of his two daughters' marriages, Louise to a distant Saxe-Coburg cousin and Stephanie to the Habsburg crown prince Rudolf, tragically remembered for having committed suicide with his lover at Mayerling in 1889. Leopold allowed Louise to be placed in an insane asylum after a love affair and disinherited Stephanie when she married a commoner in 1900. A third daughter, Clémentine, was not allowed to marry; Leopold kept her as a companion and housekeeper. In the last decades of her life, Queen Marie-Henriette rarely saw her spouse, who spent his nights with his many mistresses, eventually fathering two illegitimate children with a Parisian prostitute, Blanche Delacroix.

Once the Congo atrocities became known, Leopold was forced to turn over the colony to the Belgian government (1908). Although the black American journalist George Washington Williams wrote an indictment of the Congo Free State in 1890, effective steps toward reform began only when the Liverpool shipping agent Edmund Morel and the Irishman Roger Casement exposed the ravages taking place in the Congo, gaining wide support from such public figures of the day as Booker T. Washington and Arthur Conan Doyle. Novelist Joseph Conrad made the depravity of Leopold's "civilizing mission" the basis for *Heart of Darkness*

FIRST REPORTS OF ATROCITIES

Soldier and writer George Washington Williams (1849-1891), considered to be American's first black historian, receives credit for publishing the first accounts of the horrors in King Leopold's Congo. Williams interviewed Leopold in Belgium and then went to the Congo with the king's blessing. Apparently, Leopold believed his Congo agents would ensure that Williams saw only the benefits of Belgian control and that he would make a favorable report. If so, Leopold misjudged his man. Williams was not duped by his handlers; he talked to missionaries and saw for himself the effects of Belgian administration. In 1890, he addressed his first report—"An Open Letter to His Serene Majesty Leopold II, King of the Belgians and Sovereign of the Independent State of Congo" directly to Leopold in recognition of the king's support for the trip. Respectful but blunt, Williams accuses the agents and Belgian army of trickery, tyranny, cruelty, destruction, kidnapping, fraud, slavery, and wide-scale murder. He warns the king:

> All the crimes perpetuated in the Congo have been done in *your* name, and *you* must answer at the bar of Public Sentiment for the misgovernment of a people, whose lives and fortunes were entrusted to you by the August Conference of Berlin, 1884-1885.

Three months later, Williams published a second letter—"A Report upon the Congo-State and Country to the President of the Republic of the United States of America"—this one pointedly exposing the horrific effects of misgovernment and the ruin of the local economy in the Congo:

> In this country, destitute of a military police and semblance of constituted authority, the most revolting crimes are committed by the natives. They practice the most barbarous religious and funeral rites; they torture, murder and eat each other. Against these shocking crimes the State puts forth no effort; indeed, it systematically abandons thousands of victims to slaughter every year. Human hands and feet and limbs, smoked and dried, are offered and exposed for sale in many of the native village markets.

Thanks to Williams, Leopold's boasts of bringing civilization and Christianity to Africa began to look diabolically hypocritical.

Sources: Adam Hochschild, *King Leopold's Ghost* (New York: Houghton Mifflin, 1998). John Franklin Hope, "A Report upon the Congo-State to the President of the Republic of the United States," in *George Washington Williams* (Chicago: University of Chicago Press, 1985).

(1902), and Mark Twain satirically denounced the horror in *King Leopold's Soliloquy: A Defense of His Congo Rule* (1905).

IMPACT

Since gaining independence from Belgium in 1960, the Democratic Republic of the Congo, known as Zaire under corrupt dictator Mobutu Sese Seko (1965-1997), continued to suffer from the long-term effects of Leopold II's exploitative regime. Recurrent civil wars, poverty amid great natural wealth, political corruption, and cruelty were, in one way or another, inherited from the Congo Free State. The naked despoilation of Leopold's rule is the most notorious model of economic imperialism in Africa, and his cynical and hypocritical claims that these actions were serving noble causes leave many today suspicious of any "humanitarian interventions" on the part of Western powers.

FURTHER READING

Ascherson, Neal. *The King Incorporated: Leopold the Second and the Congo*. 1963. Reprint. London: Granta Books, 1999. Lively written account, which one reviewer called the story of unmitigated evil.

Emerson, Barbara. *Leopold II of the Belgians: King of Colonialism*. New York: St. Martin's Press, 1979. A sympathetic biography accounting for Leopold's autocratic personality in terms of his upbringing and attributing some of the horror in the Congo to his ignorance.

Ewans, Martin. *European Atrocity, African Catastrophe: Leopold II, the Congo Free State, and Its Aftermath*. New York: Routledge, 2002. A British diplomat to Africa links the destructions of the colonial era to present-day disasters in Central Africa.

Hochschild, Adam. *King Leopold's Ghost: A Story of Greed, Terror, and Heroism in Colonial Africa*. New York: Houghton Mifflin, 1998. Winner of several book prizes, a vivid account of Leopold's destruction of the Congo.

—Bland Addison

SEE ALSO: Che Guevara; Mobutu Sese Seko.

NATHAN F. LEOPOLD, JR.
American "thrill" killer

BORN: November 19, 1904; Chicago, Illinois
DIED: August 30, 1971; San Juan, Puerto Rico
ALSO KNOWN AS: Nathan Freundenthal Leopold, Jr. (full name)
MAJOR OFFENSES: Kidnapping and murder
ACTIVE: May 21, 1924
LOCALE: Chicago, Illinois
SENTENCE: Life imprisonment for murder and ninety-nine years for kidnapping; served thirty-four years

EARLY LIFE

Nathan Freundenthal Leopold, Jr. (NAY-thuhn FRUN-dehn-thawl LEE-uh-pohld), a privileged child, was born into a wealthy Chicago family. His father was Nathan Freundenthal Leopold, a manufacturer, and his mother was Florence Foreman Leopold. He was a precocious boy in certain ways, quite underdeveloped in others. He was intellectually brilliant, but his emotional and social growth was stunted. He was submissive and introverted by nature. His mind was ripe for the hero worship of a charismatic personality and, unfortunately, he eventually fell under the sway of just such a person.

Leopold attended the University of Michigan in 1921-1922 and received a bachelor's degree from the University of Chicago in 1923. He graduated at the age of eighteen. By 1922, he had written a privately published study of bird migration. He studied law in 1923-1924. His close friend, Richard A. Loeb, was seven months younger than he but was the dominant figure in the boys' relationship. Loeb, also born to wealth, had graduated from the University of Michigan at seventeen.

CRIMINAL CAREER

Leopold and Loeb carried out several petty acts of theft and arson, so as to experience the excitement of committing a crime. These were minor preparations for the act that would link the boys' names as an entity for generations thereafter. Reportedly, the teenagers read Fyodor Dostoevski's *Prestupleniye i nakazaniye* (1866; *Crime and Punishment*, 1886), a novel in which the protagonist, Raskolnikov, a poor university student who believes himself to be one of the world's extraordinary people, murders an old pawnbroker. He thinks because of his superiority to his victim he will feel no remorse, but the novel is an account of how he suffers horribly from guilt. The boys decided that in a similar circumstance they would experience no such guilt, and they set about putting their theory into practice.

They chose as the victim for their "thrill killing" (a term popularized by this crime) Bobbie Franks, a younger boy whose family was known to both the Leopolds and the Loebs. On May 21, 1924, on the south side of Chicago, they lured Franks into a rented automobile and kidnapped him. Loeb hit the youngster on the head with a

NO TURNING BACK

Paroled March 13, 1958, and freed five years later, Nathan F. Leopold recalled how he felt after the 1924 "thrill killing" in his memoirs, Life Plus Ninety-Nine Years:

"Well," I said to myself, "it's over. There's no turning back now." How on earth could I ever have got involved in this thing? It was horrible—more horrible even than I figured it was going to be. But that's behind me now. Somehow I never believed that it would happen—that we'd actually go through with it. "But it's done. And now, at least, there aren't any decisions to make. I'll be able to put all my thought on not making any slips—on staying one jump ahead of the police. But that's nonsense! Nobody's ever going to suspect me. . . ."

My motive, so far as I can be said to have had one, was to please Dick [Richard A. Loeb]. Just that—incredible as it sounds. I thought so much of the guy that I was willing to do anything—even commit murder—if he wanted it bad enough. And he wanted to do this—very badly indeed. . . .

You just couldn't figure the fellow out. Those quick alternations of mood, those sudden changes of mind. But then that was nothing compared to the real, fundamental contradiction in his character. Everybody went for the guy—and rightly so. There wasn't a sunnier, pleasanter, more likable fellow in the world. . . . I'd try deliberately to copy his mannerisms, to be consciously charming. I couldn't come close. More often than not I'd just alienate people, more so than if I hadn't made a conscious effort. But Dick didn't have to try. He just seemed able to push an imaginary button and turn on the charm. And he could be generous to a fault. But then there was that other side to him. In the crime, for instance, he didn't have a single scruple of any kind. He wasn't immoral; he was just plain amoral—unmoral, that is. Right and wrong didn't exist. He'd do anything—anything. . . .

Looking back from the vantage point of today, I cannot understand how my mind worked then. For I can recall no feeling then of remorse. Remorse did not come until later, much later. It did not begin to develop until I had been in prison for several years; it did not reach its full flood for perhaps ten years. Since then, for the past quarter century, remorse has been my constant companion. . . .

Source: Nathan F. Leopold, *Life Plus Ninety-Nine Years* (Garden City, N.Y.: Doubleday, 1958).

chisel and stuffed a gag in his mouth. Within minutes, Franks was dead. They buried the body in a railway culvert but not very well—it was soon discovered. They knew the Franks family was wealthy, so, by telephone and in writing, they demanded a ransom of ten thousand dollars.

LEGAL ACTION AND OUTCOME

Every step in the theoretical "perfect murder" was performed incompetently. The car was easily traced, and Leopold had even dropped his eyeglasses beside the body. The young supermen were quickly arrested, and just as quickly they confessed. Defending them was a formidable task as they were Jewish, rich, and homosexual, any one of which factors was sufficient to arouse prejudice in a Chicago jury in 1924. Perhaps for this reason, Judge John R. Caverly conducted a bench trial. Leopold's father hired Clarence Darrow, a lawyer who boasted that no client of his had ever faced the gallows. The boys pleaded guilty.

The trial lasted thirty-three days in July and August, 1924. Darrow defended the boys by turning the trial into an indictment of external forces—the psychological effects of their upbringing, societal attitudes, and capital punishment. The defense made extensive use of psychiatrists—"alienists" in legal terminology. Darrow concluded with an eloquent appeal against capital punishment. He secured a sentence of life imprisonment rather than execution, regarded as a victory under the circumstances. The defendants were sent to Northern Illinois Penitentiary near Joliet to serve their sentences of life plus ninety-nine years.

Loeb died in prison, but Leopold, after years as a model prisoner, was paroled March 13, 1958, on condition that he go to Puerto Rico to work as a hospital technician and never return to the continental United States. He married Gertrude Feldman, a widow, on February 5, 1961. Leopold spent the rest of his life as a respected ornithologist and medical researcher. He taught ornithology while writing books and articles on birds and their migratory practices. He earned a master of social work degree from the University of Puerto Rico in 1961 and performed social work thereafter. He also wrote about penal policies, sometimes under a pseudonym. He died of a heart attack in 1971.

IMPACT

The notorious Leopold-Loeb case had less impact upon jurisprudence than upon literature and the popular culture. In 1929, *Rope*, a stage play by Patrick Hamilton, dealt with two brilliant young thrill killers. Hume Cronyn adapted *Rope* for the screen, and the motion picture was released by Transatlantic/Warner Brothers in 1948, starring James Stewart and directed by Alfred Hitchcock. *Compulsion*, a documentary novel by Meyer Levin, appeared in 1956; only the convicts' names were changed. It so clearly identified the case that shortly after its publication, Nathan F. Leopold, Jr., sued the author for $1.5 million. His claim that Levin had unjustly appropriated his name for profit was dismissed on First Amendment grounds. In a revised version, Levin adapted his novel as a play in 1957, and *Compulsion* became a successful motion picture in 1959. Orson Welles played Jonathan Wilk (a character easily recognizable as a portrayal of Clarence Darrow).

Leopold presented his own version of the case in *Life Plus Ninety-Nine Years* (1958), and he was working on an autobiography, "Grab for a Halo," at the time of his death. A testament to the enduring interest in the case was *Teen Thrill Killers*, a television show produced by the A&E television network in 2005. It prominently featured newsreel footage of the infamous Leopold and Loeb trial.

FURTHER READING

Higdon, Hal. *Leopold and Loeb: The Crime of the Century*. Urbana: University of Illinois Press, 1999. Explores why, despite all the mass murders since, Leopold and Loeb's remains the "crime of the century."

Leopold, Nathan Freundenthal, Jr. *Life Plus Ninety-Nine Years*. New York: Doubleday, 1958. Presents the consequences of the crime and its punishment from the murderers' point of view.

Levin, Meyer. *Compulsion*. New York: Simon and Schuster, 1956. Although framed as a novel, the book is fact-based and is one of the best studies of the case.

Payment, Simone. *The Trial of Leopold and Loeb: A Primary Source Account*. New York: Rosen, 2004. A summary of what has been written about the sensational trial.

Rompalske, Dorothy. "Leopold and Loeb: The Murder That Shocked a Nation." *Biography (A&E)* 6, no. 10 (October, 2002): 26-27. A printed adaptation of the episode of the television series.

—*Patrick Adcock*

SEE ALSO: Richard A. Loeb.

JEAN-MARIE LE PEN
French politician and leader of France's anti-immigrant Front National Party

BORN: June 20, 1928; La Trinité-sur-Mer, Brittany, France

CAUSE OF NOTORIETY: Although beloved by his supporters, Le Pen is widely credited with legitimizing anti-Muslim racism in France during the late twentieth century.

ACTIVE: Beginning 1956

LOCALE: France, principally Paris and southern France

EARLY LIFE

Jean-Marie Le Pen (jahn mah-ree leh pehn) was born to a fisherman father and farm-family mother in 1928 in Brittany, a Celtic region of northwestern France known for its individualism. Even by local standards, Le Pen was argumentative and combative as child, both in school and in the streets, especially after being orphaned in 1942 following his father's death after his fishing boat struck a mine (World War II was at its height). Le Pen's teenage years were spent under his maternal grandfather's guidance until he finished high school and departed for Paris to study law.

Le Pen continued his combative ways in law school, rising to prominence in the politics of a right-wing student association and engaging in street fights with leftists. By the early 1950's, he had attracted the attention of prominent right-wing French politicians, albeit those discredited by their prior association with the regime that collaborated with the Germans in occupied France during World War II. Shortly after the right-wing campaigns in France's 1951 parliamentary elections fell flat, however, Le Pen tired of the study of law and, momentarily, French politics. In 1954, he joined the French Foreign Legion.

POLITICAL CAREER

Technically, Le Pen's political career began in 1956, when he was elected to the French Assembly as the rep-

THE FRONT NATIONAL

In 2002, Jean-Marie Le Pen, founder of France's Front National (FN), came in second to Jacques Chirac in the presidential election, gaining about 20 percent of the vote. The unprecedented success for this ultra-right political party sent shock waves through Europe and reflected a growing anti-immigrant attitude among the public—especially with regard to Muslim residents, whom many associated with the growing terrorist threat in Europe. The national populism of the FN appealed to French conservatism and nativism, touting Identité (identity), Souveraineté (sovereignty), Sécurité (security), Prospérité (prosperity), Fraternité (brotherhood), and Liberté (liberty). On his personal Web page, Le Pen lays the groundwork for the FN's agenda by appealing to his constituency's fears:

France is in a bad state, much worse than it seems. Our country is on the edge of a decline that could rapidly drive it to its disappearance. The French people, who are brainwashed by the media, don't even know it, although many of them have a fear about it.

To avoid terrible hardship, the country must react as soon as possible. The truth must help this nation to rediscover and set off again in the 21st century on the glorious route which it had followed for centuries.

Without hate, but without fear, without remorse and without repentance, each of us must now act without building castles in the sky, while keeping our eyes fixed on the end of the furrow like our ancestors in order to do what needs to be done. When the hour of the battle arrives, you close ranks and go to battle, and as Joan of Arc said: "God gives victory."

For political movements as for men, reaching the age of thirty years symbolizes the end of enthusiastic and naïve youth and introduces the age of maturity, responsibility and fulfillment. We have the opportunity to once again put the national movement, of which the National Front is the spearhead and backbone, on a straight line to victory.

The Battle of France has already begun. It's a battle of liberation, which must be won so that tomorrow, France can continue to be French. To those who dream of the future, I say: "The future is now!"

large numbers of French settlers (who had been forced out of Algeria when it acquired its independence one decade earlier) proved to be a contentious issue. To Le Pen and his compatriots, the growth of this non-French, Muslim community constituted a direct challenge to France's culture and the secular nature of the state.

The FN did not achieve instant success, as reflected in Le Pen's showing in France's 1974 presidential election, when he received only 0.74 percent of the first-round vote. By the 1980's, however, unemployment rates were soaring in France, and Le Pen slogans, such as Two Million French Unemployed Are Two Million Foreign Workers Too Many, resonated with the French. By the 1990's, his party was regularly attracting one vote in seven in France's multiparty system, and Le Pen had secured seats in the European Parliament (in 1984 and again in 1999) and was twice elected to the governing council of the Provence region of southeastern France.

The capstone of Le Pen's career was his showing in the 2002 French presidential election. With nearly 17 percent of the vote, he qualified for the two-man runoff election against the incumbent French president Jacques Chirac. Given his long record of intemperate outbursts against France's foreign communities regarding such topics as the Holocaust (he once labeled it a footnote to history), his first-round success produced considerable international notoriety. On the eve of the runoff election, French demonstrators by the thousands engaged in protests unprecedented in France's history and denounced Le Pen's candidacy. Furthermore, Le Pen's party was repudiated for its extreme proposals (such as revoking the naturalized citizenship of Muslims whenever possible) even by other anti-immigrant parties throughout Europe. When the votes were counted, Chirac had won more than 80 percent of them, enough to reelect him to the presidency.

IMPACT

In late 2005, pent-up frustrations within France's Muslim community exploded in rioting, acts of arson, and clashes with the French police, events that lasted nearly a

resentative of a small shopkeepers' party and briefly served there between and following tours of duty in Indochina, the Suez Canal, and Algeria. However, when one considers his impact on national politics, his career really began in 1972, when he and other members of the postwar, right-wing Ordre Nouveau (New Order) founded the Front National (FN) Party. Though the FN was anchored on the right by a broadly nationalist agenda, from the beginning it was defined in terms of its anti-immigrant stance. By 1972, immigrants from North Africa—whom France had recruited in the 1950's to help the country rebuild after the war—had grown quickly in numbers. Immigrant presence in those areas containing

month and encompassed most French cities. Neither Jean-Marie Le Pen nor his party was directly responsible for these riots. However, many feel that Le Pen and the FN indirectly helped build the polarized France composed of two parallel, nonintegrated societies out of which the riots grew: that of Muslim and immigrant communities and that of French-born citizens.

By electorally exploiting the foreigner issue, blaming French unemployment on France's immigrant communities, and ceaselessly defining the Muslim culture as a threat to the French way of life, Le Pen gave anti-foreigner sentiment a level of respectability in France. In turn, these attitudes condoned the discrimination encountered by France's Muslims both in society at large and in the job market. Moreover, through its success, the FN forced France's principal parties to adopt its rhetoric (French presidents have thus been known to speak of "smelly foreigners") and enact policies aimed at appeasing antiforeigner sentiment in France at the expense of preparing the French for becoming a multicultural society or effectively protecting the civil and social rights of the immigrant communities.

FURTHER READING

Davies, Peter. *The Extreme Right in France, 1789 to the Present*. New York: Routledge, 2002. In a field of few English-language sources on the topic, Davies provides a basic, brief introductory reading on Le Pen and his party, placed in historical context.

Gibson, Rachel K. *The Growth of Anti-immigrant Parties in Western Europe*. Lewiston, N.Y.: Edwin Mellen Press, 2001. This excellent analysis of anti-immigrant parties in fourteen European countries underscores Le Pen's political influence in both France and contemporary European politics.

Simmons, Harvey G. *The French National Front: The Extremist Challenge to Democracy*. Boulder, Colo.: Westview Press, 1996. Perhaps the most comprehensive examination in English of Le Pen, the FN, and late twentieth century French politics.

—*Joseph R. Rudolph, Jr.*

SEE ALSO: David Duke; George Lincoln Rockwell; John Tyndall; Hendrik Frensch Verwoerd.

MARC LÉPINE
Canadian mass murderer

BORN: October 26, 1964; Montreal, Quebec, Canada
DIED: December 6, 1989; Montreal, Quebec, Canada
ALSO KNOWN AS: Gamil Rodrigue Gharbi (birth name)
CAUSE OF NOTORIETY: Lépine, fueled by an antisocial personality and a hatred of feminists, murdered fourteen people during a shooting rampage at a university engineering school.
ACTIVE: December 6, 1989
LOCALE: École Polytechnique de Montréal, Montreal, Quebec, Canada

EARLY LIFE

Marc Lépine (lay-PEEN) was born as Gamil Rodrigue Gharbi in 1964. His father, Rachid Liass Gharbi—an alcoholic, abusive immigrant from Algeria—often said that women were slaves who should serve men. His wife, Monique, was a Québécois nurse and former nun. Rachid frequently beat his two children so severely that they bled from the ears and nose. The couple separated when Gamil was seven and were divorced in 1976. Gamil later

changed his name to Marc Lépine, adopting his mother's maiden surname.

The constant abuse as a child likely contributed to Lépine's eventually forming an antisocial personality, a trait that caused the Canadian Armed Forces to refuse his enlistment. He was also rejected by the École Polytechnique (the University of Montreal's engineering school) and was fired from a menial job in a kitchen. A narcissist, Lépine blamed feminism for his failures and admired Denis Lortie, who had murdered three people in the Quebec National Assembly in 1984.

CRIMINAL CAREER

On December 6, 1989, Lépine entered a classroom of the École Polytechnique. Speaking French, he said, "I hate feminists" and began killing people, first in the classroom and then throughout the building. He murdered thirteen people with his gun and one with a dagger; other men and women were wounded.

After seventeen minutes of killing, Lépine turned the gun on himself. A suicide letter found in his pocket expressed his hatred of feminists and listed nineteen Québécois "radical feminists" whom he had thought about murdering. Although the police arrived in the middle of the attack, they waited outside for fifteen minutes until Lépine was confirmed dead. Lépine used a Ruger Mini-14 self-loading rifle. According to the report of coroner Teresa Sourer, the particular model of rifle was unimportant, because any standard hunting rifle "probably would have had similar results."

IMPACT

Misogyny in Algerian culture was a taboo topic in public debate, although Marc Lépine's crime opened to criticism the cultural treatment of women. Many feminists argued that Lépine's crime was directed at all women and that all men were collectively guilty because masculinity fosters violence against women. Following cries for more stringent gun control, Minister of Justice Doug Lewis initially stated, "You cannot legislate against insanity." However, the Progressive-Conservative government soon began promoting gun control and in 1992 finally defeated grassroots opposition, enacting a restrictive gun law, Bill C-17.

In 1995, the new Liberal government, appealing especially to urban females by attempting to legislate against the masculine gun-and-hunting culture, passed an even more stringent law, which included mandates that all gun owners' homes are subject to unannounced, warrantless police inspections and that gun license applications may be vetoed by the applicant's former girlfriends. A government database of all firearms and their owners was also created. However, Canadian political analysts noted that a backlash against gun control likely helped Stephen Harper and his new Conservative Party oust the Liberals in the 2006 election for the leadership of the country. Since the crime, December 6 has become an annual National Day of Mourning in Canada.

FURTHER READING

Buckner, H. Taylor. *Sex and Guns: Is Gun Control Male Control?* Paper presented at the American Sociological Association Annual Meeting, August 5, 1994.

http://www.tbuckner.com/. Using a discussion of the Lépine case as part of his survey and analysis of Canadian college students who advocate gun control, the author concludes that pro-gun-control students knew very little about existing gun laws or lawful uses of firearms and favored gun control as a means of controlling male violence or sexuality or of expressing "politically correct" attitudes.

Eglin, Peter, and Stephen Hester. *The Montreal Massacre: A Story of Membership Categorization Analysis.* Waterloo, Iowa: Wilfrid Laurier University Press, 2003. Although laden with sociological jargon and the authors' praises of ethnomethodological interpretation, the book is useful for its many newspaper excerpts following the Lépine crime, such as the minister who said he was ashamed to be a male, and the arguments that college panty raids are part of the male culture of murder.

Malette, Louise, and Marie Chalouh, eds. *The Montreal Massacre.* Translated by Marlene Wildeman. Charlottetown, P.E.I.: gynergy books, 1991. Outraged Quebec feminists, following the Lépine shooting, demand the rehabilitation of males, whose misogynist death culture is based on aggressive sports, violent entertainment, and the penetration of women during sexual intercourse.

Mauser, Gary. "Evaluating Canada's 1995 Firearms Legislation." *Journal on Firearms and Public Policy* 17 (2005): 1-20. Criminologist argues that the 1995 law was symbolic and did not improve public safety.

Rathjen, Heidi, and Charles Montpetit. *December 6: From the Montreal Massacre to Gun Control—The Inside Story.* Toronto, Ont.: McClelland & Stewart, 1999. Presents the story of Rathjen, who was a student at Polytechnique during the Lépine attack and who cofounded the Coalition for Gun Control, a group that became an influential national and international voice for prohibition of almost all firearms.

—*David B. Kopel*

SEE ALSO: Baruch Goldstein; Charles Whitman.

MARY KAY LETOURNEAU
American schoolteacher and sexual offender

BORN: January 30, 1962; Tustin, California
ALSO KNOWN AS: Mary Katherine Schmitz (birth name); Mary Kay Fualaau (married name)
MAJOR OFFENSE: Child (statutory) rape
ACTIVE: 1996-1998
LOCALE: Burien, Washington
SENTENCE: Eighty-nine months in prison; suspended and then reinstated after second violation

EARLY LIFE

Mary Kay Letourneau (luh-TUHRN-oh) was the fourth of seven children born to devout Roman Catholic parents, John and Mary Schmitz. Her college professor father, reputedly one of the more conservative members of the U.S. House of Representatives, ran for president on the notably right-wing American Independent Party ticket in 1972. Her homemaker mother was an antifeminist activist who campaigned against the passage of the Equal Rights Amendment during the 1970's.

The Schmitzes' picturesque outward appearances were marred by various scandals. Letourneau's father engaged in a longtime affair with one of his former students, producing Letourneau's two half-siblings. Letourneau proclaimed that her mother's cold demeanor had prompted her father to pursue affection elsewhere. One of Letourneau's older brothers allegedly began fondling her when she was seven years old, though she later downplayed the significance of the sexual abuse. When she was eleven, her three-year-old brother drowned in the family's swimming pool while Letourneau was thought to be supervising him. Friends of Letourneau reported that she believed her parents held her responsible for the tragedy.

Despite these ordeals, Letourneau enjoyed an active social life while attending Arizona State University. At a college party, she met the man who would become her first husband: Steve Letourneau. In 1985, the two married and dropped out of college upon discovering that Letourneau was pregnant with their first child. By 1989, the couple had four children. However, the Letourneau marriage was rife with conflict, including incessant financial problems and Steve's infidelity.

After her husband took a job in Seattle, Letourneau began attending evening classes at Seattle University. Once she received her degree, Letourneau began teaching second grade at Shorewood Elementary School in Burien, Washington, where she met for the first time the student she would later refer to as her "soul mate": eight-year-old Vili Fualaau.

CRIMINAL CAREER

In 1995, Letourneau was promoted and assigned to teach fifth and sixth grades. She again had Fualaau as a student, who was now twelve years old. As his status as a favored student within the classroom solidified, Fualaau began spending time at the Letourneau residence. By the close of 1996, other teachers noted that Letourneau was acting more like a girlfriend than a mentor to Fualaau.

In the fall of 1996, Letourneau, then age thirty-four, confided in a friend that she was pregnant with Fualaau's child. Steve's suspicions that his wife was intimately involved with Fualaau were confirmed when he discovered a love letter written by Letourneau to Fualaau. Shortly after making this discovery, Steve became physically abusive toward Letourneau. Steve and Letourneau's own mother encouraged her to terminate the pregnancy.

One of Steve's cousins notified both Child Protective Services and the school district in which Letourneau

Mary Kay Letourneau. (AP/Wide World Photos)

taught about the affair. A police officer questioned Fualaau about his relationship with Letourneau, and the seventh-grader confirmed that he and Letourneau were romantically involved and that they had had sex. Many feared that Fualaau had not been Letourneau's only victim. However, investigators ascertained that she had not inappropriately touched any of her other students nor had she engaged in incest with any of her own children.

LEGAL ACTION AND OUTCOME

On February 26, 1997, Letourneau was placed under arrest for "child rape" (the term used in Washington State for statutory rape). Having undergone numerous court-ordered psychiatric evaluations following her arrest, she was eventually diagnosed with bipolar disorder. Psychotherapy and psychotropic medications were prescribed as the appropriate treatments. Four months after her arrest, Letourneau gave birth to Fualaau's daughter.

By pleading guilty on August 7, 1997, to two counts of second-degree statutory rape, Letourneau received a suspended sentence of eighty-nine months in prison. In lieu of serving the prison term, Letourneau was to serve six months in the county jail, enroll in a three-year sexual deviancy treatment program, take her psychotropic medication as prescribed, relinquish custody of her daughter with Fualaau to his mother, and permanently cease all contact with Fualaau. However, although Letourneau was released from jail in January, 1998, her freedom was short-lived. In early February of that same year, authorities found Letourneau and Fualaau in a car together. In addition to seeing Fualaau, which was a violation of her sentence conditions, she had been noncompliant with her sexual deviancy treatment program. As a result of violating these conditions of her release, Letourneau's original sentence of eighty-nine months in prison was reimposed. While serving her sentence, she gave birth to her second child with Fualaau. Both daughters were placed in the custody of Fualaau's mother. Despite being court-ordered to sever all contact with Fualaau, Letourneau continued to correspond with him from prison.

On August 4, 2004, forty-two-year-old Letourneau was released on parole. Following her release, Fualaau, by then a legal adult, had the "no contact" order lifted, enabling the two to see each another legally. On May 20, 2005, the couple married in a Seattle suburb.

IMPACT

Mary Kay Letourneau's case continued to receive media coverage and served as a reference point for subsequent female sexual offender cases involving schoolteachers. In addition to elucidating the existence of female sexual offenders, the case generated discussion regarding biological sexual differences, sexism, and gender bias as reflected in law. The case fascinated the public as it was unclear whether Letourneau's affinity for Fualaau was an aberration in the behavior of an otherwise well-adjusted woman or symptomatic of a more deep-seated pathology.

FURTHER READING

Christiansen, Alyson R., and Bruce A. Thyer. "Female Sexual Offenders: A Review of Empirical Research." *Journal of Human Behavior in the Social Environment* 6, no. 3 (2003): 1-16. Examines scientific research conducted on the characteristics of female sex offenders, the possible types of female sexual offenders, and the recommended psychosocial approaches to treatment.

Denove, Myriam S. "The Myth of Innocence: Sexual Scripts and the Recognition of Child Sexual Abuse by Female Perpetrators." *Journal of Sex Research* 40, no. 3 (August, 2003): 303-314. Reviews existing data regarding the prevalence of female sexual offending, placing specific emphasis on the ways in which conventional sexual scripts preclude official recognition of female sexual offending as a problem.

Dress, Christina, Tama-Lisa Johnson, and Mary Kay Letourneau. *Mass with Mary: The Prison Years*. Victoria, B.C.: Trafford, 2004. Dress, a close friend and former cellmate of Letourneau, chronicles Letourneau's experiences behind bars.

Letourneau, Mary Kay, and Vili Fualaau. *Un Seul Crime: L'Amour*. Paris: Robert Laffont, 1999. A tell-all book about the affair written by the participants. Written in French (the title means "the only crime, love"), it capitalizes on the sympathetic belief held by many Europeans that Letourneau and Fualaau were victims of puritanical U.S. laws.

Olsen, Greg. *If Loving You Is Wrong: The Shocking True Story of Mary Kay Letourneau*. New York: St. Martin's Press, 1999. Provides a detailed profile of Letourneau, referencing interviews with Letourneau and her friends and neighbors.

—*Christine Ivie Edge*

SEE ALSO: Sydney Barrows; Ada Everleigh; Heidi Fleiss; Virginia McMartin.

DENNIS LEVINE
American investment banker

BORN: 1953; Bayside, Queens, New York
ALSO KNOWN AS: Mr. Diamond
MAJOR OFFENSES: Insider trading, securities fraud, tax evasion, and perjury
ACTIVE: 1980-1986
LOCALE: New York, New York
SENTENCE: Two years in prison, $11.6 million in restitution, and a $362,000 fine

EARLY LIFE

Dennis Levine (leh-VEEN) was born to a middle-class family in Queens, New York. He graduated from Baruch College and worked at three investment banks as a mergers-and-acquisitions specialist. He focused his career on developing an insider trading ring of Wall Street professionals.

In the early 1980's, Levine was a managing director at Drexel Burnham, an investment bank. At the time, there was a takeover craze on Wall Street. Companies trying to acquire or take over other companies often paid more than the stock price, thereby driving it up. Because Levine knew which companies were to be acquired, he was in a position to make huge sums of money by buying the stock or options of the takeover company before the takeover was announced to the public.

CRIMINAL CAREER

Levine took advantage of every opportunity to make a profit from his inside information, knowing all the while that it was illegal. To hide his insider trading, Levine opened an account at Bank Leu, a leading Swiss bank in the Bahamas, under the name Mr. Diamond. To buy stock or options in a takeover company, Levine had his account executive at the bank, Bernhard Meier, do transactions under the name of the bank instead of his own name. After any given takeover was announced to the public and the stock price increased, Levine had the bank sell his shares. Seeing the huge profits from Levine's first trades, Meier copied Levine's trades to make himself a profit; so did a broker at Merrill Lynch, where the trades were executed.

From 1980 through 1985, Levine traded in the stock of fifty-four companies based on his inside information. His initial $100,000 grew to $12 million. Levine also defrauded the government by not reporting or paying tax on this income. The Securities and Exchange Commission (SEC) noticed signs of insider activity in the stock of takeover candidates and traced them back both to Bank Leu and to Levine and Meier.

LEGAL ACTION AND OUTCOME

After learning that the SEC would be charging him with insider trading, Levine turned himself in to the office of New York City attorney general Rudy Giuliani on May 12, 1986. On June 5, 1986, he pleaded guilty to four felony counts stemming from his insider trading activities. He faced five years in prison, but because of his cooperation with federal prosecutors, his sentence was reduced to two years.

IMPACT

Dennis Levine was the first in a line of investment bankers and traders brought down by insider trading charges. Because of scandalous abuse of power, federal prosecutors threatened inside traders with severe racketeering indictments, which was a charge that had typically been applied to organized crime, not "white-collar" criminals.

Levine's arrest and deal with the government sent a shock wave through Wall Street. His $12.6 million fine was the largest ever assessed at the time. Later, it would be dwarfed by Ivan Boesky's $100 million penalty and Drexel's $650 million penalty.

FURTHER READING

Cutler, Stephen M., and David M. Levine. "Greed Returns to Wall Street: Confidential Information Is Being Misused by a New Breed of Insider Traders." *Legal Times*, November 15, 1999, pp. 43-46. Compares the patterns, prosecutions, and types of people who were involved in insider trading during the 1980's to ten cases of insider trading in the 1990's.

Mullaney, Timothy J. "Dennis Levine: In the Hot Seat Again?" *Business Week*, June 9, 2003, p. 14. Describes an alleged violation by Levine for taking money that he did not earn.

Stewart, James B. *Den of Thieves*. New York: Simon & Schuster, 1991. An account of insider trading and other uses of unrestrained power on Wall Street during the 1980's and how violators were brought to justice.

—*Linda Volonino*

SEE ALSO: Ivan Boesky; Michael Milken.

G. GORDON LIDDY
American former political operative

BORN: November 30, 1930; Hoboken, New Jersey

ALSO KNOWN AS: George Gordon Battle Liddy (full name)

MAJOR OFFENSES: Burglary, illegal wiretapping, and conspiracy in connection with the 1972 Watergate break-in

ACTIVE: June 17, 1972

LOCALE: Washington, D.C.

SENTENCE: Twenty years in prison; served four and one-half years before his sentence was commuted by President Jimmy Carter

EARLY LIFE

George Gordon Battle Liddy (LIH-dee) was born in 1930 in Hoboken, New Jersey, to Sylvester and Maria Abbaticchio Liddy. In his autobiography *Will* (1980), Liddy described himself as a timid child who decided to use his will to confront his fears. This resolution led to some colorful stories about Liddy's youth. For example, he reports climbing a tree to confront a raging thunder and lightning storm; in another anecdote, he killed, cooked, and ate a rat in order to defeat his fear of the animals. Liddy attended a private Jesuit and Benedictine secondary school. He then enrolled at Fordham University, where he attained a B.S. in 1952. He served for two years in the U.S. Army as an artillery officer during the Korean War. Liddy then returned to Fordham in 1954 to attend law school.

LAW AND POLITICAL CAREER

Liddy graduated in 1957 with an LL.D. and joined the Federal Bureau of Investigation (FBI) that year as a special agent. He rose to become the youngest bureau supervisor at FBI headquarters before resigning from the bureau in 1962.

He went to Manhattan to practice international law and later served as a prosecutor in Duchess County, New York. At this time he led a 1966 prosecution against famed counterculture guru Timothy Leary but was unable to secure a conviction. Liddy ran unsuccessfully for the office of district attorney and then for the House of Representatives. In 1968, Liddy managed the presidential campaign of Richard Nixon for the twenty-eighth congressional district.

Liddy went on to serve the Nixon administration as assistant to the treasury secretary and later became a member of the White House Special Investigations Group. This unit was also known as "the Plumbers" because of their efforts to prevent information from leaking to the media during Nixon's reelection campaign. Liddy was also finance counsel for the Committee to Re-elect the President (CRP, known also by Nixon detractors as CREEP), a fund-raising organization headed by former U.S. Attorney General John Mitchell.

CRIMINAL CAREER

Liddy had devised some improbable schemes to attempt to embarrass, harass, or discredit the Democratic opposition, such as "Operation Gemstone," which included hiring prostitutes to entertain Democratic officials in wiretapped houseboat bedrooms in an effort to gather incriminating or embarrassing information. Although Gemstone was not enacted, a caper that involved breaking into the Democratic National Committee (DNC) headquarters was later put into action.

This break-in was not Liddy's first foray into burglary. In September, 1971, Liddy and E. Howard Hunt broke into the office of defense analyst Daniel Ellsberg's

---

LIDDY TODAY: "NO AMNESTY"

More than three decades after the Pentagon Papers and Watergate scandals, G. Gordon Liddy continued to market his brand of ultraconservative politics. In 2006, for example, the following anti-immigration petition appeared on Liddy's Web site, along with a form for his fans to sign and send to Congress:

PETITION TO THE SENATE AND HOUSE OF REPRESENTATIVES OF THE UNITED STATES

We, the undersigned, citizens of the United States of America, petition you, the members of the Senate and House of Representatives, to state that we, under no circumstances, want you to pass any law containing any provisions whatsoever for guest worker/amnesty for the millions of lawbreaking illegal aliens in our midst.

On the contrary, we ask you to pass a law that a) erects an impenetrable barrier along the entire southern border of the United States, from Brownsville, Texas to Imperial Beach, California and b) makes it a felony to knowingly hire an illegal alien to do any kind of work and c) makes the penalty for conviction of the aforesaid felony a mandatory sentence of at least one year imprisonment.

---

psychiatrist in the hope of finding information that would discredit Ellsberg, whose release of the Pentagon Papers to the press severely eroded public support for the Vietnam War.

On June 17, 1972, several men hired by CRP were apprehended while breaking into the DNC headquarters located at the Watergate building in Washington, D.C. The resulting investigation into the role of the Nixon operatives in the break-in resulted in several criminal charges against administration officials, including Liddy.

LEGAL ACTION AND OUTCOME

On January 30, 1973, Liddy was convicted of conspiring to burglarize, wiretap, and electronically eavesdrop on the Democratic Party's Watergate headquarters; burglarizing the Democratic headquarters with the intent to steal the property of another; burglarizing the Democratic headquarters with the intent to unlawfully wiretap and eavesdrop; and endeavoring to eavesdrop illegally. He faced a maximum of thirty-five years and was sentenced to twenty. However, his sentence was later commuted by President Jimmy Carter after approximately four and one-half years.

IMPACT

Since his release from prison, G. Gordon Liddy has become a popular author (his autobiography *Will* sold more than a million copies and was made into a television movie), talk show guest, actor, commentator, and syndicated radio talk show host. He continues to project a controversial and provocative presence. In 1994, for example, he was criticized for seeming to advocate the murder of federal officers (even though he is a former FBI agent himself) by advising his listeners on how to fire on agents from the Bureau of Alcohol, Tobacco, and Firearms should they come to confiscate weapons. Liddy's views are generally perceived as right-wing, with a deep streak of libertarianism.

Many people admire Liddy's steadfast refusal to cooperate with the Watergate investigation or to implicate others to spare himself prison time. Others, however, believe that Liddy's criminal actions represent a chilling abuse of governmental power and unbridled sense of entitlement by the executive branch. Liddy remains a colorful, complex, and provocative figure in the political-entertainment mixture that makes up much of the United States' cultural landscape.

FURTHER READING

Bernstein, Carl, and Bob Woodward. *All the President's Men*. 2d ed. New York: Simon & Schuster, 1994. Account of Watergate from the investigative reporters who first broke the story. Highlights the major players and provides an interesting historical look at the scandal.

Liddy, G. Gordon. *When I Was a Kid, This Was a Free Country*. Washington, D.C.: Regnery, 2002. Liddy provides his position and commentary on a variety of social, political, and cultural issues.

_____. *Will*. 3d ed. New York: St. Martin's Press, 1996. Liddy's autobiography covers his life history, formation of core beliefs, and view of the Watergate scandal.

—David R. Champion

SEE ALSO: Charles W. Colson; John D. Ehrlichman; H. R. Haldeman; E. Howard Hunt; James W. McCord, Jr.; John Mitchell; Richard Nixon.

JOHN WALKER LINDH
American Taliban

BORN: February 9, 1981; Washington, D.C.
ALSO KNOWN AS: John Philip Walker Lindh (full name); Sulayman al-Lindh; Suleyman al-Faris; Abdul Hamid; American Taliban; Johnny Jihad; Ratboy; Johnny bin Walker; John Walker
MAJOR OFFENSES: Supplying services to the Taliban and carrying an explosive during the commission of a felony
ACTIVE: c. July-November, 2001
LOCALE: Kabul and Takhar, Afghanistan
SENTENCE: Twenty years in federal prison

EARLY LIFE

John Walker Lindh (lihnd) spent the first ten years of his life in Silver Spring, Maryland, with his father, Frank, an attorney, his mother, Marilyn, and his two sisters. Lindh was a quiet child. In 1991, when his family moved to San Anselmo, California, he attended public school for one year before transferring to Tamiscal High. Tamiscal had a flexible curriculum that allowed Lindh to study Islamic and Middle Eastern culture. In 1998 he graduated early from Tamiscal after Spike Lee's film *Malcolm X* (1992) inspired him to attend the Islamic Center of Mill Valley, convert to Islam at age sixteen, and change his name to Sulayman al-Lindh. In July, he left the United States to study Arabic in Sanaa, Yemen, where he remained until May of 1999. After a brief hiatus in the United States, Lindh returned to school in Yemen in February, 2000.

MILITARY CAREER

In November, 2000, Lindh moved to Bannu, Pakistan, to attend an Islamic school. Less than six months later, he began training at a military camp in northern Pakistan and in three weeks entered Afghanistan to fight for the Taliban army in a civil war against the Soviet-supported Northern Alliance. Lindh received further military training in a government-run camp that was sponsored by known terrorist Osama Bin Laden, whom Lindh met on more than one occasion. In early September, 2001, Lindh was sent to the front lines in Takhar; it is unclear whether he fought or simply served as a guard.

Prior to October, 2001, the United States had not taken military action against the Taliban. In the wake of the terrorist acts of the previous September 11 on U.S. soil, the United States began an aerial bombing campaign designed to destroy Taliban control over Afghani-

stan. With American assistance, the Northern Alliance forced a Taliban retreat from Takhar to Herat, where Lindh's army was captured by Northern Alliance general Abdul Rashid Dostum. While captive at Mazar-i-Sharif in a makeshift prison, Lindh was questioned by two undercover Central Intelligence Agency (CIA) agents, to whom he said nothing.

Shortly afterward, the captives revolted, and a bloody confrontation forced their retreat to the basement of the compound. Lindh suffered a gunshot wound to the thigh, and one of the CIA agents, Michael Spann, was killed. The Taliban soldiers holed up without food or water for six days through aerial bombings, hand grenades, and burning oil poured into the basement. Finally, on December 1, the basement was flooded with freezing water, driving out the soldiers who were still alive, only eighty-six of the original four hundred to five hundred captives. Lindh, who was among the eighty-six, eventually asked

John Walker Lindh. (AP/Wide World Photos)

for help from Red Cross officials and American reporters and was dubbed the "American Taliban" after being filmed by CNN reporter Richard Pelton.

FBI INTERROGATION

After Lindh was discovered in Afghanistan, he remained in U.S. military custody for fifty-four days, during which the conditions of his imprisonment remain unclear. The U.S. government and primary interrogator Christopher Reimann insisted that Lindh's Miranda rights had been respected. Others, including Lindh's parents, Jesselyn Radack of the Justice Department, and a Navy medic who treated Lindh in Afghanistan, claimed that Lindh repeatedly asked for and was denied legal counsel.

Lindh's confession to an unnamed defense intelligence officer also remains in question, as the officer admitted to substituting Lindh's testimony that he trained with "al Ansar," a non-Afghani Taliban fighting force, with "al-Qaeda," the terrorist organization. Finally, several declassified accounts report that Lindh suffered mistreatment by military and intelligence personnel, including being duct-taped naked to a stretcher and left in a storage container for days with minimal food and water. Arguing that Lindh was an "enemy combatant," American officials claimed that he was outside the jurisdiction of U.S. civil law and the Geneva Conventions and was treated with as much respect as that position allowed.

LEGAL ACTION AND OUTCOME

Lindh was formally indicted on February 5, 2002, with ten counts of criminal charges, most involving aiding a terrorist organization. Lindh pleaded not guilty. After months of trial preparation, however, on July 15, 2002, he accepted a plea agreement from federal prosecutors in which he pleaded guilty to supplying services to the Taliban and to carrying an explosive during the commission of a felony. He was sentenced to twenty years in prison on October 4, 2002. In September, 2004, Lindh's lawyers appealed to President George W. Bush to have Lindh's sentence commuted.

IMPACT

Popular opinion of the "American Taliban" remains unfavorable. The capture and prosecution of John Walker Lindh heightened antiterrorist fervor in the United States in the wake of the September 11 attacks. Politicians and news media alike cited Lindh as the terror within U.S. borders in an effort to drum up support for the American War on Terror. In the years following the plea agreement, further evidence and testimony were attained that suggested Lindh never took up arms against American soldiers and never participated in terrorist activity. Furthermore, his treatment at the hands of the Federal Bureau of Investigation (FBI) and the U.S. military, under the direction of Secretary of Defense Donald Rumsfeld, raised questions about the treatment of suspected terrorist detainees at U.S. facilities around the globe.

FURTHER READING

Dobb, Edwin. "Should John Walker Lindh Go Free? On the Rights of the Detained." *Harper's Magazine* 304 , no. 1824 (May, 2002): 31-42. Dobb uses Lindh's confession to explore the intricacies of the legal system in the War on Terror and questions the interrogation techniques of CIA/FBI agents and U.S. police forces.

Kukis, Mark. *"My Heart Became Attached": The Strange Journey of John Walker Lindh*. Washington, D.C.: Brassey's, 2003. Journalist Kukis provides a biography of Lindh's personal and spiritual journey from his California upbringing to the stark landscape of Afghanistan, based on testimony from the people closest to Lindh.

Mayer, Jane. "Lost in the Jihad." *The New Yorker* 10 (March, 2003): 50-60. Mayer presents the prison interviews Rohan Gunaratna, a terrorism scholar, conducted with Lindh. She also uncovers the story of Jesselyn Radack, a whistle-blower from the Justice Department, who claims to have witnessed ethical breaches in the government's treatment of Lindh.

—*Lindsay M. Christopher*

SEE ALSO: Osama Bin Laden.

RICHARD A. LOEB
American thrill killer

BORN: June 11, 1905; Chicago, Illinois
DIED: January 28, 1936; Illinois State Penitentiary,
    Stateville, Illinois
MAJOR OFFENSES: Kidnapping and murder
ACTIVE: May 21, 1924
LOCALE: Chicago, Illinois
SENTENCE: Life imprisonment for murder and ninety-
    nine years for kidnapping

EARLY LIFE
The father of Richard A. Loeb (lohb) was a wealthy vice president of Sears, Roebuck Company. From age eleven, Richard was raised under the influence of a bright, strong-minded, orthodox governess. His reaction to her strict discipline may have produced the obsessed, ruthless, and sadistic person he became. Only the classics were prescribed as reading, but he rebelled by reading detective stories and fantasizing that he was an archcriminal. At fifteen, he was already a heavy drinker and had begun to invent stories of affairs with girls.

Loeb attended the University of Michigan at Ann Arbor, where, at age seventeen, he became its youngest graduate. His academic work came easily to him, but he was more of an athlete, outdoorsman, and dancer than he was a scholar. He and his friend Nathan F. Leopold, Jr. who was perhaps even more brilliant than he, committed a series of minor crimes (Loeb stole a typewriter from his own fraternity house), despite the fact that they were to study law in the fall of 1924. His likable, pleasant outward appearance masked the fact that he was a dangerous sociopath. Moreover, evidence presented at his trial suggested that he had seriously contemplated suicide.

CRIMINAL CAREER
Loeb and Leopold viewed themselves as young supermen, not bound by conventional norms of morality and law. They decided that as an intellectual exercise they would commit the "perfect murder," escaping detection and experiencing no feelings of remorse. They chose as their victim fourteen-year-old Bobbie Franks, whose wealthy parents were members of the Leopolds' and Loebs' social set. On May 21, 1924, on the south side of Chicago, they lured him into a rented automobile and kidnapped him. Loeb had instigated the plot, and he also committed the murder, striking Franks on the head with a chisel and stuffing a gag in his mouth. Loeb was eighteen years old, Leopold nineteen.

Leopold seems instantly to have been struck by the enormity of what they had done, but Loeb was merely exhilarated. By telephone and in writing, they demanded a ten-thousand-dollar ransom, but the body, which they had only partially buried in a railway culvert, was quickly found. After the discovery of the body, the egomaniacal Loeb contacted reporters and offered theories that might explain the crime.

LEGAL ACTION AND OUTCOME
Loeb foolishly called attention to himself, and Leopold had lost his eyeglasses in the culvert near the body. The murderers' perfect crime was amateurish at every step. They were arrested in short order and confessed immediately. Their bench trial, with Judge John R. Caverly presiding, lasted thirty-three days in July and August, 1924.

Richard A. Loeb, left, and Nathan F. Leopold, Jr., at their arraignment. (AP/Wide World Photos)

Leopold and Loeb's fourteen-year-old victim, Bobby Franks around time of murder. (Courtesy, Chicago Historical Society)

The facts of the case coupled with the overwhelming animosity of the public made the boys' situation seem hopeless. Leopold's father hired Clarence Darrow, none of whose clients had ever received a capital sentence. The defendants pleaded guilty.

Darrow was the star of the case. He had established a national reputation as a labor and criminal lawyer. He was more often associated with the defense of the downtrodden. He had attempted to free the anarchists charged with murder in the Haymarket Riot (May 4, 1886), and he had defended the labor leader Eugene V. Debs in 1894.

In the Franks case, however, Darrow welcomed the challenge of defending two spoiled Jewish homosexual boys who elicited absolutely no sympathy from any quarter. A year after defending Leopold and Loeb, he would defend John T. Scopes in the even more famous "monkey trial" at Dayton, Tennessee. He made extensive use of alienists (psychiatrists), testifying to the Freudian explanations for Loeb's aggressive, Jekyll-and-Hyde personality and Leopold's sexual and psychological submission to a dominant personality. Darrow's courtroom oratory was filled with allusions based on his wide reading, and he concluded with an impassioned appeal against capital punishment. He won for the boys a sentence of life imprisonment plus ninety-nine years, considered a victory under the circumstances.

The defendants were sent to Illinois State Penitentiary near Joliet, where Leopold became a model prisoner, but Loeb continued his troublesome behavior. On January 28, 1936, while Loeb was in the shower, his cellmate, James Day, slashed him fifty-eight times with a straight razor, and Loeb died later that day. Day was tried for the murder, but he alleged that he was defending himself against Loeb's sadistic sexual advances, and he was acquitted.

IMPACT

The Leopold-Loeb trial may have led to greater use of psychiatric testimony, both by the defense and by the prosecution, but its primary impact was upon literature and popular culture. It popularized the term "thrill killer," which has become a part of the American vernacular. In 1929, *Rope*, a stage play by Patrick Hamilton, featured two brilliant young thrill killers. The motion picture *Rope*, adapted by Hume Cronyn, was released in 1948 and starred James Stewart, with direction by Alfred Hitchcock. The superior, cocksure character John Dall is clearly based on Richard Loeb. In 1956, Meyer Levin published *Compulsion*, a documentary novel based on the case; only the names were changed. It was adapted as a play in 1957 and as a film in 1959. The character Artie Straus (played by Bradford Dillman) is a recognizable representation of Loeb; Judd Steiner (played by Dean Stockwell) is a representation of Nathan Leopold, and Jonathan Wilk (played by Orson Welles) is recognizable as Darrow. Interest in the case continued into the twenty-first century: *Teen Thrill Killers*, produced by the A&E television network in 2005, prominently features newsreel footage from the Leopold-Loeb trial.

FURTHER READING

Higdon, Hal. *Leopold and Loeb: The Crime of the Century*. Urbana: University of Illinois Press, 1999. Commemerates the seventy-fifth anniversary of the crime and discusses why, despite all the notorious murder cases following that of Leopold and Loeb, it retains the title of "crime of the century."

Levin, Meyer. *Compulsion.* New York: Simon & Schuster, 1956. Although framed as a novel, the book is fact-based and is one of the best studies of the case.

Payment, Simone. *The Trial of Leopold and Loeb: A Primary Source Account.* New York: Rosen, 2004. A guide to print accounts of the sensational trial.

—*Patrick Adcock*

See also: Nathan F. Leopold, Jr.

Huey Long
Governor of Louisiana (1928-1932) and senator from Louisiana (1932-1935)

Born: August 30, 1893; near Winnfield, Winn Parish, Louisiana

Died: September 10, 1935; Baton Rouge, Louisiana

Also known as: Huey Pierce Long (full name); the Kingfish

Cause of Notoriety: Long gained and maintained power though patronage, political machinery, and varied levels of purported coercion, which led to impeachment proceedings.

Active: 1928-1935

Locale: Louisiana

Early Life

Huey Pierce Long (HEW-ee LAWNG) was born on August 30, 1893, near Winnfield, Louisiana, the seventh of ten children born to Huey Pierce Long, Sr., and Caledonia Tyson Long. Huey Long, Sr., a farmer, provided a comfortable lifestyle for his family through the purchase and sale of real estate. The Long household was a literate and affluent one; it housed a sizable library, and Huey's father often aired his views on equal wealth distribution in frequent discussions with neighbors. Long, Jr., did not complete high school with the other students his age; instead, he left his rural home in 1910 and secured employment as a salesperson for the N. K. Fairbank Company, whose product was a lard substitute marketed under the name Cottolene. When he lost his job one year later because of company cost-cutting, he moved to Shreveport to live with an aunt. It was here that he completed his high school education. In 1913, he married Rose McConnell, and one year later, with financial and study assistance from his new bride, he entered the Tulane University College of Law and passed the bar examination after just one year of academic study. In 1915, he was admitted to the Louisiana State Bar.

Political Career

After three years practicing law, representing low-income clients seeking worker's compensation or work-related injury damages, Long ran for the post of railroad commissioner in 1918 and won by a narrow margin. During his first term, he won a victory for consumers by rejecting the 25 percent rate increase requested by the Cumberland Telephone and Telegraph Company.

When he was reelected to the commissionership in 1924, he simultaneously formulated plans to run for gov-

Huey Long. (NARA)

HUEY LONG, PRESIDENT

In 1935, looking forward to the next presidential election, Huey Long published My First Days in the White House. *Never short on chutzpah, Long predicted his own victory over President Franklin D. Roosevelt and proposed a cabinet to include Roosevelt, Herbert Hoover, and Idaho senator William E. Borah, a controversial isolationist. (Reportedly, Roosevelt was worried that Long might actually defeat him.) The book opens with Long's fantasy inauguration:*

IT HAD happened. The people had endorsed my plan for the redistribution of wealth and I was President of the United States. I had just sworn upon the Bible from which my father read to us as children to uphold the Constitution and to defend my country against all enemies, foreign and domestic. Yet standing there on the flag-draped platform erected above the East portico of the Capitol, delivering my inaugural address, it all seemed unreal. I felt that I was dreaming. The great campaign which was destined to save America from Communism and Fascism was history. Other politicians had promised to re-make America; I had promised to sustain it.

The campaign had been bitter. I was cartooned and caricatured unmercifully in some of the newspapers. . . .

As my eyes swept the throng before me, I paused in my inaugural address and looked into the face of the retiring president. He seemed worn and tired. He wore the same expression of resigned fatigue that I had observed in the face of President Hoover on Inauguration Day in 1933 when Mr. Roosevelt declared so confidently that: "The only thing we have to fear is fear itself."

And with all humility, fully conscious of the solemnity of the promise I was making, I laid aside my prepared speech and closed my inaugural address extemporaneously with these words:

"I promise life to the guaranties of our immortal document, the Declaration of Independence, which has decreed that all shall be born equal, and by this I mean that children shall not come into this life burdened with debt, but on the contrary, shall inherit the right to life, liberty and such education and training as qualifies them and equips them to take their proper rank in the pursuance of the occupation and vocation wherein they are worth most to themselves and to this country. And now I must be about my work."

ernor of Louisiana, an election to be decided that same year. In a close race, he was defeated by Hewitt Bouanchaud, who had the backing of the established "Old Regulars" political power bloc. Four years later, having honed his skills in communication, public relations, and coalition-building, Long won the governorship by a generous margin.

Using his power as chief executive of the state of Louisiana, Governor Long appointed his supporters to existing and newly created political jobs. This afforded him the opportunity to push his rigorous agenda through the state legislature with minimal obstruction. On his watch, the city of New Orleans gained access to natural gas, road improvements were implemented across the state, and students in the Louisiana school system received free textbooks. Voters approved taxes to subsidize these programs, but Long ran into problems when he attempted to impose a tax on oil. Members of this powerful industry launched impeachment proceedings against the governor, accusing Long of a palette of misdeeds ranging from payoffs to murder conspiracy. The governor responded by casting himself as victimized by "big oil." Nonetheless, varied degrees of coercion were reportedly imposed by Long and his coterie to secure anti-impeachment votes from state officials. He ultimately was acquitted, allowing him to further his agenda for improving the stature and conditions of his state.

In 1930, Long ran successfully for senator but did not assume this national office until 1932. The two-year deferment gave him a chance to handpick his replacement in the state capitol. An early supporter of Franklin D. Roosevelt's candidacy for president, Long severed ties in the light of his opinion that Roosevelt's plans for post-Depression economic recovery fell short of appropriate wealth redistribution. Long's Share the Wealth program for fiscal parity carried a slogan that also would serve as the title of his autobiography, *Every Man a King*, published in 1933.

Despite his responsibilities as U.S. senator, Long continued to participate in Louisiana legislation and, with his increased national exposure, gave serious consideration to a presidential campaign in 1940. However, Long's political adversaries, unified in groups calling themselves the "Square Deal Association" and "Minute Men of Louisiana," were unrelenting in their efforts to remove him from power. Despite his awareness of reports of a planned attempt on his life, Long attended a special session of the Baton Rouge State Legislature on September 9, 1935. Although surrounded by bodyguards, Long was felled by a bullet from the gun of Dr. Carl Austin Weiss, an ear, nose, and throat specialist and son-in-law of one of Long's political opponents. Weiss was gunned down immediately by the bodyguards. After unsuccessful emergency surgery at Our Lady of the Lake Hospital, Long passed away on September 10.

IMPACT

Huey Long's legacy to American history and politics is mixed. On the positive side, he was responsible for extensive improvements to Louisiana. Through his efforts, roads were paved, access to utilities was enhanced, state hospitals were built, and education from elementary to collegiate levels was vastly improved for the students of the state. He is also credited with innovations in campaigning. He was one of the first politicians to use printed literature, in the form of the political circular, to deliver his message, and his use of the automobile to meet voters on a one-to-one basis was revolutionary for the time. Simultaneously, however, Long is remembered for implementing two political practices that remain controversial today: the filibuster and the addition of irrelevant, previously defeated legislation to new bills up for passage.

Finally, post-Long-era instances of power-play political conspiracies and the activities that constitute them recall the brief but turbulent tenure of "The Kingfish."

FURTHER READING

Long, Huey Pierce. *Every Man a King: The Autobiography of Huey P. Long.* 1933. Reprint. Cambridge, Mass.: Da Capo Press, 1996. The Kingfish in his own words at the height of his fame, providing a showcase of the rhetoric that riveted his constituency.

Warren, Robert Penn. *All the King's Men.* 1946. Reprint. San Diego: Harcourt, 2005. A celebrated and successful fictional depiction of Huey P. Long.

Williams, T. Harry: *Huey Long.* 1969. Reprint. New York: Vintage Books, 1981. Definitive, richly annotated biography of Huey Long.

—*Cecilia Donohue*

SEE ALSO: Leander Perez; Carl Weiss.

HARRY LONGABAUGH
American bank robber and cattle rustler

BORN: Spring, 1867; Mont Clare, Pennsylvania
DIED: Possibly November 7, 1908; possibly San Vicente, Bolivia
ALSO KNOWN AS: Sundance Kid; Harry Alonzo Longabaugh (full name); Harry Long; Harry A. Place; Harry Longbaugh; Henry Long
CAUSE OF NOTORIETY: Cattle rustling, horse stealing, train robbery, and bank robbery
ACTIVE: 1887-1908
LOCALE: Western United States, Argentina, Bolivia, and Chile

EARLY LIFE

Harry Alonzo Longabaugh (LONG-bow) was born to Josiah and Annie (Place) in Mont Clare, Lancaster County, Pennsylvania. He was the youngest of five children. In 1882 Harry traveled west by covered wagon with his cousin George Longenbaugh and homesteaded for a time in Durango and Cortez, Colorado. In 1886 he headed north to work for the N-N Ranch near Culbertson, Montana.

CRIMINAL CAREER

One of the earliest reports concerning Longabaugh stems from an 1887 conviction for stealing a horse in Crook County, Wyoming. Sheriff James Ryan pursued and captured Longabaugh near Miles City, Montana. For his crime, Longabaugh served eighteen months in the jail in Sundance, Wyoming. Upon his release from jail he assumed the nickname the Sundance Kid.

Soon after Longabaugh's release from prison he was reportedly arrested for stealing eighty dollars from a man in Lusk, Wyoming, but escaped his captors. Another report has him participating in the Great Northern train robbery near Malta, Montana. Along the way, the Sundance Kid joined fellow outlaw Harvey Logan in robbing the Belle Fouche South Dakota Bank on June 27, 1897. Both were captured but escaped after only three months in prison. Soon afterward, the Sundance Kid met the outlaw Butch Cassidy and joined his famous "Wild Bunch."

One of the best-known train robberies involving the Wild Bunch took place on June 2, 1899. Butch, Sundance, and the gang's other members stopped the Union Pacific's Overland Flyer. After using explosives to separate the engine from the express car, the bandits dynamited the car door. The explosion scattered thirty thousand dollars in banknotes all over the place. After this robbery the Union Pacific Railroad hired the Pinkerton National Detective Agency and famous lawman Joe Lefors to pursue the Wild Bunch.

Harry Longabaugh (the "Sundance Kid") with Etta Place.

Butch Cassidy and the Sundance Kid robbed their last train on July 3, 1901. Shortly afterward, they decided to flee the United States to avoid capture by Lafors. For a short time they hid near Forth Worth, Texas, where Sundance began a relationship with a woman known as Etta Place, who accompanied him and Butch as they traveled to Argentina to seek new lives.

LEGAL ACTION AND OUTCOME

By 1902, Butch, Sundance, and Place were living as peaceful ranchers. In 1905 Butch and Sundance were suspected of robbing a local bank and fled to Chile. With most of their money gone, they returned to crime. In early November, 1908, in one widely accepted account of their demise, they robbed a mining company payroll and then entered the town of San Vicente, Bolivia. A man recognized the two American outlaws and informed four local soldiers. The soldiers found them in a room with only one way out. It was later reported that a short gun battle took place during which one soldier was hit and both outlaws were wounded. Witnesses then heard desperate screams coming from inside the house followed by a couple of gunshots. The next morning Butch and Sundance were found dead from gunshot wounds, suggesting they had committed suicide.

IMPACT

In their time, Butch Cassidy and Harry Longabaugh, the Sundance Kid, were treated like folk heroes. Cassidy boasted that he never killed a man, and he and Sundance freely gave their ill-gotten money to people who protected them from the law. In the end, they paid for their crimes. Today, because of numerous books, the popular motion picture *Butch Cassidy and the Sundance Kid* (1969, starring Paul Newman and Robert Redford), and television specials, they remain well-known legends of the Old West.

FURTHER READING

Meadows, Anne. *Digging up Butch and Sundance*. 3d ed. Lincoln, Neb.: Bison Books, 2003. Examines the Butch Cassidy and Sundance Kid saga, taking the reader through South America in search of evidence of their lives and reported deaths in Bolivia.

Patterson, Richard M. *Butch Cassidy: A Biography*. Lincoln, Neb.: Bison Books, 1997. A well-written book covering the lives of both Butch and Sundance.

Pointer, Larry. *In Search of Butch Cassidy*. Norman: University of Oklahoma Press, 1977. One of the most widely acclaimed books on the life of Butch Cassidy; discusses his relationship with the Sundance Kid.

—*Paul P. Sipiera*

SEE ALSO: Butch Cassidy; Robin Hood.

BILL LONGLEY
American outlaw

BORN: October 6, 1851; Mill Creek, Austin County, Texas
DIED: October 11, 1878; Giddings, Texas
ALSO KNOWN AS: William Preston Longley (full name); Wild Bill Longley; Rattling Bill; Tom Jones; Jim Webb; Jim Patterson; Bill Black; Bill Henry; Bill Jackson
MAJOR OFFENSES: Murder and robbery
ACTIVE: December, 1866-June, 1876
LOCALE: Texas, Arkansas, Missouri, Wyoming, and Kansas
SENTENCE: Death by hanging

EARLY LIFE

About one and a half years after Bill Longley (LAWNG-lee) was born to Campbell and Sarah Longley, the family moved to Evergreen, Texas. Bill attended school there and worked on the family farm. He developed a close relationship with his brother James Stockton Longley.

While still a young boy, Longley became very proficient with a pistol. By the time the American Civil War (1861-1865) ended, he had developed a deep hatred for freed slaves, Union soldiers, and carpetbaggers (Northerners who took up residence in the South and tried to exploit Southerners). Longley allegedly killed a black man on December 10, 1866, after an argument escalated between them. Longley fled and worked for a period of time as a cowboy in Karnes County, Texas.

CRIMINAL CAREER

Longley reportedly killed a calvary soldier in April, 1867. A reward of one thousand dollars was offered for his capture. On December 20, 1868, Longley and two friends killed a freed slave. By 1869, Longley had established a reputation as a daring gunslinger. He had a quick temper and was willing to pick a fight with anyone who got in his way. Trouble and killings followed Longley throughout his travels in Texas, Arkansas, Oklahoma, Kansas, and Wyoming.

During his wild escapades, Longley worked occasionally on ranches in south-central and western Texas. At various times, he was accused of stealing horses and looting homes and farms. He used a variety of aliases to avoid the law. In February, 1870, Longley and his brother-in-law, John W. Wilson, killed a black man in Bastrop County, Texas. They were also accused of kill-

ing a black woman. Longley escaped to Kansas, where he worked as a cowpuncher in Abilene and killed his trail boss after an argument. He also killed a U.S. soldier near Leavenworth and then fled to Wyoming.

On March 1, 1875, Longley gunned down a farmer, Wilson Anderson, in Lee County, Texas. In January 1876, he killed gunfighter Lou Shroyer. About six months later, he killed the Reverend William Lay in Delta County, Texas.

LEGAL ACTION AND OUTCOME

Longley was arrested for murder in 1873 in Kerr County, Texas, but was soon released when the arresting officer was paid off by one of Longley's relatives. After numerous killings in Texas, Longley hid out in Louisiana. On June 6, 1877, he was captured in DeSoto Parish, Louisiana, by Sheriff Milton Mast and returned to Lee County, Texas, for trial.

On September 5, 1877, Longley was sentenced to hang for murder. The court of appeals affirmed his conviction in March, 1878. Longley was sent to Giddings, Texas, to be hanged. The hanging took place on October 11, 1878. After the rope slipped and Longley's body fell until his feet touched the ground, Sheriff James Madison Brown made some adjustments in the rope. After eleven and a half minutes, Longley was pronounced dead.

IMPACT

Wild Bill Longley was known as one of the most dangerous, daring gunslingers in the American West. He had a reputation for being very fast on the draw and a very accurate marksman. He reportedly killed thirty-two people, ranking him second only to John Wesley Hardin for number of killings by a gunslinger.

Stories of Longley have been explored in several gunfighter texts. He was the subject of Louis Lamour's western novel *The First Draw: The Blazing Story of the First Great Gun Fighters* (1959). A television series about Wild Bill Longley titled *The Texan* aired between 1958 to 1960.

After his hanging in 1878, rumors persisted that Longley had escaped and fled to South America, appearing later in Louisiana. In 2001, his remains were exhumed from the Giddings City Cemetery. Deoxyribonucleic acid (DNA) comparison testing with a living relative proved that the body was indeed that of Longley.

FURTHER READING

Miller, Rick. *Bloody Bill Longley: A Biography*. Wolfe City, Tex.: Henington, 1996. Miller does a thorough job in separating truth from legend in explaining the life of Longley.

Rosa, Joseph G. *Gunfighters: The Outlaws and Their Weapons*. Berkeley, Calif.: Thunder Bay Press, 2006. This book provides a vivid account of the events and facts associated with the life of Longley.

Texas Historical Association. *The Handbook of Texas*. Austin: Author, 2001. Describes the adventures of Longley in detail, particularly his capture and execution.

—*Alvin K. Benson*

SEE ALSO: John Wesley Hardin.

BYRON LOOPER

American politician

BORN: 1964; Putnam County, Tennessee
ALSO KNOWN AS: Byron (Low Tax) Looper (legal name); Byron Anthony Looper (full name)
MAJOR OFFENSE: Murder
ACTIVE: October 19, 1998
LOCALE: Cookeville, Tennessee
SENTENCE: Life in prison without possibility of parole

EARLY LIFE

Byron Anthony Looper (LOOP-uhr) was born in Putnam County, Tennessee, in 1964. Looper's parents divorced when he was a teenager, and family members claim that he became deeply troubled after the divorce. Looper then moved with his mother, Reba Looper, to Georgia. In 1983, Looper attended West Point's U.S. Military Academy and was honorably discharged in 1985 because of a knee injury.

After leaving West Point, Looper lived in Georgia, where he pursued a career in politics. At age twenty-three, Looper ran for the Georgia House but did not win a term in the legislature. Following this loss, he served in the Georgia Capitol as a legislative aide to his uncle, Max Looper.

POLITICAL CAREER

When Looper returned to Tennessee, he focused his attention on the local politics of Cookeville. In 1996, Looper won the Putnam County tax assessor's seat following an extremely negative election campaign. During this campaign, Looper began asking voters to vote for "Low Tax Looper" and later legally changed his middle name to "(Low Tax)"—including the parenthetical marks—in what many considered a political stunt to win future elections.

In 1998, Looper ran for nominations in two separate races in the same primary: the Republican nomination for U.S. House of Representatives and the Republican nomination to run against Senator Tommy Burks for the Tennessee State Senate. He lost the U.S. primary and won the state nomination by default.

Looper's time in office was controversial. Within months, he was accused of unfairly firing up to twenty employees and was subsequently sued by some of them. He also brought several lawsuits against other Putnam County officials. Furthermore, Looper was facing criminal charges for trading tax favors for political gain and for the misuse of county personnel and property. Additionally, a $1.2-million lawsuit was brought against Looper by his former girlfriend concerning the illegal transfer of her property.

In October, 1998, less than one month before the election, Looper went to Burks's farm in Monterey, Tennessee, and fatally shot Burks in the head. A farm employee, Wesley Rex, saw a man matching Looper's description leaving the property after hearing a gunshot. Authorities searched for Looper for four days before arresting him at his home when he returned to Cookeville after he had fled to Little Rock, Arkansas.

LEGAL ACTION AND OUTCOME

Looper's first-degree murder trial took place from August 13 to August 23, 2000. The jury delivered a guilty verdict after less than three hours of deliberation and then recommended that Looper receive a sentence of life in prison without the possibility of parole. The death penalty was not an option for Looper because the Burks family had requested that prosecutors not ask for the death penalty.

Looper continued to appeal the verdict in his case in the years following his crime. During these postconviction appeals hearings, he contended that his legal counsel was inadequate. His 2004 appeal for a new trial was denied.

IMPACT

Because of the timing of the Burks murder, many have suggested that a little-known Tennessee law provided a motive in the case: The obscure state law required that a candidate's name be removed from the ballot if his or her death occurred within a month of the election. This law meant that Byron Looper's name was the only one left on the ballot for that election. However, Burks's supporters mounted a last-minute, write-in-vote campaign resulting in the victory of the senator's widow, Charlotte Burks, for the senate seat. Mrs. Burks later introduced legislation that changed the law that may have led to her husband's murder.

FURTHER READING

Denton, Mary Jo. "Burks, Looper Hardly Knew Each Other." *The Cookeville Herald-Citizen*, October 26, 1998. The Cookeville reporter who covered the murder of Burks and Looper's trial investigates the connection between the two men.

Reese, Krista. "High Drama in Tennessee Trial of 'Low Tax' Candidate Convicted of Killing Incumbent." *The Boston Globe*, August 27, 2000, p. A9. An account of the trial and conviction of Looper.

Shearer, John. "Two Sides of Ex-Candidate Depicted at Murder Trial." *The Atlanta Journal and Constitution*, August 15, 2000, p. 5A. Shearer reports on the conflicting testimony concerning Looper's character.

—*Kimberley M. Holloway*

SEE ALSO: Volkert van der Graaf; Dan White.

RODERIGO LOPEZ
Physician to Queen Elizabeth I

BORN: 1525; Portugal
DIED: June 7, 1594; Tyburn, London, England
ALSO KNOWN AS: Ruy Lopes
MAJOR OFFENSES: High treason and conspiracy to poison Queen Elizabeth I
ACTIVE: 1591-1594
LOCALE: London
SENTENCE: Death by hanging

EARLY LIFE

Son of the physician to John III of Portugal, Roderigo Lopez (rahd-REE-goh LOH-pehz), like many formerly Jewish "new Christians," or *conversos* (converted ones), was baptized in the Catholic faith. He studied at the University of Coimbra, completing his medical studies in 1544, and moved to London in 1559. His careful work at St. Bartholomew's Hospital earned him a respectable salary as well as a house and garden. He married the daughter of a London grocer of Portuguese Jewish extraction, and although his children were baptized Anglicans, it seems his family secretly practiced Judaism along with other émigrés.

MEDICAL CAREER

Lopez had been physician to Robert Dudley, earl of Leicester, and was appointed physician to Queen Elizabeth. Lopez is defamed in a Catholic tract as one of Leicester's henchmen, skilled in poisoning and abortions, in the aftermath of a failed conspiracy to overthrow Philip II of Spain, who had seized Portugal. One of the followers of the attempted coup approached Lopez about poisoning Dom António, the claimant to the Portuguese crown, but Lopez did not do so. Lopez next ran afoul of double agents and court intrigues both abroad and in England. He had served as physician to Sir Francis Walsingham, the head of Elizabeth's spy network, and seems to have functioned as an intermediary to urge peace talks with Spain and to secure or expel Dom António. A ring was sent to him valued at double his annuity as Elizabeth's physician. Later this ring would turn out to be incriminating, if circumstantial, evidence of his being in league with Philip II.

LEGAL ACTION AND OUTCOME

After Walsingham's death in 1591, Lopez unofficially continued his association with Spanish contacts. Robert Devereux, the earl of Essex and stepson to Leicester, wanted to fill the power vacuum at court and sought Queen Elizabeth's acknowledgment that he had saved her from danger. With the aid of the best cryptologist in London, Essex found correspondence that ultimately implicated Lopez in a plot to poison the queen. Additional letters, including one concerning donations to a synagogue in the Spanish Netherlands, made his case grim. Along with two other conspirators, Lopez was convicted of high treason and executed by being hanged, drawn, and quartered.

IMPACT

Solicitor General Sir Edward Coke, during the case for the prosecution, called Roderigo Lopez "a perjured and murderous villain and Jewish doctor, worse than Judas himself." Much was made of Lopez's secret Judaism, anathema in a time when religion was a matter of law. Capitalizing on the public response to the trial, theaters brought back Christopher Marlowe's play *The Jew of Malta* (pr. c. 1589, pb. 1633), concerning a prototypical Machiavellian villain, Barabas, who poisons wells and burns convents—thus reviving anxious myths about Jews. William Shakespeare's company premiered *The Merchant of Venice* (pr. c. 1596-1597), in which a Jewish usurer, Shylock, seeks to recover the terms of his bond of "a pound of flesh." The Lopez case contributed to the rationale for deporting foreigners, especially Jews and Africans. Not unrelated, witchcraft prosecutions increased during this volatile decade at the end of Elizabeth's reign.

FURTHER READING

Black, J. B. *The Reign of Elizabeth*. 2d ed. New York: Oxford University Press, 1994. Links the execution of Lopez to the atmosphere of panic associated with Elizabeth's fear of assassination and the anti-Catholic measures of 1593.

Green, Dominic. *The Double Life of Doctor Lopez*. London: Century, 2003. Drawing on the trial records, state papers, and previously unpublished materials, Green argues that Lopez, in addition to being a skilled medical practitioner, was a canny businessman, diplomat, spy, and secret Jew.

Katz, David S. *The Jews in the History of England, 1485-1850*. New York: Oxford University Press, 1994. Detailed reassessment of extant documents of the case, concluding that Lopez was indeed guilty of participating in a conspiracy.

Levin, Carole. *The Reign of Elizabeth I*. New York: Palgrave, 2002. Discusses the economic and political instability contributing to the discovery of the plot, and suggests that Elizabeth had doubts about Lopez's guilt.

Pelling, Margaret, with Francis White. *Medical Conflicts in Early Modern London*. Oxford, England: Clarendon Press, 2003. Looking primarily at regulatory efforts of the College of Physicians, this social history yields interesting findings about irregular medical practitioners, including Lopez.

Samuel, Edgar. "Roderigo Lopez." In *Oxford Dictionary of National Biography*. New York: Oxford University Press, 2004. Presents the subtleties of the conspiracy charges, Lopez's role as an emissary to Spanish agents, and Essex's reasons for nurturing a hatred for his former physician.

—*William E. Engel*

SEE ALSO: Moll Cutpurse; Francis Drake; Guy Fawkes; John Felton; Joan the Mad; Titus Oates; Grace O'Malley; Mother Shipton.

SEVENTH EARL OF LUCAN
English aristocrat and gambler

BORN: December 18, 1934; London, England
DIED: Declared legally dead August 11, 1999;
London, England
ALSO KNOWN AS: Richard John Bingham (birth
name); Lord Lucan; Lucky Lucan
MAJOR OFFENSE: Murder
ACTIVE: November 7, 1974
LOCALE: London, England

EARLY LIFE

Richard John Bingham was born on December 18, 1934, to George Bingham, the sixth earl of Lucan (LOO-cahn), and Kait Lucan. During World War II, Lucan and his siblings were sent first to the English countryside, then to the United States to keep them safe. Returning to England, Lucan attended the Eton School, where he developed an interest in gambling. Following a turn in the army, he joined a merchant bank. However, his penchant for gambling became his main interest. In 1960, after he won a considerable sum of money in two days, his friends began calling him Lucky Lucan. Lucan married Veronica Duncan in 1963. Veronica's sister was married to Lucan's best friend, Bill Shand Kydd.

CRIMINAL CAREER

Lucan obtained his title at the death of his father, two months after his wedding. He and Veronica (now Lady Lucan) had three children, and after each of the births, Lady Lucan showed signs of postpartum depression. Lucan tried to have his wife committed to a psychiatric hospital for depression and hallucinations, but she refused treatment. He also paid for in-home psychiatric nursing care for three months. By the early 1970's, the marriage had significant problems, and the couple lived in separate domiciles.

At 9:45 P.M. on the evening of November 7, 1974, Lady Lucan emerged from her London home at Lower Belgrave Street and entered a nearby pub; bloodstained, she claimed that an attempt had just been made on her life and screamed for someone to look after her three young children, still in the home. Soon thereafter, the children's twenty-nine-year-old nanny, Sandra Rivett, was found murdered in Lady Lucan's home, apparently bludgeoned to death with a piece of pipe. Lady Lucan later claimed to police that her husband had been the attacker.

There were many conflicting stories concerning the circumstances of the murder. The next day, Lord Lucan told a friend, Susan Maxwell-Davis, that a male stranger had entered his wife's home and that he, Lucan, had intervened. After that, Lucan disappeared. Most of Lord Lucan's friends insisted that he was not guilty of murder. However, Lucan may have made a telephone call to a family friend, Madeleine Floorman, at about 10:00 P.M. Floorman dismissed the incoherent caller as a prankster, but later blood was found on her doorstep. Two letters from Lucan were mailed to his friend Kydd; they reportedly displayed blood smears. Police found a piece of pipe similar to that of the murder weapon in Lucan's abandoned car three days later.

LEGAL ACTION AND OUTCOME

In June of 1975, a jury at coroner's court found Lord Lucan guilty of the murder of Rivett. It was the last inquest jury to name anyone as murderer, a right that ended in 1977 according to British law. Lady Lucan applied to have the legislation retrospectively applied to this case and was refused in 1978. George Bingham, Lord Lucan's son, requested a writ of summons to replace his father by taking his seat in the House of Lords. However, because there was no proof of Lord Lucan's death, Bingham was refused. Lucan's friend casino owner John Aspinwall had theorized shortly after Lucan's disappearance that Lucan probably committed suicide in order to protect his family's honor. In 1999, Lucan was declared officially dead. In 2004, the case was reopened to examine deoxyribonucleic acid (DNA) evidence, but nothing fruitful was found.

IMPACT

The mystery of where the seventh earl of Lucan is (or if he still lives) has prompted popular interest, as well as several books. Police have created a computer-generated image of him and how he might look at age seventy (as of 2005), and there have been "sightings" of Lord Lucan worldwide, but all have proved false. The well-known British novelist Muriel Spark wrote a fictional account of the disappearance titled *Aiding and Abetting* (2000). Other works based on the case include Dickon Whitfield's *Get Lucky! The Memoirs of Lord Lucan, Twenty-One Years a Fugitive* (1995), Nancy Holmes's *Nobody's Fault* (1990), and Duncan Maclaughlin's *Dead Lucky* (2003).

The British have a saying that grew out of the Lucan case, "doing a Lucan," which means to get away completely and never be seen again. The American version, "doing a Crater," refers to Judge Joseph Crater, who, similarly, disappeared in New York City in 1930.

FURTHER READING

Marnham, Patrick. *Trail of Havoc: In the Steps of Lord Lucan*. New York: Viking Penguin, 1988. A look at the Lucan case from a scriptwriter's viewpoint. The author, not whitewashing Lord Lucan, points out that Lady Lucan stated several times before the fateful night that her husband had tried to kill her by attacking her. She did not report these attacks to the police, however, and there was no physical evidence of any attack. A detailed look at the world of the elite.

Moore, Sally. *Lucan: Not Guilty*. London: Sedgwick and Jackson, 1987. A moment-to-moment look at the murder of Sandra Rivett, the evidence of Lord Lucan being seen elsewhere at the time of the murder, and reasons Lady Lucan has for lying about her husband.

Ranson, Roy. *Looking for Lucan: The Final Verdict*. London: Smith Gryphon, 1994. Written by the retired detective chief superintendent who conducted the investigation into the death of Rivett. Includes a interesting interview with Lady Lucan, who said that a stranger killed Rivett.

Wilson, Colin, and Kirk Wilson. *Unsolved Crimes*. London: Carroll and Graf, 2002. Covers ten famous unsolved murder cases of the twentieth century, including that of Lucan.

—Ellen B. Lindsay

SEE ALSO: Jeffrey MacDonald; Scott Peterson; Sam Sheppard.

TOMMY LUCCHESE
Organized crime boss

BORN: December 1, 1889; Palermo, Sicily, Italy

DIED: July 13, 1967; Lido Beach, Long Island, New York

ALSO KNOWN AS: Gaetano Lucchese (birth name); Thomas Lucchese; Tommy Brown; Three Fingers Brown

CAUSE OF NOTORIETY: Lucchese rose to power following the 1930-1931 Castellammarese War and became head of one of the five Mafia crime families. In this role, he sought new "rackets" in Manhattan's garment district and the trucking industry.

ACTIVE: 1921-July 13, 1967

LOCALE: Bronx, Manhattan, and Long Island, New York; and Scranton, Pennsylvania

EARLY LIFE

Gaetano Lucchese (loo-CHAY-zee) was born in Palermo, Sicily, Italy, and as a child who was small in stature, he learned to compensate for his size by demonstrating a combination of ruthless and aggressive behaviors. In 1910, at age twelve, Lucchese departed Italy for the United States with his parents. They resided in East Harlem, where young Lucchese joined the Ciro Terranova, 107 Street Gang. During that era, he came to appreciate the value of political connections; the ward politicians controlled the gangs to broaden their political base and influence during elections.

Lucchese lost his right index finger at age twenty in a Harlem machine shop accident and would eventually be known by the nickname Three Fingers Brown, even though four fingers remained intact. The nickname originated when a police officer, while booking Lucchese, noticed the missing index finger and was inspired by famous Chicago Cubs baseball player Mordecai "Three Finger" Brown.

MAFIA CAREER

Lucchese's only criminal conviction in his life was a three-year sentence for automobile theft in 1921. He was a model prisoner and was paroled after serving only eighteen months. After serving this jail time, Lucchese emerged as a man to be respected. He was resolute not to replicate his mistake of committing street crimes. Lucchese was capable, intelligent, and charming when necessary, a particularly valuable asset when engaging politicians. His tact, diplomacy, and political contacts served his legitimate businesses and criminal career well.

Lucchese became a suspect in numerous murders, including that of mobster Joe Pinzolo, although a grand jury failed to move the case forward to trial; he was suspected in approximately thirty other murders but was never convicted. Lucchese was arrested in the 1928 homicide of Louis Cerasulo; however, after several days the charges were dropped.

At the age of thirty-one, Lucchese became an underboss in the Gaetano "Tom" Reina family and developed a reputation for violence while playing the role. Reina was murdered in 1930, and Lucchese assumed the role of family capo, or boss. Lucchese played an important role during the so-called Castellammarese War in the early 1930's, an internal Mafia power struggle between the factions supporting bosses Salvatore Maranzano and Joe Masseria. Lucchese survived the Castellammarese War because of his aptitude for political analysis and ability to anticipate potentially dangerous situations accurately. His close association with Lucky Luciano and his capability to switch alliances at critical moments were key to his success during this period. The successive killings of Masseria and Maranzano (Lucchese was present at his death) led to the arrangement whereby five Mafia "families" of equal stature were established, one of which was the Lucchese crime family.

Lucchese made every attempt to avoid the limelight during his career, but ironically became a well-known and notorious personality. In addition, he became one of the most politically influential and successful organized crime bosses in the United States. For a time, he controlled much of New York City's garment district and took control of key union officials and trade associations. In 1952, he gained attention when he testified before the Kefauver Committee, a special Senate committee formed to learn about organized crime and ways in which to fight it. In the early 1960's, the federal government attempted to convict him of tax evasion. However, Lucchese died before the government could convict him of the charges.

Lucchese's death on July 13, 1967, from brain cancer occurred after months of medical treatment. Judges and politicians were among the thousands who came to pay their respects. Some mobsters did not attend the funeral because of ongoing Federal Bureau of Investigation (FBI) scrutiny; however, many Mafia members showed their respect by making financial contributions to the family. Mafia boss Carlo Gambino and his close associate Aniello "Neil" Dellacroce made personal appearances at the funeral.

IMPACT

Tommy Lucchese's organized crime model consisted of political support, labor racketeering, and reinvesting in legitimate businesses in order to enhance sources of fi-

Tommy Lucchese. (AP/Wide World Photos)

nancial revenues. His emphasis on legitimate business and union activities served as the foundation for success in the modern era of organized crime. Mafia white-collar crime rapidly became a new frontier in the late twentieth century, and crimes similar to gasoline tax fraud seemed to offer lucrative opportunities and a strategic shift to enterprise crime.

The legacy of the Lucchese family remains questionable following several arrests of key figures during the 1990's. After the terrorist attacks of September 11, 2001, law enforcement agencies have reorganized to meet external threats, thereby giving organized crime the opportunity to grow and find more lucrative pursuits. Organized crime opportunists and "chameleons" are always ready to reinvent, innovate, and maximize profits.

FURTHER READING

Abadinsky, Howard. *Organized Crime.* 7th ed. Belmont, Calif.: Wadsworth/Thomson Learning, 2006. The text is an in-depth analysis of organized crime from a historical and theoretical perspective.

Maas, Peter. *The Valachi Papers.* New York: Harper-

Collins Paperbacks, 2003. The original classic published in 1968, which serves as the foundation and major source for information about the Masseria and Maranzano organized crime conflict.

Raab, Selwyn. *The Five Families: The Rise, Decline, and Resurgence of America's Most Powerful Mafia Empires*. New York: Thomas Dunne Books, St. Martin's Press, 2005. The author discusses the history of the Sicilian Mafia in the United States.

Volkman, Ernest. *Five Families: Gangbusters—The Destruction of America's Last Great Mafia Dynasty*. New York: Avon Books, 1998. The book describes law enforcement operations directed at the Lucchese family and other New York organized crime families.

—*Thomas E. Baker*

SEE ALSO: Carlo Gambino; Vito Genovese; Lucky Luciano; Salvatore Maranzano; Joe Masseria.

LUCKY LUCIANO
Mafia kingpin

BORN: November 24, 1897; Lercara Friddi, Sicily
DIED: January 26, 1962; Naples, Italy
ALSO KNOWN AS: Salvatore Lucania (birth name); Charles Luciano
MAJOR OFFENSES: After eliminating the old crime bosses in New York, Luciano turned an archaic secret society called the Mafia into a modern international business conglomerate.
ACTIVE: 1916-1936
LOCALE: United States, mainly New York
SENTENCE: Fifty years for operating houses of prostitution; pardoned after ten years and deported

EARLY LIFE
Salvatore Luciano (lew-chee-AH-noh) came to New York at the age of eight years, not knowing a word of English. Unhappy in school, he made pennies a day by protecting schoolchildren from bullies who robbed them.

Angered by the flashy clothes he bought with such money, his father beat him, so he ran away from home. Confined to a truant school for four months, Luciano dropped out of school and teamed up with an Italian, Frank Costello, and two Jews, Meyer Lansky and Benjamin "Bugsy" Siegel, to form a street gang from the lower East Side, which would transform the nature of crime in the United States.

As a delivery boy for a hatmaker, Luciano was caught stashing heroin in the hatbands of ladies' bonnets. On June 25, 1916, he pleaded guilty to possession of narcotics and served a six-month sentence at Hampton Farms Penitentiary. He would not be convicted of another crime for twenty years.

CRIMINAL CAREER
The advent of Prohibition in 1920 enabled bootleggers to make big profits by selling alcohol illegally. A case of liquor costing twenty-five dollars could bring one thousand dollars. Luciano and his gang negotiated big deals for high-quality liquor from Philadelphia, Canada, and Europe. Bootlegging went beyond buying and selling. Ships anchored at sea dispensed liquor to smaller boats that sped it to warehouses for distribution to retail outlets, called speakeasies, of which there were thirty-two thousand in New York City alone. Violence was used to prevent hijacking along the way. Luciano organized bootlegging in the New York area and made a fortune.

His immense profits brought him to the attention of two major Mafia gangs, headed by Joe "the Boss" Masseria and Salvatore Maranzano, deeply sunk in internecine warfare which Luciano thought useless. After being abducted, tortured, and left for dead by Maranzano's goons, Luciano decided to kill both bosses. He lured Masseria to a restaurant to be killed by four gunmen. Maranzano was murdered in his Manhattan office by Luciano's men posing as federal agents.

Then, to make peace and money, Luciano reorganized crime. Remaining first among equals, he selected a high council that would replace rule by one man. Nine heads of the nation's twenty-four Mafia families rotated membership, meeting periodically to adjudicate disputes, approve murders, make major business decisions, and enforce Luciano's rules.

From his suite in the Waldorf Towers, Luciano directed supervisors of diversified businesses in his empire: among others, Costello, over gambling and political corruption; Arthur Flegenheimer, called Dutch Schultz, over liquor and lottery rackets; Lansky, over banking and

MURDER, INC.

Lucky Luciano, Louis Lepke, Meyer Lansky, and Frank Costello controlled the syndicate leadership council. To help enforce their decisions, they also took control of Murder, Inc., an organized squad of hired killers created in the Brownsville section of the Bronx in New York City during the 1920's by Joe Adonis. Albert Anastasia, Lepke, and, at times, Adonis ran the squad, but they acted only with the express approval of the syndicate leadership. The organization soon spread to other cities.

Its killers not only received a salary but also earned from one thousand to five thousand dollars when called on to make a "hit." There were other benefits as well, including representation by first-rate lawyers at the syndicate's expense if they were arrested. The hired killer made a hit only after the syndicate had issued a contract naming the target. The leadership was usually scrupulous about avoiding conflict of interest. For example, a member of Murder, Inc. would not be hired for a hit in his own city. Instead, a member from another city would be brought in, given a week to study the target's habits, and paid off after the murder. The method varied: strangulation; gunfire; staged accidents, such as a fall from a building's upper floor or a car crash; stabbing; beating; or drowning. Many victims disappeared without a trace.

Historians estimate that Murder, Inc. received contracts for five hundred to seven hundred murders nationally during the 1930's. Its members claimed that "we only kill our own," as high-ranking member Bugsy Siegel put it, and then only for business reasons. (Siegel himself became a victim.) A case in point was the syndicate's best-known hit: one of the ruling council's own members, Dutch Schultz. When, in 1935, he found himself under relentless investigation by New York City's district attorney, Thomas E. Dewey, Shultz demanded that the syndicate approve a hit on Dewey. Luciano, Costello, and Lansky refused; it was against their rules. Schultz then angrily announced that he would order the killing himself. Instead, the syndicate executed him first. Two of Murder, Inc.'s top assassins, Mendy Weiss and Charlie "The Bug" Workman, cornered Schultz in a bathroom and shot him through the stomach. He died a day later, steadfastly refusing to identify his killers to the police.

casinos; Albert Anastasia, over the docks and an enforcement unit called Murder, Incorporated.

In 1936, Luciano was sent to jail by an enterprising prosecutor, Thomas E. Dewey, later governor of New York and Republican presidential candidate, who made the first use of wiretaps and a new law against racketeering. After serving ten years of an unprecedented fifty-year sentence for operating houses of prostitution, Luciano was pardoned by Dewey for helping the war effort. To protect Allied shipping from Nazi submarines during World War II, the Navy had enlisted Luciano to thwart sabotage on the docks and to secure intelligence from townspeople in Sicily to facilitate the military invasion that liberated Europe.

Luciano claimed credit for the loss of the American ship *Normandie*, which, sixty days after the Japanese attack on Pearl Harbor, caught fire and capsized at its dock before the eyes of millions of New Yorkers. The press blamed the fire on Nazi sabotage, and tempers flared for war on Germany.

Although commended for aiding the war effort, Luciano was deported on February 10, 1946. The extent of his criminal career in exile remains a mystery. He visited syndicate chieftains in Cuba later that year, ostensibly to fete Frank Sinatra on his show business success or, as some say, to organize narcotics smuggling. Though arrested in his youth for possession of narcotics, Luciano denied later links with the trade. Government agents in the United States and Italy hounded him for years without making a narcotics case against him. Once he even volunteered to organize the trade and stop the flow of drugs to the United States, but his offer received no reply. The day he died, Italian officials were ready to charge him with smuggling 150 million dollars' worth of narcotics into the United States over a ten-year period.

IMPACT

Lucky Luciano had an enormous impact on crime, criminal justice, labor unions, the entertainment industry, and American society itself. By making the noble experiment called Prohibition fail, Luciano affected laws, lawmakers, and the citizenry at large. His criminal syndicate was made a permanent feature of the national landscape, and, on a deeper level, the faith of ordinary people in their established institutions was weakened.

Under Luciano's leadership, organized crime became the biggest business in the United States, with revenues greater than that of any legitimate corporation. Those funds were used to corrupt the government to an extent never known before. The criminal justice system itself had to mature to meet his challenge. Law books were rewritten to enable prosecutors to combat his sophisticated operations.

Ironically, Luciano's influence is still felt in the industries of tourism and entertainment, which he encouraged through far-flung investments in regional vice centers, most notably Las Vegas. His insights into organizing labor, first implemented in the garment district of New York, enabled the labor movement to succeed in the United States. The nation's commitment to diversity owes much to Luciano's acceptance of Jews and other minorities. He hated the old Mafia bosses for excluding non-Italians, and his political allies made such ideas about mutual respect and equality part of their agenda for the United States.

FURTHER READING

Gosch, Martin A., with Richard Hammer. *The Last Testament of Lucky Luciano.* New York: Dell, 1978. Based on confessions to the biographer in whose arms

he died, this book documents Luciano's denials of implication in prostitution and narcotics. Useful index.

Raab, Selwyn. *Five Families.* New York: St. Martin's Press, 2005. Definitive history of the rise and fall of New York's most powerful mobs. Photographs. Index. Bibliography.

Reppetto, Thomas. *American Mafia.* New York: Holt, 2004. Detailed chronicle of the rise of the Mafia in the United States from 1890 to 1951. Photographs. Excellent bibliography.

—John L. McLean

SEE ALSO: Albert Anastasia; Frank Costello; Meyer Lansky; Salvatore Maranzano; Joe Masseria; Dutch Schultz; Bugsy Siegel.

LUDWIG II
King of Bavaria (r. 1864-1886)

BORN: Customarily August 24, 1845; Nymphenburg Palace, Munich, Bavaria (now in Germany)

DIED: June 13, 1886; Castle Berg, Lake Starnberg, Bavaria (now in Germany)

ALSO KNOWN AS: Ludwig Friedrich Wilhelm (full name); Louis II; Mad King Ludwig; Dream King; Swan King

CAUSE OF NOTORIETY: Disinterested in ruling Bavaria, the eccentric Ludwig II spent huge sums on building spectacular castles.

ACTIVE: 1864-1886

LOCALE: Bavaria

EARLY LIFE

Ludwig II (LEWD-vihg) spent much of his boyhood at Hohenschwangau Castle, just north of the Austrian border. His father, King Maximilian I, had rebuilt the castle from ruins and had it decorated with a swan motif commemorating the medieval legend of the Swan Knight.

Ludwig grew to be tall, handsome, and bookish. Immersed in German literature and legend, he became as a teenager enthralled by Richard Wagner's opera *Lohengrin* (1848), which tells the story of the Swan Knight. Following his father's death, Ludwig became king of Bavaria on March 10, 1864. Immediately he sent for Wagner and began to finance the composer's personal expenses and his musical productions.

POLITICAL CAREER

In 1866 Ludwig was forced to take Bavaria into the Seven Weeks' War as an Austrian ally against Prussia. In 1871 Bavaria joined Prussia and other German states in the Franco-Prussian War. After the French were defeated, Ludwig (pressured by Prussian chancellor Otto von Bismarck) sent the crucial letter inviting the Prussian king Wilhelm to establish the German Empire and become its emperor.

Disinterested in the military, and never enjoying the work of government, Ludwig withdrew more and more into his own dreams and amusements. He built the Festspielhaus in Bayreuth in 1876 specifically as a venue for Wagner's operas, as it remains today. Ludwig often had concerts, dramas, or operas performed in various venues for himself alone, with no other audience.

Increasingly reclusive and eventually completely nocturnal, Ludwig took long coach rides about the countryside. He built one fabulous castle after another. Linderhof, modeled after the Petit Trianon at Versailles, France, included an underground Blue Grotto with a lake and a swan boat where Ludwig could watch performances of Wagner's works. Herrenchiemsee, copied from the Palace of Versailles itself, featured a Hall of Mirrors longer than the original. Neuschwanstein was a mountaintop Romanesque fantasy whose elaborate decoration and furnishings were inspired by the Germanic tales dramatized in Wagner's operas. Though he

Ludwig II.

hired architects and designers, Ludwig was intimately involved in the details. While these castles remained unfinished, he was already planning to build three more. Ludwig's huge expenditures, though largely from his inherited personal fortune, as well as his neglect of government and generally strange behavior, resulted in his removal from power in 1886.

LEGAL ACTION AND OUTCOME

In 1886, at the behest of his uncle Prince Luitpold and some government officials, a committee of physicians led by Dr. Bernhard von Gudden declared Ludwig incurably insane. He was arrested on June 8, 1886, at Neuschwanstein and taken to Castle Berg on Lake Starnberg. On June 13, 1886, Ludwig and Dr. von Gudden went for a walk. A few hours later both were found floating dead in the lake. Though theories abound, no definite conclusion about the cause of death of either man is possible.

IMPACT

Ludwig II unwillingly led Bavaria into the creation of the German Empire, but his real impact was as a patron of the musical, architectural, and decorative arts. The greatest part of his lasting fame—or notoriety—owes to his extravagantly eccentric self-indulgence, unequaled among European monarchs of his day. The annual Bayreuth festival of Wagner's works exists because of Ludwig's early support. The "Mad King's" passion also endures in his castles, especially Neuschwanstein, probably the best-known castle in the world. The Sleeping Beauty castles at Disneyland and Disney World are models of Neuschwanstein.

FURTHER READING

Blunt, Wilfrid. *The Dream King.* New York: Viking Press, 1970. A sound, readable, and lavishly illustrated biography detailing Ludwig's upbringing, his habits, his castles, and his patronage of Richard Wagner.

Eger, Manfred. "The Patronage of King Ludwig II." In *The Wagner Handbook,* edited by Ulrich Muller and Peter Wepnewski, translated by John Deathridge. Cambridge, Mass.: Harvard University Press, 1992. Gives a brief but substantial and authoritative summary and evaluation of Ludwig's support of Richard Wagner and its importance to Wagner's works.

King, Greg. *The Mad King: The Life and Times of Ludwig II of Bavaria.* Secaucus, N.J.: Carol, 1996. The best modern biography in English. Includes political context and treatment of Ludwig's relationships with his cousin the Empress Elisabeth and Wagner, as well as his homosexuality. Suggests he was more eccentric than mad.

McIntosh, Christopher. *The Swan King: Ludwig II of Bavaria.* 1982. Reprint. London: Tauris Park, 2003. An adequate and sympathetic biography covering Ludwig's personal relationships, eccentricities, political unsuitability, and extravagances, including the castles.

—*C. Herbert Gilliland*

SEE ALSO: Charles II; Christian VII.

JEFFREY LUNDGREN
American Mormon leader and murderer

BORN: May 3, 1950; Independence, Missouri
DIED: October 24, 2006; Lucasville, Ohio
ALSO KNOWN AS: Jeffrey Don Lundgren (full name)
MAJOR OFFENSES: Aggravated murder and kidnapping
ACTIVE: April 17, 1989
LOCALE: Kirtland, Ohio
SENTENCE: Death penalty for murders and five
consecutive sentences of ten to twenty-five years in
prison for kidnapping

EARLY LIFE
Jeffrey Lundgren (LUND-grihn) was the eldest of two
sons born to Don and Lois Gadberry Lundgren. Raised in
the Reorganized Church of Jesus Christ of Latter-day
Saints (RLDS), Lundgren was known as a good speaker
and writer. He acquired, primarily while in the Navy, a
vast knowledge of the Scriptures, both the Bible and the
Book of Mormon. He married Alice Keehler when he
was nineteen years old. They had four children, the eldest
of whom was involved in the murders planned by his
father.

The Church of Jesus Christ of Latter-day Saints,
founded by Joseph Smith in 1830, had an ongoing number of political and monetary problems during its fledgling years. It continually moved from one town and one
state to another in order to flee both the law and the
banks. In 1834, Smith stated that God had promised to
give these followers a prophet to lead the "saints," as they
called themselves, against their enemies, and, above all,
to redeem Zion. After his death in 1844, the time was ripe
for a new leader, and Brigham Young was both determined and charismatic. The saints went West, and the
original church stayed behind, renaming itself the Reorganized Church of Jesus Christ of Latter-day Saints.
Modern-day saints state that the promise of 1834 has not
been fulfilled. Over the decades, there have been many
men who said that they were called to be the one to redeem Zion.

From the time of Lundgren's youth, the liberal faction
of the RLDS church had been waging a battle with the
conservatives to make dramatic changes in the church,
such as having female priests and making their religion
into a mainstream American faith. Lundgren's parents
were part of the conservative movement that wanted to
make the church even stricter than it was and to restore it
to its former traditions. This is the church in which
Lundgren was raised.

CRIMINAL CAREER
In July of 1983, Lundgren received a revelation from God
that he and his family should move to Kirtland, Ohio, a
city bound up in the history of the RLDS faith. In a rift
with church officials, Lundgren withdrew his membership
in September, 1986. He then rented a large farmhouse,
where he and his family lived. Several of his followers
then joined him in Kirtland. They began to collect an arsenal, and Lundgren made plans for a "blood atonement" because five of his followers were questioning his teachings.

On April 10, 1989, Lundgren and two of his followers
began digging a pit in the barn in order to conceal
corpses. Five members of the Avery family, beginning
with the father, Dennis Avery, and including three young
daughters, were taken to the barn one by one, bound with
tape, and shot several times each. A chain saw was used
to muffle the sounds of the guns.

LEGAL ACTION AND OUTCOME
On September 17, 1990, Lundgren was convicted of five
counts of aggravated murder and five counts of kidnapping. He was sentenced to death on September 21, 1990,
and executed on October 24, 2006. Alice Lundgren was
thought to be a physically and emotionally battered wife.
When she was asked if she knew what her husband was
going to do, she replied that one would have to be a fool
not to know. Later, on the witness stand, she claimed that
everyone else involved knew but not she. Alice was
nonetheless convicted and would be eligible for parole
long after her death. The other eleven defendants received sentences ranging from 1 year to 130 years.

IMPACT
The case involving Jeffrey Lundgren was not unique:
There were two additional well-known murders involving Mormons. Mark Hoffman, an expert forger of rare
Mormon documents, murdered twice to keep his forgeries secret. Ervil LeBaron was the leader of a Mormon
fundamentalist group and killed those he viewed as his
opponents. In the years following the Lundgren murders,
the RLDS church changed its name to the Community of
Christ in order to separate itself from the Mormons of
Utah.

FURTHER READING
Earley, Pete. *Prophet of Death: The Mormon Blood-
Atonement Killings*. New York: William Morrow,

1991. Detailed description of Lundgren's beginnings in the Reorganized Church of Jesus Christ of Latter-day Saints and his efforts to keep the faith as it was in the days of Joseph Smith.

Jenkins, Philip. *Mystics and Messiahs: Cults and New Religions in American History*. New York: Oxford University Press, 2000. The author gives a humorous and detailed look at the history of various mainstream religions that were called cults when they began.

Shupe, Anson. *In the Name of All That's Holy: A Theory of Clergy Malfeasance*. Westport, Conn.: Praeger, 1995. The author, a sociologist, explores clergy who take advantage—financially, emotionally, or sexually—of their followers.

Snow, Robert L. *Deadly Cults: The Crimes of True Believers*. Westport, Conn.: Praeger, 2003. Describes the well-known and the sometimes unusual methods used by cults to recruit and keep their members. Goes into great detail about the crimes committed by the leaders and their followers.

—*Ellen B. Lindsay*

SEE ALSO: Jim Jones; David Koresh.

VICTOR LUSTIG
Czech con artist

BORN: January 4, 1890; Hostinne, Bohemia (now in Czech Republic)
DIED: March 11, 1947; Springfield, Missouri
ALSO KNOWN AS: Count Duval; Count Victor Lustig; Robert Lamar; Robert Miller; Albert Phillips; George Simon
MAJOR OFFENSES: Counterfeiting and jail escape
ACTIVE: 1934
LOCALE: New York, New York, and Paris, France
SENTENCE: Twenty years in prison

EARLY LIFE
Victor Lustig (LEWS-teeg) was born and raised in a small village in Hostinne, Bohemia, which later became the Czech Republic. His father, the local burgomaster, sent the young Lustig to boarding school in Dresden, Germany, where he studied languages. At age nineteen, he broke all connections with his family and moved to Paris.

CRIMINAL CAREER
In Paris, Lustig survived for a short time as a petty thief. He next took up gambling and apprenticed himself to the American gambler Nicky Arnstein. With Arnstein, Lustig began making Atlantic crossings on ocean liners for the sole purpose of fleecing passengers in games of chance. When the outbreak of World War I interrupted his transatlantic travel, Lustig settled in Paris for a few years before returning to the United States. In New York, he renewed his relationship with Arnstein, who helped him make connections with the American underworld.

Soon Lustig set off on his own. Posing as a displaced European aristocrat, he carried out a series of investment frauds throughout the United States and Canada in order to finance a luxurious lifestyle. In one of his most elaborate schemes, he created a fake off-track betting parlor. Relying on an accomplice who worked for Western Union, Lustig delayed the receipt of telegraphed race results long enough to place "winning" bets. The real payoff came when Lustig was able to trick an amateur gambler into betting on the wrong horse.

When Lustig needed cash quickly, he sometimes relied on a Rumanian Box, a device purported to produce exact copies of currency. In actuality, Lustig deceived his "marks" by using genuine one hundred dollar bills, one with its serial number meticulously altered to match the other. Lustig reportedly counted on his victims being too embarrassed by their greed and gullibility to press charges, and he was often successful in avoiding arrest.

EIFFEL TOWER AFFAIR
Lustig is perhaps best known for selling the Eiffel Tower to an unsuspecting Parisian businessman. In May, 1925, while staying in Paris, Lustig discovered a small newspaper article discussing the maintenance expense on the Eiffel Tower and suggesting dismantling it as an alternative. The tower, designed and built especially for the 1889 Exposition Universelle, had not been intended as a permanent installation, and it was widely regarded in artistic circles as an eyesore. Armed with the news item and forged stationery and credentials, Lustig disguised himself as a deputy director general of the Ministère des Postes et Télégraphes to a group of scrap-metal dealers to whom he had written. At a meeting in the fashionable

Hôtel de Crillon, he explained that the salvage rights to more than seven thousand tons of iron would be sold to the highest bidder. Lustig impressed upon the bidders the need to move quickly and with discretion in order to avoid public disapproval. Not only was Lustig able to convince the purchaser to deliver a certified check for the entire amount of the sale, but he also extracted a bribe from the man. Like most of Lustig's earlier victims, the businessman was too humiliated to contact authorities upon his discovery of the fraud. After one month, Lustig attempted to repeat the scheme; however, the second buyer proved less cooperative, and Lustig was forced to flee Europe for the United States.

LEGAL ACTION AND OUTCOME

Although Lustig was arrested dozens of times and found his activities and travel limited by outstanding warrants, he avoided conviction—sometimes by skipping bail, sometimes by escaping from prison, sometimes by bribery or other schemes—until his arrest in 1935. Following yet another escape, this time from a federal detention center, Lustig was convicted for counterfeiting. When his accomplice, William Watt, agreed to testify for the state, Lustig pleaded guilty. He was sentenced to fifteen years for the counterfeiting charges and an additional five for escaping from prison. After spending ten years at Alcatraz, in San Francisco, he was transferred to a medical facility in Springfield, Missouri, where he died of a brain abscess on March 11, 1947.

IMPACT

Victor Lustig never resorted to violence or threats of violence in committing his crimes, but he left many of his victims in emotional and financial ruin. He never publicly expressed remorse for his actions. Although his off-track betting scam became the basis for the plot of the 1973 Paul Newman-Robert Redford film *The Sting*, Lustig generally has not been romanticized in popular culture.

FURTHER READING

Boese, Alex. *Museum of Hoaxes*. New York: Penguin Putnam, 2002. A historical survey that examines the public's role in enabling hoaxes. Chapter 5 on the period between 1914 and 1949 discusses Lustig. Includes extensive references.

Farquhar, Michael. *A Treasury of Deception: Liars, Misleaders, Hoodwinkers, and the Extraordinary True Stories of History's Greatest Hoaxes, Fakes, and Frauds*. New York: Penguin Books, 2005. A compendium of historical facts that are thematically organized.

Johnson, James F. *The Man Who Sold the Eiffel Tower*. New York: Doubleday, 1961. A biography of Lustig by a former secret service agent involved in solving the counterfeiting case that led to Lustig's final arrest. Johnson portrays his subject as an extraordinarily clever but unfeeling villain.

Sifakis, Carl. *Hoaxes and Scams: A Compendium of Deceptions, Ruses, and Swindles*. London: Michael O'Mara Books, 1994. A reference work containing short, detailed summaries of a number of Lustig's scams.

—*K Edgington*

SEE ALSO: Lou Blonger; H. H. Holmes; Megan Louise Ireland; Henri Lemoine; Alexandre Stavisky; Joseph Weil.

TROFIM LYSENKO
Soviet agronomist

BORN: September 29, 1898; Karlovka, Poltava
Province, Ukraine, Russian Empire (now in
Ukraine)

DIED: November 20, 1976; Kiev, Ukraine, Soviet
Union (now in Ukraine)

ALSO KNOWN AS: Trofim Denisovich Lysenko (full
name)

CAUSE OF NOTORIETY: Lysenko embraced a
philosophy that placed politics and ideology ahead
of objective interpretation of data, retarding the
development of Soviet agricultural and biological
sciences.

ACTIVE: 1925-1964

LOCALE: Moscow, Odessa, and Gandzha, Soviet
Union

EARLY LIFE

Trofim Lysenko (truhf-EEM lih-SYEHN-kuh) was the
oldest of four children in a Ukrainian peasant family. He
did not learn to read until he was thirteen years of age and
never became skilled at reading and writing. He attended
schools of horticulture and agronomy, obtaining a certificate in agronomy from the Kiev Agricultural Institute in
1925.

SCIENTIFIC CAREER

Lysenko's first agronomy job was at an agricultural station in Azerbaijan, where he worked on vernalization, a
process of chilling seeds or seedlings before planting
them. In a study using winter wheat, vernalization generated an apparent increase in yield, which attracted the attention of the Soviet leaders. They were looking for successful peasants to hold up as examples of Marxism at
work. Lysenko was promoted to a position at the agricultural station in Odessa.

Lysenko's apparent success continued at Odessa.
Much later, however, his methods were judged to be de-
ficient, and his successes imaginary. For example, he
would propose a procedure to increase yield and have
peasants test it on their farms rather than carry out controlled experiments first. Results consisted of surveys in
which the peasants rated the increase in yield brought
about by the technique under study. Usually, only a frac-
tion of the surveys were returned, and conclusions were
drawn from that small and incomplete sample. Critics argued that peasants with good increases were more likely
to submit surveys than those with decreased yields. In

addition, Lysenko and his colleagues often discarded
surveys that reported decreases, arguing that in such
cases their method had not been properly applied and
thus not properly tested. With these analytical methods,
failures were made to look like successes, and Lysenko
submitted impressive reports while agricultural produc-
tivity plummeted. Before any negative impacts of Lysenko's agricultural production procedures were noticed,
Lysenko was touting another technique with great confidence and repeating his methodological tactics.

Lysenko also gained favor with Soviet leaders by convincing them that his theories and methods were consistent with Marxist philosophy while those of his opponents were antithetical to Marxist doctrine. Many of
Lysenko's opponents were exiled, imprisoned, or killed,
often with Lysenko's cooperation. The most egregious
example involved the 1940 arrest, imprisonment, and

Trofim Lysenko.

death of Nikolai Ivanovich Vavilov, an internationally known botanist and geneticist. Vavilov contributed importantly to Lysenko's early advancement. Later, he disagreed with some of Lysenko's ideas, and Lysenko supported his imprisonment.

Using these deceptive and underhanded tactics, Lysenko moved into a primary leadership role in Soviet agriculture. He was eventually appointed to membership or leadership in nearly all the important Soviet agricultural organizations. Only when Premier Nikita S. Khrushchev was removed from Soviet leadership in 1964 did Lysenko lose his position as the leader of Soviet biological sciences. He continued to hold a research appointment and to be fully supported in that position until his death.

IMPACT

Trofim Lysenko embraced the theory of acquired characteristics, first promulgated in the eighteenth entury by Jean-Baptiste Lamarck prior to the modern science of genetics, which, by Lysenko's time, was well established. Lamarck had said that characteristics developed (acquired) by an individual organism in that organism's lifetime could be inherited by the organism's offspring. This idea was replaced by the idea that genes, located on cellular structures called chromosomes, determined heredity by dictating chemical instructions for the replication of proteins that lead to the expression of traits, and these genes could not be changed by characteristics developed during the organism's lifetime. This and other aspects of Lysenko's leadership retarded Soviet biological science between the 1930's and the 1960's.

The devastating effect Lysenko's policies had on Soviet agricultural production resulted in widespread famine. Lysenko's negative influence on Soviet biology is exemplified by the term "Lysenkoism," which came to signify any situation in which politics and ideology are substituted for objective analysis in decision making.

FURTHER READING

Medvedev, Roy, and Zhores Medvedev. *The Unknown Stalin: His Life, Death, and Legacy*. New York: The Overlook Press. 2003. Roy Medvedev contributed to Lysenko's downfall; in chapter 9, titled "Stalin and Lysenko," he describes aspects of Lysenko's relationship with Stalin.

Roll-Hansen, Nils. *The Lysenko Effect: The Politics of Science*. Amherst, N.Y.: Humanity Books. 2005. More sympathetic with Lysenko than most sources but still a harsh rendering. References and discusses most other important works on Lysenko.

Soyfer, Valery N. *Lysenko and the Tragedy of Soviet Science*. New Brunswick, N.J.: Rutgers University Press. 1994. Soyfer was a biology student in Russia in the 1950's and so had firsthand experience with Lysenkoism.

—*Carl W. Hoagstrom*

SEE ALSO: Lazar Kaganovich; Nikita S. Khrushchev.

JOSEPH MCCARTHY
U.S. senator from Wisconsin (1947-1957)

BORN: November 14, 1908; Grand Chute, near Appleton, Wisconsin

DIED: May 2, 1957; Bethesda, Maryland

ALSO KNOWN AS: Joe McCarthy; Tail Gunner Joe; Joseph Raymond McCarthy (full name)

CAUSE OF NOTORIETY: McCarthy's investigation of officials and celebrities for alleged Communist activities symbolized Cold War anticommunist hysteria and set a precedent for political activity emphasizing personal destruction of one's opponents.

ACTIVE: 1950-1954

LOCALE: Washington, D.C.

EARLY LIFE

At an early age, Joseph McCarthy (mihk-KAHR-thee) exhibited intelligence, ambition, and a penchant for risk-taking. Born the fifth of nine children on his family's farm near Green Bay, Wisconsin, McCarthy quit high school to become a farmer and grocer, returned at age twenty to earn his diploma in a year, and went on to receive undergraduate and law degrees from Marquette University while working to cover his expenses. His early career as an attorney was largely unsuccessful, prompting him to supplement his earnings through gambling and politics. He also earned a reputation for heavy drinking, which would follow him for the remainder of his life.

POLITICAL CAREER

In 1939, McCarthy was elected to his first political office, a circuit court judgeship, after switching from the Democratic to the Republican Party and receiving a reprimand from the Wisconsin Supreme Court for making false claims about his opponent during the campaign. He later served in the Marine Corps during World War II as an aerial photographer and tail gunner, earning a decoration for flying with an injury that some of his fellow soldiers claimed was not received in combat. Following the war, McCarthy ran a successful campaign for the United States Senate by emphasizing his combat service.

During his first term in the Senate, McCarthy developed a reputation as an affable but mediocre legislator with tendencies toward drunkenness and questionable financial dealings. Seeking to divert attention from his personal conduct, McCarthy seized upon growing anticommunist sentiments inspired by growing tensions between the United States and the Soviet Union. He volunteered to join his fellow Republican legislators on the campaign trail in early 1950 and was assigned a series of obscure speaking engagements, beginning with an address before a women's club in Wheeling, West Virginia, on February 9. A recording of his speech by a local radio station was lost, but witnesses claim that McCarthy held aloft a piece of paper that he claimed contained the names of 205 Communist operatives within the State Department. McCarthy altered these figures in subsequent speeches, raising and lowering the number of alleged operatives to suit his audience.

McCarthy's claims were unverifiable, yet many Americans, fearing the rise of the Soviet Union and international communism, accepted them without question.

Joseph McCarthy. (Library of Congress)

"HAVE YOU NO SENSE OF DECENCY?"

In 1954, Senator Joseph McCarthy began to attack the U.S. Army with charges of inadequate security at a top-secret Army facility. The Army hired Boston lawyer Joseph Welch to represent it at the congressional hearings, and on June 9, 1954, McCarthy charged one of Welch's staff with having an association with a Communist organization. The following interchange was televised and viewed by millions of Americans:

MCCARTHY: Mr. Chairman, may I say that Mr. Welch talks about this being cruel and reckless. He was just baiting. He has been baiting Mr. Cohn [McCarthy's aide Roy Cohn] here for hours, requesting that Mr. Cohn before sundown get out of any department of the government anyone who is serving the Communist cause. Now, I just give this man's [Welch's staff attorney] record and I want to say, Mr. Welch, that it had been labeled long before he became a member, as early as 1944—

WELCH: Senator, may we not drop this? We know he belonged to the Lawyers' Guild.

MCCARTHY: Let me finish . . .

WELCH: You've done enough. Have you no sense of decency, sir, at long last? Have you left no sense of decency?

MCCARTHY: I know this hurts you, Mr. Welch.

WELCH: I'll say it hurts!

MCCARTHY: Mr. Chairman, as point of personal privilege, I'd like to finish this.

WELCH: Senator, I think it hurts you, too, sir.

MCCARTHY: I'd like to finish this. I know Mr. Cohn would rather not have me go into this. I intend to, however, and Mr. Welch talks about any "sense of decency." I have heard you and everyone else talk so much about laying the truth upon the table. But when I heard the completely phony Mr. Welch, I've been listening now for a long time, he's saying, now "before sundown" you must get these people "out of government." So I just want you to have it very clear, very clear that you were not so serious about that when you tried to recommend this man for this Committee.

WELCH: Mr. McCarthy, I will not discuss this further with you. You have sat within six feet of me and could ask—could have asked me about Fred Fisher. You have seen fit to bring it out, and if there is a God in heaven, it will do neither you nor your cause any good. I will not discuss it further. I will not ask, Mr. Cohn, any more witnesses. You, Mr. Chairman, may, if you will, call the next witness.

Source: United States Senate, transcripts of the McCarthy-Army hearings.

---

chairman of the Senate Permanent Subcommittee on Government Operations, a position that he used to broaden his investigation into alleged Communist activity in the U.S. government. He proceeded to target the Republican leadership that he had helped elect, calling numerous government employees to testify before his committee and subjecting them to hostile, intrusive questioning that was often based upon fabricated, erroneous, or nonexistent evidence. Those who refused to cooperate saw their reputations, careers, and lives destroyed as McCarthy leaked derogatory information about them to employers and the media.

He questioned the patriotism of even his mildest critics, creating an atmosphere of personal destruction and intimidation that rendered him virtually untouchable. Accused of assaulting journalist Drew Pearson in a congressional restroom, McCarthy defiantly admitted to the assault; the act went unpunished. Many Americans viewed McCarthy as a hero, and McCarthyism, as the crusade against communism came to be called, as a defense of the "American way" against an evil foe. To a growing minority, however, McCarthy and his tactics were the manifestation of an anti-American disregard for due process, civil liberties, and personal dignity.

DECLINE

McCarthy's fortunes were soon reversed as he increasingly attacked his fellow Republicans, insinuating that even Eisenhower was soft on communism. When McCarthy's investigation of the U.S. Army in 1954 led to televised hearings, during which McCarthy was revealed to have sought favors for a former staff member, the American public witnessed firsthand the inner workings of McCarthyism, and many were alarmed at the heavy-handed tactics of McCarthy and his chief counsel, Roy Marcus Cohn. Castigated in a verbal exchange with

His notoriety and influence continued to increase as his crusade intensified; several Democratic senators who questioned his claims were defeated in the 1950 election, and McCarthy's allegations that Democratic presidential candidate Adlai Stevenson was "soft" on communism led to the election of Dwight D. Eisenhower to the presidency in 1952.

McCarthy also won reelection that year and was made

Army counsel Joseph Welch, McCarthy appeared, defeated and exposed as a fraud, before a national television audience. The Senate voted to censure him in December, 1954, and he spent the remainder of his Senate career in obscurity. He died at Bethesda Naval Hospital in 1957 of liver failure precipitated by years of heavy drinking.

IMPACT

Just as his crusade against communism had brought his party to power in the early 1950's, the political demise of Joseph McCarthy contributed to Republican losses in Congress in the 1954 elections. Yet the legacy of McCarthyism continued to influence American politics and government long after the death of McCarthy. His investigations purged numerous experts on communism and communist countries from the United States government, affecting American foreign policy for decades and prompting some historians to establish links between McCarthyism and the defeat of U.S. forces in the Vietnam War. His synthesis of old-fashioned demagoguery and the fledgling medium of broadcast television created a new style of politics that emphasized skilled manipulation of information, assaults upon the patriotism and character of opponents, and appeals to emotion.

Declassified evidence indicates that a small number of the government employees whom McCarthy investigated were indeed Communist operatives. The number, however, was sufficiently small to raise questions about the propriety and competence of his investigations.

FURTHER READING

Fried, Albert, ed. *McCarthyism, the Great American Red Scare: A Documentary History*. New York: Oxford University Press, 1996. Collection of documents pertaining to McCarthyism from the late 1940's through the mid-1960's.

Ranville, Michael. *To Strike at a King: The Turning Point in the McCarthy Witch Hunts*. Ann Arbor, Mich.: Momentum Books, 1997. Story of journalist Edward R. Murrow's defense of an Air Force officer targeted by McCarthy.

Reeves, Thomas C. *The Life and Times of Joe McCarthy: A Biography*. Lanham, Md.: Madison Books, 1997. A lengthy, detailed, and scholarly biography of McCarthy.

—*Michael H. Burchett*

SEE ALSO: Whittaker Chambers; Roy Cohn; Alger Hiss; J. Edgar Hoover.

JAMES W. MCCORD, JR.
American government official and burglar

BORN: January 26, 1824; Waurika, Oklahoma
ALSO KNOWN AS: James Walter McCord, Jr. (full name)
MAJOR OFFENSES: Conspiracy, burglary, and wiretapping
ACTIVE: 1972
LOCALE: Washington, D.C.
SENTENCE: Eighteen months' imprisonment

EARLY LIFE

James W. McCord (muh-KORD), Jr., was born in Waurika, Oklahoma, on January 26, 1924, but spent most of his youth in Texas. He went to Baylor University. After obtaining a degree from George Washington University, he worked for the Federal Bureau of Investigation (FBI) during World War II. He is widely believed to have been in counterintelligence operations, fighting German spies in the United States. He also served for a time in the Army Air Force. In peacetime he returned to the FBI for a while before transferring to the Central Intelligence Agency (CIA) in 1951, working in physical security. After he left the CIA in 1970, he taught security courses and started his own security firm, McCord Associates. In 1972 he became security director for the Committee to Re-elect the President (CRP).

THE WATERGATE BREAK-IN

McCord burst onto the public scene on June 17, 1972, when he and four other men were caught breaking into the headquarters of the Democratic National Committee in the posh Watergate complex, across the Potomac River from the John F. Kennedy Center for the Performing Arts. They had come early in the morning to reposition hidden microphones ("bugs") and photograph sensitive documents, and had expected to find no one at such an hour. Instead, at 2:30 A.M. their sloppy taping of locks attracted the attention of a building security guard, who called the police.

When they were arrested, all five men gave false names. The police noted that they neither looked nor acted like typical burglars. All were dressed in suits and ties. They wore surgical gloves to prevent their leaving fingerprints. Not only were they carrying cameras, film, and electronic spying equipment, but they also were carrying large amounts of cash, including bills with sequential serial numbers.

The burglary might have been handled routinely, had *Washington Post* reporters Bob Woodward and Carl Bernstein not been covering the case. While researching McCord's background, the journalists discovered that he was also security coordinator for the Committee to Reelect the President (CRP), Richard M. Nixon's reelection campaign. From there, they meticulously followed leads that ultimately traced the entire network of corruption in CRP to the Oval Office.

LEGAL ACTION AND OUTCOME

Judge John Sirica found McCord guilty on eight counts of conspiracy, burglary, and wiretapping but suggested that his decades-long sentence could be reduced if he were to cooperate fully with the investigation into corruption in the White House. McCord then wrote a letter detailing the political pressures that were brought to bear by the Nixon administration to get its operatives to maintain their silence. He also accused administration officials of perjury, leading to a wave of confessions that rocked the administration. In return, he served only eighteen months in prison.

After his release, McCord wrote and published a memoir, *A Piece of Tape: The Watergate Story* (1974). He also went to work for the University of Michigan sports boosters and soon got in trouble for giving money from an illegal gambling operation to players.

IMPACT

The Watergate burglary led to an investigation that revealed systematic corruption and wrongdoing in the Nixon administration and ultimately brought to an end the presidency of Richard M. Nixon, the only president of the United States to have resigned from office. As a result of the name Watergate becoming so inextricably linked with the scandal, "-gate" has become a common suffix meaning "political scandal," as in Irangate, Iraqgate, Monicagate, and Zippergate. Even other countries have picked up "-gate" as a suffix for naming political scandals.

FURTHER READING

Bernstein, Carl, and Bob Woodward. *All the President's Men.* Reprint. New York: Simon and Schuster, 1994. A reissue of the best-known book on the Watergate investigation, by the reporters who broke the story.

Feinberg, Barbara Silberdick. *Watergate: Scandal in the White House.* New York: Franklin Watts, 1990. A brief history of the Watergate scandal.

Kutler, Stanley I. *The Wars of Watergate: The Last Crisis of Richard Nixon.* New York: Alfred A. Knopf, 1990. Provides a comprehensive history of the Watergate scandal.

McCord, James W., Jr. *A Piece of Tape: The Watergate Story, Fact and Fiction.* Rockville, Md.: Washington Media Services, 1974. McCord's memoir.

Schudson, Michael. *Watergate in American Memory: How We Remember, Forget, and Reconstruct the Past.* New York: Basic Books, 1992. Retrospective examination of Watergate in the popular memory.

—*Leigh Husband Kimmel*

SEE ALSO: Charles W. Colson; John D. Ehrlichman; H. R. Haldeman; E. Howard Hunt; G. Gordon Liddy; John Mitchell; Richard Nixon.

JEFFREY MACDONALD
American medical doctor

BORN: October 12, 1943; Jamaica, New York
ALSO KNOWN AS: Jeffrey Robert MacDonald (full
    name); Jeff MacDonald; Green Beret Killer
MAJOR OFFENSE: Murder
ACTIVE: February 17, 1970
LOCALE: Fort Bragg, North Carolina
SENTENCE: Three consecutive life sentences

EARLY LIFE

Jeffrey Robert MacDonald (mac-DON-ahld) was born
and grew up in New York. His high school classmates
voted him most likely to succeed. While attending
Princeton University, he married Colette Stevenson in
1963. Their daughter Kimberley was born in 1964; another daughter, Kristen, followed in 1967. During this
period, MacDonald attended Northwestern University
Medical School, from which he received his medical degree in 1968. He interned at Columbia Presbyterian
Medical Center in New York in 1968-1969.

CRIMINAL CAREER

In mid-1969, MacDonald entered the U.S. Army. He volunteered for duty with the Special Forces (also known as
the Green Berets) and moved his family to his assignment as a group surgeon at Fort Bragg, North Carolina.
On February 17, 1970, Colette (who was pregnant with a
third child), Kimberley, and Kristen MacDonald were
murdered, and MacDonald was beaten and stabbed. He
claimed that the murderers were intruders—three men
and one woman—who attacked him while he slept on the
living room couch. He also said that the woman chanted
"acid is groovy, kill the pigs" and carried a burning
candle.

Several standard investigative procedures were not
followed at the scene of the murders, including failing to
secure the premises from unauthorized entry, failing to
record the number and names of individuals who had access to evidence on the night of the murders, and failing
to order roadblocks to base exits. Despite these errors, investigators focused on MacDonald as the prime suspect
in the murders.

LEGAL ACTION AND OUTCOME

In 1970, the Army charged MacDonald with the murders
of his family. A thorough examination of the case was
launched, including psychiatric tests on MacDonald,
which determined that he had no mental illness or de-

rangement. In late 1970, an Army investigative report
stated that all charges against MacDonald were "not
true," and MacDonald was honorably discharged; he
moved back to New York. However, the Army (perhaps
illegally) continued to investigate MacDonald in his civilian life, which included surveillance after he moved in
1971 to California to accept work as an emergency room
physician.

Army attempts to bring charges against MacDonald
failed in 1972, 1973, and 1974, and charges brought in
1975 were dismissed in 1976. The Supreme Court reversed that decision in 1978, and MacDonald was convicted in 1979 of the murders of his wife and two daughters. However, the trial omitted evidence that was
uncovered through the Freedom of Information Act, and
in 1980, all charges were dismissed. MacDonald then returned to California. Moreover, also in 1980, a woman
named Helena Stockley signed a confession that she, her
boyfriend, and two other males were at the murder scene.
The judge refused to allow her testimony in subsequent
appeals, deeming her unreliable despite the fact that
Stockley passed three polygraph tests.

In 1982, the Supreme Court reversed the lower court's
decision, and MacDonald was returned to prison. In
1985, the National Association of Criminal Defense
Lawyers filed an amicus curiae (friend of the court) brief
supporting the theory that MacDonald was wrongly convicted. Throughout the 1980's and 1990's, as exculpatory evidence became known, MacDonald's attorneys
filed numerous motions asking for a new trial. All were
denied. In 1997, a motion to perform deoxyribonucleic
acid (DNA) testing on hair and blood samples found in
the victims' hands was granted. In early 2006, MacDonald was still waiting for the results of the government's
DNA testing.

IMPACT

The case of *Jeffrey R. MacDonald v. United States* has
been appealed in the United States Supreme Court more
than any other in history. Questionable prosecutorial actions and court decisions that kept possibly exculpatory
evidence from being heard by a jury defied sensibilities
and fueled a sense of injustice. Jeffrey MacDonald has
maintained his innocence for more than three decades.
To many, the impact of the case strikes at the core of the
United States justice system's admonition to "tell the
truth, the whole truth, and nothing but the truth."

FURTHER READING

McGinniss, Joe. *Fatal Vision*. New York: Penguin Putnam, 1984. The book, purporting to be the true story of MacDonald and the murder of his family, brought notoriety to the case. MacDonald sued McGinniss for fraud and breach of contract and eventually settled out of court in 1987 for $325,000.

Malcolm, Janet. *The Journalist and the Murderer*. London: Granta Books, 2004. Uses a study of MacDonald's lawsuit against *Fatal Vision* author Joe McGinniss to prove Malcolm's theory that a journalist writes his or her own interpretation of the story and not necessarily the story that the subject tries to tell through the journalist.

Potter, Jerry Allen, and Fred Bost. *Fatal Justice: Reinvestigating the MacDonald Murders*. New York: W. W. Norton, 1995. A painstakingly researched document that uses investigators' own documents uncovered through the Freedom of Information Act to detail inconsistencies in the government's case against MacDonald and to support the thesis that MacDonald did not receive a fair trial.

—*Taylor Shaw*

SEE ALSO: Seventh Earl of Lucan; Scott Peterson.

DONALD DUART MACLEAN
British spy

BORN: May 25, 1913; London, England
DIED: March 6, 1983; Moscow, Soviet Union (now Russia)
ALSO KNOWN AS: Mark Petrovich Frazer
CAUSE OF NOTORIETY: Maclean was one of the Cambridge spies, a group of men who first met at Trinity College, Cambridge University in the 1930's.
ACTIVE: c. 1935-1951
LOCALE: London, England; Washington, D.C.

EARLY LIFE

Donald Duart Maclean (DON-uhld DEW-urt muh-KLAYN) was the son of Sir Donald Maclean, a Scottish politician and public servant whose strict and authoritarian views may have encouraged a habit of duplicity in his son. Maclean attended Gresham's School in Holt and Trinity Hall College, Cambridge, in the latter of which he was regarded as an outstanding though not brilliant student. At Cambridge he joined the Apostles, a highly regarded debating society in which he met three other Cambridge personalities—Guy Burgess, Anthony Blunt, and H. A. R. (Kim) Philby—who would figure prominently in his subsequent life.

Soon after enrolling at Trinity, Maclean joined the Communist Party. He believed, as did a number of his contemporaries, that such a step was the most effective means of countering the rise of fascism. Deeply concerned with social justice, Maclean also believed that communism offered the world the best hope for an equitable society.

Donald Duart Maclean. (Hulton Archive/Getty Images)

ESPIONAGE CAREER

From the mid-1930's until 1951, Maclean followed two careers. Publicly, he downplayed his leftist political sympathies and in 1935 joined the British Foreign Office, working in London for three years. Subsequently he was posted to Paris, where he met his wife-to-be, Melinda Marling. The two were married shortly before leaving the city in advance of invading German forces. Four years later, in 1944, Maclean was posted to Washington, D.C., were he served as a secretary to the Combined Policy Committee, an Anglo-American-Canadian group dealing with the development of nuclear weapons. He was also privy to details of ongoing strategic planning between British prime minister Winston Churchill and American presidents Franklin D. Roosevelt and Harry S. Truman.

Maclean's access to the inner workings of the Western powers was crucial because secretly he had become a spy for the Union of Soviet Socialist Republics (U.S.S.R., or Soviet Union). Although his ideals prevented his accepting pay for his work, he was passing on as much sensitive information as possible to the government of Soviet dictator Joseph Stalin.

In 1948, Maclean was promoted to a challenging new position at the British embassy in Cairo, Egypt, but by now the pressure of his ongoing deception was telling on him. He had been consuming alcohol heavily for some time, and after several drunken episodes was sent home to London in 1950. Upon completion of psychiatric treatment, Maclean was promoted again, to head of the American Department. It was to be his last posting.

FLIGHT

For some time, British intelligence officials had been investigating security leaks. They believed that a "mole" (embedded double agent) code-named Homer by the Soviets had been responsible for passing information from Washington during the 1940's. Maclean was one of a handful of suspects. His interrogation was scheduled for May 28, 1951, but, incredibly enough, he was not placed under close surveillance and disappeared three days before he could be questioned. Subsequently it was determined that he and fellow spy (and former Apostle) Guy Burgess had defected to Russia, where the two eventually appeared at a news conference in 1956. British officials later explained that yet another spy and former Apostle, Kim Philby, had learned of the investigation and instructed Burgess to facilitate Maclean's quick departure.

Maclean remained true to his ideals in the Soviet Union, where he spent the remainder of his life teaching and writing. His wife joined him in 1953 but later had an affair with Philby (who had fled to the U.S.S.R. in 1963) and eventually returned home. Maclean died of a heart attack in 1983.

IMPACT

Experts differ as to the impact of Donald Duart Maclean's crimes. Some believe that information he leaked helped the Soviet Union inestimably in its atomic weapons program and in its postwar dealings with the Western powers. Others have since suggested that British intelligence had known about Maclean and his cohorts for some time and had been using them to feed "disinformation" to the Soviets.

The unmasking of the Cambridge spies damaged postwar morale in Great Britain and poisoned relations between the British and American intelligence agencies. In addition, the spies' combination of idealism, deception, and self-serving delusion has fueled a growing body of fiction and nonfiction, including novels by British writers Len Deighton, John le Carré, Graham Greene, and John Banville.

FURTHER READING

Boyle, Andrew. *The Fourth Man: The Definitive Account of Kim Philby, Guy Burgess, and Donald Maclean and Who Recruited Them to Spy for Russia.* New York: Dial Press, 1979. The first work to reveal publicly that Anthony Blunt was the fourth member of the Cambridge ring.

Cecil, Robert. *A Divided Life: A Personal Portrait of the Spy Donald Maclean.* New York: Morrow, 1989. Thoughtful consideration of Maclean and his milieu by a diplomat who worked with him.

Hamrick, S. J. *Deceiving the Deceivers: Kim Philby, Donald Maclean, and Guy Burgess.* New Haven, Conn.: Yale University Press, 2004. Argues that British intelligence knew the identity of the three spies and used them to supply misleading information to the Soviets. Extensive notes.

Modin, Yuri. *My Five Cambridge Friends: Burgess, Maclean, Philby, Blunt, and Cairncross.* New York: Farrar, Straus & Giroux, 1994. Readable, if self-serving, memoir by the Soviet agent who "handled" the Cambridge ring and engineered Burgess and Maclean's defection in 1951.

Newton, Vern W. *The Cambridge Spies: The Untold Story of Maclean, Philby, and Burgess in America.* Lanham, Md.: Madison Books, 1991. Concentrates on the period during which Maclean may have played his most damaging role.

Pryce-Jones, David. "The Usual Suspects." *New Criterion* 23 (October, 2004): 68-72. Reviews *The Private Life of Kim Philby* by Rufina Philby and *Deceiving the Deceivers: Kim Philby, Donald Maclean, and Guy Burgess* by S. J. Hamrick, above, and seconds Hamrick's evaluation of the Cambridge ring's importance.

—*Grove Koger*

SEE ALSO: Anthony Blunt; Guy Burgess; John Cairncross; Robert Philip Hanssen; Kim Philby; Joseph Stalin.

VIRGINIA MCMARTIN
American preschool operator

BORN: c. 1907; place unknown

DIED: December 18, 1995; Torrance, California

CAUSE OF NOTORIETY: McMartin, along with several family members, was charged with child sexual abuse in her preschool, causing a wave of hysteria among parents about suspected criminal intent of daycare providers. Charges against McMartin were eventually dropped.

ACTIVE: Late 1970's-early 1980's

LOCALE: Manhattan Beach, California

EARLY LIFE

Virginia McMartin (mihk-MAHR-tehn) lived in the small oceanfront community of Manhattan Beach, California, just south of Los Angeles. She opened a preschool, called the McMartin Preschool, on the main street in Manhattan Beach and hired members of her family and church to help build and run it. The school became one of the most prestigious and respected businesses in town. McMartin had earned four public citations for outstanding community service, including the city's highest honor. Applicants who wished to enroll in the McMartin Preschool usually had to wait up to six months before they could begin classes there.

TEACHING CAREER

McMartin became a defendant in one of the longest and most expensive criminal trials in the United States. The trouble for McMartin started on May 12, 1983, when Judy Johnson dropped off her two-and-a-half-year-old son at the preschool. Johnson's son was not enrolled at the preschool, but nevertheless, his mother dropped him off at the front of the school without notice and drove away. The teachers cared for him, and eventually his mother returned for him.

On August 12, 1983, Johnson called police to report that her son had reported being molested by Raymond Buckey, McMartin's grandson. A detective with the Manhattan Beach police department interviewed Johnson's son and also contacted the parents of twelve other McMartin students. Johnson's son was unable to pick out Buckey from photographs, and other McMartin parents stated that they had no reason to suspect that their children had been sexually abused. Medical examinations of Johnson's son failed to find any evidence of sexual abuse. Johnson was later diagnosed as suffering from paranoid schizophrenia.

In September, 1983, Buckey was arrested; however, prosecutors suffered from a lack of evidence. In their attempt to obtain adequate evidence for prosecution, they sent a letter to parents of McMartin students, detailing the alleged sexual abuse of Johnson's son, and asked that parents question their children to determine if they had been victimized as well. The preschoolers also underwent psychological interviews. Eventually, 360 former McMartin children were "diagnosed" as having suffered sexual abuse. In January, 1984, the McMartin Preschool closed after twenty-eight years in operation because of drastic reductions in enrollment.

LEGAL ACTION AND OUTCOME

On March 22, 1984, McMartin, Buckey, and six women associated with the preschool—including Buckey's sister and his mother, Peggy McMartin Buckey—were indicted by a grand jury on 115 counts of child sexual abuse. Two months later, the appointed district attorney for the case brought the indictment count up to 208, involving 40 alleged child victims. The defendants faced prison terms ranging from 96 years for McMartin to 776 years for Raymond Buckey. By the time the indictments were read, twenty-four parents had already filed one-million-dollar lawsuits against the preschool.

In 1985, at the end of the eighteen-month preliminary hearing, the newly elected district attorney dropped the charges against McMartin and four of the women associated with the preschool based on weak and insufficient evidence. Peggy McMartin Buckey and Raymond Buckey, however, still faced charges of child sexual abuse and conspiracy. Peggy McMartin Buckey was acquitted in 1990 after a three-year trial; Raymond Buckey was acquitted of forty counts, and a jury deadlocked on an additional eight counts against him in a second trial.

IMPACT

The McMartin Preschool trial was the costliest court case in the history of Los Angeles County: It totaled thirteen million dollars over the span of seven years. It also caused a wave of hysteria and led to several "witch hunts" of daycare providers during the 1980's—hundreds of people were arrested on the suspicion of child abuse, particularly those working in daycare centers. In part, this was because of therapists and investigators involved in the McMartin Preschool investigation who announced on national talk shows and to Congress that a network of well-financed satanic ritual abusers was operating secretly across the United States.

Following widespread criticism that investigators of the McMartin case used leading questions during interviews of the preschoolers, which in turn created "false memories" from them, prosecutors and child psycholo-gists gained an increased understanding of how to interview children in order to obtain accurate evidence. The McMartin Preschool never reopened, and the building was leveled some years after the trial.

FURTHER READING

Eberle, P., and S. Eberle. *The Abuse of Innocence: The McMartin Preschool Trial.* New York: Prometheus Books, 2003. An account of the McMartin trials.

Harris, Frann. *Martensville, Truth or Justice? The Story of the Martensville Daycare Trials.* Toronto, Ont.: Dundrun Press, 2004. Details a case very similar to that of the McMartin and Buckey case which took place in Saskatchewan, Canada, providing further insight into moral panic and the creation of false memories by investigators into suspected daycare abuse.

Nathan, D., and M. R. Snedeker. *Satan's Silence: Ritual Abuse and the Making of a Modern American Witch Hunt.* New York: Basic Books, 2001. An examination of ritual-abuse cases, including the McMartin Preschool trial, which have caused "moral panics" in the United States over the past twenty years.

—*Carly M. Hilinski*

SEE ALSO: Gilbert Gauthe; James Porter.

DANIEL M'NAGHTEN
Scottish assassin

BORN: 1814; Glasgow, Scotland
DIED: 1865; Broadmoor Hospital, Crowthorne, Berkshire, England
ALSO KNOWN AS: Daniel McNaghten; Daniel McNaughton; Daniel McNaughtan
CAUSE OF NOTORIETY: M'Naghten was acquitted for the shooting death of the secretary to England's prime minister. The verdict established the defense of not guilty by reason of insanity.
ACTIVE: January 20, 1843
LOCALE: London, England

EARLY LIFE

Daniel M'Naghten (DAN-yehl mihk-NAW-tehn) was born to a poor dressmaker and a businessman. When he was about eight years old, his mother died, and M'Naghten moved in with his father and stepmother. At age ten, he became a wood-turner apprentice to his father and was recognized for his extraordinary skills. Because his father had other illegitimate sons for whom to provide, he could not offer M'Naghten partnership in his wood shop; therefore, when M'Naghten turned eighteen, he sought work as an actor. After traveling with a theatrical group for three years, he returned to Glasgow and opened his own wood shop.

CRIMINAL CAREER

As business slowed from the economic depression in 1839, M'Naghten studied at the Mechanics' Institution in Glasgow. He involved himself in political activism and gradually came to believe that he was the target of a government conspiracy. M'Naghten believed that Prime Minister Sir Robert Peel of England (who created the first professional police force in England and for whom the "Bobbies" were named) was persecuting him and was responsible for his personal and financial difficulties. Today, M'Naghten's delusions might have led to the diagnosis of paranoid schizophrenia.

M'Naghten traveled to England to assassinate Peel. He stalked Peel for days before approaching him on a London street but mistook Edward Drummond, Peel's private secretary, for Peel. Intending to assassinate Peel, M'Naghten instead shot Drummond in the back. He was immediately apprehended by nearby policemen.

LEGAL ACTION AND OUTCOME

M'Naghten's trial began on March 3, 1843, and his attorney focused on his state of mind at the time of the murder. Nine physicians and surgeons testified at the trial, all of whom claimed M'Naghten was legally insane. A jury found M'Naghten not guilty by reason of insanity, and M'Naghten was acquitted.

While M'Naghten was not imprisoned, he was institutionalized for the rest of his life. First, he was remanded to Bethlem Royal Hospital, a mental asylum. Twenty years later, he was moved to the Broadmoor Institution for the Criminally Insane, where he died one year after his transfer.

IMPACT

The trial of Daniel M'Naghten established the defense of not guilty by reason of insanity. Public unrest followed the verdict, and Queen Victoria and the House of Lords also scrutinized the decision. Fifteen judges of common-law courts, including the judge who presided over M'Naghten's case, were assembled to discuss the law of insanity. They answered a series of questions, and the responses created a legal test to determine insanity, which came to be known as the M'Naghten Rules. The M'Naghten Rules relieve an offender from criminal liability if, at the time of the commission of the offense, the offender did not know what he or she was doing because of a mental defect or did not know what he or she was doing was wrong. Thus, the litmus test for legally right and wrong was established.

While the insanity defense was used sporadically in cases prior to that of M'Naghten, the M'Naghten case standardized this defense. The M'Naghten standard was adopted by the United States federal courts and many of the state courts in 1851 and predominantly used in the United States until the 1960's. While the insanity defense is popular in modern-day television and motion-picture crime dramas, it is rarely used and rarely successful. Probably the best-known example of a successful insanity defense is the case of John Hinckley, Jr., the man who shot President Ronald Reagan in 1981 in order to gain the attention of actress Jodie Foster. The jury found Hinckley "not guilty by reason of insanity," which proved to be an unpopular verdict among the American public.

FURTHER READING

"Daniel M'Naghten's Case." *English Reports* 8, no. 718 (1843). Trial transcript of M'Naghten's case, including the testimony of witnesses and the decisions of the judges, along with postcase discussion setting parameters for the insanity defense.

Diamond, B. "Isaac Ray and the Trial of Daniel M'Naghten." *American Journal of Psychiatry* 112 (1956): 651-656. Describes the role of scholar Isaac Ray in the M'Naghten trial and the creation of the M'Naghten Rules for a full description of the case.

Moran, Richard. *Knowing Right from Wrong: The Insanity Defense of Daniel McNaughtan.* New York: Free Press, 1981. Discusses in detail the life of M'Naghten and his trial. Includes text of the M'Naghten Rules and the House of Lords Debate, as well as M'Naghten's banking records, the post mortem report, and M'Naghten's writings.

Robinson, Daniel. *Wild Beasts and Idle Humors: The Insanity Defense from Antiquity to the Present.* Cambridge, Mass.: Harvard University Press, 1998. While the main focus is on the history of the insanity defense and its applications, this volume also provides a description of the M'Naghten case.

—Jennifer C. Gibbs

SEE ALSO: John Bellingham; John Hinckley, Jr.; Fanya Kaplan.

AIMEE SEMPLE MCPHERSON
American evangelist

BORN: October 9, 1890; Salford, near Ingersoll, Ontario, Canada

DIED: September 27, 1944; Oakland, California

ALSO KNOWN AS: Aimee Elizabeth Kennedy (birth name); Sister Aimee; Sister

CAUSE OF NOTORIETY: At the peak of her popularity, McPherson scandalized her base when she ran away with her lover, leaving everyone to think she had drowned; she explained her disappearance with a story of being kidnapped for ransom.

ACTIVE: 1926

LOCALE: Canada, California

EARLY LIFE

Aimee Semple McPherson (AY-mee SEHM-puhl muk-FURS-uhn) was the only child of Mildred Ona Pearce, a Salvation Army soldier, and James Morgan Kennedy, a farmer and devout Methodist. Mildred, known as Minnie, was hired to nurse James Kennedy's first wife, Elizabeth. After Elizabeth's death, Kennedy married the fifteen-year-old Minnie. She became a sergeant major in the Salvation Army and found joy in her service. She had taught her young daughter, Aimee, Scripture by the time she was five, considering the child a second opportunity to fulfill her own ambitions.

In December, 1907, Aimee met her first husband, Robert James Semple, a Pentecostal missionary, at a revival meeting. She converted to Pentecostalism, and after the couple married in August, 1908, they embarked on an evangelical tour of Europe and China. In Hong Kong they both contracted malaria, from which Robert died in August, 1910. Aimee, however, recovered, and her daughter, Roberta Star Semple, was born a month later. After returning to the United States with her baby, Aimee joined her mother in working for the Salvation Army. Accountant Harold Stewart McPherson became Aimee's second husband; their son, Rolf Potter Kennedy McPherson, was born in March, 1913.

RELIGIOUS CAREER

Soon after her son was born, McPherson had a near-death experience that renewed her dedication to full-time ministry. With her two children, she left her husband in 1915 and joined her mother in Canada. At a camp meeting the day after her arrival, she prayed, spoke in tongues, and found her life's work. She soon became well known as an evangelist, receiving invitations to preach in the United States and abroad. After a successful tour through the American South in her "Gospel Car" with religious slogans painted on the sides, McPherson finally settled with her mother and children in Los Angeles and founded the Foursquare Gospel Church. The large dome built to house the church, the Angelus Temple, was finished in 1923. McPherson's flamboyance and dramatic gifts drew crowds of converts and admirers. Her husband initially followed her in her religious travels but soon filed for divorce, which was granted in 1921.

In January, 1924, Sister Aimee, as she was then known, marked the temple's first anniversary by throwing a party for fifty-five hundred people, where she de-

Aimee Sempel McPherson. (Library of Congress)

FAITH AND RESOLUTION

When Aimee Semple McPherson's mother announced to a Foursquare Church congregation that her daughter was missing and feared drowned while swimming, many refused to believe it. According to a May 20, 1926, article in the *Los Angeles Times*, hundreds gathered on the beach where McPherson was last seen.

A faith as strong and deep as the ocean they watch hour after hour with aching eyes holds them there.

"She can't be dead. She can't be dead. . . ."

"God wouldn't let her die. She was too noble. Her work was too great. Her mission was not ended. She can't be dead. . . ."

The elements of tragedy and hysteria are there. They flare occasionally as some woman breaks under the vigil and sobs. Otherwise the crowd remains fixed and motionless. Few words are exchanged. . . .

But one time during the afternoon yesterday did the crowd change its position. In some manner word was spread about that promptly at 2:30 P.M. Mrs. McPherson would arise from the sea and speak to her followers. The appointed time came and many arose to look further out to sea. But it passed without the miracle which some of her followers had taken for granted.

Indeed, the story was a sensation nationwide. When McPherson surfaced five weeks later, followers and nonfollowers alike were eager to accept her story of abduction. She claimed that two men and a woman had rendered her unconscious with chloroform and spirited her away to an adobe hut in Mexico, hoping to ransom her.

Everyone loved the tale, the press above all. When inconsistencies cropped up, the scent of scandal made it even more titillating: No hut was found by police, McPherson showed no signs of the ordeal, and there was evidence that she had been in hotels with Kenneth Ormiston during the kidnap period, a man whose wife had already accused him of having an affair with McPherson.

McPherson simply ignored accusations and criticism while reveling in the publicity. "That's my story, and I'm sticking to it," she said. Legal action against her was eventually dropped, and her followers remained as faithful as ever. The Foursquare Church prospered. By 2006, its Web site claimed fifty thousand branch churches worldwide and a membership of more than five million.

Source: "Faithful Cling to Waning Hope," *Los Angeles Times*, May 20, 1926.

livered sermons on salvation, baptism, divine healing, and the Second Coming. Also in that year, McPherson became a pioneer in the new field of evangelical broadcasting and hired radio engineer Kenneth G. Ormiston to build a studio on the temple's third floor. Her station, KFSG, opened on February 6, 1924. She was the first woman to be granted a broadcast license by the Federal Communications Commission.

DISAPPEARANCE

On Tuesday, May 18, 1926, a crowd assembled in the Angelus Temple to watch McPherson's slide show of a recent trip to the Holy Land. Minnie Kennedy appeared in her daughter's stead to lead singing and narrate the show. At the end of the service, Kennedy officially announced that McPherson was missing and presumed drowned. The evangelist had gone to Ocean Beach with her secretary to swim earlier that day. For days, reporters and photographers vied with police to solve the mystery, and Kennedy preached to overflow crowds.

Ormiston, the engineer for KFSG, also disappeared around this time, but the connection went unobserved. A few months later, Kennedy received a ransom note signed "the Avengers," demanding $500,000 for McPherson's return. Los Angeles district attorney Asa Keyes investigated the case. Meanwhile, Ormiston fell under suspicion, but he arrived unexpectedly at temple headquarters on May 27 and professed no knowledge of McPherson's whereabouts.

On June 23, McPherson showed up in Douglas, Arizona, claiming she had been kidnapped, held in a shack in Agua Prieta, Mexico, tortured, and drugged. She had finally escaped, she said, and walked through the desert. Reporters arrived from all over the United States, and McPherson gave them interviews, knowing they would get out her story. Suspicion arose, however, and when sheriffs, police, and ranch hands converged in Agua Prieta to find the shack, they searched in vain.

A grand jury met in the summer of 1926, reviewed testimony, and charged McPherson and her mother with obstruction of justice. In January, 1927, District Attorney Keyes dropped all charges, citing lack of evidence. In 1931, McPherson married again, to actor and musician David Hutton; they divorced in March, 1934. During the Depression, McPherson threw her energies into creating soup kitchens and free health care clinics. In September of 1944, she died of an overdose of prescription drugs, presumed an accident.

IMPACT

Aimee Semple McPherson thrived in the cultural ebullience of the 1920's and became a symbol of that era, which adored celebrity, pageantry, and Protestantism. She had an instinctive sense of how to use the media, recognizing the possibilities of radio at a time when it was rapidly expanding, and set a precedent for the "televangelists" who now flood the airwaves. Vaudeville and Hollywood techniques helped spread her message. She practiced generic evangelical Christianity, holding credentials in such divergent branches as Assembly of God, Methodism, and Baptism. The Pentecostal Church she established did not shut out other denominations but united them. She rejected sectarianism and preached American revival ethics based on biblical Christianity mixed with a strong sense of patriotism.

McPherson's personal problems reflect women's struggle to find an outlet for their talents and ambitions. Her internal conflicts, troubled marriages, fierce devotion to her children, and drive for perfection reflect the stresses of a woman longing for personal fulfillment and determined to create a public presence. She exemplified many of the problems that would come to dominate public attention fifty years later, when American women in vast numbers rejected roles as housewives to find satisfaction in the public arena.

FURTHER READING

Bahr, Robert. *Least of All Saints: The Story of Aimee Semple McPherson.* Englewood Cliffs, N.J.: Prentice Hall, 1979. A speculative and dramatic reenactment of McPherson's life, with marvelous photos.

Blumhofer, Edith L. *Aimee Semple McPherson: Everybody's Sister.* Grand Rapids, Mich.: William B. Eerdmans, 1993. A carefully researched and detailed biography of the life of McPherson. Includes articles from her monthly magazine, *Bridal Call.*

Epstein, Daniel Mark. *Sister Aimee: The Life of Aimee Semple McPherson.* Florida: Harcourt Brace, 1993. An objective biography of McPherson.

—*Sheila Golburgh Johnson*

SEE ALSO: Jim Bakker.

TIMOTHY MCVEIGH
American terrorist

BORN: April 28, 1968; Pendleton, New York
DIED: June 11, 2001; Terre Haute, Indiana
ALSO KNOWN AS: Timothy James McVeigh (full name)
MAJOR OFFENSE: Oklahoma City bombing
ACTIVE: April 19, 1995
LOCALE: Oklahoma City, Oklahoma
SENTENCE: Death by lethal injection; executed June 11, 2001

EARLY LIFE

Timothy James McVeigh (mihk-VAY) was born on April 28, 1968, in Pendleton, New York, a small city near Buffalo. His parents were Bill, a worker at a local radiator plant, and Mickey McVeigh. Timothy was the middle sibling between two sisters.

His youth was largely uneventful except for the bullying he experienced in high school and the marital problems he witnessed between his parents, which included several separations. The marriage ended for good in 1986, a few months before McVeigh graduated from high school, when the couple divorced.

Once out of high school, McVeigh entered a local college but soon dropped out. Eventually, he became a security guard, a job that in part reflected his interest in guns, which had been sparked as a child through target shooting with his grandfather. McVeigh also became drawn to the extreme Right during this period. For example, he read Andrew Macdonald's *The Turner Diaries* (1980), a fictional account of an attack on a federal government building by a white supremacist.

McVeigh finally appeared to settle on a career in 1988 when he joined the United States Army. Eventually, he rose to the position of sergeant in the First Infantry Division and the operator of the main gun on a Bradley Fighting Vehicle. He saw combat in the 1991 Persian

Gulf War and would later mention to his biographers the traumatic impact of combat on him, particularly when he killed an Iraqi soldier. His shooting prowess was celebrated, however, and he was encouraged by the Army to audition for the Green Berets. McVeigh quickly found himself overwhelmed in this effort. He ended his attempt to join the Green Berets and soon quit the Army as well.

CRIMINAL CAREER

Back in the United States, McVeigh found it hard to blend back into civilian life and spent time with former military friends, including his chief accomplice for the Oklahoma City bombing, Terry Nichols. McVeigh also became increasingly radicalized over what he perceived as the excessive interference in everyday life by the U.S. government. He soon was selling antigovernment material at different venues and even traveled to Waco, Texas, to protest the U.S. government's 1993 confrontation with Branch Davidian cult. According to McVeigh, the final straw in his path toward his crime came with the bloody April 19, 1993, ending of the standoff at Waco. His disenchantment with the U.S. government arising out of that event would lead him to conduct an act of terrorism two years later, on the anniversary of its ending.

On that date in 1995, McVeigh drove a rental truck loaded with a massive bomb made primarily out of fertilizer to the Alfred P. Murrah Federal Building in Oklahoma City. He had selected the federal government building for the ease of access to it and because of the publicity images the attack would generate. At 9:02 A.M., the bomb exploded, killing 168 people, including 19 children. It was the worst terrorist attack on American territory up to that time.

The hunt quickly began for those responsible. McVeigh made little effort to escape capture. His name was quickly linked to the renting of the truck. By then he was already in custody, having been arrested fleeing the explosion because his car did not have a rear license plate on it. In due course, an accomplice, Nichols, who had helped him build the bomb, was also arrested, as was another man who had advance knowledge of the crime.

McVEIGH'S REASONS

On April 27, 2001, Timothy McVeigh wrote a letter of explanation to several media figures and news outlets, which reads in part:

McVEIGH: I chose to bomb a federal building because such an action served more purposes than other options. Foremost, the bombing was a retaliatory strike; a counter attack, for the cumulative raids (and subsequent violence and damage) that federal agents had participated in over the preceding years (including, but not limited to, Waco). From the formation of such units as the FBI's "Hostage Rescue" and other assault teams amongst federal agencies during the '80's; culminating in the Waco incident, federal actions grew increasingly militaristic and violent, to the point where at Waco, our government—like the Chinese—was deploying tanks against its own citizens.

Knowledge of these multiple and ever-more aggressive raids across the country constituted an identifiable pattern of conduct within and by the federal government and amongst its various agencies. For all intents and purposes, federal agents had become "soldiers" . . . and they were escalating their behavior. Therefore, this bombing was also meant as a pre-emptive (or pro-active) strike against these forces and their command and control centers within the federal building. When an aggressor force continually launches attacks from a particular base of operation, it is sound military strategy to take the fight to the enemy.

Bombing the Murrah Federal Building was morally and strategically equivalent to the U.S. hitting a government building in Serbia, Iraq, or other nations. . . . From this perspective, what occurred in Oklahoma City was no different than what Americans rain on the heads of others all the time, and subsequently, my mindset was and is one of clinical detachment.

Fox News reporter Rita Cosby interviewed McVeigh regarding his motives; here is his reply to two of her questions:

COSBY: What were some other options considered besides bombing?
McVEIGH: I waited two years from "Waco" for non-violent "checks and balances" built into our system to correct the abuse of power we were seeing in federal actions against citizens. . . . When violent action thus became an option, I considered, among other things, a campaign of individual assassination, with "eligible" targets to include: Federal Judge Walter Smith (Waco trial); Lon Horiuchi (FBI sniper at Ruby Ridge); and Janet Reno (making her accept "full responsibility" in deed, not just word).
COSBY: Lessons?
McVEIGH: Many foreign nations and peoples hate Americans for the very reasons most Americans loathe me. Think about that.

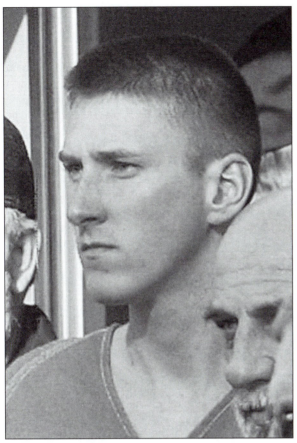

Timothy McVeigh. (AP/Wide World Photos)

LEGAL ACTION AND OUTCOME

On April 24, 1997, McVeigh's trial in federal court began. By early June he had been convicted and sentenced to death by lethal injection. He challenged the decision, but a federal court rejected his appeal in 2000, and McVeigh announced he would accept his fate. Eventually, the date for his execution at the federal prison at Terre Haute, Indiana, was set for May 16. Five days before, Attorney General John Ashcroft stayed the execution for a month because the Federal Bureau of Investigation had discovered documents related to the case that had not been shared with McVeigh's defense lawyers. In the end, a court decided that the new evidence was not significant and refused further blocks on the execution. On June 11, 2001, McVeigh became the first federal prisoner to be executed in thirty-eight years.

IMPACT

At the time of the Oklahoma bombing, the American public largely associated terrorism with foreign perpetrators, especially Middle Easterners. The fact that the worst terrorist attack on American territory had been carried out by an American citizen and military veteran made the event doubly shocking at the time. It prompted a backlash against the American far Right and increased powers for American police forces to combat domestic terrorism. Questions remain about whether others were involved beyond those, including Timothy McVeigh, who were convicted of the crime.

FURTHER READING

Bennett, David H. *Party of Fear: From Nativist Movements to the New Right in American History.* New York: Vintage, 2001. A history of the far Right, with an updated discussion of the militia movement.

Michel, Lou, and Dan Herbeck. *American Terrorist: Timothy McVeigh and the Oklahoma City Bombing.* New York: ReaganBooks, 2001. The definitive account of McVeigh's life and crime, made possible because he consented to extensive interviews with the two reporters.

Sticknew, Brandon M. *"All-American Monster": The Unauthorized Biography of Timothy McVeigh.* New York: Prometheus Books, 1996. A journalistic account written shortly after the Oklahoma City bombing.

—*Steve Hewitt*

SEE ALSO: Theodore Kaczynski; David Koresh; Terry Nichols; Eric Rudolph; J. B. Stoner; Randy Weaver.

HORST MAHLER
German terrorist and lawyer for the Red Army Faction

BORN: January 23, 1936; Haynau, Silesia, Germany (now Chojnów, Poland)

MAJOR OFFENSES: Conspiracy to commit aggravated robbery in connection with the establishment of a criminal association and inciting racial hatred

ACTIVE: 1968-2005

LOCALE: West Berlin, Germany

SENTENCE: Ten-month suspended sentence and a fine of seventy-five thousand German deutsche marks; twelve years' imprisonment plus two years for scheming the escape of Andreas Baader; nine months' incarceration for inciting racial hatred

EARLY LIFE

Horst Mahler (hohrst MAH-luhr) grew up in a middle-class family. His father was a dentist who was committed to Nazism but was still respected by his son. Mahler grew up in a very controlling environment in which his father accepted no opinions other than his own. By the time Mahler was eight years old, the Nazi regime had collapsed and the family fled, ending up in West Berlin. Later, Mahler went to the Free University of Berlin, where he joined a dueling fraternity, which he claims he joined in protest of authoritarianism; others note that his motive was linked to neo-Nazism. Upon graduation, he worked in a prominent law office in Berlin but soon began his own law firm.

CRIMINAL CAREER

Mahler led a number of demonstrations and riots before coming into contact with future members of the Red Army Faction (which was called the Baader-Meinhof Gang in its early incarnation). In the late 1960's, Germany experienced a surge in left-wing terrorist organizations, which seemed to emanate from widespread student protests that were held in Germany and elsewhere in the Western Hemisphere. The Red Faction Army was the most active of the organizations and was formed by Andreas Baader and Gudrun Ensslin, among others. It is thought to be one of the earliest groups to use violence and bombs for political purposes.

A socialist, Mahler began working with people from the Extra-Parliamentary Opposition; this radical turn limited his potential for a successful professional career in West Germany. He then defended Baader and Ensslin during their trials in 1969 for the bombing of Schneider and Kaufhof department stores in Frankfurt. On May 14, 1970, Mahler conspired with journalist Ulrike Meinhof to free Baader from prison. Following the breakout of Baader, Mahler fled to Lebanon to train with the Popular Front for the Liberation of Palestine. He also helped get weapons for the Red Army Faction.

LEGAL ACTION AND OUTCOME

In March, 1970, Mahler was sentenced to a ten-month suspended sentence for his actions relating to a violent and damaging demonstration. In June, 1970, in a civil proceeding, Mahler received a seventy-five-thousand-deutsche mark fine for damages. Mahler continued to engage in violent demonstrations, causing additional damages to public buildings.

In October, 1972, Mahler was arrested for his involvement with freeing Baader from prison. Mahler was excluded from the bar in 1974 and remained incarcerated until 1980. While in prison, he wrote a manifesto for the Red Army Faction, but the other members of the group renounced it, essentially ending his role in the group. In 1988, he was readmitted to the bar, but his license was revoked again in 2004. He was also fined for publicly supporting the terrorist events of September 11, 2001. In 2005, he was imprisoned for inciting racial hatred.

IMPACT

The Red Army Faction was the first urban guerrilla group in West Germany, and Mahler was most likely one of its founders and one of the more important theoreticians of the terrorist movement of the 1960's and 1970's in Germany. Following his release from prison in 1980, he became more involved in the country's politics. In the twenty-first century, he became active in the neo-fascist National Democratic Party (NPD) and the Deutsches Kolleg, a radically racist group that calls for a nationalist revolution in Germany. He became very public in his anti-Semitic views, calling for the destruction of Judaism.

FURTHER READING

Becker, Jillian. *Hitler's Children: The Story of the Baader-Meinhof Terrorist Gang*. New York: J. B. Lippincott, 1977. Discusses events leading up to the formation of the Baader-Meinhof Gang and its changes in membership and leadership. Provides detailed accounts of its terrorist activities and encounters with the law.

Billig, Otto. "The Lawyer Terrorist and His Comrades." *Political Psychology* 6, no. 1 (1985): 29-46. Depicts Mahler's contributions to terrorism in Germany and includes possible explanations for his actions.

Giles, Steve, and Maike Oergel, eds. *Counter-Cultures in Germany and Central Europe: From Sturm und Drang to Baader-Meinhof.* New York: Peter Lang, 2003. A collection of papers presented in 1981 that includes discussions of various forms of countercultural protest and terrorism from the 1770's until the 1990's.

Varon, Jeremy. *Bringing the War Home: The Weather Underground, the Red Army Faction, and Revolutionary Violence in the Sixties and Seventies.* Los Angeles: University of California Press, 2004. Focuses on political uprisings led by young, middle-class individuals and how they used violence to achieve their political goals.

—*Sheryl L. Van Horne*

SEE ALSO: Andreas Baader; Ulrike Meinhof.

MARY MALLON
Immigrant virus carrier

BORN: September 23, 1869; County Tyrone, Ireland

DIED: November 11, 1938; New York, New York

ALSO KNOWN AS: Typhoid Mary

MAJOR OFFENSE: A healthy carrier of typhoid fever, Mary was the first individual to be thus publicly identified in the United States.

ACTIVE: 1900-1915

LOCALE: New York, New York

SENTENCE: Quarantined and incarcerated against her will for nearly twenty-six years until her death, for protection of the public health

EARLY LIFE

Mary Mallon (MA-lon) was born on September 23, 1869, in County Tyrone, Ireland. She emigrated to the United States in 1883 and lived with her aunt in New York City. She later worked as a domestic servant, then became a cook for prominent New York families. Previously, Mallon had contracted a light case of typhoid fever. She probably never even knew she had it. Although she was asymptomatic and appeared healthy, she remained capable of spreading the disease to others.

CAPTURING MARY MALLON

Mary Mallon was a fighter. When George Soper, the man hired to track down the typhoid outbreak, tried to question her, he found that out quickly:

I had my first talk with Mary in the kitchen of this house.... I was as diplomatic as possible, but I had to say I suspected her of making people sick and that I wanted specimens of her urine, feces and blood. It did not take Mary long to react to this suggestion. She seized a carving fork and advanced in my direction. I passed rapidly down the long narrow hall, through the tall iron gate . . . and so to the sidewalk. I felt rather lucky to escape.

City authorities sent Dr. Josephine Baker next, perhaps on the theory that Mallon would trust another woman. Not so, it turned out:

Mary was on the lookout and peered out, a long kitchen fork in her hand like a rapier. As she lunged at me with the fork, I stepped back, recoiled on the policeman and so confused matters that, by the time we got through the door, Mary had disappeared. "Disappear" is too matter-of-fact a word; she had completely vanished.

She was finally discovered in a closet, hiding but undaunted:

She came out fighting and swearing, both of which she could do with appalling efficiency and vigor. I made another effort to talk to her sensibly and asked her again to let me have the specimens, but it was of no use. By that time she was convinced that the law was wantonly persecuting her, when she had done nothing wrong. She knew she had never had typhoid fever; she was maniacal in her integrity. There was nothing I could do but take her with us. The policemen lifted her into the ambulance and I literally sat on her all the way to the hospital; it was like being in a cage with an angry lion.

When finally confined to a hospital, her treatment by the staff outraged Mallon. She wrote in a letter,

I have been in fact a peep show for everybody. Even the interns had to come to see me and ask about the facts already known to the whole wide world. The tuberculosis men would say "There she is, the kidnapped woman."

Source: Judith Walzer Leavitt, Typhoid Mary: Captive to the Public's Health (Boston: Beacon Press, 1996).

DOMESTIC CAREER

Mallon worked as a cook for a number of prominent families in New York between 1900 and 1907, infecting twenty-two people during that time. After several members of one employer's household became infected, he hired George Soper, a sanitary engineer who had experience with typhoid outbreaks, to investigate. Soper proved that Mallon was the source of the infections. Mallon vehemently denied being sick or having typhoid and would not cooperate with authorities.

LEGAL ACTION AND OUTCOME

Mallon was taken into custody and quarantined for three years on North Brother Island in New York's East River. Upon her promise not to return to cooking or to work with food, she was released in 1910. Unable to make her way, she returned to cooking, the only skill she possessed by which she could earn a decent living. She then infected twenty-five people at Sloan Hospital, two of whom died. Mallon was seized again in 1915 and quarantined for the rest of her life. She died of pneumonia in 1938. At the time of her death she was found still to be contagious with typhoid bacilli.

IMPACT

The phrase "Typhoid Mary" entered the vernacular as a name given to a carrier of a contagious disease who refuses to comply with authorities to protect the public health. Mary Mallon's case involves a dilemma that has continued in the more recent emergence of infectious diseases and highlights the issue of how far authorities may go to protect the healthy population when a carrier's personal liberty is involved. The case of Typhoid Mary illuminates the human and social dimensions and dilemmas of disease control.

FURTHER READING

Bourdain, Anthony. *Typhoid Mary: An Urban Historical*. New York: Bloomsbury, 2004. This version of Mallon's case recognizes the dilemmas and dangers to both civil liberties and public health.

Gibbins, L. "Disease, Denial, and Detention." *Journal of Biological Education* 32, no. 2 (Summer, 1998): 127-132. Discusses the significance of Mallon's case in the context of emerging infectious diseases, including concepts of ethics, justice, and the role of the media.

Leavitt, Judith Walzer. *Typhoid Mary: Captive to the Public's Health*. New York: Beacon Press, 1996. Comprehensive study of Mallon's case covering the difficulties of respecting individual liberties while protecting the public's health. Extensive chapter notes with references.

—*Martha Oehmke Loustaunau*

SEE ALSO: Irish Invincibles.

WINNIE MANDELA
South African anti-apartheid activist and politician

BORN: September 26, 1936; Bizana, Transkei, South Africa

ALSO KNOWN AS: Winifred Nkosikazi Nobandle Nomzamo Madikizela Mandela (full name); Nomzamo Winifred Madikizela (birth name); Nkosikazi Nobandle Nomzamo Madikizela (full Xhosa name); Mother of the Nation

CAUSE OF NOTORIETY: Popular and well known for her decades-long struggle against apartheid, Mandela became a controversial figure because of both her use of violence against government informers and opponents and her convictions for fraud.

ACTIVE: 1960's-1990's

LOCALE: Soweto, South Africa

EARLY LIFE

The fifth of her parents' eight children, Winnie Mandela (WIH-nee man-DEH-lah) grew up in a religious family. She was trained in Johannesburg as a medical social worker and had an active working career at the Baragwanath Hospital prior to her joining the African National Congress (ANC), a center-left political party that fought against white minority rule (known as apartheid). In 1958, she married Nelson Mandela, an anti-apartheid political activist who at times resorted to violence in order to fight for equality and justice for South African black citizens. When her husband was arrested for high treason in 1962 and subsequently imprisoned for more than two decades, Winnie, the mother of two young children, embraced the anti-apartheid struggle fully. As

Winnie Mandela. (AP/Wide World Photos)

the new symbolic figure for the ANC's cause, she became a target of constant police surveillance and harassment. Her good works among the poor also won her considerable respect, and she came to be known as the Mother of the Nation.

In the late 1980's, Winnie was accused of ordering her bodyguard to assault and kidnap a fourteen-year-old ANC activist named Stompie Seipei; he was later found murdered. The murder, ostensibly carried out by the members of the Mandela United Football Club, was allegedly accomplished under the orders of Winnie. She also stood accused of eight other murders, including the assassination of her personal physician and friend Dr. Abu Baker Asvat, who witnessed the beating of Seipei and refused to side with her on the incident. Although Winnie was convicted in 1991 for the kidnapping and subsequent death of Seipei, her prison sentence was reduced to a fine, and she was never brought before the law for her alleged roles in the other murders.

POLITICAL CAREER

Winnie's political career received a boost in the decades that her husband remained in prison. However, her political activism led her to be imprisoned or banished to several locations over the years. After apartheid was dismantled in 1990 and her husband was released from jail, she was awarded with a political appointment as deputy minister for arts, culture, science, and technology in the post-apartheid regime headed by her husband.

However, her tenure as a deputy minister in the cabinet was quite turbulent, and she was fired after less than a year in office for ignoring party discipline and for allegations of corruption. Many saw her actions and rhetoric as less conciliatory toward the former white regime than that of her husband. Nelson and Winnie separated in 1992 and divorced in 1996. Winnie continued to retain her position as the head of the ANC's Women's League and her membership in parliament. However, she had to give up both positions in 2003 when she was convicted of charges of theft and fraud. The charges related to her participation in a scheme that used ANC stationery to secure loans for nonexistent Women's League employees. She appealed the conviction. In 2004, her original sentence of five years was reduced to` three and a half years, and she had the sentence suspended for five years. Her conviction for theft was also overturned. In arriving at this decision, the judge affirmed that Winnie had had a long and difficult role in public life and that she had in the past supported a cause greater than her own.

IMPACT

Winnie Mandela remained a controversial and charismatic figure. In 1997, she was arraigned before the Truth and Reconciliation Commission, which was led by Bishop Desmond Tutu, to answer to charges of terrorizing Sowetans with her bodyguards in the twilight days of apartheid. The commission had been set up by the government to investigate apartheid-era human rights violations and to promote reconciliation.

Several victims testified to the brutality that they or their loved ones had suffered at the hands of Winnie Mandela and her bodyguards. It was discovered that she had been aware of, and in several instances took part in, the terror inflicted on people by her bodyguards. Although Winnie continued to remain popular with the masses, she lost her exalted position in the ruling ANC.

FURTHER READING

Bezdrob, Anne Marie du Preez. *Winnie Mandela: A Life.* Cape Town, South Africa: Zebra Press, 2003. An in-depth biography that explores and reveals Mandela's personal and political life.

Gilbey, Emma. *The Lady: The Life and Times of Winnie Mandela*. London: Jonathan Cape, 1993. A comprehensive volume that traces Mandela's involvement in political struggles and her subsequent experiences, up to the period of being an accessory to violence.

Meltzer, Milton. *Winnie Mandela: The Soul of South Africa*. New York: Viking Kestrel, 1988. Covers the early life of Mandela and her struggles for equality.

Highlights her rise in power and gives readers a sense of her personality and political career.

Sampson, Anthony. *Mandela: The Authorized Biography*. New York: Knopf, 1999. Reflects on the life of Nelson Mandela. Draws extensively on interviews with Winnie Mandela.

—*Olutayo C. Adesina*

SEE ALSO: Eugene de Kock; Hendrik Frensch Verwoerd.

FREDERIKA MANDELBAUM
American fence

BORN: c. 1830; Hesse-Kassel, Germany
DIED: February 26, 1894; Hamilton, Ontario, Canada
ALSO KNOWN AS: Marm; Mother; Ma; Queen of Fences
CAUSE OF NOTORIETY: Mandelbaum was the largest fencer of stolen property in nineteenth century New York. She was arrested for possession of stolen property but was able to escape to Canada at a time when no extradition laws were in place.
ACTIVE: 1855-1884
LOCALE: New York, New York

EARLY LIFE

Frederika Mandelbaum (freh-deh-REE-kah MAN-dehl-bahm) was born in Germany of Jewish parents. In 1849, she emigrated to the United States with her husband, Wolfe, settling in New York City. In 1854, she and Wolfe opened a dry-goods and haberdashery store in lower Manhattan. Entertaining lavishly with her ill-gotten wealth and weighing more than 250 pounds, Mandelbaum was one of the most recognized and colorful hostesses of New York's booming criminal society.

CRIMINAL CAREER

By 1855, the haberdashery store had become a front for Mandelbaum's real business—being a fence, or a person who receives stolen goods from thieves and resells them for illicit gain. Criminals from throughout the city delivered their stolen goods to Mandelbaum and members of her gang. All items were carefully examined, and any identifying marks and labels were removed before Mandelbaum resold them. By all accounts, Mandelbaum brought an unprecedented efficiency and enterprise to the fencing racket. It is estimated that over her criminal

career, Mandelbaum fenced between seven and ten million dollars' worth of stolen property.

Some reminiscences indicate that Mandelbaum cared for her gang with motherly solicitude, in particular, the numerous pickpockets, male and female, she trained. For example, Adam Worth, known as the Napoleon of Crime, began his criminal career as part of the Mandelbaum racket, as did Sophie Lyons, a famous confidence woman. It was alleged, but not certain, that Mandelbaum financed the notorious three-million-dollar heist of the Manhattan Savings Bank in October, 1878.

LEGAL ACTION AND OUTCOME

Mandelbaum was the subject of numerous police inquiries starting in 1862. However, her system for obliterating the identity of stolen goods and moving them through her various warehouses was so efficient and her payoffs to police so extensive that no action against her was successful. Finally, in 1884, New York district attorney Peter Olney bypassed the police and employed the Pinkerton detective agency to infiltrate Mandelbaum's racket. On July 22, 1884, on the basis of the evidence accumulated by the Pinkerton detectives, Mandelbaum was arrested for possession of stolen property. She was released on a twenty-one-thousand-dollar bond. Shortly before her scheduled trial on December 4, 1884, she absconded to Toronto, allegedly with a fortune of nearly one million dollars. With no extradition law in effect, she remained in Canada and died there on February 26, 1894.

IMPACT

Frederika Mandelbaum was the most successful and notorious fence in American history. For twenty years, much of the plunder swiped by New York City's criminal elements passed through her system. Modern-day interest in the nineteenth century gangs of New York has sparked interest in the Queen of Fences. Scholarly interest has focused on Mandelbaum's prowess and capability in managing her criminal enterprise. She has also been cited for providing poor women with career "opportunities" as pickpockets and thieves and as a feminist pioneer of organized crime. Nevertheless, it seems misguided to assess Mandelbaum's impact as anything other than that of a successful criminal purveyor of stolen goods and a fugitive from justice.

FURTHER READING

Asbury, Herbert. *The Gangs of New York: An Informal History of the New York Underworld*. New York: Thunder's Mouth Press, 2004. First published in 1927, this classic account of the nineteenth century criminals of the Five Points and other sections of lower Manhattan inspired Martin Scorsese's 2002 film of the same name. It includes a vivid account of Mandelbaum's lavishly furnished New York home and soirées.

Morton, James. *Gangland: The Early Years*. London: Time Warner Books, 2003. A carefully researched, lively account of the gangs of New York, London, and Paris, and the forceful response of urban police, such as the Pinkertons.

Van Emery, Edward. *The Sins of New York: As "Exposed" by the "Police Gazette."* New York: Frederick A. Stokes, 1930. A history of crime in New York City according to its crime newspaper.

—Howard Bromberg

SEE ALSO: Adam Worth.

CHARLES MANSON
American mass murderer

BORN: November 12, 1934; Cincinnati, Ohio
ALSO KNOWN AS: Charles Milles Manson (full name); Charles Milles Maddox (birth name)
MAJOR OFFENSE: Murder
ACTIVE: August 9-10, 1969
LOCALE: Los Angeles, California
SENTENCE: Death penalty; later commuted to life in prison

EARLY LIFE

Charles Manson (MAN-suhn) was born in Cincinnati, Ohio, in 1934 and was raised primarily by his mother until the age of thirteen. His original name was Charles Maddox, but it was changed to Manson after his stepfather, who separated from Charles and his mother early in Manson's life. Manson's mother raised him in a strict religious environment, against which he rebelled, leading her to place him in a foster home. He was then moved to a boys' school in Indiana and later attempted to return to his mother.

When Manson's mother rebuffed his contact, he lived on the streets as a transient, supporting himself by committing minor crimes. When the seriousness of his crimes increased, however, Manson spent a substantial period of time in prison; he was eventually released in 1954. He married Rosalie Jean Willis, and the two

Charles Manson. (AP/Wide World Photos)

moved to California in 1955. There, Manson began committing crimes and in 1956 was again placed in prison. Manson's wife left California with another man, and Manson spent most of his time in prison over the next dozen years for a string of mostly minor crimes. He was released in 1967.

CRIMINAL CAREER

After being released from prison in 1967, Manson spent time on the streets of the Haight-Ashbury neighborhood of San Francisco, meeting a number of young women whom Manson would soon call his "Family." These young adults were bound together by their belief in antiestablishment philosophy, drug use, and a strong devotion to Manson. Indeed, many in this group believed that Manson was Jesus Christ. Manson's Family grew in the late 1960's to include nearly one hundred associated members and between twenty and thirty hard-core members after it had moved back to the Los Angeles area.

On August 9, 1969, Manson instructed four of his most loyal followers to commit murder. At around midnight, Family members Charles Watson, Patricia Krenwinkel, Susan Atkins, and Linda Kasabian arrived at the home of film director Roman Polanski and his wife, actor Sharon Tate. Manson had given the group orders to kill everyone they found inside, and upon arrival, they immediately cut phone lines and began to approach the house. At about that time, Steven Parent, a friend of a caretaker for the house, was driving out of the main entrance when he was shot and killed by Watson.

After Parent was killed, Kasabian expressed trauma over the killing and was told to remain at the car while the other three proceeded to the house. When inside the house, they gathered all four of the occupants—Jay Sebring, Wojciech Frykowski, Abigail Folger, and Tate—into the living room and began to kill them. Tate was the last to be killed, and her blood was used to write the word "pig" on the front door of the house.

The next night, Manson, Watson, Krenwinkel, and Leslie Van Houton drove to the house of Leon LaBianca and his wife, Rosemary LaBianca, in Los Angeles. Manson entered the house and tied up the couple. He then instructed the three followers to kill the victims. After killing the LaBiancas, the three Family members carved the word "war" into Leon's flesh and then used the victims'

ATWA: AIR, TREES, WATER, ANIMALS

Charles Manson continued to propagate his megalomaniacal philosophies from a Web site, http://www.mansondirect.com, as late as 2006. Here are some of his remarks about his environment-directed philosophy, ATWA, which he claims was a motivation for the actions of the Family:

All we say to each other can be true, right, and reassuring, but what good is it without ATWA? ATWA is like an earth ship and pollution is a hole in it and it is sinking as we are all playing ego roles of games that do nothing for ATWA. All live for ATWA or no one lives. All must have a one world government, money, army, all in order to bring order in fast and reset all to ATWA for life itself and all life support systems set in order, balance, and God's will. Real of it is who would want the job? No one, no one. But zero knows that without one there will be no one. Someone must pick up the one and that's what we did and it is running and rolling now. If a man stood and yelled all the names of all the bugs and bushes, wildlife and birds that are becoming extinct, gone from earth, he would be yelling all day and all night. Life is dying faster each day and there is zero, no one who will pick it up to try. The last people who picked it up to fix it was killed (swastika). Japan was running out of space and Germany's only got 15 eagles left and money cuts billions of trees each day.

Your planet is dying and so-called humans can't forgive the kids of the 60's for trying to warn you to bring change, stop the war and turn it around. . . .

Ecology, ecology, ecology is god, for without it we are dead forever—no life on earth. . . . God's coming is not for the glory of people but the kingdom of life and that's bugs, birds, bees, wildlife, trees, fish.

When you live for what others think, you're not ATWA. You're not alive. . . .

---

blood to write "death to the pigs" and "rise" on walls in the house and the misspelled "healther skelter" on the refrigerator.

The murders at the Tate residence created panic within the Hollywood community, and some noted film stars began to carry protection and add security to their homes. Law enforcement originally investigated the possibility of drug involvement in the murders of Tate and her friends and did not believe that these murders were connected to the LaBianca murders.

LEGAL ACTION AND OUTCOME

Soon after the murders, Manson and a number of his followers were arrested at the Barker Ranch in the Mojave Desert on charges unrelated to the murders. While in detention, Atkins bragged to another inmate that the Family had been responsible for the Tate and LaBianca murders and that they planned to kill more celebrities in the future. This confession, along with other interviews of Family members, led to the arrest of Manson and five of his followers on charges of murder.

Through interviews with Family members and others associated with Manson, prosecutor Vincent Bugliosi established Manson's motive for murder as centering on an attempt to begin a race war, which Manson labeled "Helter Skelter" after the Beatles' song. Manson convinced some Family members that if they could inspire a race war, black Americans would defeat the white Americans but then would have to rely on the Family for guidance on how to run the earth.

Kasabian and Atkins served as the key witnesses against Manson for the prosecution. Manson, along with Watson, Kasabian, Atkins, and Krenwinkel, was convicted and sentenced to death. This sentence was later commuted to life in prison when California abolished its death penalty.

IMPACT

The peculiar nature, habits, and loyalty of his cult members and the notorious crimes that they committed helped make Charles Manson one of the most famous criminal figures in the history of the United States. Incredibly,

well into the twenty-first century, Manson was still receiving thousands of letters in prison from fans each year. His crimes remain perhaps the most extreme and shocking occurrence of the 1960's counterculture movement, most significantly for their reflection of the way in which the youthful rebellion and moral outrage of the times could be perverted into pure evil.

FURTHER READING

Bugliosi, Vincent. *Helter Skelter: The True Story of the Manson Murders*. New York: W. W. Norton, 1974. Written by the prosecutor in the Manson case, the book provides details of the crimes and chronicles the events of the trial.

Koopmans, Andy. *Charles Manson*. San Diego, Calif.: Lucent Books, 2005. Traces Manson's life from his childhood through the Tate and LaBianca murders and into his years in prison.

Sanders, Ed. *The Family*. New York: Thunder Mountain Press, 2002. Focuses on the development of Manson's Family and its inner workings and increasingly strange behavior, which eventually led to mass murder.

—*Brion Sever*

SEE ALSO: Lynette Fromme; Charles Sobraj.

MAO ZEDONG
Chinese Communist Party chairman (1935-1976) and preeminent Chinese leader (1949-1976)

BORN: December 26, 1893; Shaoshan, Hunan Province, China

DIED: September 9, 1976; Beijing, China

ALSO KNOWN AS: Chairman Mao; Mao Tse-tung (Wade-Giles)

CAUSE OF NOTORIETY: Mao, a master politician, was instrumental in bringing the Communist Party to power in China. However, his rise to political eminence perpetrated a lifelong betrayal of his family, associates, and finally the Chinese peasant class, in whose name he led his successful but brutal Cultural Revolution.

ACTIVE: 1935-1976

LOCALE: China

EARLY LIFE

Mao Zedong (mow zuh-DOWNG) was born on December 26, 1893, in the village of Shaoshan, located in Hunan Province in south-central China. His father was a prosperous peasant by the standards of the village, although only modestly successful by Chinese national standards. Mao's father sent Mao to school hoping he would learn to read, write, and do arithmetic so he could help with the family's business accounts, but Mao wanted a far broader education. When Mao's father prohibited this, Mao threatened to commit suicide by drowning. Mao's ploy forced his father to back down. Mao's actions were a clear betrayal of his duty of filial piety according to Chinese Confucian principles.

691

Mao's early success in outmaneuvering his father may have emboldened him to begin his long betrayal of nearly every person close to him. Mao also betrayed his father by rejecting his father's arranged marriage—Mao's first of four marriages. Mao also betrayed his second wife, Yang Kai-hui, the daughter of one of his Beijing University professors. After she bore him two children, he left her with her relatives in order to begin working in the Communist Party commune in the mountains of Hunan and Jiangxi Provinces. There, he began a relationship with an eighteen-year-old peasant girl, He Zizhen. During Mao's absence, his second wife was killed by the troops of Chinese nationalist leader Chiang Kai-shek, and Mao's children disappeared. After becoming Mao's third wife, He endured commune life and accompanied Mao on the horrible three-thousand-mile trek in 1934 known as the Long March; she became a revolutionary war hero in her own right. She bore Mao six children, was wounded, and suffered other serious health problems. Under these circumstances, Mao deserted He

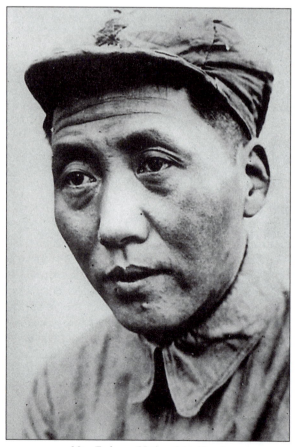

Mao Zedong. (National Archives)

for a younger woman, the modestly successful film actress Jiang Qing, who would later become his fourth wife.

POLITICAL CAREER

Mao rose to such a prominent position in the Communist Party that the party leaders felt obliged to allow him to divorce his third wife and marry Jiang Qing. The leadership made Mao promise that Jiang Qing would never be active in politics—a vow Mao also broke in the late 1960's, but not before he had tired of Jiang Qing and begun a long string of trysts with young Chinese girls at weekly (and later biweekly) "dance" parties for high Communist Party officials.

Liu Shaoqi had labored for years as Mao's confidant and revolutionary aide. However, when it served Mao's political purposes to remove Liu from his position as Mao's heir apparent in 1966, Mao launched the devastating Great Proletarian Cultural Revolution in part to depose Liu. Liu—subsequently deprived of proper food, clothing, and medicine—died in a cold, damp prison cell in 1969. Long-term revolutionary military leader Lin Biao replaced Liu as heir apparent. Despite Mao having saluted Lin as his longtime comrade in arms and heir apparent, Mao also abandoned Lin in 1971. The official story was that Lin died in a plane crash while trying to escape as a traitor to the Soviet Union, but other accounts maintain that Mao had Lin assassinated.

In the public sphere, Mao clearly betrayed the great mass of the Chinese people—the peasants who made up about 90 percent of the total Chinese population—by systematically extracting the agricultural goods they produced in order to pay for the rapid industrial production that Mao felt was necessary to make China into a great industrial power. The peasants made up the vast majority of his rebel army, and it was in their name that revolution was enacted. However, Mao was willing to sacrifice their efforts to achieve what he perceived to be the greater goal of making China a world industrial power. This situation may have been compounded by Mao's need to repay Stalinist Russia for Russian loans to China.

Nonetheless, Mao forced the Chinese peasants—more than any other Chinese group—to pay for China's industrialization. Nowhere was this more evident than in Mao's catastrophic Great Leap Forward campaign, which was designed to outstrip British industrial production in just a few years. This campaign encouraged peasants to abandon traditional farming practices in favor of building backyard iron-smelting furnaces. Following

Mao's exhortations, peasants tore up railroad tracks and threw away perfectly good steel rails (and even their own pots and pans) in order to make virtually useless pig iron. Scarce firewood and even household furnishings were thrown into fires to keep the furnaces at requisitely high temperatures.

Abandoning traditional farming practices also resulted in the largest famine in recorded history: Approximately 20 to 60 million Chinese died between 1959 and 1961. Mao said the famine was caused by the weather, noting that flooding and droughts were to blame; however, the weather was not noticeably worse in China during those years than at times when no famine had occurred. Clearly Mao's policies, however much influenced by the need to repay the Russians, were the real cause of the famine.

IMPACT

Mao Zedong fought a decades-long civil war in order to achieve a Communist revolution, which aimed at improving the economic circumstances of the Chinese and led to the promotion of a new socialist Chinese identity at the personal level: The Chinese were expected to be chaste and of the highest moral order. Mao betrayed the Communist revolution not only by failing to achieve its economic objectives but also by betraying the revolutionary ideals with his atrocious personal behavior. Indirectly, Mao's oppressive Cultural Revolution in the new Communist China may well have been responsible for more deaths than any other regime of the twentieth century, with the possible exceptions of Germany under Adolf Hitler and the Soviet Union under Joseph Stalin.

FURTHER READING

Li Zhisui. *The Private Life of Chairman Mao*. New York: Random House, 1997. From 1954 until Mao's death in 1976, Li was his personal physician. His memoir provides fascinating information about Mao's physical condition and his personal life. No other person has provided such an intimate portrait of the man. Li reviews many details of Mao's voracious sexual appetite, as well as the medical conclusion that Mao was sterile and could not have been the father of the daughter born to Mao's last long-term mistress.

MacFarquhar, Roderick, ed. *The Politics of China: The Eras of Mao and Deng*. 2d ed. New York: Cambridge University Press, 1997. Describing Chinese politics from 1949 to 1993, the book details Mao's critical role in those events. Frederick Teiwes, Kenneth Lieberthal, Harry Harding, and Roderick MacFarquhar each provide profoundly important chapters in this seminal scholarly work.

Pye, Lucian W. *Mao Tse-Tung: The Man in the Leader*. New York: Basic Books, 1976. This biography has become a classic and is especially useful for identifying the psychological characteristics of Mao from his childhood through his death.

MAO'S FABLE OF PERSEVERANCE

On June 11, 1945, Mao spoke to the Seventh National Congress of the Communist Party of China. He characterized the party's underlying policy in an adaptation of a traditional folktale:

We must first raise the political consciousness of the vanguard so that, resolute and unafraid of sacrifice, they will surmount every difficulty to win victory. But this is not enough; we must also arouse the political consciousness of the entire people so that they may willingly and gladly fight together with us for victory. We should fire the whole people with the conviction that China belongs not to the reactionaries but to the Chinese people. There is an ancient Chinese fable called "The Foolish Old Man Who Removed the Mountains." It tells of an old man who lived in northern China long, long ago and was known as the Foolish Old Man of North Mountain. His house faced south and beyond his doorway stood the two great peaks, Taihang and Wangwu, obstructing the way. He called his sons, and hoe in hand they began to dig up these mountains with great determination. Another graybeard, known as the Wise Old Man, saw them and said derisively, "How silly of you to do this! It is quite impossible for you few to dig up those two huge mountains." The Foolish Old Man replied, "When I die, my sons will carry on; when they die, there will be my grandsons, and then their sons and grandsons, and so on to infinity. High as they are, the mountains cannot grow any higher and with every bit we dig, they will be that much lower. Why can't we clear them away?" Having refuted the Wise Old Man's wrong view, he went on digging every day, unshaken in his conviction. God was moved by this, and he sent down two angels, who carried the mountains away on their backs. Today, two big mountains lie like a dead weight on the Chinese people. One is imperialism, the other is feudalism. The Chinese Communist Party has long made up its mind to dig them up. We must persevere and work unceasingly, and we, too, will touch God's heart. Our God is none other than the masses of the Chinese people. If they stand up and dig together with us, why can't these two mountains be cleared away?

Spence, Jonathan. *Mao Zedong*. New York: Viking Penguin, 1999. This insightful account by one of the greatest living China scholars provides a concise, readable biography.

Terrell, Ross. *Mao: A Biography*. New York: Harper and Row, 1980. One of the most readable, if somewhat

dated, accounts of Mao's life, written by a well-known observer of China.

—*Richard L. Wilson*

SEE ALSO: Jiang Qing.

SALVATORE MARANZANO
Organized crime boss

BORN: 1868; Castellammare del Golfo, Sicily, Italy
DIED: September 10, 1931; New York, New York
ALSO KNOWN AS: Capo di Tutti Capi (Boss of Bosses); Little Caesar
CAUSE OF NOTORIETY: Maranzano engaged in bootlegging and loan-sharking, among other crimes, and his attempts to usurp power from Joe Masseria, the reigning Mafia boss, led to the famed Castellammarese War.
ACTIVE: 1920-September 10, 1931
LOCALE: New York, New York

EARLY LIFE

His family ties and the citizens of Castellammare del Golfo, Sicily, Italy, strongly influenced the childhood development of Salvatore Maranzano (mar-ahn-ZAHN-oh). He distinguished himself early in his academic career as a scholar worthy of higher education and intellectual pursuits. Young Maranzano studied the classics, including Greek and Latin. Eventually, he would enter the seminary to become a priest; however, he lost interest in the rigors of religious life and turned to the more lucrative advantages of organized crime. He joined the Italian Mafia and became one of the few educated "men of honor." Maranzano eventually departed Italy to make his fortune in the United States; however, he never mastered the fundamentals of the English language as well as his accomplished Greek and Latin studies.

GANGSTER CAREER

Maranzano's physical stature, handsome appearance, and classical manners earned him respect in every endeavor and distinguished him as a formidable leader. He became a significant member of the Italian Mafia. Maranzano would occasionally use his formal Latin education to impress others, often leaving his less intellectually inclined listeners in a state of confusion and dismay. However, his blind ambition made the elder

Mafiosi feel threatened and earned him their hostility. In addition, the young Maranzano started to attract police attention. The combination of increased surveillance and disgruntled Mafiosi encouraged Maranzano's immigration to the United States shortly after World War I. Almost immediately, Maranzano established the Honored Society, which called as its members carefully selected criminals.

Maranzano's Honored Society Mafia faction specialized in bootlegging, loan-sharking, Italian lottery, and extorting local businesspeople. In addition, he arranged legal and illegal immigration rackets; desperate immigrants would then owe him a financial and loyalty debt. The threat of violence or deportation enhanced his power and influence; many of those he intimidated served as recruits for his emergent criminal empire.

Maranzano, a gentleman don, had disdain for direct participation in illicit activities; he preferred to remain above the ordinary fray and focus on the rewards reaped from abundant political power. Maranzano viewed people as pawns on a chessboard and attempted to checkmate the reigning Mafia boss, Joe Masseria. However, Maranzano, the challenger, lacked the power to eliminate Masseria, so he waited patiently and conspired with others until he could gain more influence.

The conflict between the two men started in 1930, when Masseria ordered attacks on Maranzano's key faction. Maranzano then ordered his supporters and thugs to hijack Masseria's bootleg liquor trucks. The hijackings and territorial encroachment for lottery and protection rackets enraged Masseria. These financial setbacks would eventually lead to a cycle of violence referred to as the Castellammarese War; numerous killings occurred on both sides.

Maranzano's strategic objective was to achieve absolute domination and become capo di tutti capi, or boss of all bosses. Maranzano deplored Masseria as an ill-mannered slob, unworthy of the American Mafia crown.

Moreover, Masseria underestimated Maranzano: He regarded him as an arrogant, pretentious status seeker, with little chance of captivating the prestigious and lucrative position as heir apparent of American organized crime.

The proverbial man in the middle of the "war," Lucky Luciano, earned his nickname after surviving an enormous beating ordered by Maranzano. The assault included torture; the resulting knife wounds to Luciano's face and chest required fifty-five stitches. The objective was to frighten Luciano into joining Maranzano's faction and use him to arrange the inside killing of Masseria. However, Luciano refused to betray Masseria under the torture, and Maranazano let him live—the biggest error of his criminal career. Luciano would survive to organize the murders of both Maranzano and Masseria.

On April 15, 1931, Luciano excused himself to use the men's room, leaving Masseria alone in the Nuova Villa Tammaro Italian restaurant. After finishing dinner and some card playing, Masseria was confronted by a hit team and was shot six times. Masseria died holding the ace of diamonds, a future symbol of a Mafia death threat.

Luciano then turned his attention to Maranzano, who was planning his execution gangland style. Maranzano hired a hit man by the name of Vincent "Mad Dog" Coll. However, Luciano conducted a peremptory strike, leaving Maranzano's contract invalid, and the Coll threat disappeared. On September 10, 1931, Meyer Lansky's associates posed as law enforcement officers, forced their way into Maranzano's office, and killed him.

Maranzano greatly admired Julius Caesar, who served as his role model for leadership. He often compared his own life with that of the great Roman conqueror and the Mafia to the Roman Empire. Unfortunately, he did not learn the prophetic lessons of Caesar's political life. He died like his hero, the victim of his own power and lust, left in a pool of blood.

IMPACT

Joe Masseria and Salvatore Maranzano failed to comprehend the discontent, anger, and rage of the younger Mafia generation born in the United States. The men's autocratic leadership and need for power and control set in motion a conspiracy to eliminate them. Their deaths provided the opportunity to set the foundation for a compromise and an adjudication system for competing factions. The Chicago meeting in the fall of 1931 set the stage for organizational change and laid the foundation for five organized crime families.

Lucky Luciano emerged as a different kind of leader: He refused the position of boss of bosses and earned considerable respect. The new Italian version of organized crime included working with other criminal groups and improving cooperation. However, the new commission would be restricted to Italians, with each member having an equal vote. Luciano would modernize the Mafia and build a business-oriented criminal organization that dominated American organized crime for decades.

FURTHER READING

Abadinsky, Howard. *Organized Crime.* 7th ed. Belmont, Calif.: Wadsworth/Thomson Learning, 2003. An in-depth analysis of organized crime from a historical and theoretical perspective.

Lyman, Michael D., and Gary W. Potter. *Organized Crime.* Upper Saddle River, N.J.: Pearson/Prentice Hall, 2004. A comprehensive textbook, including the essentials of organized crime theory and practice.

Raab, Selwyn. *The Five Families: The Rise, Decline, and Resurgence of America's Most Powerful Mafia Empires.* New York: St. Martin's Press, 2005. Discusses the history of the Sicilian Mafia in the United States.

Mass, Peter. *The Valachi Papers.* New York: HarperCollins Paperbacks, 2003. The original classic published in 1968 serves as the foundation and major source for the Masseria and Maranzano organized crime conflict.

—*Thomas E. Baker*

SEE ALSO: Vincent Coll; Meyer Lansky; Tommy Lucchese; Lucky Luciano; Joe Masseria.

JEAN-PAUL MARAT
French revolutionary journalist

BORN: May 24, 1743; Boudry, Switzerland
DIED: July 13, 1793; Paris, France
ALSO KNOWN AS: People's Friend; Wrath of the
People
CAUSE OF NOTORIETY: A member of the radical
Jacobin faction during the French Revolution,
Marat and his inflammatory publications intensified
the Reign of Terror.
ACTIVE: 1789-1793
LOCALE: Paris, France

EARLY LIFE

Jean-Paul Marat (zhahn-pawl mah-rah) was born in the
principality of Neuchâtel in Switzerland to a Sardinian
father and a Genevan mother. He studied medicine in
Bordeaux and lived in Paris and Holland before opening a medical practice in London. A prolific writing career began with his *De l'homme* (1773; *Philosophical
Essay on Man*, 1773), which attacked French philosopher Claude-Adrien Helvétius's claim that science was
unnecessary for a philosopher. The following year, *Chains of Slavery* appeared written in English, supporting popular election
of members to parliament; it was published
in French under the title *Les Chaînes de
l'esclavage* in 1793. Marat's medical pamphlets and success as a practician earned
him a position as physician to the guards of
the count of Artois and later to Charles X of
France.

In Paris, Marat published pseudoscientific theories about optics, heat, light, and
electricity but nevertheless won admiration
from American statesman Benjamin Franklin and German dramatist Johann Wolfgang
von Goethe. His interest in social issues reappeared in 1780, when he published *Plan
de législation criminelle* (plan of criminal
legislation), inspired by the Italian philosopher Cesare, marquis of Beccaria.

REVOLUTIONARY CAREER

Until the violent summer of 1789, Marat
remained more of a moderate reformer than
a radical revolutionary. However, with the
calling of the Estates-General (an assembly of several classes of French subjects),

Marat published *Offrande à la patrie* (1788; offering to
our country), arguing that the Third Estate best represented the nation. Turning to journalism, Marat began
publishing his newspaper *L'Ami du Peuple* (friend of the
people), in which his constant demagogic attacks upon
suspected traitors soon earned him his notorious reputation as a firebrand. Amid the revolutionary events of
1789, Marat, calling himself the Wrath of the People,
took up the cause of the common person, denouncing
misery and persecution of the poor and attributing such
suffering to the machinations of the rich. Marat helped
incite the insurrection of early October, 1789, when an
angry crowd forced the royal family to move from Versailles to Paris.

Marat's infamous rhetoric established his reputation
as the most bloodthirsty of the revolutionaries. On July
26, 1790, he famously declared that "peace, liberty, and
happiness" would be assured by "five or six hundred
heads chopped off." After the massacre of patriots on the
Champ-de-Mars on July 17, 1791, Marat offered to lead

Jean-Paul Marat.

two thousand revolutionaries to tear out the marquis de Lafayette's heart, burn to death the king and his ministers in the royal palace, and impale deputies of the National Assembly on their seats.

Marat's written attacks upon the Constituent Assembly, ministers, the city, the courts, Lafayette, and Louis XVI led to a call in early 1790 for his arrest, and Marat fled to London. He was forced to publish his newspapers and placards clandestinely, often hiding in dank cellars and sewers, where he contracted or exacerbated a horrible skin disease.

In April, 1792, under protection from the Cordeliers Club, Marat began denouncing the war plans of the king's Girondin ministry, which he, like revolution leader Robespierre, feared would bring about a military coup. After French forces were defeated by invading Prussians in August, 1792, Marat's press roused the sanculottes (a working-class political group) to be on guard against counterrevolutionaries in their midst. His words contributed to the frenzied slaughter of aristocrats, priests, and common criminals in prisons during the September Massacres.

Marat was then elected as a deputy to the National Convention, which was called to draw up a republican constitution. Marat became a member of the Committee of Surveillance, which was responsible for identifying enemies of the revolution. He continued to attack Girondins, and during debates on whether the king should be executed, he shrewdly moved that a roll-call vote be taken to "expose enemies of the Revolution."

On July 13, 1793, Charlotte Corday, a young woman from Caen with sympathies for the Girondins, came to Marat's home supposedly to report on counterrevolu-tionary activity. She stabbed Marat to death in his bath, where he routinely sought relief from his skin afflictions. Marat's ashes were buried in the Pantheon in 1794, only to be removed the following year by the Thermidorians.

IMPACT

From Françoise-Noël Babeuf to Leon Trotsky, revolutionary commanders have repeated Jean-Paul Marat's demands for permanent vigilance against traitors to the cause. Apologists for Marat point out that his predictions about the betrayals of the generals Lafayette and Charles-François Dumouriez were on target, as was his suspicion that the king would try to flee France to join the émigrés. Furthermore, Marat sought a social revolution not only against the aristocracy of the Old Regime but also against any aristocracy of wealth. To those horrified by the bloodshed of the Reign of Terror, Marat warned, "No one should find it odd that the people, pushed to despair, impose their own justice."

FURTHER READING

Conner, Clifford D. *Jean Paul Marat: Scientist and Revolutionary*. Atlantic Highlands, N.J.: Humanities Press International, 1997. A sympathetic biography of Marat, rehabilitating his scientific theories and establishing the reasons for his fiery accusations.

Gottschalk, Louis. *Jean Paul Marat: A Study in Radicalism*. Chicago: University of Chicago Press, 1967. A balanced study focusing on Marat's political theories.

—*Bland Addison*

SEE ALSO: Charlotte Corday; Marie-Antoinette; Robespierre.

CARLOS MARCELLO
American Mafia don

BORN: February 6, 1910; Tunis, Tunisia
DIED: March 3, 1993; Metairie, Louisiana
ALSO KNOWN AS: Calogero Minacore (birth name);
Little Man
MAJOR OFFENSES: Racketeering, mail, and wire
fraud; bribery; also suspected of involvement in a
plot to assassinate President John F. Kennedy
ACTIVE: 1947-1980
LOCALE: New Orleans, Louisiana
SENTENCE: Seven years in federal prison and $250,000
fine for fraud, bribery, and racketeering; ten years in
federal prison and $25,000 fine for bribery

EARLY LIFE
Carlos Marcello (KAHR-lohs mar-SEH-loh) was born
Calogero Minacore, the eldest son of Sicilian émigrés to
Tunisia. Within a year of his birth, the family moved to
New Orleans, Louisiana, where Carlos's father acquired
a farm and changed the family name to Marcello. As a
youth, Carlos helped deliver produce to New Orleans
markets controlled by the Mafia. After dropping out of
school at age fourteen, he began a crime spree that led to
his imprisonment for robbery when he was twenty. Four
years later, he was pardoned by the governor as a political favor to a family friend. Upon his return to New Orleans in 1934, Marcello bought a bar, from which he sold
illegal drugs. At the same time he began working as an
enforcer and entrepreneur for the New Orleans Mafia;
his diminutive stature earned him the sobriquet the Little
Man.

CRIMINAL CAREER
In 1936, Marcello was formally inducted into the New
Orleans Mafia, then controlled by Sam Carolla and his
deputy Frank Todaro, whose daughter Jacqueline married Marcello in 1938. Despite being imprisoned again
briefly in 1938 for selling narcotics, between 1934 and
1947 Marcello established a number of businesses, most
notably the Jefferson Music Company, which became a
front for distributing illegal slot machines. Though
charged four times for crimes such as assault, sale of narcotics, and tax code violations, he used his political
connections to avoid indictment. His brutal tactics in
controlling the slot machine business and his other work
for the New Orleans Mafia were rewarded in 1947, when
Marcello was named head of the organization upon
Carolla's deportation.

During the 1950's, Marcello ran many of his illegal
ventures in the open. He claimed he avoided prison by
paying off local and state government and police officials. Federal officials, however, had identified him as a
leader of underworld activity and as early as 1951 began
calling him to appear before commissions investigating
organized crime. At such hearings Marcello refused to
answer any questions, invoking his Fifth Amendment
rights. His stonewalling infuriated Robert F. Kennedy,
counsel to the 1959 McClellan Committee. When Kennedy became U.S. attorney general in 1961, he made
Marcello a primary focus of his effort to eliminate organized crime in the United States.

Marcello had never become a U.S. citizen. The federal government had been trying to deport him since
1953, but he had stymied its attempts by obtaining a
forged Guatemalan birth certificate and passport. In
1961, Kennedy had Marcello arrested and deported to
Guatemala without a hearing. Four months later, Marcello was back in New Orleans, infuriated by the treatment he had received and threatening revenge against
the attorney general and Kennedy's brother John, the
president.

John F. Kennedy was assassinated in 1963; however,
the official investigation into his death did not implicate
anyone other than Lee Harvey Oswald. Later investigations revealed Marcello's connection to Oswald and almost every other key individual involved in conspiracies
to assassinate President Kennedy, his brother Robert,
and Martin Luther King, Jr. Despite these revelations, no
charges were ever filed against Marcello in connection
with the assassinations.

During the 1960's and 1970's, several further attempts were made to deport Marcello or indict him for
crimes. He managed to avoid prosecution and continued
to expand his network of corruption throughout Louisiana and in Texas. By 1970, his operation was generating
two billion dollars annually. He was finally brought to
justice for Mafia-related activities through an elaborate
federal scheme that included planting listening devices
in his office and having an informer and two Federal Bureau of Investigation (FBI) agents infiltrate Marcello's
organization. Evidence collected in this fashion finally
allowed the government to indict Marcello—both in
New Orleans for insurance fraud and in Los Angeles for
attempting to bribe a federal judge to keep a fellow mobster out of prison.

LEGAL ACTION AND OUTCOME

Marcello was indicted under the Racketeer Influenced and Corrupt Organizations Act (RICO) in 1980 for racketeering, mail fraud, wire fraud, and bribery. He was tried in federal court in New Orleans in 1981 and found guilty. Several months later, a Los Angeles jury found him guilty of bribery. After his appeals were exhausted, Marcello entered the federal penal system in 1983 and spent nearly ten years in federal penitentiaries. He was released shortly before his death in 1993.

IMPACT

The extensive government effort to obtain evidence on Carlos Marcello's illegal operations had a chilling effect on organized crime in the United States. The tenacity and ingenuity of the FBI made it clear that the government was serious about prosecuting reputed Mafia leaders. In addition, Marcello's imprisonment led to an almost immediate shift of power in Louisiana's underworld scene; members of his organization began running his operations without his approval, and mobsters from New York and other cities moved into Louisiana to set up independent criminal networks.

FURTHER READING

Davis, John H. *Mafia Kingfish*. New York: McGraw-Hill, 1989. Provides a comprehensive, detailed account of Marcello's life of crime, focusing on his involvement with plots to assassinate President John F. Kennedy.

Raab, Selwyn. *Five Families: The Rise, Decline, and Resurgence of America's Most Powerful Mafia Empires*. New York: St. Martin's Press, 2005. Extensive history of the Mafia by an investigative reporter includes information about Marcello's activities and his links with the New York crime syndicates.

Ragano, Frank, and Selwyn Raab. *Mob Lawyer*. New York: Scribner's, 1994. A lawyer who worked for Marcello and a number of his associates reveals the inner workings of the Mafia.

Reppetto, Thomas. *American Mafia*. New York: Henry Holt, 2004. This account of the influence of the Mafia in the twentieth century and the U.S. government's attempts to eradicate its activities offers useful background for understanding Marcello's lifestyle and activities.

—*Laurence W. Mazzeno*

SEE ALSO: Lee Harvey Oswald; Clay Shaw.

FERDINAND MARCOS
President of the Philippines (1965-1986)

BORN: September 11, 1917; Sarrat, Philippines
DIED: September 28, 1989; Honolulu, Hawaii
ALSO KNOWN AS: Ferdinand Edralin Marcos (full name)
MAJOR OFFENSES: As the leader of the Philippines for two decades, Marcos plundered the country's assets and violated human rights.
ACTIVE: 1965-1986
LOCALE: Philippines

EARLY LIFE

Of Filipino, Chinese, and Japanese ancestry, Ferdinand Edralin Marcos (FAYR-dee-nahnd EHD-rah-leen MAHR-cohs) grew up in Ilocos Province before moving to Manila after his father was elected to the Philippine Congress. After completing secondary education, Marcos obtained a law degree from the University of the Philippines in 1939. Although convicted of assassinating one of his father's political rivals in 1939, he was acquitted after an appeal in 1940.

During World War II, Marcos was a Philippine army intelligence officer. In 1942, following the Japanese occupation of the Philippines, he went behind enemy lines, killed more than fifty Japanese soldiers, and destroyed mortars; he was captured and tortured by the Japanese but escaped. Captured once again, Marcos survived the Bataan Death March and escaped.

POLITICAL CAREER

After the war, Marcos used his reputation as a war hero to become involved in politics. He first became an assistant to President Manuel Roxas y Acuña. In 1949, he won the first of three terms in the House of Representatives. In 1954, he married Imelda Romualdez, who helped him win the first of two terms to the Senate in 1959 and to defeat incumbent Diosdado Macapagal to become president in 1965. He was reelected in 1969, becoming the first Philippine president to serve two terms.

During his first terms as president, Marcos accepted credit for improvements in the economic infrastructure, a

Ferdinand Marcos with his wife, Imelda, in 1965. (AP/Wide World Photos)

reduction in unemployment, and more efficient tax collection. However, unwilling to step down at the end of his second term and blaming numerous bombings in Manila on the Maoist insurgency group, the New People's Army, he declared martial law on September 21, 1972, and said that he was selected by "citizen assemblies," which allegedly ratified his "election" to another term. He claimed to be a "constitutional authoritarian" ruler, eager to build a new society. Soon, Washington, D.C., provided lavish funds to fight alleged communists and domestic Muslim separatists, but the aid was squandered by Marcos and his cronies. Opposition leaders were jailed, and the Marcos administration became a dictatorship.

Next, Marcos appointed political associates and family members, including his wife Imelda, to various government positions in order to wrest economic control from the aristocratic families that had long dominated the country. As he looted the treasury of billions of dollars,

many members of the economic aristocracy transferred assets out of the country. Some 150 blue-chip companies either were seized by the government or were bought out and awarded to political insiders.

In 1978, Marcos scheduled elections and was elected for a six-year term, though election fraud was widely assumed. His rival, opposition politician Benigno Aquino, Jr., who had been imprisoned in 1972 at the beginning of martial law, also protested the fraud but was allowed to leave the country for medical treatment in 1980. In 1981, martial law was lifted, a condition imposed by Pope John Paul II before his visit that year. Nevertheless, Marcos retained the power to rule by decree.

During the 1980's, evidence of economic crisis became increasingly obvious. Ill with lupus and needing kidney dialysis, Marcos was unable to monitor the political scene closely. In 1983, Aquino decided to return to the Philippines to garner support for another presidential contest; he was assassinated upon his arrival, and Marcos was widely assumed to have been behind the murder. General Fabian Ver and other high-ranking military officers were acquitted for the offense in 1985, a verdict that the public did not accept. In 1990, sixteen military officers were convicted of the offense.

Meanwhile, American military intelligence feared that the New People's Army was gaining increasing support. Washington authorities felt that rather than eradicating the communists, as he had pledged to do, Marcos and his dictatorial rule instead had become a rallying point both for insurgency movements (many of which were communist-leaning movements) and for increasing anti-American attitudes throughout the Philippines.

Accordingly, pressure from Washington resulted in a snap election in 1986. Marcos faced Corazon Aquino, the widow of Marcos's slain political rival. A dispute about the election outcome stimulated thousands of Filipinos to take to the streets, demanding that Marcos step down, and a widespread protest by the moderate-based opposition party, People's Power, was soon supported by the Philippine military.

American military aircraft then evacuated Marcos and Imelda to Honolulu, Hawaii, where they remained in exile until Marcos's death in 1989. After taking office, President Corazon Aquino returned several blue-chip companies to their original owners by the same means—executive orders.

RESTITUTION

Upon arrival in Hawaii, the U.S. Customs Service seized Marcos's assets of some $8.2 million and held them until his death in 1989, when his heir, Imelda, agreed to allow their return to the Philippine government.

After Marcos's departure in 1986, President Aquino appointed a commission to locate funds looted from the country by Marcos. When Marcos died, his estate went into probate and creditors came forward, but legal action was stalled on various technical grounds. Some $684 million was recovered and returned to the government from various bank accounts around the world, but millions remained to be recaptured.

Lawsuits were filed by persons who had been arrested and tortured or were the families of persons arrested, tortured, and executed during Marcos's rule. Consolidated into a class-action suit of 9,359 persons against his estate

in *Hilao v. Estate of Marcos* (1992), the plaintiffs were awarded $1.2 billion in exemplary damages and $766 million in compensatory damages. Marcos's assets in the United States were then identified and ordered frozen. Together with interest and other investments from the frozen money, the amount to be awarded by 2006 was $3.7 billion; it remained unpaid because of appeals filed in various courts.

IMPACT

Ferdinand Marcos promised to end oligarchic economic and political dominance in order to foster a new society of increased upward mobility. When his dictatorship ended, however, class divisions remained, and the country had been decapitalized. In 1998, pro-Marcos politician Joseph Estrada was elected president, only to be toppled in 2001 by another People's Power demonstration over flagrant corruption. He was succeeded by Vice President Gloria Macapagal Arroyo, who had close ties to the provincial aristocracy and financial community. The Philippine economic and political systems remained so deeply divided that Marcos was rated a better president than his four successors in a nationwide poll taken in 2005.

FURTHER READING

Aquino, Belinda. *Politics of Plunder: The Philippines Under Marcos*. Manila: University of the Philippines College of Public Administration, 1999. A political scientist analyzes how Marcos derailed the Philippine economy.

Marcos, Ferdinand. *Notes on the New Society of the Philippines*. Manila, Philippines: Marcos Foundation, 1973. Marcos's own idealistic blueprint for his country.

Seagrave, Sterling. *The Marcos Dynasty*. New York: Harper & Row, 1988. Explores the way in which, under Marcos, Manila became an international hub for moneylaundering, narcotics traffic, gambling, white slavery, and child prostitution. Also details the involvement of American business, organized crime, and high U.S. government offices.

—*Michael Haas*

SEE ALSO: Imelda Marcos; Suharto.

Imelda Marcos
First lady of the Philippines (1965-1986)

Born: July 2, 1929; Tacloban City, Philippines
Also known as: Imelda Romualdez Marcos (full name); Imelda Romualdez (birth name); Steel Butterfly
Major offense: Plundering the Philippines' assets
Active: 1972-1986
Locale: Philippines
Sentence: Pending on charges of corruption and extortion

Early Life

The daughter of an aristocratic family in the Philippines, Imelda Marcos (ih-MEHL-dah MAHR-cohs) attended St. Paul's College, where in 1949 she won a beauty contest. At age twenty-three, she went to Manila, and in 1954 she met and married Congressman Ferdinand Marcos after an eleven-day courtship. A girl from the provinces, Imelda was initially shunned by wives of other politicians.

Political Career

In 1959, Ferdinand ran for the senate, taking Imelda with him on his campaign trail. She proved to be an asset, and he was elected. In 1965, she courted votes in exchange for pesos to gain for her husband a party nomination for president, and he was again elected, in part because of her campaigning.

As president, Ferdinand told his first lady to attend to the trimmings while he set the main course. Accordingly, she embarked on a beautification program for run-down Manila, distributed seeds for backyard gardens, provided free medical care for some of the poor, and commissioned the construction of orphanages, old people's facilities, and day care centers. Imelda also settled scores with those who had snubbed her earlier. She required rich guests to bring checkbooks whenever they were summoned to a party at the presidential palace. She also demanded stock from corporations.

In 1972, Marcos declared martial law and then had presidential rival Benigno Aquino arrested. He also had the son of Vice President Fernando Lopez arrested, demanding that the Lopez family surrender the Philippines' largest utility and an influential newspaper. Imelda's brother Benjamin then headed both businesses. Crony capitalism accelerated as government regulations ruined certain businesses, which were then bought by friends and relatives of the Marcoses.

In 1973, Ferdinand introduced a new constitution that replaced the Philippine congress with a National Assembly and extended the president's term of office, with no limit on the number of terms. In 1974, Ferdinand appointed Imelda governor of Metro Manila. Soon shanties were bulldozed, an air-conditioned bus transit system began, and several multimillion-dollar Manila projects blossomed. When Ferdinand set up an Interim Legislature in 1978, Imelda was elected, and he appointed her minister of human settlements. Many Filipinos claimed election fraud, notably Aquino, who was released in 1980 for medical treatment abroad. In 1981, after lifting martial law, Marcos was reelected president in rigged voting. Aquino was assassinated when he returned to the Philippines in 1983.

As Ferdinand's health deteriorated, Imelda ran the government. When he ordered snap presidential elections in 1986, Imelda campaigned more widely than could the sickly Ferdinand. Aquino's widow, Corazon, ran against Marcos, who again attempted election fraud and then tried to retain control of the country by force. He announced a state of emergency and sought control of all media outlets and public utilities. With thousands in the streets, Defense Minister Juan Ponce Enrile and chief of staff Lieutenant-General Fidel Ramos announced they were switching loyalties and backing Corazon Aquino as president. In the face of the army mutiny, the Marcos regime was toppled. American aircraft evacuated the Marcoses to exile in Honolulu. Ferdinand died in Hawaii in 1989.

In 1991, Imelda returned to the Philippines and unsuccessfully campaigned for the presidency the following year. In 1995, she won election to the House of Representatives from her home province. In 1998, she again ran for the presidency, promising to share her husband's wealth with the Filipino people through the Marcos Foundation. After her defeat, she admitted that her husband virtually controlled the entire country's economy before parceling out corporations to cronies. In 2002, she again ran for president and lost, though she remained in the Philippines.

Legal Action and Outcome

The first action against Imelda was the seizure of cash, gold, jewelry, and other assets upon her arrival at the Honolulu International Airport in 1986. She agreed to return the assets to the Philippine government shortly after

THE REWARDS OF POWER: SHOES AND JEWELS

In 1986, after Imelda Marcos was forced to flee the Philippines with her husband, President Ferdinand Marcos, the authorities discovered an unexpected trove:

"They went into my closets looking for skeletons, but thank God, all they found were shoes, beautiful shoes," Marcos proudly told a British Broadcasting Corporation (BBC) reporter in 2001. How many shoes remains a matter of dispute. Some sources claim "thousands." Marcos dismissed such vagueness peremptorily. "I did not have three thousand pairs of shoes. I had one thousand sixty," she declared in 1987.

In 2001, Marcos opened the Marikina City Footwear Museum in Manila to display a few hundred of her favorite pairs. "This museum is making a subject of notoriety into an object of beauty. More than anything, this museum will symbolize the spirit and culture of the Filipino people," she claimed.

What Marcos could not put into a museum and what proved to be far more valuable were the jewels that she accumulated while her husband was in office. All of them, she insisted, were gifts, some of them for her dog. Impressive gifts they are, whether for dog or human. Among them are a necklace with 93 carats in diamonds centered in a single diamond of 15 carats; a 30.76-carat diamond bracelet that originally cost one million dollars; a brooch with a 20-carat emerald cabochon, 2-carat ruby cabochon, and diamonds set in white gold; a bracelet with ten 5-carat pigeon-blood rubies surrounded by smaller rubies and diamonds in yellow gold; a Persian-style necklace with more than 100 carats of canary and pink diamonds; a set of earrings with emeralds of 3 carats each and diamond droplets also of 3 carats; and her famous diamond choker with fifteen 5-carat Colombian emeralds and 50 carats of diamonds set in platinum. (A carat equals 200 milligrams; a 3-to-4-carat diamond is typical for a high quality engagement ring.) Marcos's jewelry was estimated to be worth $5.3 million in 2001. The collection is in the possession of the Philippines' Bureau of Customs.

Ferdinand's death in 1989. Once in office, President Corazon Aquino set up a commission to determine how much the country had been plundered during the Marcos years.

In 1987, a lawsuit alleged that the Marcos family confiscated private property, awarded contracts to cronies and relatives, embezzled government funds, extorted money from businesses, and routed the wealth to local and offshore bank accounts. After appeals in the case, the Philippine Supreme Court in 2003 agreed to award the amounts in frozen bank accounts, including $500 million in Switzerland. Specific assets involved were not identified fully until December, 2005, when a ten-billion-dollar case was finally remanded for trial.

In 1990, Imelda was cleared by a federal grand jury in New York of embezzling funds, and she was also exonerated in a Philippine court for misappropriation of public funds. In 1993, a Philippine court convicted her on corruption charges, sentenced her to eighteen to twenty-four years in prison, and fined her $5.1 million in damages. The judgment was overturned on appeal in 1998.

In 1992, nearly ten thousand victims of human rights abuses (including torture, illegal detention, disappearances, and summary killings) and their heirs were awarded $1.2 billion in exemplary damages and $766 million in compensatory damages in *Hilao v. Estate of Marcos*. Marcos's assets in the United States were then identified and ordered frozen. In 1995, however, Marcos and her son, Ferdinand, Jr., were found in contempt of court for using the assets and assessed a fine of $100,000 per day. Together with interest and other investments from the frozen money, the amount of the settlement to be awarded reached $3.7 billion by 2006 but remained unpaid while appeals were pending in various courts.

In 2001, Marcos was arrested on new charges of corruption and extortion, specifically stemming from the disappearance of $684 million from the Filipino treasury during the Ferdinand Marcos presidency. In 2003, the missing money was awarded to the Philippine government. Lawsuits and appeals continued, while Imelda Marcos avoided prison and was known to have retained funds in the Marcos Foundation. In March, 2006, Marcos's lawyer reported that the former first lady was open to a compromise agreement in the interest of ending years of fruitless litigation over Marcos assets.

IMPACT

Imelda Marcos's admirers have benefited from her largesse or have derived vicarious satisfaction from the way in which she became so powerful and rich. To those who did not believe the good intentions that she had articulated over the years, she was the most infamous woman in the world.

FURTHER READING

Ellison, Katherine. *Imelda: Steel Butterfly of the Philippines*. New York: McGraw-Hill, 1988. A journalistic account of Marcos, with much attention to personal and psychological elements.

Psinakis, Steve. "Two Terrorists Meet." Dobbs Ferry, N.Y.: Morgan & Morgan, 1981. Largely based on a conversation between Imelda and the author, the book reports on Marcos's megalomaniacal ambitions.

Romula, Beth Day. *Inside the Palace: The Rise and Fall*

of Ferdinand and Imelda Marcos. New York: Putnam, 1987. A firsthand account by a former Philippine foreign minister's wife about the Marcoses, their greed, their cronies, and their corruption.

—*Michael Haas*

SEE ALSO: Ferdinand Marcos.

MARIE-ANTOINETTE
Queen of France (r. 1774-1793)

BORN: November 2, 1755; Vienna, Austria
DIED: October 16, 1793; Paris, France
ALSO KNOWN AS: Marie-Antoinette-Josèphe-Jeanne d'Autriche-Lorraine (French full name); Maria Antonia Josepha Joanna von Österreich-Lothringen (German full name); Maria Antonia Josepha Johanna von Habsburg-Lothringen (birth name); Marie-Antoinette-Josèphe-Jeanne de Habsbourg-Lorraine (French birth name); L'Autrichienne; Madame Deficit; Madame Veto; Widow Capet
MAJOR OFFENSES: Self-indulgence, contempt for the common people, and treason
ACTIVE: 1770-1792
LOCALE: France
SENTENCE: Death by guillotine

EARLY LIFE

Marie-Antoinette (mah-ree ahn-twah-neht) was the daughter of Empress Maria Theresa and Holy Roman Emperor Francis I of the Habsburg line. She was beautiful as a child—blond and blue-eyed—and enjoyed court life, learning to play the harp with musical groups formed by her eleven brothers and sisters to entertain her parents. She became fluent in French but would always speak it with a German accent.

ROYAL CAREER

When she was ten, Marie-Antoinette was contracted to marry the heir to the French throne for political reasons, and on May 16, 1770, she wed the dauphin Louis, a clumsy, shy teenager. Given the long history of hostility between Austria and the Holy Roman Empire on one side and France on the other, it was little wonder that the French people were annoyed by their future queen. She was a native Austrian, a Habsburg, the daughter of a Holy Roman emperor, the sister of two others, and the aunt of the last one. She did nothing to assuage their an-

noyance. On the contrary, the crass indulgences of this spoiled teenager turned the people more firmly against her even before she became queen.

Louis ascended to the throne in 1774 as Louis XVI. His wife's lavishness made little difference to the French treasury but was widely perceived as causing massive national debt. Rumors of her sexual escapades and perversions, some of which may have been true, began almost as soon as she reached France, fueled in part by the inability of her husband to have intercourse with her until 1777 and the fact that she did not bear a child until 1778. Her detractors accused her of lesbian relationships

Marie-Antoinette. (Library of Congress)

with many of her friends, especially Marie Thérèse Louise de Savoie-Carignan, the princesse de Lamballe. The notorious "Affair of the Diamond Necklace" from 1784 to 1786 brought her allegations, probably false, of financial indiscretions with Jeanne Saint-Rémy de Valois, comtesse de la Motte, and dalliances with Cardinal Louis de Rohan.

Marie-Antoinette was indeed unfeeling toward the misery of the French peasants, but she did not utter the oblivious dismissal of their hunger that is commonly attributed to her. Legend says that, when told the starving people had no bread, she responded, "Qu'ils mangent de la brioche!" ("Let them eat cake!") The phrase, however, appears in book 6 of Jean-Jacques Rousseau's *Les Confessions de J.-J. Rousseau* (1782, 1789; *The Confessions of J.-J. Rousseau*, 1783-1790), which was written in the 1760's, before Marie-Antoinette ever saw France, but not published until 1782, when its readers could easily have thought that its antimonarchist remarks referred to her.

Her intrigues with her brothers, Holy Roman Emperors Joseph II and Leopold II, and other prominent Austrians contributed to instigate the French Revolutionary Wars, which began on April 20, 1792, with the War of the First Coalition, pitting Austria and Prussia against France.

LEGAL ACTION AND OUTCOME

Marie-Antoinette and Louis tried to escape from France but were captured at Varennes on June 25, 1791, and placed under house arrest. They were imprisoned after the French people stormed the Tuileries on August 10, 1792. The National Convention abolished the monarchy on September 21 and guillotined Louis on January 21, 1793. On August 1 Marie-Antoinette was transferred to solitary confinement in the Conciergie. At her trial before the Revolutionary Tribunal on October 14 she was convicted of treason for driving France to war with Austria. She was guillotined on October 16.

IMPACT

Marie-Antoinette's importance in the twenty-first century is mainly iconic: She is not remembered for her actual deeds so much as her symbolic significance as the most poignant symbol of the callousness of royal privilege and wealth. Imperious, mean, extravagant, or insensitive rich women since her time have been compared with her.

Even in her own time, Marie-Antoinette's public image was more powerful than her actions. She did not cre-

---

AN EXCESS OF DISSIPATION

After her daughter Marie-Antoinette had been queen of France for two years, her mother, Holy Roman empress Maria Theresa, wrote to warn her daughter of "dissipation":

My only fear for you (being so young [age twenty]) is an excess of dissipation. You have never cared to read or to apply yourself in any way; this has often troubled me, and accounts for my having tormented you so often with inquiries as to what you were reading. I was so pleased to see you devoting yourself to music. But for a year now there has been no question of either reading or music, and I hear of nothing but racing and hunting, and always without the king and with a lot of ill-chosen young people; all this troubles me very much, loving you, as I do, so dearly. Your sisters-in-law behave very differently, and I must own that all these boisterous diversions in which the king takes no part appear to me unseemly. You will say, "He knows and approves of them." I reply that he is kind and good and that that is all the more reason that you should be circumspect.

Source: Maria Theresa, letter to Marie-Antoinette dated May 15, 1776, in *Readings in European History*, edited by James Harvey Robinson (New York: Ginn, 1906).

---

ate the deficits of the late 1780's that directly caused the French Revolution, the tensions between France and Austria that led to the French Revolutionary Wars of the 1790's, or the conditions that instigated the Reign of Terror in 1793-1794, but her high visibility emphasized these deficits. Her very presence reminded the people constantly of unwanted Austrian influence in French affairs, and her obvious contempt for the common people inspired both the sansculottes and Maximilien Robespierre. Even though Louis XVI was a rather benign king, less dismissive of the people's rights than his predecessors, especially Louis XIV, her association with him hastened and intensified the revolution because the people projected their hatred of her onto him as well.

FURTHER READING

Erickson, Carolly. *To the Scaffold: The Life of Marie Antoinette*. New York: Morrow, 1991. A readable but pedestrian biography that tries to rehabilitate Marie-Antoinette's reputation but offers no new insights.

Fraser, Antonia. *Marie Antoinette: The Journey*. New

York: Talese/Doubleday, 2001. A sympathetic portrayal, emphasizing Marie-Antoinette's good qualities and reinterpreting her as a victim of circumstance.

Lever, Evelyne. *Marie Antoinette: The Last Queen of France*. New York: Farrar, Straus and Giroux, 2000. A romanticized and fanciful view that ignores politics and concentrates instead on Marie-Antoinette's personal life and aesthetic charm.

Price, Munro. *The Road from Versailles: Louis XVI, Ma-* *rie Antoinette, and the Fall of the French Monarchy*. New York: St. Martin's Press, 2003. A meticulous scholarly history that documents the many opportunities that Louis and Marie-Antoinette missed to avoid their violent demise.

—*Eric v.d. Luft*

SEE ALSO: Charlotte Corday; Jean-Paul Marat; Robespierre.

MAROZIA
Roman mistress of Pope Sergius III

BORN: c. 890; possibly Tusculum, near Rome, Papal States (now in Italy)

DIED: c. 936; Rome, Papal States (now in Italy)

ALSO KNOWN AS: Marouzia; Mariuccia

CAUSE OF NOTORIETY: Marozia's corrupt rule of Rome symbolized the era of so-called pornocracy (domination of government by prostitutes), a low point in Papal history.

ACTIVE: 920-932

LOCALE: Rome, Papal States

EARLY LIFE

Only minute factual information is available for the life of Marozia (mah-RAWT-syah). Her father, Theophylact of Tusculum, settled in Rome at the time when it was torn both by murderous factional conflicts over the papal throne and by power struggles between popular mobs and an ambitious nobility; intermittent external threats also plagued the fragmented Papal States. Theophylact became leader of Rome's nobility, with the titles of consul and senator. His forceful wife, Theodora the Elder, styled herself as a *senatrix* (senatoress). Theophylact also became financial officer to Pope Sergius III (904-911), who supposedly took the barely teenage Marozia as his mistress, thereby displaying his alliance with her parents. In firm control of Rome, Theophylact and Theodora established puppet-successors to Sergius, after whom they installed Pope John X (914-928). It was said that John X was chosen because he was Theodora's paramour; more likely it was because of his much-needed leadership abilities.

POLITICAL CAREER

John X proved an able diplomat and military leader on behalf of the battered Holy See of Rome and its central-Italian patrimony. Against the immediate threat by the raiding Saracens (who had been menacing Italy through the ninth century), John, Theophylact, and Theodora assembled an alliance that included Alberic I of Camerino, duke of Spoleto. Alberic's military aid was rewarded with marriage to Marozia. Pope John X personally led this coalition to a decisive victory over the Saracens in August, 915, thus ending their threat.

Soon after, Theodora died (c. 916), as did Theophylact (c. 920), leaving as heirs their two daughters, Marozia and Theodora the Younger. The latter lacked interest in power, but Marozia assumed the title of *senatrix* and was determined to rule Rome. Her first husband, Alberic, had ambitions of his own but was driven away by John X. With a breach opening between her and the pope, Marozia took a second husband in 927, Marquis Guy of Tuscany. When John X sought external allies, Marozia incited a mob against him in May, 928. He was deposed and imprisoned, languishing until he was murdered the following year.

Meanwhile, Marozia imposed two more stopgap occupants of the papal throne, though only to pave the way for her real choice, her eldest child, who was considered the son of Sergius III. His installation as Pope John XI deepened her family's hold on the Holy See and perhaps spawned her wider ambitions. After her second husband's death, Marozia found a third husband in Hugh of Provence, who claimed the title of king of Italy, thus promising her the co-rule of much of the peninsula. Marozia possibly hoped that John XI might then proclaim them emperor and empress of the West. Though Hugh was the half brother of her previous husband, any objections were set readily aside, and the wedding proceeded in Rome in 932.

The wedding was soon followed by disaster. Marozia had long disfavored her younger son, who was born from her first husband and named for him. In December, 932, the younger Alberic II stirred up a rebellion against his mother. The craven Hugh fled, and Marozia was seized, to be imprisoned until her death some years later.

IMPACT

Alberic II ably maintained Rome's independence thereafter. He was succeeded by his degenerate son, Octavian (by Ada, daughter of his mother's former husband Hugh). He quickly brought the pretensions of the Tusculan house of Theophylact to a climax by taking the papal title for himself as John XII (955-964).

Marozia's reputation was shaped by the bitter hostility of contemporary historian Liutprand of Cremona and then continued through much of subsequent historiography. Her contribution to debasing the Papacy within a corrupt age is undeniable, but recent scholarship has diminished the scandalous impression of this intelligent, energetic, and strong-willed woman.

FURTHER READING

Boureau, Alain. *The Myth of Pope Joan*. Chicago: University of Chicago Press, 2001. Scrutinizes the legend of a "female pope" in the 850's, an image perhaps influenced by Marozia's story.

Chamberlain, E. R. *The Bad Popes*. New York: Dorset Press, 1986. A slightly sensationalized popular survey, skipping the tenth through the sixteenth centuries, but including an ample section on "The House of Theophylact" (pp. 23-74).

Kelly, J. N. D. *The Oxford Dictionary of the Popes*. New York: Oxford University Press, 1986. A fundamental reference work, chronologically organized.

Llewellyn, Peter. *Rome in the Dark Ages*. New York: Praeger, 1971. Covers the fifth through tenth centuries, through the period of suppression of Marozia's grandson.

Partner, Peter. *The Lands of St. Peter*. Berkeley: University of California Press, 1972. A solid overview of the Papal States as a principality, with the chapter "The House of Theophylact" (pp. 77-103).

—*John W. Barker*

SEE ALSO: Alexander VI; Boniface VIII; Clement VII; Leo X; Urban VI.

JEAN MARTINET
French drillmaster of Louis XIV's army

BORN: Seventeenth century; France
DIED: 1672; Duisburg, Duchy of Cleves (now in Germany)
CAUSE OF NOTORIETY: Martinet's strict methods of training soldiers remain the basis of modern military drilling.
ACTIVE: 1662-1672
LOCALE: France and its border states

EARLY LIFE

The early life of Jean Martinet (zhahn mahr-tee-nay) remains unknown. His family was probably from Normandy, France.

MILITARY CAREER

Seventeenth century king of France Louis XIV believed that a strong military force was essential for the defense of his nation, for the expansion of its boundaries, and, most important, to make France the most powerful country in Europe. Therefore, the king created a model regular army between 1660 and 1670. In 1662, he appointed François Michel LeTellier, the marquis de Louvois, as minister of the army. Louvois set about reorganizing the army, which had been primarily composed of mercenaries who provided their own weapons and fought according to whatever methods they had acquired during their careers. Louvois sought to bring uniformity to the force. He appointed Martinet lieutenant colonel of the King's Regiment of Foot Soldiers and inspector general of the infantry.

Martinet was a strict disciplinarian and exacted total compliance with rules and regulations from his men. As a drillmaster, he was systematic, efficient, and at times even brutal. Martinet taught his soldiers precise tactics for battle. No longer were they to run helter-skelter into battle, firing at will. Martinet trained the troops to advance in a linear formation. They were to fire on command and in unison. As the muskets they used were highly inaccurate, this controlled method of firing in volleys improved the weapons' effectiveness.

Martinet also trained soldiers to stand and throw grenades. The grenades were small, sphere-shaped, and filled with gunpowder. The grenadier had to light the grenade and wait for the precise moment to throw it, so that the enemy could not return the grenade before it exploded. Grenadiers had to be extremely well disciplined to stand in the vanguard of the advancing army, light the grenades, and throw them at the precise time. Martinet first incorporated grenades into the Regiment du Roi's weaponry in 1667. Louis XIV eventually created a special company for these soldiers and gave them official status. Martinet also introduced the use of copper pontoons in warfare. Louis XIV's army used these devices to cross the Rhine River in 1672. That same year Martinet, who was by then a field marshal, was killed by his own artillery as he led the infantry into battle.

IMPACT

The methods developed and put into practice by Jean Martinet revolutionized the French army, turning it into a well-organized, disciplined, homogeneous entity. His system of training and drilling troops remains the basis for military instruction today.

History has tended to neglect Martinet. He has been overshadowed by Louvois, who, as minister of war, was responsible for all aspects of military reform. Louvois made significant contributions, including the establishment of Les Invalides, a home for invalid soldiers. However, it was Martinet's drilling methods that transformed the French army into the tactically competent force that was admired and feared by all of Europe.

The best-known legacy of Martinet is the inclusion of his name as a word in English. "Martinet" is used to describe someone who is a firm disciplinarian and demands strict compliance with rules; the word usually has a derogatory sense. His name is also often incorrectly believed to be the etymological source of the French word *martinet*, referring to a small whip formed of numerous lashes. The origin of this word traces to the French word for the black swift. The whip resembles the bird's fanned-out tail.

FURTHER READING

Chartrand, René. *Louis XIV's Army*. 1988. Reprint. Oxford, England: Osprey, 2002. Discusses the army of Louis XIV in every aspect, including uniforms, tactics, standards, training practices, and drilling procedures.

Lewis, W. H. *The Splendid Century: Life in the France of Louis XIV*. Reprint. Long Grove, Ill.: Waveland Press, 1997. Complete picture of France during the reign of Louis XIV including political, social, economic, military, and artistic ideas and practices. Chapter 5 treats the army.

Lynn, John A. *The Wars of Louis XIV, 1667-1714*. New York: Longman, 1999. Discusses operational logistics of the campaigns and their significance for France in the areas of diplomacy, economics, and politics. Chapter 3 specifically treats the army, the navy, and the art of war.

Rowlands, Guy. *The Dynastic State and the Army Under Louis XIV: Royal Service and Private Interest, 1661-1701*. New York: Cambridge University Press, 2002. Supported by extensive archival research, this work examines the army as a military, political, social, and economic institution. Discusses the administration of the army.

—*Shawncey Webb*

SEE ALSO: Alcibiades of Athens; Benedict Arnold.

JOE MASSERIA
Italian-born New York Mafia boss

BORN: 1879; Palermo, Italy
DIED: April 15, 1931; Brooklyn, New York
ALSO KNOWN AS: Giuseppe Masseria (full name); Joe the Boss
CAUSE OF NOTORIETY: Masseria emigrated to the United States and seized control of the New York Morello gang. He later clashed with another Italian-born boss, Salvatore Maranzano, in the infamous Castellammarese War.
ACTIVE: 1902-1931
LOCALE: New York, New York

EARLY LIFE

Like that of many Mafia figures, the birth date of Joe Masseria (mas-suhr-REE-uh) is not exactly known, and little more is known about his early years. He was born in Palermo, Italy, and emigrated to the United States in 1902, reportedly to escape a murder charge.

GANGSTER CAREER

Upon arrival in the United States, Masseria went to work for the Morello gang, which was the first major Mafia crime family in New York. Masseria attempted to take over the leadership of the organization by force in 1913. Masseria had taken control of the gang by 1920 after many of his opponents were either murdered or imprisoned. He overcame a challenge to his power and an assassination attempt from Morello loyalists and teamed up with the "Young Turks," a group of young gangsters that included Charles "Lucky" Luciano, Joe Adonis, Frank Costello, Carlo Gambino, Albert Anastasia, and Peter "the Clutching Hand" Morello. Masseria was eventually arrested for burglary and extortion but did not serve jail time on the charges.

Masseria was five feet, two inches tall, a stocky man with a cold temperament. He did not like Jews and disliked the younger gangsters' collaborating with Jewish criminals. He ruled with a heavy hand and took more than his share of tribute from his men. The Young Turks were therefore not terribly loyal to their boss but stayed with Masseria even when he faced a new threat in 1927 from Salvatore Maranzano, a powerful leader of immigrants from Castellammare del Golfo, Sicily.

Maranzano was considered to be an advance man for Sicilian leader Don Vito Ferro, but when Ferro was imprisoned by Benito Mussolini's fascists in Italy, Maranzano decided to become the American "boss of bosses," putting him on a direct collision course with Masseria. This conflict became known as the Castellammarese War, a bloody, drawn-out clash between the two factions between 1930 and 1931. However, Masseria's gangsters disliked both Maranzano and Masseria and wanted to operate without their Old World constraints. On April 15, 1931, Luciano took his boss out to a Coney Island restaurant, where four men shot and killed Masseria. The shooters were reportedly Bugsy Siegel, Adonis, Anastasia, and Vito Genovese. With Masseria's death, the Castellammarese War was over, but Maranzano's victory was short-lived: After proclaiming himself to be Boss of Bosses, Maranzano himself was murdered in September, 1931.

IMPACT

The end of the Castellammarese War and the deaths of old-country "Mustache Pete" bosses such as Masseria and Maranzano effectively marked the beginning of the American Mafia as a distinct entity from the Italian-Sicilian organization. The Young Turks wanted to make profits, work with other ethnic groups, and expand their wealth. They perceived the old-country bosses as unreasonably stifling and demanding, allowing their prejudices and rules to interfere with making money. The Young Turks who turned out both Masseria and Maranzano emerged as among the most influential gangsters in the history of the American Mafia and symbolize many of the cultural differences between the American Mafia and the Italian-Sicilian *cosa nostra*.

FURTHER READING

Raab, Selwyn. *Five Families: The Rise, Decline, and Resurgence of America's Most Powerful Mafia Empires.* New York: St. Martin's Press, 2005. Recounts the history of the New York crime families, focusing on major figures and events.

Reppetto, Thomas. *American Mafia: A History of Its Rise to Power.* New York: Henry Holt, 2004. Covers the historical foundations of the American Mafia organizations, starting in 1890 in New Orleans and proceeding to modern-day events.

Talese, Gay. *Honor Thy Father.* New York: World, 1971. Biographical sketch of Joe Bonanno's reign from the Castallammarese War until the infamous Banana Wars.

—*David R. Champion*

SEE ALSO: Joe Adonis; Albert Anastasia; Frank Costello; Carlo Gambino; Vito Genovese; Lucky Luciano; Salvatore Maranzano; Bugsy Siegel.

MATA HARI
Dutch spy

BORN: August 7, 1876; Leeuwarden, Holland, Netherlands

DIED: October 15, 1917; Vincennes, near Paris, France

ALSO KNOWN AS: Margaretha Geertruida Zelle (birth name); Lady MacLeod (stage name); Margaretha Geertruida MacLeod (married name); Secret Agent H-21

MAJOR OFFENSE: Passing Allied information to German intelligence during World War I

ACTIVE: 1916-1917

LOCALE: The Hague, Netherlands; Paris; and Spain

SENTENCE: Death by firing squad

EARLY LIFE

On August 7, 1876, Margaretha Geertruida Zelle, later known as Mata Hari (MAH-tuh HAH-ree), was born to a prosperous Dutch hat merchant named Adam Zelle and his wife, Antje Johannes van der Meulen. In 1899 Adam Zelle's business went bankrupt, and he abandoned his family. When she was fifteen, Margaretha's mother died, and she went to live with relatives. At eighteen she married a thirty-nine-year-old Dutch military officer, Rudolph MacLeod, who was on sick leave from service in the Dutch East Indies (Indonesia). They lived in Java and Sumatra from 1897 to 1902 and had two children. In 1899, both their children were poisoned, possibly by an angry servant; their son died. They returned to Europe, and Margaretha left MacLeod, an alcoholic and abusive husband who kept custody of their daughter.

In 1905, Margaretha moved to Paris, where she began dancing professionally, first as Lady MacLeod and finally as Mata Hari, which means "eye of the dawn" in Malay. Assuming the persona of an Eastern princess, she made her debut as an exotic temple dancer at the Guimet Museum in Paris on March 13, 1905. Her erotic strip-tease soon became popular throughout Europe. She attracted numerous lovers, including German and French military officers.

CRIMINAL CAREER

Many unanswered questions surrounded Mata Hari's alleged espionage activities during World War I. In 1916 one of her lovers, the German military attaché in Spain, suspected her of spying on him and sent radio messages to Berlin naming Mata Hari as German spy H-21, even though she had not passed sensitive military secrets to the Germans. He knew that the Allies could break the code and intercept the messages.

Mata Hari fell in love with Vadim de Masloff, a young Russian officer, and needed additional income to support her future life with her lover, so she proposed to spy for Captain Ladoux of French intelligence. Later, she claimed that the French had paid her to spy in German-occupied Belgium. British intelligence alerted the French about her activities with the German consul.

LEGAL ACTION AND OUTCOME

On February 13, 1917, the French arrested Mata Hari on charges of espionage. While she awaited trial, the military tribunal's chief investigator, Captain Pierre Bouchardon, interrogated her at least seventeen times.

On July 24-25, she was tried by a closed military court and found guilty of spying for Germany. According to

Mata Hari.

military trial rules, her lawyer could not cross-examine the prosecution's witnesses or even the defense's own witnesses. Mata Hari was accused of betraying military secrets told to her by Allied military officers. She asserted her innocence and said that she had actually worked for French intelligence. The prosecution presented the intercepted German military radio messages that identified Mata Hari as Agent H-21 of the Cologne intelligence center. On October 15, 1917, Mata Hari was executed by a firing squad.

IMPACT

Within years after her execution, Mata Hari had become a legend, often considered the greatest woman spy in history. When she was arrested, she was already a famous exotic dancer who had turned striptease into an art form. After her execution, she became the symbol of the treacherous, seductive femme fatale. However, it remained debatable whether she had actually been a dangerous double agent or German spy. In 1999, previously sealed British intelligence files were opened and provided no actual proof of her guilt. There was also no hard evidence in French military records, so it appears there was a miscarriage of justice. In 2001, the Mata Hari Foundation and the town of Leeuwarden, Netherlands, asserted that she was a scapegoat and the victim of a state conspiracy and requested a new trial and pardon from the French Ministry of Justice.

Mata Hari has been portrayed in numerous films: Asta Nielsen played her in *Mata Hari* (1920), Magda Sonja in *Mata Hari* (1927), Greta Garbo in *Mata Hari* (1931), Marlene Dietrich in *Dishonored* (1931), Jeanne Moreau in *Mata Hari Agent H 21* (1965), Zsa Zsa Gabor in the comedy *Up the Front* (1972), and Sylvia Kristel in *Mata Hari* (1985). In 2003, Maruschka Detmers starred in a television program, *Mata Hari, La Vraie Histoire*. In the twenty-first century, new books and films showed the continuing fascination with the famous femme fatale.

BEFORE THE FIRING SQUAD

"I am a woman who enjoys herself very much; sometimes I lose, sometimes I win," Mata Hari once said. This aplomb carried over even to her execution, according to an article by British journalist Henry Wales, an eyewitness to at least part of the event. At five o'clock in the morning on October 15, 1917, she was told her plea for clemency had failed, and her hour had come. Shocked at first, she quickly composed herself. Wales writes:

Never once had the iron will of the beautiful woman failed her. Father Arbaux, accompanied by two sisters of charity, Captain Bouchardon, and Maitre Clunet, her lawyer, entered her cell, where she was still sleeping—a calm, untroubled sleep, it was remarked by the turnkeys and trusties. The sisters gently shook her. She arose and was told that her hour had come.

"May I write two letters?" was all she asked.

Consent was given immediately by Captain Bouchardon, and pen, ink, paper, and envelopes were given to her.

She seated herself at the edge of the bed and wrote the letters with feverish haste. She handed them over to the custody of her lawyer.

Then she drew on her stockings, black, silken, filmy things, grotesque in the circumstances. She placed her high-heeled slippers on her feet and tied the silken ribbons over her insteps.

She arose and took the long black velvet cloak, edged around the bottom with fur and with a huge square fur collar hanging down the back, from a hook over the head of her bed. She placed this cloak over the heavy silk kimono which she had been wearing over her nightdress.

Her wealth of black hair was still coiled about her head in braids. She put on a large, flapping black felt hat with a black silk ribbon and bow. Slowly and indifferently, it seemed, she pulled on a pair of black kid gloves. Then she said calmly.

"I am ready." . . .

Mata Hari was not bound, and she was not blindfolded. She stood gazing steadfastly at her executioners, when the priest, the nuns, and her lawyer stepped away from her.

Source: International News Service, October 19, 1917.

FURTHER READING

Bentley, Toni. *Sisters of Salome*. New Haven, Conn.: Yale University Press, 2002. A former dancer, the author examines how Mata Hari and three other famous women portrayed the biblical femme fatale Salome and how their striptease performances influenced modern dance and feminism. Illustrated. Bibliography, illustrations, and index.

Coulson, Thomas. *Mata Hari: Courtesan and Spy*. 1930. Reprint. Whitefish, Mont.: Kessinger, 2004. Originally published in 1930, this biography was one of the books on which the 1931 Greta Garbo movie was based. Illustrated.

Howe, Russell Warren. *Mata Hari: The True Story*. New

York: Dodd, Mead, 1986. A readable biography based on extensive research, including access to sealed French records. The author concluded there had not been sufficient proof that Mata Hari was a spy. Index.

Ostrovsky, Erika. *Eye of Dawn: The Rise and Fall of Mata Hari*. New York: Macmillan, 1978. A well-researched portrait of the woman behind the legend and the events contributing to her transformation into the infamous Mata Hari. Bibliography, index, illustrations.

Wheelwright, Julie. *The Fatal Lover: Mata Hari and the Myth of Women in Espionage*. West Sussex, England: Collins & Brown, 1992. Asserts that wartime culture generally supported the erroneous idea of the treacherous and seductive female spy and that Mata Hari was a victim and an embodiment of this myth. Illustrated. Index, bibliography.

—*Alice Myers*

SEE ALSO: Belle Boyd; Pauline Cushman; Yoshiko Kawashima; Ethel Rosenberg.

ROBERT JAY MATHEWS
American anti-Semite

BORN: January 16, 1953; Marfa, Texas
DIED: December 8, 1984; Whidbey Island, Washington
ALSO KNOWN AS: Bob Mathews
CAUSE OF NOTORIETY: Mathews founded The Order, a white supremacist group whose fund-raising practices led to members' convictions on racketeering, conspiracy, counterfeiting, robbery, and other charges.
ACTIVE: 1983-1984
LOCALE: Washington State

EARLY LIFE
The family of Robert Jay Mathews (MATH-yews) moved to Phoenix, Arizona, when he was five years old. Mathews was a member of the Boy Scouts and the ultra-conservative John Birch Society and converted to Mormonism. He also became a staunch anticommunist, and after he left high school he founded a short-lived anticommunist group, the Sons of Liberty. During this time, Mathews was convicted of lying on a W-4 tax form—as a form of tax resistance. He was placed on probation for six months. While he was still a young man, Mathews relocated to Metaline Falls, Washington, known for its rugged beauty. There he and his father bought sixty acres of wooded property. Mathews married Debbie McGarrity, with whom he adopted a son in 1981. Mathews did not drink, smoke, or use profanity. His favorite pastime was reading.

CRIMINAL CAREER
While working to clear his land and make a small farm, Mathews began to be harassed again for the tax rebellion movement with which he had been involved in Arizona. Because of this harassment, and also as a result of his reading, which included tracts on dangers facing the white race, Mathews instigated a drive to attract whites to the Pacific Northwest. In a public letter, Mathews stated his fear that his son would grow up a stranger in his own country, where whites would be a minority. In September of 1983, Mathews founded, with eight other men, a group known as The Order, which they referred to as the Silent Brotherhood.

None of the members of The Order had previously committed violent crimes or had been in prison. Their first criminal act, whose goal was funding their new white resistance movement, was robbing a pornography shop. They branched out to robbing banks and then, in July of 1984, an armored truck. One of the members, Tom Martinez, was arrested for passing counterfeit currency.

LEGAL ACTION AND OUTCOME
Martinez testified against Mathews and others in the group. On December 8, 1984, Mathews and several others were in a small cabin on Whidbey Island in Washington. There they were surrounded by agents of the Federal Bureau of Investigation, who burned the cabin to the ground, killing Mathews. The others managed to escape.

IMPACT
In the resulting trials, charges were brought against members of The Order and others working with them. The charges included racketeering, conspiracy, counterfeiting, transporting stolen money, and robbery. Ten of

the defendants were tried for sedition but were acquitted. Two members of the group were also found guilty of violating the civil rights of controversial Denver talk-show host Alan Berg. Berg, who was Jewish, had died of a gunshot wound. No murder charges were filed in his death.

FURTHER READING

Barkun, Michael. *Religion and the Racist Right: The Origins of the Christian Identity Movement.* Chapel Hill: University of North Carolina Press, 1997. This comprehensive book concerns the ideological background of various Aryan groups that make up the loosely named Christian Identity movement.

Bushart, Howard L., and John R. Craig. *Soldiers of God: White Supremacists and Their Holy War for America.* New York: Kensington Books, 1998. A look at the complex beliefs in white supremacist organizations from the Ku Klux Klan to the smallest groups in mountain towns.

Flynn, Kevin, and Gary Gerhardt. *The Silent Brotherhood: Inside America's Racist Underground.* New York: Free Press, 1989. The story of Robert Jay Mathews, who was not part of the stereotypical anti-Semitic terrorist groups. The authors interviewed most of the key members of the Silent Brotherhood in and out of prison.

Langer, Elinor. *A Hundred Little Hitlers: The Death of a Black Man, the Trial of a White Racist, and the Rise of the Neo-Nazi Movement in America.* New York: Metropolitan Books, 2003. A thorough explanation of the neo-Nazi movement, beginning with one case in Portland, Oregon, and describing the major and minor groups across the United States.

—*Ellen B. Lindsay*

SEE ALSO: Richard Girnt Butler; Willis A. Carto; Frank Collin; David Duke; Matthew F. Hale; Tom Metzger; William Luther Pierce III; George Lincoln Rockwell; William Joseph Simmons; Gerald L. K. Smith.

GASTON BULLOCK MEANS
American civil servant and private investigator

BORN: July 11, 1879; Blackwelder's Spring, North Carolina
DIED: December 12, 1938; Springfield, Missouri
ALSO KNOWN AS: Gaston Means
MAJOR OFFENSES: Mail fraud and larceny
ACTIVE: 1924 and 1932
LOCALE: Washington, D.C.
SENTENCE: Two years' imprisonment for stealing liquor; two years' imprisonment for mail fraud; and fifteen years' imprisonment for larceny

EARLY LIFE

Born in North Carolina in 1879 to an unaccomplished family, Gaston Bullock Means (meens) apparently had three core beliefs. One was in the superiority of the Republican Party; the second was in white supremacy; and the third was that laws were made to be broken. He became a fringe figure in Republican politics and evolved into a highly unscrupulous private investigator who craved a civil service position. In 1920, Republican Warren Harding won a landslide victory in the U.S. presidential race, and Means, who knew several key players in the new Harding administration, saw an opportunity for advancement.

POLITICAL CAREER

Means befriended the ambitious and similarly amoral William J. Burns, who would be the director of the new Bureau of Investigation from 1921 to 1924. Accordingly, Burns hired Means to extort referrals and recommendations from wealthy and influential individuals. Tall, charming, and dimpled, Means succeeded at this because he made a point of knowing the guilty secrets of powerful people and threatening them with exposure. He also ingratiated himself with Harry Daugherty, Harding's corrupt new attorney general, and Daugherty's cohort Jess Smith. Smith's job was to collect extortion money from corporations and individuals whom Daugherty threatened with antitrust indictments.

Means, who at various times worked in the Justice and Treasury Departments while maintaining his own investigation business, spent most of his working hours protecting the career and reputation of President Harding. When two of Harding's mistresses threatened to publish presidential love letters unless the administration paid hush money, Means promptly broke into their homes and stole the letters.

Gradually, the weak-willed Smith fell under Means's influence. Together, they conspired to steal printing plates from the Treasury Department for counterfeiting purposes, but Means came to see Smith as a security risk. Smith was becoming increasingly erratic and unreliable, and when his sudden death in 1923 was reported as suicide, many felt Means was somehow responsible. President Harding died suddenly in San Francisco on August 2, 1923, under circumstances that many deemed strange.

LEGAL ACTION AND OUTCOME

In October, 1923, Means was indicted for the illegal removal of liquor from government warehouses. He was charged with larceny and conspiracy, but before his trial started he gave incriminating testimony to the Wheeling Committee in the Senate, which was investigating the alleged wrongdoing of Daugherty. Means was found guilty of the alcohol-related offense, as well as mail fraud in 1924, and sentenced to two years in prison for each crime and fined ten thousand dollars.

His time in prison did not reform him. Upon his release, he began work on a book (greatly aided by a ghostwriter) titled *The Strange Death of President Harding* (1930), a sleazy work that detailed Harding's adultery and stated assertively that Harding had been poisoned by his wife, Florence, a sensational and unsubstantiated charge. In 1932, Means convinced heiress and socialite Evalyn Walsh McLean that he had some inside knowledge about the 1934 kidnapping of the infant son of aviator Charles Lindbergh and persuaded her to give him $100,000 for "expenses" so he could arrange the child's release. McLean paid the money, but Means had merely perpetuated another fraud, and the baby was later found dead.

For this last wrongful act, Means was convicted of larceny and this time sentenced to fifteen years at the federal prison in Leavenworth, Kansas. He died in 1938, following gall bladder surgery at the Medical Center for Federal Prisoners in Springfield, Missouri.

IMPACT

In the years after his death, Gaston Bullock Means's name and myriad crimes were largely forgotten, perhaps due to the catastrophic world events that followed with the dawn of World War II. Perhaps his greatest legacy is the debasement and lowering of White House ethics and the many scandals that have plagued presidential administrations since.

FURTHER READING

Anthony, Carl Sferrazza. *Florence Harding*. New York: William Morrow, 1998. This biography of Mrs. Harding stresses Means's efforts to cover up the president's infidelities and repudiates Means's assertion that Harding had her husband poisoned.

Dean, John W. *Warren G. Harding*. New York: Henry Holt, 2004. This work discusses Means's book about the Hardings and dismisses it as untruthful and poorly written.

Means, Gaston Bullock. *The Strange Death of President Harding: From the Diaries of Gaston B. Means, as Told to May Dixon Thacker*. New York: Guild, 1930. Asserts that Harding was an adulterer and that he was poisoned to death by his wife, Florence.

Sobel, Robert. *Coolidge: An American Enigma*. Washington, D.C.: Regnery, 1998. Means's testimony before the Wheeler Committee, which was investigating the Harding administration, is discussed, along with Means's 1924 conviction.

—Thomas W. Buchanan

SEE ALSO: Bobby Baker; Simon Cameron; Billy Cannon; Janet Cooke; Tino De Angelis; Billie Sol Estes; Albert B. Fall; Megan Louise Ireland; Clifford Irving; Victor Lustig; Joseph Weil.

Ulrike Meinhof
German terrorist

Born: October 7, 1934; Oldenburg, Germany
Died: May 9, 1976; Stammheim Prison, Stuttgart,
West Germany (now Germany)
Also known as: Ulrike Marie Meinhof (full name)
Major offense: Attempted murder during the
freeing of a convicted prisoner, Andreas Baader
Active: May 14, 1970
Locale: West Germany
Sentence: Eight years in prison; three years into her
sentence, she hanged herself

Early Life
Ulrike Meinhof (uhl-REEK-uh MIN-hawf) was the
daughter of an art museum director and an art historian.
Both of her parents died while she was young; her father
died of cancer when she was six. To make ends meet, her
mother rented a room to an acquaintance, Renate
Riemack, whom Ulrike befriended. When Ulrike was
fifteen, her mother died of an infection following an operation for cancer. Riemack, a staunch socialist, provided Ulrike and her sister, Weinke, a place to live.

Activist Career
Meinhof became politically active in the 1950's by leading a group opposed to nuclear weapons. In 1958
Meinhof joined the Socialist German Students' Union,
published articles about the nuclear issue, and helped organize demonstrations against nuclear weapons.

In December, 1961, Ulrike Meinhof married Klaus
Rainer Röhl, who was the publisher of the left-wing
newspaper *Konkret*. She gave birth to twin girls, Bettina
and Regine, on September 21, 1962, but had to undergo
brain surgery soon thereafter. The lengthy surgery left
Meinhof with a silver clamp in her brain to relieve
pressure.

She was part of the protest movement of the 1960's
and gained notoriety as a member of the Red Army
Faction. In 1968, she was arrested for blocking the
Springer Press building with her car as part of a protest
against the newspaper's perceived anti-left slant. The
charge was dismissed in court. She also divorced her
husband in 1968.

On May 14, 1970, Meinhof played a key role in freeing Andreas Baader, one of the leaders of the Red Army
Faction, which was also known as the Baader-Meinhof
Gang. Baader, imprisoned for his activities, was allowed
to compile research for a book at the Sociological Insti-

tute in West Berlin. Meinhof entered the institute after
explaining that she was there to help Baader with his
work. Her associates arrived with tear gas and pistols;
Baader's dramatic escape was made out the library window while a getaway car waited nearby.

She spent the next two years on the run. Having escaped, Baader fled in June with Meinhof and other members of the Red Army Faction to Jordan to train with the
Popular Front for the Liberation of Palestine. By August
9, they were back in West Germany and committed a series of bank robberies, bombings, and shootings over the
following few years. Meinhof wrote a manifesto in 1971
for the Red Army Faction titled "The Urban Guerrilla
Concept," in which she coined the name Red Army
Faction.

Legal Action and Outcome
On June 15, 1972, Meinhof was arrested in Hanover and
taken to prison. Because the authorities had no fingerprints of her on file, they decided to take X rays of her

Ulrike Meinhof.

head, having learned about her operation and clamp from a lengthy article in *Stern* magazine.

In prison awaiting trial, in May-June, 1973, she and her Red Army Faction comrades who were also incarcerated went on a hunger strike to protest their conditions. On November 29, 1974, she received an eight-year sentence for the freeing of Andreas Baader and was sent to Stammheim Prison in Stuttgart in December. In Stuttgart she and other Red Army Faction members were tried for five murders, numerous attempted murders, and bank robbery.

On May 9, 1976, Meinhof was found hanging in her prison cell, dead. There is some dispute as to whether she committed suicide or the German government was responsible for her death, although most sources indicate that she did commit suicide. Her burial was attended by four thousand people.

IMPACT

One of the most famous female terrorists and political activists of the 1970's, Ulrike Meinhof is important for a number of reasons. Early in her career her name became well known when she compared the chairman of the Christian Socialist Union (CSU) to Adolf Hitler. Although her direct participation in the violent activities of the Red Army Faction are questioned by some, there is evidence that she carried weapons with her and was involved in their purchase. Meinhof's writings indicate an acceptance of violence when committed to effect societal change.

FURTHER READING

Aust, Stefan. *The Baader-Meinhof Group: The Inside Story of a Phenomenon.* London: Butler and Tanner, 1985. Provides a detailed account of the activities of numerous members of the Red Army Faction and the outcomes and legal consequences of such activities.

Becker, Jillian. *Hitler's Children: The Story of the Baader-Meinhof Terrorist Gang.* New York: J. B. Lippincott, 1977. Discusses events leading up to the formation of the Baader-Meinhof Gang and changes in membership and leadership. Provides detailed accounts of their terrorist activities and encounters with the law.

Giles, Steve, and Maike Oergel, eds. *Counter-Cultures in Germany and Central Europe: From Sturm und Drang to Baader-Meinhof.* New York: Peter Lang, 2003. A collection of papers that address various forms of counterculture and terrorism from the 1770's until the 1990's.

Slaughter, Jane, and Robert Kern, eds. *European Women on the Left: Socialism, Feminism, and the Problems Faced by Political Women, 1880 to the Present.* Westport, Conn.: Greenwood Press, 1981. Discusses a number of notable women, their beliefs, and their struggles.

Varon, Jeremy. *Bringing the War Home: The Weather Underground, the Red Army Faction, and Revolutionary Violence in the Sixties and Seventies.* Berkeley: University of California Press, 2004. Focuses on political uprisings led by young, middle-class individuals and how they used violence, both successfully and unsuccessfully, to attempt to achieve their political goals.

—Sheryl L. Van Horne

SEE ALSO: Andreas Baader; Patty Hearst; Horst Mahler.

JOSEF MENGELE
German physician and Nazi ideologue

BORN: March 16, 1911; Günzburg, Germany

DIED: February 7, 1979; Bertioga, Brazil

ALSO KNOWN AS: Fritz Ulmann; Fritz Hollmann; Andreas; Helmut Gregor; José Mengele; Peter Hochbichler; Wolfgang Gerhard; Dr. Auschwitz; Angel of Death; Todesengel

CAUSE OF NOTORIETY: Mengele tortured and murdered Auschwitz prisoners in the name of medical experimentation.

ACTIVE: May 30, 1943-January 18, 1945

LOCALE: Auschwitz (Oswiecim) concentration camp in Nazi-occupied Poland

EARLY LIFE

As the son of a prosperous industrialist, Josef Mengele (MEHN-geh-leh) had a privileged upbringing in Bavaria until, at fifteen, he was diagnosed with osteomyelitis. His health problems led to an interest in medicine, which he pursued at the University of Munich, where, as a right-wing nationalist, he joined the "Steel Helmet" (*Stahlhem*), an organization that blamed Jews for Germany's defeat in World War I. In Munich he may have met Adolf Hitler, whose racist ideas deeply influenced him. In 1935 he received his doctorate for a study of the lower jaws of four racial groups. While working at the University of Frankfurt for his doctorate in medicine under the supervision of Otmar von Verschuer in the Institute for Racial Hygiene, he joined the Nazi Party. His medical dissertation, on the genetics of cleft palate, illustrates his early commitment to use science to support Nazi ideology. He joined the Schutzstaffel (SS), Hitler's elite special security force, in 1938, the year he received his M.D.

Aspiring to an academic career, Mengele became Verschuer's assistant and married a professor's daughter, with whom he later had a son, but the outbreak of World War II in 1939 interrupted his research. As a member of the medical corps of the Waffen Schutzstaffel, he served in France, in occupied Poland, and on the Ukrainian front, where he was severely wounded. His bravery in combat earned him promotion and several decorations, including the Iron Cross, First Class.

Because his wounds rendered him unfit for combat, he was reposted to Berlin, where he resumed his scientific work with Verschuer, who was now director of the Kaiser Wilhelm Institute for Anthropology, Heredity, and Eugenics. With Verschuer's support, Mengele sought work as a doctor and researcher at a concentration camp. Heinrich Himmler, head of the SS, appointed Mengele as a medical officer at Birkenau, a supplementary camp near Auschwitz.

CONCENTRATION-CAMP CAREER

On arrival at Auschwitz on May 30, 1943, Mengele was assigned to the Gypsy camp at Birkenau (sometimes called "Auschwitz II"). Over the following twenty months he would be given increasingly powerful positions, and he became infamous for his roles as the "Great Selector" (because he chose incoming Jews and other "undesirables" for labor or extermination in the gas chambers) and as a medical experimenter on human subjects. The two roles often overlapped, as he was interested in selecting twins and prisoners with genetic abnormalities for his experiments. Committed to the Nazi policy of race hygiene, Mengele believed it was his duty to rid the Third Reich of "human garbage" and to discover how to breed a master race. He sent thousands of prisoners to their deaths because they were weak, ill, or aged, or because they had such "defects" as skin blemishes, scars, or even diminutive height.

Mengele became most notorious for his experiments on human beings, first at the Gypsy camp, then at his other Auschwitz assignments. While working with Verschuer, he had absorbed his mentor's interest in twins, and Verschuer's Berlin Institute financially supported Mengele's medical experiments, no matter how horrendous. For example, he injected chemicals into children's eyes to discover if he could permanently alter eye color. As a consequence, some children were blinded, and others died due to painful infections. Mengele even tried to create artificial conjoined twins by connecting two children's blood vessels and organs. In one experiment the joined twins screamed for three days until death ended their suffering. In other cases Mengele killed healthy twins simply because they had differently colored eyes, and he wanted these eyes to be exhibited at the Berlin Institute. People with genetic abnormalities of all kinds fascinated Mengele, and he also selected them for experimentation.

As a physician, Mengele was responsible for controlling the spread of diseases among prisoners. For example, in July, 1944, he combated a spotted fever epidemic by the monstrous method of gassing nearly four thousand men, women, and children. Mengele's work was ad-

---

MENGELE ON THE RUN

Fleeing Paraguay to escape Nazi hunters, Josef Mengele came to rest in São Paulo, Brazil. He was a lonely, frightened, broke, and depressed man, his mind still stuck in 1945. In 2004, eighty-four documents that he wrote late in life were rediscovered in the records department of the Brazilian federal police. Among them were letters and a diary written just before his death, and they show him alternately pitying himself because of his predicament and enraged about the state of the world.

He seems to have disliked everything: the climate ("the rainy weather is very depressing"), modern music ("cacophony"), theater and television ("thoughts of entrails"), modern art ("the expression of pathological mental conditions, ignorance, lack of talent, malice, or whatever"), students ("degenerate youth"), and what he read of his homeland in the newspapers ("Oh Germany, land in crisis, where is your empire?").

Commenting on these documents, German journalists Erich Wiedemann and Jens Glüsing remark on the "concert pitch of whininess" that they found. Mengele was obsessed with his health, which was worsened by his fear. The journalists write,

> At some point during the years after he fled prosecution in Germany, Mengele, terrified of being discovered, began chewing off the tips of his moustache hairs and swallowing them. After a few months, the hairs collected in his intestines into balls, blocking his digestive tract. It was a life-threatening condition.

Mengele's ferocious belief in Nazi racial theory infuses his writings; in one instance, he praises South African apartheid. He despised former Nazis who recanted. Moreover, Mengele was not completely isolated in his views. According to Wiedemann and Glüsing,

> In Mengele's view, racial confusion prevailed in his adopted country, Brazil. Nevertheless, he imagined that he was surrounded by like-minded people. In one letter . . . he wrote that he was living among families who felt largely sympathetic toward the Nazis. There was only one exception: A niece in one family was engaged to a Brazilian who had no appreciation for Aryanism. But, Mengele wrote, there will always be black sheep. From his point of view, everyone else in his social environment was intact in terms of this race-based ideology.

Source: Erich Wiedemann and Jens Glüsing, "Josef Mengele in Brazil: 'Angel of Death' Diary Shows No Regrets." *Der Spiegel*, November 29, 2004. Translated by Christopher Sultan.

---

mired by his superiors, who promoted him to the position of First Physician of Auschwitz II-Birkenau and honored him with the War Service Medal. However, early in 1945, Soviet military successes in eastern Poland forced Mengele and other Nazi officials to flee from Auschwitz to Gross-Rosen, another concentration camp, which proved to be only a temporary asylum.

LEGAL ACTION AND OUTCOME

Disguised as a regular army soldier, Mengele, after eluding the Russians and Americans, was eventually captured and held as a prisoner of war under his own name by Americans, who failed to realize that he was a war criminal until after he had escaped. With the help of family and friends, Mengele created a new identity as a farm laborer in Bavaria, before departing via Italy for Argentina in 1949. For the following thirty years Mengele lived under a variety of names in Argentina, Paraguay, and Brazil.

Despite a three-million-dollar reward and efforts by the Israeli agency Mossad and prosecutors in Frankfurt,

Mengele was never brought to justice. He was even able, in 1977, to meet with his son, who was deeply dissatisfied with his father's explanations of his Auschwitz activities. After Mengele's death from a stroke in 1979, the search for him continued, and in 1981 a court in Freiburg issued a new arrest warrant. These searches finally ended when his body was identified through the combined efforts of West German, South American, and U.S. officials in 1985.

IMPACT

Unlike many Nazi doctors who were captured, tried, and convicted during the Nuremberg Trials, Josef Mengele avoided punishment for crimes far worse than those of the prosecuted physicians. When his role in the deaths and sufferings of thousands became known to the world, he served as a symbol of all that was evil in Nazi Germany, though scholars such as Robert Jay Lifton believe it is a mistake to treat him as "purely evil." Instead, Lifton sees Mengele as a "double man" who schizophrenically compartmentalized his life into the self-sacrificial soldier and the dispassionately cruel Nazi ideologue.

Mengele's concentration-camp career has had an influence on Holocaust studies and on psychologists who study aberrant behavior. When his crimes against humanity became known, the universities of Munich and Frankfurt withdrew his degrees. The twins who survived Mengele's macabre experiments founded an organization, Children of Auschwitz Nazi Deadly Laboratory Experiments Survivors (CANDLES), in 1984 to gather evidence of his crimes and educate people about them. In 1985 a public trial was held in Israel, and Mengele was tried and convicted of war crimes in absentia.

His crimes have also had a cultural impact. In Rolf Hochhuth's controversial drama *The Deputy* (1963), the character of "the Doctor" is obviously modeled on Mengele, who serves as a symbol of Nazi evil. William Goldman's 1974 novel *Marathon Man* was made into a successful film featuring a character based on Mengele, as was Ira Levin's novel *The Boys from Brazil* (1976). The character Dorf in the 1978 television series *Holocaust* was also derived from Mengele. He was even the subject of a song, "Angel of Death," on a 1986 rock album, *Reign in Blood,* by the group Slayer. Although he saw himself as a Nazi revolutionary with a mission to remake the world, politicians, writers, religious leaders, and others see him as Hitler's "most absolutely convinced Nazi," whose incalculable atrocities must be remembered so that they will never be repeated.

FURTHER READING

Lagnado, Lucette Matalon, and Sheila Cohn Dekel. *Children of the Flames: Dr. Josef Mengele and the Untold Story of the Twins of Auschwitz.* New York: Penguin Books, 1992. This book, based largely on eyewitness accounts, tells not only the story of Mengele's experiments but also what happened to Mengele and the surviving twins after World War II.

Lifton, Robert Jay. *The Nazi Doctors: Medical Killing and the Psychology of Genocide.* New York: Basic Books, 1986. Lifton tells the story of how doctors before and during World War II became involved in killing their patients. Chapter 17 is devoted to Mengele. Extensive notes to primary and secondary sources, and an index.

Posner, Gerald. *Mengele: The Complete Story.* New York: Cooper Square Press, 2000. Based on research into previously unavailable family papers, this biography gives a detailed account of Mengele's life and work as well as an analysis of why he was never brought to justice.

—*Robert J. Paradowski*

SEE ALSO: Klaus Barbie; Martin Bormann; Léon Degrelle; Adolf Eichmann; Hans Michael Frank; Joseph Goebbels; Hermann Göring; Rudolf Hess; Reinhard Heydrich; Heinrich Himmler; Adolf Hitler; Alfred Jodl; Joachim von Ribbentrop; Baldur von Schirach; Otto Skorzeny; Julius Streicher.

MENGISTU HAILE MARIAM
Ethiopian head of state (1977-1991)

BORN: 1937; Walayata district, Kefa Province, Ethiopia

CAUSE OF NOTORIETY: Under a genocidal policy he called Red Terror, Mengistu attempted to turn Ethiopia into a communist state and ordered mass killings of Ethiopian civilians.

ACTIVE: September 12, 1974-May, 1991

LOCALE: Ethiopia

EARLY LIFE

Information on the early life of Mengistu Haile Mariam (mehng-GEES-tew HI-lee MAHR-ee-uhm) is sketchy. He was born to a humble family in 1937 in Kefa Province, southern Ethiopia, and his formal education did not go beyond middle school. He joined the Junior Signal Corps of the army in his early teens to be trained in radio

communication. Mengistu was later selected to attend the Holeta Military Academy, where he graduated with the rank of a second lieutenant in 1957. Mengistu also attended American military training programs at Fort Leavenworth in Kansas and the Aberdeen Training Grounds in Maryland. Upon his return to Ethiopia, he was assigned to the Third Army Division in Harar, where he served in the armament depot with the rank of a major.

POLITICAL CAREER

Mengistu's life took a dramatic turn in the spring of 1974, when widespread civilian protest and army mutiny shook Emperor Haile Selassie's government. Mengistu was one of about one hundred officers and enlisted men chosen by their respective military units from various parts of the country to go to Addis Ababa, Ethiopia's capital, to represent the military's grievance. The group constituted itself as the Derg (committee) and began to see itself as the official representative of the armed forces. The paralysis of the emperor's government emboldened the Derg further and catapulted it into the center stage of Ethiopian politics by the summer of 1974. Mengistu was elected chairman of the Derg. Under Mengistu's uncompromising leadership, the Derg emerged as the most powerful force of the hitherto unfocused and spontaneous movement against the discredited regime of Haile Selassie. Throughout the summer of 1974, Mengistu's group continued to make radical public demands, imprisoned key government officials, and rendered the monarchy impotent by whittling away at its institutional and structural foundation.

On September 12, 1974, with Mengistu playing the leading role, the military junta overthrew Haile Selassie and declared itself as the Provisional Military Administration Council. Aman Andom, a popular general, was elected as head of state. However, Mengistu and his fellow hard-liners in the Derg resented Andom's attempt to exercise real power and moved quickly before he had time to consolidate his authority. Under Mengistu's leadership, on November 22, 1974, the Derg ordered the execution of Andom and sixty other generals and ministers of the old regime. The fate of General Tafari Benti, Andom's successor as head of state, was no different. Mengistu saw Tafari as an obstacle to his own rise to power and succeeded in having the general and several other rivals in the Derg executed on February 3, 1977. Mengistu was declared head of state a week later.

At the same time, Mengistu waged a ruthless campaign of terror against his civilian opponents. Aided by his civilian Marxist advisers, Mengistu built a fearsome organizational apparatus of repression. Tens of thousands of youth in Ethiopia's towns fell victim to Mengistu's so-called Red Terror. Although Mengistu had become an avowed Marxist by this time, the targets of his repression were mostly the left-wing opposition to his military dictatorship.

The burgeoning secessionist movements that threatened to split the country, as well as an invasion from Somalia, allowed Mengistu to justify his murderous policy and to pose as the champion of national unity. Assisted by the Soviet Union and the Eastern bloc, he carried out a massive military buildup. Although he was able to reverse the Somali invasion in 1978, various insurgencies continued to fester throughout the country. Continuous war, persistent drought, and misguided agrarian policy

brought the country to the verge of collapse by the end of the 1980's. With the Soviet Union itself crumbling, Mengistu's regime was isolated internationally and besieged internally. An abortive coup against Mengistu in May, 1989, led to the arrest and execution of large numbers of generals and other senior military officers; the Ethiopian military crumbled in the face of massive insurgent attacks from all directions. Mengistu himself fled the country on May 21, 1991, and sought refuge in Zimbabwe. The Eritrean People's Liberation Front, which had been fighting for the independence of Eritrea, took full control of that region; its ally, the Tigrayan People's Liberation Front, which had assembled an amalgam of other ethnic guerrilla groups under it, entered Addis Ababa on May 28, 1991, and declared itself as the government of Ethiopia.

Mengistu subsequently stood accused of genocide in absentia. Although the Ethiopian government has sought his repatriation, the Zimbabwe government of Robert Mugabe has steadfastly refused to extradite him to Ethiopian authorities. Zimbabwean officials claim that they offered a safe haven for Mengistu under advice from the United States.

IMPACT

Mengistu Haile Mariam's seventeen years of Stalinistic rule were characterized by a savage repression that claimed the lives of tens of thousands of Ethiopia's educated youth. Several more thousands were tortured and imprisoned or were forced into exile. Massive war mobilization coupled with misguided agrarian policy, such as collectivization and peasant resettlements, led to the collapse of food production and massive starvation. More than one million peasants may have died as a result.

FURTHER READING

Clapham, Christopher. *Transformation and Continuity in Revolutionary Ethiopia.* Cambridge, England: Cambridge University Press, 1988. A meticulous analysis of the impact of a socialist revolution on one of the world's oldest kingdoms.

Henze, Paul B. *Layers of Time: A History of Ethiopia.* New York: Palgrave, 2000. The author was a frequent visitor to the country and was intimately acquainted with Mengistu's policy and Ethiopia's international standing during the years of the revolution.

Marcus, Harold. *A History of Ethiopia.* Berkeley: University of California Press, 1994. One of the best standard works on Ethiopia by an author with a profound grasp of Ethiopian history, both past and modern.

Mayfield, Julie. "The Prosecution of War Crimes and Respect for Human Rights: Ethiopia's Balancing Act." *Emory International Law Review* 9, no. 2 (Fall, 1995). Useful for understanding the legal proceedings against Mengistu and the challenges and complexities of prosecuting genocide and human rights violation cases.

Ottaway, David, and Marina Ottaway. *Ethiopia, Empire in Revolution*. New York: Holmes & Meier, 1978. A well-received work written at the height of the Ethiopian revolution by two keen observers of events in Ethiopia.

—*Shumet Sishagne*

SEE ALSO: Sani Abacha; Idi Amin; Omar al-Bashir; Jean-Bédel Bokassa; Samuel K. Doe; Mobutu Sese Seko; Robert Mugabe; Muhammad Siad Barre; Charles Taylor.

RAMÓN MERCADER
Spanish assassin

BORN: February 7, 1914; Barcelona, Spain
DIED: October 18, 1978; Moscow, Soviet Union (now Russia)
ALSO KNOWN AS: Frank Jacson; Jacques Mornard; Jaime Ramón Mercader del Río Hernandez (full name)
MAJOR OFFENSE: Murder of Leon Trotsky
ACTIVE: August 20, 1940
LOCALE: Coyoacán, Mexico
SENTENCE: Twenty years in prison

EARLY LIFE
On February 7, 1914, Ramón Mercader (MUR-cay-dur) was born to Eustacia Maria Caridad del Río Hernandez and Don Pablo Mercader Marina in Barcelona, Spain. However, after his parents separated, he spent most of his youth in France with his mother. He eventually became a committed Communist. By 1935, he was active in an underground Communist cell in Spain.

CRIMINAL CAREER
Recruited by his mother, who was also a dedicated Communist and a Soviet operative, Mercader traveled in 1937 to Moscow for training as an assassin. The priority of Soviet intelligence was the elimination of Joseph Stalin's great rival, Leon Trotsky. Trotsky's son and secretary had already been murdered, but so far Trotsky had escaped Stalin's wrath.

Mercader possessed a number of skills that made him suitable for the work of an assassin. He spoke several languages, was highly disciplined, had a desire to be trained, showed initiative, and enjoyed an excellent memory. He would become the top agent on a team headed by his mother, with the exiled Trotsky, based in a villa in Coyoacán, Mexico, as their target. Mercader was a Soviet "illegal," a Soviet agent operating abroad under an assumed identity. Mercader became Frank Jacson (a Soviet misspelling of Jackson), a Canadian who had fought in the Spanish Civil War.

To build his cover and begin the process of gaining access to his intended target, Mercader became romantically involved with one of Trotsky's secretaries. Every day he drove her to work in the morning and picked her up at the end of the day. Although he did not initially enter the Coyoacán compound, he soon became a familiar figure to Trotsky's numerous guards. In March, 1940, Mercader was trusted enough to enter the villa for the first time.

Although Mercader had been trained as an assassin, his initial role was one of supporting a team of assassins by serving as their scout and supplying information about the villa and its security. The hit squad struck in the middle of the night of May 24, 1940. In that attempt, Trotsky escaped unscathed, despite dozens of bullets being fired into his bedroom. Those involved in the attack either fled or were arrested.

Mercader then became the main instrument of Stalin's vengeance. A few days after the May attack, he met Trotsky for the first time, even bringing a gift for the revolutionary's grandson. Mercader made several more visits over the next few months, slowly biding his time while he won his target's trust. The day of the attack arrived on August 20, 1940, and Mercader arrived at the villa carrying three weapons: a gun, an ice pick, and a knife sewed into the lining of his jacket. He sought a private meeting with Trotsky under the pretense of discussing a magazine article. While his host leaned forward to read the article, Mercader brought the ice pick down on the back of the Russian's head. Having expected Trotsky to die without a word, Mercader was unpleasantly surprised by his victim's screams, which alerted nearby guards. Instead of escaping as he had planned, Mercader found himself beaten by the security guards and then turned over to the Mexican police.

LEGAL ACTION AND OUTCOME

Mercader was tried for Trotsky's murder, but despite offers by the Mexican authorities to reduce his sentence if he revealed who was behind the attack, Mercader kept silent. His self-imposed silence extended to his true identity. It would not be until 1953 that fingerprints revealed his real name and the fact that he was a Spaniard. Proof of ties to Soviet intelligence would not emerge until after the fall of the Soviet Union. Mercader served out his twenty-year sentence and then moved to Havana. Eventually, he traveled to the Soviet Union, where he received awards, a pension, and an apartment for his work on behalf of the Soviet state.

IMPACT

Despite the audacity of his act, Ramón Mercader is little remembered. Trotsky was already a marginalized figure, and his being a target spoke more about Stalin's paranoia than about any threat posed by the victim. By 1956, as Mercader sat in a prison cell in Mexico, Stalin and Stalinism would be denounced secretly by Nikita S. Khrushchev at a Communist Party conference. Mercader's mother would later have doubts about her role in the crime, but her son apparently did not have any regrets for what he had done.

FURTHER READING

Andrew, Christopher, and Oleg Gordievsky. *KGB: The Inside Story*. London: Hodder & Stoughton, 1990. Details Mercader's efforts against Trotsky per Gordievsky, a senior member of the KGB who defected to the West.

Andrew, Christopher, and Vasili Mitrokhin. *The Mitrokhin Archive: The KGB in Europe and the West*. London: Gardners Books, 2000. Contains a brief dis-

Leon Trotsky. (National Archives)

cussion of Mercader and his role in the Trotsky assassination uniquely based on information copied from the KGB archives by its former employee Vasili Mitrokhin.

Mahoney, Harry Thayer, and Marjorie Locke Mahoney. *The Saga of Leon Trotsky: His Clandestine Operations and His Assassination*. London: Austin & Winfield, 1998. A look at Trotsky's life and death.

West, Nigel. *The Illegals: Double Lives of the Cold War's Most Secret Agents*. London: Hodder & Stoughton, 1994. A study of leading Soviet agents by a well-known British intelligence expert.

—*Steve Hewitt*

SEE ALSO: Nikita S. Khrushchev; Vladimir Ilich Lenin; Joseph Stalin; Leon Trotsky; Vasili Vasilievich Ulrikh; Andrey Vyshinsky; Andrey Aleksandrovich Zhdanov; Grigory Yevseyevich Zinovyev.

JACQUES MESRINE
French career criminal

BORN: December 28, 1936; Clichy, France
DIED: November 2, 1979; Paris, France
ALSO KNOWN AS: Jacques René Mesrine (full name); Jean-Jacques Moreau; Bruno Dansereau; Nicolas Scaff
MAJOR OFFENSES: Kidnapping, robbery, burglary, and murder
ACTIVE: 1962-1979
LOCALE: France (mostly Paris) and Montreal, Canada
SENTENCE: Served a total of approximately five years in prison for robbery; ten years for kidnapping, served five

EARLY LIFE

Jacques Mesrine (zhahk mez-REEN), his mother, and his older sister escaped German-occupied Paris when Jacques was three, while his father was serving in the army. Even after World War II ended, Jacques felt deprived of his father's attention and failed in school. His family tried to see that he obtained an education, but in spite of his obvious talent he found more satisfaction in fighting and arguing than in studying. After being expelled from two schools he spent his days stealing cars with other teenagers. Throughout his life, his family tried to help him find a productive career, and at times he did try, but circumstances and his deep-seated desire for attention always misdirected him.

Mesrine served in French troops during the Algerian War of Independence (1954-1962). In Algeria he developed a taste for danger and brutality. He made contacts with men in the Organisation Armée Secrète (OAS) and learned many techniques of clandestine operations. These resources proved useful to him in his criminal activities.

CRIMINAL CAREER

After the excitement of army service, Mesrine found it very difficult to adjust to civilian life. In 1963, following a year in prison for committing several robberies, he made his greatest effort to find a life outside crime. With his family's help he bought a flat in Paris, enrolled in architecture courses, and found a job with a design firm. He showed talent in the work but was let go as a result of downsizing. Crime seemed to him to be the only sure way to success, and it was fame that Mesrine desired above all.

He made another effort to live a respectable life in 1967 when, with his father's help, he became an inn-keeper. He was very good in this role but found the lifestyle too drab and gradually resumed associating with the criminal side of Paris he loved.

As his criminal reputation grew, he found it costlier to live in the style he desired and spent four years in Canada, the United States, and Venezuela. In Canada he staged a spectacular kidnapping of Georges Deslauriers, for whom he had worked briefly. The plan failed when Deslauriers escaped captivity before his $200,000 ransom was paid. Although Mesrine fled to the United States, he was extradited back to Canada, where he was sentenced to ten years for kidnapping.

He escaped prison in 1972, began robbing banks, and, with an accomplice, murdered two forest rangers. Back in France in 1973, Mesrine was arrested briefly but escaped during his sentencing hearing, taking a judge as a hostage. It was four months before he was arrested again. In jail, he wrote his autobiography, which was smuggled out. In 1978 he again escaped; police shot one of his accomplices during the attempt, but Mesrine, now free, had created a national scandal. After repeated burglaries and robberies, and murders—39 by his own count—Mesrine in 1979 received six million francs for the ransom of French millionaire Henri Lelièvre.

LEGAL ACTION AND OUTCOME

By this time the police and government were under intense public criticism; the capture of French public enemy number one became their highest priority. Mesrine's prison escapes, both successful and short-lived, brought him much of the fame he desired. That fame eventually brought about his assassination, which some consider to be his final sentence. The French secretary of foreign affairs forced coordination of several law enforcement agencies, and Mesrine was eventually found. On November 2, 1979, his car was trapped between two trucks, and he was shot to death by a squad of sharpshooters.

IMPACT

Jacques Mesrine's cultured and gentlemanly demeanor created the image of a successful man-about-town. Ultimately, such a popular image must be seen in light of the harm done by a career criminal. Although a film version of his autobiography was planned for release in 2007, Mesrine's legacy is as little as that of gangster Al Capone, whom he so admired.

FURTHER READING

"The Indomitable Gaul!" *Do or Die* 9 (2001): 179-181. A summary, taken from Carey Schofield's book, includes an arresting photograph of an armed Mesrine.

Mesrine, Jacques. *L'Instinct de Mort*. Paris: Jean-Claude Lattes, 1977. Mesrine's autobiography was dismissed by police and other criminals as lies but certainly shows Mesrine's life as he saw it. In French.

Schofield, Carey. *Mesrine: The Life and Death of a Supercrook*. New York: Penguin Books, 1980. A detailed biography based on a rare personal interview and extensive research. Photographs but no references.

Wilson, Colin, and Donald Seaman. *The Encyclopedia of Modern Murder, 1962-1982*. New York: G. P. Putnam's Sons, 1983. Brief but very readable overview, with photographs of an especially grotesque incident.

—*K. Thomas Finley*

SEE ALSO: Jules Bonnot; Al Capone; Henri Charrière; George Rivas; Assata Olugbala Shakur; Jonathan Wild.

IOANNIS METAXAS
Greek dictator (1936-1941)

BORN: April 12, 1871; Ithaca, Greece
DIED: January 29, 1941; Athens, Greece
ALSO KNOWN AS: John Metaxas
CAUSE OF NOTORIETY: As dictator, Metaxas introduced strict censorship and attempted to strengthen Greek nationalism, pressuring people to swear an oath of loyalty to the government.
ACTIVE: 1936-1941
LOCALE: Greece

EARLY LIFE

Ioannis Metaxas (yo-AHN-ihs meh-TAHKS-ihs) was born and raised on the island of Ithaca in western Greece. He graduated from the Evelpidon military college in 1890 and then attended the military engineering school and the Berlin War academy. He served as a junior officer under Crown Prince Constantine, the chief of staff, in the 1897 war against Turkey, which began his relationship with the royal family leading to his conservative politics. In the Balkan Wars (1912-1913) Metaxas attained the rank of lieutenant colonel.

POLITICAL CAREER

After the pro-German Constantine, who had become king, abdicated, Metaxas was arrested with other pro-German officers and sent into exile. He returned to Greece in 1920 as a major general but resigned his commission because of his opposition to the Asia Minor campaign. Metaxas formed his own Free Opinion Party (Eleftherofronon Komma) and served in coalition governments from time to time, but his party was never strong.

During the chaos of the early 1930's, which included heightened battles between liberals and monarchists, Metaxas stood above both groups and argued for a stronger central government. In 1933, after eleven years as a republic, the monarchy resumed under Constantine's son George II.

Liberals and conservatives could not agree on a workable coalition, and the king pushed forward Metaxas, whom the parties reluctantly accepted. The prospect of a general strike led by the Communists caused the king to issue a decree handing the power to Metaxas. Numerous left-wing politicians were arrested, and the general began his dictatorial regime on August 4, 1936. What was supposed to be a temporary measure now became the permanent government. Metaxas assumed the posts of minister of foreign affairs, armed forces, and education and acted as deputy for the ministries of security, press, labor, and the economy.

In addition to the support of the king, Metaxas had the backing of the officers' corps, which had divided along party lines previously. Metaxas enjoyed no support from the civilian political leaders or the public, although they passively accepted his rule. He chose his ministers and assistants from among those whom he could trust. He strengthened the police force and destroyed the Communist Party. He introduced strict censorship and moderated schools' and universities' curricula. Metaxas banned books, including works of modern philosophy and even works of classical Greece, such as the famous funeral oration of Pericles defending democracy. He established the national youth movement, pressuring all young people to join and to swear an oath of loyalty to the state and government. His attempts to strengthen Greek nationalism included designating a standard language and supporting affiliation with the Orthodox Church, combating the tendency for regionalism.

Seeking the support of the working classes, Metaxas outlawed strikes but not unions and called for minimum-wage laws, contracts, and an eight-hour workday. Real wages actually rose under his regime. Cheap loans aided peasants, and debt reduction aided farmers. Metaxas promoted industry and also agricultural production. He improved health care and adopted a plan for public works.

Metaxas feared Italy and Bulgaria, two countries that Greece had confronted since World War I. He sought alliance with England, which responded only halfheartedly. When World War II started, Greece declared its neutrality, but Italy invaded the country in October, 1940. England was now quick to support Greece, and the Greeks drove the Italians back. Metaxas died in January, 1941, before the campaign was over. Bulgaria and Germany invaded Greece in April, and the country was occupied.

IMPACT

Ioannis Metaxas was not really a typical Fascist dictator like Benito Mussolini or Adolf Hitler in that he promoted no racist or expansionist policies. He was one of three dictators who punctuated Greek government, alternating with republics and monarchies, in the twentieth century.

FURTHER READING

Joachim, Joachim G. *Ioannis Metaxas: The Formative Years, 1871-1922.* Mannheim, Germany: Bibliopolis, 2000. A standard scholarly work on Metaxas's early life and career.

> ## PROCLAMATION OF THE FOURTH OF AUGUST RÉGIME
>
> *On August 4, 1936, Ioannis Metaxas issued his official proclamation of power in Greece:*
>
> TO THE GREEK PEOPLE,
>
> While the Parliament elected after the long domestic adventures of the Nation in January 1936, in order to redress domestic peace and order, proved itself right from the beginning incapable in this and in providing a Government to the country, and this incapacity proved later and even recently due to incurable party conflicts and personal contentions, that little interested the vast mass of the working people, Communism taking advantage of the circumstances and of the support given to it by different political groups raised its head impertinently, seriously threatening the social status of Greece. . . .
>
> My Government, above any party, having been summoned to power in April of this year and detecting right from the beginning the risks that the Greek society was taking and determined right from the beginning to take all measures . . . aiming at the moral and material improvement of all society and especially of farmers, workers and the poorer in general classes. . . .
>
> I appeal to the full and undivided contribution of all Greeks, who believe that our national traditions and our Greek culture must remain intact. . . .
>
> For this I ask from all full discipline to the State, essential for the salvation of Greek society without which discipline there cannot be real freedom. I also have to categorically declare that I am determined to exterminate by the harshest way any opposition to this national task of national regeneration.
>
> THE PRESIDENT OF THE GOVERNMENT IOANNIS METAXAS
> Athens 4 August 1936
>
> *Source:* Translated from *Ioannis Metaxas: To prosopiko tou imerologio*, edited by L. Metaxa (Athens: Gkovostes, 1970).

Popascoma, Victor. "Metaxas." In *Balkan Dictators*, edited by Bernd Fischer. London: C. Hurst, 2006. An excellent scholarly biography of Metaxas.

Vatakiotis, P. J. *Popular Autocracy in Greece, 1936-1941: A Political Biography of General Ioannis Metaxas.* London: Frank Cass, 1998. A scholarly treatment of the years of Metaxas's dictatorship.

—*Frederick B. Chary*

SEE ALSO: Benito Mussolini; Joseph Stalin; Tito.

TOM METZGER
American white supremacist

BORN: April 9, 1938; Warsaw, Indiana
ALSO KNOWN AS: Thomas Linton Metzger (full name); Thomas Byron Linton (birth name)
CAUSE OF NOTORIETY: As a politician and the founder of the racist organization White Aryan Resistance, Metzger fought against immigration and encouraged violence against minorities. A wrongful action civil suit was successfully brought against him for inciting a racist murder.
ACTIVE: 1960's-present
LOCALE: Los Angeles, California; Portland, Oregon; and Toronto, Canada
SENTENCE: Six months in prison; served forty-six days

EARLY LIFE
Thomas L. Metzger (MEHTS-guhr) was raised in Warsaw, Indiana, and served as a corporal in the U.S. Army. In 1961, he relocated to Southern California, finding em-

Tom Metzger. (AP/Wide World Photos)

ployment as an electronics technician. He and his wife Kathy married in 1964 and had five daughters, as well as one son, a boy named John who was born in 1967. During the 1960's, Metzger became involved in the John Birch Society, a conservative organization; he left it for a paramilitary organization known as the Minutemen. In 1975, he became a Christian Identity minister and also joined David Duke's Knights of the Ku Klux Klan, rising to the rank of Grand Dragon of California.

POLITICAL CAREER
In the late 1970's, Metzger led his California Klansmen on armed patrols to capture illegal Mexican immigrants crossing the border south of his base in Fallbrook, California. His strong stand against illegal immigrants helped him win the Democratic primary for Congress in his home district in the fall of 1980; the embarrassed Democratic Party subsequently threw its support to the Republican candidate, who won handily. Metzger then left the Klan and formed the White American Political Association (WAPA) in order to promote his own run for a U.S. Senate seat in the 1982 California primary, again as a Democrat. He lost, receiving only 2.5 percent of the votes.

In 1983, Metzger abandoned mainstream politics and focused on media to help spread his racist ideas. WAPA evolved into the White Aryan Resistance (WAR). He began generating a monthly newspaper, also called *WAR*, and spread his message via a telephone hotline, books, cartoons, stickers, videos, and radio and television appearances, and eventually e-mail and a Web site. In 1984, he developed a videotaped cable television series titled *Race and Reason*, which his followers successfully aired through public access in major cities throughout the country.

Metzger's media campaign found an audience in the skinheads, a disaffected youth subculture with neo-Nazi beliefs. Metzger used his son John to establish close connections with skinhead leaders in 1985. On November 3, 1988, the Metzger father-and-son team appeared on Geraldo Rivera's talk show, and their brawl there with a black activist resulted in a much-publicized broken nose for the host. Nine days later, a skinhead group in Portland, Oregon, attacked three Ethiopian immigrants, killing one of them named Mulugeta Seraw. The murder investigation revealed strong ties back to the influence of Metzger.

LEGAL ACTION AND OUTCOME

In a wrongful action civil suit brought on behalf of the Seraw family, an Oregon jury found Metzger and his organization culpable of inciting murder and awarded $12.5 million in damages. This judgment was upheld on appeal in April, 1993. Metzger's involvement in a 1983 cross-burning incident eventually led to an unlawful assembly misdemeanor conviction in 1991. Sentenced to six months in jail and three hundred hours of community service, Metzger was released from jail after forty-six days so that he could be with his chronically ill wife. In July, 1992, he illegally left the United States to attend a hate rally in Toronto and was again jailed, this time for five days, before deportation back to the United States.

IMPACT

Tom Metzger failed in his bid as a mainstream political activist for white supremacy, but he developed a mass-media outreach for his propaganda in the 1980's and 1990's using not only newsletters and fliers but also television and the Internet. He ultimately pioneered a model of racist revolt against the government known as the "lone wolf" approach: This strategy used guerrilla warfare tactics within an organization of individuals loosely interconnected via technology but performing acts of terrorism and illegal violence anonymously. The successful influence of this model was evident in the rise of a new generation of Internet-connected racists epitomized by Alex Curtis of San Diego.

The large judgment against Metzger in the Seraw case also signaled a new type of legal accountability for those who preach and advocate violence. In 1994, the Church of the Creator in Florida was ordered to pay $1 million for its support of hate crimes; in 1998, the Ku Klux Klan in South Carolina was ordered to pay $21 million for its support of arson committed against African American churches; and in 2000, the Aryan Nations in Idaho was ordered to pay $6.3 million for actively encouraging hate crimes.

FURTHER READING

Langer, Elinor. *A Hundred Little Hitlers*. New York: Metropolitan, 2003. Langer details the Portland beating and murder of Seraw, summarizes the rise of the skinhead movement, and critiques Metzger's trial.

Lee, Martin. *The Beast Reawakens*. Boston: Little, Brown, 1999. Considers the rise of neo-Nazi movements around the world and shows how Metzger connects to a larger fascist and racist network.

Phillips, John W. *Sign of the Cross: The Prosecutor's True Story of a Landmark Trial Against the Klan*. Louisville, Ky.: Westminster John Knox Press, 2000. Personal, dramatic account of the Southern California attorney who prosecuted Metzger and the Klan, tracing the ups and downs of the legal battle and the Klan's responses.

—Scot M. Guenter

SEE ALSO: Richard Girnt Butler; Willis A. Carto; David Duke; Matthew F. Hale.

MIJAILO MIJAILOVIC
Swedish assassin

BORN: December 6, 1978; Stockholm, Sweden
MAJOR OFFENSE: Murder of Anna Lindh, Swedish foreign minister
ACTIVE: September 10, 2003
LOCALE: Stockholm, Sweden
SENTENCE: Life in prison

EARLY LIFE

Mijailo Mijailovic (mih-HI-loh mih-HI-loh-vihch) was born in Stockholm, Sweden, to Serbian immigrants. Thus he was a Swedish citizen. As a child he lived for a few years in Mladenvać in Serbia, the hometown of his parents, and went to school there. After he returned to Sweden he went to high school but dropped out before graduating.

CRIMINAL CAREER

A troubled young man suffering from mental disorders, Mijailovic committed several violent crimes. After having received convictions for illegal firearms possession and threatening women, he was convicted of stabbing his father in 1997. He was placed in a psychiatric hospital, then released on September 5, 2003.

On September 10, Mijailovic felt ill and took medication to help him sleep. He then visited several shops before arriving at Stockholm's upscale Nordiska Kompaniet department store. There he saw Anna Lindh, Sweden's popular foreign minister, who was shopping there. He stabbed her several times; Lindh died the next day. Two weeks later, the police arrested Mijailovic, who at first denied committing the assault. When presented with

DNA evidence, he confessed, claiming that he did not mean to kill Lindh.

Legal Action and Outcome

Mijailovic's trial was held the following week. Remaining calm in court, Mijailovic said under examination that he was on the way out of the store when voices told him to stab Lindh. He believed the voices were those of his parents, but he also stated that Jesus was speaking to him as well. "I could not resist," he said. He told the court he did not remember the actual attack or how many times he stabbed the minister. He also claimed that he was not interested in politics and did not attack Lindh because she was the foreign minister, although he was known to obsess about famous people and expressed hatred for Lindh because of Sweden's support of the alliance against Serbia in the 1999 Kosovo war. When his defense attorney asked Mijailovic what his mood was at the time of the crime, he replied, "I felt unhappy and depressed. I was carrying a knife and wearing a bulletproof vest."

The court found Mijailovic guilty but ordered a psychiatric evaluation before sentencing him. Psychiatrists declared that Mijailovic should be held responsible for the act, and in March, 2004, the court sentenced him to life imprisonment. His attorney asked that the findings be reviewed, but the judge denied the request. Later the court also granted Mijailovic's request to drop his Swedish citizenship (most likely made because he feared retaliation in a Swedish prison), but it did not approve his petition for deportation to a Serbian prison.

An appeals court ruled that Mijailovic suffered from borderline personality disorders and should be confined to a mental hospital rather than prison. However, the prosecutors took the case to Sweden's supreme court, which, in December, 2004, reversed the decision and restored Mijailovic's life sentence. In their findings, the justices wrote that Mijailovic had used a weapon capable of killing, that he had held it with both his hands in delivering the fatal wound, and that the locations and sizes of the wounds indicate that he wished to kill Lindh. Beyond any reasonable doubt, the court declared, the act was premeditated murder.

Impact

The assassination had a profound affect on the national consciousness in Sweden, where millions followed the broadcast of Mijailo Mijailovic's trial. It also affected Swedish politics, as Lindh would most likely have become prime minister. At the time of her death, there was a prominent debate in the country on whether Sweden should adopt the Euro as its national currency. Lindh had

Swedish foreign minister Anna Lindh, Mijailovic's murder victim. (AP/Wide World Photos)

championed the Euro, but its use was not approved after her death.

Further Reading

Cooper, H. H. *The Murder of Olaf Palme: A Tale of Assassination, Deception, and Intrigue.* Lewiston, N.Y.: Edwin Mellen Press, 2003. While dealing mainly with the unsolved 1986 assassination of Swedish prime minister Olaf Palme, this book contains an appendix on the Lindh assassination.

"Sweden." *European Journal of Political Research* 43, nos. 7/8 (December, 2004): 1144-1150. Describes the effect of Lindh's death on Swedish politics.

Widfeldt, Anders. "Elite Collusion and Public Defiance: Sweden's Euro Referendum in 2003." *West European Politics* 27, no. 3 (May, 2004): 503-517. Includes a discussion of the effect of Lindh's assassination on the Euro referendum.

—*Frederick B. Chary*

See also: Said Akbar; Yigal Amir; Jean-Marie Bastien-Thiry; Nathuram Vinayak Godse; John Hinckley, Jr.; Lee Harvey Oswald; Thenmuli Rajaratnam; Beant Singh; Satwant Singh; Sirhan Sirhan; Volkert van der Graaf; Ramzi Yousef.

Stanley Milgram
American social psychologist

Born: August 15, 1933; New York, New York
Died: December 20, 1984; New York, New York
Cause of notoriety: Motivated by the Nuremberg Trials of the 1940's and by Adolf Eichmann's defense at his 1961 war crimes trial that he was merely "following orders" during the Holocaust, Milgram initiated a series of experiments on obedience to authority that involved people being asked to deliver painful electric shocks to innocent victims.
Active: 1961-1962
Locale: Yale University, New Haven, Connecticut

Early Life

The parents of Stanley Milgram (MIHL-grahm), Samuel and Adele, were European Jews who settled in New York City, where they operated a bakery. Stanley was born in New York in 1933, the second of three children. He excelled in high school, thereafter majoring in political science at Queens College. After additional coursework in psychology, Milgram was admitted to the doctoral program in the Department of Social Relations at Harvard University in the fall of 1954.

At Harvard, Milgram worked with noted social psychologist Solomon Asch, who had developed a novel technique for investigating social conformity in the face of group pressure. Milgram adapted this technique for his dissertation research. He received his Ph.D. in 1960 and obtained an assistant professorship at Yale that fall.

Scientific Career

At Yale, Milgram recruited subjects for obedience experiments from among the male citizens of New Haven, Connecticut, by advertising in the local newspaper. For their participation, volunteers were paid four dollars plus carfare. They arrived at Milgram's lab in pairs for what was advertised as an experiment on learning and memory. One volunteer was assigned the role of teacher, the other of learner. The learner was strapped into a chair, and the teacher was shown to another room and instructed on how to use a "shock generator." On the shock generator, switches were labeled in 15-volt increments, ranging from "15 volts, slight shock" to "420 volts, danger: severe shock." Two additional switches were labeled "435 volts, XXX" and "450 volts, XXX." The teacher was then told to administer the learning test. If the learner responded correctly to an item, the teacher moved on to the next item, and if not, the teacher was to

apply a "shock." Each successive error by the learner resulted in a more severe shock.

In fact, no one was shocked. The learner was an actor whose part had been carefully scripted. When 75 volts was supposedly being administered, he began to protest by grunting. At 120 volts he called out, and at 150 volts he demanded to be released from the experiment. As the "shocks" increased in intensity, his protests increased in their apparent agony, until at 270 volts he screamed in mock pain. At 300 volts the learner refused to answer the question but continued protesting until 330 volts, after which nothing further was heard from him.

If the teacher balked, the experimenter prodded him with statements like, "The experiment requires that you continue," and "You have no other choice, you must go on." In some experiments, the learner was in sight of the teacher, and in some the teacher actually had to press the learner's hand onto the shock plate. All teachers, however, complied with the instructions, and many continued the shocks up to the maximum 450-volt level. After the experiment, the teacher-subjects were interviewed and debriefed, and the true nature of the experiment was explained to them.

Milgram's reputation as a psychologist does not derive solely from the obedience experiments. In 1963 he left Yale for Harvard but was denied tenure there due in part to the controversial nature of his research. Thereafter, he took a position as professor at City University of New York, where he headed the graduate program in social psychology. He remained there until his death in 1984. During this time he conducted research on the "small world" effect (popularly known as "six degrees of separation"), the effects of violence in broadcast media, and the psychological experience of urban life.

Impact

Stanley Milgram's obedience experiments are probably the most famous experiments in social psychology, perhaps in all of psychology. Many still consider them to offer a compelling explanation of perpetrator behavior in atrocities such as the Holocaust.

Shortly after their publication in 1963, critics began raising ethical questions about the experiments. Although no one was actually shocked, ethicists raised concerns about deceiving subjects into believing they were administering painful electric shocks to innocent victims. This ultimately led to reconsideration of the ethics

AN UNEXPECTED OUTCOME

In 1974, Stanley Milgram described his experiments and some disturbing results:

Before the experiments, I sought predictions about the outcome from various kinds of people—psychiatrists, college sophomores, middle-class adults, graduate students and faculty in the behavioral sciences. With remarkable similarity, they predicted that virtually all the subjects would refuse to obey the experimenter['s instructions to administer increasingly painful shocks].... These predictions were unequivocally wrong.... [O]ne scientist in Munich found 85 percent of his subjects obedient. Fred Prozi's reactions, if more dramatic than most, illuminate the conflicts experienced by others in less visible form....

PROZI (shakes head, pats the table nervously): You see he's hollering. Hear that? Gee, I don't know.

EXPERIMENTER: The experiment requires . . .

PROZI (interrupting): I know it does sir, but I mean—hunh! He doesn't know what he's getting in for. He's up to 195 volts! (Experiment continues, through 210 volts, 225 volts, 240 volts, 255 volts, 270 volts, at which point Prozi, with evident relief, runs out of word-pair questions.)

EXPERIMENTER: You'll have to go back to the beginning of that page and go through them again until he's learned them all correctly.

PROZI: Aw, no. I'm not going to kill that man. You mean I've got to keep going up with the scale? No sir. He's hollering in there. I'm not going to give him 450 volts.

EXPERIMENTER: The experiment requires that you go on. . . .

PROZI: You accept all responsibility?

EXPERIMENTER: The responsibility is mine. Correct. Please go on. (Subject returns to his list, starts running through words as rapidly as he can read them, works through to 450 volts.)

PROZI: That's that.

EXPERIMENTER: Continue using the 450 switch for each wrong answer. Continue, please.

PROZI: But I don't get anything!

EXPERIMENTER: Please continue. The next word is "white."

PROZI: Don't you think you should look in on him, please?

EXPERIMENTER: Not once we've started the experiment.

PROZI: What if he's dead in there? (Gestures toward the room with the electric chair.) I mean, he told me he can't stand the shock, sir. I don't mean to be rude, but I think you should look in on him. All you have to do is look in on him. All you have to do is look in the door. I don't get no answer, no noise. Something might have happened to the gentleman in there, sir.

EXPERIMENTER: We must continue. Go on, please.

PROZI: You mean keep giving that? Four-hundred-fifty volts, what he's got now?

EXPERIMENTER: That's correct. Continue. The next word is "white."

PROZI (now at a furious pace): "White—cloud, horse, rock, house." Answer, please. The answer is "horse." Four hundred and fifty volts. (Zzumph!) Next words, "Bag—paint, music, clown, girl." The next answer is 'paint.'" Four hundred and fifty volts. (Zzumph!) Next word is "Short—sentence, movie. . . ."

EXPERIMENTER: Excuse me, Teacher. We'll have to discontinue the experiment.

Source: Stanley Milgram, *Obedience to Authority: An Experimental View* (New York: Harper & Row, 1974).

---

involved in the use of human subjects in psychology experiments, including use of deception.

The obedience experiments resonated even outside academic psychology. Articles quickly appeared in the popular press about them, most notably in *The New York Times* and the *St. Louis Post-Dispatch*, the latter especially being harshly critical of Milgram's treatment of naïve subjects. For most people, however, it was the shocking results of the experiments that disturbed them.

Numerous magazine articles described these results, several playwrights were inspired to incorporate them in one form or another into plays, and a made-for-television film, *The Tenth Level*, in which William Shatner played a Milgram-like scientist, appeared on CBS in 1976. Rock-and-roll lyrics were influenced when Peter Gabriel recorded "We Do What We're Told" in 1986. The experiments have influenced teaching methods in law schools and have been studied by the military.

FURTHER READING

Blass, Thomas. *The Man Who Shocked the World: The Life and Legacy of Stanley Milgram.* New York: Basic Books, 2004. A biography written by a psychologist who has continued the research on obedience begun by Milgram.

Milgram, Stanley. *Obedience to Authority: An Experimental View.* 1974. Reprint. New York: HarperCollins, 2004. Milgram's detailed description of the obedience experiments, their justification, and some of their repercussions.

Miller, Arthur G. "What Can the Milgram Obedience Experiments Tell Us About the Holocaust? Generalizing from the Social Psychology Laboratory." In *The Social Psychology of Good and Evil,* edited by Arthur G. Miller. New York: Guilford Press, 2004. Milgram argued that his experiments were relevant to explaining the failure of moral judgment that led to the Holocaust. This chapter reviews his arguments and also the opposing arguments of Milgram's critics.

Sabini, John. "Stanley Milgram (1933-1984)." *American Psychologist* 41 (1986): 1378-1379. Milgram's obituary published in a leading psychology periodical shortly after his death.

—*William B. King*

SEE ALSO: Adolf Eichmann; Laud Humphreys.

MICHAEL MILKEN

American financier

BORN: July 4, 1946; Encino, California
ALSO KNOWN AS: Junk Bond King; Michael Robert Milken (full name)
MAJOR OFFENSES: Indicted under racketeering laws for a broad range of crimes, Milken eventually pleaded guilty to a half-dozen relatively minor infractions of securities laws
ACTIVE: 1984-1986
LOCALE: Los Angeles, California
SENTENCE: Ten years in prison, subsequently reduced to thirty-four months; served twenty-two months

EARLY LIFE

Michael Milken (MIHL-kehn) grew up in Encino, California, in a middle-class Jewish family. After earning his undergraduate degree with honors at the University of California at Berkeley and a master's degree in business administration at the University of Pennsylvania's Wharton School, he joined the firm that later became Drexel Burnham Lambert in 1969 and eventually headed its high-yield bond department, where he redefined the significance of "junk bonds" (bonds with a low rating, representing greater risk but also higher yield). For a number of years in the late 1970's and early 1980's, thanks to his skill at finding buyers for his bonds, Milken exerted immense influence on the American financial community. He also earned enormous remuneration, including an astonishing half-billion-dollar bonus in a single year.

CRIMINAL CAREER

The *Wall Street Journal* reporter James B. Stewart won a Pulitzer Prize in 1988 for his reporting on the 1987 stock market crash and the insider-trading scandal. In these articles, and in his subsequent book *Den of Thieves* (1991), Stewart describes the alleged activities of Milken, Ivan Boesky, and others as well as the actions of prosecutors. Stewart's influential account has been severely criticized by Milken's supporters.

According to prosecutors, Milken conspired with Boesky and others to engage in insider trading of stocks and other illegal activities in the mid-1980's. Although originally indicted in 1989 on ninety-eight counts, Milken eventually pleaded guilty to a half-dozen "technical" violations of securities trading regulations, "violations that normally would merit only a warning letter from the [Securities and Exchange Commission] SEC," the conservative magazine *National Review* commented in 1992.

Long after Milken served his prison term, controversy about his activities continued. In 1998, though admitting no wrongdoing, he agreed to pay forty-seven million dollars to settle an SEC complaint that he had violated a ban against his participating in the securities industry.

LEGAL ACTION AND OUTCOME

In a series of so-called Fatico hearings, prosecutors were allowed to try to establish a pattern of criminal behavior to influence sentencing on the crimes to which Milken had pleaded guilty. Though their charges of bribery, manipulation, and insider trading were not considered proven, Judge Kimba Wood in November, 1990, rejected a sentence of community service, deciding that a prison term was required for purposes of "general deterrence." Milken's sentence of ten years was subsequently reduced to thirty-four months, and he actually served twenty-two months (from March, 1991, to January, 1993), in addition to paying hundreds of millions of dollars in fines and restitution.

Near the end of Bill Clinton's presidency (January, 2001), there was a campaign for a pardon for Milken, supported even by his former prosecutor, New York mayor Rudolph Giuliani, but in the end Milken was not pardoned.

IMPACT

After his release from prison, Michael Milken developed prostate cancer, and he became active in publicizing and supporting medical research relating to that illness. His activities in supporting medical research date back several decades and have, according to some accounts, significantly contributed to scientific progress. He and his family have long maintained a high profile as major philanthropists, donating tens of millions of dollars to medical research, awards for teachers, and scholarships for students. Through initiatives such as the Milken Institute, Milken exerts a force on the shaping of professional and public opinion on international financial policy and economic and educational development.

Milken's many supporters continue to insist that the crimes for which he was convicted were merely "technical" violations of the securities laws (such as having a client who failed to make required disclosures) and that similar activities were not criminally prosecuted before or since. They also hold that Milken has been unfairly equated with other notorious "greed is good" figures, such as Boesky (model for the Gordon Gekko character in Oliver Stone's 1987 film *Wall Street*). To his supporters, Milken was made a public scapegoat and required to atone for the financial excesses of the period, when in fact his "democratization of capital" had been healthy for the American economy.

Milken's numerous critics view him as a member of a group of self-seeking financiers whose activities collectively helped foster both financial crisis (for example, in the savings and loan industry) and the takeover craze that precipitated the restructuring ("downsizing") of American businesses. In their view, an unremorseful Milken has used his vast wealth, undoubted intelligence, and considerable personal charm to buy back respectability.

Michael Milken. (AP/Wide World Photos)

In November, 1996, the Brooklyn Academy of Music produced choreographer Karole Armitage's multimedia theater piece *The Predators' Ball: Hucksters of the Soul*, which speculates about Boesky's influence on Milken— a sign of the multifaceted quality of Milken's notoriety, which he continues to monitor and (through his Web site and his well-funded activities) to redefine.

FURTHER READING

Bailey, Fenton. *Fall from Grace: The Untold Story of Michael Milken*. Secaucus, N.J.: Carol, 1992. Argues that Milken's activities were not really criminal but have been misrepresented by government prosecutors and the media.

Cohn, Edward. "The Resurrection of Michael Milken." *The American Prospect* 11, no. 9 (March 13, 2000). A critique of Milken's post-conviction activity, particularly with the Milken Institute.

Fischel, Daniel. *Payback: The Conspiracy to Destroy Michael Milken and His Financial Revolution*. New York: HarperBusiness, 1995. A conservative lawyer (later dean of the University of Chicago Law School) views Milken as a financial innovator whose activities, scarcely criminal, had the effect of improving the practices of the financial community and thereby benefited the American economy.

Sobel, Robert. *Dangerous Dreamers: The Financial Innovators from Charles Merrill to Michael Milken.* Rev. ed. New York: John Wiley and Sons, 2000. A sympathetic account of Milken's contributions, set in a broader historical context.

Stein, Benjamin J. *License to Steal: The Untold Story of Michael Milken and the Conspiracy to Bilk the Nation.* New York: Simon and Schuster, 1992. Argues that the negative effects of Milken's activities far outweigh any putative benefits.

Stewart, James B. *Den of Thieves.* New York: Simon & Schuster, 1991. Pulitzer Prize winner Stewart examines insider trading.

—*Edward Johnson*

SEE ALSO: Ivan Boesky; Martin Frankel; Kenneth Lay; Dennis Levine; Jeffrey Skilling.

WILBUR MILLS
American congressman from Arkansas (1939-1977)

BORN: May 24, 1909; Kensett, Arkansas
DIED: May 2, 1992; Searcy, Arkansas
ALSO KNOWN AS: Wilbur Daigh Mills (full name)
CAUSE OF NOTORIETY: Mills left Congress in disgrace after it was revealed that he had a serious drinking problem and had been having an extramarital affair with a former stripper.
ACTIVE: 1974
LOCALE: Washington, D.C.

EARLY LIFE

A native of a small town in northern Arkansas, Wilbur Mills (WIHL-buhr mihls) grew up in a financially comfortable setting thanks to the income from a general store owned by his father, Arda Pickens Mills. Mills graduated from Hendrix College in Conway, Arkansas, before spending three years at (but not graduating from) Harvard Law School. In 1933 he returned to Arkansas, where he was admitted to the state bar association and, a year later, married Clarine "Polly" Billingsley. They had two daughters.

POLITICAL CAREER

Mills's political career began in 1934 when he won election to county and probate judge. A Democrat, he was first elected in 1938 to represent Arkansas in the United States House of Representatives, where he subsequently was assigned to the Banking and Currency Committee. Later he moved to the Ways and Means Committee, one of the most powerful panels on Capitol Hill, where he served throughout the rest of his career. In 1957 he became chairman of the committee, whose jurisdiction included such politically charged areas as tax and tariff legislation and Social Security.

The panel gained even more power by controlling member assignments to all standing committees. Mills's power was expanded yet further by his declining to divide the committee into subcommittees. This maximized his influence by forcing all decisions to be made by the entire panel, whose deliberations he always clearly dominated. In addition, Ways and Means tax bills were al-

Wilbur Mills. (Library of Congress)

ways reported to the House floor with a "closed rule." This meant that no part of such tax bills could be altered by amendments from the floor. All tax bills were subject only to straight "up or down" votes in which members either voted in favor of or against the entire measure. Hence, Mills regularly won House approval of tax measures designed largely to his specifications.

Mills quickly honed a reputation as a skilled, detailed, and hardworking legislator. His preferences in setting the nation's fiscal policies tended to dominate America's taxing and spending programs regardless of who occupied the White House. Presidents, interest group leaders, and other members of Congress all sought Mills's advice and support for their fiscal policy proposals. From the late 1950's through the early 1970's, Mills was a prominent legislator and a major political power center in Washington, D.C.

THE EARLY MORNING SWIM

In the early minutes of the morning of October 7, 1974, Mills's political and governing career came crashing down. Washington, D.C., police stopped an automobile that had been traveling erratically and with its headlights out. After the vehicle stopped, one of its three occupants left the car and either fell or jumped into the famous Washington Tidal Basin. The drenched occupant was Fanne Foxe, a nightclub stripper known popularly as the Argentine Firecracker, whose name at birth was Annabel Battistella. Also in the vehicle were Congressman Mills and a masseuse. News of the incident immediately received prominent coverage throughout the American news media. In the weeks that followed, media talk shows and late-night television comedians revisited and discussed the event at length. Jokes about swimming in the Tidal Basin circulated in offices and businesses throughout the nation.

The notoriety of the event significantly boosted the short-term fortunes of the Argentine Firecracker, whose fees skyrocketed as the "Tidal Basin Bombshell." The event simultaneously destroyed the legislative career of Representative Mills. Although Mills ironically won reelection the month following the event, the seeds of his political downfall had been planted. Mills publicly admitted to being an alcoholic and having an extramarital affair with Foxe.

The downward spiral of his political career continued throughout the following month. On December 3, Mills, complaining of exhaustion, was taken to Bethesda Naval Medical Center. The continuing ridicule directed toward Mills was a growing embarrassment for Democrats in the

House. With this in mind, the House Democratic caucus secretly voted to replace Mills temporarily as chairman of the Ways and Means Committee with Al Ullman of Oregon. On December 10, Mills resigned as committee chairman. By the end of the year, he had promised to end his alcoholism and become a teetotaler. He promised to admit himself to a clinic for a monthlong treatment of his alcoholism.

In 1975 Foxe published her biography, *The Congressman and the Stripper*. Not only did the book serve to remind the public of her affair with Mills, but the volume also included her claim that she had become pregnant by Mills and that she had ended the pregnancy by abortion. Mills declined to run for reelection in 1976. After leaving office, he became a lobbyist and tax consultant for the Washington office of a New York law firm. He retired in the early 1980's and returned to his home in northern Arkansas. He died on May 2, 1992.

IMPACT

Wilbur Mills's Tidal Basin incident remains a classic example of how misbehavior in a prominent person's personal life can destroy a career. Within a two-month period Mills went from being one of the most powerful members of the Washington establishment to a punch line in comedy acts around the United States. His rapid fall from power coincided with the demise of President Richard Nixon, who in 1974 resigned in disgrace following revelations of his behavior in the Watergate scandal.

FURTHER READING

Manley, John. *The Politics of Finance: The House Committee on Ways and Means*. Boston: Little, Brown, 1970. A study of the internal workings of the Ways and Means Committee with extensive attention paid to the crucial role played by its chairman, Mills.

_____. "Wilbur D. Mills: A Study in Congressional Influence." *American Political Science Review* (1969). Part empirical study, part political biography of Mills.

Zelizer, Julian E. *Taxing America: Wilbur D. Mills, Congress and the State, 1945-1975*. New York: Cambridge University Press, 1998. An in-depth account of the role Mills played in the evolution of U.S. policies in such important areas as Social Security, the federal income tax, and Medicare.

—Robert E. Dewhirst

SEE ALSO: Richard Nixon.

SLOBODAN MILOŠEVIĆ
President of Serbia (1989-1997) and Yugoslavia (1997-2000)

BORN: August 20, 1941; Poáarevac, Yugoslavia (now in Serbia)

DIED: March 11, 2006; near The Hague, the Netherlands

ALSO KNOWN AS: Sloba; Slobo

MAJOR OFFENSES: War crimes against humanity in Kosovo, genocide in Bosnia, and breaches of the Geneva Convention

ACTIVE: 1991-2001

LOCALE: Former Yugoslav provinces of Croatia, Kosovo, and Bosnia-Herzogovina

EARLY LIFE

Slobodan Milošević (SLOH-boh-dahn mih-LOH-sheh-vitch) was born in the same year that the Nazis attacked Yugoslavia; his birthplace of Poáarevac and all of Serbia were taken over by the Germans. He was four when the war ended and the Partisans, headed by Josip Broz (Tito), who would become Yugoslavia's postwar ruler, took control. Although Milošević was born in Serbia, his parents were Montenegrin.

Tito's Yugoslavia became communist following the war, and Milošević joined the Communist Party in 1959. He graduated from the Belgrade University Law School in 1964 while working his way up in the Communist Party apparatus. He married Mirjana Marković in 1965. She was to remain his closest confidant throughout his life.

POLITICAL CAREER

In 1980, Tito died at the age of eighty-eight, and Yugoslavia appeared to come apart at the seams. A country made up of different ethnic provinces, which Tito had held together by a combination of force and charisma, now discovered that it did not have enough in common to stay together. A year after Tito's death, Kosovo province began demanding independence; other provinces followed suit as Yugoslavia experienced successive waves of ethnic nationalist violence. Milošević took over his mentor Ivan Stambolić's position as Communist Party leader and was elected president of Serbia by the National Assembly in 1989.

By the end of the 1980's, Serbia had completed its suppression of Kosovo, forcing it under direct Serbian rule. The governments of many communist Soviet republics within Eastern Europe had fallen during this period, and Yugoslavian republics experienced a surge of nationalism. Slovenia declared independence in 1990 and was allowed to become a new state; a very small Serb presence existed within it. Macedonia declared its dependence in September, 1991. A war was fought over Croatian independence, and the West recognized Croatia as a sovereign nation in 1991.

Croatian Serbs also began campaigning for autonomy from Croatia during this period with Milošević's full support. Bosnia-Herzegovina was plunged into war in 1992, and Bosnian Serb forces soon took control of the country, committing countless atrocities in the process.

Milošević and nationalist Serbs became increasingly frustrated with the devolution process, and maintaining control over Bosnia-Herzegovina became extremely important to them. Bosnia-Herzegovina, split among Bosnian Muslims, Serbs, and Croats, became the grounds for what became known as "ethnic cleansing" of Bosnian Muslims by Bosnian Serbs who were supported by the Serbian army. It was alleged that Milošević's secret police force was at the helm of many of the massacres of Bosnian Muslims, as was Radovan Karadžić, a Bosnian Serb leader who joined forces with Milošević. Sarajevo, the capital of Bosnia-Herzegovina and an erstwhile cosmopolitan city, was bombarded relentlessly by the Serbs in the face of mounting international criticism against Milošević and Karadžić. Concentration camps were established around Bosnia to detain Muslim men; many Muslim women were raped in the camps.

By mid-1992, what remained of Yugoslavia was in grave crisis. The Serbian-controlled leadership became an international pariah both for the Bosnian massacres and for the region's ruined economy. International sanctions were put in place against Serbia, and fellow Serbs began demonstrating against Milošević.

The following year, the specter of an international war crimes tribunal was raised, and Milošević and Karadžić were listed as potential criminals. Milošević agreed to a peace plan for Bosnia developed by American diplomat Cyrus Vance and British politician David Owen. The plan was designed to divide Bosnia into several parts: three with a Serb majority, three with a Muslim majority, two with a Croatian majority, and one a blend of Muslims and Croatians. However, the plan was eventually rejected by the Bosnian Serbs.

In 1995, a peace conference was convened in Dayton, Ohio, to end the Bosnian war. Alija Izetbegović, representing the Bosnian Muslims, Franjo Tudjman, representing the Croats, and Milošević, representing the Serbs, signed the peace accord, agreeing to a multiethnic Bosnia with American and European Union troop presence in the state. This presence continued into the twenty-first century as the country was painstakingly rebuilt.

Through 1997, Milošević maintained power in Serbia through rigged elections. By this time, a rebellion led by the Kosovo Liberation Army (KLA) was starting in Kosovo, where ethnic Albanians chafed for more independence. As the situation rapidly deteriorated, Serbian-led massacres took place in Kosovo, and Milošević refused to engage the West, the North Atlantic Treaty Organization (NATO) launched air strikes against Serbia in order to force an end to the war in Kosovo. The strikes lasted three months, during which time major buildings and infrastructure in Serbia were systematically destroyed. Realizing that he had no other option left, Milošević finally agreed to a withdrawal plan from Kosovo. Although the numbers are contested, by some estimates hundreds of thousands died in the various wars that occurred during the 1990's.

LEGAL ACTION AND OUTCOME

Milošević was indicted in the United Nations International Criminal Tribunal for the Former Yugoslavia at The Hague for war crimes committed in Kosovo. To this indictment were later added two others, one for atrocities committed in Croatia in 1991-1992 and one for genocide in Bosnia. In 2000, Milošević called elections, and opposition leader Vojislav Koštunica won. Milošević was forced to step down, after initially refusing to do so, when huge demonstrations against him were held across the country. In 2001, he was arrested in Serbia for abuse of power and sent to the war crimes tribunal to stand trial for his war crimes indictments.

MILOŠEVIĆ BECOMES PRESIDENT OF SERBIA

On June 28, 1989, Slobodan Milošević delivered a speech at the six hundredth anniversary of the Battle of Kosovo (translated by the U.S. Department of Commerce), in which he warned that nationalist divisions could destroy Yugoslavia—as they did soon after:

. . . I think that it makes sense to say this here in Kosovo, where that disunity once upon a time tragically pushed back Serbia for centuries and endangered it, and where renewed unity may advance it and may return dignity to it. Such an awareness about mutual relations constitutes an elementary necessity for Yugoslavia, too, for its fate is in the joined hands of all its peoples. The Kosovo heroism has been inspiring our creativity for six centuries, and has been feeding our pride and does not allow us to forget that at one time we were an army great, brave, and proud, one of the few that remained undefeated when losing.

Six centuries later, now, we are being again engaged in battles and are facing battles. They are not armed battles, although such things cannot be excluded yet. However, regardless of what kind of battles they are, they cannot be won without resolve, bravery, and sacrifice, without the noble qualities that were present here in the field of Kosovo in the days past. Our chief battle now concerns implementing the economic, political, cultural, and general social prosperity, finding a quicker and more successful approach to a civilization in which people will live in the 21st century. For this battle, we certainly need heroism, of course of a somewhat different kind, but that courage without which nothing serious and great can be achieved remains unchanged and remains urgently necessary.

Six centuries ago, Serbia heroically defended itself in the field of Kosovo, but it also defended Europe. Serbia was at that time the bastion that defended the European culture, religion, and European society in general. Therefore today it appears not only unjust but even unhistorical and completely absurd to talk about Serbia's belonging to Europe. Serbia has been a part of Europe incessantly, now just as much as it was in the past, of course, in its own way, but in a way that in the historical sense never deprived it of dignity. In this spirit we now endeavor to build a society, rich and democratic, and thus to contribute to the prosperity of this beautiful country, this unjustly suffering country, but also to contribute to the efforts of all the progressive people of our age that they make for a better and happier world.

Let the memory of Kosovo heroism live forever!
Long live Serbia!
Long live Yugoslavia!
Long live peace and brotherhood among peoples!

Milošević was defiant throughout his trial, which began in 2002, and refused to recognize the legality of the court. He refused counsel even though counsel was appointed for him, and conducted his own defense. However, his popularity in Serbia increased during the trial, with Serbian patriotism coming to the fore and manifesting itself in sympathy for Milošević.

IMPACT

Slobodan Milošević's health deteriorated considerably during his trial, and in March, 2006, he was found dead in his cell, likely from complications related to his heart condition and diabetes. His death, which occurred with only fifty hours of testimony left before the conclusion of his trial and a verdict, left many in the region without a sense of closure: His victims felt justice had been thwarted, while his supporters were left divided over those who wanted to leave the past behind them and those who thought that Milošević was a victim of an unjust trial at The Hague.

FURTHER READING

Doder, Dusko, and Louise Branson. *Milošević: Portrait*

of a Tyrant. New York: Free Press, 1999. An in-depth account of Milošević's role in the Balkan wars written by two foreign correspondents.

Sell, Louis. *Slobodan Milošević and the Destruction of Yugoslavia.* Durham, N.C.: Duke University Press, 2002. Informative study of the dictator and the consequences of his actions.

Udovički, Jasminka, and James Ridgeway, eds. *Yugoslavia's Ethnic Nightmare: The Inside Story of Europe's Unfolding Ordeal.* New York: Lawrence Hill Books, 1995. Contains chapters on the different components of the Balkan wars.

—*Tinaz Pavri*

SEE ALSO: Radovan Karadžić; Ratko Mladić; Tito.

JOHN MITCHELL
U.S. attorney general (1969-1972) and Watergate conspirator

BORN: September 15, 1913; Detroit, Michigan
DIED: November 9, 1988; Washington, D.C.
ALSO KNOWN AS: John Newton Mitchell (full name)
MAJOR OFFENSES: Conspiracy, perjury, and obstruction of justice
ACTIVE: 1972-1973
LOCALE: Washington, D.C.
SENTENCE: Two and a half to eight years in prison; served nineteen months

EARLY LIFE

John Newton Mitchell (MIH-chehl) was born in Detroit, Michigan, in 1913, and then moved with his family to the New York City area when he was about five years old. Mitchell attended Fordham University in New York City and graduated from St. John University Law School. While attending law school, Mitchell began working in the prestigious firm of Caldwell and Raymond, where he eventually became a partner. Mitchell served as a naval officer during World War II and earned a Silver Star. He was married twice. His second wife, Martha, became known as an outspoken—some say a notorious—figure in Washington while Mitchell served as attorney general.

POLITICAL CAREER

Mitchell's involvement in national politics began after he met Richard Nixon. Mitchell had specialized in the arcane and lucrative field of municipal bonds and represented the bond sellers. Nixon, who moved to New York

after a humiliating loss in the 1962 California gubernatorial election, joined a firm that represented underwriters of such bonds. The two firms eventually merged, to become Nixon, Mudge, Rose, Guthrie, Alexander, and Mitchell.

Mitchell was instrumental in encouraging Nixon to seek the presidency in 1968 and served in Nixon's campaign during that hotly contested race. Mitchell's effective and astute management of the campaign was seen by many as a major reason for Nixon's victory. Part of Nixon's strategy in the 1968 campaign was to run on a "law and order" platform, which was critical of the "judicial activism" of the Warren Supreme Court and which also appealed to conservative white, southern voters, who had traditionally voted Democratic. This approach became known as Nixon's "southern strategy."

Mitchell served as a close adviser of the president, particularly during the early period of Nixon's first term as president. Mitchell's influence was felt even before Nixon took office; for instance, he was an advocate of Spiro T. Agnew, then governor of Maryland, for the vice presidential spot on the ticket. Agnew resigned in disgrace from that office during Nixon's second term. Mitchell was also part of the Nixon "transition team." He was appointed attorney general in 1969.

As attorney general, Mitchell also pursued a conservative agenda. He supported more extensive use of wiretapping (particularly in cases involving organized crime and national security), publicly opposed the Warren

Court's decision in *Miranda v. Arizona* (which established guidelines for custodial interrogations by police), and, at one point, actively pursued federal prosecution of the radical Black Panthers organization. Moreover, during Mitchell's tenure, the Department of Justice filed an amicus curiae brief before the United States Supreme Court opposing the busing of children in order to enhance integration.

THE WATERGATE AFFAIR

Mitchell's greatest notoriety came about because of his involvement in the Watergate affair. On Memorial Day, 1972, a group of burglars broke into the Democratic Headquarters located in the Watergate complex in Washington, D.C. At first, the event was widely viewed as merely a second-rate burglary, one that was bungled by amateurs. This view continued during the 1972 campaign, which Nixon easily won (carrying forty-nine of fifty states against Democratic contender George McGovern).

Unfortunately for the president and his associates, the Watergate cover-up soon began to unravel. Investigators discovered that Mitchell, in his role as campaign manager in the 1972 election, had approved of the initial break-in and that the initial discussion of the affair took place in his office. Not only did he support the decision to enact a burglary, but Mitchell also authorized the money to fund it (Mitchell resigned not long after as attorney general in order to concentrate on the 1972 campaign). After the burglars were caught, Mitchell also ensured that they received cash payments both to help in their defense and to keep them quiet. Mitchell also worked with others in the Committee to Re-elect the President (CRP) and in the White House to conceal his complicity (as well as that of many associates) in the burglary and the subsequent cover-up attempt.

LEGAL ACTION AND OUTCOME

In part because of the intrepid reporting of two young *Washington Post* reporters, Bob Woodward and Carl Bernstein, the American public and legal authorities learned details of the Watergate scandal, and legal proceedings began against those involved. Because of the rulings of federal judge John Sirica and the testimony before a Senate committee by John Dean (at one time a Mitchell protégé), the attempt to keep the lid on this crime imploded.

Mitchell was eventually charged with and found guilty of conspiracy, perjury, and obstruction of justice, for which he received a sentence of two and a half to eight years' imprisonment. He served nineteen months of that sentence and, after being released, was disbarred. He lived quietly in Washington until his death. Unlike many of the other actors in the Watergate conspiracy, Mitchell never wrote his memoirs or gave interviews about his activities, nor did he ever publicly criticize President Nixon. He died of a heart attack in 1988 and is buried in Arlington National Cemetery.

IMPACT

Watergate was the most notorious of the numerous "dirty tricks" played by the Nixon campaign under John Mitchell's direction. The impact of the scandal on the nation's politics was significant. Richard Nixon resigned during his second term in order to avoid impeachment, the only president to resign under such a cloud. Watergate also led to the creation of the office of special prosecutor, an office that would prove to have a checkered career in American politics. The episode also contributed to an increased cynicism on the part of the American people about politics, which continued to be felt decades later.

FURTHER READING

Bernstein, Carl, and Bob Woodward. *All the President's Men*. 1974. 2d ed. New York: Simon & Schuster, 1994. The account by the authors of how they were able to penetrate the Watergate cover-up.

Elliff, John T. *Crime, Dissent, and the Attorney General: The Justice Department in 1960's*. Beverly Hills, Calif.: Sage, 1971. An overview of Mitchell's "law and order" policies as attorney general.

Nixon, Richard. *RN: The Memoirs of Richard Nixon*. 1975. Reprint. New York: Simon & Schuster, 1990. Provides the president's view of his administration, including his interpretation of Watergate.

White, Theodore. *Breach of Faith: The Fall of Richard Nixon*. New York: Atheneum, 1975. A famous journalist's perspective on Watergate.

—*David M. Jones*

SEE ALSO: Charles W. Colson; John D. Ehrlichman; H. R. Haldeman; E. Howard Hunt; G. Gordon Liddy; James W. McCord, Jr.; John Mitchell; Richard Nixon.

RATKO MLADIĆ
Serbian general and mass murderer

BORN: March 12, 1943; Božinovići, municipality of
Kalinovik, Bosnia, Croatia (now in Republika
Srpska, Bosnia-Herzegovina)
MAJOR OFFENSES: Crimes against humanity,
genocide, and war crimes
ACTIVE: 1993-1995
LOCALE: Bosnia

EARLY LIFE

Ratko Mladić (RAHT-koh MLAH-dihch) was born in
Croatia when the country was a fascist satellite of Nazi
Germany. His parents fought as partisans in World
War II, and the Croatian government executed his father.
Mladić was reputed to be an excellent and active student
and wanted to be a surgeon or teacher before deciding on
a military career. He considered himself a Yugoslav until
1992, when he proclaimed himself a Serb.

MILITARY CAREER

Mladić was the chief of the Serbian army in Bosnia, the
right-hand man of Radovan Karadžić, the leader of the
Bosnian Serbs during the war in the 1990's. Mladić was
sent to Knin, Croatia, as commander of the Ninth Corps
of the Yugoslav People's Army in 1991. The army was
in battle with Croatia, which had broken away from
the Yugoslav confederation. On October 4, Slobodan
Milošević, the Yugoslav president, promoted Mladić to
major general. In April, 1992, he was further promoted
to lieutenant general and assigned as chief of staff and
deputy commander of the second military district in
Sarajevo, arriving there on May 9. The next day, he assumed command of the district and two days later the
command of the main staff of the Bosnian Serbian Army,
a position he held until December, 1996. In 1994, he received a further promotion to colonel general.

As commander, Mladić immediately ordered the shelling of the civilian populace in Sarajevo. He then ordered
his army to take over the towns in the Bosanski district of
eastern Bosnia, forcing thousands of Croatians and Bosniaks (Bosnian Muslims) to flee. Many were killed, and
many more confined to concentration camps. In the first
three months of 1993, Mladić's troops moved into the
Çerska district and Herzegovina. Thousands of Bosniaks
fled to Srebeniça and Žepa, then under Muslim control.

Mladić concentrated his efforts on capturing Srebeniça
as a strategic center. In 1995, with the town in his hands,
Mladić ordered the execution of seven thousand Bosniaks

in the week of July 13—almost half the number killed in
the whole fourteen months of the Reign of Terror in Revolutionary France during 1793-1794. For the rest of the
year, Mladić ordered his troops to conceal the massacre
by digging up the mass graves, exhuming the bodies, and
reburying them in isolated locations throughout Bosnia.

LEGAL ACTION AND OUTCOME

In 1995, Mladić was indicted by the Hague International
Criminal Tribunal for genocide in the siege of Sarajevo
and for the murder of thousands of Muslims in Srebeniça
in 1995. At the time, he lived in Serbia under the protection of Milošević; however, when the Serbian president
was arrested in 2001, Mladić went into hiding, although
he was seen in 2002 in a Serbian military area. The Serbian government of the post-Milošević era wished to
capture the general in order to create closer ties with the
European Union, and the authorities prepared a list of
some fifty Serbs who aided his escape. Some were arrested, but Mladić continued to evade capture.

IMPACT

Ratko Mladić's crimes, along with those of Slobodan
Milošević and Radovan Karadžić, contributed to the
breakup of Yugoslavia and the establishment of Bosnia
as an independent state, divided by the 1995 Dayton accords into three religious autonomous communities.

FURTHER READING

Glenny, Misha. *The Fall of Yugoslavia: The Balkan War*.
New York: Penguin, 1996. An excellent account of
the war by a distinguished and insightful historian.
Honig, Jan Willem. *Srebrenica: Record of a War Crime*.
New York: Penguin, 1997. Chronicles the events that
eventually proved central to Mladić's indictment by
the International Criminal Tribunal.
Isby, David C. *Balkan Battle Founds: A Military History
of the Yugoslav Conflict, 1990-1995*. Collingdale,
Pa.: Diane, 2005. An account of the war by a prolific
military historian.
Stojadinović, Ljubodrag. *Ratko Mladić: Tragic Hero*.
Translated and edited by Milo Yelesiyevich. New
York: Unwritten History, 2006. A sympathetic account with a good deal of information on the general
and the war.

—*Frederick B. Chary*

SEE ALSO: Radovan Karadžić; Slobodan Milošević.

MOBUTU SESE SEKO
President of Zaire (1965-1997)

BORN: October 14, 1930; Lisala, Belgian Congo
DIED: September 7, 1997; Rabat, Morocco
ALSO KNOWN AS: Mobutu Sese Seko Koko Ngbendu Wa Za Banga (full name); Joseph Désiré Mobutu (birth name)
CAUSE OF NOTORIETY: Mobutu became one of Africa's richest and longest-serving dictators. As president of the vast, mineral-rich central African nation of Zaire, he transformed his country into a hopelessly corrupt state characterized by large-scale inefficient patronage and acute privatization of political power.
ACTIVE: 1965-1997
LOCALE: Zaire

EARLY LIFE

Joseph Désiré Mobutu, later known as Mobutu Sese Seko (moh-BOO-too SEH-seh SEH-koh), was educated at a Roman Catholic mission school in the Belgian Congo. He joined the Belgian colonial army at the age of nineteen, where he rose to the rank of sergeant major. In the late 1950's, he joined the nationalist Congolese National Movement under the leadership of the radical nationalist Patrice Lumumba. Following the Belgian Congo's independence in June, 1960, Lumumba became the prime minister, and Mobutu became his private secretary; he soon became the army chief of staff. The subsequent power struggle between Lumumba and President Joseph Kasa Vubu would provide Mobutu with his initial foray into the political terrain.

POLITICAL CAREER

In September, 1960, Mobutu, backed by the army, temporarily suspended the government and placed Lumumba under house arrest. In November, 1965, Mobutu once again overthrew the government. He declared himself president, abolished the office of prime minister, and canceled democratic elections scheduled for 1966. In 1970, he turned his country into a one-party state under the Movement of the Revolution (MPR). In 1971, he renamed his country Zaire, and in 1972 he changed his own name to Mobutu Sese Seko in order to reflect a return to "African authenticity." He banned European names and dress and as a personal example began to wear a leopard-skin hat.

In his more than three-decade hold on political power, Mobutu violated human rights, crushed political dissent,

suppressed rebellions, and executed his rivals. He was encouraged by Western nations, which were more interested in establishing Zaire as a bulwark against the spread of communism in the region than in supporting human rights and political freedom. Moreover, Mobutu's lifestyle and assets graphically illustrated the devastating effect of corruption that he pioneered in his impoverished country. He amassed a personal fortune that included eleven castles located in Belgium and France, as well as palatial estates and residences in Spain, Italy, and Switzerland. He owned buildings in Paris and the Ivory Coast and presidential mansions in each of his country's eight provinces. Mobutu was reputed to have stashed away in his Swiss bank accounts a huge amount of money (believed to be about four billion

Mobutu Sese Seko. (Courtesy, Albert Sarlet)

dollars in the mid-1980's). He also had exclusive use or ownership of numerous ships, jet planes, and at least fifty Mercedes-Benz cars.

Mobutu bought shares in every major foreign company and banks within Zaire. A 5 percent commission from the proceeds of his country's minerals was reputedly paid into his overseas accounts. Without being subjected to any accounting, 30 percent of the country's operating budget flowed through the state house. Mobutu himself dismissed such allegations of massive corruption as fairy tales. He insisted that during his rule, he had put his personal wealth at the service of his country. However, Zaire suffered from acute inflation, an oppressive debt, and massive currency devaluations.

In 1991, the strong global currents of democratic reforms compelled Mobutu to embrace democracy, albeit superficially. Early in that year, he decreed into existence two political parties, one of which was his own, the MPR. However, this approach was rejected by the prodemocracy forces, who called for the convocation of a sovereign national conference, a forum meant to provide solutions to the chronic political and economic problems confronting Zaire. Mobutu reluctantly allowed the formation of many parties; however, he created and financed some of them in anticipation of the national conference. When the conference occurred, Mobutu succeeded, through bribery and cajoling, in infiltrating several parties; as a result, he got his cronies overwhelmingly accredited. The conference was beset with crisis from its inception. The Catholic Church, an influential social institution in Zaire, withdrew its participation because of what it perceived as unacceptable irregularities. Other members were physically manhandled by members of the National Guard who were directly answerable to President Mobutu. Eventually, the president deliberately aborted the national conference.

IMPACT

The rapacious and vicious regime of President Mobutu Sese Seko ultimately turned Zaire into a hotbed of rebellion, which consumed the entire Great Lakes region. Corruption, a thriving social industry in Zaire, left the economy in a compromised state. In 1991, both the World Bank and the International Monetary Fund (IMF) suspended further financial assistance to the country because of its ever-increasing debt, which was valued at about fifteen billion dollars at the time. Mobutu's rule was truncated by a rebellion led by a long-standing foe, Laurent-Désiré Kabila, on May 17, 1997. Kabila immediately renamed the country the Democratic Republic of the Congo (DRC) in order to obliterate the memories of more than three decades of decline and crass corruption. Mobutu died in exile in Morocco of prostate cancer later that year.

FURTHER READING

Duke, Lynne. *Mandela, Mobutu, and Me.* New York: Doubleday, 2003. A memoir of an African news reporter that takes readers across Africa and gives a detailed account of modern life in Africa. The devastation wrought by Mobutu forms an interesting portion of the book.

George, Susan. *A Fate Worse than Debt.* New York: Grove Press, 1988. A unique contribution to the understanding of the tribulations facing the Third World. It surveys the damage and human cost of the effects of IMF-imposed conditions, military spending, and political corruption in developing regions. It provides an insight into the corruption in Mobutu's Zaire.

Nzongola-Ntalaja, Georges. *The Congo: From Leopold to Kabila, a People's History.* London: Zed Books, 2002. Traces the violent and tragic history of the Congo from 1870 to the present.

Parfitt, Trevor W., and Stephen P. Riley. *The African Debt Crisis.* London: Routledge, 1989. Details the extent of corruption in Zaire and chronicles Mobutu's problems with the IMF.

—*Olutayo C. Adesina*

SEE ALSO: Sani Abacha; Idi Amin; Omar al-Bashir; Jean-Bédel Bokassa; Samuel K. Doe; Mengistu Haile Mariam; Robert Mugabe; Muammar al-Qaddafi; Muhammad Siad Barre; Charles Taylor.

MOHAMMAD REZA SHAH PAHLAVI
Shah of Iran (1941-1979)

BORN: October 26, 1919; Tehran, Iran
DIED: July 27, 1980; Cairo, Egypt
ALSO KNOWN AS: Mohammad Reza Pahlavi (birth name)
CAUSE OF NOTORIETY: After years of autocratic rule and following his contentious White Revolution, Pahlavi was overthrown by Islamic fundamentalist Ayatollah Khomeini.
ACTIVE: 1941-1979
LOCALE: Tehran, Iran

EARLY LIFE

Mohammad Reza Shah Pahlavi (mo-HAHM-ehd rih-ZAH shah PAL-uh-vee) was born to Reza Pahlavi, the Shah of Persia (name used in the West; it became Iran in 1935) from 1925 to 1941, and his second wife. As a child, he attended a Swiss boarding school and later the military college in Tehran. Although Iran was politically neutral during World War II, the Allies were alarmed at the friendly relations between the first Shah, Mohammad Reza's father, and Nazi Germany. Consequently, the Soviet Union and Great Britain staged a preemptive invasion. In September, 1941, the first Shah abdicated as a result of pressure from Iran's occupying powers. Once Mohammad Reza took over, he was amenable to suggestions offered from the West; for example, he allowed Great Britain and the United States to use Iran as a conduit to give aid to the Soviet Union.

POLITICAL CAREER

In 1953, Iran's prime minister, Mohammad Mosaddeq, nationalized the oil industry without any form of compensation for the foreign investors. Moreover, Mosaddeq entered into a close political alliance with the Tudeh Party, an Iranian communist group. This angered not only the West but also those allies that possessed either Islamic or anticommunist agendas. Mosaddeq's action led to an oil embargo on all Iranian oil exports, which weakened an economy already teetering on collapse. Many felt that the U.S. Central Intelligence Agency (CIA) and Britain's Military Intelligence Section 6 (MI6) funded and led the subsequent coup d'état against Mosaddeq. The coup, dubbed Operation Ajax, was achieved in part with the help of military forces loyal to the Shah. Initially, the coup failed, forcing the Shah to flee from Iran. After a brief exile in Italy, he was able to return as a result of a second and successful coup. Mosaddeq was arrested, tried, and put under house arrest. General Fazlollah Zahedi was elected to succeed Prime Minister Mosaddeq.

Iran has enormous oil reserves, a fact that allowed the Shah to become a powerful leader. He abolished the multiparty system of government in order to rule through a one-party state under the Rastakhiz (resurrection) Party in autocratic fashion. The Shah claimed that his actions were responses brought about by the Soviet Union funding Iranian communist militias and parties, especially the Tudeh Party. He also authorized the creation of the secret police force, SAVAK (National Organization for Information and Security), which became notorious for its ruthless persecution of dissidents.

Mohammad Reza Shah Pahlavi in 1971. (AP/Wide World Photos)

In 1963, the Shah initiated the White Revolution, a method for modernizing Iran. The revolution was meant to be a nonviolent regeneration of Iranian society through economic and social reforms, with a long-term primary goal of turning Iran into a global economic and industrial power. Part of the revolution involved granting suffrage to women, a move that caused great consternation among Islamic clergy. The revolution instituted profit sharing for industrial workers, the initiation of massive government-financed heavy industry projects, and the nationalization of forests and pastureland. Socially, the platform granted women more rights and poured money into education, especially in rural areas. Furthermore, the Shah instituted exams for Islamic theologians to become established clerics, causing great anger with clerics because of the widespread belief that the exams changed centuries-old religious traditions. Most important, the revolution allowed the Shah to curb the immense power of elite factions. This was achieved by expropriating large and mid-sized estates for the benefit of more than four million small farmers; nearly 90 percent of Iranian sharecroppers became landowners.

The Shah's reforms faced great opposition. Many Iranians did not like his pro-Western stance, seeing the United States as a nation of infidels. Many fundamentalist Muslims felt that the Shah's good relations with Israel and the United States, as well as his active support of women's rights, were valid reasons for dissent, and his regime grew more and more unpopular as time passed.

On January 16, 1979, Prime Minister Shapour Bakhtiar sought to ease the situation, suggesting that the Shah and his wife leave Iran. Bakhtiar destroyed the SAVAK and freed all political prisoners, even allowing the Ayatollah Khomeini, a fundamentalist Shiite Muslim who had been exiled to France, to return to Iran. Bakhtiar wanted Khomeini to create a Vatican-like state in the city of Qom; his pleas were ignored, and Khomeini appointed an interim government on his own. The military announced it was neutral, and, in what became known as the Iranian Revolution of 1979, the dissolution of the monarchy was completed at the hands of revolutionaries led by Khomeini.

LEGAL ACTION AND OUTCOME

The Shah, unable to return to his country, found he was an international pariah and journeyed from country to country, including Egypt, Morocco, the Bahamas, and Mexico. His non-Hodgkin's lymphoma grew worse, and he was treated in the United States—an act that caused great anger in revolutionary Iran. Muslim clerics were incensed and demanded the Shah's return to Iran to face a show trial and execution. When these demands went unmet by the U.S. government, Iranians captured a number of American diplomats, military personnel, and intelligence officers in what became known as the Iran hostage crisis. The Shah died in Egypt on July 27, 1980.

IMPACT

The Iranian Revolution, which led to the overthrow of Mohammad Reza Shah Pahlavi, was the first Islamic revolution in the modern era. It marked a period when all of the secular nations in the Middle East grew nervous about fundamentalist Islam. The Iranian Revolution inspired the creation of many new groups, including the Islamic Salvation Front in Algeria, Hezbollah in Lebanon, and Hamas among the Palestinians, all of which contributed to significant unrest in the Middle East in the following decades. Moreover, the controversy surrounding the Shah and the Iranian hostage crisis substantially influenced the U.S. presidential race of 1980, in which Ronald Reagan soundly defeated President Jimmy Carter. Many Americans felt that Carter should not have allowed the Shah into the United States and that he was not doing enough to free the American hostages in Iran.

FURTHER READING

Afshar, Haleh, ed. *Iran: A Revolution in Turmoil.* Albany: State University of New York Press, 1985. Well-written book that discusses many different aspects of the Iranian Revolution.

Harris, David. *The Crisis: The President, the Prophet, and the Shah—1979 and the Coming of Militant Islam.* Boston: Little, Brown, 2004. Details how the Shiite revolution in Iran was the forerunner of the problems experienced between the West and Islam in successive decades.

Kinzer, Stephen. *All the Shah's Men: An American Coup and the Roots of Middle East Terror.* New York: Wiley, 2003. Details the 1953 coup involving the Shah and Prime Minister Mosaddeq, as well as America's role in the coup.

—*Cary Stacy Smith*

SEE ALSO: Ayatollah Khomeini.

KHALID SHAIKH MOHAMMED
Pakistani-Kuwaiti terrorist

BORN: March 1, 1964, or April 14, 1965; probably Kuwait

ALSO KNOWN AS: Salem Ali; Abdul Majid; Ashraf Refaat Nabith Henin; Khalid Abdul Wadood; Salem Ali; Abdullah al-Fak'asi al-Ghamdior; Fahd Bin Abdallah Bin Khalid

CAUSE OF NOTORIETY: Mohammed was the alleged mastermind behind the September 11, 2001, terrorist attacks against the United States.

ACTIVE: September 11, 2001

LOCALE: New York, New York; Washington, D.C.; and Pennsylvania

EARLY LIFE

Khalid Shaikh Mohammed (kah-LEED shayk moh-HAH-mehd) is believed to have been born in Kuwait in either 1964 or 1965; his parents had moved there from Baluchistan, Pakistan, which is adjacent to Afghanistan, during the 1950's. Mohammed was one of seven children, four of whom were boys.

While Mohammed was in high school, his father died, and his older brothers became his caregivers. Through their encouragement, Mohammed became interested in the concept of the Islamic Holy War, or jihad. While still a teenager, he joined the Muslim Brotherhood, a radical Islamic organization. He especially felt sympathy for the Palestinians in their conflict with Israel.

Mohammed did well in school, and through the support of his brothers, he was accepted to graduate school in the United States. He enrolled at Chowan College, a Baptist institution in Murfreesboro, North Carolina, which several other Middle Eastern students also attended. He later attended the North Carolina Agricultural and Technical State College, from which he graduated in 1986 with a degree in mechanical engineering.

TERRORIST CAREER

From the United States, Mohammed went to Pakistan, where he became involved in the Islamic resistance against the Soviet military occupation in Afghanistan. In 1987, he fought against the Soviets in a battle that also involved Islamic fundamentalist Osama Bin Laden. Two of Mohammed's brothers would eventually die in the Soviet-Afghanistan conflict.

Once the Afghanistan War had ended, Mohammed drifted around the region in search of a career. Eventually, he turned to terrorism. His nephew, Ramzi Yousef, had a direct role in organizing the 1993 bombing of the World Trade Center in New York City. Later, in 1995, the two men moved to the Philippines and began organizing a large-scale terrorist attack against U.S. commercial airliners. However, their operation was broken up by the Filipino police, and in 1996, Mohammed was indicted in the United States for his part in the plot. He repeatedly escaped arrest, however, and began to plan new operations.

In 1996, Mohammed allegedly approached Bin Laden—by then the leader of the terrorist organization al-Qaeda—with an idea that involved the simultaneous hijacking of several jetliners in the United States. Ultimately, the concept was reduced in scale, and the decision was made to crash the airplanes into prominent American buildings. Mohammed would plan the operation, and Bin Laden would supply the men and financing. The recruits were eventually dispatched to the United States, and Mohammed, moving between Pakistan and Afghanistan, maintained operational control to the extent that he resisted pressure from Bin Laden to move up the date of the attacks.

On September 11, 2001, two hijacked jets were used to crash into the World Trade Center; one more crashed into the Pentagon in Washington, D.C., and another crashed into a field in rural Pennsylvania. Nearly three thousand people lost their lives in the attacks. Mohammed's plan had been successful.

Once the attacks occurred, Mohammed was once again on the run, this time with the U.S. government in full pursuit. He was reportedly captured in Karachi, Pakistan, in March, 2003; however, he was not seen again. Some people believe that he was not captured and remained at large. Others believe he was transferred to U.S. custody upon arrest without extradition proceedings; still others believe that he remained in Pakistani custody. He was rumored to have supplied the U.S. government with information related to terrorist operations after having been subjected to interrogation techniques. This rumor appeared to have some truth when Mohammed surfaced in March, 2006, and provided written testimony in the trial against Zacarias Moussaoui, the only person charged in the United States with the 2001 attacks.

IMPACT

Although Osama Bin Laden is the figure most associated with the attacks of September 11, it was, according to the

National Commission on Terrorist Attacks upon the United States (also known as the 9/11 Commission), Khalid Shaikh Mohammed who was the main planner. These attacks were the culmination of Mohammed's career devoted to terrorism against the United States, which included a failed effort in 1996. Mohammed's eventual fate remains unknown. As of 2006, he had not been charged with any crimes related to the September 11 attacks.

FURTHER READING

Burke, Jason. *Al Qaeda: The Real Story*. London: Penguin Books, 2004. An excellent and complex examination of al-Qaeda written by a British journalist.

Kean, Thomas H., et al. *The 9/11 Commission Report:* *Final Report of the National Commission on Terrorist Attacks upon the United States*. New York: W. W. Norton, 2004. The most authoritative account of the September 11 attacks as produced by a special U.S. government commission. Chapter 5 specifically addresses Mohammed's role in the attacks.

McDermott, Terry. *Perfect Soldiers: The Hijackers—Who They Were, Why They Did It*. New York: HarperCollins, 2005. A definitive study of the individuals involved in the September 11 attacks, including Mohammed.

—*Steve Hewitt*

SEE ALSO: Mohammed Atta al-Sayed; Osama Bin Laden; Ramzi Yousef; Zacarias Moussaoui.

MOLLY MAGUIRES
Clandestine, radical group of Irish American miners

FORMED: 1843
MAJOR OFFENSES: Murder and industrial sabotage
ACTIVE: 1860's-1877
LOCALE: Schuylkill County, Pennsylvania
SENTENCE: Death by hanging for some; others jailed

EARLY LIFE

The Molly Maguires (mah-GWI-uhrs) originated in Ireland in 1843 and served as a vigilante group, fighting Irish landlords for tenant rights. Its name is said to derive from Molly Maguire, a widow who led violent agitations after being evicted by her landlord. Some historians believe Maguire was only a mythical figure.

The ancestors of the Pennsylvanian Molly Maguires were from Ireland, particularly county Donegal, but there is little evidence that a band of Molly Maguires emigrated to the United States. In fact, the Irish miners in Pennsylvania were split into different warring secret societies, among which may have been the Molly Maguires. The secrecy of these organizations and the lack of any official documents affiliated with the Molly Maguires have given credence to the notion that Benjamin Bannan, the editor of the *Miners' Journal*, labeled some violent miners as "Molly Maguires"; the name, whether or not accurate, was subsequently used by the mine owners, the media, and the general public.

CRIMINAL CAREER

The first murder attributed to the Molly Maguires was that of mine foreman Frank W. Langdon in 1862, but charges for the crime were not brought forth until 1877. There were violent miners who committed industrial espionage and murders, but the group's membership was officially confined, for the most part, to the Ancient Order of the Hibernians (AOH). The AOH served officially as a self-help organization for Irish immigrants, and the Molly Maguires perhaps existed as a secret organization behind this front.

The first wave of violence associated with the Molly Maguires—assaults, robberies, and four murders—occurred between 1865 and 1868 and was associated with the Civil War military draft. Under the pretext of enforcing the draft, mine operators used police and the Union Army to go into the mines and remove labor activists to serve in the army; the impoverished miners did not have the money to buy their way out of the draft. The second wave began in October, 1874, and was related to cuts in the miners' wages; the unsuccessful Long Strike of 1875 followed. The miners committed acts of violence, including industrial espionage, arson, assaults, and murders, including six in 1875 alone. Most of these crimes were attributed to the Molly Maguires.

LEGAL ACTION AND OUTCOME

Many miners active in the AOH (and presumed to be Molly Maguires) were arrested for murder; the first trial began in 1876. Franklin P. Gowen, head of the Reading Railroad and the most influential mine owner in the area at the time, commissioned the Pinkerton Detective Agency to infiltrate the organization both to spy on the miners and to act as provocateurs (that is, agents who committed acts of violence that could then be blamed on the Molly Maguires). Michael J. Doyle and Edward Kelly were convicted of the murder of John P. Jones and hanged, but James Kerrigan, a third person charged with the murder of Jones, turned state's evidence, was freed, and continued to inform on other suspected murderers. His testimony and that of Pinkerton operative James McParlan were responsible for the convictions and hanging of seventeen more miners in 1877 and 1879. Other miners were convicted of lesser charges and received jail sentences.

IMPACT

The hyperbole of the media accounts of the depravity of the Molly Maguires persisted and resulted in the demise of both the Molly Maguires and the AOH. The nascent union movement, of which the Molly Maguires was a part and in which the Workingmen's Benevolent Association and the Knights of Labor played important roles, was also weakened. For the rest of the nineteenth century, violence in the workplace would be committed primarily by the owners, though there were some sporadic acts of violence committed by workers. The Molly Maguires provided a convenient label to attach to active trade unionists; the trials were designed to destroy such leaders and the unions themselves.

FURTHER READING

Bimba, Anthony. *The Molly Maguires*. New York: International, 1932. Early account explaining the collusion between the mine owners, the Pinkertons, the Irish Catholic Church, the police, and the media. Also examines the battle between capital and labor.

Broehl, Wayne G., Jr. *The Molly Maguires*. Cambridge, Mass.: Harvard University Press, 1964. Helpful discussion of the Irish roots of the Molly Maguire movement and a list of the participants in the Molly Maguire riots.

Burke, William H. *Anthracite Lads: A True Story of the Fabled Molly Maguires*. Erie, Pa.: Erie County Historical Society, 2005. Denies the existence of a Molly Maguire organization in Pennsylvania.

Kenny, Kevin. *Making Sense of the Molly Maguires*. New York: Oxford University Press, 1998. Thorough discussion of the group's agitation. Provides helpful appendixes, including an extensive bibliography and short biographies of the participants.

Pinkerton, Allan. *The Molly Maguires and the Detectives*. New York: Dover, 1973. Pinkerton's biased account of the Molly Maguire riots, the source of contemporary antiunion sentiment.

—*Thomas L. Erskine*

SEE ALSO: Black Donnellys; Irish Invincibles.

VYACHESLAV MIKHAILOVICH MOLOTOV
Soviet premier (1930-1941) and foreign minister (1939-1949)

BORN: March 9, 1890; Kukarka (now Sovetsk), Russia
DIED: November 8, 1986; Moscow, Soviet Union (now in Russia)
ALSO KNOWN AS: Vyacheslav Mikhailovich Skryabin (birth name)
CAUSE OF NOTORIETY: As the communist foreign minister of the Soviet Union, Molotov was responsible for negotiating and signing the Nazi-Soviet Nonaggression Pact, which effectively allowed Adolf Hitler to invade Poland, beginning World War II.
ACTIVE: 1930-1962
LOCALE: Soviet Union

EARLY LIFE

Vyacheslav Mikhailovich Skryabin (vyih-cheh-SLAHF mihk-KAY-loh-vihch skree-AH-bihn) was the son of a prosperous estate supervisor. While studying at university in Kazan, Russia, in 1906, he became a member of Vladimir Ilich Lenin's Bolshevik Party. Soon thereafter, the young activist adopted the pseudonym "Molotov" (meaning "hammer" in Russian), substituting it for his MAHL-uh-tawf surname. The next year, he enrolled in the St. Petersburg Polytechnic Institute and participated actively in party work with the Bolsheviks' party committee in St. Petersburg.

POLITICAL CAREER

Having withstood numerous arrests and imprisonment by czarist security organs during the remainder of the decade, Molotov then cofounded, with Bolshevik leader Lenin, the Communist Party's newspaper, *Pravda* (meaning "truth" in Russian), and played an important part in the Russian Revolution of 1917. Molotov was a staunch

From left: Vyacheslav Molotov, U.S. secretary of state James Byrnes, President Harry S. Truman, and Joseph Stalin. (NARA)

follower of Joseph Stalin, and his career rose with that of his patron. He was elevated to the Communist Party Secretariat in 1924 and to the ruling Politburo, the party's major policy-making committee, in 1926.

As a loyal Stalinist, Molotov energetically backed the removal of Stalin's chief opponents during the next decade. He was rewarded for his undying allegiance to Stalin in December, 1930, becoming the Soviet prime minister, or premier. Molotov also undertook an active role in Stalin's barbarous agricultural collectivization campaign and was later personally involved in the bloody purges of the late 1930's.

Molotov is perhaps best known for his role in negotiating and signing the treaty that brought on World War II, the Nazi-Soviet Nonaggression Pact of 1939. Throughout the 1930's, Stalin had attempted to initialize a formal alliance with Britain and France in order to restrain the German armies of Adolf Hitler. After France and Britain

consented at the Munich Conference in September, 1938, to Hitler's incorporation of the German-speaking portions of western Czechoslovakia into the German Reich, Stalin charged Molotov with the task of achieving a separate peace with his erstwhile archenemy, Hitler. Molotov's efforts gained renewed purpose after Hitler devoured the remaining portions of Czechoslovakia early the next year; it was in May of 1939 that Molotov also replaced Soviet Jewish diplomat Maksim Maksimovich Litvinov as Soviet foreign minister.

In the ensuing months, Molotov and his German counterpart, Joachim von Ribbentrop, succeeded in drawing up the broad outlines of a mutual nonaggression pact that satisfied the requirements of Germany and the Soviet Union. The agreement allowed the ill-prepared Bolsheviks to avoid war with Germany, while freeing Hitler from the need to fight a two-front war in Europe. With the public signing of the treaty by Molotov and Ribbentrop on August 23, 1939, the Soviet Union and Germany also officially divided eastern Europe into "spheres of influence"; among other considerations, the treaty's secret protocols provided for the dismemberment of Poland and Romania.

With his hands now freed in the east, Hitler's invasion of Poland in the week following the treaty-signing signaled the onset of World War II. Though the Nonaggression Pact, also known as the Molotov-Ribbentrop Pact, achieved peace between Germany and the Soviet Union for the next two years, it did not allow the Soviet Union to escape war; in June, 1941, Hitler deceived Stalin and embarked upon a massive military offensive against the Soviet regime.

During World War II, Molotov was elevated to deputy chairman of the powerful State Defense Committee. Hence, for much of the 1930's and 1940's, Molotov was the second most powerful man in the Soviet Union, after Stalin. Toward the end of his life, however, the paranoid Stalin began to distrust Molotov and removed him from his most important positions. In 1949, the virulently anti-Semitic Stalin even had Molotov's Jewish wife, Polina Semyonovna Zhemchuzhina, imprisoned in a concentration camp. It is most likely that Molotov himself would have been eliminated altogether had it not been for Stalin's demise in March, 1953.

After Stalin's death, Molotov, along with Georgi M. Malenkov and Lavrenty Pavlovich Beria, briefly formed a triumvirate that led the Soviet Union until Nikita S. Khrushchev emerged as the undisputed leader in 1955. Thereafter, however, Molotov was increasingly viewed with suspicion by Khrushchev and his supporters in the Politburo. In June, 1957, Molotov and other hard-line Stalinists attempted to overthrow the reformist Khrushchev. The leadership revolt failed, however, because of a lack of military and regional support.

Unlike Stalin before him, Khrushchev did not liquidate his opposition; instead, the members of the Anti-Party Group led by Molotov were reassigned to lowly postings or ousted from the Communist Party altogether. Indeed, Molotov's last official postings were as ambassador to Mongolia from 1957 to 1960 and as the Soviet

---

MOLOTOV'S COCKTAIL

Time may obscure Vyacheslav Molotov's role in the bloody regime of Joseph Stalin and in starting World War II, but wherever there is uprising, insurrection, terrorism, or riot, his name will live on in the Molotov cocktail. He did not invent this homemade bomb; he inspired it.

The basic Molotov cocktail, also known as a petrol bomb, consists of a glass bottle containing gasoline with an airtight screw cap or stopper and a rag tied around the mouth. The rag is soaked in a flammable liquid and set on fire. The bomb is then thrown, and when the bottle breaks upon landing, the burning rag ignites the contents in a low-intensity explosion, which leaves a patch of flames. Other material may serve as the explosive contents, such as alcohol, methanol, ethanol, or a mixture; oil or sugar is often added to make the mixture stick on its target. In any case, the emphasis is on ease of manufacture and cheapness—the poor person's napalm.

Molotov cocktails are the weapon of the underdog. The name is a wry joke based on the social convention of a pre-dinner cocktail. During the invasion of Finland by the Soviets in 1939, Molotov denied reports that his country was bombing the Finns. In radio broadcasts, he claimed that Soviet airplanes were dropping food packages. The Finns began to refer to the bombs as "Molotov picnic baskets." Vastly outmatched by the Soviet army, the Finnish army used petrol bombs as antitank weapons to great effect after concocting a special mixture: 60 percent potassium chlorate, 32 percent coal tar, and 8 percent noulee (a fuel additive). This they called the Molotov cocktail—something to use before the Molotov picnic baskets started falling. They added sulfuric acid capsules to some to make the explosion nastier. Altogether, a workforce of eighty-seven women and five men produced 542,194 Molotov cocktails to help stop the invasion and give the Soviet foreign minister an infamous reputation. Previously used during the Spanish Civil War, the petrol bomb-cum-Molotov cocktail gained greater notoriety during the Soviet invasion of Finland and thereafter was used regularly into the twenty-first century.

---

representative to the International Atomic Energy Agency from 1960 to 1961. After condemning Khrushchev's Party Program in 1962, however, Molotov was relieved from his remaining posts and expelled from the Communist Party. Thereafter, the former Soviet leader—once second in command to Stalin—lived as a pensioner in Moscow until his death in 1986 at the age of ninety-six.

IMPACT

To the extent that Vyacheslav Mikhailovich Molotov supported obsequiously and unceasingly Stalin's barbarous rise to ultimate power, he is in part responsible for the creation of one of history's most brutal totalitarian regimes. Molotov's hands were also bloodstained by his active participation in repressing and liquidating thousands of party and government officials during the savage purges of the 1930's. The weapon named after him—

the Molotov cocktail, a bomb made of bottles of flammable liquid—was made in quantity at his order during World War II. However, Molotov will be best remembered for his authorship of the Nazi-Soviet Non-aggression Pact of 1939, an agreement that ultimately led to World War II and the deaths of fifty million people.

FURTHER READING

Medvedev, Roy. *All Stalin's Men*. New York: Doubleday, 1984. Provides a clearly written and detailed overview of Molotov's political career under Stalin.

Molotov, Vyacheslav Mikhailovich. *Molotov Remembers: Inside Kremlin Politics*. Edited by Albert Resis. Chicago: I. R. Dee, 1993. Brings together interviews of Molotov by Felix Chuev.

Riasanovsky, Nicholas V. *A History of Russia*. 6th ed. New York: Oxford University Press, 2000. Discusses Molotov's role in negotiating the Nazi-Soviet Non-aggression Pact of 1939, as well as his part in the anti-Khrushchev leadership struggle following Stalin's death.

Service, Robert. *Stalin: A Biography*. Cambridge, Mass.: Harvard University Press, 2005. Details the close relationship between Stalin and Molotov and the latter's participation in virtually every major political event of the Stalin era.

—*Thomas E. Rotnem*

SEE ALSO: Lavrenty Beria; Adolf Hitler; Nikita S. Khrushchev; Joachim von Ribbentrop; Joseph Stalin.

SUN MYUNG MOON
Korean evangelist, theologian, and entrepreneur

BORN: January 6, 1920; Kwangju Sangsa Ri, Pyungan Bukedo Province, Korea (now in North Korea)
ALSO KNOWN AS: Yong Myung Moon (birth name)
CAUSE OF NOTORIETY: Moon, who claimed to have met Jesus in a vision and who was also convicted for tax fraud, founded the Unification Church, whose recruitment practices and mass weddings have been criticized.
ACTIVE: Beginning 1946
LOCALE: Washington, D.C.

EARLY LIFE

The parents of Sun Myung Moon (suhn myuhng mewn) became Presbyterian when Moon was ten. He is known to have been a quiet and devout boy. When he was sixteen, Moon said, Jesus appeared to him in a vision, telling Moon to complete Christ's work on earth.

Following the end of World War II, Moon, who had studied electrical engineering in Japan, launched his ministry in 1946. As Korea was then under Soviet control, his preaching displeased the atheist government, and Moon was sentenced to a labor camp in 1948. He was liberated two years later and fled to another Korean city, then was imprisoned for several more years in South Korea.

EVANGELICAL CAREER

Moon sent a missionary to Japan in 1958 and the following year sent a delegation to the United States, where Moon would find his greatest following. His Holy Sprit Association for the Unification of World Christianity seemed to target college-age people for recruitment, and the movement faced widespread condemnation in the 1970's for the alleged aggressiveness of its tactics. Families of some "Moonies," as Unificationists were disparagingly called, hired people to kidnap their children away from the movement and "deprogram" them, or reverse the brainwashing they had supposedly undergone to convince them of Moon's divinity.

Besides allegations of brainwashing, Moon faced scathing criticism for more tangible infractions. He served a year in federal prison in 1982 for tax fraud and conspiracy to obstruct justice. He also staged several mass weddings in Washington, D.C. In each, thousands of Unificationists were wed after having been paired by Moon. Often the bride and groom had spent little, if any, time together before their match. (Today, Unificationists reaching marriageable age are more likely to be matched with a spouse by their parents than by the Reverend Moon.)

Moon's business holdings grew to include media interests such as *The Washington Times* newspaper and *World* magazine. His assets reportedly are worth billions of dollars, thanks in large measure to the fund-raising of his followers and prudent investment of those funds. The wide range of businesses and organizations affiliated with Moon became a source of unease for critics, who saw in such diversity an attempt to influence culture in the United States and abroad.

The Reverend Sun Myung Moon concludes a 1982 mass marriage ceremony in Manhattan. (AP/Wide World Photos)

THE UNIFICATION CHURCH

Some Unificationists believe that Moon represents the second coming of Christ and that Moon and his wife, Dr. Hak Ja Han Moon, are the "True Parents" of humanity. Others see Moon as a revealer or messenger of a messiah yet to come. The True Parents notion plays into the Unificationists' understanding of the divine as possessing both masculine and feminine qualities. As the group's name implies, the unification of humanity is a key element of its doctrine. One way this goal is pursued is through the deliberate blending of nationalities and ethnicities in Unificationist small groups and marriages.

Moon, a former Soviet subject, is anticommunist. He centers his operations in the United States, citing the suitability of American democracy as the environment into which to beckon the messiah. Millennialism, the belief that this physical world can be made perfect or restored, underpins much of Moon's thinking and writing. According to him, humanity must be unified and purified before the era of perfection can arrive. During Christ's lifetime, disbelief prevented him from establishing such perfection on earth. Therefore, reparations for the sin of that disbelief must be made, says Moon, who has taken on the mantle of humanity's new leader. Politically, Moon and his followers tend to be extremely conservative.

IMPACT

For scholars of religion, the Unification movement offers a unique opportunity to observe the formation of a faith and see its leaders attempt to make a marginalized religion into a mainstream one. The cult scare of the 1970's, of which Sun Myung Moon's movement was such a large part, raised important cultural questions for Americans, such as when it is appropriate for people to intervene in someone else's religious practices and whether faith can be coerced.

FURTHER READING

Bednarowski, Mary Farrell. *New Religions and the Theological Imagination in America.* Bloomington: Indiana University Press, 1989. Examines six new religious movements, pairing Unificationism with Mormonism, saying, in part, that both are aggressively American and sharply focused on family and community.

Hong, Nansook. *In the Shadow of the Moons*. Boston: Little, Brown, 1998. One of a large number of exposés by former Unificationists. This author, who was wed to one of Moon's sons when she was fifteen, chronicles abuse and her departure from Moon's family and movement.

Moon, Sun Myung. *Divine Principle*. 2d ed. Washington, D.C.: Holy Spirit Association for the Unification of World Christianity, 1984. Moon sets out his think-

ing on Christian theological categories such as creation, the Fall, and predestination.

Sontag, Frederick. *Sun Myung Moon and the Unification Church*. Nashville, Tenn.: Abingdon Press, 1977. The author, a Christian theologian, explores the reasons Moon was so strongly feared and hated in the 1970's. Sontag interviews a number of Moon's followers and Moon himself to probe these issues.

—*Elizabeth Jarnagin*

SEE ALSO: Marshall Applewhite; Jim Bakker; L. Ron Hubbard; David Koresh; Bonnie Nettles.

BUGS MORAN
American mobster

BORN: August 21, 1891; St. Paul, Minnesota
DIED: February 25, 1957; Leavenworth Federal Penitentiary, Leavenworth, Kansas
ALSO KNOWN AS: Adelard Cunin (birth name); George Clarence Moran (full name); George Gage; George Morrissey
MAJOR OFFENSES: Robbery and conspiracy to counterfeit and cash sixty-two thousand dollars' worth of American Express checks
ACTIVE: 1924-1945
LOCALE: Primarily Chicago, Illinois
SENTENCE: Ten to twenty years in Ohio State Prison; five years in Leavenworth Prison

EARLY LIFE
Bugs Moran (buhgz MOHR-an) was born Adelard Cunin, the son of Jules and Marie Diana Gobeil Cunin, French Canadians who had emigrated to St. Paul, Minnesota, where Moran was born. He attended Creighton, a private school administered by the Christian Brothers. While in school, he joined a local juvenile gang; he left school when he was eighteen. For a short time, he was employed as a driver by the Elmquist Brothers, but he and a friend were caught robbing a St. Paul store; Moran was sent to the state juvenile correctional facility at Red Wing. After escaping from Red Wing, he fled to Chicago. Meanwhile, the rest of his family moved to Winnipeg, Manitoba, Canada.

In September of 1910, Moran was wounded and apprehended while trying to rob a warehouse and was

sentenced to one to ten years' imprisonment in Joliet Prison. On June 18, 1912, he was paroled under the custody of a Bloomington, Illinois, businessman, but he became part of a horse-stealing ring and was again caught, receiving another prison sentence, one to ten years. Four years later, he was freed but was again arrested for taking part in a robbery in which a police officer was killed. This time, he was exonerated, but in a brawl later that year he received a knife wound that resulted in a four-inch neck scar. When he got out of the hospital, he joined a gang led by Charles "the Ox" Reiser. Other prominent members of the gang were Dion O'Banion, Hymie Weiss, and Vincent Drucci, all of whom later became well-known mobsters. Moran was arrested on November 18, 1917, for robbing a freight car; he made bond but jumped bail. He was arrested on February 1, 1918, and was sent to the Cook County Jail.

CRIMINAL CAREER
Moran's serious Mafia career began with Prohibition, which was enacted on January 16, 1920, and made illegal the manufacture, sale, import, or export of alcohol. O'Banion, who had taken control of the North Side Gang in Chicago, secured Moran's release from prison on March 16, 1921, and got his conviction reversed. When Moran was charged with burglary on June 1, 1921, the jury—which O'Banion had bribed—found him not guilty. Moran then married Lucille Logan and adopted her son, who became known as John George Moran.

While Moran was in St. Paul visiting his mother in

1924, O'Banion was killed by members of Johnny Torrio's gang. Moran became second in command to Weiss. To avenge O'Banion's death, on January 25, 1925, Weiss and Moran attempted to kill Torrio, who escaped death only because Moran's gun misfired and Moran had no more bullets. Torrio subsequently retired, turning his operation over to Al Capone, and thus began the turf wars between Capone and Weiss and Moran—known as the Bootleg Battle of the Marne. While Capone supplemented his bootlegging income with prostitution rings, Moran, a professed devout Roman Catholic, took the "higher ground" and refused to deal in prostitution. The battles, conducted on the street and in the press, escalated, and on September 20, 1926, Moran and his men attempted to kill Capone at his headquarters at the Hawthorne Inn in Cairo, Illinois. More than one thousand shots were fired at the inn and at a nearby restaurant in the unsuccessful effort to kill Capone. In retaliation, Capone had his minions kill Weiss on October 11, leaving Moran in charge of the gang. Moran responded by having Pete and Frank Gusenberg attempt to kill Jack McGurn, one of Capone's top henchmen. While Capone was conveniently in Florida, his men staged the most famous of all gangland killings on February 14, 1929. The St. Valentine's Day Massacre, as the killings were immortalized, was led by McGurn and cost Moran the lives of seven of his best people. As a result, he moved his operations—which included breweries, union racketeering, and slot machines—to Lake County, where he operated until 1936. His wife divorced him in 1930, and in 1931 he married Evelyn Herrell, who was more comfortable with his criminal activities. In 1938, he turned to counterfeiting and was arrested in April of that year.

LEGAL ACTION AND OUTCOME

On April 30, 1939, Moran was convicted of conspiracy to make and cash sixty-two thousand dollars' worth of American Express checks. Freed on appeal when he posted a bond, he fled but was captured and not released until December 21, 1943. In 1945, he went to Owensboro, Kentucky, and was thought to have robbed three banks; he was likely involved in even more bank robberies.

On July 6, 1945, Moran was arrested for robbery, found guilty, and sentenced to ten to twenty years in the Ohio State Prison. There, he had two hernia operations and a hemorrhoidectomy and nearly died of pneumonia. After his release, he was tried in 1957 for a robbery in Ansonia and found guilty; he was sentenced to five years in Leavenworth Prison in Kansas. A month later, on February 25, 1957, he died of lung cancer in Leavenworth.

IMPACT

Bugs Moran's claim to fame was that he outlived his criminal contemporaries and was "the man who got away" from Al Capone. He gained notoriety for having survived the St. Valentine's Day Massacre. In 1947, the *Chicago Tribune* offered him fifty thousand dollars for his story, and Hollywood gossip columnist Louella Parsons reportedly offered him $100,000 for film rights to his story.

FURTHER READING

Dretske, Diana. *Lake County, Illinois: An Illustrated History*. Carlsbad, Calif.: Heritage Media, 2002. Details Moran's activities in upstate Illinois after the St. Valentine's Day Massacre.

Helmer, William J., and Art Bilek. *The St. Valentine's Day Massacre: The Untold Story of the Gangland Bloodbath That Brought Down Al Capone*. Nashville: Cumberland House, 2004. Detailed account of the events leading up to the St. Valentine's Day Massacre and the ensuing repercussions of the killings.

Keefe, Rose. *The Man Who Got Away: The Bugs Moran Story*. Nashville: Cumberland House, 2005. Thorough scholarly treatment of Moran's life, containing photos, a comprehensive bibliography, and the context in which Moran operated.

—*Thomas L. Erskine*

SEE ALSO: Al Capone; Dion O'Banion; Hymie Weiss.

SIR HENRY MORGAN
Welsh buccaneer

BORN: c. 1635; Llanrumney, Glamorgan (now in
Cardiff), Wales

DIED: August 25, 1688; probably Lawrencefield,
Jamaica

ALSO KNOWN AS: Harry Morgan

CAUSE OF NOTORIETY: Morgan's pirate raids against
the Spaniards were known for their extreme
cruelty.

ACTIVE: 1654-1688

LOCALE: The West Indies and the Americas, primarily
Panama

EARLY LIFE

Little is known about the earliest years of Henry Morgan
(MOHR-guhn). It is likely that he was born in Llanrumney, Glamorgan (now in Cardiff), Wales. His father's name was probably Robert Morgan. Morgan later
disputed a report that he had gone to Barbados as an in-
dentured servant. His uncles, Thomas and Edward Morgan, fought on opposite sides during the English Civil War.

When Morgan was nineteen, he joined a
British expedition to the West Indies, under
the leadership of General Robert Venables
and Vice Admiral William Penn. After they
failed to capture the island of Hispaniola from
the Spaniards, they seized the smaller, de-
fenseless Jamaica. At the time, Spain dominated trade with its mainland ports along the
Caribbean and Gulf of Mexico, known collectively as the Spanish Main. Because of its strategic location, Jamaica became an important
base from which the British launched attacks
against the Spaniards.

PIRATING CAREER

Morgan remained in Jamaica and joined the
local militia. The governor, Sir Thomas Windsor, also gave Morgan a commission, which
authorized him to use a private vessel to attack
Spanish interests on behalf of England. In return, Morgan was entitled to the seized riches.
Known as a "letter of marque," the commission gave Morgan the status of "privateer." He
was therefore not a pirate, whose activities
were illegal. He also became known as a
"buccaneer," a term that originated from the

French *boucanier* and initially applied to illegal cattle
hunters. Eventually, "buccaneer" came to include sea
raiders.

Morgan captained a private vessel in 1660 when he
participated in Commodore Christopher Myngs's successful raid on Santiago del Cuba. They overcame a fort,
Castillo del Morro, and returned with six prize ships.
During the next several years, Morgan plundered towns
in the Americas, including Campeche and Villahermosa
in Mexico and Gran Granada in Nicaragua. By 1666, he
had returned to Jamaica and wed his first cousin, Mary
Elizabeth Morgan, the daughter of his Uncle Edward.

When he was thirty-two, the Brethren of the Coast, an
association of buccaneers, elected Morgan to be their
admiral after their leader, Edward Mansfield, was killed
by the Spaniards. In 1668, then-governor Sir Thomas
Modyford granted Morgan a "privateering" commission
in order to circumvent a suspected Spanish plot to attack
Jamaica. Morgan raided Puerto del Principe, Cuba;

Sir Henry Morgan.

there, his men reportedly locked citizens in churches and refused to feed them for a week while holding them for ransom.

Morgan also plundered Portobello, Panama, in 1668. His men paddled twenty-three canoes up the Guanches River and captured several forts along the way. The buccaneers reportedly tortured citizens in order to make them reveal where they had hidden their valuables. It is disputed as to whether they used nuns and monks as a human shield against Spanish attack. They returned to Jamaica with 250,000 pesos, including 100,000 pesos that they received from Panamanian officials to refrain from burning Portobello.

In 1669, Morgan's flagship, *Oxford*, exploded and sank near Cow Island off Hispaniola after a powder keg was set afire during a rowdy party. Although several hundred men were killed, Morgan survived and raided Maracaibo and Gibraltar in Venezuela the same year.

THE SACKING OF PANAMA CITY

Morgan's most famous raid occurred in 1670-1671 on Panama City, which was very rich from the influx of silver and gold from Peru. Starting with thirty-six ships and eighteen hundred men, the buccaneers first recaptured Old Providence Island, then took Fort San Lorenzo on the Chagres River and trekked through a mosquito-infested jungle for eight days. With a force of twelve hundred, they ultimately defeated a larger Spanish militia.

It is disputed whether Morgan or the Spaniards set the city ablaze. By the time of Morgan's arrival, many of the riches were on fleeing ships. His men spent three weeks ransacking the city, holding drunken orgies, and torturing the inhabitants, including hanging men by their testicles. Some buccaneers suspected Morgan of taking more than his share of the booty.

On returning to Jamaica, Morgan learned that the sacking of Panama City occurred after England and Spain had signed a treaty. To appease Spain, Morgan was sent back to England under arrest. Never imprisoned or formally put on trial, he made influential friends and even wrote a memorandum about military issues for King Charles II. In 1674, the king appointed him lieutenant governor of Jamaica and gave him a knighthood. It was there that he died fourteen years later, after a new governor took power, probably from complications of alcoholism.

IMPACT

While Sir Henry Morgan's personal reputation may have been questionable, his leadership and military skills were undeniable. His victories gave England greater access to the New World. Morgan spent his remaining years on Jamaica as a politician and wealthy plantation owner. His 1688 death was triggered by excessive drinking. Officials honored him with a twenty-two-gun salute at his funeral.

There is no doubt that Morgan's raids were fraught with violence. However, the nature and extent of his atrocities were exaggerated in *The History of the Bucaniers in America* (1684), a popular book written by Alexandre Olivier Exquemeling, a participant in some of the raids. Morgan was so outraged by certain passages about his life that he brought the first successful libel suit in history. By that time, however, the public had embraced Exquemeling's representation of Morgan.

FURTHER READING

Breverton, Terry. *Admiral Sir Henry Morgan: King of the Buccaneers*. Gretna, La.: Pelican, 2005. Presents Morgan as a brilliant leader who should be remembered as a hero. Contends that Morgan's reputation was unfairly blemished by Exquemeling.

Petrovich, Sandra Marie. *Henry Morgan's Raid on Panama: Geopolitics and Colonial Ramifications, 1669-1674*. Lewiston, N.Y.: Edwin Mellen Press, 2001. Suggests that Morgan's raid on Panama prompted England to develop a stronger colonial policy. Proposes that events in New World colonies affected European foreign relations.

Pope, Dudley. *Harry Morgan's Way*. London: Secker & Warburg, 1977. Examines the era's volatile political climate and portrays Morgan as a complex individual who was a product of his times.

Rogozinski, Jan. *A Brief History of the Caribbean from the Arawak and Carib to the Present*. Rev. ed. New York: Facts On File, 1999. Provides an excellent overview of Caribbean history, with tables and maps. Describes the islanders and natural resources. Also addresses European settlements, trade, and piracy.

—*Diane S. Carter*

SEE ALSO: Samuel Bellamy; Stede Bonnet; Anne Bonny; John Rackham; Mary Read; Bartholomew Roberts; Dominique You.

SIR OSWALD MOSLEY
Founder of the British Union of Fascists

BORN: November 16, 1896; Staffordshire, England
DIED: December 3, 1980; Orsay, near Paris, France
ALSO KNOWN AS: Oswald Ernald Mosley (full name)
MAJOR OFFENSE: Treason
ACTIVE: 1931-1940
LOCALE: England
SENTENCE: Three years in prison

EARLY LIFE

Oswald Mosley (MOHZ-lee) was born into an old British landed family. Educated in private schools, he entered Sandhurst, Britain's premier military school, in the summer of 1914. A month later, World War I broke out, and Mosley was commissioned an officer. Elected to Parliament in 1918 from a conservative constituency, he was its youngest member. King George V attended Mosley's first wedding, to Cynthia Curzon—daughter of the first earl of Curzon of Kedleston, viceroy of India—but Mosley, a brilliant orator, was impatient with the political establishment. He soon became an Independent and subsequently joined the opposition Labour Party. His primary concern was the economy. Unemployment remained high, and Britain's foreign trade had declined. Overproduction was believed to be the cause, and the orthodox remedy was deflation, including reducing wages. Mosley, like British economist John Maynard Keynes, claimed that the economic problems were a result of underconsumption, necessitating a reduction in interest rates and an increase in production through government planning and investment.

POLITICAL CAREER

Mosley became a popular figure in the Labour Party, and when the party took power in 1929, he joined the cabinet. However, the party's doctrinaire socialism and hidebound leadership proved inadequate to deal with the impact of the Great Depression. When Mosley's advocacy of a public works program under centralized leadership was rejected, he resigned his cabinet office. In early 1931, he abandoned the Labour Party and with a handful of followers established the New Party. With the party lacking support in the press, Mosley's public speeches became the major vehicle in spreading the party's message, and when Mosley was heckled by left-wing opponents, young recruits were organized to protect the speaker—some compared them with "storm troopers."

In the 1931 election, the New Party failed disastrously. In the aftermath, Mosley visited Italy to view fascism at first hand. He was not impressed with Italian leader Benito Mussolini but claimed that fascism was solving Italy's economic problems. In his mind, liberal capitalism had failed and communism was too destructive; he took the fascist alternative and established the British Union of Fascists (BUF) in October, 1932. Its emblem was the fasces (a bundle of rods with an ax emerging from them) of ancient Rome, replaced later by a lightning bolt in a circle, symbolizing action in unity. Black shirts became the official garb.

The initial BUF rallies were peaceful, and fascism seemed almost respectable in Britain. Mosley debated Prime Minister Clement Atlee at Oxford University and exchanged letters with President Franklin D. Roosevelt. Unlike Adolf Hitler's racial fascism, Mosley's was committed mainly to economic reform, favoring national autarchy and managed capitalism. By 1934, there were fascist weddings, fascist funerals, and fascist soccer teams; black uniforms substituted for black shirts. BUF membership, which peaked in 1934, numbered about forty thousand, or the same as Britain's Communist Party.

Mosley was anti-Semitic but probably little more so than most British citizens of his social class. However, anti-fascist demonstrations at BUF rallies increased Mosley's anti-Jewish statements, and his condemnation of finance capitalism had anti-Semitic references. He suggested in 1936 that Jews be deported. Later, he claimed that his opposition to Jews was not based upon race or religion but because of Jews' policy of pushing Great Britain into a European war against Hitler's Germany.

Confrontation was part of the BUF mystique and reflective of Mosley's own personality and philosophy, and hecklers were violently expelled from his rallies. By the 1936 Public Order Act, BUF activities were severely limited, including the banning of uniforms. Mosley's second marriage seemed to confirm his fascist commitment. Cynthia Mosley had died in May, 1933, and in 1936 in Berlin Mosley married Diana Mitford, whose sister Unity was devoted to Hitler. The German führer even attended a luncheon given for the newlyweds.

Mosley opposed British involvement in World War II, favoring a policy of isolation and national self-sufficiency. He believed that Hitler should be allowed to expand into Eastern Europe, Italy into Africa, and Japan into northern China. He claimed that if Hitler invaded Britain, he would fight for Britain. He continued to advocate peace in order to safeguard Britain and the British Empire even after war began in September, 1939.

LEGAL ACTION AND OUTCOME

By May, 1940, Mosley's position had become untenable. The government, claiming that the BUF was a potential fifth column in the event of a German invasion, arrested him on May 2, 1940, and Diana on June 29, 1940. Whether Mosley was legally a traitor is a problematic argument, but given the circumstances, incarceration was not unexpected. Mosley's health declined while in prison, and in November, 1943, Prime Minister Winston Churchill released both Mosleys on humanitarian grounds.

After World War II, Mosley attempted to return to politics, writing books, and delivering speeches. With prewar fascism dead, Mosley advocated the formation of a nation of Europe, with Africa as its empire, as a counterweight to the Soviet Union. He waited for the summons to power, but it never came. In 1959, he ran for Parliament from a London constituency but received only 8 percent of the vote. *My Life*, Mosley's autobiography, was published in 1968, receiving largely favorable reviews. He died in 1980.

IMPACT

Many considered Sir Oswald Mosley to be one of the most brilliant young men of his generation, but in the maelstrom of the Great Depression, Mosley, like many others, turned to radical alternatives to liberal capitalism.

Some became communists, and some turned to fascism; both ideologies proved to be gods that failed. World War II destroyed fascism, as Mosley's postwar career indicated. He picked up the mantle of Europeanism and probably would have felt vindicated by the creation of the European Community (EC) in 1993, but the evolution of the EC owed nothing to Mosley, and he would have condemned both globalization and the decline of his neo-Keynesian economics.

FURTHER READING

Cannadine, David, ed. *History in Our Time*. New Haven, Conn.: Yale University Press, 1998. Brings together essays on twentieth century Britain, including an excellent commentary on Mosley.

Laybourn, Keith. *Fifty Key Figures in Twentieth Century British Politics*. London: Routledge, 2002. Includes an insightful discussion of Mosley and his career.

Lewis, David Stephen. *Illusions of Grandeur*. Manchester, England: Manchester University Press, 1987. A comprehensive analysis of Mosley and British fascism.

Mosley, Sir Oswald. *My Life*. London: Nelson, 1968. Mosley's well-written autobiography, self-serving but revealing of his motivations.

Skidelsky, Robert. *Oswald Mosley*. London: Macmillan, 1990. First published in 1975, this revised edition remains the standard biography.

—*Eugene Larson*

SEE ALSO: Jacques Doriot; Julius Evola; William Joyce; Benito Mussolini; Anastase Vonsiatsky.

Mou Qizhong
Chinese businessman

Born: 1940 or 1941; Wanxian or Chongqing, Sichuan
Province, China
Also known as: Mu Qizhong
Major offense: Foreign exchange fraud
Active: 1974, 1983, and 1995
Locale: Northeastern China
Sentence: Life imprisonment, commuted to eighteen
years' imprisonment

Early Life

Mou Qizhong (moh shee-jewng) was born in 1940 or
1941, during China's war against Japan, either in Wanxian or Chongqing in Sichuan Province. His father,
Mou Pingzi, was a powerful financier, and Mou grew up
in a privileged environment. After the Communist takeover in 1949, his family was denounced, and he became a
farmer.

Criminal Career

During China's Cultural Revolution of 1966-1976, Mou
wrote and published a series of critical pamphlets and a
book, *Where Is China Going?* This earned him the wrath
of Mao Zedong's authorities, and in 1974 he was sentenced to death for counterrevolutionary activities.
Mao's death in 1976 and the reform program of Deng
Xiaoping saved Mou, whose conviction was overturned
in 1979; Mou was released from death row.

Now, with thirty-six dollars, Mou set up one of the
People's Republic of China's first private businesses,
dealing in alarm clocks. In 1983, he was convicted of tax
evasion and sentenced to one year in jail. Mou rebounded
upon his release: in 1992, he traded surplus pork, clothing, and electrical appliances for four Tupolev Tu-154
airplanes from Russia, which he sold to Sichuan Airlines,
making a profit of eleven million dollars. With the
money, he founded Nande Group, reorganized as the
Land Economic Group in 1993.

As Mou's business prospered, he sponsored soccer
clubs and hosted a new year's banquet for the Chinese
Ministry of Culture in 1994. He donated $360,000 to-
ward China's first North Pole expedition in 1995 and
$120,000 toward space exploration, tied to his business
in satellite communications. His net worth approached
$240 million.

Later in 1995, Mou faced a serious cash-flow problem. Because his private company could not apply for
credit in Communist China, he turned to alternative

means of raising money. On the basis of a forged import
contract with an Australian company, he asked managers
of the public Hubei Light Industrial Import and Export
Company to apply for a state credit of seventy-five million dollars, which was granted. Of this sum, Mou borrowed twenty-two million dollars at high interest rates.

At around this time, his wife objected to Mou's relationship with her sister Xia Zongwei. She divorced Mou
and took their son to the United States. From there, in
1996, she denounced his business practices to China's
authorities.

Legal Action and Outcome

In January, 1999, Mou was arrested at gunpoint and jailed.
Authorities charged him with obtaining the seventy-five-
million-dollar credit of 1995 through an intermediary
with fraudulent documents and causing losses to the state
of thirty-five million dollars, a foreign exchange crime
because of the Australian company involved. On May
30, 2000, Mou was sentenced to life imprisonment by the
Intermediate People's Court of Wuhan City, stripped of
political rights for life, and fined $625,000. On August
22, 2000, Hubei Provincial Higher People's Court upheld Mou's conviction. Languishing in jail but supported
by Xia Zongwei, on April 12, 2004, Mou saw his sentence commuted to eighteen years' imprisonment.

Impact

Mou Qizhong's trials in 2000 drew international attention, highlighting a darker side of China's emerging
market economy. His trials were part of a public anti-
corruption campaign meant to show official resolve.

Mou's sympathizers pointed out the difficulty for
Chinese private enterprises in obtaining business credit
in the 1990's. It was widely held that the first post-Mao
entrepreneurs operated in legal limbo and had to rely on
the support of high party officials. When this support was
withdrawn, often in the light of extravagant entrepre-
neurial behavior, the road to conviction was politically
hastened. Indicative of the uncertain, politically charged
atmosphere, Mou's sympathizers pointed out that two of
his judges were convicted and jailed for taking bribes in
2002.

Further Reading

Doebele, Justin. "China's Fifty Richest Businessmen."
Forbes Global, November 15, 1999. Lists Mou as the

sixteenth-richest man in China and warns of his impending trial.

Fishman, Ted. *China, Inc.* New York: Scribner, 2005. Optimistic review of China's transition to a market economy; mentions challenges faced by early entrepreneurs like Mou (who is not mentioned).

Kitamura, Yutaka. "The Precarious Perch of China's

Wealthy." *Sumitomo Corporation: Economic Trends* 168 (June, 2003): 2-3. Sympathetic account of Mou's fall as symptomatic of Chinese entrepreneurs' need not to run afoul of Communist officials.

—*R. C. Lutz*

SEE ALSO: Mao Zedong.

ZACARIAS MOUSSAOUI
Terrorist and co-conspirator in the September 11, 2001, attacks on the United States

BORN: May 30, 1968; France

ALSO KNOWN AS: Shaqil; Abu Khalid al-Sahrawi; Twentieth Hijacker; Zuluman Tangotango

MAJOR OFFENSES: Conspiracy to commit international terrorism, conspiracy to destroy aircraft, and conspiracy to use weapons of mass destruction

ACTIVE: 1998-2001

LOCALE: United States

SENTENCE: Life in prison without parole

Zacarias Moussaoui. (AP/Wide World Photos)

EARLY LIFE

Zacarias Moussaoui (zak-uh-REE-uhs moo-SOW-ee) was born and raised in France by his Moroccan mother. There was no religious education within the family. He earned a master's degree from Southbank University in the United Kingdom. French authorities began monitoring Moussaoui in 1996, when they observed him with Islamic extremists in London. He carried letters indicating that he was a marketing consultant in the United States for Infocus Tech, a Malaysian company.

In April, 1998, Moussaoui spent time at the al-Qaeda-affiliated Khalden training camp in Afghanistan. He then traveled to Chicago from London in February, 2001. He enrolled in a flight school in Norman, Oklahoma, but was such a poor student that he dropped out. He then traveled to Minnesota and enrolled in another flight school but was unable to learn to fly. In June, 2001, Moussaoui purchased flight training videos for the Boeing 747 Model-400 and the Boeing 747 Model-200 from an Ohio pilot store. In mid-July, 2001, he made credit card payments to the Pan Am International Flight Academy in Minneapolis for a simulator course in commercial flight training. He attended this course between August 13 and August 15, 2001.

CRIMINAL CAREER

On August 17, 2001, Moussaoui was arrested on immigration charges and interviewed by federal agents in Minneapolis. He attempted to explain his presence in the United States by falsely stating that he was simply interested in learning how to fly. Federal Bureau of Investigation (FBI) agents were worried about why Moussaoui was taking flight training. They tried to get permission to search his laptop computer in order to discern what his plans were, but the agents' request was turned down because they lacked sufficient probable cause for the search. Moussaoui was still being held in prison on September 11, 2001, when the terrorist attacks on the World Trade Center in New York City and on the Pentagon in Washington, D.C., took place, all by commercial airplanes.

LEGAL ACTION AND OUTCOME

As of 2006, Moussaoui was the only person in the United States charged in connection with the September 11 attacks. He was charged with six counts of conspiracy: conspiracy to commit international terrorism, to commit aircraft piracy, to destroy aircraft, to use weapons of mass destruction (namely, airplanes intended for use as missiles, bombs, and similar devices), to murder U.S. employees, and to destroy property. After his arrest, sometimes he chose to represent himself; other times he insisted on having a defense lawyer.

The terrorist attacks on September 11, 2001, provided the evidence that the FBI needed to get a search warrant for Moussaoui's computer and other belongings. The agency learned that Moussaoui had had a Hotmail.com e-mail account when he disclosed that information in a motion filed with the court in July, 2002. However, after thirty days of inactivity, Hotmail accounts are erased; after ninety days of account dormancy, records are unable to be retrieved. Therefore, by the time agents learned of Moussaoui's Hotmail e-mail account, it was too late to find it. Moussaoui also used the alias Zuluman Tango-tango to register pilotz123@hotmail.com, another Hotmail e-mail account. The FBI confirmed Moussaoui had used that account to contact the two flight schools, according to a floppy disk seized along with Moussaoui's laptop.

On December 11, 2001, a federal grand jury indicted Moussaoui for conspiring with al-Qaeda leader Osama Bin Laden and other al-Qaeda members "to murder thousands of innocent people in New York, Virginia and Pennsylvania." Moussaoui was regularly called the Twentieth Hijacker in American media reports. On April 22, 2005, Moussaoui pleaded guilty to the six counts of conspiracy in the indictment, admitted helping al-Qaeda carry out

---

THREE ASSESSMENTS OF THE MOUSSAOUI TRIAL

On May 24, 2006, following Zacarias Moussaoui's sentencing three weeks earlier, the Arab news agency Aljazeera reported a taped message from someone purporting to be Osama Bin Laden. The speaker said that Zacarias Moussaoui was not involved in the September 11, 2001, attacks on the United States, because he (assumably Bin Laden) had personally assigned to the nineteen hijackers who were involved their various terrorist tasks:

The truth is that he [Moussaoui] has no connection whatsoever with the events of September 11. I am certain of what I say because I was responsible for entrusting the 19 brothers . . . with the raids. . . . I call to memory my brothers the prisoners in Guantanamo, may Allah free them all, and I state a fact, about which I am also certain: All the prisoners of Guantanamo, who were captured in 2001 and the first half of 2002 . . . had no connection whatsoever to the events of September 11.

Moussaoui himself described his trial as a

. . . wasted opportunity for this country to understand and to learn why people like me and people like Mohamed Atta and the rest have so much hatred for you. You don't want to hear, America. You will feel. We will come back another day. . . . God curse America. God save Osama Bin Laden. You'll never get him. . . . America, you lost! I won!

U.S. president George W. Bush commented that

. . . Mr. Moussaoui got a fair trial. The jury convicted him to life in prison, where he will spend the rest of his life. In so doing, they spared his life, which is something that he evidently was not willing to do for innocent American citizens. It is really important for the United States to stay on the offense against these killers and bring them to justice.

---

the September 11 hijackings, and stated that he understood he could be given the death penalty for his role in the deadliest terrorist attack in U.S. history. By pleading guilty, he ended his trial, and the jury had to decide his penalty.

During the penalty phase of the trial, Moussaoui claimed that the terrorist plot had been to fly planes into U.S. buildings, including the White House, and insisted that he was not one of the September 11 hijackers but rather that he had his orders directly approved by Bin Laden to attack the White House on an unspecified future date. During the course of the trial and sentencing period, Moussaoui uttered deliberately provocative remarks and, as one of his defense attorneys put it, proved to be the most difficult client he had ever had to defend.

On May 3, 2006, a jury in Virginia sentenced Moussaoui to life in prison without parole for conspiracy to commit international terrorism, conspiracy to destroy aircraft, and conspiracy to use weapons of mass destruction. Moussaoui irrationally claimed that he had "won" the case and America had lost. At his formal sentencing, he cursed America and declared that Osama Bin Laden would never be captured. U.S. District Judge Leonie Brinkema responded: "You came here to be a martyr and die in a big bang of glory . . . instead you will die with a whimper."

IMPACT

The jury decided on life in prison without parole for Zacarias Moussaoui because three of the jury members did not agree that his offenses required the death sentence. There were strong and emotional reactions to this verdict, both pro and con—even among those whose family members were killed during the events of September 11, 2001. Some believed that the death penalty, if justified in any case, was justified in this one, since Moussaui was deemed to have had information that could have halted the attacks. Others believed that the life imprisonment sentence demonstrated to the world that the United States—even though it remained one of the few nations that allowed the death penalty—was a fair nation governed by the rule of law. Several Americans expressed confidence in the American justice system, noting that even in such a highly emotionally charged case, a jury could look beyond revenge and render a fair verdict; some, in addition, pointed out that Moussaui was not primarily responsible for the September 11 attacks (calling him an al-Qaeda "wannabe" who lacked the ability to plan them) and wondered why, for example, the architect of the attacks, Khalid Shaikh Mohammed (who was in U.S. custody), was not similarly brought to justice.

There are several potential positive impacts of the Moussaoui trial on a global level, not the least of which was the possibility that other nations would be more likely to support extradition of suspected terrorists to the United States for trial, having just witnessed the integrity of the American jury system. Finally, by rejecting death

for Moussaoui, the jury denied him want he claimed he wanted: to become a martyr for al-Qaeda. Instead, he would enter prison as a relatively young man and spend twenty-three hours a day in solitary confinement for the remainder of his life.

FURTHER READING

Frank, Mitch. "Terror Goes on Trial." *Time*, March 7, 2005 (U.S. edition), 34. Discusses how, following September 11, 2001, lawyers used preemptive prosecution to break up suspected terrorist groups before they could strike.

Markon, Jerry, and Timothy Dwyer. "Moussaoui Unfazed as 9/11 Attacks Detailed; Defendant Smiles as Prosecutor Describes Doomed Flight During Death Penalty Trial." *The Washington Post*, March 8, 2006, p. A-7. An account of how prosecutors triggered strong emotions from September 11 victims' family members by reading detailed accounts of each hijacked flight in court.

Moussaoui, Abd Samad, and Florence Bouquillat. *Zacarias Moussaoui*. New York: Seven Stories Press, 2003. A book written by Moussaoui's brother (and translated into English) about Zacarias's early family life and how he became a terrorist.

National Commission on Terrorist Attacks. *The 9/11 Commission Report*. New York: W. W. Norton, 2004. The final report of the commission that investigated the time line and dynamics of the September 11, 2001, terrorist attacks on the United States. It is also available for download from http://www.9-11commission.gov/.

Thomas, Evan, Daniel Klaidman, and Michael Isikoff. "Enemies Among Us." *Newsweek*, June 7, 2004, 4-8. A discussion of the politics and fear surrounding terrorist threats in America and how they are handled by law enforcement.

—*Linda Volonino*

SEE ALSO: Mohammed Atta-al-Sayed; Osama Bin Laden; Khalid Shaikh Mohammed.

ROBERT MUGABE
Prime minister (1980-1987) and executive president (1987-   ) of Zimbabwe

BORN: February 21, 1924; Kutama, Southern Rhodesia (now Zimbabwe)

ALSO KNOWN AS: Robert Gabriel Mugabe (full name)

CAUSE OF NOTORIETY: Mugabe's autocratic rule and repressive policies generated political and economic crises and turned his country into a pariah state.

ACTIVE: Beginning 1980

LOCALE: Zimbabwe, Africa

EARLY LIFE

Robert Gabriel Mugabe (moo-GAH-bay) was born on February 21, 1924, at Kutama Mission near Salisbury (now Harare), the capital of Southern Rhodesia (now Zimbabwe). He was endowed with a restless spirit and a voracious reading habit. After acquiring a teaching diploma in 1945, he attended Fort Hare University College in apartheid South Africa, where he learned of Marxism and Gandhian principles of resistance. Having obtained a bachelor's degree in English and history from Fort Hare, he returned to Southern Rhodesia in 1952. He then acquired degrees in education and economics by correspondence from the University of South Africa and London University between 1952 and 1958. From 1958 to 1960, he taught at a teachers' college in Accra, the capital of Ghana, which was the first independent black African country. It was there that he met his first wife, Sally Hayfron.

POLITICAL CAREER

Mugabe returned to Southern Rhodesia in 1960 to take part in the independence struggle against white settler minority rule. He joined the National Democratic Party (NDP) and the Zimbabwe African People's Union (ZAPU), both led by veteran nationalist Joshua Nkomo. In 1963, Mugabe founded the Zimbabwe African National Union (ZANU), essentially constituted by the majority Shona (an ethnic group), with the Reverend Ndabaningi Sithole and Herbert Chitepo. Mugabe became the first secretary general of ZANU. In 1964, British premier Ian Smith's minority government detained Mugabe and other nationalist leaders for the next ten years.

After his release in 1974, Mugabe relocated to Mozambique, a Portuguese colony that attained independence in 1975, from where he led the Zimbabwe African National Liberation Army (ZANLA), the military wing of ZANU. Following a split in ZANU, Mugabe headed the militant faction of the organization that ultimately eclipsed Sithole's moderate faction.

Military pressure from Mugabe's ZANLA and Nkomo's Zimbabwe People's Revolutionary Army (ZIPRA, the armed wing of ZAPU), as well as diplomatic pressure from South Africa and Britain, forced Smith to accept that white minority rule would have to come to an end in Southern Rhodesia. However, an attempt to hand over power to moderate black leaders—Bishop Abel Muzorewa and Sithole—to the exclusion of Mugabe and Nkomo proved futile. Eventually, an agreement in September, 1979, which was brokered by Britain in response to Nigeria's nationalization of British Petroleum (BP) assets, led to an all-inclusive election on March 4, 1980. Mugabe's ZANU won fifty-seven of the eighty seats contested by the majority African parties.

Southern Rhodesia was now Zimbabwe, and Mugabe was the prime minister of the country from 1980 to 1987.

Robert Mugabe. (AP/Wide World Photos)

He formed a broad-based government, which included ministers from ZANU, Nkomo's ZAPU, and the white minority party. Mugabe sought to absorb ZAPU into ZANU, and ZIPRA into the new national army dominated by ZANU cadres. Such bridge-building efforts unraveled when Nkomo's supporters in Matabeleland revolted. Nkomo was dismissed from the government, and the army's Fifth Brigade brutally suppressed the uprising between 1982 and 1985. The crisis ended with a negotiated settlement in 1987. ZANU and ZAPU were merged to create the ZANU-Patriotic Front (ZANU-PL), and Nkomo was appointed as one of the country's two vice presidents.

REPRESSIVE RULE AND NATIONAL DECLINE

Mugabe's assumption of power as executive president in 1987, after amending the constitution, sealed his slide into autocracy. Having merged the two dominant black parties, he was bent on creating a one-party state. He proceeded to suppress or eliminate opposition within the party and state. To consolidate his regime, he placed his cronies in high-ranking positions. He embarked on an austerity program in 1991 in response to international pressure and a deepening economic crisis. However, the volatile issue of land redistribution, initially tackled under a "willing buyer, willing seller" scheme, defied solution; it proved to be his trump card when his political hold was threatened in 2000.

Mugabe had proposed some constitutional changes, which were defeated by referendum following strong opposition by disenchanted urban Zimbabweans. He then unleashed war veterans on the white-owned farms to effect their expropriation. In April, 2000, he railroaded his rejected constitutional amendments through the Parliament, which legalized the seizure of white-owned farms. The seizures were a political maneuver intended to retain the loyalty of his rural supporters in Mashonaland. They led to the flight of white farmers and the collapse of what had been a flourishing agricultural sector. Zimbabwe turned from an exporter to an importer of foodstuffs.

In March, 2002, Mugabe was challenged at the polls by Morgan Tsvangirai, leader of the Movement for Democratic Change (MDC), the most credible opposition to Mugabe's rule since 1980. However, owing to a high turnout in his rural strongholds and the intimidation of the opposition, Mugabe won 56 percent of the votes to Tsvangirai's 42 percent. Thereafter, Mugabe continued to consolidate his one-man rule and to abridge the human rights of Zimbabwe's citizens, including a curb on press freedom.

In June, 2005, Mugabe ordered the police to evict 200,000 squatters from urban shantytowns, ostensibly to "drive out trash." However, this move was a political strike at the urban strongholds of the opposition. It was also an inhumane operation that attracted international condemnation. Meanwhile, the country's economic downslide was compounded by prolonged drought and official corruption.

IMPACT

Robert Mugabe's excesses provoked a backlash from the international community. In March, 2003, the United States imposed economic sanctions on him and his associates. The Commonwealth, an association of former British colonies, suspended Zimbabwe in 2003. When the suspension was extended for an additional eighteen months in December, 2003, Mugabe pulled Zimbabwe out of the Commonwealth. The European Union placed a travel ban on him and his officials, a move that put Mugabe's Zimbabwe in the same class with Sani Abacha's Nigeria as a pariah nation.

FURTHER READING

Chan, Stephen. *Robert Mugabe: A Life of Power and Violence*. London: I. B. Tauris, 2003. A detailed study of Zimbabwe under Mugabe's rule following independence in 1980.

Meredith, Martin. *Our Votes, Our Guns: Robert Mugabe and the Tragedy of Zimbabwe*. New York: PublicAffairs, 2002. An account of Mugabe's leadership written by a journalist.

Norman, Andrew. *Robert Mugabe and the Betrayal of Zimbabwe*. Jefferson, N.C.: McFarland, 2004. A critical and trenchant examination of Mugabe's rule.

—*Ayodeji Olukoju*

SEE ALSO: Sani Abacha; Idi Amin; Omar al-Bashir; Jean-Bédel Bokassa; Samuel K. Doe; Mengistu Haile Mariam; Mobutu Sese Seko; Muammar al-Qaddafi; Muhammad Siad Barre; Charles Taylor.

ELIJAH MUHAMMAD

African American leader of the Nation of Islam (1934-1975)

BORN: October 7, 1897; Sandersville, Georgia
DIED: February 25, 1975; Chicago, Illinois
ALSO KNOWN AS: Elijah Poole (birth name); Gulam Bogans
CAUSE OF NOTORIETY: Muhammad, best known for his leadership of the controversial Nation of Islam, also created notoriety with his refusal to be inducted into the U.S. Army, charges of sedition filed against him, and his paternity of thirteen children with teenage girls.
ACTIVE: 1934-1975
LOCALE: Chicago, Illinois
SENTENCE: One to five years in prison for violation of the 1940 Selective Training and Service Act; released after three years on conditional parole

EARLY LIFE

Elijah Poole, who would later change his name to Elijah Muhammad (eh-LI-jah moo-HAM-mehd), was born in Sandersville, Georgia, in October, 1897, to William and Mariah Poole, working-class African Americans in the segregated South. His maternal grandmother was a mulatto and slave whose master had raped her. His father came from a long line of Georgia ministers. Elijah was raised in a Christian church and, as much as possible, his parents tried to shield him from the harsh realities of the Jim Crow South.

Nevertheless, at the age of ten, Elijah witnessed the lynching of a young black man whom he knew. The eighteen-year-old victim had been accused of raping a white woman, a charge often levied against black males but seldom substantiated. At the age of sixteen, Elijah moved to Macon, Georgia, where he found employment. The Poole family had briefly relocated to Cordele, Georgia, where two more black males were lynched, prompting a mass exodus both from the town and from the state of Georgia beginning in 1916.

Between 1916 and 1923, Elijah worked in a number of jobs, including as a laborer in Georgia's lumber industry and as a brick maker. However, an experience with a racist, white farmer who threatened to beat him forced Elijah to migrate out of the state. In April, 1923, Elijah and his young wife, Clara, and two children took the train to Detroit, Michigan, accompanied by his parents and other close relatives.

ACTIVIST CAREER

By 1928, Elijah was employed in the growing Detroit auto industry, but his asthma soon forced him to quit. While employed, though, Elijah often discussed racial issues with fellow employees who were members of the Moorish Science Temple of America (MSTA). Timothy Drew, later renamed Drew Ali, founded the MSTA in

---

ELIJAH MUHAMMAD ON THE RACES

In his Message to the Blackman in America *(1965), Elijah Muhammad set forth his understanding of the origins and relationship between the "Adamic" (white) and "Muslim" (black) races:*

According to the Bible (Gen. 3:20-24), Adam and his wife were the first parents of all people (white race only) and the first sinners. According to the Word of Allah, he was driven from the Garden of Paradise into the hills and caves of West Asia, or as they now call it, "Europe," to live his evil life in the West and not in the Holy Land of the East. . . . The sword of Islam prevented the Adamic race from crossing the border of Europe and Asia to make trouble among the Muslims for 2,000 years after they were driven out of the Holy Land and away from the people, for their mischief-making, lying and disturbing the peace of the righteous nation of Islam. . . .

The Adamic race is still the enemy of the Muslims (the black man). Nevertheless, Allah did not deprive the Adamic race right guidance through His prophets, whom they persecuted and killed. The Adamic white race's history is proof that they are the enemies of God and the righteous, for they never did sincerely accept a prophet of God. Can they now claim to be the chosen race of God? Why would God limit their time of rule? Why did God send His prophets to warn them that He was going to destroy them? Holy Qur'ān (7:14): "He said (the devil) respite me until the day when they are raised up." Those that are referred to as being "raised up" refer to the resurrection of the black man into the knowledge of the white race as being the devils, the enemies of Allah (God) and the black nation. "He as (the devil) said: Thou hast caused me to remain disappointed, I will certainly lie in wait for them in Thy straight path" (Holy Qur'ān 7:166). What Allah disappointed the devils in was the limiting of their rule over the nations and making it manifest to the world of black man that they are the enemies and great deceivers of the righteous.

The white race is not, and never will be, the chosen people of Allah (God). They are the chosen people of their father Yakub, the devil.

1913 as an offshoot of a group called the Ahmadiyya. The Detroit branch of the MSTA was one of the largest among seventeen chapters. Ali preached black nationalism and emphasized black religion.

Elijah and his family relocated again in 1931, this time arriving in Chicago, where thousands of southern blacks had already preceded them. Elijah and his wife began attending meetings led by a man who called himself Wallace Fard Muhammad (also known as Wallace Dodd Fard), the founder of the Nation of Islam. Three of Elijah's brothers, already strongly influenced by Muhammad, had joined the Nation of Islam. Elijah decided to join too. A religious and sociopolitical organization that set as its goal the "resurrection" of the condition of black Americans, the Nation of Islam considered itself a form of Islam. However, its divergence from traditional doctrine caused many Muslims to call the organization blasphemous. Moreover, its radical black nationalism and assertions of white inferiority furthered racial tensions with white Americans.

In 1931, Muhammad renamed Elijah Poole as Elijah Muhammad, and Elijah soon became one of Muhammad's trusted lieutenants. Elijah thus began his forty-four-year career with the Nation of Islam; he would spend approximately forty-two years as leader of the black Muslims. By the time Wallace Muhammad disappeared in 1934, there were some eight thousand black Muslims in Chicago.

SEDITION CHARGES

As World War II escalated, Elijah and thirty-seven other black Muslims were arrested for refusing induction into the United States Army. Elijah received draft notices in September, 1942. Citing his religion and his opposition to the United States' involvement in the war, he rejected the summons to appear. Elijah was also arrested in a raid in Chicago on October 5, 1942, and charged with eight counts of sedition and supporting the enemy (the Japanese) through his writings. It appeared that the U.S. government used the sedition charges against Elijah and dozens of other black Muslims, as well as the charge of conspiracy to commit sedition, in order to weaken the movement.

In the mid-1950's, rumors of Elijah's infidelity surfaced. Although no one challenged him regarding these affairs, tales of his associations persisted into the late 1950's. According to several scholars and Federal Bureau of Investigation (FBI) records, between January 17, 1960, and August 28, 1967, seven underage girls, all black Muslims who acted as Elijah's personal secretar-

ies, gave birth to thirteen children. Some of the teenage girls were relocated to California, where they filed paternity suits in state court.

LEGAL ACTION AND OUTCOME

Elijah pleaded guilty to three accounts of refusing induction into the army. He had violated the 1940 Selective Training and Service Act and was sentenced to one to five years in prison. He entered the federal facility in Milan, Michigan, on July 23, 1943, and was released on August 24, 1946, with a conditional parole, meaning any additional violations would result in another two years in federal prison. The eight counts of sedition, already weak when they were issued, were dropped by the federal prosecutor handling the case because the draft refusal charges were much stronger. Moreover, although child paternity suits were filed by lawyers representing most of the teenage girls, Elijah was never charged with rape or any related crime concerning the underage girls.

IMPACT

The Nation of Islam, under the leadership of Elijah Muhammad from 1934 until his death in 1975, became a potent black nationalist organization. Counting more than twenty-five mosques and a membership of twenty thousand staunch members (and several thousand more supporters), the black Muslims stood as a pillar in many urban ghettos, especially in the northern states. With the ownership of farmland, grocery stores, shopping malls, and other real estate holdings valued in the millions of dollars, the Nation of Islam also built a strong economic base by providing jobs and other opportunities for lower-class black Americans. Elijah spoke on a nationwide network of 150 radio stations, and his newspaper, *The Messenger*, often attacked and criticized the actions of white police departments around the nation, garnering support from many African Americans but spurring ire among white Americans. Elijah's stature brought the black Muslims increasing attention not only from the FBI but also from congressional committees. His success even created envy among some non-Muslim black leaders.

Overall, Elijah and the Nation of Islam offered African Americans an alternative to the Christian-based Civil Rights movement led by Dr. Martin Luther King, Jr., and others. Although Elijah tempered his antiwhite position after 1960, he still remained a hero to many African Americans.

FURTHER READING

Evanzz, Karl. *The Messenger: The Rise and Fall of Elijah Muhammad.* New York: Pantheon Books, 1999. This detailed work makes good use of FBI documents and previously unused sources to unravel the life of Elijah Muhammad.

Gregg, Claude A. *An Original Man: The Life and Times of Elijah Muhammad.* New York: St. Martin's Press, 1997. This biography provides a good, balanced account of Elijah's life.

Lincoln, C. Eric. *The Black Muslims in America.* Trenton, N.J.: Africa World Press, 1961. For more than thirty years, Lincoln's volume remained the definitive account of the Nation of Islam and Elijah Muhammad.

Ogbar, Jeffrey. *Black Power: Radical Politics and African American Identity.* Baltimore: Johns Hopkins University Press, 2004. Ogbar provides a synthesis of previous works on Elijah Muhammad, offering good insight into his sometimes elusive personality.

—*Jackie R. Booker*

SEE ALSO: Wallace Dodd Fard; Father Divine; Huey Newton.

JOHN ALLEN MUHAMMAD AND LEE BOYD MALVO
American snipers

JOHN ALLEN MUHAMMAD

BORN: December 31, 1960; New Orleans, Louisiana
ALSO KNOWN AS: Beltway Sniper; D.C. Sniper; Tarot Card Killer; John Allen Williams (birth name)

LEE BOYD MALVO

BORN: February 18, 1985; Kingston, Jamaica
ALSO KNOWN AS: Beltway Sniper; D.C. Sniper; Tarot Card Killer; John Lee Malvo; Malik Malvo

MAJOR OFFENSE: Murder
ACTIVE: October 2-22, 2002
LOCALE: Maryland, Virginia, and Washington, D.C.
SENTENCE: John Allen Muhammad received the death sentence for one homicide in Virginia and six consecutive life sentences for six homicides in Maryland; Lee Boyd Malvo was sentenced to life in prison without parole for a Virginia homicide and six life sentences without parole for six Maryland homicides

EARLY LIVES

John Allen Muhammad (mew-HAHM-ehd) was born John Allen Williams. His father was a railroad porter who was mostly absent from John Allen's life. His mother, Myrtis, got breast cancer and moved in with family in Baton Rouge. She died when John Allen was only three; he was then raised by aunts. He had a son, Travis, with a girlfriend. In 1981 he married his first wife, Carol, and fathered a son, Lindberg. In 1987 he and Carol divorced. One year later he married his second wife, Mildred.

He served in the Louisiana National Guard from 1975 to 1985 and was in the U.S. Army from 1985 to 1994, during which time he fought in the Gulf War. In 1994 he and his wife moved to Tacoma, Washington, where they started a car repair business. In 1999 the couple separated, and Mildred filed for divorce. In 2000 she filed a restraining order against him because he had threatened her. In October, 2001, he changed his name to Muhammad, to reflect his conversion to Islam.

Lee Boyd Malvo (MAL-voh) was born in Jamaica to Una James, a seamstress, and Leslie Samuel Malvo, a mason. His parents were never married; their relationship ended when Lee was an infant. He rarely saw his father, and his mother traveled a great deal, trying to find work. Lee was often left with relatives and friends. When he was fourteen years old, he and his mother moved to Antigua. She eventually left him there and went to Florida to live. Malvo moved in with Muhammad and Muhammad's three children in Antigua. In 2001 he converted to Islam. He began calling Muhammad "Dad."

CRIMINAL CAREERS

During three weeks in October, 2002, Muhammad and Malvo shot more than a dozen people, ten of whom died. Although not charged for it, they reportedly also killed at least three others before the October shootings: the daughter of Muhammad's ex-wife's friend at her home, a pizzeria owner in Maryland who was locking up his store, and a liquor store clerk in Alabama during a robbery. On October 2, 2002, the first of the Beltway area shots by Muhammad and Malvo was fired around 5:00 P.M. in Maryland; no one was hurt. Less than one

Lee Boyd Malvo. (AP/Wide World Photos)

hour later the shooter hit a customer in a supermarket parking lot. Over the following two and a half weeks, additional shots were fired from relatively long ranges at gas stations, in store parking lots, near a bus station, at people walking down the street, and at a middle school. The victims apparently were selected at random.

LEGAL ACTION AND OUTCOME
After receiving two tips from citizens, police arrested both Muhammad and Malvo at a highway rest stop in Maryland on October 24, 2002. Despite pleading not guilty by reason of insanity, on March 10, 2004, Malvo was sentenced to life in prison without parole for the death of the Federal Bureau of Investigation analyst Linda Franklin. During the same trial, Malvo was also convicted of unlawful use of a firearm. On April 22, 2005, Muhammad was sentenced to death by a Virginia court for his conviction of capital murder, homicide with intent to terrorize the government or public, conspiracy to commit murder, and the illegal use of a firearm.

Muhammad was also tried in Maryland for the six deaths from the shootings committed there. He was convicted on May 30, 2006, and sentenced on June 1, 2006, to six consecutive sentences of life imprisonment with-

out the possibility of parole, with the help of testimony from Malvo. Malvo pleaded guilty to those six murders. He testified that the reason for their actions was to create havoc so that Muhammad could easily kidnap his three children and so they could extort money from the government. Muhammad planned next to train homeless men to use weapons to cause chaos in cities across the United States. On November 9, 2006, the twenty-one-year-old Malvo was sentenced to six additional, consecutive life sentences for the six Maryland murders.

IMPACT
The Beltway Sniper shootings had a significant impact on American society. Americans, especially on the East Coast, experienced a heightened fear for personal safety. These events had an even broader impact on the criminal justice system, especially in terms of profiling. Criminal justice professionals agreed that it must be a crazed white man who committed such atrocities. Both John Allen Muhammad and Lee Boyd Malvo, however, were black. The benefits of profiling as well as the understanding of spree killers was therefore called into question. Additionally, once Muhammad and Malvo were captured, there was significant debate as to which jurisdiction should try the offenders. Virginia was the first state, followed by Maryland. Finally, the case inspired a film and multiple books were produced.

FURTHER READING
Cannon, Angie. *Twenty-Three Days of Terror: The Compelling True Story of the Hunt and Capture of the Beltway Snipers.* New York: Pocket Books, 2003. The author, a journalist, profiles the shooters and discusses the victims of the shootings, providing a detailed account of the events of those three weeks.

Horowitz, Sari, and Michael E. Ruane. *Sniper: Inside the Hunt for the Killers Who Terrorized the Nation.* New York: Ballantine Books, 2004. The authors describe the actions and histories of Malvo and Muhammad and how the events in Maryland, Virginia, and the District of Columbia occurred.

Moose, Charles A., and Charles Fleming. *Three Weeks in October: The Manhunt for the Serial Sniper.* New York: Signet, 2004. Highlights the police chief of Montgomery County's hardships and accomplishments related to prosecuting the shootings.

—*Sheryl L. Van Horne*

SEE ALSO: Marc Lépine; Charles Whitman.

JOAQUÍN MURIETA
California bandit

BORN: c. 1832; Sonora Province, Mexico
DIED: July 25, 1853; probably San Benito County, California
ALSO KNOWN AS: Joaquín Murrieta; Joaquín Murrietta; Joaquín Botellier; Joaquín Carrillo; Joaquín Ocomorenia; Joaquín Valenzuela; Mexican Robin Hood; Robin Hood of El Dorado; Napoleon of Banditry; the Ghost of Sonora
CAUSE OF NOTORIETY: Murieta became a legendary California bandit during the California gold rush by engaging in robberies, cattle rustling, and murder.
ACTIVE: Early 1850's
LOCALE: Northern Sierra Nevada, California

EARLY LIFE
Most historians believe that Joaquín Murieta (hwah-KEEN moo-ree-AY-tah) was born in the Sonora province of southern Mexico, was a miner by trade, and emigrated to California as a young man. With passage of California's foreign miners' tax in the early 1850's, Anglo-American prospectors had begun to drive out miners who were Chinese and Mexican, ethnicities that were not considered "American." Murieta and his bride, after living in and around several towns in the gold foothills of California, began working gold mines in the Sonora-Murphy area. Murieta invited his brother, Jésus Murieta, and three of his bride's brothers to join them. Murieta borrowed a mule from his brother, who had started a mule train business; however, two San Franciscans said the mule was stolen, and Murieta's brother was tied to a tree and publicly horsewhipped. Although accounts vary, Murieta's brother was later hanged when he stepped outside a tent to help Joaquín, and Murieta's wife was disrobed, beaten, and gang raped. The lynch mob reportedly laughed and humiliated Murieta. Murieta later told the sheriff about the incident but was told that he and his family were Mexicans, not citizens, and nothing could be done. Murieta and his bride moved to Niles Canyon in Contra Costa County, where he began catching wild mustangs.

CRIMINAL CAREER
Murieta supposedly transformed himself into a justice-seeking avenger. Joined by family and sympathizers, he tracked down and killed the five men involved in the rape of his wife. The horsemanship of Murieta and his gang kept them ahead of the law. Anglo lawmen considered Murieta's gang to be the worst bandits ever to appear in California. The gang, some of whom were family members, robbed stagecoaches, stole gold, rustled horses, and killed several prospectors. A growing Hispanic population in and around Los Angeles saw Murieta as a kind of Robin Hood, stealing from the rich and giving to the poor. Stories were told of a Hispanic bandit named Joaquín Murieta (dubbed the Napoleon of Banditry or the Ghost of Sonora) racing on horseback to steal back gold that had been taken illegally from poor Mexican miners. Newspapers often used the name Joaquín Carrillo, not Murieta, which led to more confusion. Carrillo was the name of Murieta's mother by a first marriage and frequently was used by Murieta himself. The name confusion subsequently led to numerous variations of his surname.

LEGAL ACTION AND OUTCOME
In spring, 1853, California governor John Bigler offered a one-thousand-dollar reward for the capture of Mu-

Joaquín Murieta. (Courtesy, California State Library)

rieta's gang. The legislature, pressured by continuing newspaper accounts of robberies, cattle rustling, and killings (many blamed on Murieta), authorized a State Company of Mounted Rangers (later known as the California Rangers) to arrest Murieta and members of his gang. The warrant listed five surnames of Joaquín (names from newspapers and circulated stories): Joaquín Botellier, Joaquín Carrillo, Joaquín Ocomorenia, Joaquín Valenzuela, and Joaquín Murieta. Under the command of Captain Harry Love, a Texan who had served in the Mexican War and a former deputy sheriff in Los Angeles, a posse of approximately twenty men was formed. Within three months' specified time and upon capture of Murieta, they would receive a five-thousand-dollar reward (plus the one thousand dollars offered by the governor).

With one month remaining, Love and the California Rangers came upon a group of Mexican males near Panoche Pass in San Benito County. One of the Rangers shouted, "There's Murieta!" and quick gunfire took place. Two Mexicans were killed. One was positively identified as Three Finger Jack (Manuel Garcia), a member of the gang. The other was thought to be Murieta. Because both bodies were riddled with bullets and mutilated, the Rangers cut off the head of Murieta and the hand of Three Finger Jack, stuck them in bottles filled with brandy and alcohol, and took them back to Sacramento, the state capital. A priest identified Murieta, but later reports said that Murieta's sister did not recognize the "pickled" head of Murieta because it did not display his scar. Love displayed the jars at several county fairs and exhibitions in California, but as crowds dwindled, the head and hand were sold and put on exhibit at the Pacific Museum in San Francisco for one "Yankee" dollar. Both disappeared in the 1906 San Francisco earthquake.

IMPACT

The legend of Joaquín Murieta endured from the time of his death and into the twenty-first century thanks in part to several depictions in literature and film. The first novel ever to be published in California was a biography of Murieta titled *The Life and Adventures of Joaquín Murieta: The Celebrated California Bandit* (1854). Written by Cherokee native John Rollins Ridge, who

used the pen name Yellow Bird, it is also believed to have been the first novel written by an American Indian. Ridge became a successful newspaperman with the *Sacramento Bee* and *San Francisco Herald*. Murieta's colorful exploits as told by Ridge caught the imagination of the "dime novel" circuit. Historians have called the book inaccurate despite the claim by Ridge that it was factual. The *California Police Gazette* serialized Ridge's story, but to avoid having to license copyright, it published it using an anonymous writer. Translations were published in Spain, Chile, Mexico, and France. Many of these translations depict Murieta as an avenger of justice, in a flowing cape and mounted on a swift horse.

In the twentieth century, more literary works followed, including a play written by Chilean author Pablo Neruda titled *Fulgor y muerte de Joaquín Murieta* (pb. 1967; *Splendor and Death of Joaquin Murieta*, 1972) and a silent film from director D. W. Griffith titled *Scarlet Days* (1919). The fictional character of Zorro is said to be loosely based on the life of Murieta; the motion picture *The Mask of Zorro* (1998) blended Murieta's persona into that of Zorro.

FURTHER READING

Burns, Walter Nobel. *The Robin Hood of El Dorado: The Saga of Joaquín Murrieta, Famous Outlaw of California's Age of Gold*. Albuquerque: University of New Mexico Press, 1999. As part of the Historians of Frontier and American West Series, this collection brings together stories of the exploits of Murieta.

Ridge, John Rollins (Yellow Bird). *The Life and Adventures of Joaquín Murieta: The Celebrated California Bandit*. 1854. Reprint. Norman: University of Oklahoma Press, 1977. The first published novel about the life of Murieta.

Thornton, Bruce. *Searching for Joaquín: Myth, Murieta and History of California*. San Francisco: Encounter Books, 2003. A California historian's account of Murieta's life; considered most accurate by researchers.

—*William Bourns*

SEE ALSO: Salvatore Giuliano; Robin Hood; Pancho Villa; Emiliano Zapata.

BENITO MUSSOLINI
Italian dictator (1922-1945)

BORN: July 29, 1883; Predappio, Emilia-Romagna, Italy

DIED: April 28, 1945; Giulino di Mezzegra, near Dongo, Como, Italy

ALSO KNOWN AS: Il Duce (the Leader); Benito Amilcare Andrea Mussolini (full name)

CAUSE OF NOTORIETY: Dictator and founding member of the Fascist Party, Mussolini allied Italy with Germany in the shadow of World War II.

ACTIVE: 1922-1945

LOCALE: Italy and its African colonies

EARLY LIFE

Benito Mussolini (beh-NEE-toh mew-soh-LEE-nee) was born in Predappio, Italy, to a father who was a blacksmith and socialist journalist and a mother who was a primary school teacher. Mussolini received a solid education and graduated with a teaching diploma. He then migrated to Switzerland, where he worked at various odd jobs. Mussolini read the philosophical works of Georg Wilhelm Friedrich Hegel, Immanuel Kant, Karl Marx, Friedrich Nietzsche, and Georges Eugène Sorel. In addition to his reading, Mussolini became politically active. In speeches, he called for strikes and the use of violence against the ruling elite.

Returning to Italy, Mussolini taught for a short time and eventually married. His political activities brought him imprisonment as well as fame among radicals. Proving to be a gifted journalist, Mussolini eventually became editor of the Italian Socialist Party newspaper. Although the Socialist Party opposed Italy's entrance into World War I, Mussolini called for involvement. As a result, he was removed as editor and expelled from the party. Assuming control of a non-Socialist newspaper, Mussolini promoted his nationalist and interventionist message. Mussolini was called to serve in the military, then wounded at the battlefront. He returned from the war with a renewed commitment to alter Italian politics radically.

POLITICAL CAREER

Mussolini's extreme nationalism became a central message in a new political movement called Fascism (from the Latin word *fasces*, referring to an ancient Roman symbol of authority), which was supported by veterans, industrialists, bankers, and, in general, members of the middle class. Besides ardent nationalism, Fascists held in common the fear of Marxist revolution and contempt for parliamentary leaders unable to meet the perceived postwar crisis.

Gifted with oratorical skills and an uncanny ability to assess the political climate, Mussolini was a key figure in the Fascist Party from its origins in 1919 to his assumption of national political power. While calling on Fascists to attack Marxist-influenced unions and seize political power, Mussolini skillfully maneuvered behind the scenes, eventually achieving national power through legal means. After accepting the position of prime minister offered by King Victor Emmanuel III in 1922, Mussolini undermined Italy's constitution and centralized author-

A U.S. war poster depicting Mussolini. (NARA)

MUSSOLINI ON THE WAR'S PROGRESS

In a speech before the Chamber of Fasces and Corporations given in Rome, Italy, June 10, 1941, Benito Mussolini reported the status of Italy's cooperation with Germany and Japan (the Tripartite Pact):

Collaboration between the powers of the Tripartite Pact is under way. But above all, collaboration between Germany and Italy is under way. . . .

Added to this Japan . . . is in perfect line with the Tripartite Pact. The Japanese are a proud and loyal people who would not remain indifferent in the face of American aggression against the Axis powers.

With the other powers adhering to the Tripartite Pact, namely, Hungary, Slovakia, Rumania and Bulgaria, relations are more than cordial even where special political accords do not exist.

Regarding Turkey, that country has until now refused to all English solicitations. President Inonu has seen the tragic fate that awaits all nations which in any way trust themselves to Britain. But I wish to take this occasion to say to President Inonu that Italy intends to follow toward Turkey that policy of comprehension and collaboration which was inaugurated in 1928 and which for us is still in effect.

If Spain and Turkey are out of the fighting there is one transoceanic State which seems likely to enter it. It is well that it be known that American intervention does not bother us excessively. A specific declaration of war would not change the present situation, which is one of de facto war, if not de jure. American intervention, when employed completely, would be late, and if it were not late, would not remove the terms of the problem. American intervention will not give victory to Britain but will prolong the war; will not limit the area of war but will extend it to other oceans; will change the United States regime into an authoritarian, totalitarian one in comparison with which the European forerunners—Fascist and Nazi—will feel themselves far surpassed and perfected. . . .

How long it may last cannot be known, but it is certain that resistance will be protracted to the limits of human possibility.

Even the whole conquest of the empire by the English has no decisive importance toward the ending of the war. This is a vendetta of strictly personal character which could have no influence on the results of a war which has dug even deeper chasms between Italy and Britain. I cannot tell you today when or how, but I affirm in the most categoric manner that we shall return to that land bathed by our blood and—Our dead shall not go unavenged.

ordered Italian troops to the Austrian border to defend that small republic from a Nazi-inspired German annexation.

Mussolini might have held on to popularity and power had he not made fundamental errors in Italian foreign policy. Dreaming of empire, Il Duce turned against Ethiopia in 1935. Italy conquered that mountainous nation by the use of new technologies such as airplanes and mechanized units. The addition of Ethiopia to Italy's colonial holdings of Libya, Somalia, and Eritrea was denounced by numerous nations, many of which, ironically, were colonial powers. The League of Nations declared sanctions against Italy, but Mussolini held his ground. He distanced his regime from democratic states by sending troops to aid Francisco Franco in his struggle against the Spanish republican forces.

Mussolini watched with alarm as Adolf Hitler's bellicose actions brought Europe closer to World War II, but, faced with increased international isolation and growing German power, Mussolini allied Italy with Germany. This alliance was especially welcomed by Hitler, for the German dictator had long admired Mussolini and considered him his mentor and friend. When Germany finally attacked France, Mussolini sent in Italian military forces alongside the Germans. After Hitler invaded Romania and the Soviet Union without consulting Italy, Mussolini ordered troops into Greece. Eventually Hitler dispatched forces to Greece and North Africa to aid the Italians. Soon after the defeat of Italian-German forces in North Africa, the Allies invaded Sicily. Fascist Party leaders dismissed Il Duce, and Mussolini was imprisoned.

German commandos freed Mussolini and transported him to northern Italy, where the establishment of a new Fascist republic was declared. Fighting between anti-Fascist Italian partisans and Germans exploded throughout northern Italy, and Allied forces moved relentlessly forward. Though determined to make a stand, Mussolini

ity in his own hands. By 1925 Mussolini had created a dictatorship popular among many Italians and foreign leaders such as England's Winston Churchill, who believed that a return to order was imperative.

To Mussolini's domestic and foreign admirers, the outlawing of all political parties but the Fascist Party was not significant because now, under Mussolini, strikes no longer hindered daily life, the threat from the Marxist Left was eliminated, and economic stability promised to return. In 1934, Mussolini found himself widely applauded by foreign democratic figures after he had

was abandoned except for a handful of men. He was captured and executed by partisans in 1945.

IMPACT

As Europe's first Fascist leader, Benito Mussolini set the stage for a new form of dictatorship based on a totalitarian philosophy supported by the classes which most feared radical revolution from below. Hitler and other right-wing dictators learned from Mussolini's early example. However, the promotion of extreme nationalism led to foreign imperial ventures and worldwide war. Though Mussolini was eventually toppled, his legacy still lives in the extreme nationalist and neofascist political organizations found throughout the modern world.

FURTHER READING

Cardoza, Anthony L. *Benito Mussolini: The First Fascist*. New York: Pearson Longman, 2006. Presents a thoroughly researched summary of Mussolini's influence and shows how Fascism worked to transform politics in the first half of the twentieth century.

Clark, Martin. *Mussolini*. New York: Pearson Longman, 2005. A respected scholar of modern Italian history offers a thorough assessment of Mussolini as a political leader in this well-written biography.

Kirkpatrick, Ivone. *Mussolini: A Study in Power*. New York: Hawthorne Books, 1964. A seminal book. This British diplomat's early review of the life of Mussolini is still most valuable.

Mack Smith, Denis. *Mussolini*. New York: Vintage Books, 1981. Considered by many to be the finest English scholar of Italian history, Mack Smith offers a traditional interpretation of Mussolini.

Moseley, Ray. *Mussolini: The Last Six Hundred Days of Il Duce*. Dallas: Taylor, 2004. Presents an intriguing story of when the once-powerful dictator became a Nazi pawn and ultimately a prisoner executed by Italian partisans.

_____. *Mussolini's Shadow: The Doubled Life of Count Galeazzo Ciano*. New Haven, Conn.: Yale University Press, 1999. Presents an unusually intimate view of the inner circles of power from the perspective of the colorful son-in-law of Mussolini.

Neville, Peter. *Mussolini*. London: Routledge, 2003. This study is an important contribution to the debate over the central role played by Mussolini in directing Italian domestic and foreign policy.

—*Pietro Lorenzini*

SEE ALSO: Francisco Franco; Adolf Hitler; Saparmurat Niyazov; Getúlio Vargas.

NADIR SHAH
Shah of Persia (1736-1747)

BORN: October 22, 1688; Dastgird, Persia (now in Iran)

DIED: June 19, 1747; Fathabad, Persia (now in Iran)

ALSO KNOWN AS: Nadr Kuli; Nader Shah; Tahmasp Kuli Khan; Nadir Shah Afshar; Nadir Qoli Beg; Nadr Qoli Beg

CAUSE OF NOTORIETY: Nadir Shah was a brutal warlord and a bandit leader on an international scale.

ACTIVE: 1708-1747

LOCALE: Afghanistan, India, Iran, Iraq, and Uzbekistan

EARLY LIFE

In the twilight years of Safavid Iran, Nadir Shah (NAY-duhr shah) rose to fame through his skills as a border raider. A local celebrity by the age of twenty, he quickly caught the attention of provincial authorities, who inducted him into an elite military unit.

Between 1723 and 1726, Persia nearly collapsed as Ottoman, Afghan, and Russian armies marched across the land. Nadir fought numerous battles and skirmishes during this period, building on his reputation as a leader who produced victory. Shah Tahmasp II invited Nadir to join the imperial army and promoted him to khan. However, this was only a temporary alliance, as Nadir deposed Tahmasp in 1731. Over the next five years, Nadir claimed to act as regent for the infant prince Abbas, while simultaneously building a collection of allies in the court, armed forces, and government. Then, from January to March, 1736, Nadir organized a grand congress of Iranian notables, a *quriltai*.

MILITARY AND POLITICAL CAREER

Nadir's *quriltai* featured thousands of tents, parties, feasts, and—despite the Islamic proscription against consuming alcohol—plenty of wine. Nadir used the latter to loosen tongues and had spies listen for negative opinions. If too loud in their complaints, such critical men disappeared or were murdered. Rank was no cover, for even Persia's chief religious figure, the Mullah Basha, was killed at this bloody conclave. The end result was Nadir's election as Persia's next shah.

Nadir's interests were purely military; he had little time or interest in civil functions. His only efforts in such were designed to raise money for support of his large army. Indeed, most of his military campaigns seemed more like massive looting expeditions, very much in the tradition of fourteenth century warlord Tamerlane (Timur), whom Nadir admired and claimed as kin.

Following in his "ancestor's" footsteps, Nadir took his army eastward in 1737-1738, invading Afghanistan, then the Mughal Empire. Very wealthy but not especially well organized, the Mughals failed to stop Nadir's formidable army and asked for terms. Wily Nadir agreed to negotiate, using diplomacy to cover a successful kidnapping of the Mughal emperor, Muhammad Shah. Next, Nadir surrounded the Mughal army in camp and made clear that their food supply was at his mercy.

Having immobilized the Mughal army and incapacitated the government, Nadir marched into the Mughal capital, Delhi, one of the most prosperous cities on the subcontinent. In February, 1739, Nadir began collecting "taxes" and "gifts." Within a month, he acquired 6.5 million gold tumans (more than three times the total cost of this campaign). Resulting riots brought fierce suppression and heavy fines and allowed Nadir's soldiers to loot the more prosperous neighborhoods. So much came from these new requisitions that Nadir remitted taxes back home for the next three years and paid all his soldiers a bonus worth six months of salary.

Still not finished, Nadir forced a Mughal princess to marry his son and then collected an additional 3.5 million tumans for her dowry. Finally ready to leave, Nadir politely freed Muhammad Shah, gave him back his now bankrupt state, and marched home. According to one source, Nadir and his men carried back so much loot that the river and mountain passes were full of furniture, carpets, and other goods too difficult to carry home.

Nadir returned to Persia, displaying vast quantities of spoils, including the 105-carat Koh-i-noor diamond and the jewel-encrusted Peacock Throne, which became the symbol of legitimacy for every subsequent government. Mayhem and looting expeditions next moved to Central Asia, then to Iraq, and finally ended in 1747, when a cabal of army officers, disgruntled over their pay, murdered Nadir Shah.

IMPACT

The reputation of Nadir Shah has undergone a variety of interpretations over the years. He has been seen as the last great Asian conqueror, spun from the traditions of Amir Timur and Genghis Khan; as the "Napoleon of Iran"; and as one of history's most successful bandit leaders. Modern scholarship tends to support the latter view of Nadir Shah, who ruled Persia badly for ten years.

FURTHER READING

Abraham, Erwants'i. *History of the Wars, 1721-1738.* Translated and edited by George Bournoutian. Costa Mesa, Calif.: Mazda, 1999. A essential source on the wars that propelled Nadir to power.

Axworthy, Michael. *Sword of Persia: Nadir Shah, from*

Tribal Warrior to Conquering Despot. London: I. B. Tauris, 2006. Solid scholarship and a good supplement to Lockhart.

Lockhart, Laurence. *Nadir Shah.* London: Luzac, 1938. Although dated, still considered one of the best biographies of Nadir.

—*John P. Dunn*

SEE ALSO: Genghis Khan.

NE WIN
Burmese military dictator (1962-2002)

BORN: May 24, 1911; Paungdale, Burma (now Myanmar)

DIED: December 5, 2002; Yangon, Myanmar

ALSO KNOWN AS: Shu Maung (birth name); Bo Ne Win; U Ne Win

CAUSE OF NOTORIETY: In Burma, Ne Win led a brutally repressive socialist regime that persecuted all opposition. Considered responsible for the murders of three thousand to ten thousand demonstrators in 1988, Ne Win fought tribal minorities and wrecked the country's economy.

ACTIVE: 1949-2002

LOCALE: Burma (Myanmar)

EARLY LIFE

Ne Win (neh wihn) was born Shu Maung on May 24, 1911, in Paungdale in central Burma, then a British colony. The son of a Chinese Burmese tax collector and a businesswoman, he studied biology at Rangoon University from 1929 to 1931, until failing his exams. He joined the anticolonialist Dobama Asiayone ("We Burmans Association") in the 1930's. In 1941, he was one of the "Thirty Comrades," a military unit trained by the Japanese on China's Hainan Island. Made a general in the Japanese-controlled Burmese Independence Army founded on December 26, 1941, he changed his name to Bo Ne Win ("Commander Brilliant Sun"), shortened to Ne Win.

MILITARY AND POLITICAL CAREER

Ne Win entered Burma with the Japanese during World War II in early 1942, as British troops were retreating. In 1943, he became chief of staff of the Burmese National Army (BMA). Japanese policies in Burma were not seen favorably by the Burmese; after the British re-invaded in

1945, the BMA, including Ne Win, switched allegiances and sided with the victorious British. After Burma won its independence on January 1, 1948, Ne Win rose to commander in chief of the armed forces (February 1, 1949) and deputy prime minister, home minister, and minister of defense (April 1, 1949). Throughout the 1950's, he fought tribal separatists and Communists.

In 1958 Ne Win, having been asked to serve as prime minister in the face of ethnic insurgencies, formed a military government. He returned power to the former prime minister, U Nu, in April, 1960, and democracy was restored. On March 1, 1962, however, Ne Win seized power again. He established a Marxist military dictatorship that nationalized businesses, expelled foreigners and seized their enterprises, brutally repressed all internal opposition, and fought tribal minorities. He became chairman of the Burma Socialist Program Party (BSPP).

In Rangoon on July 7, 1962, Ne Win ordered shots fired at student demonstrators opposed to the junta, killing about one hundred of them. The next morning the historic Rangoon University Student Union building was dynamited by the military. Throughout the 1960's and 1970's, Burma's economy deteriorated, and human rights were repressed.

In 1972-1973 Ne Win and his associates adopted a new constitution, institutionalizing the one-party rule. Ne Win became president on March 5, 1974. On November 9, 1981, he resigned but continued as BSPP chairman. In 1987 he admitted some economic mistakes and on July 23, 1988, resigned as BSPP chairman. This did not calm the "Rangoon Spring" of 1988, inspired by activist Aung San Suu Kyi. The August 8, 1988, uprising was repressed with Ne Win's consent, resulting in the deaths of three thousand to ten thousand demonstrators.

Ne Win continued to control the military government,

locked in a power struggle with Aung San Suu Kyi's National League for Democracy. Aung San Suu Kyi, though placed under house arrest, was awarded the Nobel Peace Prize in 1991. International opposition to the military regime, however, did not dislodge Ne Win's generals in the 1990's.

LEGAL ACTION AND OUTCOME
On March 7, 2002, Ne Win and his favorite daughter, Sandar Win, were suddenly placed under house arrest and charged with complicity with Sandar's husband and their three sons in a planned coup. On September 12, Ne Win's guards were sentenced to fifteen years in jail. On September 26, his four relatives were sentenced to death for high treason; their sentences were soon commuted to life imprisonment. Ne Win died, without having been charged, on December 5, 2002. He was cremated without a state funeral.

IMPACT
Ne Win's rule over Burma proved devastating. His Marxist economic policies had turned Burma into one of the world's poorest nations by 1987. He established a nightmare dictatorship likened to George Orwell's totalitarian state in the novel *Nineteen Eighty-Four* (1948). Ne Win's fight against tribal leaders kept Burma intact, but at a high price in blood.

Ne Win's culpability for the notorious suppression of the Rangoon Spring is generally accepted, and his personal antagonism toward Aung San Suu Kyi prevented political reconciliation. In Burma, Ne Win's personal corruption, flamboyant lifestyle, and nurturing of a generation of military cronies turned him into a secretly despised dictator. Few mourned his death.

FURTHER READING
Aung San Suu Kyi. *Letters from Burma*. London: Penguin, 1998. Fifty-two moving letters by the Nobel Peace Prize winner and antagonist of Ne Win highlight negative effects of his notorious rule. Includes map.

Fink, Christina. *Living Silence: Burma Under Military Rule*. London: Zed Books, 2001. A perceptive analysis of Ne Win's notorious rule is summarized in chapter 2. Illustrated, with maps, notes, index, and bibliography.

Larkin, Emma. *Finding George Orwell in Burma*. New York: Penguin Press, 2005. Harrowing account of military dictatorship of Ne Win and his successors; the author is fluent in Burmese and protected by a pen name.

—*R. C. Lutz*

SEE ALSO: Than Shwe.

BABY FACE NELSON
Bank robber

BORN: December 6, 1908; Chicago, Illinois
DIED: November 27, 1934; Niles Center (now Skokie), Illinois
ALSO KNOWN AS: Lester Joseph Gillis (birth name); George Nelson
MAJOR OFFENSE: Attempted robbery
ACTIVE: Arrested in 1931
LOCALE: Chicago, Illinois
SENTENCE: One year to life in prison; escaped within one year

EARLY LIFE
Baby Face Nelson (NEHL-suhn) was born Lester Gillis in Chicago, Illinois, on December 6, 1908. The courts convicted Lester, a skillful car thief by age fourteen, and sentenced him to serve time in an infamous Chicago

boys' home. Arrested only five months after his release for robbing a department store, Gillis was remanded by the courts back to the boys' home.

CRIMINAL CAREER
Released from the boys' home for a second time in 1926, Gillis returned to Chicago and organized a protection racket with known criminal associates. His exploits captured the attention of Mafia boss Al Capone, who recruited the young hoodlum to work for him as an enforcer. Gillis's inclination for violence quickly alienated Capone, who preferred peaceful arrangements when possible. Angry and unemployed, Gillis began robbing jewelry shops throughout Chicago. The 1930 robbery of a gem dealer in Wheaton, Illinois, earned Gillis five thousand dollars, his biggest heist so far.

LEGAL ACTION AND OUTCOME

Gillis's arrest in 1931 for the attempted robbery of another Chicago-area jeweler earned him a sentence of one year to life in the Joliet Penitentiary. However, after his arrival at Joliet, a witness identified Gillis as the perpetrator of the Wheaton robbery. A conviction for that crime could have sentenced him to an additional twenty-five to thirty years. On February 17, 1932, while being transported back from a pretrial hearing for the Wheaton case, Gillis managed to escape detectives and fled with his wife, Helen, to California.

Gillis began working for Sicilian mob boss Giuseppe Parente in California, who labeled Gillis with the sobriquet Baby Face, after a popular song. Gillis, not flattered by his new nickname, adopted the alias George Nelson, after a Depression-era prizefighter whom he admired. Nelson quickly grew tired of working for Parente and moved his family to Long Beach, Indiana, with dreams of following the legacy of his idol, bank robber John Dillinger.

Nelson assembled a gang and began robbing banks throughout the Midwest. He eventually formed a partnership with Dillinger, his idol, a partnership that Dillinger would later regret. Federal Bureau of Intelligence (FBI) agents staked outside a Chicago movie house shot and killed Dillinger on July 22, 1934.

Nelson would not get to bask in the limelight of his new status as public enemy number one. On November 27, 1934, FBI agents ambushed his car as he was traveling to Chicago with his wife and longtime friend John Chase. Nelson shot and killed two agents during a violent exchange; however, agents riddled his body with seventeen bullets. Nelson had vowed never to be taken alive; he succumbed to his wounds later that evening. His wife and friend dutifully removed his body from the scene and placed him near a cemetery in Niles Center, Illinois, where he was found the next day.

IMPACT

Baby Face Nelson remains an infamous name in American history. Remembered mostly for his exploits as a bank robber, he also worked for some of the United States' most notorious organized crime figures, including the emerging Chicago boss Capone. Nelson's partnership with Dillinger led to the federal government's passing new anticrime legislation. The federal statutes specified that bank robbery, the transport of stolen goods, and the flight of a felon across state lines to avoid prosecution are federal crimes. Prior to that time, state agencies could not pursue criminals across state borders.

Nelson is also one of several Depression-era desperadoes whose exploits have left an indelible imprint on American popular culture. Romanticized by some and demonized by others, Nelson's life has been the subject of numerous books, television programs, and feature films.

FURTHER READING

Nickel, Steven, and William J. Helmer. *Baby Face Nelson: Portrait of a Public Enemy*. Nashville, Tenn.: Cumberland House, 2002. Provides a factual account of Nelson's life and times.

Owen, Richard, and James Owen. *Gangsters and Outlaws of the 1930's: Landmarks of the Public Enemy Era*. Shippensburg, Pa.: White Mane, 2003. Includes biographies of notorious Depression-era outlaws as well as photographs of crime scenes associated with infamous robberies, shoot-outs, and jailbreaks from the public enemy era.

Reppetto, Thomas. *American Mafia: A History of Its Rise to Power*. New York: Henry Holt, 2004. Provides a comprehensive history of the American Mafia.

—*James C. Roberts and Thomas E. Baker*

SEE ALSO: John Dillinger; Pretty Boy Floyd; J. Edgar Hoover.

LESLIE NELSON
American murderer

BORN: September 26, 1957; Haddon Heights, New
Jersey
ALSO KNOWN AS: Glen Nelson (full name); Mabel
MAJOR OFFENSES: Murder and aggravated assault
ACTIVE: April 20, 1995
LOCALE: Southern New Jersey
SENTENCE: Death for murders of two police officers
and five to ten years in prison for aggravated
assault; death sentence was overturned and changed
to life imprisonment

EARLY LIFE
Glen Nelson (NEHL-suhn) was an emotionally disturbed
young boy by the age of five. He was harassed by other
children during his childhood. His father nicknamed him
"Uriney" for his bed-wetting problem and "Mabel" when
he became fearful of using public bathrooms in elementary school. Nelson eventually believed that his gender
was the basis of all of his problems. He became very introverted when he reached puberty, suffered from depression, and had no friends in high school. In his teens, he
started to dress in women's clothing and shaved his legs.

In his late twenties, Nelson started taking female hor-
mones. Later, he was threatened by a man with a knife in
Philadelphia, an event that plunged him deeper into depression. As a result, he bought a handgun and bullets,
cutting an *X* in the top of each bullet with a knife. Shortly
thereafter, Nelson was arrested on unlawful weapons
charges and received a term of probation. During a court-
mandated psychological interview, it was reported that
Nelson was in love with his gun. He was diagnosed with
several mental illnesses. In 1988, after writing a suicide
note, he was involuntary committed to a psychiatric facility for nearly three weeks. Although he had a history of
mental illness, he again began estrogen treatments in
1989 as a precursor to gender-reassignment surgery.
Finally in 1992, Nelson had the surgery, changed his
name from Glen to Leslie, and began to live as a woman.

CRIMINAL CAREER
In the beginning of 1995, Nelson was very reclusive and
lived with her mother. She continued her fascination with
firearms and accrued a collection, including handguns and
an AK-47. However, she was still suffering from mental
illness and believed that the guns were her children.

During the morning of April 20, 1995, following an
allegation that Nelson may have abused a child, Haddon

Heights detectives Robert Griffith and Richard Norcross, Camden County prosecutor-investigator John Mc-
Laughlin, and Division of Youth and Family Services
employee Carmelo Garcia arrived at Nelson's home to
investigate. McLaughlin and Garcia entered the home to
talk to Nelson, at which time McLaughlin noticed bullets
in her bedroom. To prevent the situation from escalating,
the officers left the home and returned at 2:00 P.M. with a
no-knock search warrant. When the officers advised Nelson's mother that they had a search warrant, Nelson ran
upstairs and opened fire with her AK-47 assault rifle. In
her delusional state, Nelson did not want the officers to
take her "children." McLaughlin was fatally shot, and
Norcross was severely wounded. Norcross was able to
escape the house; however, Nelson began shooting from
her second-story bedroom window and fatally shot
Norcross's brother, police officer John Norcross. After a
fourteen-hour standoff, Nelson finally surrendered.

LEGAL ACTION AND OUTCOME
In 1997, Nelson was found guilty of murdering Mc-
Laughlin and John Norcross and of the aggravated assault of Richard Norcross. She was sentenced to death
and was the only woman among fourteen men on New
Jersey's death row. However, in 1998, the New Jersey
Supreme Court overturned her death sentence because of
her mental illness and changed it to life imprisonment.
Nelson was admitted into New Jersey's Edna Mahan
Correctional Facility, where she began serving her thirty
years to life sentence and her five to ten years' imprisonment for the aggravated assault. Her sentence was upheld
in March, 2001, following a retrial.

IMPACT
Leslie Nelson gained notoriety for being the only female
on New Jersey's death row; she was housed in a ward
with fourteen men before her original sentence was overturned. The issue of Nelson's mental instability raised
concerns over her punishment for the murders. Because
she killed two law enforcement officers, many called for
absolute punishment on death row. However, Nelson
was afforded her constitutional rights and ultimately not
subjected to a punishment that was cruel and unusual.

FURTHER READING
McGraw, Seamus. *Leslie Nelson: Deadly Transsexual.*
Court TV Crime Library, 2006. http://www.crime

library.com. An in-depth, online account of Nelson's story.

Mansnerus, Laura. "Top Court Again Rejects Sentence of Death." *The New York Times*, July 31, 2002, p. B5. A short article that helps explains the complex legal issues of Nelson's case.

The New York Times. "Jury Votes Death in Murder of Officer by Irate Woman." May 14, 1997, p. B7. A news account of the original trial.

—*Cassandra L. Reyes*

SEE ALSO: Antoinette Frank; Assata Olugbala Shakur.

NERO
Roman emperor (r. 54-68 C.E.)

BORN: December 15, 37 C.E.; Antium, Latium (now Anzio, Italy)

DIED: June 9, 68 C.E.; Rome (now in Italy)

ALSO KNOWN AS: Lucius Domitius Ahenobarbus (birth name); Nero Claudius Caesar Augustus Germanicus (adopted imperial name); Nero Claudius Caesar Drusus Germanicus (full name)

CAUSE OF NOTORIETY: Few past figures provoke as much negative fascination as Nero, epitomizing what was wrong with imperial Rome. His conduct was unbecoming for an emperor or even a Roman patrician in his chariot racing, professional musicianship, and nocturnal thuggery. He was behind the assassinations of his mother, Agrippina, and his royal wife Octavia. He abandoned state duties, especially oversight of the army, and his extravagance ended in Rome's near bankruptcy.

ACTIVE: 54-68 C.E.

LOCALE: Rome and Neapolis (now Naples, Italy), Roman Empire, and province of Greece

EARLY LIFE

Nero (NEE-roh) was the son of Gnaeus Domitius Ahenobarbus, former consul, and Agrippina the Younger, both patricians. His mother, Agrippina, was descended by birth and adoption from Caesar Tiberius (Tiberius Julius Caesar Augustus) by Germanicus (Nero Claudius Germanicus), also father of the emperor Gaius Caligula (Gaius Julius Caesar Germanicus). Nero's noble but exiled childhood was outside Rome, and he was later tutored by the philosopher-playwright Seneca (Lucius Annaeus Seneca). Claudius Caesar married Agrippina in 48 C.E. and in 50 adopted Nero as guardian of his son Britannicus. In 53 Nero married Octavia, daughter of his stepfather (and uncle) Claudius the emperor and his first wife, the notorious Messallina, but this was not by his own choice. His adolescent life was dominated by his mother, Agrippina.

IMPERIAL CAREER

On the death in 54 (likely by Agrippina's poisoning) of his stepfather, the Emperor Claudius, the imperial will was not read publicly or confirmed by the Senate but said

Bust of Emperor Nero, c. 60 A.D. (Courtesy, Capitoline Museums, Rome)

NERO'S IDEA OF FUN

According to the Roman historian Suetonius, Nero started bad and quickly grew vicious:

Although at first his acts of wantonness, lust, extravagance, avarice and cruelty were gradual and secret, and might be condoned as follies of youth, yet even then their nature was such that no one doubted that they were defects of his character and not due to his time of life. No sooner was twilight over than he would catch up a cap or a wig and go to the taverns or range about the streets playing pranks, which however were very far from harmless; for he used to beat men as they came home from dinner, stabbing any who resisted him and throwing them into the sewers. He would even break into shops and rob them, setting up a market in the Palace, where he divided the booty which he took, sold it at auction, and then squandered the proceeds. . . .

Little by little, however, as his vices grew stronger, he dropped jesting and secrecy and with no attempt at disguise openly broke out into worse crime. . . .

Besides abusing freeborn boys and seducing married women, he debauched the vestal virgin Rubria. The freedwoman Acte he all but made his lawful wife, after bribing some ex-consuls to perjure themselves by swearing that she was of royal birth. He castrated the boy Sporus and actually tried to make a woman of him; and he married him with all the usual ceremonies, including a dowry and a bridal veil, took him to his house attended by a great throng, and treated him as his wife. And the witty jest that someone made is still current, that it would have been well for the world if Nero's father Domitius had had that kind of wife. . . .

He so prostituted his own chastity that after defiling almost every part of his body, he at last devised a kind of game, in which, covered with the skin of some wild animal, he was let loose from a cage and attacked the private parts of men and women, who were bound to stakes. . . .

Source: C. Suetonius Tranquillus, *The Lives of the Twelve Caesars*, translated by J. C. Rolfe (New York: Macmillan, 1914).

by Agrippina to declare Nero as emperor rather than the emperor's own son Britannicus. Nero immediately gave a funerary oration for Claudius and blunted criticism and speculation by dispersing a huge gift of money from the Roman treasury to soldiers in the Roman army. Because he was only seventeen years old, it was clear that his mother, Agrippina, was, or tried to be, the real power behind the imperial throne for several years.

Britannicus died by poisoning little more than a year later, in 55, either by Agrippina's or Nero's hand or by that of both together. Nero spent little or no time with his wife, the princess Octavia, because he had a succession of older lovers, including a Greek former slave named Acte and then Sabina Poppaea, whom he eventually married against the will of the Roman people after divorcing Octavia, also murdered in 63. At first, in the years 55-

59, while separating himself from his mother and relying instead on his close advisers, his tutor Seneca and an old retired procurator, Sextus Afranius Burrus, Nero seemed to follow the Augustan way of peace by letting imperial administration take care of itself in the able hands of Seneca and Burrus.

However, after the assassination of his mother in Naples in 59, the sudden death of Burrus in 62, and Seneca's resignation in 62, Nero became more independent. His absence from duties became pronounced, with lack of policy and appointments of bad advisers like Tigellinus or officials who were mostly incompetent or corrupt. If Nero did not start the great fire in Rome in 64, during which legend says he composed or played music to the burning, he certainly profited by confiscating property in the valley between the seven hills to build his palatial Golden House (Domus Aurea) with acres of lakes and gardens, where he was said by the Roman historian Tacitus to have used Christians as nocturnal torches.

Nero did little to quell rebellions in Britain in 61 and Judaea in 66-67, preferring instead during the latter to tour Greece and play at concerts at Delphi, where, as elsewhere in Greece, he competed victoriously on his kithara while joined by his huge entourage of thousands of paid applauders. Because Nero was commonly perceived as a murderer, the historian Suetonius suggested Nero avoided asking for initiation into the Eleusinian Mysteries for fear of rejection. He put down the Pisonian conspiracy against him in 65, forcing old Seneca to commit suicide as a coconspirator, and then had many senators and able governors and generals executed in 65-68.

Nero's reign grew increasingly repressive and his appointments usually weak, with the exception of governors such as Servius Sulpicius Galba and Titus Flavius Vespasianus, both of whom had been chosen by Burrus and Seneca and who succeeded Nero as emperor in 68 and 69, respectively. His endless parties were scandalous for destroying priceless imported mineral glasses (myrrhina) thrown against walls. He often refused to walk on any surface not covered by rose petals and threw fits if he could not drink pearls ground up in goats' milk. Hated by every Roman class by 68, partly because he freed Greeks from taxation that Italians had to pay, Nero fled Rome and was forced to commit suicide outside Rome, where the Praetorian Guard found him dying. His last words were reputedly, "What a great artist dies here."

IMPACT

Nero almost caused the Roman Empire's breakup with his dereliction of imperial duties and demonstrated in his last years the danger of absolute rulers. His name has also been reviled as a persecutor of Christians. While he proved to be amoral toward members of his family as well as to most Romans, he was capable of being flattered and manipulated by sycophants and dominated by his mother, Agrippina, who tried to rule in his name. Seeking the adoration of Rome for his artistry, Nero alienated Romans. His infamy ended the Julio-Claudian Dynasty and resulted in a pattern for later emperors who either were first proclaimed by Roman armies—especially through the Praetorian Guard and legions

abroad—or were not even members of the patrician class and possibly not even Italian. Whether or not Nero was the worst of Roman emperors, he did vivify the depth of corruption and is probably the most infamous Roman in history.

FURTHER READING

Holland, Richard. *Nero: The Man Behind the Myth*. London: Sutton, 2000. A fair, even generous, assessment of Nero's life.

Suetonius. *The Twelve Caesars*. Reprint. Edited by Michael Grant. Translated by Robert Graves. London: Penguin Classics, 1989. An excellent contemporary biography of the emperor.

Wiedemann, T. E. J. "Tiberius to Nero" and "Nero to Vespasian." In vol. 10 of *Cambridge Ancient History*. New York: Cambridge University Press, 1996. A scholarly survey of Nero's period.

—*Patrick Norman Hunt*

SEE ALSO: Caligula; Commodus; Domitian; Elagabalus; Fulvia; Galerius; Justin II; Phalaris; Polycrates of Samos; Lucius Cornelius Sulla; Theodora.

BONNIE NETTLES
American cult founder

BORN: 1924; Houston, Texas
DIED: June, 1985; Dallas, Texas
ALSO KNOWN AS: Bonnie Lu Trusdale Nettles (full name); Peep; Ti; the Battery
CAUSE OF NOTORIETY: With Marshall Applewhite, Nettles co-founded the Heaven's Gate cult.
ACTIVE: 1974-1985
LOCALE: Western United States

EARLY LIFE

Little is known about Bonnie Nettles (NEH-tuhls) during her early years. Raised as a Baptist, she married young and had four children. She worked as a registered nurse in Houston, but where and when she studied nursing are unknown. In the 1950's, she supposedly began to channel the spirit of Brother Francis, a nineteenth century Franciscan who provided her with astrological information, which she used for a column in a Houston newspaper. She was active in the Theosophical Society, whose members believe that all major religions are derived

from an ancient religious philosophy. Most believe in spiritualism, and Nettles's group in Houston performed weekly séances. Twice, she said, a mysterious man communicated with her, whom she later identified as Marshall Applewhite.

RELIGIOUS CAREER

In March, 1972, Nettles met Applewhite at the hospital where she worked. Applewhite was depressed over the end of his marriage and the ruin of his career as a professor of music. At the time Nettles's marriage was also ending. Nettles and Applewhite immediately became inseparable, although they described their relationship as platonic. They founded the Christian Arts Center at a Houston church but soon were forced to give it up because of rumors that they held séances there. About this time, Nettles and her husband were divorced.

Both she and Applewhite claimed to receive messages from beings on unidentified flying objects (UFOs), who told the pair that they must abandon their ordinary life. Applewhite began to refer to himself as the "Mouth-piece" and Nettles as the "Battery." In January, 1973, Nettles and Applewhite left on what they called a trip into the wilderness to find their calling. After a year of aimless wandering, their mission was revealed to them: They would soon be martyred, rise from the dead, and be taken by UFO to another planet. Those who wished to join them in the journey to the new world would have to undergo a metamorphosis, which they called the Process. Celibacy was required of followers, because sex took too much energy away from the Process, which would be complete only when they boarded the UFO.

In 1974, Applewhite spent four months in jail for failing to return a rental car, and Nettles returned to Houston, where she lived with her mother. When Applewhite was released, she went with him to Los Angeles, where they began to win converts, largely from another UFO group. Applewhite and Nettles became known as Bo and Peep, as they were now the "shepherds" of a "flock." In late 1975 they received a revelation that a spaceship would come to collect them and their followers in Colorado. Some fifty followers joined them in making the trek there. The UFO failed to appear, and the number of cult members dropped to about twenty.

The two leaders now called themselves Do and Ti, notes in the celestial harmony, and they spent the following ten years wandering the western states, often dashing to meet a UFO, only to be disappointed. In 1983, Ti had an eye removed in the course of treatment for cancer. The cancer spread, and she died in Dallas in June, 1985. In Do's words, she had left her earthly vessel and gone to the next level. In 1997 Do took the appearance of Comet Hale-Bopp as a marker from Ti that the arrival of a space-ship "to take us home" was imminent. He and thirty-eight others committed suicide in a rented house in the affluent San Diego suburb of Rancho Santa Fe.

IMPACT

Bonnie Nettles earned notoriety as the cofounder of Heaven's Gate (the name of the cult she and Applewhite had established) when its members committed suicide in 1997, although there is no reason to believe that she would have approved. She demonstrated the close connection between Theosophy, spiritualism, and the belief in UFOs that contain benign aliens who intend only the best for humanity. Such beliefs have usually baffled both civil authorities and ordinary people, but they have an appeal to some, especially those who have difficulty finding meaning in their lives.

FURTHER READING

Balch, Robert. "Bo and Peep: A Case Study of the Origins of Messianic Leadership." In *Millennialism and Charisma*, edited by Roy Wallis. Belfast: Queen's Unversity, 1982. Balch and another sociologist joined Bo and Peep's group as observer-participants for two months in 1975, and this article provides information on Nettles's background and early beliefs.

_____. "The Evolution of a New Age Cult: From Total Overcomes Anonymous to Death at Heaven's Gate." In *Sects, Cults, and Spiritual Communities*, edited by William Zellner. Westport, Conn.: Praeger, 1998. This article, by a prominent sociologist of charismatic leadership, follows the story of Heaven's Gate to the suicides of 1997.

Wessinger, Catherine. *How the Millennium Comes Violently: From Jonestown to Heaven's Gate*. New York: Seven Bridges Press, 2000. Contains a valuable section on Heaven's Gate, with details about Nettles's life.

—Frederic J. Baumgartner

SEE ALSO: Marshall Applewhite; L. Ron Hubbard; Jim Jones; David Koresh; Charles Manson; Sun Myung Moon; Charles Sobraj.

FLORENCE NEWTON
Irish witch

BORN: Date and place unknown
DIED: Probably 1661; probably Youghal, County
  Cork, Ireland
ALSO KNOWN AS: Witch of Youghal (also Youghall);
  Goody Newton; Gammer (Grandmother) Newton
MAJOR OFFENSES: Bewitching a serving maid and
  causing the death of a prison guard through
  witchcraft
ACTIVE: December, 1660-1661
LOCALE: Youghal, County Cork, Ireland
SENTENCE: Imprisonment

EARLY LIFE
Nothing is known of Florence Newton (NEW-tuhn) before she was charged with witchcraft.

SORCERY CAREER
Although Florence Newton was a real woman, the accounts of her notorious activities are shrouded in legend:
At Christmas in 1660, Newton, by then an old beg-
garwoman, approached serving maid Mary Longdon,
asking her for a piece of beef. Longdon refused to give
away her master's beef, and Newton went away, mutter-
ing under her breath. About a week later, Newton went to
Longdon and kissed her violently, asking that the two be
friends. Shortly after, Longdon was visited by the spirit
of a little man and the image of Newton. The maid refused to follow the devil and for many weeks was tormented by violent fits during which she vomited needles,
bent pins, wool, and straw. Stones would fall upon her or
seem to be thrown at her, but the stones could never be
found. All this she attributed to Newton's having bewitched her by kissing her. On March 24, 1661, Newton
was committed to Youghal Prison.

LEGAL ACTION AND OUTCOME
Newton was put on trial for witchcraft in the case of
Mary Longdon at Cork assizes on September 11, 1661.
During her trial at Cork, Newton underwent examinations by the noted witch finder Valentine Greatrakes
(Greatrix) and local men of importance. A number of
commonly known methods of identifying witches were
employed in addition to the interrogation. Among these
were a version of pricking or prodding with a sharp instrument, in this case a shoemaker's awl, which was used
to lance both of Newton's hands. That one hand bled and
the other did not seemed to implicate Newton as a witch.

Newton's inability to recite the Lord's Prayer, which
she attributed to being old and having a poor memory,
harmed her case, as did Longdon's continuing accusations and fits.

Newton did not admit to bewitching Longdon but said
she had "overlooked" her; the former implied the use of
magic to cause harm, while the latter simply meant a
forceful wish for some ill to befall the serving maid.
Newton admitted—after first denying it—that during her
time in prison she had been visited by her familiar in the
form of a greyhound. She also apologized for causing
any harm to Longdon.

The court subsequently charged Newton with the
death of prison guard David Jones. After his attempts to
teach her the Lord's Prayer, Newton had kissed his hand
through the prison bars. Jones died fourteen days later,
claiming Newton had bewitched him. No record of the
verdict survives, and Newton's fate is unknown.

IMPACT
Florence Newton's trial is the only recorded account of a
witchcraft trial in seventeenth century Ireland. It was so
significant during its time that the Irish attorney general
prosecuted the case. Newton is now generally considered
an unfortunate old woman and victim of the influx of
Anglo-Protestantism and the changing face of social and
legal custom.

FURTHER READING

Curran, Bob. *A Bewitched Land*. Dublin: The O'Brien
  Press, 2005. Contextualizes the history of witchcraft
  prosecution in Ireland by looking at major cases of interest. Explicates the recorded text of Newton's trial
  and suggests a psychological and sociopolitical interpretation of the events.
Fuller, James F. "Trial of Florence Newton for Witchcraft in Cork, 1661." *Cork Historical and Archeo-
  logical Society* 10, no. 63 (July-September, 1904):
  174-183. Fuller's article reprints the text of the pam-
  phlet published subsequent to Newton's trial giving a
  firsthand account of the events and witnesses' statements.
Klaits, Joseph. *Servants of Satan: The Age of the Witch
  Hunts*. Bloomington: Indiana University Press, 1985.
  A comprehensive study pursuing the evolution and
  impact of the European witch-hunts of the sixteenth
  and sixteenth centuries, focusing on prosecutions (in-

cluding methods of torture) and religious and sexual politics.

O'Dowd, Mary. *A History of Women in Ireland, 1500-1800*. Harlow, England: Pearson, 2005. A general study looking at the economic, political, and religious circumstances of women during the period of English settlement and changing laws.

Seymour, St. John D. *Irish Witchcraft and Demonology*. Baltimore: Norman, Remington, 1913. Classic study

offering a corrective to the long-held belief that the witch-hunt craze did not affect Ireland. Assesses and largely recounts the original records of Newton's trial.

—Jennie MacDonald

SEE ALSO: Tamsin Blight; Mary Butters; Margaret Jones; Lady Alice Kyteler; Dolly Pentreath; Elizabeth Sawyer; Mother Shipton; Joan Wytte.

HUEY NEWTON
African American cofounder of the Black Panther Party

BORN: February 17, 1942; Monroe, Louisiana
DIED: August 22, 1989; Oakland, California
ALSO KNOWN AS: Huey Percy Newton (full name)
CAUSE OF NOTORIETY: As leader of the Black Panther Party, Newton encouraged Bay Area black citizens to arm themselves against police harassment and supported programs to improve the well-being of African Americans. However, he also faced criminal charges numerous times, including for voluntary manslaughter and embezzlement of Black Panther funds.
ACTIVE: March, 1967-August, 1989
LOCALE: Oakland, California
SENTENCE: Two to fifteen years' imprisonment for voluntary manslaughter; served three years

EARLY LIFE

Huey Newton (HEW-ee NEW-tuhn) was the youngest of seven children born to Armelia and Walter Newton, a Baptist minister and struggling sharecropper who was active in the National Association for the Advancement of Colored People (NAACP). When he was a child, his family moved from rural Louisiana to Oakland, California. Despite attending school, Newton did not learn to read until his early teen years, when he taught himself.

Newton turned to crime and was arrested several times for minor offenses as a teenager. He attended Merritt College—where he met his friend and Black Panther cofounder, Bobby Seale—and later studied law at Oakland City College and San Francisco Law

School. By his own admission, he studied criminology and law only to be a better criminal and to oppose the police. Newton dropped out of school before graduating and made his living through robbery.

Huey Newton (right) and Bobby Seale in 1967.

THE BLACK PANTHER PARTY PLATFORM

In 1966, the Black Panther Party announced its ten-point plan for society, largely written by Huey Newton. As he explained in a speech at Boston College, it was not reformist:

It is a survival program. We, the people, are threatened with genocide because racism and fascism are rampant in this country and throughout the world. And the ruling circle in North America is responsible. We intend to change all of that, and in order to change it, there must be a total transformation. But until we can achieve that total transformation, we must exist. In order to exist, we must survive; therefore we need a survival kit: the Ten-Point Program.

Here is the Panthers' ten-point plan:

- We want freedom. We want power to determine the destiny of our black and oppressed communities.
- We want full employment for our people.
- We want an end to the robbery by the capitalists of our black and oppressed communities.
- We want decent housing, fit for the shelter of human beings.
- We want decent education for our people that exposes the true nature of this decadent American society. We want education that teaches us our true history and our role in the present-day society.
- We want completely free health care for all black and oppressed people.
- We want an immediate end to police brutality and murder of black people, other people of color, all oppressed people inside the United States.
- We want an immediate end to all wars of aggression.
- We want freedom for all black and oppressed people now held in U.S. federal, state, county, city and military prisons and jails. We want trials by a jury of peers for all persons charged with so-called crimes under the laws of this country.
- We want land, bread, housing, education, clothing, justice, peace and people's community control of modern technology.

Source: The Huey P. Newton Reader (New York: Seven Stories Press, 2002).

ACTIVIST CAREER

While in college, Newton became attracted to revolutionary politics and joined the Afro-American Association, where he succeeded in getting the campus to establish the first black studies course. Newton became a supporter of Malcolm X, gravitated toward the thought and works of revolutionaries such as Che Guevara and Mao Zedong, and later, in 1971, traveled to China, where he met with Premier Zhou Enlai. In 1974, Newton earned a bachelor's degree from the University of California, Santa Cruz.

Newton cofounded the Black Panther Party for Self-Defense in 1966, served as its minister of defense, and produced the party's platform and principles. Deter-

mined to stop the Oakland Police Department from harassing blacks, Newton encouraged black self-defense and formed armed patrols to monitor the police. Such actions earned the organization a reputation as an antiwhite, extremist group and resulted in an effort by the Federal Bureau of Investigation (FBI) to monitor and disrupt the Black Panthers' activities. In 1967, Newton captured national media attention for leading an armed Black Panther march on the California State Capitol.

The Black Panthers also organized a free breakfast for poor children, a sickle-cell disease program, and other community-based and educational projects. Newton's beliefs were far more than simply kneejerk radicalism. He advocated structural changes in the American economic system in the service of the have-nots and saw capitalism as exploitation by corporations of poor blacks. Newton emerged as a figurehead for urban black youth frustrated by harsh inequalities, and, although shy, he gave voice to black nationalism through his inspired oratory, written word, and signature black beret and black leather jacket.

LEGAL ACTION AND OUTCOME

Newton spent most of his adult life in trouble with the law. After numerous charges of burglary, he was arrested in 1967 after a confrontation with police. Later that same year, Newton was indicted for the murder of police officer John Frey and attempted murder of officer Herbert Haines. In 1968, Newton was sentenced to two to fifteen years in jail on voluntary manslaughter, but the sentence was reversed in 1970 and Newton was freed after serving three years in prison.

By 1972, most of the Black Panther leaders had been killed, imprisoned, or expelled from the party, and the organization's influence waned. Newton again faced a lengthy prison sentence when, in 1974, charges were filed against him for murdering Kathleen Smith, a seventeen-year-old prostitute, and for beating Preston Callins. After Newton failed to appear in court, his bail was revoked, and a warrant was issued for his arrest (his name appeared on the FBI's "most wanted" list). Newton fled to Cuba, where he spent three years in exile; he later returned to the United States to face his charges but was acquitted of murder when the jury deadlocked.

In 1985, Newton was again arrested, this time for embezzling state and federal funds from the Black Panthers. He was also arrested in 1988 for drug possession and convicted in 1989 of embezzling funds from a school run by the Black Panthers. However, shortly after his conviction, Newton was shot and killed by a drug dealer in Oakland. Official accounts remain vague, but some suggest he was involved in drug dealing and was shot during a drug deal. Newton's efforts were undermined, in part, by his own contradictions: relationships with drug dealers and prostitutes and his addiction to drugs and alcohol.

IMPACT

Huey Newton's legacy remained as founder and leader of the Black Panthers and as icon of the counterculture and black nationalist movements of the 1960's. His Cuban exile, arrests, and prison sentences led to highly visible Free Huey rallies, which only furthered his stature as a revolutionary hero. The Dr. Huey P. Newton Foundation continued his work into the twenty-first century. A one-man stage play about Newton's life, written by Roger Guenveur Smith, debuted in 1996 and inspired the 2001 television film *A Huey P. Newton Story*, directed by Spike Lee; it was nominated for two Image Awards, given by the NAACP.

FURTHER READING

Morrison, Toni, ed. *To Die for the People: The Writings of Huey P. Newton*. 1972. Rev. ed. New York: Writers and Readers Press, 1999. Edited by noted author Toni Morrison, this collection of Newton's writings and speeches is updated from the first publication in 1972.

Newton, Huey P. *Revolutionary Suicide*. New York: Writers and Readers Press, 1995. Discussions include the author's frank assessment of his life as a hustler, the Black Panthers, and America's penal system.

_____. *War Against the Panthers: A Study of Repression in America*. Reprint. New York: Harlem River Press, 2000. Newton's rereleased scholarly examination of inequality and racism, which draws on historical examples and revolutionary leaders.

Seale, Bobby. *Seize the Time: The Story of the Black Panther Party and Huey P. Newton*. 1970. Rev. ed. Baltimore: Black Classic Press, 1997. Written by the Panthers' cofounder, this sympathetic assessment of Newton and the organization discusses the party's founding and struggles.

—Robert P. Watson

SEE ALSO: Wallace Dodd Fard; Che Guevara; Patty Hearst; Mao Zedong; Elijah Muhammad; Assata Olugbala Shakur.

CHARLES NG
American murderer

BORN: December 24, 1960; Hong Kong
ALSO KNOWN AS: Charles Chitat Ng (full name); Mike Kimoto
MAJOR OFFENSES: Serial murders
ACTIVE: 1979-1985
LOCALE: Oahu, Hawaii; Calgary, Canada; and San Francisco and Wilseyville, California
SENTENCE: Death penalty

EARLY LIFE

The father of Charles Ng (eeng)—a self-made, middle-class man—punished Charles harshly, trying to motivate him. The young Ng was a loner, who often clung to and overwhelmed potential friends. During his school years, Charles became fascinated with martial arts, weapons, and Molotov cocktails. He also loved origami and drawing. He was dismissed from boarding school in England after stealing from classmates.

In 1978, with a student visa, Ng enrolled in Notre Dame College, in San Mateo County, California. He left his schooling to join the U.S. Marines; he lied on his enlistment form and was admitted to the Marines despite his lack of citizenship or permanent residency. Generally a good soldier, he practiced martial arts and made some friends. However, in October, 1979, at Kaneohe Marine Corps Air Station in Oahu, Hawaii, he masterminded plans to steal from the armory. Rather than face court-martial, he fled but was caught a month later by military police and taken to jail to await trial. He escaped from prison, however, and eventually returned to California.

CRIMINAL CAREER

Ng met Leonard Lake and Lake's wife Cricket in 1981 through Mark Novak, a survivalist who disdained Lake but felt Lake's isolated ranch in Philo, California, would hide Ng. Lake and Ng collected weapons and practiced shooting, at which Ng excelled. They also probably burglarized stores for guns. In San Francisco, Ng raped a prostitute that Lake hired, marking the beginning of one of history's most successful serial-killer teams.

In 1982, police arrested Ng for his theft in Hawaii and Lake for having illegal weapons. Lake fled, and Ng made a plea bargain and was sent to prison in Ft. Leavenworth, Kansas. There, he told fellow inmates about his fantasies of torturing women. He also corresponded with Lake, who sent him photos both of seminude women and of the bunker he was building in Wilseyville, California.

In July, 1984, Ng was released. He visited a woman who had written to him in prison, and they had a tryst. Then he joined Lake and Cricket in Wilseyville. The two men began a string of crimes that acted out Lake's sexually sadistic and murderous fantasies.

Two days after joining Lake, Ng killed Donald Giuletti. Ng's coworkers at a moving company, Jeff Gerald and Clifford Peranteau, were his next murder victims; Michael Caroll, another victim, had known Ng in Leavenworth.

Most damningly, Ng appeared in videos with two kidnapped women, Brenda O'Connor and Kathy Allen, Caroll's girlfriend. Ng taunts them and threatens them with a stun gun; he removes their clothing and his own. Lake and Ng kept the women as sex slaves and then murdered them. A brief videotaped scene showed Ng transporting two corpses.

LEGAL ACTION AND OUTCOME

Ng was caught shoplifting with Lake in June, 1985. Ng fled, and Lake committed suicide shortly after his arrest while in police custody. While searching for Ng, police excavated the Wilseyville property and found the partial or complete remains of at least twenty-four bodies. Remains continued to be found at that location until 1992. A month later, as he was being arrested for shoplifting food

in Calgary, Alberta, Canada, Ng shot and injured security guard John Doyle. After a long debate about his extradition, Ng was sent to California in 1991.

Ng had learned how to manipulate the legal system while serving time in prison. His eight-month trial, ending in June, 1999, cost twenty million dollars, at the time one of the longest and most expensive trials in California. The case dragged on as Ng hired and fired attorneys. Despite defense attempts to blame Lake, Ng was convicted of murdering six men, three women, and two children. The jury deadlocked on one count, which was dropped. Ng was sentenced to death, a judgment that he continued to appeal into the twenty-first century.

IMPACT

Authorities debate Charles Ng's responsibility for the crimes. Many question whether he was a dependent follower of a depraved mentor or an equal partner; his own previous actions and fantasies displayed his willingness to participate in criminal acts. His personality has also presented a fascinating case study to criminologists. Furthermore, the trial highlighted the way in which the meticulous use of law could prevent justice; in the Ng case, rules to protect the accused became tools of delay and misdirection.

FURTHER READING

Harrington, Joseph, and Robert Burger. *Justice Denied.* New York: Plenum, 1999. Covers Ng's trial and its publicity; somewhat sensationalistic but informative.

Henton, Darcy, and Greg Owens. *No Kill, No Thrill.* Calgary, Alta.: Red Deer Press, 2001. Covers Ng's background, crimes, and trial; factually accurate but interpretations are biased against Lake.

Lassiter, Don. *Die for Me.* New York: Pinnacle Books, 2000. Devoted equally to Lake and Ng; includes a detailed and objective depiction of Ng's background, crimes, and trial.

—*Bernadette Lynn Bosky*

SEE ALSO: Kenneth Bianchi; Angelo Buono, Jr.; Leonard Lake.

MADAME NHU
Sister-in-law of South Vietnam's first president

BORN: 1924; Hanoi, Vietnam

ALSO KNOWN AS: Tran Le Xuan (maiden name); Madame Ngo Dinh Nhu

CAUSE OF NOTORIETY: Nhu's reference to the self-immolation of Buddhist monks in Saigon as a "monk barbecue" helped turn world public opinion against the anti-Communist administration of her brother-in-law.

ACTIVE: 1963

LOCALE: South Vietnam

EARLY LIFE

Madame Nhu (new) was born Tran Le Xuan in Hanoi in 1924, the second of three children. Her father, Tran Van Chuong, was a Paris-educated lawyer, and her mother, Nam Tran Chuong, was a descendant of the Vietnamese emperor Dong Khanh. Even though they remained Buddhist, her family thoroughly embraced French culture, and Xuan grew up speaking more French than Vietnamese. As teenager, she enjoyed life in Hanoi and married librarian Ngo Dinh Nhu in 1943, thus becoming Madame Nhu. Upon marriage she converted to Roman Catholicism, the religion of her husband. They settled in the South Vietnamese resort town of Dalat and had four children.

POLITICAL CAREER

When Vietnam gained independence from France in 1954, Nhu's bachelor brother-in-law, Ngo Dinh Diem, set up an American-supported government in South Vietnam and appointed her husband chief of security and leader of his political party. Madame Nhu quickly styled herself as first lady of South Vietnam. During coup attempts in November, 1960, and in February, 1962, she steeled President Diem's heart against any compromise with the insurgents.

Emboldened by her success, Nhu became known for her strong will and flamboyant behavior. As a member of South Vietnam's National Assembly, Nhu pushed through a series of conservative reforms limiting divorce and outlawing contraceptives, dancing, and other perceived vices. She also founded a Women's Solidarity Movement that advocated paramilitary education in Vietnam and was famously photographed at pistol shooting practice.

Nhu's most noted moment came in response to the self-immolation of the Buddhist monk Thich Quang Duc on a Saigon street on June 11, 1963, in protest against Diem's anti-Buddhist policies. When four more monks, filmed by foreign journalists, burned themselves to death in August, Nhu referred to the events as a "monk barbecue show." Her comment was quoted in the August 19, 1963, issue of *Newsweek* magazine. International public outrage did little to soften Nhu's anti-Buddhist stance or prevent her from making similar remarks, such as that she would gladly provide the gasoline if the monks wanted to hold another barbecue.

Nhu dissuaded President Diem from compromise with the restive Buddhists, whose opposition led to a se-

Madame Nhu. (AP/Wide World Photos)

vere decline in his vital American support. In October, 1963, Nhu and her oldest daughter, Le Thuy, embarked on a goodwill tour of the United States. On October 11, the two appeared on the cover of *Life* magazine. On October 13, Nhu was interviewed by the National Broadcasting Company, reiterating her suspicion that the Central Intelligence Agency was conspiring against her husband and brother-in-law.

On November 2, 1963, while she was in Los Angeles, Nhu's husband and President Diem were murdered in Saigon when their government was overthrown. Distraught, she blamed the Americans. When American president John F. Kennedy was assassinated on November 22, 1963, Nhu remarked to his wife, Jacqueline Kennedy, "Now you know what it feels like."

The following year, while Nhu was living in exile in Paris, her oldest daughter, Le Thuy, died in a car crash. Two years later, in a dispute over his inheritance, Nhu's brother Tran Van Kiem strangled their parents on November 1, 1986, and was arrested in Washington, D.C. On the following day, Nhu blamed the Americans for haunting her family, declaring "I spit on the world." As of 2006, she was living on the French Riviera.

IMPACT

By 1963, exasperated American officials in Saigon saw Madame Nhu and her brother as key impediments to anti-Communist success in Vietnam. Americans were wont to say "no Nhus is good news." Journalists called her the "Dragon Lady." From that point on in American public opinion, Nhu's anti-Buddhist intransigence was widely blamed for fueling South Vietnam's eventual fall to Communism. Her staunch support for repressing a faith held by 90 percent of the Vietnamese population in favor of a small Roman Catholic elite is seen as a severe political misjudgment.

FURTHER READING

Catton, Philip E. *Diem's Final Failure*. Lawrence: University Press of Kansas, 2002. Blames Madame Nhu for intensifying President Diem's isolation.

Goldstein, Lawrence. "Madame Nhu, Woman and Warrior: A Reading of 'Le Xuan, Beautiful Spring.'"

MADAME NHU'S BARBECUE

On June 11, 1963, Buddhist monk Thich Quang Duc protested the Diem administration's killing of eight South Vietnamese monks in the spring of that year by setting himself on fire. New York Times *reporter David Halberstam witnessed the scene:*

Flames were coming from a human being; his body was slowly withering and shriveling up, his head blackening and charring. In the air was the smell of burning human flesh; human beings burn surprisingly quickly. Behind me I could hear the sobbing of the Vietnamese who were now gathering. I was too shocked to cry, too confused to take notes or ask questions, too bewildered to even think. . . . As he burned he never moved a muscle, never uttered a sound, his outward composure in sharp contrast to the wailing people around him.

Madame Nhu ridiculed the protests:

What have the Buddhist leaders done comparatively . . . the only thing they have done, they have barbecued one of their monks whom they have intoxicated, whom they have abused the confidence, and even that barbecuing was done not even with self-sufficient means because they used imported gasoline.

Source: David Halberstam, *The Making of a Quagmire* (New York: Random House, 1965). Madame Nhu quoted in "Vietnam: A Television History," on the PBS program *The American Experience* (Boston: WGBH Educational Foundation, 1963).

Callaloo 28, no. 3 (Summer, 2005): 764-770. Examines Nhu's place among Vietnamese women.

Karnow, Stanley. *Vietnam: A History*. 2d ed. New York: Viking Press, 1997. Covers Nhu's contribution to U.S. disenchantment with Diem.

—*R. C. Lutz*

SEE ALSO: Eva Braun; Magda Goebbels; Jiang Qing; Imelda Marcos; Eva Perón; Winifred Wagner.

NICHOLAS I
Czar of Russia (r. 1825-1855)

BORN: July 6, 1796; Tsarskoye Selo (now Pushkin), Russia

DIED: March 2, 1855; St. Petersburg, Russia

ALSO KNOWN AS: Nikolay Pavlovich (birth name)

CAUSE OF NOTORIETY: As czar, Nicholas I proved a conservative, even autocratic ruler whose policies hastened the coming of revolution in Russia.

ACTIVE: 1825-1855

LOCALE: St. Petersburg and Moscow, Russia

EARLY LIFE

Nicholas (NIHK-uh-luhs) was born on July 6, 1796, son of Emperor Paul I and grandson of Catherine the Great. Because he was the emperor's third son, no one expected that Nicholas would ascend the throne. When Nicholas was five years old, his father was murdered by a group of Russian nobles and officers of the royal guards. His eldest brother, Alexander I, became czar and ruled from 1801 to 1825.

As a young child Nicholas disliked schoolwork and was easily distracted, though his teachers were some of Russia's leading scholars. Instead, Nicolas was fascinated with all things military. He and his younger brother Michael frequently played army and could be found building forts out of palace furniture. Nicholas became a general in the Russian army in 1808, although he was inactive until 1814, the year after the repulse by Alexander I of Napoleon's invading army.

IMPERIAL CAREER

Nicholas ascended the throne December 26, 1825, during a time of grave uncertainty. His eldest brother, Alexander I, had died unexpectedly on November 19, 1825, without any male heirs. According to the rules of succession, Nicholas's older brother, Constantine, would normally have become the next czar. However, Constantine had secretly abdicated his privilege in 1820 upon marrying a Polish countess and taking up residence in Poland. Unknown to Nicholas, Alexander I had named Nicholas as heir apparent in a sealed document in 1823, with multiple copies housed in various state institutions. Nicholas elected to accede to the throne under protest, telling Constantine in a series of letters that he would take the crown only if Constantine officially and publicly abdicated. Constantine refused.

This protracted sequence of events, coupled with the secrecy of the proceedings, provided the opportunity for a group of Russian noblemen and military members to revolt in what became known as the Decembrist movement. The Decembrists wanted Constantine to become czar so they could force him to institute sweeping reforms in Russia and modernize a nation that in many ways was still feudal in character. The day of Nicholas's coronation as czar in St. Petersburg arrived; when the time came to recite the oath of allegiance to Nicholas I, some three thousand troops on the main square of the city refused to swear allegiance and announced their stand with the Decembrists.

Nicholas was reluctant to use military force to suppress the revolt, although his advisers encouraged it. He did not want his first day as a Russian ruler to end in bloodshed. He mounted his horse and led his loyal royal guards to put down the revolt. When the revolutionaries refused to yield, however, Nicholas acted decisively and directed cannon fire on them. Many were killed, and

Nicholas I.

other Decembrists were arrested in St. Petersburg, Moscow, and throughout Russia. After the events, a commission of inquiry established for the purpose delivered to Nicholas a report on the entire affair and the reasons behind it. Several conspirators were sentenced to death; more than one hundred others were exiled to Siberia, some for life.

As czar, Nicholas did not intend to modernize Russia, as some previous rulers had attempted, but to preserve the absolutism of monarchal power and retain serfdom as core elements of the Russian imperial system. Nicholas stopped further implementation of the constitution that his brother Alexander had drafted and rescinded those aspects of the constitution that had already been implemented. Because the Decembrist revolt had made him distrust the noble class that made up the government service, the czar created an entire network of secret government agencies and committees to bypass all usual government channels. Throughout his reign Nicholas held the fear that people were trying to usurp his power; his paranoia led him to create Russia's first police state. Anything that Nicholas perceived as a threat or possible threat was quickly suppressed.

Nicholas prohibited Russians from traveling abroad and in 1850 created twelve censorship agencies. These censorship agencies banned such subjects as foreign languages from school curricula, no longer allowed the study of philosophy in college, and supervised the press and literature. Nicholas believed that everything not Russian was dangerous to Russia. Anti-Semitism was not only state sanctioned but also encouraged. Nicholas's oppressive rule extended beyond his Russian subjects; he rescinded the autonomy that Poland had enjoyed for decades. He attempted to wipe out Polish culture and transferred ownership of all Catholic Church lands to the state.

Nicholas is most remembered for the Crimean War, having sent troops into the Ottoman Empire in 1853 to "protect" the rights of Christians. Early in the war Russia experienced victory after victory. After Britain and France entered the war on the side of the Ottomans to stop what they saw as Russia's expansionist intentions, the Russians began to suffer their first military defeats in centuries. Nicholas died March 2, 1855, of natural causes, a year before the Crimean War ended.

IMPACT

Nicholas I's reign affected those of the two Russian czars who would follow him; the police state Nicholas established created great hostility toward the monarchy. The military losses in the Crimean War dealt a swift blow to national morale. The continued suppression of the common people under public and private serfdom helped sow the seeds for the October Revolution of 1917, as the peasant population grew steadily disenchanted with the exercise of imperial power that in the past had generally been viewed as benevolent.

FURTHER READING

Lincoln, W. Bruce. *Nicholas I: Emperor and Autocrat of All the Russians.* DeKalb: Northern Illinois University Press, 1989. A detailed look into Nicholas's rise to power, his policies, his reign, and his legacy.

_____. *The Romanovs: Autocrats of All the Russians.* New York: Dial Press, 1967. An examination of the line of succession and reign of the Romanovs, from Ivan the Terrible to Nicholas II.

Troubetzkoy, Alexis S. *Imperial Legend: The Mysterious Disappearance of Tsar Alexander I.* New York: Arcade, 2002. The book investigates the legend that Alexander I staged his own death and reappeared in Russian society as a wanderer. It also describes the confusion following Alexander's death and the crowning of Nicholas I.

—Carol A. Cheek and Dennis W. Cheek

SEE ALSO: Vladimir Ilich Lenin; Konstantine Petrovich Pobedonostsev; Grigori Yefimovich Rasputin; Leon Trotsky; Grigory Yevseyevich Zinovyev.

TERRY NICHOLS
American terrorist

BORN: April 1, 1955; Lapeer, Michigan
ALSO KNOWN AS: Terry Lynn Nichols (full name)
MAJOR OFFENSE: Conspiracy to bomb a federal building, involuntary manslaughter in the deaths of eight federal law enforcement officers, and first-degree murder for the deaths of 161 persons
ACTIVE: April 19, 1995
LOCALE: Oklahoma City, Oklahoma
SENTENCE: Life in prison without parole on federal conviction; 161 counts of first-degree murder in state conviction

EARLY LIFE
Terry Nichols (NIH-kohlz) was born on April 1, 1955, in Lapeer, Michigan, to Robert Nichols and Joyce Wilt. He was raised a Christian and appeared to have a normal childhood with his three siblings. Nichols graduated from Lapeer High School with a 2.6 grade point average and attended Central Michigan University; he withdrew from college in the late 1970's in order to assist his father with the family farm. In 1981, Nichols married Lana Padilla and fathered a son, Josh. He worked a variety of jobs to support his family, including selling life insurance, performing carpentry work, and managing a grain elevator. Nichols divorced his wife in 1988.

CRIMINAL CAREER
In 1988, Nichols joined the U.S. Army and was assigned to the First Infantry Division in Fort Riley, Kansas. During basic training, Nichols became friends with Timothy McVeigh, and both shared an interest in guns, survivalist training, and white supremacy. Nichols and McVeigh also shared a strong hatred for the federal government. After Nichols's discharge from the Army in 1991, he continued to maintain a close friendship with McVeigh. The two men often traveled together, attending gun shows and reinforcing each other's hatred for the federal government.

In 1991, Nichols was married for a second time, to Marife Torres, a seventeen-year-old woman from the Philippines, who was already six months pregnant from a previous relationship. Nichols had been introduced to his second wife in Cebu City, Philippines, through a mail-order bride service out of Scottsdale, Arizona. Nichols would father two more children with his second wife, a daughter and a son.

Nichols and McVeigh together watched television coverage of the standoff between the federal government and the Branch Davidians in Waco, Texas, on April 19, 1993. After the confrontation at the Branch Davidian compound ended with the deaths of eighty people, the two became outraged by the actions of government agents. In September, 1994, Nichols and McVeigh began purchasing ammonium nitrate fertilizer and stocking it in storage facilities around the country; they planned to bomb the Alfred P. Murrah Federal Building in Oklahoma City, Oklahoma. Nichols rented the storage space and registered the material using an alias.

Two days prior to the Oklahoma City bombing, Nichols drove to Oklahoma to pick up McVeigh and then brought him to Kansas. Nichols and McVeigh assembled the bomb at an isolated location near Geary State Lake, a few miles from Nichols's home in Herington. On the morning of April 19, 1995, Nichols was seen by his neighbors applying fertilizer to his lawn at his home in Herington. At this time, McVeigh had parked a Ryder rental truck containing five thousand pounds of explo-

Terry Nichols. (AP/Wide World Photos)

sives outside the Alfred P. Murrah Federal Building and walked away from the truck after igniting a timed fuse. After the explosives detonated, 168 persons were killed, including a number of children located in the building's day care center; hundreds more building employees and visitors were injured in the domestic terrorist attack. After McVeigh was arrested in connection with the bombing, authorities then focused on Nichols, who voluntarily surrendered on April 21, 1995.

LEGAL ACTION AND OUTCOME

In May of 1995, Nichols was formally charged with having assisted McVeigh in planning to carry out the terrorist attack. On June 4, 1998, Nichols was convicted in federal court on eight counts of involuntary manslaughter for the deaths of eight law enforcement officers, as well as conspiring to bomb a federal building. He was sentenced to life in prison and was sent to a super-maximum security prison in Florence, Colorado. Nichols also was tried for murder by the state of Oklahoma, and a jury found him guilty on August 9, 2004. Nichols received 161 counts of first-degree murder, the sentence to be served in conjunction with the federal life sentence. The juries in both the federal and the Oklahoma trials spared Nichols the death penalty.

IMPACT

The Oklahoma City bombing created widespread support for passage of the Victims' Rights Clarification Act (VRCA), passed by Congress and signed into law by President Bill Clinton in 1997. The legislation provides victims of federal crime and their relatives the legal right to be present at a criminal trial, as well as the right to testify during the penalty phase of the trial. Proponents of the legislation argued that the victims of the Oklahoma City bombing would receive psychological benefits if they were able to observe the trials of Timothy McVeigh and Terry Nichols.

The Oklahoma City bombing also produced a variety of conspiracy theories. For example, people theorized that McVeigh supposedly met with a white supremacist group, the Aryan Republican Army, in northern Arkansas in the months leading up to the bombing. Others have attempted to draw a link between Islamic terrorists located in the Philippines and the fact that Nichols spent a considerable amount of time in Cebu City, Philippines, where he met his second wife. Cebu City is considered a base for several militant groups, including al-Qaeda. Finally, some have argued that the federal government was involved in the bombing because the attack provided an excuse to crack down on right-wing extremists. However, no credible evidence exists to support allegations of a wider conspiracy beyond that between McVeigh and Nichols.

FURTHER READING

Dyer, Joel. *Harvest of Rage: Why Oklahoma City Is Only the Beginning.* Boulder, Colo.: Westview Press, 1998. Dyer, an investigative journalist, analyzes the relationship between the farm crisis of the 1980's and hatred for the federal government in the 1990's. Dyer argues that inspiration for the Oklahoma City bombing grew out of frustration from citizens in rural America who had become disenfranchised and powerless.

Jones, Stephen, and Peter Israel. *Others Unknown: Timothy McVeigh and the Oklahoma City Bombing Conspiracy.* New York: PublicAffairs, 2001. The defense lawyer of McVeigh, Stephen Jones, documents his experience defending McVeigh. Jones and Israel also explore the conspiracy side of the bombing by asking the question whether others, such as Islamic terrorists who may have associated with Nichols in the Philippines, were involved in the bombing.

Padilla, Lana, and Ron Delpit. *My Blood Betrayed: My Life with Terry Nichols and Timothy McVeigh.* New York: HarperCollins, 1995. Padilla, the first wife of Nichols, documents her relationship with him and her limited experience with McVeigh.

—*Scott P. Johnson*

SEE ALSO: David Koresh; Timothy McVeigh; Randy Weaver.

ELIGIUSZ NIEWIADOMSKI

Polish modernist painter, art critic, political activist, and assassin

BORN: December 1, 1869; Warsaw, Poland, Russian
  Empire (now in Poland)
DIED: January 31, 1923; Warsaw, Poland
MAJOR OFFENSE: Assassination of Poland's first
  president, Gabriel Narutowicz
ACTIVE: December 16, 1922
LOCALE: Warsaw, Poland
SENTENCE: Death by firing squad

EARLY LIFE

Eligiusz Niewiadomski (ehl-EE-gyoosh nyehv-yuh-
DOHM-skee) was born in Warsaw, Poland (under Russian occupation), on December 1, 1869, to Wincenty and
Julia Niewiadomski. His father was a writer, military
veteran, and laborer at the Warsaw minting house. His
mother died when Niewiadomski was two years old, and
his older sister Cecylia took over the maternal duties of
the family. After graduating from a Warsaw trade school
in 1888, Niewiadomski went to St. Petersburg and later
to Paris to study art. Upon his return to Warsaw, he began
teaching sketch drawing at the Warsaw University of
Technology and wrote for a number of Warsaw-based art
journals and newspapers as an art critic. During this period, he also began his radical political career as a supporter of the National League (Democratic Party) and
taught history and art courses at various institutions of
higher learning. He later served in the Polish army during
the Polish-Soviet War (1919-1921). It was after Niewiadomski's return from his military service—when he
regained his esteemed position of director of painting
and sculpture for the Regency Council of Warsaw—that
he began to realize his true discontent with the direction
of the Polish government.

CRIMINAL CAREER

After not receiving his requested budget allocations for
his art department, Niewiadomski resigned his post as director with the Regency Council. His anger and frustration with the Russian-Communist influence on the new
Polish government became heightened. The December,
1922, election of Gabriel Narutowicz as the first president of Poland sparked a national revolt (led by the
Democratic Party) throughout much of Poland. Although Narutowicz's election was supported by leftist,
centrist, and peasant deputies, right-leaning deputies rebelled against the election because they claimed that the
group of deputies who supported Narutowicz included

Jews. The National League took to calling Narutowicz
President of the Jews.

The election of Narutowicz seemed to send Eligiusz
over the edge of reason. On December 16, 1922, Narutowicz was present at an opening of an art exhibition at
an art gallery in Warsaw. Niewiadomski, a frequent
guest at such events, approached Narutowicz, bran-
dished a small-caliber pistol, and shot the president-elect
three times at close range. Narutowicz died immediately.

LEGAL ACTION AND OUTCOME

On December 30, 1922, Niewiadomski was arrested and
subsequently sentenced to death, a penalty some scholars
believe he proposed to the high court himself. At trial, he
also openly admitted that he had intended to kill the chief
of state, Józef Piłsudski, but was not given an adequate
amount of time to carry out his plan. Niewiadomski was
convicted on the assassination charge, and his death sentence was carried out by firing squad in Warsaw, Poland,
on January 31, 1923. His funeral was attended by an estimated ten thousand people. His body was then laid to rest
at Powąki Cemetery in Warsaw.

IMPACT

Niewiadomski, although an acclaimed modernist painter,
art critic, writer, and activist of the late nineteenth and
early twentieth centuries, regrettably gained his notoriety and place in historical annals as the assassin of
Poland's first president. The murder of President Narutowicz brought to light the political unrest between the
Communist and democratic parties of the Polish government. Even decades after his execution, many right-wing
media representatives and political figures presented
Niewiadomski as a national hero and political martyr for
the National League.

FURTHER READING

Davies, Norman. *Heart of Europe: The Past in Poland's
  Present*. New York: Oxford University Press, 2001.
  Takes an in-depth historical look at Poland beginning
  in 1945 but examines the country's past in order to
  understand the history and politics of a proud yet
  oppressed and continually conquered people.
Wandycz, Piotr. *Soviet-Polish Relations, 1917-1921*.
  Cambridge, Mass.: Harvard University Press, 1969.
  Offers a detailed account leading up to the assassina-
  tion of Poland's first president and the Polish-Soviet

War. An unbiased look at the problems between the two nations and their sometimes varied views of political ideology.

Zimmerman, Joshua. *Poles, Jews, and the Politics of Nationality: The Bund and the Polish Socialist Party in Late Czarist Russia, 1892-1914.* Madison: University of Wisconsin Press, 2003. Although predominantly focusing on the role of the Jewish people in Polish

politics, this text provides a tremendous understanding of the escalating political turmoil in czarist Poland.

—Paul M. Klenowski

SEE ALSO: Sante Jeronimo Caserio; Leon Czolgosz; Charles Julius Guiteau; Fanya Kaplan; Ramón Mercader; Puniša Račić.

RICHARD NIXON
President of the United States (1969-1974)

BORN: January 9, 1913; Yorba Linda, California
DIED: April 22, 1994, New York, New York
ALSO KNOWN AS: Richard Milhous Nixon (full name); Dick Nixon; Tricky Dick
CAUSE OF NOTORIETY: Although praised by many as a statesman, President Nixon became notorious when he was forced to resign the presidency in the wake of the Watergate scandal.
ACTIVE: 1960's-1970's
LOCALE: Washington, D.C.

EARLY LIFE
Richard M. Nixon (NIHK-sehn) was the thirty-seventh president of the United States, serving from 1969 to 1974. Before being elected president, he served two terms as vice president under President Dwight D. Eisenhower, from 1953 to 1961.

Nixon rose to these high offices from modest beginnings. He was born in Yorba Linda, California, and grew up in the then largely rural area of Whittier, California. His father, Francis Nixon, owned a small store that sold groceries and gasoline. His mother, Hannah Milhous Nixon, was a devout member of the Society of Friends (Quakers) who reared her son in the Quaker faith and hoped that her son would grow up to be a Quaker missionary.

Nixon attended Whittier College, winning election as student-body president. After graduation, he went on to law school at Duke University on a full scholarship. During World War II (1941-1945), he volunteered for the Navy, despite his pacifist upbringing, and served in the South Pacific.

POLITICAL CAREER
After the war, Nixon ran for the U.S. House of Representatives, defeating his opponent, Jerry Voorhis, in a cam-

paign that suggested that Voorhis had communist connections. Nixon used a similar tactic in successfully running for the Senate in 1950, when he accused the other candidate, Helen Gahagan Douglas, of having communist sympathies. While in Congress, Nixon used his stance against communism to win public attention when he played a leading role in the investigation of former State Department official Alger Hiss.

Richard Nixon. (NARA/Nixon Presidential Materials)

THE FIRST RESIGNATION OF A PRESIDENT

On August 8, 1974, President Nixon became the first U.S. president to resign, delivering this speech to the American public:

I have never been a quitter. To leave office before my term is completed is abhorrent to every instinct in my body. But as President, I must put the interest of America first. America needs a full-time President and a full-time Congress, particularly at this time with problems we face at home and abroad.

To continue to fight through the months ahead for my personal vindication would almost totally absorb the time and attention of both the President and the Congress in a period when our entire focus should be on the great issues of peace abroad and prosperity without inflation at home. . . . Therefore, I shall resign the Presidency effective at noon tomorrow. Vice President Ford will be sworn in as President at that hour in this office.

By taking this action, I hope that I will have hastened the start of that process of healing which is so desperately needed in America. . . .

Sometimes I have succeeded and sometimes I have failed, but always I have taken heart from what Theodore Roosevelt once said about the man in the arena, "whose face is marred by dust and sweat and blood, who strives valiantly, who errs and comes short again and again because there is not effort without error and shortcoming, but who does actually strive to do the deed, who knows the great enthusiasms, the great devotions, who spends himself in a worthy cause, who at the best knows in the end the triumphs of high achievements and who at the worst, if he fails, at least fails while daring greatly."

When I first took the oath of office as President five and half years ago, I made this sacred commitment, to "consecrate my office, my energies, and all the wisdom I can summon to the cause of peace among nations."

I have done my very best in all the days since to be true to that pledge. As a result of these efforts, I am confident that the world is a safer place today, not only for the people of America but for the people of all nations, and that all of our children have a better chance than before of living in peace rather than dying in war.

In 1952, the still youthful Nixon was elected vice president under Republican president Dwight D. Eisenhower. During the election, he came under attack for allegedly having a slush fund from business sources. In response, Nixon made his famous televised "Checkers" speech, in which he defended his ethics but acknowledged that his family had received a small dog, named Checkers, as a gift from supporters. He said that he would not return the dog because of his daughters' attachment to it. Nixon was apparently a skillful vice president but did not have close relations with President Eisenhower.

Nixon's presidential aspirations seemed to have come to nothing when he was defeated by Democratic candidate John F. Kennedy in 1960. In 1962, his entire politi-

cal career appeared to be over when he lost a run for governor of California. Nevertheless, he was able to stage a comeback and received the Republican nomination for president in 1968. Saying that he had a secret plan to end the unpopular Vietnam War, Nixon became the thirty-seventh president.

Nixon and his chief adviser, Henry Kissinger, attempted to take the United States out of the Vietnam War by turning over more of the war effort to South Vietnam, which the United States supported, and by using massive bombing to pressure North Vietnam into negotiation. In one of their most controversial actions, Nixon and Kissinger began secretly bombing neighboring Cambodia, an officially neutral nation, where North Vietnamese troops were taking refuge.

THE WATERGATE AFFAIR

In 1972, Nixon sought and won reelection against the Democratic candidate, Senator George McGovern. However, on June 17, 1972, five men were arrested for breaking into Democratic campaign headquarters at the Watergate Hotel in Washington, D.C. The Watergate burglars were eventually linked to President Nixon's campaign fund-raising committee, and in 1973 the U.S. Senate created a committee to investigate whether the White House had connections to the burglary and whether people around the president had been trying to prevent a full investigation of the incident.

The discovery of secret audio tapes set up by the president to record White House conversations raised further suspicions, especially when it was found that a crucial part of a tape had been mysteriously erased. The Senate was preparing impeachment proceedings against President Nixon when he announced his resignation on April 8, 1974.

IMPACT

Richard Nixon's role in history continues to be ambiguous. Some historians and commentators on politics have seen him as a far-sighted statesman. They praise his achievement of normalization of diplomatic relations with the People's Republic of China, his negotiation of the Strategic Arms Limitation Talks (SALT I) and the Anti-Ballistic Missile Treaty with the Soviet Union, and other accomplishments in office. In the years following his resignation of the presidency, Nixon often played the part of a respected elder statesman, advising his Republican and Democratic successors in office. By most accounts, he was one of the most intelligent and insightful politicians ever to occupy the office.

Despite his contributions, however, notoriety will undoubtedly continue to haunt Nixon's legacy and many aspects of his career will continue to be controversial. Nixon's characterizations of his early political opponents as communist sympathizers continued to strike a number of historians as ruthless and cynical. The journalist William Shawcross and many others have seen the 1969 bombing of Cambodia as an immoral attack on a neutral country that led to social chaos in that nation.

The most controversial aspect of Nixon's career, though—and one that threatens to overshadow his accomplishments—is the Watergate scandal. This affair is undoubtedly the most lasting source of Nixon's notoriety and perhaps his most substantial legacy. As a result of the Watergate scandal, for the first time an American president resigned his office out of fear of impeachment and acknowledging that remaining in office would be more harmful to the nation than stepping down. If President Gerald Ford had not issued a pardon and granted Nixon immunity, Nixon could easily have faced criminal prosecution.

Most important, Nixon's actions resulted in an erosion of the office of president that would last for decades after he left office: The popular perception of corruption at the highest levels of government undermined public faith in the presidency and in the electoral process. The word "Watergate" became so closely associated with political scandal that scandals afterward were routinely labeled with the "-gate" suffix. When President Ronald Reagan's administration secretly sold arms to Iran in the 1980's, for example, the affair became known as "Irangate." After Watergate, the U.S. presidency, and Americans' trust in their highest elected officials, was eroded by a cynicism that did not exist before 1973.

Further Reading

Morgan, Iwan W. *Nixon.* New York: Oxford University Press, 2002. Morgan takes recent historians' more balanced view of Nixon, challenging previous notions that his career is overshadowed by Watergate. Walks the line between condemning his career entirely and overemphasizing his positive achievements.

Olson, Keith W. *Watergate: The Presidential Scandal That Shook America.* Lawrence: University Press of Kansas, 2003. Olson, a professor of history at the University of Maryland, provides a succinct yet engaging account of the Watergate break-in and subsequent Senate proceedings. Clearly details the actors, their roles, and the outcomes, offering a useful overview from the perspective of thirty years later.

Reeves, Richard. *President Nixon: Alone in the White House.* New York: Simon & Schuster, 2001. A deft and extremely detailed portrayal of the evolution of Nixon's presidency, from his aspiration to provide moral leadership to his siege mentality before and during Watergate. Takes full advantage of one of the most thoroughly documented presidencies on record, ironically in the context of one of the most insular presidencies in U.S. history. More than an analysis of a president, this is an exposé of an anguished mind.

Shawcross, William. *Sideshow: Nixon, Kissinger, and the Destruction of Cambodia.* 1979. Rev. ed. Boulder, Colo.: Cooper Square Press, 2002. Using memoranda and taped meetings, relates what went on behind the scenes regarding what was arguably the second most notorious action of the Nixon presidency, the invasion of Cambodia. Shawcross brings historical context to the events of 1969 by comparing the words of other presidents (including Abraham Lincoln) in somewhat similar circumstances.

—*Carl L. Bankston III*

See also: Charles W. Colson; John D. Ehrlichman; H. R. Haldeman; E. Howard Hunt; G. Gordon Liddy; James W. McCord, Jr.; John Mitchell.

SAPARMURAT NIYAZOV
Dictator of Turkmenistan (1985-   )

BORN: February 19, 1940; Kipchak, near Ashgabat, Turkmenistan

ALSO KNOWN AS: Turkmenbashi (Father of the Turkmen); Saparmurat Atayevich Niyazov (full name)

CAUSE OF NOTORIETY: The sole governmental power in Turkmenistan, Niyazov subjected his people to repressive rule as well as deteriorating health and economic conditions.

ACTIVE: Beginning 1985

LOCALE: Turkmenistan

EARLY LIFE

Saparmurat Niyazov (sah-PAHR-mew-raht NEE-yah-zof) was born to a working-class family near Ashgabat. His father died in battle in World War II; other family members died in the region's devastating 1948 earthquake. Niyazov spent the remainder of his youth partly in an orphanage and partly with distant relatives. Nonetheless, he graduated in engineering from the prestigious Leningrad Polytechnic Institute in 1966.

Beginning his career as an engineer, Niyazov soon rose through Soviet administrative ranks, becoming chairman of the Supreme Soviet of Turkmenistan in 1990; thus he occupied the top administrative post in his country upon Turkmenistan's independence from the Soviet Union in 1991.

POLITICAL CAREER

Niyazov inherited a country a little larger than California, home to 4.5 million people, with many problems and one notable asset: its enormous reserves of natural gas. Manipulating that resource produced most of the country's revenue and provided its government with leverage in world affairs. Niyazov used this leverage to strengthen his position. None of the major foreign powers competing for Turkmenistan's gas showed a willingness to challenge Niyazov's repressive domestic policies.

After his election as president-for-life in 1999, Niyazov subjected his country to increasingly arbitrary personal rule characterized by complete suppression of all political dissent, extreme nationalism, disastrous economic and social policies, and a cult of personality rivaling that of former Soviet premier Joseph Stalin. Niyazov's portrait appeared on currency and stamps, and grandiose statues of the "Turkmenbashi" rose up throughout Turkmenistan. In 2001, he published *Rukhnama*

(*Rukhnama: Reflections on the Spiritual Values of the Turkmen*, 2005), a rambling, paranoid exposition of political and religious philosophy that became required reading in all schools in Turkmenistan.

By periodically purging subordinates, Niyazov could ensure that no one became capable of challenging him. Such purges usually involved charges of complicity with organized crime and drug trafficking. With the fall of the Taliban in Afghanistan in 2002, opium cultivation skyrocketed, and Turkmenistan became the main conduit through which that opium reached Russia. Some observers believe that Niyazov was involved in the drug trade.

High unemployment in Turkmenistan fueled this crime wave. Discriminatory laws closed many professions to people who were not ethnic Turkmen (about 15 percent of the country's population in 2006) or those who had obtained their education outside Turkmenistan. Systematically removing the best-educated and most cosmopolitan people from medicine and education progressively limited access to the associated resources while degrading their quality. The effect on the medical field quickly became evident in rising infant mortality rates, lowered life expectancy, and a resurgence of deadly infectious diseases, including bubonic plague.

Niyazov disbanded the national symphony, opera, ballet, and circus and banned the public performance of recorded music. Religious freedom deteriorated after Turkmenistan's independence. Only the Sunni sect of Islam and the Russian Orthodox Church were recognized, and these were subjected to obnoxious state controls. Other sects were banned, their adherents subject to arrest.

The exact prison population of Turkmenistan, while unknown, was considered to be high and increasing steadily. Mortality rates were high in prisons and labor camps, where torture was routinely used to extract confessions, making trials a travesty of justice.

IMPACT

Turkmenistan became a paradigm of a country sinking into barbarism because of irresponsible government policies, for which Saparmurat Niyazov was primarily responsible. As of 2006, Niyazov's reign of terror in his own country showed no signs of abating. Critics did not dismiss the possibility of Niyazov being an international threat. His rhetoric of extreme nationalism and racial superiority recalled Adolf Hitler and Benito Mussolini. In a politically unstable region, bordered by populous nations with which Turkmenistan had strong historical ties, the potential for escalating conflict posed a significant threat to world peace, especially as the whereabouts of the former Soviet Union's nuclear arsenal remained unknown.

FURTHER READING

Burghart, Daniel L., and Teresa Sabonis-Hall, eds. *In the Tracks of Tamerlane: Central Asia's Path to the Twenty-First Century.* Washington, D.C.: Center for Technology and National Security Policy, National Defense University, 2001. Contains chapters on drug trafficking and oil and gas export policies.

Cummings, Sally N., ed. *Power and Change in Central Asia.* New York: Routledge, 2002. This contrasts reactionary Turkmenistan with its more progressive neighbors.

Peimani, Hooman. *Failed Transition, Bleak Future? War and Instability in Central Asia and the Caucasus.* Westport, Conn.: Praeger, 2002. Emphasis on economic difficulties and common patterns of failed transition following independence.

Turkmenbashy, Saparmyrat (Saparmurat Niyazov). *Rukhnama: Reflections on the Spiritual Values of the Turkmen.* Ashgabat, Turkmenistan: State Publishing Service Turkmenistan, 2005. Niyazov's statement of his philosophy.

—*Martha A. Sherwood*

SEE ALSO: Adolf Hitler; Saddam Hussein; Benito Mussolini; Joseph Stalin.

MANUEL NORIEGA
Military leader and dictator of Panama (1983-1989)

BORN: February 11, 1938; Panama City, Panama
ALSO KNOWN AS: Manuel Antonio Noriega Moreno (full name); Cara de Piña (Pineapple Face)
MAJOR OFFENSES: Drug trafficking, money laundering, and racketeering
ACTIVE: 1967-1989
LOCALE: Panama
SENTENCE: Forty years in prison; subsequently reduced to thirty years

EARLY LIFE

Manuel Antonio Noriega Moreno (MAN-wehl an-TOH-nee-oh noh-ree-AY-gah moh-REH-noh) was born the illegitimate son of Ricaurte Tomás Noriega and the Noriega family's maid, María Moreno. Noriega's father was a lower-middle-class civil servant who worked as an accountant. Noriega's mother left the Noriega family and went back to her hometown, Terraplén. She became ill with tuberculosis and was eventually forced to give Noriega away to his godmother, Luisa Sanchez, who raised him.

As a child, Noriega was described by acquaintances as introverted and studious. When he attended the Instituto Nacional, he met one of his older brothers, Luis Carlos Noriega Hurtado, who influenced Noriega to become more political. Luis was a student political leader and became Noriega's mentor and confidant. Luis also helped Noriega secure a scholarship at the Chorrillos Military School in Lima, Peru.

CRIMINAL CAREER

During his time at military school, Noriega became involved with the Central Intelligence Agency (CIA) and received his first payment from the United States in 1958. Noriega's job was to provide reports to the CIA on any leftists or any teachers within the academy who supported Cuban leader Fidel Castro. In 1967, Noriega began to work in the Panama National Guard under General Omar Torrijos Herrera. Noriega supported Torrijos during the 1968 coup d'état against Arnulfo Arias Madrid, after which Torrijos took power.

As the Panamanian leader, Torrijos promoted Noriega to lieutenant and then in 1970 to lieutenant colonel and chief of military intelligence. At this point, Noriega was given command of the G2 intelligence branch of the National Guard. He traveled to France, England, and Israel to arrange the purchase of weapons for the expanding guard. He also became a member of the counterintelligence and counterespionage organization, which was part of an international network of intelligence agencies. In 1970, Noriega became the official liaison with the CIA. In 1971, the U.S. Bureau of Narcotics and Dangerous Drugs (BNDD), the predecessor of the Drug Enforcement Administration (DEA), arrested and tried Him González Joaquín for smuggling heroin and cocaine to the United States from South America. BNDD agents were informed by González that Noriega was also directly involved in drug trafficking, but American agents chose to ignore this information.

General Torrijos died in 1981 and was succeeded by Rubén Darío Paredes. Noriega succeeded Paredes and assumed power in August, 1983. He manipulated the 1984 and 1989 elections in order to secure the continuation of the military in power. During this time, Noriega helped the left-leaning Nicaraguan ruling party, the Sandinistas. However, he later helped anti-Sandinista armed insurgents, the Contras, smuggle weapons—first into Panama from Cuba, Israel, and the United States and then from Panama into Nicaragua. Although aware of this situation, the United States government did not take any legal action against Noriega at the time, as the Shah of Iran, Mohammad Reza Shah Pahlavi—an ally of the United States—was living in exile in Panama. Both times, with the firearms and drug smugglings, the United States either owed Noriega a favor or chose to turn a blind eye in the name of foreign policy. Noriega was also presumed to be responsible for the 1985 torture and decapitation of Panamanian doctor Hugo Spadafora, who openly criticized his dictatorship.

Manuel Noriega. (AP/Wide World Photos)

LEGAL ACTION AND OUTCOME

In June, 1986, Seymour M. Hersh of *The New York Times* wrote an article titled "Panama Strongman Said to Trade in Drugs, Arms, and Illicit Money," which linked Noriega to drug trafficking. Colonel Roberto Díaz Herrera, second in command of the Defense Forces, retired in May, 1987, and disclosed Noriega's corruption. More Panamanians involved in illegal activities were either caught or turned themselves in; in order to reduce their own sentences, they disclosed more information about Noriega's involvement with the Medellín and Cali drug cartels. Noriega was given the option by authorities to retire and live in exile in Spain; he refused.

In December, 1989, one U.S. marine was shot by members of the Panama Defense Force (PDF), and this incident became a pretext for an intervention by American military forces, which was dubbed Operation Just Cause and had already been planned. The American-led attack on Panama began on December 19, 1989. During the confrontation, twenty-three U.S. soldiers and hundreds of Panamanians died. Noriega turned himself in to the U.S. military on January 3, 1990, and was brought to Miami, where he was charged with drug trafficking, money laundering, and racketeering. He was found guilty on all charges and sentenced on September 16, 1992, to forty years in prison. His sentence was reduced to thirty years in 1999, and he would be eligible for parole in 2029.

IMPACT

It is difficult to determine what finally led the U.S. military to intervene and to end Manuel Noriega's dictatorship. The U.S. government was aware of the corruption involved with Noriega, namely, the money revenue from drug trafficking, money laundering, and the murder of Spadafora. However, the United States held back an intervention because Noriega had collaborated with the CIA and had been on its payroll since 1958. Noriega had also supported U.S. activity from Panama, including facets of the Iran-Contra operation led by Lieutenant Colonel Oliver North. Ultimately, however, most analysts believe that Noriega held intelligence that could affect the United States adversely, which led to his downfall at the hands of the U.S. military. Because of Noriega's power as military leader, he became increasingly autonomous and noncompliant with the U.S. government. The rise and fall of Noriega's military dictatorship attests the corruption and manipulation of information among unethical leaders of states to perpetuate their power.

FURTHER READING

Dale, Peter Scott, and Jonathan Marshall. *Cocaine Politics: Drugs, Armies, and the CIA in Central America.* Berkeley: University of California Press, 1998. Dale and Marshall develop an in-depth analysis of the U.S. war on drugs and its impact both on the United States and on Latin American countries. It includes extensive interviews and secondary sources.

Dinges, John. *Our Man in Panama: The Shrewd Rise and Brutal Fall of Manuel Noriega.* New York: Random House, 1991. Dinges writes an objective and thorough investigation of the rise and fall of Noriega, giving the reader plenty of detailed information to assess Noriega's military career.

Webb, Gary. *Dark Alliance: The CIA, the Contras, and the Crack Cocaine Explosion.* New York: Seven Stories Press, 1999. Webb examines the role of the U.S. government in drug trafficking and its revenues.
—*Kim Díaz*

SEE ALSO: Fidel Castro; Ferdinand Marcos; Anastasio Somoza García.

NOSTRADAMUS
French astrologer, physician, and writer

BORN: December 14, 1503; Saint-Rémy-de-Provence, France

DIED: July 1 or 2, 1566; Salon-de-Provence, France

ALSO KNOWN AS: Michel de Nostredame; Michaletus de Nostra Domina; Michel Nostredame; Michel de Notradame; Michel Notredame (birth name)

CAUSE OF NOTORIETY: Author of a series of almanacs, Nostradamus was thought to have predicted the death of the king; from that arose his fame as wealthy clients sought his counsel and horoscopes.

ACTIVE: 1549-1566

LOCALE: France and throughout Europe

EARLY LIFE

Michel de Nostredame, or Nostradamus (nohs-truh-dah-muhs), as he later became known, was the son of Jaume de Nostredame, a middle-class merchant of Jewish ancestry from Avignon, and of Reynière de Saint-Rémy, the granddaughter of a physician-astrologer from the town of Saint-Rémy-de-Provence. Nostradamus left his hometown of Saint-Rémy-de-Provence at an early age to study in nearby Avignon, where he apparently developed an interest in medicine and pharmacy. From 1521 to 1529, he traveled extensively as a wandering apothecary, collecting firsthand knowledge in the use of common medicinal herbs and remedies. Then, in October of 1529, he enrolled as a student at the renowned Medical School of Montpellier. While there is no record of his graduation anywhere, his future secretary, Jean-Aim de Chavigny,

maintains that he received a doctorate in medicine soon afterward.

From about 1533 to 1546, Nostradamus led an itinerant lifestyle, stopping to practice medicine and observe the craft of experienced healers in various southern

Nostradamus.

NOSTRADAMUS PREDICTS HIS END

In a letter to King Henry II of France, Nostradamus discussed the broad outlines of the future. Here are excerpts and his first two prophetic quatrains:

I readily admit that all proceeds from God and render to Him thanks, honor and immortal praise. I have mixed therewith no divination coming from fate. All from God and nature, and for the most part integrated with celestial movements. It is much like seeing in a burning mirror, with clouded vision, the great events, sad, prodigious and calamitous events that in due time will fall upon the principal worshippers. First, upon the temples of God; secondly, upon those who, sustained by the earth, approach such a decadence. Also a thousand other calamitous events which will be known to happen in due time.

After that Antichrist will be the infernal prince again, for the last time. All the Kingdoms of Christianity will tremble, even those of the infidels, for the space of twenty-five years. Wars and battles will be more grievous and towns, cities, castles and all other edifices will be burned, desolated and destroyed, with great effusion of vestal blood, violations of married woman and widows, and sucking children dashed and broken against the walls of towns. By means of Satan, Prince Infernal, so many evils will be committed that nearly all the world will find itself undone and desolated. Before these events, some rare birds will cry in the air: Hui, Hui [Today, today] and some time later will vanish.

After this has endured for a long time, there will be almost renewed another reign of Saturn, and golden age. Hearing the affliction of his people, God the Creator will command that Satan be cast into the depths of the bottomless pit, and bound there. Then a universal peace will commence between God and man, and Satan will remain bound for around a thousand years, and then all unbound. . . .

> Sitting alone at night in secret study;
> it is placed on the brass tripod.
> A slight flame comes out of the emptiness and
> makes successful that which should not be believed in vain.

> The wand in the hand is placed in the middle of the tripod's legs.
> With water he sprinkles both the hem of his garment and his foot.
> A voice, fear: he trembles in his robes.
> Divine splendor; the God sits nearby.

Source: Nostradamus: The Complete Prophecies, edited and translated by Henry C. Roberts (Brooklyn, N.Y.: Nostradamus Inc., 1962).

lished a permanent residence in Salon-de-Provence, where he married his second wife, Anne Ponsarde, on November 11, 1547.

CAREER

Nostradamus acquired international fame as an astrologer when he began publishing astrological almanacs variously titled *Pronostications* (forecasts), *Almanachs* (almanacs), or *Presages* (predictions) in the 1550's. Similar to the well-known *calendriers des bergers* (shepherds' calendars) popular in France since the fifteenth century, Nostradamus's almanacs typically included a calendar of important dates, discussion of significant astronomical events, and forecasts for the coming year. While there are no known copies of his almanacs for 1550, 1551, or 1556, it appears nonetheless likely that he prepared at least one for publication each year from 1549 until his death in 1566. He saw some of them translated into English, Italian, or German during his lifetime. His final almanac, written for the year 1567, appeared posthumously.

In 1555 he published a compilation of recipes for the preparation of cosmetics, jams, and elixirs under the title *Excellent & moult utile opuscule* (*The Elixirs of Nostradamus*, 1996). This popular book was reprinted five times in as many years and was translated into German in 1572.

Affecting the gift of clairvoyance, he also published in 1555 the first installment of *Les Prophéties de M. Michel Nostradamus* (pb. 1555-1568; *The True Prophecies or Prognostications of Michael Nostradamus*, 1762), a collection of prophetic verse in which he predicted future world events up to the year 3797. In the near-complete edition of 1568, *Les Prophéties* contained a total of 942 quatrains clearly attributable to the author, along with additional quatrains and *sixains* (six-line stanzas) of questionable authenticity.

Summoned to appear before King Henry II of France in the summer of 1555, he came into contact with important members of the royal entourage and appears to have made a favorable impression on the queen consort, Catherine de Médicis, before returning home. By June, 1558, he completed the last three hundred quatrains of *Les Prophéties* and dedicated them to the king. In the

French localities, including Narbonne, Toulouse, and Bordeaux. Very little is known about his first wife and children, who are said to have succumbed to an epidemic in the town of Agen during those years. Following Nostradamus's study and treatment of plague victims in Marseille (1544) and Aix-en-Provence (1546), he estab-

wake of the king's tragic death one year later, curious minds quickly discovered in the seer's obscure quatrains enough elements to convince themselves that he had foreseen the event. Thus, on the eve of the French Religious Wars, people throughout Europe began to take note of his predictions.

Working at his home in Salon-de-Provence, he produced elaborate horoscopes for several heads of state, a common practice in his day. Wealthy clients from France and abroad sought his counsel on matters pertaining to health, business, marriage, politics, even the location of hidden treasure and that of missing relics—and they paid him well for it. In 1564, during a tour of the nation, King Charles IX of France conferred upon Nostradamus the honorable title of Councilor and Physician in Ordinary to the King. Nostradamus died about two years later, at the age of sixty-two.

IMPACT

Over the four and a half centuries following his death, in particular during times of crisis or in the wake of momentous events, credulous devotees of Nostradamus, amateur scholars, shrewd publishers, and merchants of disinformation have vigorously entertained the myth of his prophetic powers. Their creative minds have read into *Les Prophéties*, usually after the fact, visions of such historical moments as the execution of King Charles I of England (1649), the Great Fire of London (1666), the French Revolution (1789-1799), the advent of Napoleon Bonaparte (1804) and that of Adolf Hitler (1933), the election of French president François Mitterrand (1987), the destruction of the World Trade Center (2001), and the Asian tsunami of December 26, 2004.

As critics point out, Nostradamus's prophetic quatrains have been able to generate so much attention because they are as highly suggestive as they are obscure. They are filled with descriptive paraphrase, metaphors,

and fanciful grammar. They follow no chronological order and only 0.5 percent of them are clearly dated. In addition to historical acumen, a high degree of reader participation is required to make any sense of them at all. Scores of Nostradamian writers have deceived their readers and often themselves with ever-ingenious interpretations purported to reveal the seer's true prophetic visions. In the absence of historical perspective, however, such interpretations risk disclosing more about the writers' own hopes and fears than anything Nostradamus himself could have possibly imagined.

FURTHER READING

Brind'Amour, Pierre. *Nostradamus astrophile*. Ottowa, Ont.: Presses de l'Université d'Ottowa, 1993. An in-depth study of astrological thought in the works of Nostradamus; written in French.

Leroy, Edgar. *Nostradamus: Ses Origines, sa vie, son œuvre*. 1972. Reprint. Marseille, France: Laffite Reprints, 1993. An authoritative biography based on archival records. In French.

Randi, James. *The Mask of Nostradamus. The Prophecies of the World Most Famous Seer*. Buffalo, N.Y.: Prometheus Books, 1993. Exposes some of the methods and myths embraced by Nostradamian writers.

Wilson, Ian. *Nostradamus: The Man Behind the Prophecies*. New York: St. Martin's Press, 2003. A judicious, well-researched biography; includes discussion of salient Nostradamian fallacies.

Yafeh, Maziar, and Heath Chip. "Nostradamus's Clever Clairvoyance.'" *Skeptical Inquirer* 27 (2003): 36-40. Evokes briefly some of the reasons for Nostradamus's continuing appeal as a writer of prophetic literature.

                                                                                                                                              —*Jan Pendergrass*

SEE ALSO: Adolf Hitler; Leo X; Roderigo Lopez; Mother Shipton.

TITUS OATES
English dissembler

BORN: September 15, 1649; Oakham, Rutland, England

DIED: July 12 or 13, 1705; London, England

CAUSE OF NOTORIETY: Oates fabricated the so-called Popish Plot in order to overthrow England's Protestant government and restore Catholicism as the state religion. Rumors of the fictional plot fueled preexisting anti-Catholic hysteria, violent purges, and passage of anti-Catholic legislation.

ACTIVE: 1678-1681

LOCALE: London, England

SENTENCE: Fined £100,000 for slander; defrocked and sentenced to life imprisonment, with whippings and pillory, for perjury; later pardoned

EARLY LIFE

Titus Oates (TI-tuhs ohtz), son of an Anabaptist preacher, was born at Oakham, England. An unpromising student, he was expelled from Merchant Taylors' School, London and from Caius College, Cambridge. Subsequently enrolled at St. John's College, Cambridge, he left abruptly in 1669 without a degree.

CAREER

After leaving Cambridge, Oates became an Anglican curate but in 1673 was ejected by his parishioners. He next went to Hastings, where involvement in his father's quarrel with a local family resulted in a charge of perjury, so he left hurriedly in May, 1675, to become chaplain on a boat bound for Tangier. Accused of sodomy, he was soon dismissed.

Back in London in 1676, he was installed as Protestant chaplain in the household of the Roman Catholic earl of Norwich. Shortly afterward, Oates was converted to Roman Catholicism. From 1677 until June, 1678, he was a candidate for the priesthood in Jesuit seminaries, first at Valladolid, Spain, and then at St. Omer, France, from which he was dismissed for deficiency in Latin, scholastic inadequacy, and suspect motivation.

In London again in summer, 1678, Oates was embittered by his most recent failure with the Jesuits. He joined forces with an acquaintance, Israel Tonge, who had long been obsessed with a conviction that the Jesuits planned to kill King Charles II, install his brother James, Duke of York in his place, and so restore Roman Catholicism to England.

THE POPISH PLOT

In September, 1678, Oates, swearing under oath, read the Privy Council a paper of eighty-one articles in which he implicated Edward Coleman, chaplain to the duchess of York, and Sir George Wakeman, the king's physician, among others, in a plot to kill the king. That night Oates accompanied soldiers assigned to arrest those he had accused of treason. After that, Oates testified repeatedly and expansively to the existence of the conspiracy, which soon included the duke of York and Charles II's queen among the major plotters. The king did not believe Oates's stories, but he was unable to overcome the Whigs, who were happy to encourage anything that could prevent the duke of York from succeeding to the throne. As the plot thickened and boiled, Oates, self-proclaimed savior of the nation, was rewarded with an apartment in Whitehall and a generous annual pension.

Between 1670 and 1681, the plot led to legislation that allowed Roman Catholics to be impoverished, fined, imprisoned, and banished. In addition, no fewer than sixteen innocent men were executed as traitors. By 1681, however, the plot had cooled, doubts about Oates's truthfulness were expressed, the king remained alive, and Oates's pension was drastically reduced.

LEGAL ACTION AND OUTCOME

In 1684 Oates was arrested for having called the duke of York a traitor. He was unable to pay the fine of £100,000 and consequently was thrown into debtors' prison. In 1685, immediately after James became king, Oates was indicted for perjury. On May 16 of the same year, he was defrocked and sentenced to stand in the pillory, to be whipped annually, and to be imprisoned for life. This sentence was enforced until December, 1688, when James was overthrown.

In March, 1689, Oates petitioned Parliament to reverse his conviction and to award him damages. After a temporary reimprisonment for fraudulently claiming to have received a doctorate from the University of Salamanca, he was pardoned by William III, James's successor. Shortly afterward, William awarded Oates a pension. In August, 1693, although most likely a homosexual, Oates married a wealthy widow. For a time, until his popularity vanished, he was a successful Baptist preacher. Oates died, impoverished and virtually ignored, on July 12 or 13, 1705.

Impact

The Popish Plot was the direct cause of the imprisonment and execution of a number of innocent Roman Catholics. This bogus plot was responsible for the passage of the Papists' Disabling Act in 1678, a law that excluded Roman Catholics from sitting in Parliament. It was finally repealed in 1829. The failure of the Whig faction to exclude James, duke of York, from the succession after the Popish Plot led the Whigs to attempt the assassination of both Charles II and his brother in 1683. The discovery of this actual Rye House Plot resulted in the trial and execution of a number of prominent Whigs, the same men who had endorsed the judicial murder of the innocent victims of the Popish Plot. Perhaps the only positive result of the Popish Plot was the passage of the Habeas Corpus Act, one of the pillars of modern liberty.

Titus Oates is still a subject of interest to scholars of late seventeenth century English history and to students of political intrigue and espionage. The Whig historian Thomas Babington Macaulay displayed considerable sympathy for Oates on account of the whippings and imprisonment to which he was sentenced, but to other writers and thinkers—including John Dryden, Voltaire, David Hume, Samuel Taylor Coleridge, Herman Melville, Stephen Crane, Bertrand Russell, and George Bernard Shaw—Oates remained the archetypal rogue, liar, and perjurer.

Further Reading

Black, Jeremy, ed. *Culture and Society in Britain, 1660-1800.* Manchester, England: Manchester University Press, 1997. Contains Paul Hammond's essay on Oates's homosexuality.

Greene, Douglas G., comp. *Diaries of the Popish Plot . . . Including Titus Oates's "A True Narrative of the Horrid Plot (1679)."* Delmar, N.Y.: Scholars' Facsimiles and Reprints, 1977. Includes an introduction and index by Greene.

Kenyon, J. P. *The Popish Plot.* London: Heinemann, 1972. Readable account of Oates's role in the plot. Bibliography.

Lane, Jane. *Titus Oates.* 1949. Reprint. Westport, Conn.: Greenwood Press, 1971. The authoritative biography, including an exhaustive list of authorities consulted (pp. 365-370).

—Margaret Duggan and Clifton W. Potter, Jr.

See also: Guy Fawkes.

Dion O'Banion
American gang leader

Born: July 8, 1892; Maroa, Illinois
Died: November 10, 1924; Chicago, Illinois
Also known as: Charles Dean O'Banion (full name)
Major offenses: Bootlegging, theft, carrying concealed weapons, and possibly murder
Active: 1909-1924
Locale: Chicago, Illinois
Sentence: Six months in prison for theft; three months for carrying concealed weapons

Early Life

Born in a small town southwest of Chicago, Dion O'Banion (DEE-ahn oh-BAHN-yuhn) was the son of Charles O'Banion, a barber, and his wife, Emma Brophy, who died of tuberculosis in 1901. Leaving his daughter with an aunt, Charles O'Banion moved his two sons to Chicago. There they made their home in Little Hell, a North Side area noted for its crime, vice, and poverty. Charles and his older son worked in a factory. Dion attended Catholic schools from 1901 to 1907. He worked as a newsboy, selling papers; his lifelong limp may have been the result of an accident that occurred during this time. At sixteen, he became a singing waiter in the notoriously violent McGovern's Saloon and Cabaret; the saloon was closed by reformers.

Criminal Career

O'Banion next joined the violent circulation wars between William Randolph Hearst's *American* and Robert McCormick and Joseph Medill Patterson's *Tribune.* Both sides paid young hoodlums to hijack opposition trucks, destroy opposition papers, and rough up newsboys and dealers who refused to carry only the employer's papers. By 1913, at least twenty-seven news dealers had been shot. Politicians similarly hired young men to intimidate political opponents and voters. O'Banion found more money and excitement in violence than in newspaper sales and waiting tables.

Possessed of a quick mind, considerable daring, an easy smile, and a charismatic personality, he was mentored by racketeers such as Charles "Ox" Reiser (born Frederick Schoeps) and quickly gathered his own followers. These included Hymie Weiss (born Earl Wajciechowski), George "Bugs" Moran, Vincent "Schemer" Drucci (born Victor di Ambrosia), and labor racketeer "Dapper" Day McCarthy. As eager for excitement as for wealth, O'Banion committed crimes for the thrill of it; his followers attempted to tame his impulsiveness. They were partly successful in that O'Banion was convicted of only two offenses, both while he was still a juvenile. In 1909, he was sentenced to six months in the House of Corrections for theft. In 1911, he received a three-month sentence for carrying concealed weapons.

By the start of Prohibition in January, 1920, O'Banion was trained for gang leadership. His political importance was such that he could deliver the vote of Chicago's North Side; this assured him political protection. His experience with the newspaper wars had taught him techniques that would serve him well during Prohibition. He hijacked his first liquor truck on December 30, 1919, before Prohibition began. He sold the hijacked liquor through Samuel "Nails" Morton (born Samuel Markovitz), a Jewish gang leader with contacts on the Canadian border that allowed the illegal importation of liquor. Morton offered his contacts in return for the use of O'Banion's gang. The merger allowed O'Banion to take control of liquor supplies to Chicago's North Side, where he insisted on marketing a quality product in contrast to the dangerously unsanitary and contaminated liquor sold by competitors.

During the period between 1920 and 1924, O'Banion was regarded as the second most important gangster in Chicago; he was second only to the mob headed by Johnny Torrio, soon to be headed by Al Capone. Chicago Police Chief Morgan Collins claimed O'Banion to be responsible for twenty-five murders. O'Banion began to dress like a successful businessman. On February 5, 1921, he married Helen Viola Kaniff. He and Nails Morton bought an interest in the William F. Scofield flower shops, and O'Banion worked in the shop on North State Street across from Holy Name Cathedral, designing extravagant displays for gangster funerals.

His success, his unpredictability, and his violence threatened other gang leaders. He delighted in challenging the authority of Torrio and other competitors. His most daring caper occurred when he offered to sell Torrio and Capone his share in the Sieben Brewery. O'Banion said he wanted to retire and move west. The men agreed and made plans to be at the brewery in time for the first delivery under the new management. O'Banion knew, as the other two did not, that the brewery was to be raided, making the property worthless and guaranteeing Torrio a prison sentence because it would lead to Torrio's second conviction. In the wake of the arrest, O'Banion walked off with the money, leaving a furious Torrio and Capone.

Up to that point, O'Banion was protected by Mike Merlo, head of the Unione Siciliana. Merlo, much respected, apparently foresaw the bloodbath that would follow if O'Banion were killed. Merlo died of cancer on November 8, 1924. Two days later, O'Banion was shot to death in his flower shop, probably by John Scalise, Albert Anselmi, and Frankie Yale (born Francesco Uale), or Mike Genna.

IMPACT

Hymie Weiss, determined for revenge, took over leadership of Dion O'Banion's gang. Weiss was a businessman, but revenge became his primary goal. His first attempted murder of Capone took place on January 12, 1925. On January 24, Torrio was seriously wounded by Weiss and Moran. A series of murders and attempted murders followed. Weiss's attacks increased in frequency and intensity. Capone was behind the October 11 murder of Weiss, who was succeeded as gang leader by Vince Drucci. Drucci was killed while in police custody on April 5, 1927; Bugs Moran became gang leader.

The end of O'Banion's gang came with the St. Valentine's Day Massacre of February 14, 1929, almost certainly set up by Capone to put an end to Moran's threats to Capone's leadership. That massacre became a legend. In 1927, screenwriter Ben Hecht based one of the characters of his script for *Underworld* on O'Banion. A distorted portrayal of O'Banion was filmed in 1931, starring James Cagney as *Public Enemy*. Seventy-two years later, O'Banion remained a potent enough figure to be at the center of novelist Michael O'Rourke's *O'Banion's Gift* (2003).

FURTHER READING

Bergreen, Laurence. *Capone: The Man and the Era.* New York: Touchstone, 1994. Treats rivalry between O'Banion's and Torrio's gangs and O'Banion's death; well documented.

Binder, John J. *Images of America: The Chicago Outfit.* Charleston, S.C.: Arcadia, 2003. Pictorial history covering O'Banion only briefly but correcting errors in earlier Chicago crime literature.

Keefe, Rose. *Guns and Roses: The Untold Story of Dean O'Banion, Chicago's Big Shot Before Al Capone.* Nashville, Tenn.: Cumberland House, 2003. Readable and reliable biography.

Kobler, John. *Capone: The Life and World of Al Capone.* 1971. Reprint. Cambridge, Mass.: Da Capo Press, 2003. Includes O'Banion's attempted challenge to Capone and Torrio.

—*Betty Richardson*

SEE ALSO: Al Capone; Bugs Moran; Hymie Weiss.

GRACE O'MALLEY
Irish pirate

BORN: c. 1530; Connaught, Ireland
DIED: c. 1603; probably Rockfleet, Ireland
ALSO KNOWN AS: Gráinne Ní Mháille (Gaelic name); Grainne Mhaol; Granuaile; Grace the Bald
CAUSE OF NOTORIETY: In the late sixteenth century, O'Malley was notorious for captaining a pirate fleet operating off the coast of Ireland.
ACTIVE: 1566-1603
LOCALE: Ireland

EARLY LIFE

Grace O'Malley (oh-MAL-ee) was the daughter of Owen (Dubhdarra, or Black Oak) O'Malley, a Connaught chieftain. She may have been his only legitimate child. One story says that as a child, she cut her hair to disguise herself as a boy in order to stow away on one of her father's ships as it was leaving for Spain. Her nickname Granuaile came from Grainne Mhaol (Grace the Bald); it is probably a corruption of Gráinne Ní Mháille, the Gaelic form of her name.

In about 1546, O'Malley married Donal O'Flaherty, also known as Donal-an-Chogaidh (Donal of the Battles). Donal had extensive lands and was, in the Gaelic succession system of tanistry, the designated successor to the O'Flaherty clan. The couple lived at O'Flaherty's castle of Bunowen and had two sons, Owen and Murrough, and a daughter named Margaret. However, they do not seem to have been happy, and O'Flaherty's position as tanist heir was compromised when he murdered Walter Burke, the heir to a Burke chieftainship, so that O'Flaherty's nephew Richard-an-Iarainn (Iron Dick) Burke (later to be O'Malley's second husband) could move into the position instead.

PIRATING CAREER

With O'Flaherty's position weakened, O'Malley emerged from the shadows and began to secure the loyalty of his followers for herself. Soon she was leading them on legitimate trading expeditions to Spain and Portugal and also on pirate raids. At some unknown point around this time, O'Flaherty died, and O'Malley returned to her father's territory, where she continued her pirating career from a castle on Clare Island, off the West Coast of Ireland. On one expedition, she rescued a young man and took him as her lover, but he was murdered; O'Malley killed those responsible.

Around 1566, she married Burke, her first husband's nephew, perhaps in a Gaelic "trial" marriage of one year; O'Malley is said to have ended it after she had secured Burke's castle of Rockfleet. The marriage produced one son, Tibbot-na-Long (Theobald of the Ships); legend declares that O'Malley fought an action at sea the day after his shipboard birth. In 1574, the British deputy led an expedition against her, but she prevailed. In 1576, she kidnapped and held for ransom the son of the heir to Howth Castle, near Dublin.

In 1577, O'Malley was finally captured and imprisoned in Limerick for eighteen months. She was then sent to Dublin, but she negotiated her release, possibly as an attempt to control Burke, who was rebelling against the government; she then returned to Connaught. In 1580, Burke became clan leader and was knighted in 1581, but he died in 1583. O'Malley seized his lands, but the new British governor Sir Richard Bingham broke her power and killed her son Owen. Only a rescue by her son-in-law saved O'Malley from death. In 1593, O'Malley took the astonishing step of sailing to London to complain about Bingham to Queen Elizabeth I, who, equally astonishingly, supported O'Malley and recalled him. In 1597, around the age of sixty-seven, she was recorded as leading an attack at sea. She probably died around six years later.

IMPACT

Grace O'Malley challenged every contemporary norm of women's behavior and spawned a lasting legend. In subsequent centuries, musicians, novelists, and playwrights have been inspired by her life to create notable works. A musical play, titled *The Pirate Queen* and based on O'Malley's life, was created in 2006 by Alain Boublil and Claude-Michel Schönberg. Its production at the Chicago Cadillac Palace Theater was announced in November, 2005.

FURTHER READING
Chambers, Anne. *Granuaile: The Life and Times of Grace O'Malley, c. 1530-1603.* Dublin, Ireland: Wolfhound Press, 1997. Chambers's book, which first introduced O'Malley to the wider world, remains the definitive account and provides copious background detail.
Siegfried, Brandie R. "Queen to Queen at Check: Grace O'Malley, Elizabeth Tudor, and the Discourse of Majesty in the State Papers of Ireland." In *Elizabeth I: Always Her Own Free Woman*, edited by Carole Levin, Jo Eldridge-Carney, and Debra Barrett-Graves. Burlington, Vt.: Ashgate, 2003. Points to similarities between O'Malley and Elizabeth I and traces the importance of O'Malley in English and Irish writing of the time.
_____. "'To the Queen's Most Excellent Majesty': Grany ny Mally of Conaught to Elizabeth Tudor." In *Reading Early Women: Texts in Manuscript and Print, 1500-1700*, edited by Helen Ostovich and Elizabeth Sauer. New York: Routledge, 2004. Offers transcriptions and analysis of letters from O'Malley to Queen Elizabeth and from the queen to Sir Richard Bingham, situated in the context of early modern women's writing.

—Lisa Hopkins

SEE ALSO: Charlotte de Berry; Anne Bonny; Cheng I Sao; Mary Read.

ARTHUR ORTON
English impostor

BORN: March 20, 1834; Wapping, England
DIED: April 2, 1898; London, England
ALSO KNOWN AS: Thomas (Tom) Castro; Sir Roger Charles Doughty Tichborne; Tichborne claimant
MAJOR OFFENSES: Posing as heir to the Tichborne estate and perjury
ACTIVE: 1865-1885
LOCALE: Australia and England
SENTENCE: Fourteen years in prison; served ten

EARLY LIFE
Arthur Orton (OOR-tuhn) was a butcher's son from Wapping, England. He traveled in South America to avoid being imprisoned for horse theft and other crimes, and while there he began using the name Tom Castro.

Sir Roger Tichborne, the eldest son of a baronet and heir to a family fortune, disappeared when his ship was lost at sea in the spring of 1854. His mother refused to accept that her favorite son was dead. She sent inquiries all over the world, and one of the replies concerned possible survivors of the shipwreck. Some of the crew and passengers may have been saved by a ship headed for Australia. Maritime law, then and now, stated that the families of the survivors must be notified immediately and the survivors taken to the nearest port. The Tichborne family had received no such notification.

CRIMINAL CAREER
Orton had nothing in common with the aristocratic Sir Roger Tichborne. He spoke not a word of French (Tichborne's native language), weighed approximately two hundred pounds more than the svelte man he was impersonating, had brown eyes to Tichborne's blue, and had little education. He was far from a fool, however. A clever man with a near-photographic memory, he researched the well-known Tichborne family. He sent letters, through his attorney, to Lady Tichborne, claiming to be her son. Also, a former family servant named Andrew Bogle, living in Australia, offered his services to Orton for a percentage of the inheritance. In return, he gave Orton considerable information about Sir Roger and the family.

On February 25, 1866, Lady Tichborne accepted him as her son before she even met Castro. After meeting him, she believed unreservedly that her son had returned to her. The rest of the Tichborne family, however, saw no reason for this obvious impostor to inherit Sir Roger's vast holdings.

LEGAL ACTION AND OUTCOME

Investigators from various parts of the world were hired to see just who this Thomas Castro was. They found that he was actually Arthur Orton, who had worked in several places as a butcher. Orton was denied his claim to the estates of Sir Roger's father, Sir James Tichborne. Two trials were held between 1867 and 1874; in the first it was decided that Orton was an impostor, and in the second, he was found guilty of perjury. He was sentenced to fourteen years in prison, of which he served ten. Orton confessed and then repudiated his confession shortly afterward when he realized that he could make some money on the music-hall circuit by continuing to pose as Tichborne.

IMPACT

Arthur Orton's trial was England's longest legal action to date. Orton was only one of the world's well-known impostors. Edward Kenealy, Orton's attorney, was disbarred for his unwarranted attacks on the Tichborne family, the judges, and the prosecution. The Tichborne baronetcy ended in the 1960's. In Wagga Wagga, Australia, Orton is considered a hero because he made the city famous.

FURTHER READING

Bondeson, Jan. *The Great Pretenders: The True Stories Behind Famous Historical Mysteries*. New York: W. W. Norton, 2004. A detailed look at a series of unsolved historical mysteries. Aside from the Tichborne claimant, it covers the lost dauphin, Kaspar Hauser, and several others.

Chessman, Clive. *Rebels, Pretenders, and Imposters*. New York: St. Martin's Press, 2000. A detailed book describing some lesser-known impostors, not only those who rewrote a family history in order to insert themselves but also those who assumed the identity of real personages.

Maugham, Sir Frederick H. *The Tichborne Case*. Westport, Conn.: Hyperion Press, 1936. Discusses the upper classes of England, especially the family of Baronet Sir Roger Daughty Tichborne. This insightful book begins with the family in the late 1700's and goes through the entirety of the two trials of the claimant.

—*Ellen B. Lindsay*

SEE ALSO: Frank W. Abagnale, Jr.; Billy Cannon; Cassie L. Chadwick; Susanna Mildred Hill; Megan Louise Ireland; Clifford Irving; Victor Lustig; Alexandre Stavisky; Joseph Weil.

LEE HARVEY OSWALD
American assassin

BORN: October 18, 1939; New Orleans, Louisiana
DIED: November 24, 1963; Dallas, Texas
ALSO KNOWN AS: Alex Hidell; Leon Oswald; O. H. Lee
CAUSE OF NOTORIETY: Considered by the Warren Commission to be the lone assassin of President John F. Kennedy, Oswald was arrested for allegedly murdering Dallas police officer J. D. Tippit as well as the Kennedy assassination.
ACTIVE: November 22, 1963
LOCALE: Dallas, Texas

EARLY LIFE

The childhood of Lee Harvey Oswald (AHZ-wahld) was characterized by loneliness. Oswald's mother, Marguerite, was a self-absorbed woman who neglected her children. Oswald's father, Robert Oswald, died of a heart attack two months before Oswald was born. As a young child, Oswald spent a brief time in an orphanage with his older brothers. Oswald had one full-blooded brother, Robert, and a half brother, John Pic. Oswald's brothers both joined the military at a young age, which left him to be raised exclusively by his mother. He spent much of his childhood alone watching television, reading books, and attending a variety of schools from New Orleans to New York City.

In New York, Oswald was picked up by police at the Bronx Zoo and given a truancy hearing. A psychological evaluation found that Oswald was above average in intelligence but demonstrated a passive-aggressive personality with a great deal of hostility toward his mother and society because he was deprived of affection. He also appeared to have delusions of grandeur that were somewhat detached from reality, such as fantasizing about having power over people. As a teenager, Oswald supposedly was handed Marxist literature by someone on the street during the Ethel and Julius Rosenberg trial; he thus began to develop an interest in communism and a hatred for capitalism.

CAREER

Oswald joined the Marines when he was seventeen. As a Marine, he began teaching himself the Russian language. He was stationed at a U.S. airbase in Atsugi, Japan, where he worked as a radar operator on the U-2 spy plane project. Oswald became resentful about reprimands from military superiors, and he applied for an honorable discharge. After his discharge, Oswald defected to the Soviet Union with the promise of turning over military secrets. After the Soviets granted him a six-day visa, Oswald applied for citizenship to the Soviet Union but was denied; he subsequently attempted suicide by slitting his wrist. Because the Soviet Union sensed an international controversy, Oswald was admitted with a work visa and given employment at a radio factory in Minsk.

He lived in the Soviet Union from 1959 to 1962 and was supplied with a stipend and a nice apartment by the Soviet government. He dated many Russian women and ultimately married Marina Pruskova in 1961.

Oswald eventually became disillusioned by the communist system in the Soviet Union because the party elites maintained all of the advantages. He also was disappointed to find that the brand of communism practiced in Russia had abandoned Marxist principles. Oswald returned with his wife and daughter, June, to the United States in 1962.

From June, 1962, to November, 1963, Oswald worked for a commercial photography business, a coffee company, and, finally, the Texas School Book Depository in Dallas. In March, 1963, Oswald purchased a rifle and a revolver from a mail-order company. In April, he allegedly attempted to assassinate General Edwin Walker, a right-wing extremist. Because of his interest in Cuban leader Fidel Castro, Oswald started a chapter of the Fair Play for Cuba Committee in New Orleans. In August, Oswald was arrested twice in disturbances with anti-Castro Cubans and later appeared on radio talk shows to express his Marxist views. In September, Oswald took a bus trip to Mexico City, where he visited the Soviet and Cuban embassies in an attempt to obtain a visa to enter Cuba. After he was denied entrance into Cuba, Oswald returned to his family in Texas and obtained employment at the Book Depository.

THE ASSASSINATION

On November 22, 1963, Oswald allegedly shot three times with his rifle at President Kennedy's motorcade from the sixth floor of the Book Depository; his third shot struck Kennedy in the head and killed him. Oswald fled the depository and fatally shot Dallas police officer J. D. Tippit in an attempt to escape arrest. Oswald was eventually arrested in a Texas theater. While in custody, Oswald claimed that he was a "patsy."

Less than forty-eight hours after his arrest, Oswald was murdered by a Dallas nightclub owner, Jack Ruby, who shot Oswald in the basement of the Dallas city jail. The murder of Oswald by Ruby was aired live on national television and caused a majority of Americans to believe that the assassination of Kennedy involved a conspiracy. In 1964, the Warren Com-

Lee Harvey Oswald in custody. (AP/Wide World Photos)

mission concluded that Oswald had acted alone in the assassination, portraying him as a disconnected Marxist with few friends. However, in 1979, the House Select Committee on Assassinations concluded that the assassination was probably the result of a conspiracy. The select committee recommended that the Justice Department reopen the investigation, but as of 2006, it had not done so.

IMPACT

The Kennedy assassination significantly affected the American people, who lost a young and popular president. However, the assassination created momentum for the passage of the Civil Rights Act of 1964. President Kennedy had supported civil rights for African Americans, but he was unable to get legislation passed in Congress because of Republicans and southern Democrats who opposed civil rights. The assassination also exposed flaws in the Secret Service's methods of protecting the president and led to major changes in presidential security. Finally, the Kennedy assassination created an environment for conspiracy theories and political alienation among the American public as well as a lack of trust in government, arising from the inconclusive results of the investigations by the Warren Commission as opposed to the House.

FURTHER READING

Clarke, James W. *American Assassins: The Darker Side of Politics*. 1982. Rev. ed. Princeton, N.J.: Princeton University Press, 1990. Clarke develops a typology for analyzing political assassins throughout American history.

Mailer, Norman. *Oswald's Tale: An American Mystery*. New York: Random House, 1995. Mailer examines the life of Oswald in an attempt to understand Oswald and also to understand who killed Kennedy.

Posner, Gerald. *Case Closed: Lee Harvey Oswald and the Assassination of JFK*. New York: Random House, 1993. Posner makes the argument that Oswald acted alone in the assassination of Kennedy.

Warren Commission. *The Official Warren Commission Report on the Assassination of President John F. Kennedy*. Garden City, N.Y.: Doublesay, 1964. The report provides a comprehensive analysis of Oswald and presents compelling evidence that Oswald acted alone in the assassination.

—*Scott P. Johnson*

SEE ALSO: John Wilkes Booth; Leon Czolgosz; Charles Julius Guiteau; Jack Ruby.

OSWALD RE-CORPSED

Of all the conspiracy theories surrounding the assassination of President John F. Kennedy, one of the earliest and most byzantine came from a British author. In *The Oswald File* (1977), Michael Eddowes insisted that Lee Harvey Oswald did not kill the president. Instead, he claimed, a Russian agent did it, a "look-alike" for Oswald. Eddowes adduced various bits of evidence for his argument, but his principal claim was that the autopsy performed on the man killed by Jack Ruby did not match the Marine Corps medical records for Oswald. Ergo, Russia was involved.

Eddowes was persistent. He proposed that a reexamination of Oswald's body would prove him right. After several legal battles with medical officials in Texas and wrangles with Oswald's brother Robert, Eddowes managed to get the widow, Marina Oswald Porter, to agree to an exhumation of the body. On October 3, 1981, it took place, paid for by Eddowes. Backhoes uncovered the inexpensive coffin, buried seventeen years earlier. It was found to have cracked and let in water, and the corpse was in advanced decomposition. Nonetheless, forensic specialists Linda E. Norton, James A. Cottone, Irvin M. Sopher, and Vincent J. M. DiMaio performed a detailed examination the next day at Baylor Hospital of Dallas. They published their findings in the *Journal of Forensic Sciences* (January, 1984). They conclude unequivocally,

> A news conference was held at approximately 3:00 P.M. (CDT) on 4 Oct., 1981, at Baylor Medical Center for the examination team to announce that based upon the forensic science examination conducted that date, "the remains in the grave marked as Lee Harvey Oswald are indeed Lee Harvey Oswald." This conclusion was based upon comparison of the postmortem dental findings with existing antemortem dental charts and radiographs. The left mastoidectomy defect also correlated with the antemortem medical records.

However, Eddowes's conspiracy theory had grown too popular to be refuted simply by expert testimony. Soon enthusiasts were claiming that robbers had broken open the coffin before the exhumation and taken away the Russian agent's body, or at least its head, and replaced it with Oswald's. The conspiracy grew ever more fanciful but never died.

EUSAPIA PALLADINO
Italian medium

BORN: January 21, 1854; Minerva-Murge, near Bari
(now in Italy)
DIED: May 16, 1918; Naples, Italy
ALSO KNOWN AS: Eusapia Maria Palladino (full
name)
CAUSE OF NOTORIETY: Palladino was a well-known
spiritualist whose admirers continued to believe in
her powers even after she was caught faking
paranormal phenomena at numerous séances.
ACTIVE: 1872-1918
LOCALE: Italy, England, France, and the United
States

EARLY LIFE
When Eusapia Palladino (YEW-say-pee-uh pahl-ah-
DEE-noh) was born, her mother died in childbirth. Palladino's father, who placed her in the care of friends, was
allegedly murdered while she was still young. After
working at various jobs, she obtained a position as nurse-
maid with a family in Naples. Her supposed talents as a
medium were identified in 1872 by an Italian psychic investigator named Damiani, who was allegedly guided to
her by directions that his English wife had received from
the spirit of one John King during a London séance.
Palladino made slow but significant progress in her new
trade, contriving the spectral manifestations that made
her famous in the late 1870's. John King—whose rein-
carnated daughter she was supposed to be—remained
her spirit "control," communicating by means of raps
and trance-induced speech (but never in his supposedly
native English—a language that the illiterate Palladino
never mastered).

SPIRITUALIST CAREER
Palladino was an exceptionally histrionic medium. As
she manipulated nearby objects, and especially when
moving furniture, her hands bound, she put on considerable shows of suffering. She was also obliging, usually
managing to produce the phenomena urgently demanded
by her clients. She was recruited by the credulous investigator Ercole Chiaia in 1891 to assist him in convincing the famous proto-psychologist Cesare Lombroso of
the reality of spiritualism. Lombroso was suitably impressed—although he subsequently observed her faking
on numerous occasions—and Palladino became famous.
She reportedly married one Raphael Delgaiz, but he
remained a near-invisible presence in her public life.

As a result of Lombroso's interests, Palladino was investigated by a panel of scientists in Milan, including the
astronomers Giovanni Schiaparelli and Carl du Prel. After convincing this company of her ability to touch them
with a living hand while her own were apparently bound,
she began exhibiting her skills more widely. The English
investigators Oliver Lodge and F. W. H. Myers observed
her in 1894 and returned a favorable report to the Society
for Psychical Research (SPR). Criticism by Richard
Hodgson and others, on the basis that all the phenomena
could be explained if she could free one hand from her
bonds, was turned aside.

Hodgson and the stage magician J. N. Maskelyne
were both invited to séances held at Myers's house in
Cambridge, where they observed "much conscious and
deliberate fraud, of a kind which must have needed long
practice to bring it to its present level of skill." Palladino's supporters immediately leapt to her defense and
began to arrange further examinations by more sympathetic investigators, some of whom alleged that she released her hand only reflexively, to touch her aching
head. In 1898 a series of séances was arranged in Paris
for the specific purpose of redeeming her reputation, including some held at the home of the French astronomer
Camille Flammarion, the most prestigious popularizer of
spiritualism in that era. Palladino was investigated in
Genoa in 1901 and again in Paris in 1905-1907, with
Marie and Pierre Curie among the observers. Fraud was
repeatedly detected, but this did not deter many of the
observers from reporting that genuine phenomena also
occurred. By 1908 the SPR skeptics had recanted. Palladino was invited to the United States in 1909; she was
caught cheating at several séances held there, but her
champions remained adamant in her defense.

IMPACT
Eusapia Palladino was the most important of all the me-
diums of the late nineteenth century. No other was subjected to such intense scrutiny by investigators, and the
results of that scrutiny proved very revealing as to the
intensity of her fans' desire to believe in her abilities, no
matter how often she was caught cheating. Many
convinced spiritualists believed then—and many still
believe—that Palladino provided the best evidence
available for the reality of psychic phenomena. Skeptics
concurred but disagreed sharply in their opinion of the
import of the evidence.

FURTHER READING

Carrington, Hereward. *Eusapia Palladino and Her Phenomena*. New York: B. W. Dodge, 1909. A significant popularization of Palladino's career, written from a credulous viewpoint, which adopts a polemical tone in proclaiming Palladino to be a fine advertisement for spiritualism.

Doyle, Arthur Conan. "The Career of Eusapia Palladino." Chapter 1 in *The History of Spiritualism*. Vol. 2. 1926. Reprint. New York: Arno Press, 1975. Doyle is as credulous as Carrington but strikes a rather different pose, pretending greater objectivity and paying more attention to the supposed significance of the tests to which Palladino was subject.

Feilding, Everard. *Sittings with Eusapia Palladino, and Other Studies*. New Hyde Park, N.Y.: University Books, 1963. Extracts from the *Proceedings of the Society for Psychical Research* 23 (1909), which offer a detailed account of the SPR's investigation of Palladino, along with other similar inquiries.

Flammarion, Camille. *Mysterious Psychic Forces*. Boston: Small Maynard, 1907. One of Flammarion's many popularizations of spiritualism, including an elaborate account of his own observations of Palladino and the endorsements offered by his fellow astronomers.

—*Brian Stableford*

SEE ALSO: Billy Cannon; Susanna Mildred Hill; Megan Louise Ireland; Clifford Irving; Victor Lustig; Arthur Orton; Alexandre Stavisky; Joseph Weil.

BONNIE PARKER
American robber and murderer

BORN: October 1, 1910; Rowena, Texas

DIED: May 23, 1934; near Gibsland, Bienville Parish, Louisiana

ALSO KNOWN AS: Bonnie Elizabeth Parker (full name); Bonnie of "Bonnie and Clyde" (with Clyde Barrow)

CAUSE OF NOTORIETY: Parker, along with Clyde Barrow, enacted a violent crime spree of robbery and murder.

ACTIVE: 1932-1934

LOCALE: Southern, midwestern, and southwestern United States

EARLY LIFE

Bonnie Elizabeth Parker (PAHR-kuhr) was born into a loving but utterly destitute family. Her father, a bricklayer, died when Bonnie was young, leaving her often unemployed mother alone to rear three children. In desperation, Emma Parker moved her family to Cement City, Texas, a suburb of Dallas, to live with her parents. Young Parker was a bright and popular child and excelled in the creative arts. Favoring colorful clothes and usually wearing a hat, the strawberry blond petite girl (she was under five feet tall and weighed less than one hundred pounds) was often the center of attention. At age sixteen, she married Roy Thornton, a petty career criminal who was sentenced to five years in prison in 1929. Although Parker and Thornton never were divorced, their relationship ended at this time.

Parker found work as a waitress at Marco's Café in east Dallas. Personable and proficient, she did well and earned good tips, but the restaurant soon closed. Bored, alone, and again poverty-stricken, Parker seemed to be aimless when, in January, 1930, her life took a criminal turn.

CRIMINAL CAREER

Parker met Clyde Barrow through mutual friends in Dallas. Their mutual attraction was immediate, and they were quickly inseparable. Barrow was from Telico, Texas, one year older than Parker, and already a hardened career criminal. From a sharecropping family, he never showed any predilection for hard work or education, dropping out of school after the fifth grade. The Barrow family moved to Dallas in 1921, and Barrow, often accompanied by his older brother Buck, became progressively more involved in criminal activity, such as selling stolen goods. Shortly after meeting Parker, Barrow was arrested and taken to Denton and then to Waco to face a variety of charges, including car theft.

Parker's career in crime apparently began when she smuggled a Colt pistol to Barrow, who promptly used it to escape. Fleeing to Ohio without Parker, Barrow was caught in Middletown and sentenced to fourteen years in prison. Hating both work and incarceration, Barrow had several of his toes cut off with an ax to avoid chain-gang labor. His mother wrote a sincere letter of apology on her son's behalf, and that, accompanied by his crippling injury, led to his release in February, 1932.

Bonnie Parker. (Library of Congress)

New Mexico, and allegedly several other states. The role Parker played in the mayhem has been debated, but most accounts portray her as an active participant.

In March, 1933, while hiding in Joplin, Missouri, the gang was taken by surprise by the local police, who had mistaken them for bootleggers. They managed to escape, although Jones and Barrow were wounded. Shortly thereafter, Parker was seriously injured in a flaming car wreck in Wellington, Texas, suffering a shattered leg that never fully healed. Buck Barrow was shot in the head in another fight at Platte City, Missouri, and then killed in yet another confrontation.

Parker was always fatalistic and knew by early 1934 that Barrow's and her demise was near. Nevertheless, they continued their criminal activity, freeing Hamilton from prison in a burst of fire from a machine gun that left a guard dead. Texas governor Miriam Ferguson put together a task force led by former Texas Ranger Frank Hamer and charged it with bringing Barrow and Parker to justice. While being chased by Hamer, Barrow killed another three law officers.

At some point, in exchange for a pardon for his son, Methvin had told Hamer where the gang was located and what road Barrow used while traveling between the Methvin farm and nearby Black Lake, Louisiana. With this information, Hamer located Barrow and Parker. After waiting in ambush for seven hours, the posse killed the couple in an avalanche of 167 rounds of steel-coated, high-velocity bullets on May 23, 1934.

IMPACT

Bonnie Parker has often been portrayed as a fascinating, romantic, nonconforming figure. The fact that she was a small, beautiful, and intelligent woman in a field dominated by abhorrent male career criminals—and her gift for self-promotion—made her something of a heroic figure to some. Her main legacy, however, was her example that women could be as violent and as bloodthirsty as any man. In the years following her death, she was often characterized as a sympathetic figure, the victim of poverty, circumstances, and bad influences. Many historians counter, however, that Parker was always the victimizer.

Barrow tried very briefly to go straight but quickly abandoned the idea, picked up Parker, and resumed his criminal behavior. The police caught them in Kaufman, Texas. Barrow escaped in a shoot-out, but Parker was captured and held for two months while prosecutors tried without success to build a case against her; she was ultimately released. While Parker was in jail, Barrow was implicated in the murder of John Butcher, a jewelry store owner. Later, two police officers in Oklahoma were murdered as they approached the car in which Barrow and Parker were sitting. By this point, the couple had pledged never to be taken alive again.

Parker and Barrow robbed grocery stores, gas stations, and small banks—targets that they believed would be lightly guarded. They developed a reputation for gratuitous violence, often targeting law enforcement officers. Sometimes joined by fellow criminals W. D. Jones, Raymond Hamilton, Henry Methvin, and Barrow's brother Buck, the Barrow gang terrorized the law and business communities in Texas, Oklahoma, Missouri,

FURTHER READING

Barrow, Blanch Caldwell. *My Life with Bonnie and Clyde*. Norman: University of Oklahoma Press, 2004. A firsthand source written by the widow of Buck Barrow. Not surprisingly, the author is protective and defensive toward Buck and disparaging toward her perceived rival, Parker.

Flowers, H. Lorraine, and R. Barri Flowers. *Murder in the United States: Crimes, Killers, and Victims of the Twentieth Century*. Jefferson, N.C.: McFarland, 2001.

An accurate overview of Parker's criminal career, related in substantial detail.

Steele, Phillip W., and Marie Barrow Scoma. *The Family Story of Bonnie and Clyde*. Gretna, La.: Pelican, 2000. A sympathetic account of the Barrow gang's criminal activities. It reiterates in some detail Barrow's and Parker's devotion to their respective families.

—*Thomas W. Buchanan*

SEE ALSO: Clyde Barrow.

ANTE PAVELIĆ
Croatian dictator (1941-1945)

BORN: July 14, 1889; Bradina, Bosnia
DIED: December 28, 1959; Madrid, Spain
ALSO KNOWN AS: Anton Pavelitc; Ante Plavelitch; Pedro Gonner; Butcher of the Balkans
CAUSE OF NOTORIETY: To Serbs, Pavelić is known as the butcher of the Balkans because of his culpability in the deaths of 500,000 Serbs, 80,000 Jews, and 30,000 Gypsies. He is considered responsible by some for the elimination of Croatian Orthodox Christians.
ACTIVE: 1941-1945
LOCALE: Croatia

EARLY LIFE

Ante Pavelić (AHN-teh PAH-veh-lihch) was born on July 14, 1889, in Bradina, Bosnia. From an early age, Pavelić nurtured strong Croatian nationalistic sentiments and advocated an independent sovereign state. The Treaty of London (April, 1915), in effect, divided Croatia and Slovenia between Italy and Serbia. Pavelić strongly objected to Croatia's union with Serbia in 1918, resulting in the first Yugoslav state, which Pavelić considered illegal. His own vision was that of a Croatian independent state whose territory would stretch from the Drava River to the Adriatic Sea.

POLITICAL CAREER

Pavelić in 1928 founded the militant and separatist organization known as Ustaše (Insurrection, from the Croatian word *ustanak*, meaning "uprising"). That same year, he became head of the Croat Party of Rights. In 1929 Pavelić went into exile in Italy as a result of his anti-Yugoslav activity. There he enjoyed the protection of Benito Mussolini's Fascist regime, which provided

training camps for Pavelić's Ustaše followers. Mussolini declared Pavelić a *poglavnik* ("leader" or *führer)*. Pavelić would reward Mussolini for his support when, in 1941, he ceded to Italy Yugoslavia's entire Dalmatian Coast.

From Italy, Pavelić and his organization plotted the assassination of King Alexander I of Yugoslavia, whose regime Pavelić considered a dictatorship. Alexander I was responsible for the assassination in 1928 of Stjepan Radić, the leader of the Croatian Peasant Party. In the aftermath of Radić's murder, Pavelić became head of the Croat Party of Rights and began a campaign of terror, including bombings inside the Yugoslavian kingdom. Mussolini provided not only sympathy but also financial support to the increasingly powerful Ustaše.

To offset the Italian Fascist support of the Croatian Ustaše movement, the Yugoslav king sought to improve his ties with France; he needed French support in the face of Mussolini's ambition toward the Adriatic coast. Toward this end, Alexander went to Marseilles to meet with the French foreign minister. There Alexander was assassinated on October 10, 1934, by the Ustaše, in collaboration with the Macedonian Revolutionary Organization (IMRO). IMRO leader Dido Kvaternik, along with Pavelić, was placed under arrest in Italy, but the two were soon released. In France, where the foreign minister, Louis Barthou, had been killed in the same violent act, both were sentenced in absentia to death.

On April 6, 1941, Pavelić went back to Croatia, along with the Nazi-Fascist troops of occupation, and proclaimed the Nesavisna Država Hrvatske (NDH), or Independent State of Croatia. The NDH was not supported by the leader of the Croatian Peasant Party, Vlatko Maćek (1878-1964), or Croatian archbishop (later cardinal)

PRINCIPLES OF THE USTAŠE MOVEMENT

Ante Pavelić, in "Principles of the Ustaše Movement" (translated by Sinisa Djuric, 1929), set forth Ustaše's goals:

1. The Croatian nation is an independent ethnic and national unit. . . .

7. The state of Croatia was already formed when many other nations lived in complete chaos. The Croatian nation preserved its state through the centuries until the end of the World War, and never abandoned it, not by any act or by any legal resolution, nor did it give away its rights to anyone else, but at the end of the World War foreign forces prevented the Croatian people from exercising their sovereign right to form their own CROATIAN STATE.

8. The Croatian nation has the right to revive its sovereign authority in its own Croatian State in its entire national and historical area, that is to say to re-constitute a complete, sovereign and independent Croatian state. This re-constitution may be accomplished by any means, including force of arms.

9. The Croatian nation has the right of happiness and prosperity, and every single Croat has that right as a part of the Croatian nation. . . .

10. The Croatian nation is sovereign, therefore only it has the right to rule an independent state of Croatia and to manage all state and national affairs.

11. In the Croatian state and in the national affairs of a sovereign and independent state of Croatia no one can make decisions who is not by origin and by blood a member of Croatian nation. . . .

12. The Croatian nation belongs to western culture and to western civilization.

13. The peasantry is not only the foundation and source of life, but it alone constitutes the Croatian nation. . . .

14. All classes of the Croatian people constitute one unified whole, defined by their Croatian blood. . . . In ninety-nine out of a hundred cases someone in Croatia who does not originate from a peasant family is not a Croat at all, but a foreign immigrant. . . .

17. Balanced breeding, the promotion and perfection of these virtues and branches of national life is the goal of all public welfare and of state authority as such, because they have guaranteed survival for centuries of existence and will guarantee the prosperity of future generations of the Croatian nation and existence of that security in the independent Croatian state.

Alojzije Stepinac (1898-1960), who both considered the Ustaše state a puppet government of Germany and Italy.

In a speech on July 22, 1941, Mile Budak, the deputy leader (*doglavnik*) of the NDH, stated that the goal of the Croatian regime was to expel a third of the non-Croatian population, convert a third to Catholicism, and murder the remaining third. A concentration camp off Jasenovac was established for the Ustaše Black Legion's purposes in order to carry out the murders. In 1942, German and Italian troops had to intervene to stop the slaughter of the Ustaše Black Legion. After the fall of Mussolini in 1943, the Ustaše state began to fall apart, yet the killings continued until 1945.

This formally independent state of Croatia lasted until 1945, when Tito and his partisans occupied Croatian territory. At that point, the Ustaše state collapsed. Many Croatian nationalists escaped to Austria, hoping that the occupying British would spare their lives. The British, however, sent them back to Yugoslavia, where many of them were condemned and executed. Pavelić managed to escape in August, 1945, to Austria's American zone and then to Italy in 1946, where he enjoyed the protection of the Vatican in the monastery of San Girolamo until 1948. He moved on to Argentina with the help of a Catholic priest, Krunoslav Draganovic, by means of the famous "Ratline" which had arranged the escape of many criminals, including Nazis Klaus Barbie and Adolf Eichmann.

In Buenos Aires, Pavelić formed a new Ustaše movement with other NDH fugitives, called the Croatian Liberation Movement. Following an attempt on his life on April 10, 1957, by unknown assailants suspected of being Tito's emissaries, Pavelić went to Spain, where he died stateless in Madrid on December 28, 1959, a result of wounds he suffered in that shooting. His assassin later identified himself as Blagoje Jovovic, an émigré from Montenegro. Jovovic dictated the events of the ambush to a journalist, Tihomir-Tiho Burzanovich, whose resulting book is titled *Two Bullets for Pavelić* (2003).

IMPACT

According to the Simon Wiesenthal Center in the United States, the Ustaše regime murdered 30,000 Jews, 29,000 Roma Gypsies, and 500,000 Serbs. The United States Holocaust Memorial Museum estimates the number of Serbs killed to be between 330,000 and 390,000.

Croatia became an independent and sovereign country on October 7, 1991, having declared its dissociation from Yugoslavia and having been recognized by the international community. Many Croatians consider Pavelić the father of Croatia's independence and are willing to overlook his bloody history. They are well conscious of the fact that the opposing side engaged in similar deeds upon its return to power in 1945 and in the subsequent bloody history of the region until January 15, 1992, when the European Community gave Croatia its official recognition as an independent sovereign state. Pavelić remains, however, a war criminal.

FURTHER READING

Banac, Ivo. *The National Question in Iugoslavia*. Ithaca, N.Y.: Cornell University Press, 1984. A thorough historical analysis of the national question of Yugoslavia, focusing on the years 1918-1921, when the kingdom of the Serbs, Croats, and Slovenes was formed. Provides a study of the origins of the subsequent tragic history of these lands.

Burzanovich, Tihomir-Tiho. *Two Bullets for Pavelić: The Story of Blagoje Jovovic*. Translated by Sinisa Djuric. Banja Luka, Bosnia: The Pavelic Papers, 2003. An autobiographical account and confession by the man who claims to have shot Pavelić in front of his residence in Buenos Aires in 1957.

Mačeck, Vladko. *In the Struggle for Freedom*. Translated by Elizabeth and Stjepan Gazi. University Park: Pennsylvania State University Press, 1957. An autobiographical and historical account of the Croatian question from World War I to the creation of Yugoslavia. The author was the leader of the Croatian Peasant Party.

Pavelić, Ante. *Putem hrvatskog dr avnog prava: Čanci, gorovi, izjave*. 1942. Reprint. Buenos Aires: Domovina, 1977. Pavelic's account of the events, the personalities, the speeches, and the facts making up the road map for "the national rights" and the creation of the Ustaše movement (1918-1929).

—*Giuseppe Di Scipio*

SEE ALSO: Adolf Hitler; Radovan Karadžić; Slobodan Milosević; Benito Mussolini; Račić Puniša; Tito.

CHARLES PEACE
English burglar and murderer

BORN: May 14, 1832; Sheffield, England
DIED: February 25, 1879; Armley Prison, Leeds, England
ALSO KNOWN AS: Charles Frederick Peace (full name); John Ward
MAJOR OFFENSES: Numerous burglaries and two murders
ACTIVE: 1850-1878
LOCALE: England
SENTENCE: Death by hanging

EARLY LIFE

Charles Peace (pees) was born in Nursery Road, Sheffield, the son of a shoemaker. He had little schooling and was barely literate, but accounts of his early life given in the fictionalized biographies published immediately after his death claim that he had a remarkable talent for music, especially playing the violin. Whatever truth there may be in these claims, he was apprenticed at the local steel mill, where he suffered two serious accidents. One cost him three fingers (which must have severely inhibited his musical endeavors), and another left him with a permanent limp. In spite of these handicaps—or perhaps because of them—he began to cultivate a new career as a burglar.

CRIMINAL CAREER

Like most famous cat burglars, Peace was small and slender and showed little initial aptitude for the business. He was imprisoned for the first time at age eighteen and was returned to jail frequently in the 1850's. In 1859 he met Hannah Ward, a widow with a young child; she and Peace had a daughter of their own and a son who died in infancy. They lived a peripatetic existence, moving on from the scenes of Peace's more successful crimes, but returned to Sheffield in 1872, where Peace set up shop as a picture framer and seller of musical instruments.

If Peace's intention was to go straight, it was ruined when he began an affair with a young neighbor, Katherine Dyson. After he threatened her husband, Arthur, with a gun in the course of a violent quarrel, a warrant was issued for Peace's arrest, and he fled the city in 1876. During a robbery in Whalley Range, Manchester, in August of that year he shot and killed a policeman, Nicholas Cock—a murder for which another man, William Habron, was subsequently convicted. In November Peace returned to Sheffield, where he shot and killed Arthur Dyson. He fled again, now wanted for murder.

In Nottingham, Peace acquired another mistress, Sarah Grey (whose name is given in the fictionalized biographies as Susan Thompson). Grey traveled with Peace—who was now calling himself John Ward—and Hannah Ward to London. There Peace and Sarah posed as man and wife, while Hannah played the part of their housekeeper. In October, 1878, however, he was ambushed by two policemen during a burglary in Blackheath. Although he contrived to shoot one of them, Edward Robinson, in the arm, he was overpowered.

LEGAL ACTION AND OUTCOME

When John Ward was convicted of the attempted murder of Edward Robinson, Sarah Grey revealed his true identity, apparently in order that she might claim a one-hundred-pound reward. Peace was sent back to Yorkshire to stand trial for Arthur Dyson's murder. He escaped by jumping off the train while being transferred but was later found unconscious, lying in the snow next to the line. After a short delay occasioned by his injuries, Peace was convicted of Dyson's murder. He confessed to the Whalley Range murder before being hanged at Armley Prison in Leeds.

IMPACT

Charles Peace's exploits established him as the most famous career criminal of his era, but the legendary tradition that had made romantic antiheroes out of such celebrated bandits as Dick Turpin and Jack Sheppard had fallen into some disrepute under the repressions of Victorianism. Although a sensational "penny dreadful" serialized work appeared, making as much melodramatic

capital as possible out of his exploits, Peace excited more disdain than sympathy in his own era. The late twentieth century vogue for "true crime" stories renewed interest in him, however, and accounts of his career based on the fictionalized sources are prolifically distributed on the World Wide Web.

FURTHER READING

Charles Peace: Or, The Adventures of a Notorious Burglar. London: G. Purkess, 1880. A text originally issued as a serialized work in one hundred parts; an interesting example of a late "penny dreadful" attempting to revive the tradition of eighteenth century broadsides and sensationalist pamphlets in a typically Victorian format. Like earlier works in the tradition, it claims—falsely, one supposes—to be based on confessions made by Peace before his execution.

The Master Criminal: The Life Story of Charles Peace. London: Fredonia Books, 2003. A print-on-demand publication reprocessing a digest of the fictionalized biography for modern "true crime" aficionados.

Shore, W. Teignmouth, ed. *Trials of Charles Frederick Peace*. Edinburgh: William Hodge, 1926. A not-altogether-successful attempt to correct and counterbalance the fictionalized biography, which retains too much sensationalism to be reckoned historically scrupulous.

Ward, David. *King of the Lags: The Story of Charles Peace*. Foreword by Richard Whittington-Egan. 1964. Reprint. London: Souvenir, 1989. A journalistic account based on the fictionalized biography.

—*Brian Stableford*

SEE ALSO: Jack Sheppard; Dick Turpin.

THOMAS JOSEPH PENDERGAST
American machine politician

BORN: July 22, 1872; St. Joseph, Missouri
DIED: January 26, 1945; Kansas City, Missouri
MAJOR OFFENSE: Two counts of income tax evasion
ACTIVE: January 22, 1935-October 23, 1936
LOCALE: Chicago, Illinois; Kansas City, Missouri
SENTENCE: Fifteen months in a federal prison, five years of probation, and a ban on political activity; served twelve months

EARLY LIFE

Thomas Joseph Pendergast (PEHN-dehr-gast) was born into a large Irish Catholic family in St. Joseph, Missouri, on July 22, 1872. James Pendergast, his oldest brother, moved to Kansas City, Missouri, in 1876. When Thomas permanently moved there in 1894, James was a prosperous saloon keeper, gambler, and Democratic alderman.

POLITICAL CAREER

Pendergast soon became a political protégé of James. Like other rapidly growing, major American cities in the late nineteenth and early twentieth centuries, Kansas City and the surrounding Jackson County experienced machine politics. A political machine is a powerful yet informal system of politics and government in which the private interests of politicians and their constituents are served through a mutual exchange of favors. For example, a machine's poor and working-class constituents vote for machine-endorsed candidates in exchange for patronage jobs, welfare, and other government favors. Businesspeople bribe or politically support machine politicians in exchange for favorable governmental decisions on local taxes, regulations, and public contracts. Machine politics, therefore, often encourages and protects corruption and illegal vices, such as gambling, prostitution, and, when prohibited, liquor.

Pendergast quickly learned how to practice machine politics and use it to benefit his and his family's economic interests, especially in liquor, gambling, and construction. Unlike his brother James, Pendergast was not satisfied with controlling one ward in Kansas City politics. He wanted to dominate Kansas City's government and Democratic Party.

Pendergast was never elected mayor of his city. Instead, he dominated local, county, and, occasionally, state politics through his ability to deliver large blocs of votes to machine-supported candidates. The Pendergast machine's wealth and power benefited from general prosperity, widespread disobedience of the federal prohibition of alcohol, and the rise of organized crime during the 1920's. Nonetheless, in an effort to attract middle-class voters in Kansas City and rural Jackson County, the Pendergast machine promoted the political career of Harry S. Truman, who developed a reputation for honesty and efficiency on the county court. With Pendergast's support, Truman was later nominated and elected U.S. senator in 1934 and eventually became U.S. president in 1945.

During Franklin D. Roosevelt's first term as president (1933-1937), Pendergast received preferential treatment for Kansas City and Jackson County in the use of New Deal programs and funds. By the mid-1930's, however, Pendergast's power was increasingly threatened. Americans in general were shocked and outraged by nationally publicized news about election-day beatings and ballot fraud in Kansas City and its reputation as a safe haven for notorious gangsters. As his health declined and his obsessive gambling increased, Pendergast neglected political affairs and needed more money to pay huge gambling debts.

LEGAL ACTION AND OUTCOME

In 1935 and 1936, Pendergast traveled to Chicago several times and received a total of $440,000 in bribes to influence a legal decision on an insurance case in Missouri. U.S. attorney Maurice Milligan, the Federal Bureau of Investigation (FBI), and federal tax officials began to investigate Pendergast in 1938. After a sensationalized trial that revealed details of Pendergast's wealth, corruption, and gambling debts, Pendergast pleaded guilty to income tax evasion on May 22, 1939. In addition to the payment of fines and taxes owed, Pendergast was sentenced to fifteen months in prison, five years of probation, and a ban on political activity.

IMPACT

Thomas Pendergast served twelve months of his sentence and was released from prison on May 30, 1940. He died of a heart attack in a Kansas City hospital on January 26, 1945. The most prominent mourner at Pendergast's funeral service was Vice President Truman. The efforts of federal and state officials and local reformers ensured that Pendergast's machine died with him.

FURTHER READING

Dorsett, Lyle W. *The Pendergast Machine.* New York: Oxford University Press, 1968. A history of the development and power of the Pendergast machine.

Larsen, Lawrence H., and Nancy J. Hulston. *Pendergast.* Columbia: University of Missouri Press, 1997. A detailed political biography of Pendergast.

Reddig, William M. *Tom's Town: Kansas City and the Pendergast Legend.* Columbia: University of Missouri Press, 1986. A reprint of a journalist's 1947 account of Kansas City politics under the Pendergast machine.

—*Sean J. Savage*

SEE ALSO: Leander Perez; William Marcy Tweed.

DOLLY PENTREATH
Cornish witch

BORN: c. 1675; Cornwall, England
DIED: December, 1777; Paul, Cornwall, England
ALSO KNOWN AS: Dorothy Pentreath; Dorothy Jeffery; Dorothy Jefferies; Fish-Wife of Mousehole
CAUSE OF NOTORIETY: Known for her drinking, smoking, cursing, and witchcraft, Pentreath is also considered to be the last known native speaker of the Cornish language.
ACTIVE: c. 1687-1777
LOCALE: Paul, Cornwall, England

EARLY LIFE

The year in which Dolly Pentreath (DAHL-ee PEHN-treeth) was born has been debated. The register for the parish of Paul has her year of death as 1777, and the legend claims she lived to be 102. Therefore, her birth year would be approximately 1675. However, she was baptized in 1714, and some scholars claim she was ninety when she died.

Throughout her life, Pentreath lived in the parish of Paul, near the fishing village of Mousehole in Cornwall, England. She was the daughter of Nicholas Pentreath, a fisherman. At the age of twelve she was sent to sell fish on the streets of Penzance and took advantage of the naïve. Pentreath later married a fisherman named Jeffery.

LEGENDARY CAREER

Pentreath lived in a small hut on a narrow lane in Paul. She sold fish, drank beer, smoked a pipe, and cursed loudly in Cornish. She was also known for performing witchcraft and having knowledge of astrology. Pentreath once saved a man from being hanged by hiding him in her chimney and fooling the naval officers when they came to question her. Pentreath would sit at a table by the window at the Keigwin Arms pub, drink, smoke, and yell to the fishermen when they came into port.

Pentreath is considered to be the last person who spoke fluent Cornish. Cornish is a part of the Celtic language family, which also includes Welsh, Irish, Scottish Gaelic, Manx, Cumbric, and Breton. Cornish is most similar to Welsh and Breton. Pentreath was discovered by Daines Barrington, who interviewed her in 1768 and subsequently wrote an article published in *Archceologia*, volume 3. At the time of the interview Barrington claimed Pentreath was about eighty-two years old. Some say that the Cornish language died with Pentreath and that any revival of the language is actually a synthetic language that only resembles original Cornish. Others have disputed the idea that Pentreath was the last living native Cornish speaker, citing that William Bodener, John Nancarrow, and John Davey also spoke Cornish and lived after Pentreath's death in 1777.

While she was short in stature and partially deaf, even at an advanced age Pentreath had an excellent intellect and memory, and she could walk six miles in bad weather. The English translation of Pentreath's last words before dying is, "I will not speak English, you ugly black toad!"

IMPACT

Prince Louis Lucien Bonaparte, a descendant of Napoleon, visited Paul to research the disappearance of the Cornish language. While there in 1860, he erected a monument in Dolly Pentreath's honor in the churchyard at Paul Church. The gravestone was a granite obelisk with a Maltese cross on top. Inscribed in both Cornish and English was the biblical Fifth Commandment: "Honor thy father and thy mother, that thy days may be long upon the land which the Lord thy God giveth thee." The monument was purportedly placed by the wrong grave and was subsequently moved to its present location in 1882.

FURTHER READING

Harris, J. Henry. *Cornish Saints and Sinners.* 1906. Reprint. Kila, Mont.: Kessinger, 2003. A collection of fascinating stories about three men traveling through the Cornwall region and the people and places they experience along the way.

Nettle, Daniel, and Suzanne Romaine. *Vanishing Voices: The Extinction of the World's Languages.* New York: Oxford University Press, 2000. A documentation of the extinction of many world languages (including Cornish) and a tribute to their last speakers.

Trenhaile, John. *Dolly Pentreath, and Other Humorous Cornish Tales.* 1854. Reprint. Newcastle upon Tyne, England: F. Graham, 1968. A collection of Cornish stories attributed to both Dolly Pentreath and Trenhaile.

—Kathryn Vincent

SEE ALSO: Tamsin Blight; Mary Butters; Margaret Jones; Lady Alice Kyteler; Florence Newton; Elizabeth Sawyer; Mother Shipton; Joan Wytte.

LEANDER PEREZ
American politician and segregationist

BORN: July 16, 1891; Jesuit Bend, Plaquemines Parish, Louisiana

DIED: March 19, 1969; Belle Chasse, Plaquemines Parish, Louisiana

ALSO KNOWN AS: Leander Henry Perez (full name); Judge Perez

CAUSE OF NOTORIETY: As a political boss in south Louisiana, Perez leased governmental land at low cost in order to profit personally, spurring charges of corruption. He also became a vocal opponent of racial integration. He was investigated but never convicted of various types of fraud.

ACTIVE: 1919-1969

LOCALE: Plaquemines Parish, Louisiana

EARLY LIFE

Leander Perez (lee-AN-duhr PEHR-ehz) was one of thirteen children born to Roselius "Fice" Perez and Gertrude Solis. Fice was a successful farmer elected to the parish police jury and served for twenty-four years; he also served on the Lafourche Levee Board for thirty-five years. However, there are few records of his being perceived as a powerful politician.

Leander attended Our Lady of Holy Cross College and Louisiana State University in Baton Rouge, although he did not graduate. However, he had enough credits to enter Tulane Law School, from which he graduated in 1914. Perez then began a small law practice and in 1916 ran for the state House of Representatives against the powerful local political boss John Dymond, Jr. Although he was defeated, Perez caught the attention of reform-minded politicians such as Louisiana governor-elect John Parker and rising political star Huey Long. In 1917, Perez married Agnes Octavee Chalin.

POLITICAL CAREER

When Twenty-ninth Judicial District judge Robert Hingle died in 1919, Perez was appointed to fill the final year left in Hingle's term of office. Perez then won a bitterly contested election by a slim margin to gain a four-year term to the judgeship. Though he never served on the bench again, he was known as Judge Perez for the rest of his life. He was elected district attorney for the Twenty-fifth Judicial District in 1924, and he was continuously elected to that office until he died.

While seen as an ally to Long in his bids for the governorship of Louisiana (in which Long was defeated in 1924 but victorious in 1928), Perez was not known for delivering a significant number of votes to Long. However, when Long faced impeachment, Perez was the leader of Long's legal defense team. This team developed what was labeled the Round Robin strategy, whereby fifteen senators signed a document stating that they would not consider any charges against Long. With this document, it was evident that no attempt to impeach Long would succeed.

His defense of Long made Judge Perez a figure of statewide prominence. His relationship with Long was cemented when Long received more than 90 percent of the Plaquemines vote in his election for governor, and the "Long ticket" of endorsed candidates shared years of incredible electoral support there. Among the most interesting situations was the 1932 gubernatorial primary, in which 3,152 votes were cast for the Long-supported

O. K. Allen and none for Allen's four opponents. Down the ticket, all other Long opponents officially received zero votes as well. For several elections held from the 1930's through the 1950's, ridiculous election returns came in from St. Bernard and Plaquemines Parishes. On some occasions, more votes were recorded than the actual number of voters registered.

Although his salary never exceeded seven thousand dollars per year, Perez amassed a significant fortune. By the early 1930's, he had established a complex web of businesses to make money from the mineral wealth of the lands belonging to the school board, parish, and levee board. Contracts to develop this land were awarded by the police jury, which was supervised by the district attorney. Specific companies were awarded the rights to lease governmental land at very low cost. The companies would immediately sublease the lands to a company that would extract the oil and mineral riches of the land. Perez was frequently insulated from accusations of corruption because he served as the attorney for these companies rather than as owner of them. Instead, family members and close associates who owned the companies, located in various regions of the country, paid significant amounts of their revenue to Perez to serve as their attorney.

Perez's political power also was used to promote racial segregation. Although blacks constituted generally one-third of the population of Plaquemines Parish, few voted throughout Perez's term of office. For a time in 1952, no blacks were registered to vote in the entire parish. Numerous references cite Perez's address to the White Citizens' Council in 1960, in which he contributed to inciting a riot with such incendiary statements as "Don't wait for your daughter to be raped by these Congolese. Don't wait until the burrheads are forced into your schools. Do something about it now."

Perez was active in the states' rights and racial segregationist movements. Nearly all politically powerful people in Louisiana were Democrats for the first three-quarters of the twentieth century; however, while Perez was a Democrat and heavily involved as a member of the state central committee, on a national level he publicly opposed all of the Democratic presidential candidates, from Harry S. Truman in 1948 to Hubert Humphrey in 1968. Moreover, Perez was excommunicated from the Roman Catholic Church for his public defiance of the order from New Orleans archbishop Joseph Rummel to desegregate the region's Catholic schools throughout the late 1950's and early 1960's.

At the age of seventy-seven, Perez died of a heart at-

tack at his fishing camp. His excommunication from the Church was quietly lifted shortly before his death, and his funeral mass was held at the Holy Name of Jesus Church in New Orleans. More than one thousand people attended his funeral, representing a virtual who's who of powerful southern politicians.

IMPACT

Louisiana has always had a reputation for corrupt politicians, which has led to significant mistrust of large corporations investing in the state, as well as federal allocations of block grants. Leander Perez was accused of mishandling numerous contracts that would have led to billions of dollars of revenue for the state of Louisiana. His intractability in negotiating state royalties for offshore oil leases led to the state of Louisiana receiving virtually no money. Moreover, the legacy of the local controls of the levee board may have significantly contributed to a lack of federal support in gaining adequate maintenance and care for the numerous levees in Louisiana. This lack of coordination demonstrated itself when the levees failed in New Orleans after Hurricane Katrina hit in late summer, 2005.

Perez's excommunication from the Catholic Church is frequently referenced in order to challenge Catholic politicians who defy certain Church doctrines, including those regarding abortion. Many Catholic politicians, including 2004 presidential candidate John Kerry, have been subject to threats of excommunication for supporting political issues such as the right to choose an abortion.

FURTHER READING

Boulard, Gary. *The Big Lie: Hale Boggs, Lucille May Grace, and Leander Perez in 1951.* Gretna, La.: Pelican, 2001. A detailed description of the way in which Perez exercised political power throughout the state of Louisiana in the 1950's.

Conaway, James. *Judge: The Life and Times of Leander Perez.* New York: Alfred A. Knopf, 1973. An independent biography describing Perez as a political power.

Jeansonne, Glen. *Leander Perez: Boss of the Delta.* Baton Rouge: Louisiana State University Press, 1977. An independent biography that details many aspects of Perez's life.

—*John C. Kilburn, Jr.*

SEE ALSO: Theodore G. Bilbo; David Duke; Huey Long; Thomas Joseph Pendergast; Carl Weiss.

EVA PERÓN
Argentine leader, workers' advocate, and philanthropist

BORN: May 7, 1919; Los Toldos, Argentina
DIED: July 26, 1952; Buenos Aires, Argentina
ALSO KNOWN AS: María Eva Duarte (birth name);
María Eva Duarte de Perón (full name); Eva Duarte
de Perón; Evita; Lady of Hope
CAUSE OF NOTORIETY: Perón was the mistress, first
wife, and main political counselor of Argentine
president and military dictator Juan Perón. Eva
ardently supported the lower classes and earned the
ire of the upper classes, creating an ambiguous
relationship with her public and leading to the
formation of a mythic figure in Argentine history.
ACTIVE: 1944-1952
LOCALE: Argentina

EARLY LIFE

María Eva Duarte, later known to the world as Eva Perón
(AY-vah peh-ROHN), was born to Juan Duarte, a land-
owner, and his mistress, Juana Ibarguen, in rural Los
Toldos. When Eva was seven, her father died, and she
worked with her mother and sisters as a cook. During this
time, she observed the injustices and great disparities of
wealth in her society. At fifteen, Eva ran away to the Argentine capital, Buenos Aires, to become an actor.

After several years of struggle, she became a radio
actor and began to have relationships with powerful,
wealthy men. In 1944, she met Colonel Juan Domingo
Perón at a fund-raiser. Perón led a group of officers who
had gained control of Argentina after a coup in 1943. Eva
became his mistress, influencing him to adopt populist,
pro-labor policies that would increase his support among
the lower classes. She softened Perón's image as an
antidemocratic militarist who expressed support for the
Axis Powers during World War II. After the war, a democratic uprising threatened Perón's power, and some of
his fellow officers resented Eva's increasing influence.
They plotted against Perón and even had him arrested,
but Eva cleverly orchestrated an overwhelming display
of support from laborers, police, and loyal elements of
the army. She ultimately reversed the situation so that
Perón was released and restored to power. He married
Eva on October 18, 1945, and became president in 1946.

POLITICAL CAREER

Although Eva never held an official government office,
her power matched that of her husband, who depended
on her for public relations, political advice, organiza-

tional skills, and her powerful oratory. She was especially active in the ministries of labor and health, and she
appointed her family members to high positions. Re-
membering her earlier life of poverty, she used her power
to settle old scores, both personally and in general terms.
She never forgot the throngs of laborers and acted to improve their economic conditions. They responded enthusiastically, shouting "Evita" as an affectionate, informal
version of her name as she traveled the country and
showered gifts on them. She created the philanthropic
Eva Perón Social Aid Foundation, supported by compul-
sory donations. She built schools, hospitals, and large
housing projects for the poor, who called her the Lady of
Hope. She was, however, despised and resented by many
members of the upper classes.

In many ways, she took on her celebrity and political
power as an ongoing dramatic role, refining her own
public character and projecting her values of nationalism, social justice, and women's rights into a kind of
religious quest. She simplified her clothing and cultivated a consistent visual impact with her dyed blond hair
pulled back, adding an inspiring air of self-sacrifice to
her physical beauty.

Eva also fought for women's rights, and her very existence threatened the established social order. Among the
elite, wives were usually chosen from the same social
class, while mistresses came from lower levels; this hierarchy was carefully maintained. Eva's own mother had
been part of this system, and as her father's illegitimate
child, Eva's only social connection to him was her use of
his surname, Duarte. However, because Perón actually
married Eva, a former mistress was transformed into a
wife. Her prominence as Argentina's first lady further
alarmed upper-class married women and simultaneously
inspired women of the lower classes. Concurrently, her
outspoken political activism violated the norms of ma-
chismo (a strong sense of masculinity prevalent in Latino
cultures). However, Eva's "feminist" agenda was not
merely symbolic; she wanted constitutional changes so
that women could vote.

Eva was nominated for vice president in 1951, but resistance from military circles was too great. On July 26,
1952, her political career and young life were cut short by
terminal cancer, and the nation went into intense mourning. Without her presence, her husband's dictatorship
eventually collapsed, and Juan Perón was deposed in
1955.

IMPACT

Despite her humble origins, Eva Perón tried fanatically to transform Argentina through a combination of legislation, advocacy, and agitation, as well as by projecting herself as a role model for women. In response to disapproval from social conservatives, she positioned herself as an idealistic nationalist and a savior of the poor; she subsequently became a heroine to the masses. After her death, the idealization and mythmaking intensified. On August 2, 1952, the food workers union appealed to the Roman Catholic pope to begin Eva's canonization. Although the Vatican refused, hundreds of thousands of people continued to have shrines honoring "Saint Evita." However, to her enemies, Eva was a vindictive tyrant who would not tolerate any opposition. Her influence was so persistent that after Juan Perón was deposed, Eva's body was shipped to Milan, Italy, by the new government, which feared a Perónist resurgence.

Eva became a legend and icon, whose fascinating and often scandalous story became part of international popular culture and media in the twentieth century. In 1978, *Evita*, a musical by Andrew Lloyd Webber and Tim Rice, premiered in London and was an immediate success. A 1996 film version was made with pop singer Madonna, an international icon herself, portraying Eva. The musical and film were candid in presenting Eva's numerous early love affairs and the chaotic events in Argentine politics and captured some of the ambiguities in Eva's relationship with the public.

FURTHER READING

Fraser, Nicholas, and Marysa Navarro. *Evita: The Real Lives of Eva Perón*. London: André Deutsch, 2003. A well-researched and fascinating biography which examines the reality versus the legend of Eva Perón. Illustrated.

Guillermoprieto, Alma. *Looking for History: Dispatches from Latin America*. New York: Pantheon Books, 2001. The first essay, "Little Eva," is a vivid portrait with profound reflections on Eva Perón and her historical significance. Illustrated.

Ortiz, Alicia Dujovne. *Eva Perón*. Translated by Shawn Field. New York: St. Martin's Press, 1997. This international best seller is a well-researched, complete biography based on declassified materials and other rare sources. Illustrated; bibliography.

Perón, Eva. *Evita: In My Own Words*. Translated by Laura Dail. New York: New Press, 2005. Brings forth the first English translation of "My Message," Eva Perón's controversial deathbed manuscript found in a government archive thirty years after her death. Photos, chronology, and facsimile of the manuscript.

Taylor, J. M. *Eva Perón: The Myths of a Woman*. Chicago: University of Chicago Press, 1981. An anthropologist, the author examines the causes and history of the myths surrounding Eva Perón: revolutionary, prostitute, and saint. Illustrated; bibliography.

—*Alice Myers*

SEE ALSO: Juan Perón; Jorge Rafael Videla.

EVITA'S POSTMORTEM ODYSSEY

Eva Perón dead was nearly as dangerous to her political enemies as she was alive. The poor and the working classes adored her. In fact, she was as much a symbol of social betterment for them as a leader. To the conservative elite, as long as her corpse could be seen and revered, Evita would inspire the underclasses. For a time, the corpse was visible to Argentineans: General Perón hired Dr. Pedro Ara of Spain to embalm Evita in lifelike fidelity. After a series of ceremonies to mourn her death, the corpse was moved to the top floor of the Peronist trade union headquarters, and people streamed in to pay their last respects. There were plans to build a towering monument to the *descamisados* (shirtless ones, or laborers; the word also came to refer to followers of Perón) and install Evita's body in the base on permanent display.

This fanfare was too much for the Argentine military. When generals overthrew Juan Perón in 1955, they had Evita's body secretly moved to Milan, Italy, and buried in a crypt under the name María Maggi. There she stayed for sixteen years. In 1971, she was moved to Spain and Juan Perón's villa, her body still perfectly preserved. Perón returned to Argentina in 1973 and to the presidency in October of that year. He died in July, 1974. His third wife, Isabel, a great admirer of Evita, had her corpse returned to Buenos Aires and displayed next to Perón's body. Another plan for a monument, this time to them both, also had to be abandoned because of political turmoil. Evita was secretly reburied in the Recoleta Cemetery, the resting place of Argentina's social elite. Behind stout walls and in a deep compartment under two sets of trap doors lies her coffin, at rest at last and reputably safe from even a direct bomb blast.

Meanwhile, Juan Perón's corpse did not fare so well. Two years after his death, the military junta removed the body from the presidential palace and interred it in his family estate. Vandals broke open the coffin in 1987 and cut off Perón's hands; their motive remains a mystery.

JUAN PERÓN
President of Argentina (1946-1955, 1973-1974)

BORN: October 8, 1895; Lobos, Buenos Aires
Province, Argentina

DIED: July 1, 1974; Buenos Aires, Argentina

ALSO KNOWN AS: Juan Domingo Perón (full name)

CAUSE OF NOTORIETY: Despite earning widespread
political approval in his early presidency from
Argentina's labor unions, Perón lost support when a
series of economic crises arose and he resorted to
dictatorial measures in an attempt to maintain his
power.

ACTIVE: 1946-1974

LOCALE: Argentina

EARLY LIFE

Juan Domingo Perón (wawn doh-MIHN-goh peh-
ROHN) , the son of Mario and Juana Perón, was abandoned by his father when he was five years old. At the
age of ten, he went to live with his uncle in Buenos Aires.
In 1911, Perón enrolled in the Military Academy of Argentina; he graduated in 1913 as a second lieutenant in
the infantry division.

Perón occupied diverse military positions in Argentina and wrote several texts that discussed morals in the
military. By 1930, he was already a member of the military hierarchy in Argentina, reaching the rank of lieutenant colonel in 1936 and serving as the Argentine military
attaché in Chile in the same year. Along with other military officers, he was sent in 1938 to Germany and Italy in
order to study the military organizations of those countries. He became an admirer of the Italian dictator Benito
Mussolini and in early 1941 returned to Argentina with
the rank of colonel. On his return to Argentina, Perón immediately became a member of the Group of United Officers, whose primary goal was to foment and support nationalistic ideals.

POLITICAL CAREER

On June 4, 1943, Perón, leading the Group of United Officers, participated in a military revolution, which ended
the corruption that had existed in the military government under President Ramón Castillo. Castillo's forced
exile led to a three-year military regime in Argentina in
which Perón functioned first as secretary of work and social welfare and later, in 1945, as vice president and minister of war.

On October 9, 1945, as a result of another civil and
military coup, Perón was imprisoned. However, because

of the efforts of his mistress, Eva (Evita) Duarte, and
some union leaders, he was freed. In his subsequent
speech, transmitted to more than 300,000 people, Perón
promised to lead the people to victory and prosperity
in the forthcoming presidential elections. He married
Evita—who was adored by Argentina's poor and working classes and provided her husband with significant
political capital—and won the presidential elections in
February, 1946, with 56 percent of the popular vote. He
took office as president of Argentina on June 4, 1946.

Because of the popularity of his wife, Perón garnered the support of the Argentine labor unions, whose
members' lives he improved by raising their wages and
providing them with paid holidays, medical benefits,
and vacation days. As president, Perón founded the Peronista movement (eventually the Peronista Party) and
initiated vigorous national reforms. In 1949, the constitution was reorganized, incorporating the new social reforms and granting the vote to women, thereby extending, almost exponentially, his political support within
the country. Perón's fame, fueled both by Evita's popularity and by the loyal support of the laborers, was so
widespread that in 1951, by 62 percent of the popular
vote, he was reelected as president for an additional six
years.

Evita's death from cancer in 1952 affected Perón's
popularity: She had been the catalyst who successfully
rallied the support of the people for her husband's presidency. Argentina was also undergoing a series of economic crises caused primarily by Perón's original reforms. He attempted to ameliorate the situation both
by reversing his original reforms and by instituting oppressive dictatorial policies, which ultimately divided
his supporters and his opponents. He tried to curtail
the power of the labor unions and incurred the wrath of
the Roman Catholic Church, which excommunicated
him after he exiled two of its priests. The labor unions
then turned against him when he moved financial and
other resources from the agricultural sector to other projects.

DOWNFALL AND RESURRECTION

After an attempted military coup in 1955, Perón declared
a state of siege on September 3, 1955. A second and successful coup on September 16 led to his downfall; he was
exiled for the next eighteen years, first to Paraguay and
then to Spain. During his exile, Argentina underwent a

Juan and Eva Perón. (AP/Wide World Photos)

background. He founded the populist Peronista Party, which continued to hold an important role in modern-day Argentine politics. In 1990, for example, Carlos Saúl Menem, the Peronista candidate, won the election for the presidency, thus demonstrating the ongoing popularity of Perón's political ideologies. Although Perón instituted labor reforms, which raised the living standards of the working poor of Argentina, his political tactics ultimately worked against them. Peronism was originally designed to help the lower classes but ended up heavily taxing the upper class and then giving the money back to the rich. In the end, his corruption and his loss of support from the military proved to be his undoing.

series of difficult economic crises culminating in a limitation of the power of the labor unions. A gradual pro-Perón movement began to form in the country, and on June 20, 1973, Perón returned to Argentina as a popular hero. Upon Perón's return, the current president, Hectór Cámpora, resigned, and Perón ran for the presidency with his third wife, Isabel Martínez de Perón, as his choice for vice president.

On September 23, 1973, Perón was elected president of Argentina for the third time, with 62 percent of the electoral vote. He attempted to institute some reforms while trying to appease the opposition, but this tactic led to more economic trouble for the country. In addition, Perón's poor health forced him to forgo many public appearances, thereby decreasing his popularity with the people. Perón died on July 1, 1974, and was succeeded to the presidency by his widow, Isabel; she was ousted by a military coup in 1976.

IMPACT

Juan Perón is one of the few presidents in Latin America who was democratically elected to the presidency for three terms, although he came from a strong military

FURTHER READING

Alexander, Robert. *Juan Domingo Perón: A History.* Boulder, Colo.: Westview Press, 1979. The author provides insights into the life and times of the Argentine leader and delineates the effects of Peronism on modern-day Argentina.

Romero, Luis Alberto. *History of Argentina in the Twentieth Century.* Translated by James P. Brennan. University Park: Pennsylvania State University Press, 2002. One of Argentina's leading historians chronicles a century of history, providing good contextual information about the Perón years.

Turner, Frederick C. *Juan Perón and the Reshaping of Argentina.* Pittsburgh, Pa.: University of Pittsburgh Press, 1983. An investigation of the life of Perón and an account of his three terms as president of Argentina, as well as a discussion of how Peronism shaped current Argentine history.

—*Víctor Manuel Durán*

SEE ALSO: Leopoldo Galtieri; Eva Perón; Augusto Pinochet Ugarte; Alfredo Stroessner; Getúlio Vargas.